Richard Cobden

Speeches on Questions of Public Policy

Richard Cobden

Speeches on Questions of Public Policy

ISBN/EAN: 9783742806963

Manufactured in Europe, USA, Canada, Australia, Japa

Cover: Foto ©Thomas Meinert / pixelio.de

Manufactured and distributed by brebook publishing software
(www.brebook.com)

Richard Cobden

Speeches on Questions of Public Policy

SPEECHES

ON QUESTIONS OF PUBLIC POLICY

BY

RICHARD COBDEN, M.P.

EDITED BY

JOHN BRIGHT

AND

JAMES E. THOROLD ROGERS

IN TWO VOLUMES

VOL. I.

FREE TRADE, PEACE, GOOD WILL AMONG NATIONS

London
MACMILLAN AND CO.
1870

PREFACE.

THE Speeches contained in these two volumes have been selected and edited at the instance of the Club which was established for the purpose of inculcating and extending those political principles which are permanently identified with Cobden's career. They form an important part of that collective contribution to political science, which has conferred on their author a reputation, the endurance of which, it may be confidently predicted, is as secure as that of any among the men whose wisdom and prescience have promoted the civilisation of the world.

These Speeches are not in any sense compositions. Cobden was, in the strictest meaning of the words, an extempore speaker. He pretended neither to rhetoric nor to epigram, though the reader will find passages in these volumes the unaffected grace of which is as pleasing as the highest art, and illustrations which have all the force of the liveliest humour. But, as a rule, the speech is, as Sir

b

Robert Peel called it, when the speaker's career was in its beginnings, 'unadorned.' The style is homely, conversational, familiar, and even garrulous. But it is always clear, and invariably suggests such a comprehension of the subject which is discussed, as gives the exposition all the force of a debate. So cogent and exhaustive was Cobden's reasoning, that, in almost every case, they who attempted to resist the effect of his conclusions, were constrained to betake themselves to some irrelevant issue, or to awaken some prejudice against him. What he said, too, was stated with great geniality and kindliness. If it was difficult to refute the speaker, it was impossible to quarrel with the man. He was as popular as he was wise. His manner was as modest as his speech was lucid.

There is no subject which Cobden treated, which he did not take care to know perfectly well. He was never unprepared, for he never spoke on any topic with which he was not thoroughly conversant. He read up everything which he talked about. Hence his facts were as indisputable as his inferences were precise. He was never obliged to repudiate a principle which he had once adopted or announced, for he never accepted a compromise on any question of public policy. Hence he has done more than any other statesman to make the administration of public affairs an exact science. And for the same reason, as he entered into Parliament in the full maturity of his powers, he never had to abandon a single position which he accepted, maintained, and affirmed.

Cobden's name is principally identified with the agitation which led to a Free Trade in Food. This is not the place to enter into the history of that great financial reform, because an examination of all the statements which were made in defence of that restrictive policy to which the Corn-laws were the coping-stone, would require, in itself, the space of a special treatise. Most of them, it will be found, are taken and refuted in the Free-trade speeches with which these volumes commence. A quarter of a century after the final overthrow of the system, we can have no conception of the warmth and vindictiveness with which that system was defended, and of the courage, readiness, and learning which were needed in order to combat protective theories, and finally to overthrow them.

The immediate object of the organisation with which Cobden was associated, was the repeal of all protective taxes. For the purpose of carrying out this work, Cobden sacrificed fortune and health. The labours which he undertook during the campaign against the Corn-laws, materially injured a constitution, which, like that of all his family, was never robust. The unremitting attention which he gave to the details of an agitation, which confronted such vast and such angry interests, left him no leisure for conducting the affairs of his own manufacture. But once embarked in political life, Cobden could not abandon it, or retreat from it. He knew very well, that after he had organised and carried out the campaign against the Corn-laws, there were other violations of economical laws, which characterised the social system of this country, the correction of which was only less important than the repeal of those monopolies, though the machinery for correcting them was by no means equally available.

He saw, for example, that no ultimate benefit would ensue to the mass of the people by the abolition of all taxes on food, unless what he called by a pardonable metaphor, Free Trade in Land, were also established. By this he meant the removal of that artificial scarcity of marketable land, which is directly traceable to certain usurpations in the real or presumed interest of the aristocracy, by which the devolution of land is regulated according to the custom of primogeniture, and by which estates are restrained from alienation under the covenants of a strict settlement. Thus, in the last year of his life, and in the last speech which he made, he regretted his age and failing physical energies, since he was now debarred from entering on an agitation for the abolition of those customs and privileges which make land the monopoly of the rich, and condemn the English peasantry to hopeless labour.

The same anxiety to carry out Free Trade to its legitimate consequences made Cobden an advocate of Financial Reform, and thus induced him to suggest the extension of one part, which is as yet the least equitable part of our financial system, and even to urge the absolute abandonment of the other part. He wished to see the United Kingdom a free port, rightly recognising that the more fully such a result could be obtained, the greater might be the industry, and the greater must be the affluence of his countrymen. Hence he advocated direct instead of indirect taxation.

Again, Cobden had the greatest anxiety to improve the moral and material condition of the people, and he had certain very definite views as to the machinery by which the improvement could be effected. He was one of the earliest advocates of a system of National Education. But, in the face of facts, he saw that it could be universal, only if it were permanently freed from the risk of denominational intrigue. He knew, again, that excessive taxation presses with increasing weight on those whose income supplies the narrowest margin above the necessaries of life. By far the largest part of the public expenditure is levied for the maintenance of the Services, and he was never weary of demanding that the cost of these Services should be materially reduced. He saw that the apology for these Services was to be found in the Foreign Policy of this country; and from the earliest days of his political career he urged the country to adopt the principle of non-intervention. He clearly understood, that if the people of England busied themselves solely with their own defence, the charges on the revenue might be so reduced, that the industry and enjoyments of the people would be vastly augmented.

But he founded his arguments on behalf of international amity, justice, and peace on far higher

grounds than the material interests of society. He
strongly held to the opinion that there is a retri-
bution for national crimes, and he believed that the
Foreign Policy of this country had been constantly
immoral. He was persuaded that no advantage
which can be obtained by War is equal to the
loss, misery, and demoralisation which inevitably
accompany it; and he knew that every end which
warfare aims at, can be safely, honourably, and
cheaply obtained by arbitration. He denounced
War as barbarism, and he saw that the stimulants
to War are almost invariably supplied by those
violent and self-seeking partisans, who appeal to
professional prejudice or a sordid patriotism in order
to achieve their personal objects. After all means
of averting War had failed, after every appeal to
international law and public faith had been exhausted, a defensive War might, he held, be just
and necessary; and defence, he very easily recognised, was far stronger than attack, far cheaper than
aggression.

With the same end, he strove to do away with one
of the professional incentives to War, the custom of
confiscating unarmed vessels, belonging to the subjects of a belligerent Power, on the high seas. The
retention of such a custom by a nation whose mercantile marine is larger than that of any other community, was, he saw, an act of astonishing folly, or
still more amazing ignorance. To those who argued
that the risk of loss by such a nation is a powerful
preventive of War, he answered, that War is never

desired by a people, but by politicians and military men, whose ambition and cupidity are fired by the prospect of advancement or profit, and that it is in the interest of such persons that the present custom is retained. The experience of the late American War has taught us that this barbarous and indefeasible practice has other and more serious consequences.

In the same spirit, and with the same purpose, he dissected the motives which induce Governments to contract, and money-dealers to negotiate, Public Loans. He saw that these obligations were generally created in order to subserve some aggressive or tyrannical policy; and he contrasted the inconsistency of the public conscience, which was always ready to sympathise by demonstration with an oppressed people, and yet did not scruple to lend money to the oppressor, in order to enable him to outrage humanity with safety. He held that the men who lend money to profligate Governments, occupy exactly the same place with those who make advances for infamous purposes, and that, until such time as the public conscience scouts their proceedings, they should at least be denied sympathy and assistance in recovering principal or interest from their defaulting debtors.

To these views of Mr. Cobden on War Expenditure and Foreign Policy, his opponents had nothing to answer, except by charging him with advocating peace at any price. It is almost superfluous to say that the charge was false, and nearly as superfluous to state, that they who made it knew it to be false. The reader of these Speeches will find sufficient proof, that the speaker put no limit to the necessary cost of defence—that he simply wished to take away the motives and materials of aggression.

It was a common saying about Cobden, that his range of political action was narrow. A glance at the topics treated in these volumes, a little reflection on their magnitude, will be a sufficient proof that this charge also is unfounded. But Cobden's political speeches cover only a small number of the subjects on which his opinions were strongly and clearly formed. They who had the advantage of his familiar intercourse, and who regularly corresponded with him, know how universal was his knowledge on political subjects, how lucid and sagacious were his interpretations of political events. When, in time to come, his correspondence is given to the world, it will be found to be a copious and profound history of his public life, and of the facts to which he contributed, or which he witnessed. There was hardly a subject of social interest on which he had not thought deeply, on which he did not speak and write wisely. But clear and wise as he was, his manner was inexpressibly gentle and modest.

There is one misstatement which was freely made against Cobden during his lifetime, and which has been reiterated since by such shallow people as form their opinions at secondhand. He was supposed to have been very moderately informed, to have ridiculed all learning, to have despised culture, and to have overvalued the educational importance of modern politics. At the time when it was first promulgated, the calumny was convenient and ingenious. It was intended to discredit Cobden's reputation as a statesman among educated persons. To repeat it now, is to be guilty of an act of gross carelessness,—an act of which no responsible and competent person would be guilty.

What Cobden did comment on, once and again, in terms of increasing severity, is the utter ignorance, on subjects of great political importance, which prevails among young men who have graduated at the older Universities, and who, under the peculiar parliamentary institutions of this country, are presented to seats in the House of Commons, or purchase admission into it, or succeed to analogous positions in the House of Lords. The system which introduces these personages to the Legislature, puts them also into the Administration. Now, Cobden used to argue that the particular knowledge which the older Universities impart to such people, is of absolutely no use to them in the responsible place which they occupy, and that, considering the magnitude of the interests with which they deal, it is of paramount importance that they should have some knowledge of their own country and its history, and should furthermore gain similar information about those other countries with which their own has relations. He commented also on the danger which this

country runs by incompetence and ignorance on
the part of Ministers and Members of Parliament,
and he might, had he wished to strengthen his
case, have pointed to the absurd and mischievous
misconceptions which prevailed among statesmen
and politicians of the academical type as to the
circumstances of the American War. Now, Cobden
did not stand alone in this judgment. One of the
commonest charges against the English is what
foreigners call their insular habits, by which is
probably meant, a boisterous self-complacency, and
a contemptuous disregard for the opinions of other
nations. There are persons who consider this coarse
and ignorant pride, patriotic.

But, on the other hand, no man honoured with
a more generous and modest deference that culture
which he confessed to lack, but which he saw
made in certain cases, as it always should be made,
the substratum and method of practical experience.
The scholarship which was coupled with a knowledge of modern facts, and which was made the
means for arranging and illustrating such facts, was
in Cobden's eyes an invaluable acquisition. For
pedantry he had a hearty contempt. For learning,
which is of no age or country, he had an exaggerated respect. But the difference between pedantry and learning lies in the fact, that the former
is satisfied with a narrow portion of the facts which
constitute the history of the human mind, while
the latter. grasps all the inductions of social philosophy, or at least strives to do so.

If exact and careful knowledge of history constitutes learning, Cobden was, during the years of his political career, the most learned speaker in the House of Commons. Dealing as he did with broad questions of public policy, he got up his case accurately and laboriously. His facts, culled from all sources, were judiciously selected, and were never challenged. A cautious student of political economy, he knew that this science, the difficulty of which he fully recognised, was or ought to be eminently inductive, and that an economist without facts is like an engineer without materials or tools.

It was originally intended that all the Speeches contained in these volumes should have had the advantage of Mr. Bright's revision. Mr. Bright has done this service to those which are contained in the first volume. But, after he had given the same assistance to a few sheets in the second, he was unhappily seized with illness, and has been unable to give his further supervision to the work. It is hoped that this loss will not detract too much from the value of this publication.

A few of the Speeches were corrected by the speaker himself. But not a few, delivered on the spur of the occasion, have been extracted from newspaper reports, and have sometimes required the corrections of conjectural criticism. Mr. Cobden was a rapid speaker, and, as his voice became feebler, he was not always easy to report accurately.

The thanks of the Editors are due to the Proprietors of the *Manchester Examiner and Times,* who were good enough to put the files of this influential paper at their disposal.

JAMES E. THOROLD ROGERS.

OXFORD, *April* 14, 1870.

CONTENTS OF VOL. I.

FREE TRADE

FINANCE.

FREE TRADE.

FREE TRADE.

I.

HER MAJESTY'S SPEECH.—AMENDMENT ON THE ADDRESS.

HOUSE OF COMMONS, AUGUST 25, 1841.

[Mr. Cobden was returned to Parliament for the first time in August, 1841, as Member for Stockport. He had previously, in 1837, contested this borough. In the debate on Mr. Baring's Budget, who was Chancellor of the Exchequer in Lord Melbourne's Government, Lord John Russell avowed that it was the intention of the Government to propose a moderate fixed duty on corn, in lieu of the sliding-scale. These duties were announced on the 7th of May, to be 8s. on wheat, 5s. on rye, 4s. 6d. on barley, and 3s. 6d. on oats. On May 27th, Sir Robert Peel moved a resolution of want of confidence. This resolution was carried by a majority of 1 (312 to 311). On this, Lord Melbourne appealed to the country. When the new Parliament met, Mr. Wortley moved and Lord Bruce seconded an amendment to the Address, to the effect that the Administration did not enjoy the confidence of the country. The amendment was carried by a majority of 91 (360 to 269), and Sir Robert Peel came into office. This statesman continued in office till he repealed those Corn-laws which he took office to maintain.]

I FEEL some difficulty in attempting to treat the question before the House, as there does not seem to be a good understanding of the position in which the House stands with regard to it. Different opinions have been expressed as to the object for which hon. Members have been sent here, and as to the nature of the late general election. It has been said that the elections were not a test of public opinion in reference to the monopolies, but merely in reference to the

question of confidence in her Majesty's Ministers. That
opinion has been expressed by the right hon. Gentleman
the Member for Tamworth (Sir R. Peel), and a disposition
has been evinced by his followers to take it as his dictum.
But we are not then sent here to represent monopoly, and
strange would it be did the majority of this House authen-
tically announce that they have been sent here for such a
purpose by what is called the 'people of England.'

A recommendation has been made by the Executive to this
House, advising us to set about the immediate reduction of
taxation; and it is accompanied by an assurance that not only
will that reduction not impair the revenue, but increase the
resources of the national Exchequer. That, after all, is the
nature of the message upon which the late Parliament was
dissolved. But how can Gentlemen opposite, notwithstanding
what has been said for them, come to this House to maintain
taxation in all its inordinate vigour and mischievousness, because they wish for taxation in order to protect monopoly, as
well as for the purposes of the State? It is really well that
all people have not become enamoured of monopoly.

There is another difficulty in addressing the House on
the present occasion. We are told that the question is not
whether the Corn-laws shall be repealed or monopoly abated,
but whether the amendment upon the Address shall be agreed
to; and hon. Gentlemen opposite, in discussing that question,
talked of the wars in Syria and China, and of the affairs of
Canada and New York, but never once touched upon those
questions which had been recommended to their consideration,
and with a view to a diminution of the burdens of the people.
But while I give hon. Gentlemen opposite credit for their
discretion in excluding those important topics from the discussion, I see no reason why hon. Gentlemen on my side of the
House, who feel that such questions as the Corn-laws are of
greater interest to the people than the Chinese or Syrian wars,
or any other remote subject of the kind, should not declare

their views upon those questions; or why, if the speeches from my side of the House are to meet with no response on the other, we should not discharge our duty towards the people, and pay that respect and deference to her Majesty to which she is entitled, by calmly considering those questions and stating our opinions upon them. I believe it was customary, under the old *régime*, particularly with the Conservative party in this House, to treat the Speech from the Throne as something very nearly appertaining to monarchical dignity. I do not think it was customary, unless with very great reason, to drag in the Ministers of the day, but rather to respond to the Speech from the Throne as something connected with royal dignity, and entitled to that calm discussion which hon. Gentlemen opposite are not willing to accord to the most gracious and, since the time of Alfred, the most popular monarch of these realms.

It has been said that the people of England are not sincere in seeking for a total repeal of the food tax. With all sincerity, I declare that I am for the total repeal of those taxes which affect the price of bread and provisions of every description, and I will not allow it to be said without denying it, that the three millions of people who have petitioned the House for the total repeal of those taxes are not sincere in their prayer. What are those taxes upon food? They are taxes levied upon the great body of the people, and hon. Gentlemen opposite, who show such sympathy for the working classes after they have made them paupers, cannot deny my right to claim on their behalf that those taxes should be a primary consideration. I have heard them called protections; but taxes they are, and taxes they shall be in my mouth, as long as I have the honour of a seat in this House. The bread-tax is a tax primarily levied upon the poorer classes; it is a tax, at the lowest estimate, of 40 per cent. above the price we should pay if there were a free trade in corn. The report upon the handloom weavers puts down 10*s.* as the estimated weekly

earnings of a family, and states that in all parts of the United
Kingdom that will be found to be not an unfair estimate of the
earnings of every labourer's family.   It moreover states, that
out of 10s. each family expends 5s. on bread.   The tax of
40 per cent. is, therefore, a tax of 2s. upon every labouring
man's family earning 10s. a week, or 20 per cent. upon their
earnings.   How does it operate as we proceed upwards in
society?   The man with 40s. a week pays an income-tax of
5 per cent.; the man of 250l. a year pays but 1 per cent.;
and the nobleman, or millionaire, with an income of 200,000l.
a year, and whose family consumes no more bread than that
of the agricultural labourer, pays less than one halfpenny in
every 100l.   [Laughter.]   I know not whether the laugh is
at the monstrous character of the case, or the humble individual who states it; but I repeat that the tax upon the
nobleman is less than one halfpenny per cent., while upon the
poor man's family it was 20l. per cent.   I am sure there is
not an hon. Member in the House who would dare to bring in
a bill to levy an income-tax on all grades of society upon a
scale similar to this, and yet I maintain that the bread-tax is
such a tax, and is levied not for the purposes of the State, but
for the benefit of the richest portion of the community.   That
is a fair statement of the tax upon bread.   I can sympathise
with the incredulity of hon. Gentlemen opposite, but if they
knew the case as it really is, and felt it as they would if they
did know it, they would also feel that they could not lie down
to rest in comfort or safety if they voted for such a tax.   With
the exception of England and of Holland, in no country has
any Government, however distressed, ever yet resorted to the
monstrous injustice of levying a tax upon bread.   Gentlemen
will point to the laws affecting the importation of corn in
France, Spain, and the United States of America; but in
those countries they export corn upon an average, one year
with another, and therefore no import duty could operate with
them as with us.

But it is said that the working classes have some compensation—some protection extended to them by this law. Hon. Gentlemen on the other side have talked largely at the hustings of their determination to protect the poor; and the noble Lord (Stanley) opposite, at the election for North Lancashire, eagerly propounded this doctrine of protection. I have heard the noble Lord with my own ears; his case of protection to the labourer was that which I will now unfold. The noble Lord said that the manufacturers wanted to repeal the Corn-laws because they wanted to reduce the rate of wages; that, unless by the repeal of the bread-tax they reduced wages, they could not be better able to compete with foreigners; and that if they did, it could be no benefit to the working man. Let me remind the House, that the parties who have so patiently struggled for three years past for a hearing at your bar, have never been allowed to state their case; that the hon. Member for Wolverhampton (Mr. Charles Villiers)—for whose great and incessant services I, in common with millions of my fellow-countrymen, feel grateful—when he proposed that the case of those millions should be heard at the bar, had the proposition scouted and spurned; and that, when they had denied them a hearing, they proceeded to misrepresent their motives. I will state the case as given by the noble Lord himself. If he can be in error in appreciating the merits of the question, with all his brilliant talents, other hon. Gentlemen opposite will excuse me if I believe that they also are in error. The case was stated by the noble Lord thus:—Those who advocate a repeal of the Corn-laws have again and again announced that their object is to exchange the produce of their industry for the productions of all other countries, and that all duties for protection (so called) levied upon articles in the manufacture of which they are engaged, should be likewise removed, and a free and unfettered intercourse established between all the countries of the earth, as was clearly the design of nature. But we were told by the noble lord the Member for North

Lancashire that this means the reduction of wages. If I
know anything, it means increased trade, and the claim of a
right, besides, to exchange our manufactures for the corn of
all other countries, by which we should very much increase
the extent of our trade. How can this be done, unless by an
increased amount of labour? How can we call into requisition an increased demand for labour without also increasing
the rate of wages?

Another prevailing fallacy was mixed up with the noble
Lord's statement. The object, he said, was to reduce wages,
so as to enable our manufacturers to compete with foreigners.
I maintain that we do now compete with them; that we now
sell our manufactures in neutral markets in competition with
other countries; that we now sell them, in New York, for
instance, in competition with all the other countries of the
earth. You talk of protection to the home producer, but it
should ever be remembered that it is the foreign market
which fixes the price of the home market. Would any man
think of sending to a distance of 3,000 miles articles for
which he could find a better market at home? I see in this
fallacy of wages that which is at the bottom of all the opposition to the repeal of the Corn-laws. There are many conscientious upholders of the present system who support them
in the supposition that they maintain the rate of wages. I
see no relation between the price of food, or of any other
article of consumption, and the price of labour, in its wholesome, natural state. In Cuba, or in the slave-holding states
of America, I can imagine the price of labour to be affected
by the price of food. I can imagine the slave-holder sitting
down and estimating the value of herrings and rice. In his
case, the price of labour at his command is affected clearly by
the price of provisions.

There is another stage in the labour market—I refer to
labourers in the agricultural districts—where the amount of
wages has reached the very minimum, according to their

habits of life. These unfortunate men are told that their wages will rise as the price of provisions advances. Why? Is it because the high price of provisions increases the demand for labour, or is it done from pure charity? But I come to that state of the labour market under which—and God knows how long it will continue under such legislation—the various products of our manufacturing industry are called into existence, and there, I assert, without fear of contradiction, that the rate of wages has no more connection with the price of food than with the moon's changes. There it depends entirely on the demand for labour; there the price of food never becomes an ingredient in testing the value of labour. There the labour market is, happily, elastic, and will become more so, if you leave it unfettered. But if you continue to legislate in the spirit by which you have so long been animated, you will succeed at last in bringing our commercial and manufacturing population down to the same pitch to which you have reduced our agriculturists, and then these merchants and manufacturers may come forward and give alms to the wretched men in their employment; then it will perhaps be said that 'with the increase in the price of food arises an increase in the rate of wages.' It will be doled out as an alms, as a mere act of charity, and not because the working man, as a free agent, is entitled, in return for his labour, to a decent subsistence.

I will now dismiss the question of wages, though it is one which I must say should be again and again mooted in this House. I now come to the consideration of that all-important subject—the existing state of our manufacturing and agricultural labourers—which has already called forth your sympathy, and to which I must again direct your attention. I have lately had an opportunity of obtaining, by peculiar means, access to a report about the state of the labouring population in all parts of the country. A highly important Convocation was held in Manchester a week ago, consisting entirely of the ministers

of religion. [Ironical cheers.] I understand those cheers.
I will not pause in my statement of facts, but will say a word
upon that subject when I have done. I have seen at Manchester
a body of ministers of all religious persuasions—not 620, as
has been stated, but 650 in number—assembled together from
all parts of the country, at an expense of from 3,000*l.* to
4,000*l.*, which was borne by their respective congregations.
Those clergymen gathered, not from Yorkshire or Lancashire
only—not from Derby or Cheshire only—but from every county
of Great Britain—from Caithness to Cornwall,—and stated the
most important facts relating to the labouring population in
their various districts. I have had an opportunity of examining those statements. I will not trespass on the time and
attention of the House by going into those statements in
detail; but I will state generally, that, from both the manufacturing and agricultural districts, there was the most un-
impeachable testimony that the condition of the great body
of her Majesty's labouring subjects had deteriorated wofully
within the last ten years, and more especially so within the
three years last past; and furthermore, that in proportion as
the price of the food of the people had increased, just so had
their comforts been diminished. I have seen statements derived
from the reports of infirmaries and workhouses, from savings'
banks and prisons; and all alike bore testimony, clear and
indubitable, that the condition of the great mass of her
Majesty's subjects in the lower ranks of life is rapidly deteriorating; that they are now in a worse condition, and
receiving less wages; and that their distress and misery
result in a greater amount of disease, destitution, and crime
than has ever been witnessed at any former period of the
history of this country.

One word in reference to the jeers with which the mention
of this Convocation has been received. I do not come here to
vindicate the conduct of those Christian men in having
assembled to take this momentous subject into their con-

sideration. The parties who will more fitly judge them are
their own congregations. At that Convocation we had
members of the Established Church and of the Church of
Rome, Independents, Baptists, members of the Church of
Scotland, Seceders, Methodists, and every other denomination with which I am acquainted. If hon. Gentlemen are
disposed to impugn the character of those reverend individuals, they will be at the same time casting a reproach and a
stigma on the great body of dissenting Christians in this
country.

It may be thought that these reverend persons were travelling
out of their province. But when I heard these worthy men
telling their tales of saddening misery—when I heard them
state that members of their congregations would keep away
from their places of worship in the morning, and steal out
to the house of God at night, wrapped up in a cloak or an
outside coat, when a shade was thrown over their misery—
when I heard that others were unfitted to receive spiritual
consolation because of their being so plunged in physical
destitution; that the Sunday-schools were falling off, because
their congregations could not attend—when I heard these
things, and was further assured that the provisions monopoly
is at the bottom of all the misery under which these poor
people labour, I cannot conscientiously say that those ministers
were out of their place. When they who sit in high places
are oppressive and unjust to the poor, I am glad to see that
there are men amongst us who, like Nathan of old, can be
found to come forward and exclaim, 'Thou art the man!'
The religious people of the country have revolted against the
infamous injustice of that bread-tax, which is condemned by
the immutable morality of the Scriptures. They have prepared and signed a petition to this House, in which they
declare that these laws are a violation of the will of the
Supreme Being, whose providence watches over His famishing
children. You may rely upon it that the time abounds with

momentous signs. It is not those 650 ministers only, but
1,500 ministers of the Gospel, whose letters have been read at
the Manchester meeting, and who send up their prayers to
Heaven daily and hourly that it may be the will of Him who
rules both princes and potentates to turn their hearts to justice
and mercy.

And now, having told you what has been done by these
men, and in what spirit they have proceeded, we cannot for a
moment doubt that these men were in earnest; neither can
we doubt that these are men to make very efficient emissaries
in this great cause. Remember what has been done in the Anti-
Slavery question. Where is the difference between stealing a
man and making him labour, on the one hand, or robbing
voluntary labourers, on the other, of the fruits of their labour?
The noble Lord opposite (Lord Stanley) knows something of
the ability of these men to give efficacy to their strong convictions. When the noble Lord proposed his Emancipation
Bill in 1833, he broadly stated, that from the moment that
the religious community took up the question, from that
moment it was settled. I believe that the result will be the
same here.

Let me remind hon. Members of the qualities which pervade the minds of their countrymen. They have great
deference for power and rank, and respect for wealth—
perhaps too much; they have a most profound attachment
to the laws and institutions of the country. But it must be
remembered that there is another attribute peculiar to the
minds of Englishmen—a veneration for sacred things, far
beyond their deference to human authority. Once infringe
upon that, and their respect for you and yours will vanish
like chaff in the whirlwind. What must be the feeling of
the country when they find upon this occasion that the most
kind, and benevolent, and generous recommendation of her
Majesty, that you should take the Corn-laws into your wise
consideration, with a view to relieving the heavy burdens

under which her poor people suffer, of diminishing labour
and insufficient food—what will be said by the country at
large when they find this gracious recommendation from the
Crown scouted and scorned by the majority of this House?
What will be their feelings of indignation when they find a
question of this magnitude treated as of secondary importance
to the question whether a gentleman with a white hat, on
that side, or a gentleman with a black hat, on this side of the
House, shall hold the patronage of office? The people of
this country will regard the transaction—if Parliamentary
language will permit me to say so—as the most factious
proceeding which has ever characterised the conduct of this
House.

If I turn to a declaration made elsewhere—in a place
which, in conformity with the rules of the House, I will not
particularise—when I find an illustrious Duke stating that
the condition of the labouring population in this country is
enviable compared with that of any other population in
Europe, and that every labouring man in this country, who
has industry and sobriety to recommend him, can attain to a
competence—what, I ask, will be the feelings of the country
at large upon hearing such a declaration? Are hon. Gentlemen disposed to respond to that sentiment, and accept it as
their own? Let them remember that about ten years since
the same illustrious individual stated that the old borough-
mongering Parliament, under which we then suffered, was the
perfection of human wisdom. Yes; and I shall not be surprised if this doctrine of yesterday, meeting a similar and
still more remarkable fate, may be the forerunner of a far
greater change than that contemplated by her Majesty's
Ministers.

Let me, before I sit down, say one word to the right hon.
Baronet (Sir R. Peel) opposite. I have heard some allusions
made here to the opinions of Mr. Huskisson. The right
hon. Baronet the Member for Tamworth is fond of appearing

under the sanction of that distinguished statesman. I am most
anxious that he should not fall into the error of appearing in his
cast-off garments, and fancying himself arrayed in his mantle
—that when he gives us the last will and testament of that
distinguished statesman, he should know that an important
codicil was added to that will, which I will now present him.
I heard Mr. Huskisson's opinion in 1828 quoted. It is
deeply to be lamented that after that period he sanctioned, by
joining the Duke of Wellington's Administration, a line of
policy to which he had strongly objected. But when he
spoke last in the House on the subject of the Corn-laws, on
the 25th of March, 1830, upon the occasion of Mr. Poulett
Thomson's motion on the subject, Mr. Huskisson gave his
opinion in these terms:—' It is my distinct conviction that
we cannot maintain the present Corn-laws, and at the same
time maintain the permanent prosperity and prevalent contentment of the country. That those laws may be repealed
without injury to our landed interests is my firm belief.'
Here is the last codicil to the will of Huskisson. I protest
in his name, in many respects illustrious, though not of
uniform brightness, against the misrepresentation of his
opinion. When Mr. Huskisson spoke in 1830—and I would
strongly recommend the whole of that speech to hon.
Members' attentive perusal—there was by no means the
same amount of distress prevalent as that from which the
country is now suffering, nor was there anything like the
same gloom in her prospects. But if Mr. Huskisson spoke
so despondingly then, what would he have said had he
lived in 1841, and seen the accumulated difficulties under
which the country now labours,—if, instead of the Bank of
England, with 10,000,000l. or 12,000,000l. of treasure, and
money in abundance at 3 per cent., he saw scarcely half that
amount of treasure, and the interest raised to 5 per cent.?
What would have been his opinion of the Corn-laws, had he
lived to see all those things accomplished? I am earnestly

impressed by a desire to record his solemn conviction on this
subject.

The right hon. Baronet opposite possesses at this moment
the power to do immense service to his country. Let the
right hon. Baronet refer back to 1830, and consider what
were then the circumstances of the country, compared with
what they are now. What is the cause of our elevation from
that prostration to which the country had fallen in 1830?
It was clearly not a natural or legitimate trade which then
sprung up. From 1831 to 1836 the increase of our exports,
compared with our imports, amounted to 20,000,000*l.* official
value. But all these goods were sent to America, where they
were neither sold nor consumed, but despatched in exchange
for bank and railway shares, and State bonds. That is not
legitimate trade; it is over-speculation; the goods are not
paid for.

It should be borne in mind, too, that from the period of
1831 to 1836 there was an extension of the banking system
in this country, increasing the number of banks by nearly
100, and extending their capital by nearly 60,000,000*l.* The
increase of the export and home trade thus factitiously
created, accompanied with a fortuitous series of unexampled
harvests, created a state of prosperity which enabled the
Government of the day to move tranquilly on in carrying
the Reform Bill and amending the Poor-law; but it was a
fictitious prosperity.

Has the right hon. Baronet, then, any plan—I will not
ask him to divulge it at present—but has he any plan by
which, in 1841, he can raise up a real prosperity in the
country? If not, can he hope even to raise up a factitious
prosperity? If so, it will only lead to a recoil which will be
infinitely more disastrous than that under which we are now
suffering.

Thank God, Ministers in this country require money, and
glad I am that they cannot get it but through the prosperity of

the trading and manufacturing interests. The landholder who spends his money in Paris or Naples cannot find revenue for the Minister. The revenue flourishes when the trading and commercial community are prosperous, and when the farmers are crying out under excessive distress; and, on the other hand, just in proportion as the landowner feels prosperous on account of the starvation of the millions, the revenue of the State falls off.

Having made these few remarks, though not, I must be allowed to say, in a party spirit (for I call myself neither Whig nor Tory; I am a free-trader, and such I shall always be ready to avow myself), I have only, in conclusion, to observe, that while I am proud to acknowledge the virtue of the Whig Ministry in coming out from the ranks of the monopolists, and advancing three parts out of four towards my own position, yet, if the right hon. Baronet opposite advances one step farther, I will be the first to meet half way and shake hands with him.

FREE TRADE.

II.

CORN-LAWS.—MR. VILLIERS' ANNUAL MOTION.

HOUSE OF COMMONS, FEBRUARY 24, 1842.

[On Feb. 18, 1842, Mr. Villiers proposed his annual motion, to the effect,
'that all duties payable on the importation of corn, grain, meal, and flour,
do now cease and determine.' After five days' debate, the motion was negatived by a majority of 303 (393 to 90), on Feb. 24. Mr. Cobden was one of
the tellers. The majority of the Conservative party voted or paired; but 108
of the Opposition were absent. On the last day of the debate, Mr. Ferrand,
Member for Knaresborough, made a violent personal attack on Mr. Cobden.
In explanation, Mr. Cobden stated, once for all, that he intended never to
be driven into personal altercation with any Member of the House. He
was advised by Mr. Byng, then the senior Member of the House, to be
utterly indifferent to Mr. Ferrand's personalities. Shortly after the rejection of Mr. Villiers' motion, Sir R. Peel made certain alterations in the
sliding-scale, the maximum duties on wheat, barley, rye, oats, pease, and
beans, from foreign countries, being 20s., 11s., 11s. 6d., 8s., and 11s. 6d.
the quarter, and from British colonies, 5s., 2s. 6d., 3s., 2s., and 3s.; a
shilling duty being payable when wheat rose to 73s., barley to 37s., oats to
27s., rye, pease, and beans, to 42s., if the corn was of foreign origin, while,
if colonial corn were imported, the shilling duty commenced on wheat at
58s., and a 6d. duty on barley at 31s., oats at 33s., rye, pease, and beans at
34s. Similar duties were to be levied on meal and flour.]

IF the hon. Gentleman (Sir Howard Douglas) who has just
sat down will give the House another promise, that when he
speaks he will always speak to the subject, the House will
have a more satisfactory prospect of his future addresses. I
have sat here seven nights, listening to the discussion on
what should have been the question of the Corn-laws, and

I must say that I think my hon. Friend the Member for Wolverhampton (Mr. C. Villiers) has just grounds for complaint, that in all those seven nights scarcely two hours have been given to the subject of the bread-tax. Our trade with China, the war in Syria, the bandying of compliments between parties and partisans, have occupied our attention much and often, but very little has been said on the question really before the House. I may venture to say that not one speaker on the other side of the House has yet grappled with the question so ably propounded by my hon. Friend, which is—How far, how just, how honest, and how expedient it was to have any tax whatever laid upon the food of the people? That is the question to be decided; and when I heard the right hon. Baronet (Sir R. Peel) so openly express his sympathy for the working classes of this country, I expected that the right hon. Baronet would not have finished his last speech on this question without at least giving some little consideration to the claims of the working man in connection with the Corn-laws.

To this view of the subject I will therefore proceed to call the attention of the Committee; and I call upon hon. Gentlemen to meet me upon neutral ground in discussing the question in connection with the interests of those working classes, who have no representatives in this House. While I hear herein strong expressions of sympathy for those who have become paupers, I will ask hon. Gentlemen to give some attention to the case of the hard-working man before he reaches that state of abject pauperism in which he can only receive sympathy. In reading the debates upon the passing of the first stringent Corn-law of 1814, I am much struck to find that all parties who took part in that discussion were agreed upon one point,—it was that the price of food regulated the rate of wages. That principle was laid down, not by one side of the House, but by men of no mean eminence on each side, and of course of opposite opinions in other respects.

Mr. Homer and Mr. Baring, Mr. F. Lewis, the present Lord
Western, Mr. (now Sir) G. Philips, were all agreed on that
head, though some advocated and others opposed the measure.
One of the speakers, indeed, went so far as to make a laboured
computation to show the exact proportion which the price of
food would bear to the rate of wages. The same delusion
existed out of doors too. A petition was presented to the
House in 1815, signed by the most intelligent of the manufacturing and working classes, praying that the Corn Bill
might not be passed, because it would so raise the rate of
wages, that the manufacturers of this country would not be
able to compete with the manufacturers abroad. In reading
the debates of that date, I have been filled with the deepest
sorrow to find how those who passed that measure were
deluded. But I believe that they were labouring under an
honest delusion. I firmly believe, that if they had been
cognisant of the facts now before the House, they would
never have passed that Corn Bill. Every party in the House
was then deluded; but there was one party, that most interested, the working classes, who were not deluded. The
great multitude of the nation, without the aid of learning,
said—with that intuitive and instructive sagacity which had
given rise to the adage, 'The voice of the people is the voice
of God'—what the effect of the measure would be upon
wages, and therefore it was, that when that law was passed
this House was surrounded by the multitudes of London,
whom you were compelled to keep from your doors by the
point of the bayonet. Yes, and no sooner was the law passed
than there arose disturbances and tumults everywhere, and
in London bloodshed and murder ensued; for a coroner's jury
returned a verdict of wilful murder against the soldiers who
were called out and fired upon the people. The same hostility
to the measure spread throughout the whole of the north of
England; so that then, from the year 1815 down to 1819,
when the memorable meeting was held at Peter's-field in

Manchester, there never was a great public meeting at which
there were not borne banners inscribed with the words 'No
Corn-laws.'

There was no mistake in the minds of the multitude then,
and let not hon. Gentlemen suppose that there is any now.
The people may not be crying out exclusively for the repeal
of the Corn-laws, because they have looked beyond that question, and have seen greater evils even than this, which they
wish to have remedied at the same time; and, now that the
cries for 'Universal Suffrage' and 'The Charter' are heard,
let not hon. Gentlemen deceive themselves by supposing that,
because the members of the Anti-Corn-law League have
sometimes found themselves getting into collision with the
Chartists, that therefore the Chartists, or the working men
generally, were favourable to the Corn-laws. If one thing is
more surprising than others in the facts which I have mentioned, it is to find in this House, where lecturers of all things
in the world are so much decried, the ignorance which prevails upon this question amongst hon. Members on the other
side of the House. [Oh! oh!] Yes, I have never seen their
ignorance equalled amongst any equal number of working
men in the north of England. Do you think that the fallacy
of 1815, which I heard put forth so boldly last week, that
wages rose and fell with the price of bread, can now prevail
in the minds of working men, after the experience of the last
three years? Has not the price of bread been higher during
that time than for any three consecutive years for the last
twenty years? And yet trade has suffered a greater decline
in every branch of industry than in any preceding three years.
Still there are hon. Gentlemen on the other side of the House,
with the Reports of Committees in existence and before them
proving all this, prepared to support a bill, which, in their
ignorance—for I cannot call it anything else—they believe
will keep up the price of labour.

I am told that the price of labour in other countries is so

low that we must keep up the price of bread here, to prevent
wages going down to the same level.   But I am prepared
to prove, from documents emanating from this House, that
labour is cheaper here than in other countries.   I bear a
sound of dissent; but I would ask those who dissent, do they
consider the quality of the labour?   By this test, which is
the only fair one, it will be proved that the labour of England
is the cheapest labour in the world.   The Committee on
machinery, last session but one, demonstrated that fact beyond all dispute.   They reported that labour on the Continent
was actually dearer than in England in every branch of
industry.   Spinners, manufacturers, machine-makers, all
agreed that one Englishman on the Continent was worth
three native workmen, whether in Germany, France, or
Belgium.   If they are not, would Englishmen be found in
every large town on the Continent?   Let us go to any populous place, from Calais to Vienna, and we should not visit
any city with 10,000 inhabitants without finding Englishmen who are earning thrice the wages the natives earn,
and yet their employers declare that they are the cheapest
labourers.   Yet we are told that the object of the repeal of the
Corn-laws is to lower wages here to the level of continental
wages.

Have low wages ever proved the prosperity of our manufactures?   In every period when wages have dropped, it has
been found that the manufacturing interest dropped also;
and I hope that the manufacturers will have credit for taking
a rather more enlightened view of their own interest than to
conclude that the impoverishment of the multitude, who are
the great consumers of all that they produce, could ever tend
to promote the prosperity of our manufacturers.   I will tell
the House, that by deteriorating that population, of which
they ought to be so proud, they will run the risk of spoiling
not merely the animal but the intellectual creature, and that
it is not a potato-fed race that will ever lead the way in arts,

arms, or commerce. To have a useful and a prosperous people, we must take care that they are well fed.

But to come to the assumption that the manufacturers do want to reduce the rate of wages, and that the Corn-law will keep them up, we are still going to pass a law which will tax the food of our industrious and hard-working people; and what must be the result? The right hon. Baronet, in answer to a fallacy so often uttered on the other side of the House, said, 'We do now compete with the foreigner: we export to the extent of 40,000,000*l*. or 50,000,000*l*. a year.' That is true; but how? By taxing the bones and muscles of the people to double the amount of good supposed to be done to them by the Corn-laws. A double weight being put upon them, they are told to run a race with the labourers of Germany and France. We exult in a people who can labour so; but I would ask, with Mr. Deacon Hume, Whose are the energies which belonged to the British people, their own property or that of others? Think you, that for giving them an opportunity merely to strive and struggle for an existence, you may take one-half of what they earn? Is that doing justice to the high-mettled racer? You do not treat your horses so; you give them food, at all events, in proportion to their strength and their toil. But Englishmen, actually, are worse treated; tens of thousands of them were last winter worse off than your dogs and your horses.

Well, what is the pretence upon which you propose to tax them? We have been told by the right hon. Gentleman that his object is to fix a certain price for corn; and hearing that proposition from a Prime Minister, and listening to the debates, I have been almost led to believe that we are gone back to the times of the Edwards, when Parliament was engaged in fixing the price of a table-cloth, or a napkin, or a pair of shoes. But is this House a corn-market? Is not your present occupation better fitted for the merchant and the exchange? We do not act in this way with respect to cotton,

or iron, or copper, or tin. But how are we to fix the price of
corn ? The right hon. Baronet, taking the average of ten
years at 56s. 10d., proposes to keep the price of wheat at
from 54s. to 58s. Now Lord Willoughby D'Eresby will not
be content with less than 58s. Some hon. Members opposite
are for the same price at the lowest ; and I see by the
newspapers that the Duke of Buckingham, at a meeting of
farmers held at Aylesbury on the preceding day, said the
price ought to be 60s. But there is one hon. Gentleman,
whom I hope I shall have the pleasure to hear by-and-
by go more into detail as to the market price which he
intends to secure for his commodity in the market. I see in
that little but very useful book, the *Parliamentary Companion*,
which contains most accurate information, and in which some
of the Members of this House give very nice descriptions of
themselves, under the head of Mr. Cayley, M.P. for North
Yorkshire (p. 134), the following entry :—' Is an advocate for
such a course of legislation, with regard to agriculture, as will
keep wheat at 64s. per quarter, new milk cheese at from 52s.
to 60s. per cwt., wool and butter at 1s. per lb. each, and other
produce in proportion.'

Now it is all very amusing, exceedingly amusing, to find still
that there are gentlemen, at large, too, who will argue that
Parliament should interpose and fix the price at which they
should sell their own goods. That is very amusing indeed ;
but when we find the Prime Minister of this great country
coming down to Parliament and avowing such a principle, it
becomes anything but amusing. I will ask the right hon.
Baronet, is he prepared to carry out this principle in respect
to cotton and wool? I pause for a reply.

[Sir R. Peel : ' I have said that it was impossible to fix the
price of food by any legislative enactment.']

Then upon what are we now legislating? I thank the
right hon. Baronet for that avowal. Will he oblige me still
further by not trying to do it ? But supposing he will try,

all I ask of him is—and again I shall pause for a reply—will
he try to legislate to keep up the price of cottons, woollens,
silks, and such like goods? There is no reply. Then we
have come to this, that we are not legislating for the universal people. Here is the simple, open, avowal, that we are
met here to legislate for a class against the people. I do not
marvel, therefore, though I have seen it with the deepest
regret and indignation, that the House has been surrounded
during this debate by an immense body of the police force.
(A laugh.) I cannot let this subject drop with a laugh. It
is no laughing business to those who have no wheat to sell, and
no money to purchase food to sustain life.

I will refer the House to the great fall in the price of
cotton. At this day, in Manchester, the price of that article
is 30 per cent. less than it was ten years back. It is the
same with respect to ironmongery. During the average of the
last ten years it has also fallen 30 per cent., and yet with this
great reduction of price the man engaged as an ironmonger
is to take his goods and to exchange them with the agriculturist for the produce of the land at the present high price
of corn. Is this fair and reasonable? Can it be called legislation at all? Sure I am that it is not honest legislation. It
is no answer to this argument, if the Prime Minister of this
country comes forward and declares that he has not the power
to obviate this evil; yet it is not too much to assert that
the man placed in that high and responsible situation should
stop forward to stay the progress of such unjust and partial
legislation.

I have only yet touched the skirts of the question. I
would remind the House that it will not be a laughing
question before it is settled. I would ask the right
hon. Baronet whether, whilst fixing the scale of prices for
wheat, he intends to introduce to the House a sliding scale
for wages as well? I know only one class of the community whose wages are secured by the sliding scale, and

those are the clergy of this country. I would ask what
is to be done with the artisan? I know that I shall be
told that a resolution has been passed declaring that the
scale of wages cannot be kept up. I am well acquainted
with the answer which the poor distressed hand-loom
weavers got when they addressed the House and claimed
its protection. They were told that the House had been
studying political economy, and that the weavers had entirely
mistaken their position, and that their wages could not be
maintained up to a certain price. That was the answer which
those poor men received. Why, I will ask, should a law be
passed to keep up the price of wheat, whilst you admit that
wages cannot be also sustained at a certain price? It is not
complicated statistics, learned references to authorities, or
figures nicely dovetailed, that will satisfy the starving people
of this country, and convince them that a band of dishonest
confederates had not been leagued together for the purpose of
upholding the interests of one body against the general good
of the country.

We have been told that the land of this country is subjected to peculiarly heavy burdens. But what is the nature
of those burdens? A facetious gentleman near me has
attempted an explanation of this matter, and has declared
that ' the heavy burdens ' meant only heavy mortgages. The
country has a right to expect that the right hon. Baronet
will inform the House what those burdens are to which the
landed interest is exposed. When questioned on this point,
the right hon. Baronet states that there exist a variety of
opinions on the subject; and that is the only explanation
that can be obtained. I boldly declare that for every
one burden imposed on the land I am able to show ten
exemptions.

I will refer to the speech of the hon. Member for Renfrew-
shire (Mr. Stewart). He complained of the delay which had
occurred in obtaining a return moved for some time back

with reference to the land-tax to which the land abroad was
subjected. I should like to know why our Consuls abroad
have not made some official return on the subject. They
surely might have forwarded the Government the desired
information. Being without any official intelligence on this
point, it will not be in my power to give the House any
explicit information on the subject. With reference to the
land-tax in France, it has been stated by M. Humann, in the
Chamber of Deputies, that the land-tax paid in France was 25
per cent. upon the value of the soil, and equal to 40 per cent.
of the whole revenue of the country. In this country the
land-tax amounts to 1,900,000l., and the value of the landed
property, as stated by one of your own men, Mr. Macqueen,
was about 230,000,000l. This tax is but a mere fraction
compared to the duty levied in this country on the poor man's
tobacco. I think that if the right hon. Baronet does not
soon propound his views on this subject to the House, he will
be treating them with great disrespect.

I look back to the past debate with feelings not altogether
devoid of satisfaction. Many important admissions have been
made. I never heard it admitted, until the right hon. Baronet
made the admission, that the tax upon food actually contri-
butes to the revenue of the proprietors of the land. What
are the peculiar burdens imposed on land which led to the
introduction of the present tax on corn? I have a right to
demand an answer on this point. The only plea for levying
such a tax is to benefit one class of society.

It has been admitted by the head of the Government that
this country never can be entirely independent of the foreign
grower of corn; that our state was a kind of supplementary
dependence; that in some years we must look abroad for a
supply of food, and that this is when we want it. I perfectly
agree with the right hon. Baronet, that corn ought only to be
admitted free of all restrictions when it is 'wanted.' That is,
the particular moment or crisis when it is desirable to open

our ports for the admission of foreign corn. But I would
ask the House and the Government of the country, who are to
decide when the corn is wanted? Is it those who need food
and are starving, or those who fare sumptuously every day
and roll in all the luxuries of life? What right has the right
hon. Baronet to attempt to gauge the appetite of the people?
It is an inordinate assumption of power to do so. Such a
thing cannot be tolerated under the most monstrous system
of despotism which the imagination of man has ever conceived. Do we sit here for the purpose of deciding when the
people of this country want food? What do the Members of
this House know of want? It is not for them to say when
the starving people of this country ought to have food doled
out to them. The people are the best judges upon that
point.

The right hon. Baronet has been guilty of having made
contradictory statements with reference to the condition of the
hand-loom weavers. What is the state of the poor in Ireland?
I refer to the work of Mr. Inglis. That gentleman declared,
at the conclusion of his publication, that one-third of the
people of Ireland are perishing for want of the common
necessaries of life.

I have heard other admissions during the debate, some of a
very startling character, with reference to which I will make
an observation. It has been affirmed by the right hon.
Baronet the Paymaster of the Forces (Sir E. Knatchbull),
that a tax upon corn is necessary in order to enable the
landed interest to maintain their rank in society. I do
not think that the noble Lord (Stanley) who sits near the
right hon. Baronet the Paymaster of the Forces, is dealing
fairly by the people of England. It was very justly observed some years ago by the *Times* newspaper, that the
Corn-laws were nothing but an extension of the Pension
List; but it might have been added that it was also an
extension of a system of pauperism to the whole of the

landed aristocracy. If this country is to be ground down by an oligarchy, we had better at once adopt the system pursued in ancient Venice, where the nobles entered their names in the Golden Book, and took the money directly out of the people's pockets. It would be more honest to imitate those nobles openly, than do so in a covert manner. But one class will not submit to be heavily taxed, whilst the other lives in opulence and splendour.

The right hon. Baronet is not ignorant of the state of the commercial and manufacturing interests of the country. He is not legislating in the dark. I will tell the right hon. Baronet, that bad as trade is now, it will soon be much worse. The Government must be aware that the measure proposed for the settlement of the Corn-law question will not extend the commerce of the country. The House has been told that the measure must be pushed forward without any delay, and this is the result of a communication which the right hon. Baronet has received from the corn-dealers. But I would ask, why there should not be corn-merchants as well as tea-merchants? Why should not the corn-merchant be able to bring back, in exchange for other commodities, a cargo of corn, as well as a cargo of sugar or of tea? If something is not done, we shall see our large capitalists struggling against bankruptcy. In the last speech which the right hon. Baronet addressed to the House, he adopted an apologetic tone of reasoning. An excuse might be offered for the right hon. Baronet if he had been placed in his present position by the people, or by the Queen; but he has placed himself in his present situation.

With reference to the proposition of the noble Lord (J. Russell) the Member for the City of London, I must say that, although it is not good, it is infinitely better than the measure submitted to the House by the hon. Gentleman opposite. The right hon. Baronet has been reconstructing his party ever since the carrying of the Reform Bill. He must know that

his party is composed of monopolists in corn, tea, sugar,
timber, coffee, and the franchise. Out of that band of monopolists the right hon. Baronet has formed the party which
supported him, and which formed his Government. They
bribed, they intimidated, until they got possession of office.

I will say a word to the noble Lord and his right hon.
associates on this (the Opposition) side of the House, who,
whilst advocating generally Free-trade principles, have manifested a squeamishness in supporting the motion for a total
and immediate repeal of the Corn-laws. With all deference
to them, that shows too great sympathy with the few, and
too little with the many who are suffering. I would ask
them, if they had had the power of rescinding the Corn-law
Bill by their votes in 1815, would they then have talked of
compensation, or of a nine or ten years' diminishing duty?
No, they would not. Why then, I would ask, do they now
think that twenty-seven years' unjust enjoyment entitles them
to an increased benefit in the shape of compensation? I have
frequently known the difficulty met before. I give hon.
Gentlemen and noble Lords on my side of the House full
credit for sincerity, but, for their benefit, I will state the
answer I once heard given to the difficulty on the hustings,
an answer which was most satisfactory to my mind. On the
hustings, there was a great difficulty amongst Whiggish
gentlemen. They were arguing on the danger and hardship
which might follow the immediate repeal of the Corn-law,
when a poor man in a fustian jacket said, 'Why, mon, they
put in on all of a ruck.*' I may explain, for the benefit of
those unacquainted with the Lancashire dialect, that the
meaning was, all at once; and so the Corn-laws were. They
were put on in 1815 at once, and against the remonstrances
of the people. Let them, then, abolish the law with as little
ceremony.

---

* 'Ruck,' in the Lancashire dialect, means 'heap'; they put it on all in a
heap, or all at once.

I will not further detain the House.   The question resolves itself into a very narrow compass.   If you find that there are exclusive burdens on the land, do not put a tax upon the bread of the people, but remove the burdens.   If you are not prepared to ameliorate the condition of the people, beware of your own position—nay, you must take care that even this House may not fall under the heap of obloquy which the injustice you are perpetuating will thrust upon you.

FREE TRADE.

III.

DISTRESS OF THE COUNTRY.

HOUSE OF COMMONS, FEBRUARY 17, 1843.

[The Queen's Speech, read Feb. 2, 1843, 'regretted the diminished receipt from some of the ordinary sources of revenue, and feared that it must be in part attributed to the reduced consumption of many articles, caused by the depression of the manufacturing industry of the country which has so long prevailed.' On this statement Lord Howick moved, on Feb. 13, that the House be resolved into a Committee of the whole House, to consider this part of the Speech. Lord Howick's motion was rejected by 115 votes (306 to 191). The peculiarity of the debate, however, was, that Sir Robert Peel imagined that Mr. Cobden had charged him with being personally responsible for the distress of the country. Sir Robert Peel had been greatly affected by the murder of his private secretary in the preceding month (Jan. 14), who was shot by one Macnaghten. It was believed that the secretary was shot by mistake for the Minister. Mr. Cobden disclaimed using the term 'individually or personally responsible' in any other sense than that of Ministerial responsibility. It should be added that the allusion to 'an eminent and learned Lord,' is to Lord Brougham, who insinuated that the attempt of Macnaghten was stimulated by the language of the League. His words were 'that ministers of religion did not scruple to utter words—calculated to produce fatal effects (he would not say had produced them), but calculated to produce the taking away of innocent life.']

We have heard much objection made to the form of this motion. We have heard it charged as being a party motion. Now, Sir, I can, at all events, say it is not a party motion as far as I am concerned. I was absent from town when it was

put on the books. I am no party man in this matter in any
degree; and if I have any objection to the motion it is this,
that whereas it is a motion to inquire into the manufacturing
distress of the country, it should have been a motion to inquire into manufacturing and agricultural distress. If the
motion had been so framed, we should not have had the
words 'manufactures' and 'agriculture' bandied between the
two sides of the House, but we should have had the Gentlemen
on the other side of the House put in their proper position as
defendants, to justify the operation of the law as it affects
their own immediate interests.

I ask you, are the agricultural districts of the country in
such a state now, that you are entitled to say that this law—for
this has been made a Corn-law debate—that this law, which injures the manufacturers, has benefited the agriculturists? There
is the hon. Member for Dorsetshire (Mr. Bankes), one of the
most clamorous assailants of the Anti-Corn-law League, he
will probably speak on this question—there is plenty of time,
the debate may be adjourned, if necessary—and when he speaks
he can answer me, and correct me if I am wrong. Take the district of Dorsetshire which the hon. Gentleman represents. Take
his own property. I ask him, are the labourers on his estates
receiving more than the miserable pittance of 8*s.* a week at
this moment? I ask him to contradict me, if he can, when
I state that the labourers in his neighbourhood are the worst
paid, the worst clad, and the most illiterate portion of the
population of this country. I tell him that the peasantry on
his own estates, earning these 8*s.* a week, if their families
average the usual number of five, that then the head of each
of these families is sustained at less cost than the cost of the
maintenance of each person in the county gaol of Dorsetshire, and I ask you—you with your peasantry at your own
doors, living worse than paupers and felons—I ask you, are
you entitled to assert, and will you maintain, that the present
state of things is for the benefit of the agriculturists? I put

you on your defence—I call on you to prove the benefit which
this law confers on the agriculturists. Mind, I do not call you
agriculturists. The landlords are not agriculturists; that is
an abuse of terms which has been too long tolerated. The
agriculturists are they who cultivate the land, who work at
it either with their hands or their heads, and employ their
capital on it; you are the owners of the land, who may be
living at London or Paris : to call yourselves agriculturists is
just as absurd as if shipowners were to call themselves sailors.
I deal with the agriculturists, and not with the landowners—
not with the rent-owners; and I tell you that you cannot
show me that the labouring classes on farms are as well off as
the much-deplored manufacturing population.

I myself employ a number of men ; my concern is in the
country, like your own. I have a number of labourers like
yours ; unskilled labourers, as unskilled as your own. I employ them in washing, cleansing, wheeling, and preparing
materials, and I pay them 12*s*. a week ; but I have no protection. Take Devonshire, Sussex, Wiltshire, Oxfordshire,
and other agricultural counties, which send up their squires
to this House to support this odious system, and any of these
counties will show you a larger ratio of paupers than the
manufacturing districts. Take Dorset ; there has just been
laid on the table of the House a Return of the population and
revenue, and here we find, that in the year 1840, the very
year in which we were blessed with wheat at 66*s*. a quarter,
one out of every seven of the population in Dorsetshire was a
pauper. And if we go to Sussex and the rest of the counties
which send representatives to support this system for the
benefit of the agriculturists, there we shall invariably find the
largest amount of pauperism.

I will turn to the farmers. The hon. Gentleman, and other
hon. Gentlemen, are pleased to designate me as the arch
enemy of the farmers. Sir, I have as good a right as any
hon. Gentleman in this House to identify myself with the

order of farmers. I am a farmer's son. The hon. Member
for Sussex has been speaking to you as the farmers' friend; I
am the son of a Sussex farmer; my ancestors were all yeomen
of the class who have been suffering under this system; my
family suffered under it, and I have therefore as good or a
better right than any of you to stand up as the farmer's
friend, and to represent his wrongs in this House. Now, I ask
you, what benefits have the farmers had from this protection
of which you speak so much? I put you on your defence,
and I again call on you to show how the farmers can possibly
derive higher profits from your law to enhance the price of the
produce of the soil of this land? You must answer this
question; this has not been shown yet at any of your agricultural meetings, where you tell the farmers that you must sink
or swim together, and that you both row in the same boat.
But the time is coming, and on the next quarter-day you
will be called upon to show the farmer—upon whom some
little enlightenment is now creeping—to show how he hitherto
has gained, or can gain, any benefit from this legislation.
You will have to answer this question from the intelligent
farmer :—

'If there be more farmers than farms, then will not the competition amongst
us for your farms raise the rent of land ? and will there not be a proportionate
value of the produce to whatever value you may give it in your Acts of
Parliament !'

The same intelligent farmer may tell you:—

'If there were more farms than farmers, and if you raised the value of your
produce, you would be bidding against each other for farmers, and then I
could understand how the farmers could get some benefit in the shape of
extra profit, for you would be compelled to pay them better for cultivating
your farms.'

Now all this has been made as clear as noon-day.

The hon. Member for Dorsetshire has maligned the Anti-
Corn-law League, as an association for disseminating, not
useful but disagreeable knowledge. Every farmer in Dorset-

shire has had a packet; every county voter of Dorsetshire
has received a packet, containing about a dozen little tracts.
This has not been left to casual distribution; it has not even
been entrusted to the Post-office; but special agents have
gone from door to door, climbing the mountains and pene-
trating the valleys. There is not a freeholder in the country
who does not know as much about the matter as we ourselves. Do you think we shall hear next year, at the agricultural meeting at Blandford, the hon. Member for Dorsetshire
telling his hearers that ' the Corn-law is the sun of our social
system; that it gilds the spire of the church, the dome of the
palace, and the thatch of the cottage '? There will be some
black sheep, who will shout out, ' and the chimney of the
landlord.' We have had during this debate a great deal of
criminating language cast at this body. Far be it from me
to enter into such extraneous matter as the objects and proceedings of that body. I shall not think it necessary to answer
the very amusing gossip in a stage coach which has been re-
lated to us. But attacks have been made upon this body at
other times. The right hon. Baronet (Sir R. Peel) made a
dark insinuation against it at the close of last session, when
there was no one to answer it; and we have had the cry raised
since, ' that the Anti-Corn-law League is an incendiary and
revolutionary body.' We took no pains to refute that charge.
How have the public treated your accusations? The shrewd
and sagacious people of England and Scotland have given bail
for the morality and good conduct of the maligned body to
the amount of 50,000*l.*; and let the same slander go forth
another year, and I am sure that the people will then enter
into recognizances for the same body to the extent of 100,000*l.*
No, it is not necessary that I should enter into the defence of
such a body.

There has been an attempt, an alleged attempt, made to
identify the members of this body with a most odious—a most
horrible—I might say, a most maniacal transaction which has

lately occurred. An attempt has been made in another place
—reported to have been made—to suggest that the proceedings
of the League were to be connected with that horrible transaction. I do not—I cannot—believe that this report is a correct one; I cannot believe that either the language or the spirit
of the remarks attributed to an eminent and a learned Lord
(Brougham) are founded on anything that really took place. If
they were uttered, I can only attribute them to the ebullition of
an ill-regulated intellect, not to a malicious spirit. This trick
of charging the consequence of injustice upon the victims of
injustice is as old as injustice itself. Who does not remember
that, when this infamous law was enacted in 1815, Mr. Baring,
now Lord Ashburton, was charged, in this House, by one of
the Ministers of the day, with having caused all the riots,
murders, and bloodshed which ensued in the metropolis,
merely because he had been one of the most pertinacious
opponents of the law, denounced it in the House as a mere
scheme to raise rents at the expense of the commercial classes,
and the welfare of the community. Sir, if there be anything
which can add to the gratification I feel at having taken an
active part in this body, it is the high character of those
with whom I have been associated. Yes, tested by their
utility, tested by their public character and private worth,
they might justly be compared to the Members of this House,
or of another more illustrious assembly. But enough of this
subject.

I will now turn my attention to the question before the
House. Last session the Anti-Corn-law party put the
question, What was to be done for the country? That is
the question I now put. I say to the Government—I say
to the right hon. Gentleman opposite—What do you now
think of the condition of our trade, and the condition of the
country? I gather from what has fallen from hon. Members
on the other side, that this motion is to be resisted. The
motion is to be resisted; but what are the reasons for resisting

it? How is the question met by the Government? It is alleged that there is a great discrepancy of opinion on this side of the House. I admit it. There is such a discrepancy between some Gentlemen on this side and myself, between the noble Lord (Worsley), the Member for North Lincolnshire, and myself; there is as great a difference of opinion as between me and the Gentlemen on the other side. The party on our side is as the hon. Gentleman opposite described it—it is broken into atoms, and may never be reunited. But does that diminish the responsibility of the Government, which is strong in proportion as the Opposition is weak? Are we never to escape from this mode of evading responsibility—this bandying of accusations about Whigs, Tories, and Radicals, and their differences of opinion? Is that cry always to be repeated and relied on? How long, I ask, is this course to be continued? How long is the argument to be used? If it be continued, what defence will it be for the Government? There always have been differences of opinion on both sides of the House, but that can be no excuse for the right hon. Baronet at the head of the Government, who took the reins of power into his hands on the avowed responsibility of bringing forward measures to meet the exigencies of the moment. But there is not one measure of importance adopted by the Government which has not been taken out of the school of the Free-traders. The colleagues of the right hon. Baronet who have spoken on this occasion have introduced the Corn-laws into this debate, and have discussed that subject in connection with the present distress. But what says the right hon. Member the Vice-President of the Board of Trade (Mr. Gladstone)? Why, he says that there are not two opinions on the subject of free-trade. What says the right hon. Baronet (Sir R. Peel) at the head of the Government? Why, he says that on this point we are all agreed. And the right hon. Baronet the Secretary of the Home Department (Sir J. Graham) says that the principles of free-trade are

the principles of common sense. And last night, to my amazement, the Chancellor of the Exchequer (Mr. Goulburn) said,
there are not two opinions on the subject, and there never was
any dispute about it. The noble Lord the Member for North
Lancashire (Stanley), who has not yet spoken, will, I believe,
justify by his vote the same principles. Again, the right hon.
Gentleman the Paymaster of the Forces (Sir E. Knatchbull)
must adopt the same course. That right hon. Gentleman, and
that noble Lord, may not have avowed free-trade principles; but
they must, as men of morality, carry those principles into effect,
for both of them have averred that the Corn-laws raise rent.
The right hon. Gentleman the Paymaster of the Forces has
expressly declared in this House that the Corn-laws were
passed to maintain country gentlemen in their station in the
country. The noble Lord the Member for North Lancashire
has said that the Corn-laws raise the price of food, and that
they do not raise wages; the noble Lord, therefore, says that
the landed gentlemen increase their rents at the expense of
the profits of the middle classes. They must carry their principle into their conduct. Now, taking the four Members of
the Cabinet who have avowed free-trade principles, and assuming that the two others by their addresses must be favourable to them, I ask, why do they not carry their principles
into effect? How am I met? The right hon. Gentleman
the Vice-President of the Board of Trade admits the justice
of the principles of Free Trade. He says that he does not want
monopoly; but then he applies these just principles only in
the abstract. Now, I do not want abstractions. Every moment
that we pass here, which is not devoted to providing for the
welfare of the community, is lost time. I tell the hon. Member that I am a practical man. I am not an abstract Member, and I ask what we have here to do with abstractions?
The right hon. Gentleman is a free-trader only in the abstract.
We have nothing, I repeat, to do with abstractions here. The
right hon. Gentleman used another plea. He said that the

system has been continued for centuries, and cannot now be abandoned. If the Attorney-General be in the House (and I hope he is), what would he say to such a plea in an action of trover? Would he admit the plea? Would he say, ' I know that you have right and justice on your side in the abstract, but then the unjust possession has been for so long a time continued that it cannot be at once abandoned?' What would be the verdict in such a case? The verdict would not be an abstract verdict, but one of restitution, of total and immediate restitution. The right hon. Gentleman has made the admission that these principles must be carried out, and he says that the Corn-laws are temporary. I ask why the Corn-laws are temporary? Just laws are not temporary. It is the essence of just laws to be eternal. You have laws on your statute-book against murder and robbery, and no man says they should not be continued. Why, then, are the Corn-laws to be temporary? Because the Corn-laws are unjust; because they are neither right nor expedient. They were passed to give a benefit to the country gentlemen, and raise them in society at the expense of the rest of the community.

The hon. Member for Bridport (Mr. Baillie-Cochrane) made last night a declaration against the Anti-Corn-law League, but he pronounced it with such gentle accents, he put so much sweetness into his denunciation, that he deprived it of its effect. That hon. Member is a young man, and perhaps is not aware of the force of what he said. But that hon. Gentleman, too, made an admission which will not sustain your system. The hon. Member said, that if the Corn-laws were repealed, the aristocracy would be forced to reduce their rents, and could not live as an aristocracy. The Gentlemen who make those admissions are the real incendiaries, the real revolutionists, and the real destroyers of the aristocracy. I must put the honest part of the aristocracy on their guard against them, and must tell them not to allow themselves to be included with those who fear destruction from the repeal of the Corn-laws. They

must know that an aristocracy cannot maintain its station on
wealth moistened with the orphans' and the widows' tears,
and taken from the crust of the peasant. The question has
been brought before the country, and the decision must be
adverse to them. The people are well aware of their conduct.
They may talk about an increase of one or two mills, or of the
increase of joint-stock banks, but I call attention to the condition of the country, and I ask you if it is not worse now
than it was six months ago? It has been going on from bad
to worse. And what is the remedy you propose? what are
the proceedings by which you propose to give relief to the
country? Is it an abstraction? You cannot say that we are
at the close of the session, or that you are overloaded with
public and private business. Never before were there so few
measures of importance under the consideration of Parliament
at such a period. Have you devised some plan, then, of giving
relief to the country? If you have not, I tell you emphatically that you are violating your duty to your country; you
are neglecting your duty to your Sovereign if you continue
to hold office one moment after you can find no remedy for
the national distress. The right hon. Gentleman, however,
proposes nothing. The measures which he has brought forward since he has held office have not remedied the distress
of the country. It may be said of me, that I am a prophet
who fulfils his own prophecy; but I tell you your proceedings
will lead from bad to worse; that more confusion will come;
there are germs of it sown in the north of England. Yes, not
in the cotton district. The danger which menaces you will
come from the agricultural districts, for the next time there
is any outbreak, the destitute hands of the agricultural districts will be added to the destitute hands of the manufacturing districts.

Does the right hon. Gentleman, who must know the state
of the country, doubt whether this be the fact? I receive
correspondence from every part of the country—but what is

my correspondence to his?—and he must know that what I say is the fact. It is time, then, to give up bandying the terms 'Whig' and 'Tory' about from one side of the House to the other, and to engage in a serious inquiry into the present condition of the country. The right hon. Baronet cannot conceal from himself what is that condition: capital is melting away, pauperism is increasing, trade and manufactures are not reviving. What worse description can be given of our condition? and what can be expected, if such a state of things continues, but the disruption and dissolution of the State? When the agitation was begun for the repeal of the Corn-laws, four years ago, the right hon. Baronet met our complaints by entering into many details, showing that our commerce was increasing, that the savings'-banks were prospering, that the revenue was improving, and that consumption was augmenting. When a deputation of manufacturers waited upon him to represent the hopeless state of trade, he refused to listen to their representations, or he met them with details of an extraordinary increase in the consumption of the people and in the revenue, and with many official statements full of hope. I ask the right hon. Baronet, can he take the same ground now? Can he tell the country and his Sovereign when this state of things is likely to terminate; or what other remedy has he for this than that we propose? Can he find a better?

If you (Sir Robert Peel) try any other remedy than ours, what chance have you for mitigating the condition of the country? You took the Corn-laws into your own hands after a fashion of your own, and amended them according to your own views. You said that you were uninfluenced in what you did by any pressure from without on your judgment. You acted on your own judgment, and would follow no other, and you are responsible for the consequences of your act. You said that your object was to find more employment for the increasing population. Who so likely,

however, to tell you what markets could be extended as those
who are engaged in carrying on the trade and manufactures
of the country ? I will not say that the mercantile and
manufacturing body, as a whole, agree with me in my views
of the Corn-laws; but the right hon. Baronet must know
that all parties in the manufacturing and commercial districts
disapprove of his laws.   I do not speak of the League—I
speak of the great body of commercial men ; and I ask, where
will you find on any exchange in England, Scotland, or Ireland, where ' merchants do congregate,' and manufacturers
meet, twelve men favourable to the Corn-law which you
forced on the community, in obedience to your own judgment,
and contrary to ours? You passed the law, you refused to
listen to the manufacturers, and I throw on you all the responsibility of your own measure.   The law has not given the
promised extension to our trade : it has ruined the Corn-law
speculators. (A laugh.) You may laugh; but is it a triumph
to ruin the corn-dealers, or cause a loss of £2,000,000 of
money ? When you have ruined the corn speculators, who
will supply you with foreign wheat? The Corn-law is in
such a state that no regular merchant will engage in the
corn trade. Ask any merchant, and you will find that no
man, let his trade be what it will, sends abroad orders for
corn as he sends abroad orders for sugar and coffee. No merchant dares to engage in the corn trade. I was offered, or
rather the Anti-Corn-law League was offered, a contribution
of wheat from one of the Western States of America, on condition that we should pay the expense of transport down the
Mississippi. On calculating the cost of transport, we found it
would not pay the expense of carriage. On taking the 20s.
duty into consideration and the expense of carriage, we found
that when it was sold here there would not be one farthing
for the League ! When such is the case, how can such merchants as the Barings, or the Browns of Liverpool, send out
orders for corn, when there is no certainty whether they shall

have to pay 20s. duty, or any less sum, when it arrives? Such a law defies calculation, and puts an end to trade.

Take, again, the article sugar. The right hon. Gentleman by his tariff reduced the duties on 700 articles, and he carefully omitted those two articles which are supplied by North and South America, the only two countries the trade of which can resuscitate our present declining manufactures. Yes, the right hon. Baronet altered the duties on 700 articles. He took the duty off caviare and cassava powder, but he left corn and sugar oppressed with heavy monopoly duties. The right hon. Baronet reduced the charges on drugs, which was not unimportant, but ho excluded those two vital commodities which the merchants of the country know can alone supply any extension to our trade. I will not say that this was done with a design of injuring our trade, but it was done. The right hon. Baronet acted on his own judgment, and he retained the duty on the two articles on which a reduction of duty was desired, and he reduced the duties on those on which there was not a possibility of the change being of much service to the country. It was folly or ignorance. (Oh! oh!) Yes, it was folly or ignorance to amend our system of duties, and leave out of consideration sugar and corn. The reduction of the duties on drugs and such things was a proper task for some under-Secretary of State, dealing with the sweepings of office; but it was unworthy of any Minister, and was devoid of any plan. It was one of the least useful changes that ever was proposed by any Government. There is also the case of timber. I admit that the reduction of the duty on timber is a good thing; but you reduced the duty when there are 10,000 houses standing empty within a radius of twenty miles of Manchester, and when there are crowds of ships rotting in our ports. At the same time, you denied our merchants the means of traffic, by refusing to reduce the duties on the two most bulky articles which our ships carry. You reduced your timber duties when there were no factories to build, and when

there was no employment for ships. That is the scheme of the
right hon. Baronet—the only plan which he has to propose
for the benefit of the country. Can he not try some other
plan? Does he repudiate that which has been suggested by
the hon. Member for Whitehaven (Mr. Attwood)? and will he
have nothing to do with altering the currency, to which he
is invited by the hon. Member for Birmingham (Mr. Muntz)?
The hon. Member for Shrewsbury (Mr. Disraeli), too, and the
organs of his party in the press, have plans, but he will adopt
none of them. It is his duty, he says, to judge independently,
and act without reference to any pressure; and I must tell
the right hon. Baronet that it is the duty of every honest
and independent Member to hold him individually responsible
for the present position of the country.

I am not a party man. Hon. Members know that I am
not. But this I will tell the right hon. Baronet, that let
who will be in office, whether Whigs or Tories, I will not
sit in the House a day longer than I can, in what I believe
to be the interest of my constituents, not vote for or against
Whigs or Tories, as I may think right. I tell the right
hon. Gentleman that I, for one, care nothing for Whigs or
Tories. I have said that I never will help to bring back
the Whigs; but I tell him that the whole responsibility of
the lamentable and dangerous state of the country rests with
him. It ill becomes him to throw that responsibility on any
one at this side. I say there never has been violence, tumult,
or confusion, except at periods when there has been an excessive want of employment, and a scarcity of the necessaries
of life. The right hon. Baronet has the power in his hands
to do as he pleases. If he will not, he has the privilege,
which he told the noble Lord (Palmerston), the late Secretary for Foreign Affairs, he had, namely, that of resigning the
office which gives him the power. I say that this is his duty.
It is his duty to resign office the moment he finds he has not
power to carry out to the fullest extent those measures which

he believes to be for the benefit of the country. But whether
he does so or not, I have faith in the electoral body—I have
faith in the middle classes, backed by the more intelligent of
the working classes, and led by the more honest section of the
aristocracy—I have faith in the great body of the community
that they will force the Government, whether of the right
hon. Gentleman or of any other party, to the practical adoption of those principles which are now generally believed to
be essential to the welfare of this country. The right hon.
Gentleman has admitted the justice, the policy, and expediency of our principles. He has admitted, then, that they
must in the end be triumphant. I repeat, I trust in the
middle classes, in the electoral body, in the better portion of
the working classes, and in the honester part of the aristocracy, to force the right hon. Baronet, or his successors, to
put in practice those principles, the justice, policy, and rea-
sonableness of which he has himself admitted.

FREE TRADE.

IV.

HOUSE OF COMMONS, MAY 15, 1843.

[Spoken during the debate on Mr. Villiers' annual motion. After the discussion had been carried on for five nights, the motion was negatived by a majority of 156 votes (381 to 125).]

I THINK we may fairly consider the speech of the hon. Member for Birmingham (Mr. Muntz) as an episode in this debate. I was going to remark, that by hon. Gentlemen opposite, and by many upon this side of the House, although we have had five nights' debate, the question proposed by the hon. Member for Wolverhampton (Mr. Villiers) has been scarcely touched: that is, How far you are justified in maintaining a law which restricts the supply of food to be obtained by the people of this country.

In supporting the present Corn-law, you support a law which inflicts scarcity on the people. You do that, or you do nothing. You cannot operate in any way by this law, but by inflicting scarcity on the people. Entertain that proposition. In fact, you cannot escape it. And if it is true, how many of you will dare to vote for the continuance of the present law? You cannot enhance the price of corn, or of any other article, but by restricting the supply. Are you justified in doing this, for the purpose of raising your prices?

Without attributing motives to hon. Gentlemen opposite, I tell them (and they may rely upon it as being true) that they are in a false position when they have to deprecate the imputation of motives. We never hear of a just judge on the Bench fearing the imputation of motives. But I will not impute motives, although they have been imputed by hon. and right hon. Gentlemen opposite. Dowries, settlements, mortgages, have all been avowed as motives from the benches opposite; but I will take things as I find them. Upon what ground do you raise the price of corn? For the benefit of the agricultural interest. You have not, in the whole course of the debate, touched upon the farmers' or agricultural labourers' interest in this question. No; hon. Gentlemen opposite, who represent counties, instead of taking up the old theme, and showing the benefit of this law to farmers and to farmers' labourers, have been smitten with a new light. They have taken the statistics of commerce and the cotton trade to argue from. Will the hon. Member for Shoreham, who took the statistics which the right hon. Baronet (Sir R. Peel) four years ago cast aside, tell the House how it is you do not take the agricultural view of the question, and show the farmers' interest in it? There is something ominous in your course. Shall I tell you the reason? Because the present condition of the farmers and labourers of this country is the severest condemnation of the Corn-laws that can possibly be uttered. During the whole operation of this law, or during that time when prices were highest under this law, the condition of the agricultural labourers was at the worst. An hon. Gentleman opposite says 'No.' Has he looked at the state of pauperism of this country in the last Return which was laid before the House? There he will find, that up to Lady-day, 1840, the proportion of paupers in the different counties in this country, showed that the ten which stood highest in the list were ten

of the purely agricultural counties, and that after your law
had for three years maintained corn at 67s. per quarter. If
anything could have benefited the labourer, it should have been
three years of high prices, and after trade had suffered the
greatest depression in consequence of your law. If the agricultural labourer had not prospered up to the year 1840, what has
been his condition since? The returns of pauperism show
an increase in the number of the poor; and what is the present condition of the labourer in the agricultural districts?
Is not crime increasing in the same proportion as pauperism
has increased? I heard it stated that the actual returns of
your petty sessions and your assizes furnish no criterion as to
the state of demoralisation in your districts; nay, I heard
that such was the extent of petty pilfering and crime, that
you were obliged to wink at it, or you would not be able to
carry out the business of your criminal courts. I hear that
both in Somersetshire and in Wiltshire. Hon. Gentlemen
may cry 'No, no,' but there is an intelligent audience outside
which knows that I am stating the truth. And what are the
crimes these poor people are brought up for? Why, one old
woman for stealing sticks of the value of 1½d. was sentenced
to a fine of 15s. Another case was a charge for stealing
turnip-tops; and at Chichester an individual has been con-
victed of stealing mould from the Duke of Richmond. Such
is the state of poverty and distress, that they are glad to
steal the very earth. Again, what was the fact urged by the
hon. Member for Dorsetshire (Mr. Bankes), in extenuation of
the condition of his labouring poor, but this: that he allowed
them to gather up the sticks that were blown from the trees in
his park? It was brought forward as a proof of the hon.
Member's benevolence, that he allowed his labourers to gather
the crows' nests which were blown from the trees. And
what does all this argue? Why, it argues that which you
cannot deny, namely, that the agricultural peasantry of this
country are in a state of the deepest suffering at this moment,

and that, if there has been any benefit from the Corn-laws, they, at least, have not derived one particle of a share of it.

I now come to the farmer; and I ask how it is that you, who support this law, have not adduced the case of the farmer? Are there no farmer's friends present who will state his condition? You know that his capital is wasting away —that he cannot employ his labourers—and why? Because that money which should go to pay them is absorbed in your rents. Hon. Gentlemen opposite cry 'No, no;' but the farmers of this country will corroborate me, and that you well know. Does the hon. and gallant Member for Sussex (Col. Wyndham) say 'No'? If so, I leave the farmers of Sussex to say whether I am uttering the truth or not. The hon. and gallant Member tells me to go to Sussex. I mean to do so, and perhaps the hon. and gallant Member will meet me there. Now, I want to ask what benefit the farmer ever derived from the Corn-laws? I have asked the question of hundreds, nay, thousands of farmers; and, as I am now in the presence of landlords, I ask it of you. I ask you to go back to the Corn-law of 1815. What was the object of the Corn-law of 1815? Why, to keep up the price of wheat at 80s. per quarter. Did it ever produce that effect? No; for in 1822, seven years afterwards, wheat was sold as low as 42s.; and yet your agents and valuers valued to your tenants upon the calculation that they would get 80s. per quarter for their wheat. You cannot deny that. And what was the consequence? Why, in 1822, the farmers were ruined by hundreds and thousands. One newspaper in Norwich contained 120 advertisements of the sale of stock in one day. The farmers then came to ask you for another law. You appointed Committees, you went through the farce of inquiring into agricultural distress, and you passed another law, that of the year 1828, giving the sliding-scale protection, to secure them 64s. per quarter for their wheat; and then, again, the red-tape men went about to value your farms, on the calculation that the price obtained would be 64*s*. Another seven years elapsed, and then wheat was selling at 36*s*. Then came general distress again, and an application for a fresh Committee. You gave them another Act; and I now come to the Act passed in 1842 by the right hon. Baronet at the head of the Government; and now the farmers are again distressed, and blame the right hon. Baronet for deceiving them. They do blame, and they are justified in blaming the right hon. Baronet, and I will tell you why. The right hon. Baronet, in the speech in which he proposed that law, said that he intended it to give to the farmer, as far as legislation could give it, 56*s*. per quarter for his corn. Now, the right hon. Baronet will remember that I called his attention at the time to that point. I saw the importance of it then, and I see it now, and I wish the House to see clearly how the matter stands. The right hon. Baronet said, that on taking a comprehensive view of the cost of production and the then state of the country, he thought, if he could secure the farmer a price not rising higher than 58*s*., nor going lower than 54*s*., that these were about the prices the farmer ought to obtain. It is true that afterwards, in the course of the same speech, the right hon. Baronet said that no legislation could secure that price.

Now I do not charge the right hon. Baronet with intending to deceive the farmers; I do not attribute motives to the right hon. Baronet; but this I do say, that in dealing with plain and simple men—men accustomed to straightforward and intelligible language, this was certain, however intended, to mislead the farmers in their calculations. But it was a most convenient thing for the landlords to go to the tenant with a promise to secure him 56*s*. per quarter for his wheat, and it was very convenient for the right hon. Baronet to say, at the same time, that though the law purports to give you 56*s*. per quarter, still I have not the power to secure it to you. And now, what is the price? 45*s*. or 46*s*. instead of 56*s*.

The right hon. Baronet distinctly says now he never intended
to maintain the price, and that he could not maintain it.
Now, then, I ask, what is this legislation for? I ask what it
means?—what it has meant from 1815 downwards? I will
not say what the motives of its promoters have been; but
the effect has been one continued juggle played off upon the
farmers, in order to enable the landlords to obtain artificial
rents. These being paid out of the farmer's capital, loss falls
on him, while the landlords are enabled to profit by it, owing
to the competition among tenants for farms.

We will not separate this night until we have a perfect
understanding of what you do propose to do for the farmer.
I ask the right hon. Baronet opposite, when he talks of the
prices which the farmers should obtain, whether he can prevent wheat from falling as low as 36s.?—whether he can
ensure it from falling as low as 30s.? As the right hon.
Gentleman says nothing, I will assume that this House cannot
secure to the farmer a price of even 30s. per quarter. Let this
go forth; let there be, if you please, no ambiguity on the
point—no more deception; let the farmer perfectly understand
that his prosperity depends upon that of his customers—that
the insane policy of this House has been to ruin his customers,
and that Acts of Parliament to keep up prices are mere frauds
to put rents into the landlord's pockets, and enable him to
juggle his tenants. Now we shall soon be able to dispose of
some other sophistries upon the Corn-laws. We are told that
the Corn-laws are intended to compensate certain parties for
excessive burthens; that is to say, that the landowners, who
have had the absolute command of the legislature of the
country, and who, to a late period, did not permit a man to
vote in this House unless he swore he was a landowner, have
been such disinterested angels (for no human beings would do
as much) as to lay excessive burthens upon their own shoulders;
and when they find it necessary to readjust taxation and relieve
themselves, they do it by passing a Corn-law, and then come

forward and confess that the law is inoperative. Now, in the first place, I say that the disinterestedness of the landlords on this presumption surpasses all human perfection; it is perfectly angelical.

But, unfortunately, the contrary to the proposition of excessive burthens falling on land is so notorious, that to say a word upon the subject would be a work of supererogation. Let a copy of the statutes be sent, if it were possible, to another planet, without one word of comment, and the inhabitants of that sphere would at once say, 'These laws were passed by landlords.' The partiality of your legislation is notorious; but, if you had been really so disinterested, is it not likely, when you found out your real condition, that you would have put taxation fairly upon the shoulders of the people, instead of substituting a clumsy law, which you admit does not reimburse you at all?

Now we come to another view of this question. We have the confessions of the right hon. Baronet the Paymaster of the Forces (Sir E. Knatchbull), and of the hon. Member for Wiltshire (Mr. Bennett); the one to the effect that the Corn-law goes to pay marriage settlements, and the other that it goes to pay mortgages. Now, if it goes to pay these, how can it pay the farmer? And if you cannot insure the operation of the law, if, after you have passed it, you are obliged to confess that you cannot insure its operation, who then pays the dowries and the settlements? Surely, in that case, they must be paid out of the pockets of the farmers. You have confessed that a law cannot secure prices, but as mortgages and settlements are paid, then I say that you have confessed that the money comes from the farmers; and surely this is sufficient to account for their distress. I contend, then, that if this law creates a profit at all, that profit passes into rent. And this proposition rests on more than the admission of the Paymaster of the Forces, or of the hon. Member for Wiltshire. We have other acknowledgments of the fact coming from still higher authority. See a transaction of Mr. Gladstone, of Fasque, in Kincardineshire, of which I have an account in a paper in my pocket. Mr. Gladstone was applied to to reduce his rents, and he writes a letter to his agent telling him—and his confession is worth something, as coming from a prudent and sagacious merchant—telling him that he does not look at the alteration in the Corn-law as calculated to reduce prices, and that consequently he does not feel himself bound to reduce his rents. Now this is a clear admission that the benefit from the law goes into the shape of rent. But this is not all. There is his Grace the Duke of Richmond. The other day he was visiting his tenants in Scotland, dining with them, and looking over his estates, and in one of his speeches he told them, whilst speaking of the alteration in the Corn-law, that he was not the man to hold his tenants to any bargain they had made under circumstances which had been altered, and that if they wished it he was willing that they should throw up their leases and return their farms into his hands. Now what does that amount to? Why, merely that the Corn-law influences the rent. It means that or nothing; although I must say such a speech shows very little care for the farmer, who perhaps a dozen years ago purchased stock and went into his farm, and is now told, when probably the price of his stock has fallen 40 per cent., that if he pleases he may sell off, leave his farm, retire from his connection with the noble Duke, and get another landlord where he may. All this shows, then, that if the Corn-law operates to cause a profit at all, it also operates to put that profit into the pockets of the landlord.

Now do not suppose that I wish to deprive you of your rents; I wish you to have your rents; but what I say is, don't come here to raise them by legislative enactments. I think you may have as good rents without a Corn-law as with it; but what I say is this, that when you come here to raise the price of corn under the pretence of helping the

farmer and the farm-labourer, whilst in reality you are only
going to help yourselves, then, I say, you are neither dealing
fairly by the farmer, nor yet by the country at large; and,
mind me, this is just the position in which you stand with
the country. You have deceived the farmers, and, feeling that
you have deceived them, they have a right to ask, how you
intend to benefit them? Nay, more, they have a right to
inquire into your rentals, and find out how you have benefited
yourselves. Yes, I say they have a right to inquire into your
rentals. The hon. Member for Sussex (Colonel Wyndham)
laughs, and truly it would be laughable enough were he to
come to me to inquire into the profits of my business; but,
then, he should remember that I do not ask for a law to
enhance the profits of my business. He, on the contrary, is the
strenuous supporter of a law, which, in its effect—whatever
may be its intention—benefits his own class and no other class
whatever. This language, I dare say, is new to the House.
I dare say it is strange and unexpected in this place; but it
is the language I am accustomed to use on this subject out of
doors, and I do not wish to say anything behind your backs
that I am not prepared to say before your faces.

And here let me ask what progress has been made in rents?
Since 1793, rents in this country have doubled. I have returns in my pocket sent in by the clergy of Scotland, from
which it appears that the rental of that country has increased
in the same time threefold. In England, rents have not increased to that extent; but I can say with safety that they
have more than doubled; and there is something beyond even
this. You have had a considerable advance in rents since
1828. There has been a great rise since that year. I hold
in my hand a return of the rents of the corporation lands of
the city of Lincoln since 1828. I see the hon. Member for
Lincoln (Colonel Sibthorp) in his place. Now I have a return
of the property of the city corporation; it is nearly all agricultural property, and I find that that rental has increased

50 per cent. since the year 1829. Now I do not say that the whole rental of the kingdom has increased in the same proportion, but I do say that we have a right to inquire what is the increase in that rental. The hon. Member for Lincoln says he won't tell me; but I will tell him that nothing is so easy to learn as the history of rents in this country, for there is scarcely a village in England in which there is not some old man who can tell what was the price of land in his parish through many succeeding years. I say it is the business of the farmer and the poor labourer to know the progress which rents have made since the Corn-law passed, and if they find that whilst in the one case they are losing all their capital, and in the other their condition is deteriorating, and they are obliged to put up with a potato diet—if they find, I say, that whilst this has been going on, rents have increased and are increasing. then, I contend, they will have a proof that this law was passed for the landlords, and that it operates for their benefit, and their benefit only. I know that this is a sore subject; but I am bound to make it known that this is not the only way in which you have profited by political delusions.

I will now show you another view of the question. You have made the Corn-law the subject of political outcry in the counties. You have made it a Church and State question, and at the same time you have made the farmers your stepping-stones to political power. And for what has this been done? I will take the last general election. At the last election the 'farmers' friends' were running through the country, and, with the purest and most disinterested intentions, no doubt, were making all sorts of promises to the agriculturists. Well, here are some of them, sitting in this House. Here they are, some of them sitting on the Treasury Bench. The right hon. Baronet at the head of the Government (Sir R. Peel), made a speech at Tamworth as the 'farmers' friend.' The hon. Member for Essex (Sir

John Tyrell) says he quoted it repeatedly, but I don't think he quotes it now. As for the right hon. Baronet, however, with all his ability, and with his thirty years' Parliamentary experience, he might probably have obtained the situation he now holds whatever might have been the circumstances of the time. The post was due to him, perhaps, for his talents; so of him I shall say no more just now. But there is another right hon. Baronet very near him—I mean the Paymaster of the Forces (Sir E. Knatchbull). There is no disturbing force in him. The right hon. Member is the 'farmers' friend.' There he sits. O, I was struck, the other night, at the fervour with which the hon. Member for Wallingford (Mr. Blackstone) apostrophised this 'farmers' friend,' when, with clasped hands and uplifted eyes, he said, 'O if the Paymaster of the Forces were himself again! A few years back, he would not have treated the farmer so.' [Question!] Ay, it is not a very pleasant one, certainly; but it is the question. I do not complain of the Paymaster of the Forces; I have no reason. He has made a speech which is more to the point, which is better calculated to serve the cause which I uphold than anything that has occurred in this debate, excepting, perhaps, his own explanation. I don't complain of him; I pass on. There is a noble Duke (Newcastle) who is a 'farmers' friend,' and he has a son (Lord Lincoln) in the Woods and Forests. The noble Lord, I dare say, performs his duty efficiently; but I want to show the farmers of England—of whom there is not one genuine specimen in this House—who they are who profit by this law. Well, then, there is a noble Duke (Buckingham) who is the 'farmers' friend' *par excellence.* He has reached the summit of rank already. He has no son requiring a place under Government. But one prize he had not, and that he soon obtained—I mean the blue riband. Now these are but the outward and visible signs of the gains of this triumph; but whilst all this patronage, and all these honours, have been showered on the 'farmers' friends,' what have the farmers got themselves? You think this is not the question; but I can tell you we have no hope of the salvation of the country but by showing the farmers how you have cajoled them. You taught the farmers to believe, that if they elected you, their 'friends,' to Parliament, you would speedily repay them for their trouble. They allowed themselves to be driven to the poll by their landlords, who raised this cry: they believed the landlords could keep up the price of corn by Act of Parliament. Will you now confess that you cannot? You have confessed by your silence that you cannot guarantee the farmer even 30s. a quarter. That delusion is at an end.

How is it, now, that the farmers cannot carry on their business without political intermeddling, like other people? 'Throw the land out of cultivation,' by removing the Corn-law! who say that? The worst farmers in the country,—the landlords, rather, of the worst-farmed land. Who tells us that the land will not be thrown out of cultivation? The landlords of the best-farmed land. I put one prophecy against the other. Let the question be decided, as other matters are, by competition. I object to your pretences for keeping up the price of corn. Those who are most rampant for protection are the landlords, I repeat, of the worst-farmed land—the Members for Wilts, Dorset, Bucks, Somersetshire, and Devonshire—where you may see the worst farming in the kingdom; and why is it so? Not because the tenants are inferior to those elsewhere—Englishmen are much the same anywhere; but the reason is, because they are under political landlords,—men who will not give their tenants a tenure, but with a view to general elections. You say 'No,' but I will prove it. Go into the country yourselves, and where you find the best-farmed land there you will find the longest leases. The Lothians, Northumberland, Norfolk, Lincoln. [No.] What, no leases in Lincolnshire?

[Colonel Sibthorp: 'Not long leases.']

Exactly; I mentioned Lincoln last, as being nearer south.
Well, on the estates of the Duke of Northumberland, for
example, you will find no long leases, and the worst farming;
and you will find with long leases good farming, even in the
midst of bad; and *vice versâ*. This is unpalatable, of course.
Hon. Gentlemen say it is not true. I ask them if they expect
farmers to farm well without long leases? Can you really
expect tenants to lay out capital in draining and improvements without long leases? I should feel insulted if anybody
offered me a farm, expecting me to lay out money, without
the security of a lease. What is the language of the farmers
themselves? You must not treat them now as if they believed you the ' farmers' friends.' Did you hear the petition
I presented from Dorsetshire, agreed to at a meeting of 3000
farmers and others, and signed by the chairman, a landholder,
for the total repeal of the Corn-laws?

But this cannot be treated as a farmers' question. We shall
have it put upon a proper footing from this very night. The
Corn-law, if it does anything, raises rents. I do not come
here to tell you it does so. I do not think you understand
your own interests. But I know this, that you inflict the
greatest possible amount of evil upon the manufacturing and
commercial community, and do no good either to the farmer
or the farmer's labourer. It may be a very unpalatable
question; but what, I ask, are the terms which you wish
to make, under the new law, with your tenants? I do not
like the language I have heard upon the subject from landowners. The right hon. Baronet (Sir R. Peel) said, the protection had been reduced; but I have heard little talk, at
least in public, about reducing rents. However, I have heard
a great deal about the farmers ' improving and curtailing
their expenses.' What says the Member for Worcestershire
(Mr. Barneby)?—

' I have been in Yorkshire, and the worst land there produces as much as
the best in this country.'

What, again, was the language of a noble Earl (Verulam) at St. Alban's?—

'You must no longer sit before your doors, with your pipes in your mouths, and drinking your ale ; but you must at once bestir yourselves.'

What said the Member for Somersetshire (Mr. Miles), who sometimes appears here in the character of the 'farmers' friend?'—that

'In Scotland they have double our crops, and that this might be secured in this country by improved husbandry.'

Now, this is not fair language on the part of landowners to farmers ; for if protection be reduced, the farmers have a right to reduced rents ; and if not, let us hear what is the intention of the Corn-law?

We have heard a great deal of ambiguous language during the debate from the right hon. Vice-President of the Board of Trade (Mr. Gladstone), but we have not yet heard what the Corn-law and the tariff have done.   At one time, we hear an avowal of reduced prices ; next (like putting forward one foot, and then withdrawing it, and advancing the other to erase the foot-trace), we hear that credit was not taken for that.   This might not be intended, but it certainly is calculated to deceive the farmers.   But the right hon. Gentleman said, ' Whether the tariff has reduced prices or not, prices had been reduced, and there has been no reason to complain.' This sort of ambiguity is not the way now to deal with the farmers.   Gentlemen must not regard this as a battle between the farmers and the manufacturers.   We propose to make good friends with the farmers.   Yes ; we are their best friends, their only friends, their best customers ; and I can tell you this, they are beginning to be sick of the political landlords.

There is a small section of this House now setting themselves up as the real farmers' friends, upon the ruins of the old friendship : and I can say this, that so badly have they

been treated, that they are now inclined to suspect even these
new friends; and they say, 'What are they after? Don't you
think they want to get up a party? Are they not wishing to
make themselves troublesome to the Minister, that he may
fancy it worth while to offer them something?' The farmers
are now disposed to distrust everybody who promises them
anything; and the reason they are ready to look on us with
friendly eyes is, that we never promised them anything. We
tell them distinctly that legislation can do nothing for them.
It is a fraud. They must never allow bargaining for leases
and rents to be mixed up with politics. They must deal with
their landlords as with their wheelwrights and saddlers, with a
view to business, and business alone.

I am fully aware that I have said more than may be quite
agreeable to hon. Gentlemen opposite. I think it is but fair
to exculpate ourselves from the imputations that have been
cast upon us by the right hon. Gentleman (Sir R. Peel), and
the Vice-President of the Board of Trade, that we are seeking
a monopoly for ourselves, as well as to deprive others of their
monopoly. But what I have to say is this—we want no
monopoly; and this I know, that the moment I go amongst
the farmers, and say we are for free trade in coffee, in sugar,
in manufactures, in everything, that the farmers, like honest
and just men as they are, will at once exclaim, 'That is right,
that is fair!' Now I not only say this, but I complain of
something else. There was a singular evasion of the question
by the right hon. Baronet (Sir R. Peel), when he talked of
colonial manufactures and colonial produce, and mixed them
up with the corn question. But what we want is a free
trade in everything. The policy of the right hon. Gentleman
amalgamated duties for the purposes of protection, and duties
for the purposes of revenue, and he would have it believed
that we could not carry free trade without interfering with
the Custom-house duties. Now, we do not want to touch her
Majesty at all by what we do. We do not want to touch

duties simply for revenue; but we want to prevent certain
parties from having a revenue which is of benefit to themselves, but advantage to none else.   On the contrary, what
we seek for is the improvement of her Majesty's revenue;
what we wish to gain is that improvement.   We say that
your monopoly gives you a temporary advantage—a temporary, not a permanent advantage, and that you thereby
cripple the resources of the revenue.

What is the amount of all these protecting duties?   This
morning I went through the whole of those revenue returns,
and how much do you think they amounted to?   To two
millions per annum, and this included the timber duties, and
every other article to which you for your own views give protection.   This is the entire question.   What is, I ask, the
difficulty of abolishing protecting duties on manufactures?
How much do they produce to the Customs?   Less than
350,000l. a-year.   Then the right hon. Gentleman has spoken
of the cotton trade.   How much is paid, think you, for the
protection of cotton goods?   By the last returns, 8150l.
a-year.   There is no difficulty in a Prime Minister, in a
Minister of capacious mind, of enlarged views, of one whose
genius leads him to deal with something better than caviare
and other trifling articles.   Such a Minister would, I say, find
no difficulty in sweeping away the protecting duties.

Then the right hon. Gentleman spoke of subverting the
whole of our colonial system.   What does he mean by subverting the whole of our colonial system?   We do profess to
subvert the colonial monopolies.   It is true that we would do
that; but that is not subverting the colonial system.   What
we would do must benefit the revenue, and not injure.   The
equalization of the duty on sugar would increase the revenue,
as it has been proved by Mr. M'Gregor, to an amount of not
less than 3,000,000l. a-year.   Take away the monopoly, and
you benefit the revenue.   You might, too, do the same with
coffee.   You might increase the revenue to the amount of

300,000*l.* a-year by the equalization of the duty on coffee. Would it be an injury to the colonies that you left them to all the enjoyments of a free trade? Where is the value of our possessions, if they are not able to supply us with articles as cheap and as good as come from other countries? They pay us the same price for our cottons as other countries, and no more. If they cannot supply us with sugar, surely they can supply us with something else.

There can, then, be no difficulty in the way of the Exchequer which need prevent you from carrying the principle of free trade. I want the Anti-Corn-law League to be known as the Free-trade League. I know that hon. Gentlemen opposite think that all we want to do is to take away the corn monopoly. The public mind is urged on by us against that key-stone in the arch of monopoly; but I can tell hon. Gentlemen opposite, that that organization never will be dispersed until there is a total abrogation of every monopoly. There has been a great deal of talk of free trade being theoretically and in the abstract right. Does the right hon. Gentleman know what that would lead to? If free trade be theoretically right—if it is as old as truth itself, why is it not applicable to the state and circumstances of this country? What! truth not applicable; then there must be something very false in your system, if truth cannot harmonise with it. Our object is to make you conform to truth, by making you dispense with your monopolies, and bringing your legislation within the bounds of justice. I thank you for the admission that we have a true cause, and, armed with the truth of that cause, I appeal to the friends of humanity, I appeal to those on the other side who profess and practise benevolence, I appeal to certain Members on the other side of the House, and I appeal especially to a certain noble Lord (Lord Ashley), and I ask him, can he carry out his schemes of benevolence if he votes for any restriction on the supply of the people's food? If he should vote against the present motion, I ask him, will not he and his friends be viewed with suspicion in the manufacturing districts?

We often hear a great deal about charity, but what have we to do with charity? Yes, I say, what have we to do with charity in this House? The people ask for justice, and not charity. We are bound to deal out justice; how can charity be dealt out to an entire nation? Where a nation is the recipients, it is difficult to imagine who can be the donors. I, therefore, exhort the advocates of religion, the advocates of education, the friends of moral and physical improvement, to reflect upon the votes which they are about to give. I ask, what will the country say if such Members, patching up a measure of detail, are found voting in the approaching division against the motion of the hon. Member for Wolverhampton? I call upon them, therefore, to separate themselves from those with whom they are accustomed to act, unless they are prepared to lose all the influence which they have laboured so hard to acquire in the manufacturing districts. I call upon them to support the present measure if they hope to be useful.

There are 7,000,000 or 8,000,000 people without wheaten bread. If the people continue to descend in the scale of physical comfort, and to eat potatoes, the hope of moral improvement which the friends of humanity indulge must be altogether disappointed. The right hon. Gentleman the President of the Board of Trade said, that the importation of 600,000 quarters of wheat would be a national calamity; but how otherwise are the people to be supported? The Poor-law Commissioners told them that they must add a county as large as Warwick to the territorial extent of the country, or the population of the land must descend to a lower scale of food. They will go on multiplying; no scheme has yet been devised to stop that. You have attempted to bring down the population to the supply; but the evil which you sought to inflict upon them has recoiled upon yourselves.

I have now a word to say to the noble Lord (J. Russell) the Member for London. The noble Lord will not vote for this motion; he says he objects to the repeal of the Corn-laws, but prefers a fixed duty to the sliding-scale. Now, I think the noble Lord has not treated the great party on this side of the House, nor the country, well, in not stating explicitly the grounds on which he would retain any portion of this obnoxious law. He talked of the exclusive burdens to which he said the land was subject; but he did not specify those burdens. I have the greatest respect for the noble Lord, but I venture to tell him that I think it is due to his own reputation, and to the party which acknowledges him for its leader, that he should distinctly state the grounds on which he advocates the imposition of a duty on the importation of corn. As far as I know the feeling out of doors, whatever may be the fate of the motion, however small the numbers in its favour may be, it will not have the slightest effect upon the progress of public opinion on the question. The League will go on as they have hitherto done. In the course of our agitation we may probably dissolve Parliaments and destroy Ministries, but still public opinion upon the subject cannot be checked by the division, whatever it may be, and, if there be any force in truth and justice, we shall go on to an ultimate and not distant triumph.

FREE TRADE.

V.

LONDON, SEPTEMBER 28, 1843.

[The systematic agitation for the repeal of the Corn-laws commenced with a meeting held at King-street, Manchester, on Dec. 20th, 1838. In course of time considerable funds were collected, in order to carry on the movement. In 1843, the League hired Covent Garden Theatre, and employed it for the purpose of metropolitan meetings, besides organising a complete staff of lecturers throughout the country, and establishing a newspaper which should report speeches and disseminate information on the subject. In the speech printed below, when Mr. Cobden said that the League had resolved to petition the House of Commons no longer, the audience, almost in one mass, rose and burst into a series of the most enthusiastic cheers, which lasted for several minutes, accompanied by waving of hats and handkerchiefs, and other tokens of satisfaction.]

IT would be no impeachment of the nerves of the most practised speaker if he felt a little daunted at such a meeting as this. I thought our last gathering at Drury Lane a most imposing one, but that could not be compared with the sublime spectacle which now presents itself before me. My business to-night is purely of a practical nature, and I am glad it is so, for I am altogether a practical man. I do not know that I should have deemed it necessary to trouble you with one word of argument on the general question of the Corn-laws or Free Trade; but we meet at the present moment under rather different circumstances from those under which we last parted, and I will, therefore, detain you for a

moment before I enter into the practical details which I have
to bring before you. You will have observed in the monopolist
newspapers that our opponents place considerable reliance, in
seeking to make out a case, upon the recent revival of trade
and manufactures, for they tell you that this revival will not
only terminate our agitation, but that it is the best possible
refutation of the truth of our principles. Now I tell them
that it will not put an end to our agitation, and I am prepared to show them and you that it is a triumphant proof of
the truth of our principles. I admit the partial revival of
trade and manufactures; I wish I could say it was a general
revival. I wish I could say it was half as extensive as these
monopolist exaggerations represent it to be.

What is the cause of the revival? I am not in the habit
of troubling such meetings as this with reading statistical
documents — they are generally most inappropriate — but by
way of showing you what the cause of the recent revival
of trade is, as an illustration better than any other I could
give you of the truth of our principles, I will just ask
your attention to one short statistical statement. The
average price of wheat in the three years, 1839, 1840, and
1841, was 67s. 1d.; the price in 1839 being 70s. 6d., the
price in 1840, 66s. 4d.; and the price in 1841, 64s. 5d. These
three years were years of unparallelod suffering and distress in
this country. Last autumn Providence blessed us with an
abundant harvest, and this, in connection with an importation
of foreign corn to the extent of three millions, so reduced the
price of wheat, that the average price of that article for the
first six months of the present year has been only 47s. 7d.
Now, if there had been no revival of trade, under such circumstances, I should not have dared to appear before you.
I should have deserved, indeed, the character of an im-
postor, as to all that I have said on this subject, had
there been no revival of trade under such circumstances.
You will have observed from what I have said, that

wheat was about 20s. a quarter less for the first six months
of the present year than for the three years, 1839, 1840, and
1841; and while there was this reduction in the price of
wheat, there was, at the same time, a reduction in the price
of all other kinds of grain by 8s. a quarter.

In order to understand the magnitude and importance of
the subject with which we have to deal — there are some
who think we over-estimate its importance; I think that
up to the present time we have under-estimated it — in
order to understand the matter better, I will mention, that
the estimated consumption of grain per annum in this
country is twenty million quarters of wheat, and forty
millions of quarters of all other kinds of grain. It follows,
therefore, that the additional cost of grain in each of the
three years of distress was, say—twenty millions of quarters
of wheat, at 20s. a quarter, twenty millions sterling; forty
millions of quarters of all other kinds of grain at 8s., sixteen millions sterling; together, thirty-six millions sterling. But grain is not the only article of agricultural produce, though grain governs the price of the other articles.
It is estimated that the consumption of potatoes, meat,
cheese, and all other articles of agricultural produce, is equal
to the same quantity of grain (sixty millions of quarters);
and the price of the one being, as I have said, governed
by the other, taking the advance in price as equal to 8s.
a quarter, here is a further addition of twenty-four millions
sterling, making a total of sixty millions sterling per annum,
or thirty millions for the half year, or five millions per month.
All this difference in price was left in the pockets of the
people the first six months of the present year; which saving,
after supplying food and other articles of agricultural produce,
they were thus able to spend in other ways, in buying articles
of linen and cotton manufacture, hats, bonnets, and so forth.
This accounts for the increased demand we have noticed for
the labour of those who make linen and cotton goods, hats,

bonnets, and so forth; and this accounts, too, for the people
being able to buy an extra quantity of tea, sugar, and other
articles in the cheap year, beyond what they consume in
dear years, and this again accounts for the foreign trade in
those articles also improving.

This, I say, accounts for the partial revival we have observed in our trade; but, then, this revival has been accompanied by a corresponding depression of the agricultural
interest. The agricultural and the manufacturing interests
would seem to be like the two buckets in a draw-well, the one
going down empty as the other comes up full. In proportion as there is a revival of manufactures, consequent upon
moderate prices in food, we hear the cry of agricultural distress. This has always been so much the case, that I challenge
any one to point out an instance, ever since these Corn-laws
were introduced, wherein the agriculturists and the manufacturers have had simultaneous prosperity. Now, I ask, is this
a natural state of things? Is this alternation of distress—
this intermittent fever, now attacking the one great portion
of the body politic, and then the other—this distress falling
on the farmer at a time when Heaven has blessed him with
an abundant harvest—is this a natural state of things? And
yet in every instance where the farmers have been plunged in
the greatest distress and suffering, it has been in the midst of
the most bountiful harvest, and in the most genial seasons.
Any man who takes these facts alone must have a very undue
and irreverent notion of the great Creator of the world, if he
supposes that this is a natural or a designed state of things.
No; there is an unnatural cause for this unnatural state of
things, and that unnatural cause is the law which interferes
with the wisdom of the Divine Providence, and substitutes
the law of wicked men for the law of nature.

During the three years to which I have been adverting, the
owners of the soil might have expected to have suffered in
consequence of the bad seasons; but what has been the fact?

The landlords have been revelling in prosperity—in a bloated and diseased prosperity—at the very time when the people have been suffering the greatest privations and want of food. Rents have been rising. I say it boldly—it cannot be denied —rents have been generally, if not universally, raised during the three years of which I have been speaking. How stands the case of the landowner during the years of short crops and suffering to the whole community? He then extorts his rents from the distress of the operative, from the capital of the employer, or from the savings of those who are living upon the accumulations of themselves or their forefathers. And when the season is favourable—when Heaven smiles upon the fields, and our harvests are again abundant—the landlord extorts his rent from the distress and the capital of the farmer. Nobody can deny that for a series of years the landowners have been raising their rents, not from the legitimate prosperity of the tillers of the soil, or the prosperity of the manufacturing classes. They have been raising their rents from the capital and the labour of the trading community, or from the capital of their own deluded victims, the farmers. The landowners— Oh, shame upon the order! I say shame upon the landowners and their order, unless they shall speedily rescue themselves from this pitiable — if they deserve pity — this degrading dilemma. The landowners will very soon be ashamed to hold up their heads and own themselves to be English landowners and members of our aristocracy in any enlightened and civilised country in Europe.

Do I seek to injure the landowners even pecuniarily? I have never owned it where I should have been most ready to tell them my opinions to their face—in the House of Commons. The landowners have nothing pecuniarily, they have nothing ultimately, to dread from a free trade in corn. But under Free Trade, instead of extorting their rents from the distress of every class in the country, they would be thrown back upon their own resources. Now there are riches slum-

bering in the soil—if the owners employ their capital and
their intelligence, as other classes are forced to do, in other
pursuits—there are undeveloped bounties even on the surface of the earth, and there are ten times more beneath the
surface, which would make them richer, happier, and better
men, if they would cast aside this monopoly. Last week, in
addressing the farmers of Cheshire, I said I would bring a
jury of Scotch agriculturists before the House of Commons—
if their verdict could be taken there—who would state upon
oath that the surface of Cheshire would, if properly cultivated, yield three times the amount of its present produce.
If you were travelling by the railroad, and marked the country from Stafford to Whitmore, and then from Whitmore to
Crewe, and thence the thirty miles to Manchester, I challenge
all England to show such a disgraceful picture—three-fourths
of the finest fields left to the undisputed dominion of rushes—
not a shilling spent in draining, although it is now universally
acknowledged that draining is the means of doubling the productions of such soils—hedge-rows of every imaginable shape
but a straight line, and fields of every conceivable form but
the right one. And these are the men who content themselves
with sluggish indolence, and draw from the impoverishment
of the people; who pick the pockets of the handloom weavers
rather than by a right application of their intellect and their
capital, double the quantity of grain, or butter, or cheese,
which the land is capable of providing. And thus, if Free
Trade did compel them to sell their articles at a less price,
it would be the means of enabling the people of the country
to have a double supply of food. The home market for food
would be doubled, and the landowner might become an honest
politician.

We are now told that the present state of the manufacturing
and trading classes will put an end to the agitation for the
repeal of the Corn-laws. Why, gentlemen, I think we have a
few mementoes left yet to remind us that we have a Corn-law

monopoly in the shape of an income-tax ; in our extra poors'-rates, extra county-rates, extra taxation for the five thousand troops which were added to the army in 1839, on the first outbreak consequent upon the famine which overspread the land. We have these, and other memorials of monopoly; and if some of us have survived the hurricane, can we forget the thousands and tens of thousands who fell victims to the distress of 1839, 1840, and 1841 ? Shall we forget that 500,000 of our countrymen have, since the August of 1838, expatriated themselves from their native soil, to seek in more hospitable lands the food denied them here? Can we forget the hundreds who have dropped into a premature grave, famine-stricken, since that time ? Can we forget the scores who, by the records of the coroners' courts, have died by their own hands, to escape a lingering death by starvation ? No; if we could be selfish enough—we, who have braved the storm and outlived the hurricane—ourselves to forget these things, we ought to be reminded of these events. But that we are not going to forget them, and that we will make this the occasion for redoubling our exertions, the plan which I shall have the pleasure of laying before you, and submitting to your approbation as the plan of the League for future proceedings, will be sufficient to demonstrate.

You have heard that we have distributed a vast amount of useful knowledge on the subject of the existing monopoly. We should be bad husbandmen if we allowed the harvest which is ripening around us to be overspread by weeds or gathered by others than by ourselves.

The League proposes to take another step in giving a direction to the legislative power of this country. We propose to draw the bonds more closely between the League and the electoral body of the country, by the course of proceedings which I shall submit to you. We regard the electors of the country as possessing in their own hands absolute dominion within these realms. The laws of the country, whether good or bad, are but the breath of their nostrils. It is not our fault if the electoral body is not exactly as we should have wished to have found it—we must work with the instruments we have, unless others will find us better ones. We are not in fault if the electoral body is so distributed as to give by its scattered and detached fragments the greatest advantages to our enemies, who are the enemies of the human race, in meeting us in the field of combat. We must make the best use we can of it as it is. The plan of the League is to bring the more powerful sections of the electoral body into a union with the more vulnerable portions. What is the use of Manchester and Birmingham, and Glasgow and Edinburgh, possessing an overwhelming majority—which no monopolist will dare to face at another election—if their voices are to be counterbalanced, probably by the intriguers living in some small borough which has for electoral purposes the same weight as Manchester or Birmingham? But we will bring the great majority of the electors in the large boroughs into union with those in the smaller ones. Do you suppose that because the small boroughs have not always resisted the influences exercised upon them, they are without sympathy with the condition of other bodies of their countrymen? I have the means of knowing the reverse to be the case. I have been to your cathedral cities and to your rural boroughs, which are now represented by monopolists; and I have heard upon the best authority that three-fourths of the inhabitants are heart and soul Free Traders.

We propose—we, the League, propose a plan. And don't suppose that means a few men from Manchester. The League is composed, I hope, of this meeting to begin with. It contains a great majority of the electors in the great towns and cities I have mentioned. This is the League, and before long I hope it will comprise every man in the country, unless he either believes that he has an interest in monopoly, or

because the marks of stupidity are so strongly imprinted on
his countenance as to hold out a continual running invita-
tion, 'Come rob me.' We propose to provide a copy of every
registration-list for every borough and county in the United
Kingdom, as soon as the present registration shall have been
completed. We intend to bring these registers to a central
office in London. We then propose to open a correspondence
the most extensive that ever was contemplated, and that
ever, I am sure, was undertaken. Those electors amount to
800,000; but I will take 300,000, excluding those in the
already safe boroughs, as forming the number necessary to
constitute the returns of a majority in the House of Commons.
We propose to correspond with these 300,000 to begin with.
And when I say correspond, don't let any timid, cautious
friends fancy that we are going to commit them by forming
ourselves into a 'Corresponding Society.' I am going to
tell you what we mean to correspond about. We propose
to keep people well informed as to the progress of our question by means of the penny postage, which has not yet been
sufficiently used. I may say, in a parenthesis, that the
Duke of Buckingham presided at a public meeting at Salt
Hill, to celebrate the defeat of the Great Western Railway.
He was a sagacious man, for the railways and the penny
postage will pull down his monopoly. We intend, then, to
keep the constituencies well informed by means of the penny
postage, enclosing the useful information connected with the
question, and tracts bearing the most recent illustrations of
it together. What could be more desirable than to-morrow
to send to those 300,000 electors copies of the newspapers containing the best reports of this meeting? But
we propose to send them one letter a week, and that will
cost twopence for the stamp and the enclosure. That will
be 2500*l.* I mention this by way of illustration and preface
to what I am going to tell you before I conclude. Besides
this correspondence, we intend to visit every borough in the

kingdom, not by agents—we will go ourselves, because we
want the thing well done. We will specially invite the
electors to meet such deputations without distinction of party
—we know nothing of party in this agitation,—and having
met the electors, we shall have a little business to transact
with them. In the first place, we shall urge upon our friends
to organise themselves, and to commence a canvass of their
boroughs to ascertain the number of Free Traders, and in
every case where it is possible to obtain a majority of the
electors in favour of Free Trade; that majority to memorialise their members, where they have not voted rightly,
to vote in favour of Mr. Villiers' motion, which will be
brought on early next session. Besides that, the deputation
will urge upon the electors to have a Free-trade candidate
ready to supplant every monopolist who still retains a seat
for a borough; and the League will pledge itself, where a
borough constituency finds itself at a loss for a candidate,
to furnish it with one, and to give to every borough in which
a vacancy occurs an opportunity for its electors to record
their votes in favour of Free-trade principles. [A Voice:
'The City.'] We'll talk of that by-and-by.

Now, it may be objected to us—and it has been objected—
that by such means no good can be accomplished. If it
cannot be accomplished by such means, it cannot be righte-
ously accomplished at all. But it can be accomplished by
such means, and we have hitherto been unfairly dealt with
in our struggle with the constituencies. The last general
election disclosed an amount of bribery, corruption, and
intimidation, involving brutal violence, even to homicide;
and the present Parliament is the creature of that vile system.
And shall such a system be continued? No; not against
the League. Whenever we have a voice—and we will have
one in every borough when an election takes place—we will
see if we cannot put down this system of bribery, and I
think we may manage effectually to muzzle the intimidators.

The system itself got its death-blow at the last election. It was found, in the first place, too costly. The rents would not stand such an experiment again for either party. In the next, Mr. Roebuck's exposure—and thanks to him for making it—shamed even shameless men in the House of Commons. In the next, Lord John Russell's new law—I wonder they ever let him pass it—presents the means of putting down bribery, if fairly used; but beyond that we have a better and a wiser resort than any. Hitherto the bribers and the bribees have been suffered to escape with impunity. They have been brought before the House of Commons, a Committee has decided upon the case, the petitioner has had the satisfaction of unseating the member, and was saddled with the same expense, and was at liberty to stand again; but the House of Commons took no steps to punish those by whose guilt the system was carried on. By that means they were accessories after the fact; and little better, indeed, could be expected from such a House of Commons. Now, we will try the experiment of a criminal court against these gentry. The man who bribes, or offers a bribe, is guilty of a misdemeanour, and liable to a heavy fine, and also liable to a severe imprisonment. I have heard an objection made that you cannot obtain a conviction in such a case. You cannot obtain a conviction! why not? Will a jury of our countrymen find a verdict of guilty against the hapless wretch who steals a morsel of bread for his famishing children, and will they not convict those whose guilt was of tenfold criminality—who would buy and sell that franchise upon which the bread of that poor creature depends? I say, yes. The juries of this country are precisely the class which will convict in such cases; and it is upon a jury of the country that we mainly rely for putting down bribery, and abating the flagrant system of intimidation for the future. Yes, a jury of our country saved our liberties in times past from a despotic monarchy, and again from corrupt and tyrannical administrations; and it will save us from the worse danger to our liberties—from the taint that has been eating into the electoral bodies of the kingdom.

It is not the intention of the League to recommend any further petitioning to the House of Commons. So soon as the proceedings in reference to the electoral body to which I have alluded shall have reached such a point as to warrant the step, the Council will recommend the electors, not to petition Parliament—of that enough has been done already—but to memorialise the Queen, that she will be pleased to dissolve the present Parliament, which, like everything generated in corruption, must necessarily be short-lived, and to give to the electors an opportunity of sending men to make laws, with the advantages of the lights and experience which they have acquired, since, under a delusion, they were induced at the last election to return the majority of the present House of Commons.

I have now told you the plan which we have to submit to you, the sanction of which we have to ask you to-night; and as a means of carrying on these proceedings, and to furnish the money for doing so, the Council are resolved to raise the sum of 100,000l. Yes, it may save a waste of ink to-morrow, by telling the monopolist scribes that the money will be raised, and that hereafter, as heretofore, the men who have taken the greatest amount of labour, and who will continue to do so in the cause, and who did so before they were ever heard of beyond the precincts of their own localities, will, as they did from the beginning, lead the van in the amount of their subscriptions for the great object which we have in view. We offer to every one the opportunity of registering his name, or her name, on this muster-roll of commercial freedom; and we do so with the perfect assurance that it is the last time we shall have to call upon our friends for a sacrifice in the cause. I feel bound, in making this statement, to take care that there shall be no misunderstanding in the minds of any party as to the money which shall be subscribed, or the conditions on which it shall be raised. We ask no one to give us money unless they are fully convinced that we are in earnest in the principles which we advocate. We ask none to contribute unless they believe that the characters, personal, private, and public, of the men who shall be hereafter taking the responsible part in this agitation, are such as they can approve and trust; and we do not ask anybody to join us now who will not be prepared, when the time shall come, to give full effect to his opinions and convictions by standing firm to the principles upon which the League is founded. Let there be no misunderstanding as to that. This is not a party move, to serve any existing political organisation; we care nothing for political parties. As they at present stand, there is very little indeed to choose between the two great parties. Let a statesman of established reputation, of whatever side in politics, take the step for perfect freedom of trade, he shall have the support of the League. We have given but a slight specimen of what we shall be able to do when a Minister, whether Whig or Tory, shall adopt such a course. He shall have the support of the League to carry such a measure, whatever his other political opinions may be.

We do not seek to interfere with any man's political opinions; there are no ulterior objects in the view of this Association. I say it solemnly, on behalf of the men with whom I am daily associating, that they have no second or collateral object in view that I am acquainted with. The single and undisguised object of the League is to put down commercial monopoly; but that cannot be done by saddling upon our backs a fixed duty on corn, which means a differential duty on sugar, on coffee, and monopoly in every other article. The Corn-law is the great tree of Monopoly, under whose baneful shadow every other restriction exists. Cut it

down by the roots, and it will destroy the others in its fall.
The sole object of the League is to put an end to and extinguish, at once and for ever, the principle of maintaining
taxes for the benefit of a particular class. The object is
to make the revenue what it ought to be—a stream flowing
into the Queen's Exchequer, and not a penny of it inter-
cepted by the Duke of Buckingham, or Sir E. Knatchbull,
to pay off their endowments or their settlements; by Lord
Mountcashel to discharge his burthens or his mortgages; or
by any other person, or for the maintenance of any object
whatsoever.

I have told you the object of the League; but it is no
fault of ours if our enemies, by their opposition to our just
demands, give rise to a struggle on other points with which
this agitation has nothing to do. It is no fault of ours
if with this agitation should be mixed up the question of
rents, and should mingle in a degree that would render it
difficult to separate the rights of property from the claims
of those who labour under the grievance of these intolerable
exactions. It is no fault of ours if the nobility of this
country should become as much detested at their own baronial
hall doors as were the noblesse of France previous to the
Revolution. We are responsible for none of these things.
The fault lies with those who support monopoly, who are
deaf to reason and justice, and who place themselves upon
a pedestal of injustice; a pedestal which is always liable to
fall, and always certain to bring down those who stand upon it.

Gentlemen, I have said my say. There are others to
follow me, and I will only say, unfeignedly, that we are
engaged in an agitation which has no ulterior views, and
that, while so engaged, we are utterly regardless of the
imputations that may be cast upon us by our opponents.
I could spare the monopolist prints oceans of ink, and great
midnight labour in preparing their vituperations, if I could
only make them believe that their attacks upon me fall as

harmless as the water-drops from the sky do. We have no
desire to be politicians. I say it, without affectation, that
there is not a man amongst us who aims at making a
political life his profession. We are aware that this great
question must be carried in Parliament, not by us, but by
some statesman of established reputation; but while we possess
the power that we do possess out of doors—and it is nothing
to what it will be twelve months hence—the cause shall never
be surrendered to any Minister, to promote the purpose of
any political party; and, so far as the labour goes, so long
as I am blessed with health, I shall give it cheerfully; nay,
I shall consider it a privilege to labour in the cause. If
I were not convinced that the question comprises a great
moral principle, and involves the greatest moral world's
revolution that was ever yet accomplished for mankind, I
should not take the part I do in this agitation.

Free Trade! What is it? Why, breaking down the
barriers that separate nations; those barriers, behind which
nestle the feelings of pride, revenge, hatred, and jealousy,
which every now and then burst their bounds, and deluge
whole countries with blood; those feelings which nourish
the poison of war and conquest, which assert that without
conquest we can have no trade, which foster that lust for
conquest and dominion which sends forth your warrior chiefs
to scatter devastation through other lands, and then calls
them back that they may be enthroned securely in your
passions, but only to harass and oppress you at home. It
is because I think I have a full apprehension of the moral
bearing of this question, that I take a pride and gratification
in forming one in the present agitation; and I invite you
all to take a part in it, for there is room and glory and
fame enough for all as soon as we have achieved the great
triumph of the downfall of the Corn-laws.

FREE TRADE.

VI.

LONDON, OCTOBER 13, 1843.

[After the death of Sir Matthew Wood, and, consequently, on a vacancy in the representation of the City of London, two candidates—Mr. Pattison, Free Trader, and Mr. Thomas Baring, a Protectionist—came forward as rival candidates. Mr. Pattison was returned by a narrow majority, and the victory was deemed significant. The day after this meeting, the League resolved to raise 100,000l., 12,6col. of which was subscribed in Manchester in a single day.]

WE do not seek to disguise the fact that our object here is to discuss with you—to entreat with you—to canvass you on the important election about to take place. Our meetings, gentlemen, are always canvassing meetings; we have no other object in our meetings than to influence the electoral voice, and every voter of the City of London has received a circular, requesting his presence here. The question we have to submit is not very well fitted for declamatory appeals; and if we would make a good use of the short time we have, to address ourselves to your judgments, we must beg your attention to what may appear very dry matter. We have come here to ask you to consider whether you will give your votes in favour of Monopoly or Free Trade. Now, by free trade I do not mean the throwing down of all custom-houses. One of your candidates, Mr. Baring—in pure ignorance, I presume, for I

VOL. 1.   o

will not suppose he would insult you by inventing such a
statement—actually says that free trade means the abolition
of all custom-house duties. We have said, thousands of times,
that our object is not to take away the Queen's officers from
the custom-house, but to take those officers away who sit at
the receipt of custom to take tithe and toll for the benefit of
peculiar classes.

There is something so obviously honest and just in what
we advocate, that there has been no writer, seated in the
quietude of his closet, who has discussed the matter—there is
no writer, I say, with a name having pretensions to last
beyond the year of the publication of his works, who does not
agree with us in our doctrines. Nay, we have lived to see
practical statesmen, while they hold office, actually driven by
the force of argument and the intelligence of the age, to admit
the justice of our principles, while they have basely con-
descended to practise their direct opposite. Nay, more, your
candidates, both of them, stand upon the same ground as to
avowal of principle. The difference is, that one will honestly
and consistently carry out his opinions—the other refuses to
do so. Now, our business is to ask you, whether you will
take a man for your representative who, acknowledging free
trade to be just—though I confess I believe he does not know
much about it—yet refuses to act up to his professions? Will
you take him, or a man who, after avowing our principles,
will go into Parliament pledged and determined to carry
them out?

Our chairman has said that Mr. Baring admits our principles to be true in the abstract—that is, that his own principles are untrue in the abstract. Did you ever hear of a
father teaching his children to obey the Ten Commandments
—in the abstract? Did you ever know the plea to go down
at the Old Bailey, after a verdict of guilty had been returned
of 'Oh, I did steal the pocket-handkerchief—but only in the
abstract?' Is monopoly an abstraction? If it be, I have

done with Mr. Baring and this election; but the abstraction presents itself in bodily form under the shape of certain monopolists, who diminish, by one-half, your supply of sugar, and cut off large slices from your loaves. Now, that is no abstraction.

Let us for a moment condescend to meet the arguments of our opponents, although, in point of fact, these gentlemen have put themselves out of court by their own admission. What are the grounds upon which they refuse to carry into practice principles which they admit to be true in theory? Why (they say), to start with, that, if you do give up monopoly, it will be impossible for you to raise the national revenue. Now, if I understand this, it is, that we have so much taxation to pay to the Queen for the support of our naval, military, and civil establishments, that we never can get on unless we place a burden of nearly equal weight on our shoulders in the shape of contributions payable to the Duke of Buckingham and Co. What does it mean, if it does not mean that? It is a poor compliment to the present age that this argument was never discovered until our own day; for when monopoly was first established, nobody thought of making use of that argument.

Now, let us see how the imposition of monopolies can aid the revenue. Take corn, and go back only to the time of your own memory. During the four years of 1834, 1835, 1836, and 1837, the average price of corn was 45s. It so happened that the Chancellor of the Exchequer had, during these years, a surplus of revenue; he could afford to come forward and remit taxation. But then we had the four years of 1838, 1839, 1840, 1841, when monopoly did its worst for the people, but when, according to the arguments of its supporters, it should have done its best for the revenue. And what was the result? Why, a declining revenue. And when corn cost 65s. per quarter, the Premier admitted that the ability of the working classes to pay any more taxation was exhausted, and that he had no

alternative but to levy an income-tax upon the middle classes.
Now, I like to go to facts and experience, in preference to
authority; and I take this experience, as a much better
guide in forming my opinions, than anything Mr. Baring
can say.

And now then for sugar. Here we have another great
monopoly. And let me remind you, citizens of London, that
you are fighting sugar monopolists in the City rather than
bread monopolists—that aristocracy of the sugar-hogshead, to
which I have so often referred—that is the monopoly which
you have now to deal with — a most ignoble oligarchy.
Mincing-lane cries aloud for protection. And what has
sugar done for the revenue? What is the price of sugar
in bond? 21s. per cwt. What do you pay for it? 41s.
per cwt. Here you have 20s. additional on three or four
millions of cwts.; an item worth fighting for, is it not?"
And you, the shopkeepers, butchers and bakers, grocers and
drapers of London, what good do you obtain from this monopoly? There is this mysterious character, Monopoly, sitting
at your tea-tables, and for every lump of sugar put into your
cup, presto!—there is another taken out of the basin. And
when your wives and children look up, and ask for the
lump of sugar which they have earned, and which they
think fairly belongs to themselves, this mysterious assailant,
Monopoly, says he takes it for your protection. Well, now,
what does the revenue lose by sugar? Mr. Macgregor,
the Secretary to the Board of Trade, in his evidence before
the Import Duties Committee in 1840, showed that, if the
monopoly in sugar were abated, the people would have double
the quantity at the same price, and that three millions of
money additional would be poured into the Exchequer. Mr.
Macgregor is still the Secretary of the Board of Trade, and
most fit he is to fill the situation. Such was his evidence,
and in it is published to the world our condemnation of the
present system.

Now, what is the pretence for monopoly in sugar? They cannot say that it benefits the revenue; neither is it intended to benefit the farmer in England, or the negro in the West Indies. What, then, is the pretence set up? Why, that we must not buy slave-grown sugar. I believe that the ambassador from the Brazils is here at present, and I think I can imagine an interview between him and the President of the Board of Trade. His Excellency is admitted to an interview, with all the courtesy due to his rank. He delivers his credentials; he has come to arrange a treaty of commerce. I think I see the President of the Board of Trade calling up a solemn, earnest, pious expression, and saying, 'You are from the Brazils; we shall be happy to trade with you, but we cannot conscientiously receive slave-grown produce.' His Excellency is a good man of business (most men are who come to us from abroad to settle commercial matters); so he says, 'Well, then, we will see if we can trade together in some other way. What have you to sell us?' 'Why,' returns the President of the Board of Trade, 'cotton goods; in these articles we are the largest exporters in the world.' 'Indeed,' exclaims his Excellency, 'cotton, did you say? Where is cotton brought from?' 'Why,' replies the Minister, 'hem!— chiefly from the United States;' and at once the question will be, 'Pray, is it free-grown cotton, or slave-grown cotton?' Now, I leave you to imagine the answer, and I leave you also to picture the countenance of the President of the Board of Trade. [At this moment something gave way at the back of the stage, and a trifling interruption ensued.] Do not be afraid (continued the hon. Gentleman), it is only a form which has fallen; it is symptomatic of the fall of the monopolists. Now, have any of you had your humanity entrapped and your sympathies bamboozled by these appeals against slave-grown produce? Do you know how the law stands with regard to the sugar trade at present? We send our manufactures to Brazil, as it is; we bring back Brazilian sugar; that

sugar is refined in this country—refined in bonded warehouses, that is, warehouses where English people are not
allowed to get at it—and it is then sent abroad by our
merchants, by those very men who are now preaching against
the consumption of slave-grown sugar. Ay, those very men
and their connections who are loudest in their appeals against
slave-grown sugar have bonded warehouses in Liverpool and
London, and send this sugar to Russia, to China, to Turkey,
to Poland, to Egypt; in short, to any country under the sun ;
to countries, too, having a population of 500,000,000; and
yet these men will not allow you to have slave-grown sugar
here. And why is it so? Because the 27,000,000 of people
here are what the 500,000,000 of people of whom I have
spoken are not—the slaves of this sugar oligarchy. Because
over you they possess a power which they do not over others.
Oh, hypocrites! The Mahometans have gradations of punish-
ment in a future state for different kinds of sins, and the very
lowest depth of all is assigned to hypocrites. I should not
wonder, when the Turks hear of Mr. Baring, and the arguments uttered in the House of Commons, if they were to offer
up prayers for the poor hypocrites of this country. And these
are the grounds on which, in this eighteen hundred and forty-
third year, you are called upon to return a man to Parliament
to uphold monopoly, in order that a few men in the City may
sell you your sugar 20s. per cwt. dearer than the natural
price of the market of the world. It is a dirty, a base and
sordid conspiracy. I have said it before, and I will say it now, I
would rather be governed for a time by a despot like Mehemet
Ali—a despot, yet a man of genius—than I would knuckle
down to a sordid aristocracy, such as the sugar oligarchy.
Thus the men who maintain monopoly by such arguments are
the men from whom you might expect to hear complaints,
that we, happening to have for half the year our domiciles
in Lancashire, should presume to have a voice in the election
here.

I see by to-day's paper that Mr. Baring says that we have
no direct interest in this election. What, is there a law passed
which I am not called upon to obey in Lancashire as well as
here? Does the sugar oligarchy content itself with plunder-
ing its own constituents and neighbours? No, they plunder
Lancashire too. And oh, this comes well from the monopolists. It is but consistent that the men who would cut us off
from the intercourse of the world, should attempt to cut off
Middlesex from Lancashire. The project shows the extent
and range of their intellects. It is carrying out their principles; it is letting us know fully and clearly what they
would be at. But when I speak of these men, do not let me
be misunderstood as having implied that the larger, or even
a large portion of the merchants of your city, are on the
side of restriction. I deny that the monopolists of the
City have the best or richest men in their ranks. I
can appeal to the declarations and writings of some of
the most eminent and wealthy men among them for proof
that they possess different sympathies from the monopolists,
and very different grades of intelligence. There are men in
the City who know well the direct and the immediate connection between the prosperity of the great manufacturing
districts and this great metropolis. There was one man in
particular—I allude to Mr. Rothschild—who was a man
possessing an intellect that would have made him great in
any walk of life, and who saw and grasped the commercial
operations of the world. He knew well that he, sitting here
in London, was but the minister, the passive instrument for
effecting the exchange between the manufacturing districts
and the great producing countries of the Continent. In his
evidence before the Bank Committee in 1832, are these
words :—

' What I receive in large sums, other people receive in small sums ; I buy on
the Exchange bills drawn from Liverpool, Manchester, Newcastle, and other
places, and which come to every banker and merchant in London. I purchase
60,000l. or ;000l., and sometimes 10,000l. of those bills in a week, and I send

them to the Continent to my houses; my houses purchase against them bills upon this country, which are purchased for wine, wool, and other commodities.'

Mr. Rothschild, had he been living now, would not have come forward and said, 'Lancashire, I have no sympathy with you;' and I am happy to add that one bearing his name, and I believe his son, is one of the warmest supporters of Mr. Pattison.

There is another gentleman in the City, who, if wealth commands respect, has riches enough, and who, if intelligence has any claim on your admiration, can bear comparison with any that can be opposed to him—I allude to Mr. Samuel Jones Loyd. In a pamphlet written by this gentleman in 1840, he says:—

'Who can fail to feel an interest in that great hive of industry? That noble, though new-born metropolis of trade, which presents so splendid a concentration of the most ennobling qualities of man—honesty, industry, intelligence, energy, enterprise, steadiness of purpose, freedom of thought, liberality of sentiment. As an Englishman, I may be proud of the town and trade of Manchester. Again, the prosperity of Manchester is another expression for the well-being of England. When that great town, and the immense population dependent upon it, cease to advance in prosperity and wealth, the star of England has culminated. Failing trade will soon undermine the foundation on which every other interest rests. Our teeming population, deprived of employment, will soon convert this fair and happy land into a warren of paupers. Nor can the retrograde movement stop even at this stage. A dense population, maddened by disappointment, and rendered desperate by irremediable want, will soon fall into a state, from the contemplation of which one may well turn away.'

I am reading the opinion of one entitled to take his place with the wealthiest and, I opine, with the most intelligent of your City merchants and bankers; but this is not a question which has to be settled by great, rich merchants only. Are there not other classes as deeply interested in the matter as are these?

I see in this election a disposition to make it a property election; and, by way of stimulating the zeal of men of property, we are told that this is an Anti-Corn-law League election, and that the men of the League have a disposition to subvert property; and I am specially charged with having said something calculated to loosen the bonds which bind men to observe the rights of property. Now, gentlemen, I think, if anybody in the country can say he is the advocate of the rights of property, I am the man. Why, my whole labour in public, for the last five years, has been to restore the rights of property to those unjustly deprived of them. As there is one particular property which Mr. T. Baring seems to have lost sight of, I don't know that I could do better than refer him to Adam Smith. That writer says :—

'The property which every man has in his own labour, as it is the original foundation of all other property, so it is the most sacred and inviolable. The patrimony of a poor man lies in the strength and dexterity of his hands, and to hinder him from employing this strength and dexterity in what manner he thinks proper without injury to his neighbour, is a plain violation of the most sacred property. It is a manifest encroachment upon the just liberty both of the workman and of those who might be disposed to employ him.'

Now, having thus the countenance of Adam Smith for the assertion, I must say I think that Mr. T. Baring, his aiders and abettors, in so far as they support the Corn-laws and other monopolies, violate the right of property in the labouring man; and by so doing, I tell them now, as I did at the last meeting, that they thus undermine the rights of property of all kinds.

But allow me, gentlemen, to recall your attention for a moment to the interests of the great body of the electors in the metropolis. I will leave these millionaires to take care of themselves, which they can do very well; but will take the shopkeeper, skilled artisan, and labourer, and ask what interest they can have in any support of monopoly? Can you, in the metropolis, be any longer hoodwinked by those who say that the abolition of the corn and sugar monopoly is a manufacturers' question? I should like to ask the shop-keepers what kind of trade they have had for the last five years? I would ask them, when communing with their wives and families, what do they calculate as the return of the

year and the prospect of the next? They may not have felt
the revulsion as soon as the manufacturers; but how, I should
like to know, how long was it after our first deputation of 1839
that the cause which was at work with us began to prey on
their interests? Why, is there a trade you carry on in the
metropolis, of the wholesale and manufacturing kind, that has
not the best customers in the manufacturing districts? Take
the bookselling trade, which appeals to the minds of the
people. I venture to say that one-half of the popular literature that is furnished by London finds its way into the manufacturing districts. I take the distillers, the brewers, the
wholesale chemists, the silversmiths and jewellers; and
do you find that the travellers of those houses go to the
county of the Duke of Buckingham for orders?—are they not
rather packed off straight for Manchester, or Glasgow, or
Liverpool, or some such emporium of manufactures? Well,
take again your domestic trade. Do you depend for customers
on the half-score of gentlemen who are sugar monopolists, or
on the general passers-by before your doors? How often do
you see one of those sugar lords in your shop; and when you
do, do they give you twice the price for your goods that they
make you pay for their sugar? Your traders are supporters
of traders; but not a twentieth, or fiftieth, or one hundredth
of those who uphold trades and manufactures are landlords or
sugar lords, who, nevertheless, cause all the mischief they can
to the community. And when that mischief has gone so far
that it reaches the revenue, your business is overhauled—you
have a tax upon income to meet, and pleasant surcharges, in
order to make up what the great monopolists have taken from
the Queen's Exchequer. Will you have again skilled artisans
—men who surpass all other workmen in the more delicate
and refined manufactures, and whose full employment can be
alone secured by a full demand in the manufacturing as well
as in other districts? How can any one, then, have the
impudence, the effrontery to draw a distinction between the

interests of the people of London and of the people of Lancashire? I will take your most fashionable streets—Regent-
street, if you choose—and I will ask, do the shopkeepers in
that street number amongst their best customers the landlords
or the sugar lords? I called on a jeweller there the other day,
and I asked him what sort of season he had. 'Very poor,'
he replied. 'How is that,' said I, 'rents are pretty good
this year?' 'I don't care,' said he, 'if I never see a lord
come into my shop, for even if they buy they don't pay me.
The people we rely on for custom are,' added he, 'those
brought up by the Birmingham Railway; but there lately
have not been so many as there used to be, and our trade will
never be what it was until we get these summer birds again
to pluck.'

But I should only waste your time if I adduced any
arguments to prove that your interest, or any interest in the
community save that of the monopolists, is not benefited by
monopoly. And the object of this meeting is to call upon the
electors to vindicate your rights, and to assert the interests of
the whole community. Now how are you to do that? Why,
first, every voter will, I hope, promptly register his vote in
favour of Mr. Pattison. Oh, what a bright muster-roll of
votes we shall have against monopoly! I trust that those
who live at a distance will make a pilgrimage in the cause
of Free Trade. If you who have not votes live outside the
City districts, look up the Liverymen, and see that they
vote in favour of Free Trade. I see, by the papers, that
the Attorney-General has turned canvasser. Well, now, I
should think that any of our friends of the League will
make as good a canvasser as the Attorney-General. It is
not merely Lancashire that looks to you. This meeting is an
unique mode of canvassing. The attention of the civilised
world is fixed upon our struggle. A friend of mine went
to America some time ago, for the purpose of indoctrinating
the people there with a horror of slavery. The first

thing he saw in the newspapers was a denunciation of his proceeding, and a desire expressed that he should go home and emancipate the white slaves of England, who were taxed in their food. What does Commodore Napier say as to his reception in Egypt by the shrewd old Turk, Mehemet Ali? 'Our system,' said he, 'may be a bad one, but we have grown under it; and when I send wheat to England I find I cannot sell it at a profit, for there is a monopoly in bread there.' In the *National* I was reading the other day this statement (and that, be it remembered, is the ultra-Liberal journal of France): 'You' (speaking of England) 'should erase from your standard the lion, and place in its stead the starving operative craving a morsel of bread.' This is the way that foreigners speak of us; this is the way in which our missionaries are met. It is now for you, the voters of London, to decide whether you will submit your necks voluntarily to this bondage—whether you will bow before this Juggernaut, or, by an effort worthy of yourselves and of the occasion, strike off for ever the fetters that have manacled this country.

Gentlemen, it may be done, and it will be done. I tell you it is a winning game. It is a 100 to 1, if we all exert ourselves, that we shall succeed; but our opponent, on this occasion, is one who, if we credit reports, either by himself or his agents, resorted, in another place, to practices which we must not allow in the City of London. Now, we must all know what was done in Yarmouth in 1835. I may be told that our present candidate knew nothing about it. The question naturally arises, who did it? It is my firm belief that no corruption ever takes place but that the candidate knows it and pays for it. I say that, after having been a candidate myself. I never paid 10l. without knowing for what; and I don't think that 12,000l. would be advanced by a candidate without value received. Now, I see by the newspapers that the same practice is likely to be resorted to in a small portion of London. Considering that it is the largest, it is one of the

honestest constituencies in the kingdom; but there is a slight
canker eating into one of the extremities of the metropolis.
But I think it right to warn all parties likely to be impli-
cated of the danger which they will run now, beyond what
they ever did before, in taking bribes or treats. In the first
place, if a poor voter bo told 'Let it be: it will be all right,
when the time fixed by law after the election is over;' I must
tell him that there is no time after the election for head-
money or any other money. The League is determined on
putting down bribery as one of its noble objects; and the plan
we have determined on for effecting this purpose we mean to
put in force at the present election. It is our intention to
prosecute criminally every one against whom we think can be
established the charge of taking, offering, giving, or offering
to take a bribe. It is, in the next place, the intention of the
League to offer a reward of 100*l.* for such evidence as may
lead to the conviction of such parties as are charged with those
acts. Let, therefore, the poorest voter know, that if he offers
his vote for a sum of money, it is an indictable offence; and if
any one offers money to him, that is also an indictable offence.
Indeed, if any one should offer a poor voter money, I should
recommend him instantly to seize him by the collar, hand
him over to a police-officer, and take him before the nearest
magistrate, seeing that he does not destroy any papers, or
take anything out of his pocket by the way. But I think
we shall succeed in putting down bribery in the City.

I shall not say anything about petitions to unseat a candidate, because we do not intend that Mr. Baring shall win;
but whether he win or lose, every man against whom a charge
can be established of taking a bribe, giving a bribe, or offering
a bribe, shall be prosecuted criminally in a court of law. The
penalty has been, in ordinary cases, that the culprit should
kick his heels for twelve months within the four walls of a
gaol. Now we should much prefer to prosecute the man who
offers a bribe, to him who receives it; and, therefore, I advise

the poor elector, who may get 30s., to keep a sharp look-out
and see if he cannot honestly get 100l. Why, is it not
astonishing that we should have Acts of Parliament on Acts of
Parliament, that we should have hundreds of them, in fact, one
after another, until they have become a laughing-stock in the
House of Commons, and that yet no one should have thought
before of this plan of putting down bribery? An anecdote is
told of Chancellor Thurlow, before his elevation to the peerage,
that, defining bribery very minutely, and after the fashion of
technical lawyers, some wag said of the display, 'he has
taken a great deal of pains to define what bribery is, as if
there was anybody in the House that did not understand it.'
And this, gentlemen, is our plan for putting an end to bribery
—not going to a Committee of the House of Commons, but
straight to a jury of our countrymen. We will do that in
every place where bribery is carried on; and we have a list,
and pretty minute particulars, of all the transactions that took
place at the last election.

Can any man deny that the object we seek is as pure as
the means by which we hope to effect it? They may talk as
they please of our violence, and of the revolutionary character
of our proceedings. Why, our tactics from the first have been
most peaceable. We have been accused of being, on that
account, somewhat lukewarm, and that, having some property,
and belonging to the middle classes, we did not appeal sufficiently strong to the physical force of the country. I can
forgive a candidate at a losing election for some fictions; but
Mr. Baring has not exhibited a very brilliant fancy in his
inventions. When he talked of the guillotine and a san-
guinary revolution, it was but a poor travestie of a travestie
acted in the House of Commons—the assassination farce.
Gentlemen, our object is what I have always declared it—the
benefit of the whole community. I admit that some may
suffer a temporary loss from the abolition of a monopoly, but I
venture to say that, in the end, there will be no class that will

not be permanently benefited by the removal of those unjust laws.

Mind you, I do not come here as the opponent of the farmers and agriculturists; I come charged with the authority of twenty-five county meetings in the open air, every one of which pledged itself to seek the abolition of those laws. I say, therefore, that, in voting for Free Trade, you will not be merely promoting your own interest, but the best interests of every class. With such an object, I expect you will act like men having justice and humanity to guide and direct you; and the next time I appear before a London audience, I hope I shall have to congratulate you on that triumph which will be hailed through the length and breadth of the land; for the result of your contest will be as a knell of despair throughout the kingdom, or the proud signal of a speedy triumph.

FREE TRADE.

VII.

MANCHESTER, OCTOBER 19, 1843.

After many wanderings in distant counties, I really feel myself revived on finding myself once more amongst my old friends, with the same smiling faces, the same hearts in the same places, and in this cradle of the agitation of the Anti-Corn-law League. You have heard something said of the labours which some of us have undergone for this cause. I don't know—if we could have foreseen, five years ago next month, the arduous duties upon which we were entering—whether we should have had the moral courage to undertake them. I believe we are all now willing to admit that, when we commenced the agitation of the Anti-Corn-law League, we had not the same comprehensive views of the interests and objects involved in the agitation that we now have. I am afraid, if we must confess the truth, that most of us entered upon this struggle with the belief that we had some distinct class interest in the question, and that we should carry it by a manifestation of our will in this district against the will and consent of other portions of the community. I believe that was our impression. If there is one thing which more than another has elevated and dignified and ennobled this agitation, it is that, in the progress of the last five years, we have found,

gradually but steadily, that every interest and every object,
which every part of the community can justly seek, harmonises
perfectly with the views of the Anti-Corn-law League.

I cannot help referring to the remarks which have been
made by my friend Mr. Pearson, upon a subject which does
not usually come under our consideration; but if there was
one point which might be considered more than another likely
to be a stumbling-block in the way of Free Traders, it is that
question which he has so ably handled to-night; and as I
know that monopoly has been drawing upon the humane feelings of the community in order to sustain its sugar monopoly,
by pretending commiseration for the slaves, I am very glad
indeed that this ground has been so completely and effectually
cut from under them by one whose motives must be above
suspicion, for he took a part in the abolition of slavery many
years ago. But how few of us there were who, five years ago,
believed that, in seeking the repeal of the Corn-law, we were
also seeking the benefit of the agriculturists! And if we had
not had the five years' experience we have—if we had not
persevered for the five years that we have been in existence
as a League—we should not have had the opportunity of de-
monstrating the benefits which agriculture will receive from
the adoption of the principles of Free Trade. This only proves,
gentlemen, that what is true requires but time to establish it
in men's minds. Time and truth against all the world. But
you must have time; and that time which destroys everything
else only establishes truth. We had at the commencement of
our career to encounter the agriculturists, flushed with prosperity from high prices; and they believed that their prosperity would be permanent, as many of us believed that our
adversity would be permanent. But it has been found that
what then injured us reacted upon those who thought that
they had an interest in injuring us. There is nothing inconsistent in our position to say that the agriculturists have
derived no benefit from the injury inflicted upon us.

We are told sometimes that we are inconsistent, because we
don't admit that the agriculturists benefit by our injury.
It would be very monstrous indeed, in the moral government of this world, if one class of the community could permanently benefit at the expense of the misery and suffering of
the rest. But, gentlemen, here is this important distinction
to be borne in mind, that although agriculturists may not
benefit themselves ultimately, that is no reason why they
should not inflict great misery upon us. You may strike a
blow, and, though that blow may be mortal to another, its
recoil may be mortal to yourselves; but it is no less a mortal
blow to him you strike, because you strike yourselves also.
Now, we required this experience to show the agriculturist
that his permanent interest is in the prosperity of his customers, and if we have done nothing else in the five years
that we have been in existence than to show the agriculturists
what is their true interest, and to show them also what they
are capable of doing upon the soil, we should have spent all
our money and all our labour to very good purpose. I have
been into most parts of the country amongst the agriculturists,—I may say, by the way, that I have been exceedingly well received by the great body of the agriculturists—
that I have no reason to complain of the courtesy either of
the landowners or the farmers in any part where I have
been—that I have found men, noblemen and gentlemen,
directly opposed to me and my views, who have yet not hesi-
tated on many occasions to take the chair at our meetings,
and to secure a fair hearing and fair play for all parties; and
this I venture to say, that there is not a county in England
where I have been to address a meeting, where I should not
be as well received at any farmers' market ordinary, as any
landowner professing to be a 'farmer's friend' in that
county.

Well, I have naturally taken some interest since my return
in what has been going on in the counties that I have visited;

and I say that, if our agitation has had no other advantage
than in the stimulus it has given to the agricultural community, our money and our time will have been well expended.
I never take up a newspaper now from the agricultural districts, containing a report of one of their agricultural meetings
(and this is the period of the year when they are holding them
in all parts), but I find, mingled with occasional apprehensions
of what the League is going to do, one universal cry—'Improve your agriculture.' There is not one of the Members of
Parliament, who sit on the monopolist benches, and who has
gone amongst his constituents to attend their agricultural
dinners, but has carried with him some one panacea or other
that is to enable farmers to brave the rivalry which they now
see is inevitable with foreign countries. One says, 'Subsoil
your land;' another, 'Thorough-drain your land;' another,
'Grub up your fences;' another, 'Take care and improve
the breed of stock;' another, 'You have not good farmsteads
for your manure;' and one worthy gentleman of my own
county, Sussex, Sir Charles Burrell, has gone back to the
nostrum, that the farmers must take to growing white carrots.
Well, it is something, at all events, to find that there is
now acknowledged to be room for improvement in British
agriculture.

But we have further acknowledgments, which are very
important indeed in our case. I took up a newspaper—I had
one sent to me yesterday—from Essex. There I find that a
meeting has been held in Colchester, and the gentleman who
presides (the president of the East Essex Agricultural Society)
is the gentleman who signed the printed circular that was
sent round throughout that division of the county, begging
the farmers and agriculturists generally to come up and put
me down when I visited Colchester. Now, I'll give you the
opinion of this gentleman upon the Corn-law:—

'Mr. Rawtry said he had no pretensions to be a prophet; but if so, he
should predict that, at no very distant period, agriculture would be left to

stood upon its own legs—that the adventitious protection which it now derived from legislative enactments would be withdrawn; and, therefore, the question for the farmers was, how should they be best prepared to meet the crisis!'

Well, what is his remedy?—

'He thought it would be at once admitted that their sole consideration must be to make up the deficiency in the value of agricultural produce, by increasing the amount of production.'

Now, gentlemen, this is an important admission—that they have not hitherto done as much as they might have done to improve the cultivation; and it is an admission, too, that they are only now stimulated to make by our agitation.

But what can be done? I don't come here to talk agriculture to you on my own knowledge; but I quote from the speeches of gentlemen opposed to us at their agricultural meetings. What then can be done? I see that a Mr. Fisher Hobbes (and I may tell you that Mr. Fisher Hobbes wrote a letter in the newspapers against me in Essex, and that he is one of the most eminent agriculturists there) says, at the same dinner,—

'He was aware that a spirit of improvement was abroad. Much was said about the tenant-farmers doing more. He agreed they might do more: the soil of the country was capable of greater production, if he said one-fourth more, he should be within compass. But that could not be done by the tenant-farmer alone: they must have confidence; it must be done by leases; by draining, by extending the length of fields, by knocking down hedgerows, and clearing away trees which now shielded the corn. They did not want trees, which, if they stood for forty years, were not in a much better position, but were only worth, perhaps, 1s., while at the same time they were reducing the value of the crop from 10s. to 30s. a-year.'

Well, gentlemen, here is some homage paid, at all events, to the Anti-Corn-law agitation—the admission, by one of the highest authorities in Essex, that the land can produce one-fourth more than it has produced. I see at the meeting of the Liverpool Association, Lord Stanley makes a similar statement; and a Mr. Binns, who was one of the judges of stock, at the same meeting declares that the land is capable of pro-

ducing double as much—as much again as it now produces.
Well, now, let us take the lowest estimate—let us suppose
that one-fourth more can be produced. We produce only
about twenty million quarters of wheat; it appears, now, that
the land can produce, and ought to produce, five million
quarters of wheat more. That would have saved us all the
famine we went through for four years after the beginning
of our agitation. Why has this not been produced? Lord
Stanley says, in his speech at Liverpool, 'The farmers must
not, now-a-days, stand, as their fathers and grandfathers
did, with their hands behind their backs, fast asleep.' But
I want to ask Lord Stanley why the farmers' fathers and
grandfathers stood fast asleep, with their hands behind their
backs? I charge Lord Stanley, who came down to Lancaster
and talked about Tamboff being able to send here an enormous
quantity of wheat—a man who, knowing better (I cannot
charge him with ignorance)—a man who, knowing better all
the while, pandered to the very ignorance he is now complaining of in the farmers, by telling them that a single province in Russia could send 38,000,000 quarters of corn here
to swamp them. I charge it upon Lord Stanley, and others
of his class and order, the politicians, who tell the farmer not
to rely upon his own exertions, but upon Parliamentary protection; I charge it on these men that they are responsible for
the farmers having stood with their hands behind their backs.

Well, gentlemen, then it seems that one of the effects of
the agitation of the League is, that agriculture is to improve,
and we are to have at least one-fourth more corn produced
at home—we may have double; with all my heart, and we
may then do very well without going 3000 or 4000 miles for
corn; but, in the name of common sense and common justice,
I say, don't starve the people here till your prating statesmen,
that come down once a year to talk at their agricultural dinners, have devised some plan by which the people may be fed
at home, according to their notions of production—don't pre-

sume entirely to stop any inlet for corn from abroad which
the people here may require to keep them from starvation. I
have never been one who believed that the repeal of the Corn-
laws would throw an acre of land out of cultivation. But not
only now does it appear that land is not to be thrown out of
cultivation, but, if we may take the testimony of these gentlemen themselves, all that is required is free trade in corn, in
order that they may produce one-fourth more than they do
now. And that, recollect, when we are told by the very same
parties — and their newspapers are now rife with the same
arguments—that our object is to bring agricultural labourers
into the manufacturing districts in order to reduce wages
there. But what do these very gentlemen admit? That you
must increase cultivation, and that increased cultivation, as
they well know, can only go on by additional employment of
labour upon the soil. You must have more labour to lay down
the draining tiles of which Lord Stanley speaks, and which he
recommended to the landowners of Yorkshire and Lancashire.
You cannot grub up hedges, you cannot grub up thorns, you
cannot drain or ditch, or make any improvement, but you
must call into employment more agricultural labour. Our
object, therefore, is not to diminish the demand for labour in
the agricultural districts, but I verily believe, if the principles
of Free Trade were fairly carried out, they would give just as
much stimulus to the demand for labour in the agricultural as
in the manufacturing districts. Oh, but it is pleasant to find
gentlemen who have been asleep (for they have been quite as
much asleep as the farmers have), going down to their agricultural dinners, and paying these tributes to the men of
Manchester, who, by these fly-flappers, have managed to rouse
them into a little activity. These squires at dinner remind
me of the story of Rip Van Winkle, who awoke from his
thirty years' sleep, rubbing his eyes, and looking about him
for his old scenes and old connections, and wondering where
he was. So these squires are rubbing their eyes, and opening

them, for the first time, to a sense of their real situation.
Having worked round our agitation to this point, I think
that, so far as argument goes, our labours are nearly at an
end.   I think the whole case, so far as discussion goes, is
given up, by the reports of the late agricultural meetings.

We are the great agricultural improvers of this country.
Amongst the other glories which will attach to the name of
Manchester will be this, that the Manchester men not only
brought manufactures to perfection, but that they made the
agriculturists also, in spite of themselves, bring their trade
to perfection.   Now, though the agriculturists have much to
learn, and many improvements to make, they are doubtless
very much in advance of most of the agriculturists in other
countries.   The only fault is, that they don't keep so much in
advance as the manufacturers do.   But that they are in advance of most other countries I think we have sufficient proof;
and I was reading an American paper this very morning
which gives an illustration of that in a way that must be
quite consolatory to those squires who are afraid that they
cannot compete with the Americans.   I see that at an
agricultural meeting in the State of New York, held at
Rochester, on the 20th September, Mr. Wadsworth, their
president, in the course of his speech, said, in speaking of
this country,—

' We have tried the English in the field of war and on the ocean, and the
result had been such that neither might be ashamed.   But there was a more
appropriate field of contest—the ploughed field—and while England could
raise forty bushels on an acre, whilst we could raise but fifteen, we must acknowledge that she was pretty hard to whip, meet her where we may.'

Well, then, gentlemen, we are constantly met and taunted
with this objection : — ' If you are not going to get corn
cheap, what's the advantage to be? — how are you to be
able to reduce wages, and so compete with the foreigner?'
Now, you know this has been a weak invention of the
enemy, in order to lead the working classes upon a wrong

scent; but I think the experience of the last twelvemonth
has had one good effect, at all events, that of convincing the
working people in this district that lower-priced food does not
mean also employment at lower wages. The object of Free
Trade is not to take foreign corn, and to prevent the home-
grown corn from being sold; but we have gone upon the
assumption—I don't know whether we are correct or not, but
I am afraid we are—that the people of this country have
never been sufficiently fed with good wheaten bread. We
have had a notion that, to four millions at least in Ireland
(and Ireland has its Corn-law as well as England), wheaten
bread is a luxury only seen occasionally, and never tasted;
and we have a notion that there are one and a half or two
millions at the least in this country, who eat a great deal too
much of that root, against the use of which I join somewhat in
Cobbett's prejudice—the potato—unless it is accompanied with
a good joint of roast beef,—and too little wheaten bread. Well,
the object of the Free Traders is (it may be very trite to tell
you, but we must reiterate these old arguments, for they are
always the best arguments), that these people may all be able
to get a bit of wheaten bread if they like to work for it. And
this, without preventing the farmers at home from sending
their corn to market, but by enabling the whole of the working classes to purchase more of the necessaries and comforts
of life. Now I heard this case put at Doncaster the other
day, by Mr. Wrightson, the member for Northallerton — a
most estimable man and a large landed proprietor in the West
Riding of Yorkshire—as properly as I have heard it put for a
long time. He says:—

'The great delusion of our landed gentry is this: they think, if they can
prevent the hand-loom weaver exchanging his web for the corn of America,
that they keep that man at home, a customer to themselves. Now (he says)
that is our greatest delusion. If we would allow that man to exchange his
web for American corn, he would then have a considerable surplus of earnings
to lay out with us for fresh meat, for vegetables, for butter, milk, cheese, and
other things. But if we prevent that man exchanging his web for the corn

of America, we deprive ourselves of him as a customer for those articles, and we are obliged to subsist him altogether as a pauper.'

And, gentlemen, I may say it is a matter of proud congratulation to us that we find in this country men of the stamp of Mr. Wrightson, and of that noble Earl who joined him on that occasion at the meeting at Doncaster. It is a subject of proud congratulation for us that we have men of that stamp belonging to our landed aristocracy. I have myself always had the impression that we should find such men come out to join us. It is something peculiar to the English character, to individuality of character, that you will find men, whatever may be their apparent motives for going with their order, who will have the moral courage to come out and join the people; and I augur well from the presence of Lord Fitzwilliam at our meeting. I hope Lord Spencer will be the next to follow. I hope that such a manly example as has been set by Mr. Samuel Jones Loyd in London,—for most manly it was in a gentleman of his reputation, and of his notorious wealth, to join the League at the very moment that it was suffering under the opprobrium attempted to be fastened upon it by a millionaire of the City,—a most manly act it was of Mr. Samuel Jones Loyd at that time to throw himself into the ranks of the Leaguers; and, I say, I hope the example of such men as my Lord Fitzwilliam and Mr. S. J. Loyd will be followed by others nearer home, in Manchester.

I can make allowance for, and can duly appreciate, the causes which may deter gentlemen of influence—gentlemen to whom parties look up, whom a wide circle respect and follow in every movement; I can make allowance for the caution with which they may hesitate to join such a body as the Anti-Corn-law League; but I put it to them, whatever their political opinions may be, whether the time is not now come at which they can with safety and propriety join us as a body, and whether we have not given them guarantee sufficient, by the prudence and the caution, and, I will say, the self-denial

with which we have carried on our proceedings, that they
will run no risk, whatever opinions they may have on other
subjects than that of Free Trade, of having those opinions in
the slightest degree offended, or prejudiced in any way by
joining us forthwith in this agitation.

Gentlemen, I think our proceedings have now been brought
to that point where we have disseminated sufficient knowledge
through the country, that we see the harvest now ripening for
the sickle, and we must be prepared with the husbandman to
gather in the harvest. It has been under that impression that
the Council of the Anti-Corn-law League has determined on
a course of action which I will just now briefly refer to,
as the course which we intend to pursue in future. It has
been thought that we have distributed information sufficient
amongst the electoral body to have given us a very considerable and preponderating strength among the electors. The
next step must be to organise and render efficient that
strength amongst the electors. Now, we have gone to work
in this agitation with the full conviction that we may carry
out the principles of Free Trade with the present constitution
of Parliament. We may be right, or we may be wrong ; we
are not responsible for the Parliament as it exists ; we did not
make the present constituencies as they are ; we did not distribute the franchise as it is distributed ; but as we find the constituencies, we, as practical men, must go to work upon them;
and through the constituencies, through the electoral body,
is the only righteous and just means of carrying the repeal of
the Corn-laws. Now, I have never doubted that the object
may be gained through the present electoral body. I have
always found, on looking back to the history of past events,
that public opinion, when well expressed, could carry its end
in this country, even when the constituency was not one-
hundredth part so favourable to the expression of public
opinion as it is now. Well, on looking at the present state
of the constituencies of this country, the Council of the

League remembered that we have certain very large constituencies, which are generally favourable to Free Trade. We
have such places as Manchester, Glasgow, Birmingham, and
a great many others, where there will never be another contest on the subject of Free Trade. I venture to say, too, that
not one of the boroughs in Scotland will have to fight a battle
in favour of Free Trade. But the representatives of these large
boroughs are countervailed in Parliament by the votes of
smaller constituencies, like St. Albans and Sudbury. How
do you get over that difficulty? Why, do you believe that
the electors of Sudbury and St. Albans are more favourable to
monopoly in their hearts than the electors of Manchester or
Birmingham? No; they are just as intelligent, just as
rightly disposed as we are; but they are not placed in such
a favourable position for giving expression to their opinions.
How is that to be remedied? I say, lay Manchester and
Birmingham alongside of St. Albans and Sudbury, and you
will give them a moral influence and support, and, by persevering in a local way, you will beat down the influence of
the local monopolist squire who has been hitherto able to
domineer over the inhabitants of those small boroughs. I
speak of these boroughs merely as a type of others, where
there has been no countervailing power to step in and prevent
the neighbouring tyrants from domineering over the constituencies.

The Council of the League have, therefore, determined that
their future operations shall be strictly electoral. You have
heard that we intend to arrange in London a collection of all
the registration lists as soon as they are published in December; we will have in a central office in London every registration list in the United Kingdom. We will have a ledger,
and a large one, too, and we will first of all record, in the
very first page, the City of London, provided it returns
Mr. Pattison; and if not, we will have Manchester first. In
this ledger we shall enter first, in due succession, each in a

page, every borough that is perfectly safe in its representation
for Free Trade.   There will be a second list—a second class—
those boroughs that send Members to Parliament who are
moderate monopolists, who have notions about differential
duties and fixed duties; and we will have another class, for
those who are out-and-out monopolists. Well, we may tick off
those boroughs that are safe; we go to work in the next place
in those boroughs that are represented by moderate monopolists, to make them send Free Traders, and we will urge upon
them in particular to canvass the electors, and send up a
majority of their signatures requiring their Members to vote
for Mr. Villiers' motion at the beginning of next session.
We will make a selection of so many boroughs as shall
be sufficient to give us a majority in the House; and I
take it that those boroughs will not require to have more
than 300,000 electors, and upon those 300,000 electors
we will begin our fire. We will give them, through the
penny postage, full acquaintance with all our proceedings;
we will furnish them with arguments, put them in possession of the latest tactics of the enemy, so that they shall
have the refutation of the youngest-born fallacy always at
their fingers' ends. We intend to visit them by deputation.
If my friend Bright takes one set, and I take another, we may
get over a great many of them. And we will take somebody
else with us. We will convene these meetings from London;
we will send our circulars from London; there shall be no
party work, the business shall not go into the hands of local
cliques at all. We will take a room, and meet the electors
by appointment there, without the co-operation of any local
leaders, so as to excite no jealousy on either side. And when
we have got them there, we shall try and put this Free Trade
question upon neutral grounds, and see if we cannot find
honest men in all parties who will join us in putting down
monopoly. We will organise them; we will not go without
leaving traces behind us, and we will leave an organisation to

work after we are gone; and we shall take care to bring away with us a list of the best men in the borough, with whom we may correspond on particular business. I was told by an old electioneerer in London, one who had dipped his fingers pretty deep into the system we are going to put down,—' You will frighten them more than anything, if you carry out that part of your plan of going down to see the electors.' It is the very thing we intend to do; and we will do it ourselves, too. It is not merely intimidation we have to contend with in these small boroughs; the system of bribery at the last election was carried out to an extent which few people in this Hall, perhaps hardly one, have ever dreamt of even in your worst suspicions. The boroughs were literally put up to auction at the Carlton Club—ay, and at the Reform Club, too—at the last general election; a price was fixed upon them; and men went up to London to these cliques and coteries to know how much they could buy boroughs for. We have got an alteration of the law, which enables any public body that determines to take that patriotic task in hand, to prosecute these bribers in a way that they very little dreamt of when they passed that law. Now, we intend, as one of the glorious objects of the Anti-Corn-law League, to put down for ever the system of bribery in this country. We can expose the intimidators, and raise a pretty loud cry against them; and we will expose them wherever they are found exercising their tyrannical acts. But the bribers we can and will put down by a jury of our countrymen.

I have often expressed my astonishment that no society was ever formed similar to the Anti-Felony Societies in the agricultural districts for the prosecution of sheep-stealers, whose object was to put down bribery. Nothing is so simple; it ought to be done in London by the House of Commons. But what is the process now? A man gets into Parliament by bribery; the defeated candidate petitions the House to unseat him; a Committee is appointed to examine into the

case; the whole system of bribery is laid bare in that Committee; the scoundrels who have been the actors in it are
there, blocking up the lobbies of the House, enough to make
a man's blood run chill as he passes them; there they are,
day after day, exposing their acts of perjury and subornation;
while the result is, the Committee declares the sitting Member
unseated; the candidate who petitioned has to pay just the
same expense as the man who is unseated, and he may go and
stand again if he likes, and go through the same ordeal for his
pains. What does a Committee of the House of Commons do
when these men are proved guilty of the worst crime that can
be conceived,—for what crime can be more heinous than buying and selling the franchises, by which the laws of this
country are framed? If a man has his pocket picked of his
handkerchief, if the felony is made public, he is bound to
prosecute, otherwise he is held to be an accessory after the
fact; and if he had taken his passage to America, the
magistrates would make him stop and prosecute the felon.
Yet the House of Commons allows all these nefarious practices
to go on under its own roof, and never takes one step to vindicate its character with the country. I told them in the
House, on the occasion of Lord Dungannon's exposure,—Sir
Robert Peel was present,—' If you do not order your Attorney-
General to prosecute these men, I will belong to a society out
of doors that shall undertake that task for him.'

The thing can be done; you may put down bribery. It
has been practised to an extent of which you are perfectly unconscious. With the exception of some of the new boroughs—
and even some of them have been touched with this canker—
there is hardly a pure borough to be found in the south
of England. To put the system down there will require a
vigorous effort; and the plan that the League has now
adopted in London will, I hope, do more than anything else
that could be done to convince these traffickers in seats that
we are in earnest. There is a placard now spread throughout

London, headed with the Queen's arms, offering a reward of
100*l.* for the evidence that shall go to convict any one who is
guilty of either offering or taking a bribe.   The course is by
indictment in a criminal court, and a conviction ensures the
offender twelve months' imprisonment, at least; and I hope
that we shall manage to bring some high game before a jury
of our countrymen.   You will not convict men before a
Committee of the House of Commons.   There was Lord
Dungannon, who wrote a cheque for 700*l.*, and sent to his
agent; that agent was proved to have just handed over the
money to the men who voted for Lord Dungannon; Lord
Dungannon is unseated, he is incompetent to sit again during
this Parliament, and yet the Committee declared there is no
proof that bribery was practised with the cognizance of Lord
Dungannon.   Now, I would like to see some of these Lord
Dungannons brought before a jury—an honest jury—of
twelve of our countrymen.   Well, gentlemen, the object we
have in view is to remove a mighty injustice, and the effort
that it will require will be commensurate.   But the effort will
be made, and of its success I entertain no doubt whatever.

FREE TRADE.

VIII.

LONDON, FEBRUARY 8, 1844.

SINCE I last had the pleasure of meeting you here, I have had the honour of addressing many large assemblies of my fellow-countrymen; but I can assure you I return to this magnificent gathering with increased surprise and gratification at the ardour and enthusiasm that I see to prevail in the metropolis. I am told that we are favoured this night with the attendance of many visitors who are neither very well informed, nor, of course, very much convinced on our question. Now, will you, who sit on the front form in our seminary, condescend to make a little allowance if I give to these young pupils a lesson in the elementary principles of Free Trade, and endeavour to send them away as efficient missionaries as doubtless you have been in our cause? But then, I hope our good friends the reporters will spare their fingers, that they may not convict me of tautology. We will begin at the beginning. Now, we are 'Free Traders;' and what is Free Trade? Not the pulling down of all custom-houses, as some of our wise opponents the dukes and earls have lately been trying to persuade the agricultural labourers; I should think it would do with nobody else. By Free Trade we mean the abolition of all protective duties. It is very possible that our children, or at all events their offspring, may be wise enough to dispense with custom-house duties altogether. They may think it prudent and economical to raise their revenues by direct taxation, without circumventing their foreign trade. We do not propose to do that; but there are a class of men who have taken possession of the Custom-house, and have installed their clerks there, to collect revenue for their own particular benefit, and we intend to remove them out of the Custom-house.

Now, I want to impress on our new friends, these students in Free Trade, to remind them of that which I have frequently dwelt upon, and which cannot be too often repeated, that this system of monopoly is analogous in every respect to that which existed 250 years ago under the Tudors and the Stuarts, when sovereigns granted monopolies to the creatures of their courts for the exclusive sale of wine, leather, salt, and other things, and which system our forefathers, at great labour and heavy sacrifice, utterly extirpated. One by one these monopolies were abolished; and, not content with destroying the existing monopolies, they passed a law, which became, as it were, a fundamental principle in our Constitution, that no sovereign, thenceforth or for ever, should have the power of granting a monopoly to anybody for the exclusive sale of any necessary commodity of life. Now, what I want to impress on our young learners is this, that that which sovereigns cannot do, a band of men united together—the selfish oligarchy of the sugar-hogshead and the flour-sack — have done. They have got together in the House of Commons, and by their own Acts of Parliament have appropriated to their own classes the very privileges, the self-same monopolies, or monopolies as injurious in every respect to the interests of the people as those monopolies were which our forefathers abolished two centuries and a half ago. There is no difference whatever in the effect of a monopoly in the sale of sugar held by a few men, the owners of those specks of land in the West Indies (for specks they are compared with the South American continent, the East Indies, Siam, China, the Indian Archipelago, and those other countries from which sugar might be supplied); there is no earthly difference in its effect on the community, whether a body of men in London take to themselves a monopoly in the sale of sugar, or whether Queen Victoria granted that monopoly to one of the noblemen of her court. Well, our forefathers abolished this system; at a time, too, mark you, when the sign manual of the sovereign had somewhat of a divine sanction and challenged superstitious reverence in the minds of the people. And shall we, the descendants of those men, be found so degenerate, so unworthy of the blood that flows in our veins, so recreant to the very name of 'Englishmen,' as not to shake off this incubus, laid on as it is by a body of our fellow-citizens?

I believe some of our visitors here to-night are of what is called ' the agricultural interest.' They are probably curious to know why it is that we, professing to be Free Traders in everything, should restrict the title of our association to that of ' The National Anti-Corn-Law League.' I will explain the reason. We advocate the abolition of the Corn-law, because we believe that to be the foster-parent of all other monopolies; and if we destroy that—the parent, the monster monopoly—it will save us the trouble of devouring all the rest. We have had now, for more than twenty years, a succession of Cabinets, every one of them claiming the merit in the eyes of the people of England of being Free-trade Administrations; from the year 1823, when Mr. Huskisson proposed his extensive changes in our commercial system,—when he became installed, as it were, the very lion of the aristocratic coteries of London, as a Free Trader—a Free Trader in silks and ribbons, French lace, and the like,—from that time to this we have never wanted a Government willing to take the credit to themselves of being Free Traders. If I wanted an argument to convince you that we are right in the title

that we have taken, and the direction we have given to our
agitation, I would show it in the conduct of Sir Robert Peel
two years ago. He then boasted that he had propounded the
largest measure of commercial reform of any Minister in this
country; he brought in his tariff with an alteration of 500
or 600 articles therein. I looked over it again and again,
expecting to find corn there, but was disappointed. The right
hon. Baronet was asked why corn was not there? and his
reply was, ' It has always been customary in this country
to treat corn differently from every other item in the tariff.'
In that significant reply of the Prime Minister do we find a
justification for the title of our agitation, and the direction
in which we carry it. You will have reform enough in
colonial asses, caviare, fiddlesticks, and other equally important matters. You will have all those items very diligently
attended to. Do you look after corn, and corn will take
care of all the rest. Thus have I told our new visitors what
' Free Trade' means, and why we almost exclusively advocate the repeal of the Corn-laws, instead of taking a wider
purpose.

Now, what are the objections alleged against the adoption
of Free-trade principles? First of all, take the most numerous
body—the working class—by far the most important in the
consideration of this question : for probably nine-tenths of all
the population of this country are dependent on labour, either
the hard work of hands, or the equally hard toil of heads. I
say, take their case first. We are told this system of restriction
is for the benefit of the labourers. We are informed by the
earls, dukes, and the squires, that the price of corn regulates
the rate of wages; and that, if we reduce the price of corn by
a free trade in that article, we shall only bring down the rate
of wages. Now, I see a good many working people in this
assembly, and would ask them whether, in any bargain ever
made for labour in London, the question of corn or its price
was ever made an element in that agreement? Why, look at

your hackney-coach and watermen's fares, and at your ticket-
porters' charges. Your own Corporation, in their bye-laws
and Acts of Parliament regulating the wages of a variety of
labourers in this metropolis, have been strangely oblivious of
this sliding scale of corn, when they have fixed a permanent
rate of wages. I think I have heard lately something about
women who

> 'Stitch—stitch—stitch!
> For three half-pence a shirt.'

I want to know whether the wages of those poor creatures
are regulated by the price of corn.   I thought I had
settled that matter, as far as regards the working man, at
the time Sir Robert Peel brought in his Corn Bill two
years ago.   I then moved an amendment to this effect:—
' Resolved, That before we proceed to pass a law having for
its object to raise, artificially, the price of bread, it is expedient and just that we should first of all consider how far it
is practicable to raise in proportion the wages of labourers in
this country.' I was determined I would stop that gap for
the monopolists for ever; and accordingly I brought on my
amendment; and was then informed by Sir Robert Peel,—
' It is quite impossible we can fix the rate of wages in this
country. Parliament has no power to settle the rate of wages;
that must be settled by the competition of the world's market.'
I forced the monopolists to a division on this matter, determined that it should not be a sham motion; and we accordingly had a division.   The right honourable Baronet and all
his friends walked out at one door, and I had some twenty or
thirty who accompanied me out at the other.   We had not
been back again in the House five minutes before this body of
innocents were busy passing a law to prevent the price of
their corn being settled by 'the competition of the world's
market.'   I shall not be surprised some night, perhaps when
my friend Mr. Villiers brings forward his next motion, in
going down to St. Stephen's, to see a bit of paper fixed to the

door of that place with something of this kind written upon
it : 'Corn and cattle-dealers to be found within. No competition allowed with the shop over the water.'

Now, the first and greatest count in my indictment against
the Corn-law is, that it is an injustice to the labourers of this
and every other country. My next charge is, that it is a
fraud against every man of capital engaged in any pursuit,
and every person of fixed income not derived from land. I
will take the trader   I am a manufacturer of clothing, and I
do not know why, in this climate, and in the artificial state of
society in which we live, the making of clothes should not be
as honourable—because it is pretty near as useful—a pursuit
as the manufacture of food. Well, did you ever hear any
debates in the House to fix the price of my commodities in
the market ? Suppose we had a majority of cotton-printers
(which happens to be my manufacture) in the House: and if
we had a majority I have no doubt we should find Sir Robert
Peel quite willing to do our work for us : he is the son of a
cotton-printer, and I dare say he would do it for us as well as
any one else. Let us suppose that you were reading the
newspaper some fine morning, and saw an account of a
majority of the House having been engaged the night before
in fixing the price at which yard-wide prints should be sold :
' Yard-wide prints, of such a quality, 10d. a yard ; of such a
quality, 9d. ; of such a quality, 8d. ; of such a quality, 7d.,'
and so on. Why, you would rub your eyes with astonishment! You would clear your spectacles, if you wore any, and
you would doubt your own senses! The very boys in the
streets leading to Parliament, and the cabmen and omnibus-
drivers, would hoot and hiss us out of the metropolis! Now,
did it ever occur to you that there is no earthly difference
between a body of men, manufacturers of corn, sitting down
in the House, and passing a law enacting that wheat shall be
so much, barley so much, beans so much, and oats so much?

Why, then, do you look at this monopoly of corn with

such complacency? Simply because you and I and the rest of us have a superstitious reverence for the owners of those sluggish acres, and have a very small respect for ourselves and our own vocation. I say the Corn-law monopolists, who arrogate to themselves power in the House of Commons, are practising an injustice on every other species of capitalists. Take the iron trade, for example—a prodigious interest in this country. Iron of certain qualities has gone down in price, during the last five or six years, from 15l. 10s. to 5l. 10s. per ton. Men have seen their fortunes—ay, I have known them—dwindle away from 300,000l. till now they could not sit down and write their wills for 100,000l. Well, did any man ever hear in the House of Commons an attempt made to raise a cry about these grievances there, or to lodge a complaint against the Government or the country because they could not keep up the price of iron? Has any man come forward there proposing that by some law pig-iron should be so much, and bar-iron of such a price, and other kinds of iron in proportion? No; neither has this been the case with any other interest in the country. But how is it with corn? The very first night I was present in the House this session, I saw the Prime Minister get up, having a paper before him, and he was careful to tell us what the price of corn had been for the last fifty years, and what it was now. He is employed for little else but as a kind of corn-steward, to see how the prices may be kept up for his masters.

What are the grounds on which this system is maintained? The farmer is put forward—the interests of the farmer and the farm-labourer are put forward — as the pretext for maintaining this monopoly. I have heard the admission made at agricultural meetings by landlords themselves, that there are twenty farmers bidding for every farm, and that they excuse themselves to the farmers at these very meetings that they let their land at the full value, and they cannot help it. It is not their fault because there are these twenty farmers bidding for every farm that is vacant. Now, I would ask you, or the merest tyro in this question, if there be twenty farmers bidding for every farm, and the law can raise the price of the produce of that farm, do you think that one out of those twenty farmers will get the benefit of that rise in price? Will not the other nineteen take care that it is brought down by competition to the ordinary profit of trade in this country? The farmers have been too long deluded by the mere cry of 'Protection.' We read of it now in every meeting—'Protection to the farmers.' It is destruction to the farmers. The word should be changed from 'protection' to 'destruction,' and it would then be more expressive of the effect of the Corn-law on the farmers.

With respect to the farm-labourers, our opponents tell us that our object in bringing about the repeal of the Corn-laws is, by reducing the price of corn, to lower the rate of their wages. I can only answer upon this point for the manufacturing districts; but, as far as they are concerned, I state it most emphatically as a truth, that, for the last twenty years, whenever corn has been cheap wages have been high in Lancashire; and, on the other hand, when bread has been dear wages have been greatly reduced. Now, I distinctly put this statement on record, and challenge any one to controvert it. Wages may possibly be affected by the price of food in the agricultural districts, and rise and fall in proportion ; but if they do, it is simply for this reason—that they have reached their minimum, or the point at which they verge towards what you might call slave labour, when a man gets in the best of times only as much as will keep him in health. When corn rises, equal food must be given to the labourer to eat, just upon the same principle as farmers or others give an equal quantity of corn to their horses in dear years as they do in periods of cheapness, in order that they may be maintained in health, and be equal to the amount of labour which is wanted of them. But whenever the value of labour rises and falls in the agricultural

districts with the price of food, it must be because those wages
have previously sunk to that point which is next in degree to
the wages which slaves obtain for their labour. Now, let me
be fully understood as to what Free Traders really do want.
We do not want cheap corn merely in order that we may have
low money prices.   What we desire is plenty of corn, and
we are utterly careless what its price is, provided we obtain
it at the natural price. All we ask is this, that corn shall
follow the same law which the monopolists in food admit
that labour must follow; that 'it shall find its natural level
in the markets of the world.'

And now, what would be the process of this equalisation of
prices? I think I can give you the rationale of it. The
effect of free trade in corn will be this: It would increase the
demand for agricultural produce in Poland, Germany, and
America. That increase in the demand for agricultural produce would give rise to an increased demand for labour in
those countries, which would tend to raise the wages of the
agricultural labourers. The effect of that would be to draw
away labourers from manufactures in all those places. To
pay for that corn, more manufactures would be required from
this country; this would lead to an increased demand for
labour in the manufacturing districts, which would necessarily
be attended with a rise of wages, in order that the goods
might be made for the purpose of exchanging for the corn
brought from abroad. Whether prices would be equalised,
according to the opinion expressed by my Lord Spencer, by a
rise in the price of bread abroad to the level at which it is here,
or whether it would be by a fall in the prices here to the
level at which they now exist on the Continent, would not
make the least earthly difference to the Free Traders; all they
ask is, that they shall be put in the same position with others,
and that there should be no bar or hindrance to the admission
of food from any quarter into this country. I observe there
are narrow-minded men in the agricultural districts, telling

us, 'Oh, if you allow Free Trade, and bring in a quarter of corn
from abroad, it is quite clear that you will sell one quarter less
in England.' Those men, fellow-countrymen, who utter such
nonsense as this, are a sample of the philosophers who are now
governing this country. What! I would ask, if you can
set more people to work at better wages—if you can clear
your streets of those spectres which are now haunting your
thoroughfares begging their daily bread — if you can depo-
pulate your workhouses, and clear off the two millions of
paupers which now exist in the land, and put them to work
at productive industry—do you not think that they would
consume some of the wheat as well as you; and may not
they be, as we are now, consumers of wheaten bread by millions, instead of existing on their present miserable dietary?
Mark me: these philosophical men, so profoundly ignorant of
what is immediately around them, but who meet us at every
turn with prophecies of what is going to happen in future,
will tell us, forsooth, that Free Trade will throw their land
out of cultivation, and deprive their labourers of employment.

Now, we put against the prophecies of these selfish, ignorant beings the predictions of the most eminent and skilful in
agriculture in this land. I will take my Lord Ducie, who
confessedly stands at the head of the arable farmers of this
country, and my Lord Spencer, who is admitted to be the
first of the grazing farmers of England; I will take the
biggest-headed and shrewdest farmers and tenants in every
county; and if the monopolists will give me a Committee of
the House of Commons, which I intend to move for, they
shall be examined before it; and these practical men will,
every one of them, predict what I have also predicted
(although I claim to be no authority), that, with free trade
in corn, so far from throwing land out of use or injuring the
cultivation of the poorer soils, free trade in corn is the very
way to increase the production at home, and stimulate the
cultivation of the poorer soils by compelling the application

of more capital and labour to them. We do not contemplate
deriving one quarter less corn from the soil of this country ;
we do not anticipate having one pound less of butter or
cheese, or one head less of cattle or sheep: we expect to have
a great increase in production and consumption at home ;
but all we contend for is this, that when we, the people
here, have purchased all that can bo raised at home, we shall
be allowed to go 3000 miles—to Poland, Russia, or America
—for more; and that there shall be no let or hindrance put
in the way of our getting this additional quantity.

Now, we are met by the monopolists with this objection :—
If you have a free trade in corn, foreigners will send you their
wheat here, but they will take nothing in return. The argument employed, in fact, amounts to this, if it amounts to
anything—That they will give us their corn for nothing. I
know not what can exceed the absurdity of these men, if they
be honest, or their shallow and transparent knavery, if they
be dishonest, in putting forward such an argument as that.
If there be a child here, I will give him a lesson which
will make him able to go home and laugh to scorn those
who talk about reciprocity, and induce to make fools'-caps
and bonfires of the articles in the *Morning Post* or *Herald.*
Now, I will illustrate that point. I will take the case
of a tailor living in one of your streets, and a provision-
dealer living in another, and this busybody of a reciprocity-
man living somewhere between the two. He sees this tailor
going every Saturday night empty-handed to the provision-
dealer, and bringing home upon his shoulder a side of bacon,
under one arm a cheese, and under the other a keg of butter.
Well, this reciprocity-man, being always a busybody, takes
the alarm, and says, 'There is a one-sided trade going on
there, I must look after it.' He calls on the tailor, and says,
' This is a strange trade you are doing! You are importing
largely from that provision-dealer, but I do not find that you
are exporting any cloths, or coats, or waistcoats, in return ?'

The tailor answers him, 'If you feel any alarm at this, ask the provision-dealer about it: I am all right, at all events.' Away goes the reciprocity gentleman to the provision shop, and says, 'I see you are doing a very strange business with that tailor; you are exporting largely provisions, but I do not see that you import any clothes from him: how do you get paid?' 'Why, man, how should I?' replies the provision-dealer, 'in gold and silver, to be sure!' Then the reciprocity-man is seized with another crotchet, and forthwith begins to talk about 'the drain of bullion.' Away he flies to the tailor, and says, 'Why, you will be ruined entirely! What a drain of the precious metals is going on from your till! That provision-dealer takes no clothes from you: he will have nothing but gold and silver for his goods.' 'Ay, man,' replies the tailor, 'and where do you think I get the gold and silver from? Why, I sell my clothes to the grocer, the hatter, the bookseller, the cabinet-maker, and one hundred others, and they pay me in gold and silver. And pray, Mr. Busybody, what would you have me to do with it? Do you think my wife and family would grow fat on gold and silver?' Now, if there is any little girl or boy in this assembly, I hope they will go home, and for exercise write out that illustration of reciprocity, and show it to any of their friends who may be seized with this crotchet respecting reciprocity and the drain of gold, and see if they cannot laugh them easily out of their delusions.

Well, now, my friend, Mr. Villiers, has alluded to the subject of revenue. I need not go into that point, for he has completely exhausted it; but it was a most impudent pretence which the monopolists set up, and set up in the face of the income-tax, levied upon us, as it were, to be a scourge of thorns to remind us of our sins of ignorance and our neglect of our interests. To think of their having the impudence to tell this to us, with this fact, not staring in our faces, but visiting us in our pockets; to think that this should ever be

advanced again—that the monopolists keep up the revenue—
is to me the most monstrous piece of impudence I ever heard
of in my life. Now, we want the farmers to understand
precisely what the National Anti-Corn-law League is, and
what its objects are. We are not going to allow the landlords
to carry off the farmers with the old stale watchword and the
threadbare arguments again. Why, they had not anything
new to offer them, and, therefore, they have started this
about the revenue; their agitators are all the old hacks over
again; there has not been even a young aristocrat come forward to show a modicum of talent in support of the system.
There they are! the same men and the same arguments, and
the whole being summed up in 'Protection.' That word
'protection' reminds me of another word that was used by a
character in the 'Vicar of Wakefield,' I mean Mr. Jenkinson,
who, if ever he wanted to take in anybody, had some talk
to them about the 'cosmogony' of the world; and with
that word he took in poor Moses with his green spectacles,
and actually imposed upon poor Dr. Primrose himself in the
same way. Now, this 'protection' is, to my ear, very much
like the 'cosmogony' of good Mr. Jenkinson; and I think
the men who use it have just about as honest objects in view
as Mr. Jenkinson had.

I do not like to turn these meetings into scolding assemblies, for we are too majestic a body to scold any person; but
I do like, if possible, to extract a little amusement out of our
opponents in this matter; and certainly, when I look through
their speeches and read what they have been saying, I must
confess I have enjoyed more laughter about these statements
than this question has afforded me ever since we began our agitation five years ago. We are going to prepare a pamphlet—I
am not sure whether it will not grow into a volume—of elegant
extracts from monopolists' speeches! There shall be separate
headings to the several extracts. One head shall be, 'argument;'
another, 'wit;' a third, 'humour;' a fourth, 'manners;' and a

fifth, ' morals ;' and you shall see choice specimens of every one
of them.   There is one worthy gentleman, who, in speaking of
the League, has given such a bouquet of flowers of oratory,
that I think we ought to put him as a frontispiece to this
volume.   This gentleman, in the course of about twenty lines,
manages to apply about as many abusive epithets to the
League :—We are mere ' Jacobins,' ' Jonathan Wilds,' and
' Jack Shepparda.'   We are a ' scratch pack of hounds ;' and
he condescends to explain that that phrase means the odds
and ends, or a pack collected from the whole county.   The
elegant gentleman winds up with the choice appellation of
' ragamuffins.'   That is the effusion of Sir Charles Knightley ;
and I think we must have his portrait for a frontispiece to our
volume.

I observe one noble Lord has inquired very innocently, in
alluding to our agitation, ' What does all this bobbery mean ?'
Now, they have let us into a secret in this agitation of theirs.
We did not think—I am sure I did not—that there was so
much titled ignorance or coroneted vulgarity in the land as I
find there is.   I confess I did not expect to find the strongest
argument coming from such a source, but had hoped to meet
with something like decency of manners !   Why, who would
belong to such a set ?   If that is the best language they can
put out in public, what sort of talk must it be theirs in
private ?

And then for ' violence'—why, we were charged with
violence at one time ; and I really believe we used to be
somewhat violent.   Five years ago, when we began, we were
small and insignificant, and very poor ; fighting our way up
in the world.   We were really almost compelled to make a
noise to attract a hearing.   All small things, you know, are
generally very noisy ; it is the order of nature.   See how the
little dog barks at the stately steed as he goes along your
streets ; but the horse takes no notice of him.   There was
some excuse for us ; our cause appeared a desperate one.

Now, they must have an excuse, too, for their violence, and I suspect it is the very same we had—they feel their cause to be a desperate one. But I want, in this stage of our agitation, to impress on our friends the necessity of taking warning by the spectacles which our opponents now present, and that they should resolve not to imitate such a bad example. We have got up in the world; we can pay our way. We have the nobles and the gentles of the land in our ranks, and we ought to be very decorous. We can afford to be condescending, even. I should not wonder if we soon begin to ballot for members, and not admit people unless they happen to be ' of the superior kind.'

Our opponents, I presume, intend to spend their money in something like the same way as we have expended ours,—that is, in giving lectures and distributing tracts. How I should like to attend one of their first meetings ! Fancy a meeting like this ! An orator introduced to deliver a magnificent— magniloquent, I should say—lecture in behalf of starvation ! Only think of his exordium and his peroration, with such an inspiring topic! We have heard much boasting of these meetings ; we have been told that they are ' farmers' meetings ;' but we have not seen the names of any farmers who have made these vulgar speeches of which I have been speaking. Now, as having something like an hereditary right to identify myself with farmers, I do rejoice to say, that, in scanning over all the proceedings of these monopolist gatherings, I have not seen a single instance of vituperation, or anything approaching to vulgarity of language, on the part of the *bona fide* tenant-farmers. The monopolists of corn— the landlords—are the monopolists of all the vulgarity of language ! There have been one or two individuals paraded, who have been called ' farmers,' and who have made long speeches ; but I have taken pains to inquire a little of their whereabouts, and I find that they are all auctioneers and land-valuers ; and it is a remarkable fact, that I have never met

with a protectionist orator at the meetings I have attended
in the agricultural districts, but he has always turned out an
auctioneer or a land-valuer. The land-valuers are a body of
men—I mean the land-valuers and auctioneers—who represent
the landlord in his very worst aspect; they are persons that
have an interest in this system which causes perpetual change
and a constant rise in rent; for the more changes there are, or
the more failures there are, the more valuing there is for the
valuer, and the more selling there is for the auctioneer: though,
if you had a system by which prices were steadied, and leases
were granted, the land-valuers and auctioneers would not
be known in the land; in fact, they are a tribe hardly to be
met with in Scotland at the present time.

Now, we expect our opponents will meet us fairly in this
matter. We have avoided, although we have been often
pressed to do so, interfering with any of their meetings. I
hold it to be unjust in this country, wherever meetings are held
avowedly upon one side of the question, and to make a demonstration, that anybody should go and interfere with such a
meeting, or attempt to put counter-resolutions. I say I hope
they will deal fairly with us, but, judging by their conduct in
past times, I do not expect they will. I know that monopolist
money has been paid for the hire of men to attend and interrupt our meetings ever since we began our agitation. I am
now suffering under a hoarseness from an encounter of this
kind in the great Town-hall of Birmingham on Monday last.
When I arrived in that town I found huge yellow placards
posted all over the walls, the cost of which a printer there
told me must have been many pounds, professing to emanate
from the O'Connor Chartist agitators, calling upon the working men to 'assemble in all their might, and upset these mill
tyrants, and drive them out of the town.' Now it is remarkable that there was no printer's name to these placards, therefore there is every reason to suppose they were imported from
a distance. The Town-hall was thrown open. A fair public

meeting had not been held in Birmingham for six years previously; and I was glad of an opportunity of making my first
experiment upon the good sense of the working people of that
district. The magnificent building of which I have spoken
was crammed, and four-fifths of the audience were working
men; for it was in the morning of holiday Monday. About
fifty men, however, of another description, were packed in the
centre of that meeting. A most notorious individual was
placed in the organ-loft by the side of us, who acted as fugle-
man to the rest. Their object evidently was to prevent the
deputation of the League from being heard. While my friend
Colonel Thompson—who is even hoarser than I am myself—
was speaking, they kept up a continued clamour. When my
turn came, I appealed to the 4000 working people, and asked
them whether they would allow themselves to be tyrannised
over by a handful of men, who, with liberty on their lips, had
despotism at heart? In less than five minutes the most dis-
orderly among them were removed from the hall; and the
remainder, when they saw two or three of their number
carried out by the working men, showed—what such fellows
will always show—that they were as great cowards as they
had previously shown they were bullies. They were as peaceable as mice in a church for the rest of the meeting; and, I
will venture to say, it is the last appearance of that body in
the Town-hall of Birmingham.

I know that monopolist money in former times has been so
spent and taken by men who have degraded the name they
have borne—that is, men of a political party seeking for
liberty. I reverence men who make honest efforts, who seek
for freedom in any form; but I say that these persons have
degraded the sacred name under which they have pretended to
work. They have been for the last three years doing nothing
but trying to help the aristocracy in maintaining the Corn-
laws. Look, I say, at their organ of the press, and you will per-
ceive the character of its leading articles for the last two years.

Has it been advocating the object which it professed to be
established to promote? No. The staple of its articles are
just the counterpart of what you will find in the *Morning Post.*
Look at its leaders—who are they? Men who are ever found
trying to thwart us in our honest, single-minded effort to pull
down this giant monopoly. Well, then, I say, those men who
have been hitherto paid for this work—though I admit that some
of them have been fools enough to do the work for nothing—but
as they have been paid, I suspect that some of the money that
has been raised recently by the monopolists will find its way
into the same channel, and that there may be further attempts
made of the kind I have alluded to. But I think a body that
had the temerity to come into this theatre with such an object
would look twice before it made the essay. There may be
an attempt made even to interrupt the orderly proceedings of
these most important gatherings; for if these meetings continue, and are carried on with the same numbers, order, and
decorum with which they are now, speaking a voice that is felt
throughout Europe — yes, I know they are felt throughout
Europe, and one of the first things inquired for when intelligent foreigners come here is to have an opportunity of seeing
such unparalleled demonstrations — I say, if these meetings
continue, do you think it will be long before their influence
will be found in another place whose locality will be nameless,
not far from Parliament-street?

Then, I say, fair play. Let every man follow his own bent
in this free country—free, at all events, to hold meetings like
this. Let every man attend his own meeting, call together
his own, and promote whatever legitimate objects he pleases.
We will neither intrude into the meetings of others, nor allow
intrusion into ours. If a meeting be held to take the sense of
a district, it is the duty of every man to attend; and the votes
should be taken to see what the sense of the majority of that
district may be. Now, I give notice to the monopolists, that
in all my meetings in their counties I invite all comers to

oppose me ; I will consider their doing so no intrusion. Talk
of their meetings! Why, I have been in every county in which
they have held them, and I have no hesitation in declaring,
that for every hundred they have had gathered together I
have had a thousand on every occasion. Take their largest
number—in Essex, where it is said they had 600 gathered—
we had 6000 at Colchester! Ay, and I promise them that,
when the weather comes that is favourable for open-air meeting, I will visit their counties again, and take the opinion of
their population. I call my meetings in the same place where
their own high authorities always convene theirs — in the
county towns, such as Winchester and Salisbury. I could
gather ten times the number to hear me as at these recent
meetings, though perhaps they may have ten Dukes, fifteen
Earls, or a dozen Members of Parliament.

But when I have taken the sense of such meetings in favour
of Free Trade, what have the monopolists said upon the subject? That we have carried our resolutions merely by 'the
rabble of the towns.' Now, mark this fact : I have observed in
every instance that their own organs of the press declare that
I am indebted to ' the rabble of the town' for carrying my
resolutions. But, now it is this same 'rabble' which they
pretend to tell us is opposed to the Anti-Corn-law League !
They throw it in our teeth that we are not supported by this
very rabble, which they formerly said was our whole support
at our open-air meetings. They go down to Birmingham and
hire fifty, certainly of the dirtiest and most unintelligent
fellows they can find, and try to get them to break up the
meeting, and then boast that ' the rabble of the town,' as they
condescend to call you, are against us.

I will not disguise from you my opinion, that the time
is approaching when it will require every effort on the part
of Free Traders to carry out the objects which we have in
view. I am not one who would, and I never did, underrate the power or the importance of our opponents. There is

much work for us to do, but the work shall and will be done.
There are men now brought out by this very agitation in every
borough and large town that I have visited—new men—not
the old hacks of party, but persons drawn out with a solemn
and earnest conviction, with a craving after justice and truth
in this matter, who are diligently at work in every part of the
kingdom. And if we were to be taken off this scene, in
which we have been and are now most prominent, and were
unable to continue our effort, the question has gone beyond
the stage from which it can recede. It only requires that you
should continue to disseminate the knowledge which you have,
and increase the interest which is felt in London upon this
subject, that this question will ultimately be brought to a
triumphant issue. It cannot be carried *pro* or *con.* by such
insignificant boroughs as Devizes. Give us the large constituencies—give us, as we will have when another election
comes (and you cannot carry this question without a dissolution), every borough in South Lancashire and the West Riding
of Yorkshire, give us Birmingham, Edinburgh, Glasgow,
Leeds, Hull, Bristol, and all the large constituencies; give
us Liverpool—ay, and give us London—and there is no
Minister to be found who can maintain office to carry on a
system of monopolies upon the strength of a mere numerical
majority of the House of Commons, and by the aid of the
representatives of such places as Devizes or St. Albans;
there is no Minister who would dare to do it, though the
monopolists would be glad to find their tool, if they could, in
the face of the united expression of opinion of the great constituencies of this kingdom. But from the moment that you
are right in the metropolis—and we are right in all the large
towns—that moment the Corn-laws are repealed!

Still, you have work to do in London. I observe that your
beaten candidate, who I thought was silenced for ever, at one of
his meetings, either by himself or by his chairman, denominated
those who voted for Mr. Pattison at the last election as ' the

rabble of the City.' Now it so happens that I am entitled to
register myself as a voter for the City of London, but have
neglected so to do; but I intend at the next revision to
register, in order that I may have the honour of joining
that 'rabble' which rejected Mr. Baring. Be diligent
therefore in disseminating knowledge on this question. The
repeal of the Corn-laws will be carried when men understand
it. And when you understand it, if you are honest men, you
will feel it; if you feel it, at least as I have, you will not be
able to be quiet without doing something to put down this
great injustice. I exhort you each in your several circles to
spread abroad light on this subject. Knowledge is the
power—knowledge alone—by which we shall bring this foul
system to the dust.

—»→+◆✦✦◆►+++—

FREE TRADE.

IX.

EFFECT OF PROTECTIVE DUTIES.

HOUSE OF COMMONS, MARCH 13, 1844.

[On March 13, 1844, Mr. Cobden brought forward his motion for a Select Committee to inquire into the effects of Protective Duties on Imports on the Interest of the tenant-farmers and farm-labourers of the country. The debate is interesting, partly from the fact that the reply to Mr. Cobden on the part of Ministers was entrusted to Mr. Gladstone, partly because a considerable part of the debate was occupied with the question as to the proportion which rent bears to cost. The motion was rejected by 91 (133 to 224). Messrs. Cobden and Bright were the tellers.]

THE motion which I have to make is one of a nature which I believe is not ordinarily refused; it is for a Select Committee to sit upstairs, to take evidence on a question that excites great controversy out of doors, and which I believe is likely to cause considerable discussion in this House. It may be thought that my motion might have been appropriately placed in other hands. I am of that opinion too. I think it might have been more properly brought forward by a Gentleman on the other side of the House, particularly by an honourable Member connected with the counties of Wiltshire or Dorsetshire. But, although not myself a county Member, that does not necessarily preclude

me from taking a prominent part in a question affecting
the interests of the tenant-farmers and farm-labourers of this
country, for whom I feel as strong a sympathy as for any
other class of my countrymen; nay, I stand here on this
occasion as the advocate of what I conscientiously believe
to be the interests of the agriculturists.   We have instances
of Committees being appointed to take evidence as to the
importation of silk, the exportation of machinery, the navi-
gation-laws, and on questions of similar importance.   It must
also be admitted that such Committees have been appointed
without the parties more immediately concerned having in
the first instance petitioned the House for their appointment.   On the appointment of the Committee relative to
the exportation of machinery the motion was granted, not
at the instance of manufacturers who had a monopoly of
the use of machinery, but by parties whose interests were
concerned in the making and exporting of machinery.   I
do not therefore anticipate that my motion will be resisted on the ground that no petitions have been presented
demanding it.

I shall now state what my views will be on entering
the Committee.   I shall be prepared to bring forward important evidence showing the effects of 'protection,' as it
is called, on the agriculturists by the examination of farmers
themselves.   I will, in fact, not bring forward a single
witness before that Committee who shall not be a tenant-
farmer or a landed proprietor, and they shall be persons
eminent for their reputation as practical agriculturists.   The
opinion that I shall hold on entering the Committee is, that
'protection,' as it is called, instead of being beneficial, is
delusive and injurious to the tenant-farmers; and that
opinion I shall be prepared to sustain by the evidence of
tenant-farmers themselves.   I wish it to be understood I do
not admit that what is called protection to agriculturists has
ever been any protection at all to them; on the contrary,

I hold that its only effect has been to mislead them. This
has been denied both in this House and out of doors. I have
recently read over again the evidence taken before the Committees which sat previous to the passing of the Corn-law
of 1815, and I leave it to any man to say whether it was
not contended at that time that sufficient protection could not
be given to the agriculturists unless they got 80s. a quarter
for wheat. I wish to remind the hon. Member for Wiltshire
(Mr. Bennett) that he gave it as his opinion before the Committee of 1814, that wheat could not be grown in this
country unless the farmers got 96s. a quarter, or 12s. a bushel,
for it, while now he is supporting a Minister who only proposes to give the farmers 56s. a quarter, and confesses he
cannot guarantee even that. It is denied that this House
has ever promised to guarantee prices for their produce to
the farmers. Now what was the custom of the country
from the passing of the Corn-law in 1815? I will bring
old men before the Committee who will state that farmers
valued their farms from that time by a computation of wheat
being at 80s. a quarter. I can also prove that agricultural
societies which met in 1821, passed resolutions declaring that
they were deceived by the Act of 1815, that they had taken
farms calculating upon selling wheat at 80s., while, in fact,
it had fallen to little more than 50s. In the Committee
which sat in 1836, witnesses stated that they had been
deceived in the price of their corn; and I ask whether at
the present moment rents are not fixed rather with reference
to certain Acts that were passed than the intrinsic worth of
farms? In consequence of the alteration that was made in
the Corn-law of 1842, the rent of farms has been assessed
on the ground of corn being 56s. a quarter. I know an
instance where a person occupying his own land was rated
at a certain amount, viz. at the valuation of corn being 56s.
a quarter, while, in fact, it was selling at 47s.; and, upon
his asking why he had been so rated, he was told that the

assessors had taken that mode of valuation in consequence of
what the Prime Minister had stated was to be the price of corn.
['Oh! oh!'] Hon. Gentlemen may cry 'Oh! oh!' but I will
bring forward that very case, and prove what I have stated
concerning it.

What I wish in going into Committee is, to convince
the farmers of Great Britain that this House has not the
power to regulate or sustain the price of their commodities.
The right hon. Baronet opposite (Sir R. Peel) has confessed that he cannot regulate the wages of labour or the
profits of trade. Now, the farmers are dependent for their
prices upon the wages of the labourer and the profits of
the trader and manufacturer; and if the Government cannot
regulate these—if it cannot guarantee a certain amount of
wages to the one, or a fixed profit to the other—how can
it regulate the price of agricultural produce? The first point
to which I should wish to make this Committee instrumental
is to fix in the minds of the farmers the fact that this House
exaggerates its power to sustain or enhance prices by direct
acts of legislation. The farmer's interest is that of the whole
community, and is not a partial interest, and you cannot
touch him more sensitively than when you injure the manufacturers, his customers.

I do not deny that you may regulate prices for awhile
—for awhile you have regulated them by forcing an artificial scarcity; but this is a principle which carries with
it the seeds of self-destruction, for you are thereby under-
mining the prosperity of those consumers upon whom your
permanent welfare depends. A war against nature must
always end in the discomfiture of those who wage it. You
may by your restrictive enactments increase pauperism and
destroy trade; you may banish capital and check and ex-
patriate your population; but is this, I will ask, a policy
which can possibly work consistently with the interests of
the farmers? These are the fundamental principles which

I wish to bring out, and with this primary view it is that I ask for a Committee at your hands.

With regard to certain other fallacies with which the farmers have been beset, and latterly more so than ever, the farmer has been told that if there was a free trade in corn, wheat would be so cheap that he would not be able to carry on his farm. He is directed only to look at Dantzic, where corn, he is told, was once selling at 15s. 11d. per quarter, and on this the Essex Protection Society put out their circulars stating that Dantzic wheat is but 15s. 11d. per quarter, and how would the British farmer contend against this? Now, I maintain that these statements are not very creditable to the parties who propagate such nonsense, nor complimentary to the understandings of the farmers who listen to and believe them. It would be no argument against Free Trade, but quite the contrary, if wheat could be purchased regularly at Dantzic at that price; but the truth is, that in an average of years at that port it has cost much more than double; and the truth, I suppose, is what all men desire to arrive at. The farmer will be very easily disabused on this and other points if you will grant me the Committee I seek. We know what the price has been in the Channel Islands, where the trade is free. These islands send the corn of their own growth to this country whenever it is profitable to do so, and they receive foreign corn for their own consumption duty free. Sir, without pretending to look into futurity, I know of no better test of what the price of corn in this country would be in a state of free trade, than the prices in the island of Jersey afford, taken, not like the Essex Protection Society for a single week or month, but for a number of years, comprising a cycle of high and low prices in this country. We know that the fluctuation of prices in this country embraces the fluctuation of the whole of Europe. We have papers on the table showing what the prices of corn were in Jersey in the ten years from 1832 to 1841 inclusive.

The average price was in those ten years 48s. 4d. What do you think was the average price in your own markets in those years? It was 56s. 8d. Now, I have taken some pains to consult those who best understand this subject, and I find it to be their opinion, that a constant demand from England under a free trade would have raised the level of European prices 2s. or 3s. a quarter during the above period. If this be a fair estimate, it brings the price up to within 5s. or 6s. a quarter of our own average. Was this difference in price to throw land out of cultivation, annihilate rent, ruin the farmer, and pauperise the labourers? But in years of high prices the farmers do not receive the highest price for their corn. On the contrary, they sell their corn at the lowest prices, and the speculator sells his at the highest.

A short time ago I met a miller from near Winchester, who told me the prices which he paid every year for the corn which he purchased before the harvest and after the harvest during five years. That statement I beg to read to the House :—

									Load of 5 qrs.		
1839	August	Wheat	.	.	.	.	.	.	£19	10	0
	November	,,	.	.	.	.	.	.	16	0	0
1840	August	,,	.	.	.	.	.	.	18	0	0
	October	,,	.	.	.	.	.	.	14	5	0
1841	August	,,	.	.	.	.	.	.	19	0	0
	October	,,	.	.	.	.	.	.	15	0	0
1842	August	,,	.	.	.	.	.	.	17	0	0
	September	,,	.	.	.	.	.	.	12	0	0
1843	July	,,	.	.	.	.	.	.	15	15	0
	September	,,	.	.	.	.	.	.	12	10	0

Thus in these five years there had been a difference of 3l. 10s. a load, or 15s. a quarter, between the prices of wheat in July and August and in October and November in each year, showing, beyond dispute, that the farmer did not sell his corn at the highest, but at the lowest of the markets.

Now, Sir, there is another point upon which as much misrepresentation exists as upon the one I have just stated, namely, the price at which corn could be grown abroad.

The price of wheat at Dantzic during those ten years to
which I have referred averaged upwards of 40s. a quarter;
and if you add to it the freight, it will corroborate the statement I have made with regard to the price at which wheat
has been sold at Jersey. Another point upon which misrepresentation has gone abroad, relates to the different items
of expenditure in bringing wheat to this country. We have
had consuls' returns from various ports, of the charges for
freight at various periods, but we have not had full accounts
of the other items of expenditure. It would be important to
elicit as much information as possible upon this subject, and
the best means of arriving at it would be to examine practical
men from the City before a Select Committee of the House as
to the cost of transit. As far as I can obtain information
from the books of merchants, the cost of transit from Dantzic,
during an average of ten years, may be put down at 10s. 6d.
a quarter, including in this, freight, landing, loading, insurance, and other items of every kind. This is the natural
protection enjoyed by the farmers of this country. I may
be answered, that the farmers of this country have the cost of
carriage to pay also, as, for instance, from Norfolk to Hull or
London. But I beg to remind hon. Gentlemen that a very
small portion of home-grown corn is carried coastwise at all.
Accurate information upon this point might be got before a
Select Committee of this House. From information which
I have obtained, I am led to believe that not more than
1,000,000 of quarters are carried coastwise at all, or 5 per
cent. of the yearly growth of the country; the rest is carried
from the barn-door to the mill. This is an important consideration for those who say that there is no natural protection
for the farmer, inasmuch as it gives a farmer here the constant
protection of half-a-guinea.

But hon. Gentlemen ought to bear in mind that the
corn which is brought from Dantzic is not grown on the
quays there, any more than it is grown on the quay of

Liverpool. On the contrary, it is brought at great expense from a very long distance in the interior. I have seen a statement made by an hon. Member from Scotland, who said that the rafts on which the corn was brought down the river to Dantzic were broken up and sold to pay the cost of transit. I have not been able to verify that statement in the course of my inquiries. These are points which might all be cleared up by practical men before the Committee; and thus, instead of resorting to prophecy, we should be able to judge from facts and past experience as to the ability of the English farmers to compete with foreigners.

Hon. Gentlemen would do well to consider what happened in the case of wool. Every prediction that is now uttered with regard to corn, was uttered by Gentlemen opposite with regard to wool. If hon. Gentlemen visited the British Museum, and explored that Herculaneum of buried pamphlets which were written in opposition to Mr. Huskisson's plans for reducing the duty on wool twenty years ago, what arguments would they find in the future tense, and what predictions of may, might, could, would, should, ought, and shall! But what was the result? Did they lose all their sheep-walks? Had they no more mutton? Are their shepherds all consigned to the workhouse? Were there no more sheep-dogs? I have an account of the importation of wool and the price of wool, and the lesson I wish to impress on Gentlemen opposite is this, that the price of commodities may spring from two causes—a temporary, fleeting, and retributive high price, produced by scarcity; or a permanent and natural high price, produced by prosperity. In the case of wool, you had a high price springing from the prosperity of the consumers. It so happens, in the case of this article of wool, that the price has been highest when the importation has been most considerable, and lowest in the years when the importation has been comparatively small. I beg to read a statement which illustrates this fact :—

								Imported lbs.
1827	.	.	.	10d. per lb.	.	.	.	29,115,341.
1829	.	.	.	7d. per lb.	.	.	.	31,516,649.
1836	.	.	.	18d. per lb.	.	.	.	64,739,000.
1841	.	.	.	11d. per lb.	.	.	.	56,170,000.
1842	.	.	.	10d. per lb.	.	.	.	45,833,000.

From this statement it appears, that in every instance where the price has been highest, the English farmer has had the largest competition from foreign growers, and that the price was lowest where the competition was least.

Well, that is the principle which I wish to see applied in viewing this much-dreaded question of corn. You may have a high price of corn, through a prosperous community, and it may continue a high price; you may have a high price through a scarcity, and it is impossible in the very nature of things that it can be permanent.

Now, put this test of wool in the case of cattle and other things that have been imported since the passing of the Tariff. I want this matter to be cleared up. I do not want Gentlemen to find fault with the Prime Minister for doing what he did not do. I do not think his Tariff caused a reduction of one farthing in the price of articles of consumption. But I must say, with all deference to him, that I think he himself is to blame for having incurred that charge by the arguments which he brought forward in support of the Tariff; for assuredly he took the least comprehensive or statesmanlike view of his measures when he proposed to degrade prices, instead of aiming to sustain them by enlarging the circle of exchanges. It is said that the Tariff has caused distress among the farmers. I don't believe there has been as much increase in the imports of cattle as would make one good breakfast for all the people. Did it never enter the minds of hon. Gentlemen who are interested in the sale of cattle, that their customers in large towns cannot be sinking into abject poverty and distress, without the evil ultimately reaching

themselves in the price of their produce? I had occasion,
a little time ago, to look at the falling-off in the consumption
of cattle in the town of Stockport. I calculated the
falling-off in Stockport alone, for three or four years, at
more than all the increase in the importation of foreign
cattle. It appears, therefore, that the distress of that town
alone has done as much to reduce prices as all the importation
under the Tariff. It has been estimated that in Manchester,
40 per cent. less of cattle was consumed in 1842
than in 1835; and it has also been estimated that the cotton
trade was paying 7,000,000*l*. less in wages per annum in
1842 than in 1836. How could you then expect the same
consumption? If you would but look to your own interests
as broadly and as wisely as manufacturers look to theirs,
you would never fall into the error of supposing that you
can ruin your customers, and yet, at the same time, prosper
in your pursuits. I remember hearing Lord Kinnaird, whose
property is near Dundee, state, that in 1835 and 1836, the
dealers from that town used to come and bespeak his cattle
three months in advance; but in 1842, when the linen
trade shared the prostration of all the manufactures, he had
to engage steam-boats three months in advance to bring
his cattle to the London market. Hon. Members who live
in Sussex and the southern counties, and who are in the
habit of sneering at Manchester, should recollect that they
are as much dependent upon the prosperity of Lancashire as
those who live in its immediate neighbourhood. If graziers,
on looking at the *Price Current*, find they can get a better
price for their cattle in London than in Manchester and
Stockport, will they not send their cattle up to London, to
compete with the southern graziers?

The point, therefore, which I wish to make known is, that
the Tariff has not caused any reduction in prices. There is
nothing which I regret more than that the Corn-law or the
Tariff should have been altered by the right hon. Baronet at

all. Without this alterntion, I feel confident we should have
had prices as low at least as they are; our lesson would then
have been complete, the landlords and tenants would have
been taught how dependent they are on their customers, and
they would then have united with the manufacturers in
favour of Free Trade. But, if the late alterations in the Corn-
law and Tariff are now to be made the bugbear for frightening the farmers from the path of Free Trade—if they are
to be told that those measures have reduced their protection
30 per cent.,—then I think those political landlords who
were returned to this House as ' farmers' friends,' pledged
to defend ' protection ' as it stood, and who betrayed their
trust, ought to do something more if they are sincere; they
ought to reduce their rents in proportion to the amount
of protection which they say they have withdrawn from the
farmer—they ought to do this, not for one rent-day, but
permanently; and they should do it with penitence and in
sackcloth and ashes, instead of hallooing on the poor farmers
upon a wrong scent, after the Anti-Corn-law League, as the
cause of their sufferings.

Now, with regard to the low prices having been caused
by the change in the Tariff, I do not know whether a
noble Lord happens to be present who illustrated this
very aptly, by stating that the farmers in the West of
Scotland had been ruined by the reduction in the duty
on cheese. There could be nothing more unfortunate than
that statement, as there happens, in that respect, to have
been no alteration; and yet, I believe, cheese fell in price
as much as any other article. It is well known that
whilst the price of cheese has fallen in the home market,
the importation from abroad has been also considerably
diminished. There is another subject upon which I must
entreat hon. Members' forbearance, for it is an exceedingly
tender point, and one which is always heard with great
sensitiveness in this House: I refer to the subject of rent.

We have no tenant-farmers in this House. I wish we had, and I venture here to express a hope that the next dissolution will send up a *bona fide* tenant-farmer. I know nothing more likely than that to unravel the perplexity of our terminology—nothing more likely to put us all in our right places and to make us speak each for himself on this subject. The landowners—I mean the political landowners, those who dress their labourers and their cattle in blue ribbons, and who treat this question entirely as a political one—they go to the tenant-farmers, and they tell them that it would be quite impossible for them to compete with foreigners, for, if they had their land rent-free, they could not sell their produce at the same price as they did. To bear out their statement, they give a calculation of the cost per acre of growing wheat, which they put down at 6*l.* Now, the fallacy of that has been explained to me by an agriculturist in the Midland Counties, whom I should exceedingly like to see giving his evidence before the Committee for which I am moving. He writes me, in a letter which I have received to-day :—

'You will be met by an assertion, that no alteration in rent can make up the difference to the tenant and labourer of diminished prices. They will quote the expense on a single crop of wheat, and say how small a proportion the rent bears to the whole expense, but that is not the fair way of putting it. Wheat is the farmer's remunerating crop, but he cannot grow wheat more than one year in three. The expense, then, of the management of the whole farm should be compared with the rent, to estimate what portion of the price of corn is received by the landlord. I have, for this purpose, analysed the expenses of a farm of 400 acres—130 arable, 170 pasture.

'The expenses are :—

Parish and county rates . . .	£90
Interest of capital	150
Labour	380
Tradesmen's bills	80
Manure and lime	70
Wear of horses	20
	790
Rent	800
	£1,590

So that on this farm, which is very fairly cultivated, the rent is 80ol., the other expenses 70ol. Now, if it requires 55s. per quarter in an average year, to enable the tenant to pay the rent and make 150l. profit, it is obvious that without any rent he would be enabled to pay his labourers and tradesmen as well, and put the same amount of profit into his pocket, with a price of 30s., supposing other produce to be reduced in the same proportion. But I do not anticipate that wheat will be reduced below 45s., even by free trade, and meat, butter, and cheese will certainly not fall in the same proportion.'

This, then, is a very important statement from a competent authority, and the gentleman who makes it I should be very glad to have examined before the Committee, if the House grant one. I believe that the writer will have no objection to his name being published : he is Mr. Charles Paget, of Ruddington Grange, near Nottingham.

Allow me now to state the method by which I calculate the proportion which rent bears to the other outgoings on a farm. I ascertain first what amount of produce the farmer sells off his farm in the year, and next I inquire how much of the money brought home from market goes to the landlord for rent. I take no account in this money calculation of the seed-corn, stock manure, horse-keep, or other produce of the land used or consumed upon the farm, because these things are never converted into money, and cannot, therefore, be used in payment of rent, taxes, &c. Now I am prepared to prove before a Committee, by a Scotch farmer, that one-half of the disposable produce from a Lothian farm goes to the landlord for rent—that 26s. out of every 52s. for a quarter of wheat is rent; and that consequently, if they had their land rent free, and sold their wheat at 26s. a quarter, they would do as well, pay as good wages, and everybody about the establishment be as well provided for as they are now, when paying rent and getting 52s. for their wheat. With such a margin as this, I think we need not be in much fear of throwing land out of cultivation in Scotland !

I believe many hon. Gentlemen opposite have never made a calculation of what proportion of the whole of the saleable produce goes for rent. It must be borne in mind

that every acre of a farm pays rent, although probably not
more than one acre in three, and in the best farming not more
than one in four, is in the same year devoted to the growth of
wheat, whilst a part of the farm is generally in permanent
pasture. My mode of calculation, then, is this : ascertain the
money value of the whole produce of every kind sold in a year,
find how many quarters of wheat it is equal to at the price of
the year, and next divide the total number of quarters by the
number of acres in the farm, and the result will give you the
quantity of wheat sold off each acre in the year. I have made
the calculation, and in doing so have had the opinions of those
who have taken pains upon the subject ; and these are the
conclusions to which I have come :—I calculate that an arable
farm, on an average, does not yield for sale, of every kind of
produce, more than equivalent to ten bushels of wheat per
acre ; so that a farm of 500 acres would not dispose of more
than what is equivalent to 5000 bushels. In many parts I
believe that this estimate is too high, and that the farmer does
not dispose of more than one quarter per acre. And the result
of the inquiry would show that in Scotland (where much of
the labour on the farm is paid in kind) one-half of the produce taken to market goes to the landlord as rent, whilst in
England it will average more than 20s. a quarter upon the
present price of wheat. With regard to cheese, I am prepared
to bring witnesses to prove that more than half of the produce
goes to the landlord, owing to the fact of there being less paid
in wages upon dairy farms. For every 5d. received for cheese,
more than 2½d. is paid in rent ; and upon grazing farms, also,
for every 5d. received for a pound of meat, at least 2½d. is
paid to the landlord. This is, after all, the important point in
the consideration of this question, because, it being settled,
the public would no longer labour under the apprehension,
that if free trade were adopted the farmers would suffer, or
that land would be thrown out of cultivation.

This is a point upon which I should not have entered, had

not the investigation been challenged by my opponents. It must not be imputed to me that I entertain the opinion that free trade in corn would deprive the landowners of the whole of their rents. I have never said so—I have never even said that land would not have been as valuable as it is now, if no Corn-law had ever existed. But this I do mean to say, that if the landowners prefer to draw their rents from the distresses of the country, caused by their restrictive laws to create high prices through scarcity of food, instead of deriving an honourable income of possibly as great, or even greater amount, through the growing prosperity of the people under a free trade, then they have no right, in the face of such facts as I have stated, to attempt to cajole the farmer into the belief that rent forms an insignificant item in the cost of his wheat, or to frighten him into the notion that he could not compete with foreigners if he had his land rent free.

I shall now touch upon another and more important branch of this question, I mean the interests of the farm labourer. We are told that he is benefited by a system of restriction which makes the first element of subsistence scarce. Do you think posterity will believe it? They will look back upon this doctrine, in less than twenty years, with as much amazement as we do now upon the conduct of our forefathers when they burnt old women for witchcraft! To talk of benefiting labourers by making one of the main articles of their consumption scarce! The agricultural labourers live by wages; what is it which regulates the wages of labour in every country? Why, the quantity of the necessaries and comforts of life which form the fund out of which labour is paid, and the proportion which they bear to the whole number of labourers to be maintained. Now, the agricultural labourer spends a larger proportion of his wages in food than any other class. And yet, in the face of this fact, do you go on maintaining a law which makes food scarce in order to benefit the agriculturist. I hold in my hand a volume which has been

presented to the House relating to the state of the agricultural
population of this country, and which, I think, ought to have
been brought under the notice of the House, by some one
competent to deal with the subject, long before now.

Last year a Commission was appointed to inquire into the
state of women and children employed in agriculture. I beg
to make a few observations before proceeding further upon the
manner in which this inquiry has been conducted. Some years
ago the House will recollect that a Commission was appointed
on the condition of the hand-loom weavers. That Commission
sat two years; its inquiries have since been directed to the
state of other manufacturing interests, and it is still, I believe,
in existence. The inquiry upon the state of the labourers
employed in our manufactures, therefore, will have been very
fully gone into. But when an application was made to a
member of the Cabinet to allow the same Commission to
institute a similar inquiry into the state of the labourers
employed in husbandry, he refused to do so; but afterwards
he agreed that an inquiry should be made by the Assistant
Poor-law Commissioners, but that only thirty days could be
allowed for such inquiry. The volume which I hold in my
hand is, therefore, the work of four gentlemen during only
thirty days; one of these gentlemen, Mr. Austin, set forward
on his task, and consumed two days in travelling. He had
thus only twenty-eight days to inquire into the condition of
the agricultural population in four counties in the south of
England. We have, however, some facts elicited on that
inquiry, which ought to have drawn forth remarks from
hon. Gentlemen opposite as to the condition of their own
constituents.

Before I allude to the condition of the agricultural
labourers, I wish to state that, whatever may have been the
animus which influenced others in investigating the condition
of the manufacturing districts, I am actuated by no invidious
feeling whatever towards the agriculturists; for bear in mind

that my conduct has been throughout marked by consistency
towards both. Had I ever concealed the wretched state of the
manufacturing operatives, or shrunk from the exposure of
their sufferings, my motives might have been open to suspicion in now bringing before your notice the still more
depressed condition of the agricultural poor. But I was one
of that numerous deputation from the North which, in the
spring of 1839, knocked in vain at the door of this House for
an inquiry at your bar into the state of the manufacturing
population. I was one of the deputies who intruded ourselves
(sometimes five hundred strong) into the presence of successive Prime Ministers, until our importunities became the subject of remark and complaint in this House. From that time
to this we have continued without intermission to make public
in every possible way the distress to which the manufacturers
were exposed. We did more : we prescribed a remedy for that
distress; and I do not hesitate to express my solemn belief
that the reason why, in the disturbances which took place,
there was no damage done to property in the manufacturing
districts, was, that the people knew and felt that an inquiry
was taking place, by active and competent men, into the
cause of their distress, and from which they had hoped some
efficient remedy would result. Now I would impress upon hon.
Members opposite, as the result of my conviction, that if the
labouring poor in their districts take a course as diabolical as
it is insane—a course which I am sorry to see they have
taken in many agricultural localities—of burning property to
make known their sufferings—if I might make to those hon.
Gentlemen a suggestion, it would be this—that if they had
come forward to the House and the country as we, the manufacturers, have done, and made known the sufferings of the
labouring population, and prescribed any remedy whatever—
if that population had heard a voice proclaiming their distresses, and making known their sufferings—if they had seen
the sympathies of the country appealed to—I believe it would

have had such a humanising and consoling effect upon the
minds of the poor and misguided people, that in the blindness
of despair they would never have destroyed that property
which it was their interest to protect. I have looked through
this volume, which is the result of Mr. Austin's twenty-eight
days' travels through the agricultural districts, and I find
that during that period he visited Somersetshire, Devonshire,
Wiltshire, and Dorsetshire. He has given the testimony of
various respectable gentlemen in these several localities, as to
the condition of the agricultural labourers. Some of these
accounts are highly important. The first that I shall refer to
is the evidence of the Rev. J. Guthrie, the vicar of Calne, in
Wilts. He says (speaking of the agricultural labourers in
that district) : —

'I never could make out how they can live with their present earnings.'

Dr. Greenup, M.D., Calne, says : —

'In our union, the cost of each individual in the workhouse, taking the
average of men, women, and children, is 1s. 6d. a week, for food only ; and,
buying by tender and in large quantity, we buy at least 10 per cent. cheaper
than the labouring man can. But, without considering this advantage, apply
the scale to the poor, industrious family. A man, his wife, and two children,
will require, if properly fed, 6s. weekly ; their rent (at least 1s.) and fuel will
very nearly swallow up the remainder ; but there are yet things to provide—
soap and candles, clothes and shoes ; shoes to a poor man are a serious expense, as he must have them strong, costing about 12s. a pair, and he will
need at least one pair in a year. When I reckon up these things in detail,
I am always more and more astonished how the labourers contrive to live
at all.'

Thomas King, Esq., surgeon, Calne, Wilts, says : —

'If women and boys who labour in the field suffer in their health at all, it is
not from the work they perform, but the want of food. The food they eat is
not bad of its kind, but they have not enough of it ; and more animal food
would be most desirable, but with the present rate of wages it is impossible.
Their low diet exposes them to certain kinds of diseases, more particularly to
those of the stomach.'

Mr. Robert Bowman, farmer, and vice-chairman of the
Board of Guardians, Calne Union, deposes : —

'In the great majority of cases, the labourer has only the man's wages (7s.

or 9s. a week) to live on. On that, a man and his wife, and family of four, five, or six children, must live, though it is a mystery to me how they do live.'

This was the evidence of a farmer. Mrs. Britton, wife of a farm labourer, says :—

' We could eat much more bread, if we could get it.'

Mrs. Wiltshire, wife of a farm labourer at Cherill, Wilts, in her own pathetic way, says :—

' Our common drink is burnt-crust tea. We also buy about half-a-pound of sugar a week. We never know what it is to get enough to eat. At the end of the meal the children would always eat more. Of bread there is never enough ; the children are always asking for more at every meal. I then say, "You don't want your father to go to prison, do you ?"'

That is a specimen of the evidence collected in the south of England, in the purely agricultural districts, by Mr. Austin. I have myself had the opportunity of making considerable observations in the agricultural districts, and I have come to this conviction, that the farther you travel from the much-maligned region of tall chimneys and smoke, the less you find the wages of labourers to be ; the more I leave behind me Lancashire and the northern parts of England, the worse is the condition of the labourers, and the less is the quantity of food they have. Does not this, I will ask, answer the argument that the agricultural labourer derives protection from the Corn-laws? Now, what I wish to bring before the Committee is not merely that, in the abstract, and as a general principle, the working class can never be benefited by high prices occasioned by scarcity of food, but, that even during your casual high prices, caused by scarcity, the agricultural labourers always suffer. Pauperism increases as the price of food rises ; and, in short, the price of the loaf is in a direct ratio proof of the increase of pauperism. An hon. Gentleman says 'No, no.' I hope I shall have him on the Committee, and, if he will only hear me out, I am sure I shall persuade him to vote for the Committee.

With regard to the condition of the agricultural labourer, I have taken some pains to ascertain what has been the relative progress of wages and rents in agricultural districts. I know that this is a very sore point indeed for hon. Members opposite; but I must tell them that in those very districts of Wilts and Dorset the wages of labour, as measured in food, are lower now than they were sixty years ago, while the rent of land has increased from two-and-a-half to threefold. Mind, I do not pretend to decide whether, with a free trade, rents might not have advanced even fivefold, but I do contend that, under those circumstances, the increased value of land could have only followed the increased prosperity of every portion of the industrious community; and so long as you maintain a law for enhancing prices by scarcity, and raising artificial rents for a time, and by the most suicidal process, out of the privations of the consumers, you must not be surprised if you are called upon to show how the system works upon those for whose benefit you profess to uphold the law. I find that the following were the ordinary wages of the common agricultural day-labourers previous to the rise of prices after 1790, taken from the accounts of the respective counties drawn up for the Board of Agriculture; not including hay-time and harvest :—

Average price of wheat . . . . 44s. 6d.

Devonshire .	. . . 6s. to 7s. 6d. per week.
Wiltshire .	. . . 6s. to 7s.	„
Somersetshire	. . . 7s. to 9s.	„
Dorset	. . . 6s. to 6s. 6d.	„

(With wheat at 5s. per bushel.)

Gloucester . . . . 7s. to 10s. per week.

Since that period, money wages have hardly increased in those districts; and wages, computed in food, have certainly declined, while rent has progressed from 200 to 250 per cent. I will mention another fact, illustrative of the relative progress of rents and wages. When lately attending a meeting at Gloucester, I heard a gentleman say publicly that he had

recently sold an estate which had belonged to his great-grand-
father, and which brought him ten times the price his ancestor
had given for it. But what, in the same time, has been the
course of wages?   It is stated in a work attributed to Justice
Hale, published in 1683, upon the condition of the working
classes, that the wages of a farm-labourer in Gloucestershire
were 10s. a week; and he remarks :—

'Unless the earnings of a family, consisting of the father, mother, and four
children, amount to that sum, they must make it up, I suppose, by begging or
stealing.'

Wheat was then 36s. a quarter.   Now that wheat is 40 per
cent. higher, the average wages in Gloucestershire are only
8s. to 9s., and in many cases 7s. and 6s.   And Mr. Hunt, a
farmer in Gloucestershire, who is also a guardian of the poor,
stated publicly at the same meeting, that in his district it was
found, when relief was applied for, that in many instances
families, who were endeavouring to exist on wages, were,
taking the number of the family into account, only obtaining
one-half the amount which their maintenance would cost in
the workhouse.   Mr. Hunt also stated that, directions having
been received by the guardians of the union to keep the poor
who were inmates of the workhouse upon as low a diet as the
able-bodied labourer and his family could obtain out of it,
they were, on inquiry, startled at the small quantity of food
upon which, from the low rate of wages, the labouring population were forced to subsist; and upon referring the point to
the medical officer of the union, he reported that it would not
be safe to feed the able-bodied paupers upon the scale of food
which they were getting out of the workhouse.
Hitherto I have spoken of the food of the agricultural
population; and when we speak of food, it implies lodging,
clothing—it implies morality, education, ay, and, I fear, religion, and everything pertaining to the social comforts and
morals of the people.   I have informed the House in what
manner that population is fed; but there is another point

in the volume before me which most especially calls for the
attention of hon. Gentlemen opposite—I refer to the lodging
of the agricultural poor. That is a point that more nearly
concerns, if possible, the character of the landowner than,
perhaps, the question of food. Mr. Austin, in the report from
which I have before quoted, in reference to the four counties
I have enumerated, says :—

'The want of sufficient accommodation seems universal. At Stourpain, a
village near Blandford, Dorset, I measured a bed-room in a cottage. The
room was 10 feet square, not reckoning the two small recesses by the side of
the chimney, about 18 inches deep. The roof was the thatch, the middle of
the chamber being about 7 feet high. Eleven persons slept in three beds
in this room. The first bed was occupied by the father and mother,
a little boy, Jeremiah, aged one year and a half, and an infant, aged four
months; second bed was occupied by the three daughters—the two eldest,
Sarah and Elizabeth, twins, aged twenty, and Mary, aged seven; third bed
was occupied by the four sons—Silas, aged seventeen, John, aged fifteen,
James, aged fourteen, and Elias, aged ten. There was no curtain or any kind
of separation between the beds.'

Mr. Phelps, an agent of the Marquis of Lansdowne, says :—

'I was engaged in taking the late census in Bromhill parish; and in one
case, in Studley, I found twenty-nine people living under one roof; amongst
them were married men and women, and young people of nearly all ages. In
Studley it is not at all uncommon for a whole family to sleep in the same room.
The number of bastards in that place is very great.'

The Hon. and Rev. S. Godolphin Osborne, rector of Bryan-
ston, Dorset, says :—

'Within this last year I saw in a room about 13 feet square, three
beds : on the first lay the mother, a widow, dying of consumption; on the
second two unmarried daughters, one eighteen years of age, the other twelve;
on the third a young married couple, whom I myself had married two days
before. A married woman, of thorough good character, told me a few weeks
ago that on her confinement, so crowded with children is her one room, they
are obliged to put her on the floor in the middle of the room that they may
pay her the requisite attention; she spoke of this as to her the most painful
part of that, her hour of trial.'

Mr. Thomas Fox, solicitor, Beaminster, Dorset, in his
evidence to Mr. Austin, says :—

'I regret that I cannot take you to the parish of Hook (near here), the
whole parish belonging to the Duke of Cleveland, occupied by a tenant of

the name of Rawlins, where the residences of the labourers are as bad as
it is possible you can conceive; many of them without chambers, earth floors,
not ceiled or plastered; and the consequence is, that the inhabitants are the
poorest—the worst off in the country.'

Ho is asked :—

'Are you of opinion that such a want of proper accommodation for sleeping
must tend very much to demoralize the families of the labouring population?
—There can be no doubt of it; and the worst of consequences have arisen
from it.'

Mr. Malachi Fisher, of Blandford, Dorset, says :—

'That in Milton Abbas, on the average of the late census, there were
thirty-six persons in each house. It is not an uncommon thing for two
families, who are near neighbours, to place all the females in one cottage,
and the males in another.'

And Mr. Austin, in his report, says :—

'The sleeping of boys and girls, young men and young women, in the same
room, in beds almost touching one another, must have the effect of breaking
down the great barriers between the sexes: the sense of modesty and decency
on the part of women, and respect for the other sex on the part of the men.
The consequences of the want of proper accommodation for sleeping in the
cottages are seen in the early licentiousness of the rural districts—licentiousness
which has not always respected the family relationship.'

I am by no means desirous of using excitable language or
harsh terms in anything I may have to address to the House
upon this subject; but I should not do justice to my own
feelings if I failed to express my strong indignation at the
conduct of those owners of land who permit men, bred on
the soil, born on their territory, to remain in the condition
in which the labouring population of Dorsetshire appear, not
occasionally, but habitually to exist. [Lord Ashley : 'Hear!']
I am glad to hear that cheer from the noble Lord; I should
have expected as much. You talk to us about the crowding
together of the labouring population in the manufacturing
towns, and charge that upon the manufacturer and the mill-
owner, forgetting that the crowding together in towns cannot
come under the cognisance of particular individuals or employers; but in the agricultural districts we find the large

proprietors of land, who will not allow any other person to
erect a stick or a stone, or to build a cottage upon their
estates, nevertheless permitting men, for whose welfare they
are responsible, to herd in this beastly state in dwellings
worse than the wigwams of the American Indians. When
we see these things, I repeat, that the persons by whom
they are permitted to continue, deserve to be visited with
the most unqualified reprobation of this House. It was well
said by the late Mr. Drummond, 'that property has its duties
as well as its rights,' but these duties are grossly neglected
when a Commissioner from the Government can find people
living in such pigsties—or worse than pigsties—as have been
described.

I have alluded to the evidence of the Rev. Godolphin
Osborne. I have not the honour to be acquainted with that
gentleman, and I have no doubt that in political matters we
differ 'wide as the poles,' but I cannot but admire him or
any other man who will come forward and express his opinion,
and make public the state of a population so degraded. That
gentleman, in a letter lately written, says :—

'Our poor live on the borders of destitution . . . From one year's end to
another, there are many labouring families that scarcely touch, in the way of
food, anything but bread and potatoes, with now and then some bacon.
Bread is in almost every cottage the chief food of the children, and, when
I know of what that bread is often made, I am not surprised at the great
prevalence amongst the children of the labourers, of diseases known to proceed
from an improper or too stinted diet . . . The wages paid by farmers I do not
find exceeding 8s., except, perhaps, in the case of the shepherd or carter.
In many parishes only 7s. a week are paid . . . A clergyman in this union
states to me, that he had lately had four blankets sent to him to dispose of.
In making inquiry for the most proper objects, he found in fifteen families
in his parish, consisting of eighty-four individuals, there were only thirty-three
beds and thirty-five blankets, being about three persons to one bed, with one
blanket. Of the thirty-five blankets, ten were in good condition, having
been given them within the last four years, the other twenty-five were mere
patched rags.'

Bear in mind that I am describing no sudden crisis of
distress, such as occasionally takes place in the manufacturing

districts, but the ordinary condition of the people. The strikes
and tumults of which you hear so much in those districts, are
the struggles of the operatives against being reduced from
their comparatively comfortable earnings to the deplorable
condition in which the agricultural population have sunk
unconsciously, and, I am afraid to think, contentedly.
Speaking of the union of Tarrant Hinton, the same rev.
gentleman says :—

'In Tarrant Hinton parish, a father, mother, married daughter and her
husband, an infant, a blind boy of sixteen, and two girls, occupying one
bed-room; next door, a father, mother, and six children, the eldest boy
sixteen years of age, in one bedroom ; two doors below, a mother, a daughter
with two bastards, another daughter, her husband and two children, another
daughter and her husband, one bedroom and a sort of landing, the house in
a most dilapidated state! It is not one property or one parish alone, on or
is which such cases exist; the crowded state of the cottages generally is
a thing known to every one who has occasion to go amongst the poor. In
one or two cases whole villages might be gone through, and every other
house at least would tell the same tale; and I know this to be true out
of this union as well as in it; and in some of these worst localities, a rent
of from 3*l.* to 5*l.* yearly is charged for a house with only one room below and
one above. It may serve to corroborate what I have stated of the crowding
of the villages to add, that I have now a list before me of forty families
belonging to other parishes in the union, who are now actually residing in
the town of Blandford.'

Now, mark ! the progress of the evil is this. The landowner
refuses to build up new cottages, and permits the old cottages
to fall down; and I speak advisedly when I say, that this
is the course adopted systematically in Dorsetshire, and the
people are driven to Blandford and other towns. And what
a population they are thus sending to the manufacturing
districts ! And what are these villages but normal schools
of prostitution and vice ? Oh, do not then blame the manufacturers for the state of the population in their towns, while
you rear such a people in the country, and drive them there
for shelter, when the hovels in which they have dwelt fall
down about them.

I wish to be understood, that in speaking of the condition
of the agricultural labourer, and of the wages he receives,

I do not intend to cast imputations upon any individual.
I attack not individuals, but the system. Although I hold
the proprietor to be responsible for the state of lodging
on his own land, I do not hold him responsible for the rate
of wages in his district. I never held the farmers responsible
for the want of employment or the price of labour, although
it has been foolishly said of me that I did so. I challenge
the Argus-eyed opponent I have to deal with to show that
I have ever done so. But, so far from that being the case,
I have, in every agricultural district which I have visited,
told the labourers, ' that the farmers cannot give what wages
they please—wages are not to be looked upon as charity—
the farmers are in no way responsible for low wages—it is
the system.' I have thus spoken of the food and lodging
of the agricultural labourers, and shall content myself with
one extract from Mr. Austin's description of their clothing :—

' A change of clothes seems to be out of the question, although necessary
not only for cleanliness, but saving of time. It not unfrequently happens,
that a woman on returning home from work is obliged to go to bed for an hour
or two, to allow her clothes to be dried. It is also by no means uncommon
for her, if she should not do this, to put them on again next morning nearly
as wet as when she took them off.'

Now, what kind of home customers do hon. Gentlemen
opposite think these people are to the manufacturers? This
is the population, who, according to those hon. Gentlemen,
are our best customers. I should be glad for a moment to
call the attention of the right hon. the Home Secretary to
the present working of the New Poor Law in Wilts. I have
observed in a Wiltshire paper a statement which I will read
to the House :—

' In Potterne, an extensive parish on the south-west side of Devizes, in
which reside two country gentlemen, who are magistrates, considerable landowners, and staunch advocates of the Corn-laws, besides other gentlemen
of station and of wealth, this plan of billeting the labourers has been adopted ;
and the following are the prices which are put on those poor fellows who
cannot get work at the average rate of 7s. a week, and of whom, we understand,
there are, or lately were, about forty :—Able-bodied single men, 1s. 6d. a

week: ditto married men, 4s.; ditto with two or three children, 5s.; ditto with large families, 6s. a week. At these rates then—fixed with reference to the number of mouths to be fed, and not according to the ability of the parties as workmen, the object clearly being to reduce the poor's rate—may any person in the parish, or out of it either, we presume, command the services of any of these forty unfortunates. We may command, for these independent labourers, "bold peasantry, their country's pride," have no voice in the matter; they have not even the option of going into the Union-house while any one can be found willing to use up their sinews and their bones at this starvation price.'

I have seen this in the Independent Wiltshire newspaper, and have taken it down, and had the names of the parties sent to me corroborating it.   And is not this, I will ask, quite inconsistent with what is the understood principle of the Poor Law?   Here is a sliding tariff of wages beginning at 2s. 6d., and ending at 6s., the men who are the victims of the system having no more voice in the matter than the negro slaves of Louisiana!

Now, I put it to you who are the supporters of the Corn-law—Can you, in the face of facts like these, persist in upholding such a system?   I would not, were I in your position, be a party to such a course—no, nothing on earth should bribe me to it—with such evidence at your doors of the mischiefs you are inflicting.   I have alluded to the condition of the people in four of the southern counties of England—in Wiltshire, Dorsetshire, Somersetshire, and Devonshire; and what I have stated in regard to those places would apply, I fear, to all the purely rural counties in the kingdom, unless you go northward, where the demand for labour in the manufacturing districts raises the rate of wages on the land in the neighbourhood.

The hon. and gallant Member for Lincoln says 'No;' and I will concede to the hon. and gallant Member, for I have no wish to excite his temper by contradicting him, that it is not so in Lincolnshire; I admit there is an exception to the general rule in regard to that county—there, I believe, both the labourers and farmers are in a much better

condition than in the south. But I am referring to the
condition of the agricultural population generally; and when
we look at the orderly conduct of that population, at the
patience exhibited by them under their own sufferings and
privations—fortified, as it were, by endurance so much, that
we scarcely hear a complaint from them, I am sure such a
population will meet with the sympathies of this House, and
that the noble Lord, the Member for Dorset (Lord Ashley)
whom I see opposite, and whose humane interference on
behalf of the factory labourers is the theme of admiration, will
extend to the agricultural population that sympathy which
has been so beneficial in ameliorating the condition of a large
portion of the labouring people. But where are the Scotch
county Members, that they have nothing to say? In that
country there is an agricultural population, that, as far as
their conduct is concerned, would do honour to any country.
Yet I find the following description of the diet of these
labourers in a Scotch paper:—

' In East Lothian, the bread used by hinds and other agricultural labourers
is a mixture of barley, peas, and beans, ground into meal; and you will understand its appearance when we inform you that it is very like the rape and oil
cakes used for feeding cattle and manuring the fields; and it is very indi-
gestible, coarse food.'

And I have received from a trustworthy person a letter,
giving me the subjoined account of the peasantry of the
county of Forfar :—

' In this county (Forfarshire), the mode of engaging farm-servants is from
Whitsunday to Whitsunday; in some cases the period of engagement is only
for half a year. The present average rate of wages is 11l. per annum, or a
fraction more than 4s. per week, with the addition of two pecks or 16lbs.
of oatmeal, and seven Scotch pints of milk weekly. The amount of wages
may be stated thus :—

	s.	d.
Money	4	0
Oatmeal, two pecks at 10d. . . .	1	8
Seven pints of milk at 2d. . . .	1	2
Total weekly wages	6	10

'That is the current weekly wages of an able-bodied agricultural labourer. An old man — that is, a man a little beyond the prime of life—if employed at all, his wages are considerably lower. The universal food of the agricultural labourers in Forfarshire is what is locally called " brose," which is merely a mixture of oatmeal and boiling water; the meal is not boiled, only the boiling water poured on it. There is no variation in this mode of living: butcher's meat, wheaten bread, sugar, tea, or coffee, they never taste. The outhouses they live in are called "bothies," and more wretched hovels than these bothies are not to be found among the wigwams of the uncivilised Africans.'

It really would appear, from the slight notice taken here of the state of suffering in the rural districts, that the County Members were sent up to this House to conceal rather than to disclose the condition of the people they left behind them. Then there is the case of Wales. There can be no excuse for ignorance as to the state of the Welsh people, for during the time of the recent disturbances we had the accounts given by the *Times'* reporter, corroborated by persons living in the locality, showing clearly what was the condition of both the farmer and the labourer in that country. In one of those accounts it was stated :—

'The main cause, however, of the disturbances, is beyond question the abject poverty of the people. The small farmer here breakfasts on oatmeal and water boiled, called " duffrey" or " flummery," or on a few mashed potatoes left from the previous night's supper. He dines on potatoes and buttermilk, with sometimes a little white Welsh cheese and barley bread, and, as an occasional treat, has a salt herring. Fresh meat is never seen on the farmer's table. He sups on mashed potatoes. His butter he never tastes; he sells it to pay his rent. The pigs he feeds are sold to pay his rent. As for beef or mutton, they are quite out of the question—they never form the farmer's food.'

Then as to the labourer :—

'The condition of the labourers, from inability in the farmers to give them constant employment, is deplorable. They live entirely on potatoes, and have seldom enough of them, having only one meal a-day ! Being half starved, they are constantly upon the parish. They live in mud huts, with only one room for sleeping, cooking, and living—different ages and sexes herding together. Their cottages have no windows, but a hole through the mud wall to admit the air and light, into which a bundle of rags or turf is thrust at night to stop it up. The thinly-thatched roofs are seldom drop-dry, and the mud floor becomes consequently damp and wet, and dirty almost as the road ; and, to

complete the wretched picture, huddled in a corner are the rags and straw
of which their beds are composed.'

I have now glanced at the condition of the agricultural
population in England, Scotland, and Wales. You have too
recently heard the tales of its suffering to require that I
should go across the Channel to the sister island with its
two millions and a half of paupers; yet bear in mind (for we
are apt to forget it), in that country there is a duty this day
of 18s. a quarter upon the import of foreign wheat. Will it
be believed in future ages, that in a country periodically on
the point of actual famine—at a time when its inhabitants
subsisted on the lowest food, the very roots of the earth—
there was a law in existence which virtually prohibited the
importation of bread! I have given you some idea of the
ordinary condition of the agricultural labourers when at
home: I have alluded to their forced migration from the
agricultural districts to the towns; and I will now quote from
the report of the London Fever Hospital, a description of the
state in which they reach the metropolis:—

'Dr. Southwood Smith has just given his annual report upon the state of
the London Fever Hospital during the past year, from which it appears that
the admissions during the period were 1461, being an excess of 418 above that
of any preceding year. A large portion of the inmates were agricultural
labourers, or provincial mechanics, who had come to London in search of
employment, and who were seized with the malady either on the road or
soon after their arrival, evincing the close connexion between fever and
destitution. These poor creatures ascribed their illness, some of them to the
sleeping by the sides of hedges, and others to a want of clothing, many of
them being without stockings, shirts, shoes, or any apparel capable of defending
them from the inclemency of the weather; while the larger number attributed
it to want of food, being driven by hunger to eat raw vegetables, turnips, and
rotten apples. Their disease was attended with such extreme prostration as
generally to require the administration of an unusually large proportion of
wine, brandy, ammonia, and other stimulants. The gross mortality was
15½ per cent. An unprecedented number of nurses and other servants of the
hospital were attacked with fever, namely, twenty-nine, of whom six died.'

I have another account from the Marlborough-street police
report, bearing upon the same point, which is as follows :—

' Marlborough Street.—The Mendicity Society constables and the police have brought a considerable number of beggars to this court recently. The majority of these persons are country labourers, and their excuse for vagrancy has been of the same character—inability to get work from the farmers, and impossibility of supporting themselves and families on the wages offered them when employment is to be had. It is impossible to describe the wretched appearance of these men, most of whom are able-bodied labourers, capable of performing a hard day's work, and, according to their own statements, willing to do so, provided they could get anything to do. A great many of these vagrant agricultural labourers have neither stockings nor shoes on their feet, and their ragged and famished appearance exceeds in wretchedness that of the Irish peasantry who find their way to this metropolis. The magistrates, in almost every instance, found themselves obliged to send these destitute persons to prison for a short period, as the only means of temporarily rescuing them from starvation. Several individuals belonging to this class of beggars were yesterday committed.'

You have here the condition of the agricultural labourers when they fly to the towns. You have already heard what was their condition in the country, and now I appeal to honourable Members opposite, whether theirs is a case with which to come before the country to justify the maintenance of the Corn-laws? You are nonsuited, and put out of court; you have not a word to say. If you could show in the agricultural labourers a blooming and healthy population, well clothed and well fed, and living in houses fit for men to live in—if this could be shown as the effects of the Corn-laws, there might be some ground for appealing to the feelings of the House to permit an injustice to continue while they knew that they were benefiting a large portion of their fellow-countrymen. But when we know, and can prove from the facts before us, that the greatest scarcity of food is to be found in the midst of the agricultural population, and that protection does not, as its advocates allege, benefit the farmer or the labourer, you have not a solitary pretext remaining, and I recommend you at once to give up the system, which you can no longer stand before the country and maintain.

The facts I have stated are capable of corroboration. Before a Select Committee we can obtain as much evidence as we want to show the state of the agricultural population. We

may get that evidence in less time and more satisfactorily
before a Select Committee than through a Commission.
Though I by no means wish to undervalue inquiries conducted by Commissions, which in many cases are very useful,
I am of opinion that an inquiry such as I propose would be
carried on with more satisfaction and with less loss of time by
a Select Committee than by a Commission. There is no tri-
bunal so fair as a Select Committee; Members of both sides
are upon it, witnesses are examined and cross-examined,
doubts and difficulties are removed, and the real facts are
arrived at. Besides the facts I have stated, if you appoint a
Committee, the landlords may obtain evidence which will go
far to help them out of their own difficulty—viz. the means
of giving employment to the people. The great want is employment, and if it is not found, where do you suppose will
present evils end, when you consider the rapid way in which
the population is increasing? You may in a Committee
receive valuable suggestions from practical agriculturists—
suggestions which may assist you in devising means for
providing employment. There may be men examined more
capable of giving an opinion, and more competent to help you
out of this dilemma, than any you could have had some years
ago. You may now have the evidence of men who have given
their attention as to what can be done with the soil. Drain-
tiles are beginning to show themselves on the surface of the
land in many counties. Why should they not always be
placed under the surface, and why should not such improvements give employment to labourers?

You do not want Acts of Parliament to protect the
farmer—you want improvements, outlays, bargains, leases,
fresh terms. A farmer before my Committee will tell you
that you may employ more labourers by breaking up land
which has lain for hundreds of years in grass, or rather
in moss, to please some eccentric landowner, who prefers
a piece of green turf to seeing the plough turning up

its furrows. This coxcombry of some landlords would disappear before the good sense of the Earl of Ducie. You may derive advantage from examining men who look upon land as we manufacturers do upon the raw material of the fabrics which we make—who will not look upon it with that superstitious veneration and that abhorrence of change with which landlords have been taught to regard their acres, but as something on which to give employment to the people, and which, by the application to it of increased intelligence, energy, and capital, may produce increased returns of wealth.

But we shall have another advantage from my Committee. Recollect that hitherto you have never heard the two sides of the question in the Committees which have sat to inquire into agricultural subjects; and I impress this fact on the notice of the right hon. Baronet opposite as a strong appeal to him. I have looked back upon the evidence taken before these Committees, and I find that in none of them were both sides of the question fairly stated. All the witnesses examined were protectionists—all the members of all the Committees were protectionists. We have never yet heard an enlightened agriculturist plead the opposite side of the question. It is upon these grounds that I press this motion upon hon. Gentlemen opposite. I want to have further evidence. I do not want a man to be examined who is not a farmer or landowner. I would respectfully ask the Earl of Ducie and Earl Spencer to be examined first; and then hon. Gentlemen could send for the Dukes of Buckingham and Richmond. I should like nothing better than that — nothing better than to submit these four noblemen to a cross-examination. I would take your two witnesses and you would take mine, and the country should decide between us. Nothing would so much tend to diffuse sound views as such an examination. But you have even Members on your own side who will help me to make out my case. There is the hon. Member for Berkshire (Mr. Pusey); he knows of what land is capable—he knows

what land wants, and he knows well that in the districts
where the most unskilful farming prevails, there does pauperism exist to the greatest extent. What does he say to you?
He advises that—

'More drains may be cut; more chalk be laid on the downs, the wolds, and
the clays; marl on the sand, clay on the fens and heaths, lime on the moors—
many of which should be broken up. That old ploughs be cast away, the
number of horses reduced, good breeds of cattle extended, stock fattened where
it has hitherto been starved, root-crops drilled and better dunged; new kinds
of those crops cultivated, and artificial manures of ascertained usefulness
purchased.'

It almost appears from the testimony of your own side, that
you are doing nothing right. There is nothing about your
agriculture that does not want improving. Suppose that you
could show that we are wrong in all our manufacturing processes—suppose the theorist could come to my business, which
is manufacturing garments, and which, I take it, is almost as
necessary, and why not as honourable, in a civilised country
and with a climate like ours, as manufacturing food; suppose,
I say, a theoretical chemist, book in hand, should come to me,
and say, ' You must bring indigo from India, madder from
France, gum from Africa, and cotton from America, and you
must compound and work them scientifically, so as to make
your gown-pieces to be sold for 3s. each garment.' My
answer would be, ' We do it already.' We require no theorist
to tell us how to perform our labour. If we could not do this,
how could we carry on the competition which we do with
other nations? But you are condemned by your own witnesses; you have the materials for the amelioration of your
soils at your own doors: you have the chalk and clay, and
marl and sand, which ought to be intermingled, and yet you
must have people writing books to tell you how to do it.

We may make a great advance if we get this Committee.
You may have the majority of its Members protectionists, if
you will; I am quite willing that such should be the arrangement. I know it is understood—at least, there is a sort of

etiquette—that the mover for a Committee should, in the event of its being granted, preside over it as chairman. I waive all pretensions of the sort—I give up all claims—I only ask to be present as an individual Member.

What objections there can be to the Committee I cannot understand. Are you afraid that to grant it will increase agitation? I ask the hon. Baronet the Member for Essex (Sir J. Tyrell), whether he thinks the agitation is going down in his part of the country? I rather think there is a good deal of agitation going on there now. Do you really think that the appointment of a dozen Gentlemen, to sit in a quiet room up-stairs and hear evidence, will add to the excitement out of doors? Why, by granting my Committee you will be withdrawing me from the agitation for one. But I tell you that you will raise excitement still higher than it is, if you allow me to go down to your constituents—your vote against the Committee in my hand—and allow me to say to them, ' I only asked for inquiry; I offered the landlords a majority of their own party; I offered them to go into Committee, not as a Chairman, but as an individual Member; I offered them all possible advantages, and yet they would not—they dared not grant a Committee of inquiry into your condition.' I repeat to you, I desire no advantages. Let us have the Committee. Let us set to work, attempting to elicit sound information, and to benefit our common country. I believe that much good may be done by adopting the course which I propose.

I tell you that your boasted system is not protection but destruction to agriculture. Let us see if we cannot counteract some of the foolishness—I will not call it by a harsher name—of the doings of those who, under the pretence of protecting native industry, are inviting the farmer not to depend upon his own energy and skill and capital, but to come here and look for the protection of an Act of Parliament. Let us have a Committee, and see if we cannot elicit facts which may counteract the folly of those who are persuading the farmer to prefer Acts of Parliament to draining and subsoiling, and to be looking to the laws of this House when he should be studying the laws of nature.

I cannot imagine anything more demoralising—yes, that is the word—more demoralising, than for you to tell the farmers that they cannot compete with foreigners. You bring long rows of figures, of delusive accounts, showing that the cultivation of an acre of wheat costs 6*l*. or 8*l*. per year. You put every impediment in the way of the farmers trying to do what they ought to do. And can you think that this is the way to make people succeed? How should we manufacturers get on, if, when we got a pattern as a specimen of the productions of the rival manufacturer, we brought all our people together and said, 'It is quite clear that we cannot compete with this foreigner; it is quite useless our attempting to compete with Germany or America; why, we cannot produce goods at the price at which they do.' But how do we act in reality? We call our men together, and say, 'So-and-so is producing goods at such a price; but we are Englishmen, and what America or Germany can do, we can do also.' I repeat, that the opposite system, which you go upon, is demoralising the farmers. Nor have you any right to call out, with the noble Lord the Member for North Lancashire—you have no right to go down occasionally to your constituencies and tell the farmers, 'You must not plod on as your grandfathers did before you; you must not put your hands behind your backs, and drag one foot after the other, in the old-fashioned style of going to work.' I say you have no right to hold such language to the farmer. Who makes them plod on like their grandfathers? Who makes them put their hands behind their backs? Why, the men who go to Lancashire and talk of the danger of pouring in of foreign corn from a certain province in Russia, which shall be nameless—the men who tell the farmers to look to this House for protective Acts, instead of their own energies—instead of to those capabilities which, were they

properly brought out, would make the English farmer equal
to—perhaps superior to—any in the world.

Because I believe that the existing system is worse for the
farmer than for the manufacturer—because I believe that
great good to both would result from an inquiry—because I
believe that the present system robs the earth of its fertility
and the labourer of his hire, deprives the people of subsistence,
and the farmers of feelings of honest independence—I hope,
Sir, that the House will accede to my motion for—

. ' A Select Committee to inquire into the effects of protective
duties on imports upon the interests of the tenant farmers and
farm-labourers of this country.'

FREE TRADE.

X.

LONDON, MAY 1, 1844.

FORTUNATELY for me, the phrenologists, who have examined my head, tell me that I have neither the organ of self-esteem nor that of love of approbation: if I had, I am sure you would spoil me. At this late hour of the meeting I should not have intruded myself at all upon you were it not for a consciousness of the duty we owe to our visitor to-night— the noble Lord (Kinnaird) who has so kindly consented to fill the chair upon the present occasion, who, possessing great nobility and courage of nature, is the second individual who has come forth from his Order to preside at our meeting, who has furnished us with so many additional arguments, and who is thereby able to cheer us on in the pursuit of our great cause. Had it not been for the duty we owe to his lordship and to the gentleman (Mr. Somers) who has just sat down, who is an occupier of land, and who, I may tell you, holds the situation of acting chairman of the board of guardians of the Bridgwater Union—if it had not been, I say, for the purpose of paying a tribute to this noble Lord and the Somersetshire farmer, I am sure I should not have trespassed upon your time at this late hour of the evening.

We have here again another answer to his Grace of Richmond, who stated in the House of Peers that the farmers to a
man are with the monopolists. I tell the noble Duke, ' Well,
you have not yet answered the speeches of Messrs. Hunt and
Lattimore, and now are you willing to reply to that of
Mr. Somers?' We will call upon his Grace to notice these
men, and to say whether, in the counties of Gloucester, Hert-
ford, and Somerset, from whence these three farmers severally
came, there can be found more unexceptionable witnesses, in
point of talent, character, morality, and fitness in every respect; whether there could have been better witnesses brought
from the counties I have named than those gentlemen. These
are not the description of men the Protectionists put forward
at their meetings as ' farmers;' their farmers generally consist
of lawyers, land-valuers, and auctioneers—mere toadies and
creatures of the landlords. They are men who stand towards
the real farmers in a far worse relation than the landlord himself; for they do the dirty work on the tenant which the landlord personally would scorn to do. I will tell you what kind
of people these land-valuers and auctioneers are. I was once
travelling in Scotland upon the banks of a loch, between Tay-
mouth and Killeen. A Highlander rode with me in the car
who was a firm believer in witches and ghosts. He said his
father had seen many of these ghosts, and he himself had seen
some ; that they were exceedingly mischievous, for they actually put stumbling-blocks in the way of people going home on
a dark night, and often bewitched the cattle; ' in fact,' said
he, reasoning the matter out, ' I believe they are worse than
the Evil One that sends them. Just, you see, as the factor
over there,' pointing in the direction of the marquis's factor
or land-agent's mansion, ' just as the factor there is waur than
the laird.' Now, we do not bring forward these land-valuers
and auctioneers. Mind you, the talking men in the farming
districts generally are these auctioneers and land-agents. We
have not too wide a choice among farmers who are Free Traders,

and who can speak at public meetings like this; but this I can tell you from my own experience: wherever you find in any county of the kingdom a man of original thought and independent mind, and who has wherewithal to make him independent, and enable him to stand erect in the world, that man is almost invariably in favour of Free Trade.

But, upon the general argument of Free Trade, what am I to say to you, since you are all agreed on the subject? I can only congratulate you, that during this present week we have not been without evidence of a progress in high quarters on our question. We have had a budget—I cannot say it is a Free-trade one, because, when we Leaguers get into power, we will bring forward a much better budget than that. But still there were some little things done in the budget on Monday night, and everything that was done was in the direction of Free Trade. What have the Duke of Richmond and the Protection Society been about? Why, I thought they had organised themselves, and assembled in his Grace's parlour, and had declared that their Prime Minister had gone so far that he now should go no farther. But it is quite clear to me that the Prime Minister does not dread those carpet-knights much who sit in the drawing-room of his Grace; he is not very much alarmed at that chivalry. I think he has a great deal more reliance upon us than dread of them. There is one thing done by the present Government which has been well done, because it was totally and immediately done — I mean their abolition of the protection upon wool. Twenty-five years ago there was an uprising of all the Knatchbulls, Buckinghams, and Richmonds of that day, who said, we insist on having a 6d. duty laid on foreign wool, to protect our own growth. They obtained what they asked. Five years afterwards, Mr. Huskisson said he had been informed by the Leeds manufacturers, that if that duty was not greatly altered, and almost taken off, all the woollen manufactures would be lost, and then the English farmers would have no market for their

wool at all. By dint of great management and eloquence on
his part, Mr. Huskisson was enabled to take off at that time
5*d.* of the 6*d.* which had been laid on. And during the past
week we have got rid of the other 1*d.* When it was proposed
to take off this duty, the agriculturists—I mean the Knatchbulls and Buckinghams of the day—declared (I have often
quoted from their pamphlets upon that subject before), that
if the duty was repealed, there would be no more shepherds
employed, but that they would all go to the workhouse;
that there would be no mutton in the land, and that all the
shepherds' dogs might be hanged. If you had heard them
talk in those days, you would have thought the poor sheep,
instead of carrying merely its own wardrobe on its back, bore
the entire wealth and prosperity of the whole nation. Now
they are going to carry on the trade of sheep-rearing and
wool-selling without any protection.

Why should they not conduct the business of raising and
selling corn upon the same principle? If it is unreasonable
to 'totally and immediately' abolish the duty on corn, why
has their own Prime Minister and Government 'totally and
immediately' abolished the protection on wool? We find
encouragement and good argument in favour of our principles
by every step that is taken, even by our professed opponents.
Take the article of coffee; a reform in that is not entirely, but
it is half done. The duties on coffee formerly were—indeed, at
this moment, are—4*d.* per lb. duty on colonial, and 8*d.* per
lb. on foreign. That meant just 4*d.* per lb. monopoly to the
colonial growers, because they were thereby enabled to sell
their coffee at just 4*d.* more than they otherwise would have
done. Sir Robert Peel has reduced the duty on foreign coffee,
but not on colonial, leaving the latter with 2*d.* per lb. less
protection than it formerly had. I cannot say that is rightly
done, but it is half done, and we will have the other half by-
and-by. Now, the next matter is sugar. Ladies, you cannot
make your coffee without you have sugar; at least, with all

your most honeyed smiles, you cannot make it sweet. Now, we are in a little difficulty about this sugar; for there are scruples of conscience which have come over the Government of this country. They cannot take foreign sugar, because it is tainted with slavery. Now observe, I am going to let out a secret. There is a secret correspondence going on between the Government of this country and that of Brazil to this effect. You know that statesmen sometimes write private letters and instructions to their agents, which are not published till about one hundred years after they are written, when they become curiosities. I will just give you one that will be published one hundred years hence respecting our Government and the Brazils. The present Ministry turned out the late Administration on the question of sugar. Lord Sandon, when he moved an amendment to the Whig proposition to allow foreign sugar, rested his argument on the ground that it was very impious to consume slave-grown sugar. But he said nothing about coffee; the rest I will explain in the words of the supposed secret letter from our Government to their ambassador in Brazil :—

' Inform the Brazilian Government that we stand pledged to the country, as regards this article of sugar, and, when we bring in our budget, we shall be obliged to tell the people of England, who are very gullible, and who will believe anything we tell them from our places in the House of Commons, that it will be very improper to encourage slavery and the slave trade by taking Brazilian sugar; but, to convince the Brazilian Government that we do not mean to do them any harm in this matter, we will preface our remarks about sugar by a declaration that we will admit their coffee at 2d. per lb. reduction on the former duty; and as four out of five of the slaves who are employed in Brazil are engaged in the coffee plantations, and as three-fifths of all the exports from the Brazils are coffee, and as sugar forms comparatively an insignificant item in their production and exports (of all which the people

of England are profoundly ignorant), this will convince them
that we do not mean any injury to the Brazilian planters, and
that we are not in earnest when we propose to stop the slave
trade; we are simply bound to exclude the sugar by the
exigencies of our party and our peculiar position. But tell
them, at the same time, how cleverly we have tripped up the
heels of the Whigs by the manœuvre.'

That is the description of despatch which will be published
one hundred years hence, as having been sent by our present
Government to their envoy extraordinary and minister pleni-
potentiary at Brazil.

No doubt there are people who have been taken in by this
cant about slave produce: honest, well-meaning philanthropists, if I must call them so, although I find it difficult to
treat men as philanthropists who merely revel in the enjoyment of an unreasoning conscience, because true philanthropists have always a real ground of reason by which to guide
their benevolence. There is a class of individuals who have
come into considerable notoriety of late in this country, who
wish to subject us, not to the dictates of an enlightened benevolence, but to the control of mere fanaticism. They are men
who, under the plea of being anti-slavery advocates, petition
the Government that they should not allow the people of this
country to consume sugar, unless they can prove that it had
not 'the taint of slavery,' as they call it, upon it. Is there
anything in morals which answers to the principle in material
nature that there should be one thing which is a conductor
of immorality, and another a non-conductor? that coffee is a
non-conductor of the immorality of slavery, but that sugar is
a conductor, and therefore you must not take it? I have
personally met with some of these unreasoning philanthropists,
and have been called upon by them to meet their objections
relative to slave-grown sugar. I remember in particular one
very benevolent gentleman in a white muslin cravat, with

whom I discussed this question.   I met him this way :—
'Before you say another word to me on the subject, strip that
slave-grown cotton from your neck.'   He replied, that it was
not practicable to do so.   I rejoined, 'I demand it; it is practicable; for I know one gentleman who has dispensed with
wearing cotton stockings in the summer, and will not allow his
garments to be put together with cotton thread, if he knows it.'
It is, I assure you, a fact, that I know one philanthropist who
has made that sacrifice.   'But,' said I, 'if it is impracticable
for you, who stand up before me now with slave-grown cotton
round your neck, to abstain from slave-grown commodities,
is it possible for the people of England to do it?   Is it practicable for us as a nation to do so?   You can, if you please,
pass a law prohibiting the importation of slave-grown sugar
into England, but will that accomplish your object at all?
You receive free-grown sugar in England; that leaves a
vacuum in Holland and elsewhere, which is filled up with
slave-grown sugar.'   Before men have a right to preach such
doctrines as these, and call upon the Government and the
nation at large to support them, they ought to give evidence
of their sincerity by the self-denying practice of abstaining
from those articles which are already consumed in this
country.

What right have a people who are the largest consumers
and distributors of cotton goods to go over to the Brazils with
their ships full of cotton, then turn up the whites of their
eyes, shed crocodile tears over the slaves, and say, 'Here we
are with a cargo of cotton goods, but we have qualms of conscience, religious scruples, and cannot take your slave-grown
sugar in return for our slave-grown cotton?'   In the first place,
the thing is inconsistent, and in the next it is hypocritical.
Mark me, clever knaves are using fanatics in order to impose
upon the people of England a heavy burden.   That is just
what it amounts to.   Cunning and selfish men are tampering
with the credulity of what used to be the reasoning benevo-

lence of the people of England. We must put down this sort
of dictatorship, which has no rational judgment to guide it.
Will they venture to assert that I am an advocate for the continuance of slavery because I maintain the principle of Free
Trade? No; I assert here, as everywhere, that one good,
sound, and just principle never can be at war with another
of a similar character. If you can show me that Free Trade
is promotive of slavery, and that it is calculated to extend or
perpetuate it, then I should doubt, pause, and hesitate whether freedom of trade and personal freedom are equally consistent and just in their principles; and, as I say, *primâ facie*,
there can be no question but that the possession of human
beings as goods and chattels is contrary to the first Christian
precept, therefore I say at once that slavery is unjust; and,
if you can show me that Free Trade would promote that
diabolical system, then I should be prepared to abandon Free
Trade itself.

But I have always been of the same opinion with the most
distinguished writers who have ever treated upon this subject—such men as Adam Smith, Burke, Franklin, Hume, and
others, the greatest thinkers of any age—that slave labour
is more costly than free labour—that if the two were brought
into fair competition, free labour would supersede slave labour.
I find this view so strongly put and clearly borne out by a
body of men whom I should think ought to be considered
as authorities on this matter—I mean the anti-slavery body
themselves — that I will venture to read just three or four
lines out of this volume, which is a record of the proceedings
of the General Anti-Slavery Convention, called by the committee of the British and Foreign Anti-Slavery Society, and
held in London in 1840. It was denominated the 'World's
Convention of Anti-Slavery Delegates,' for its members
assembled from all parts of the globe. They appointed a
most intelligent committee to make a report as to the relative value of free and slave labour, and here is their decla-

ration, unanimously agreed to by the conference, with Thomas
Clarkson at their head. They say,—

' Resolved—That, upon the evidence of facts to which the attention of this
Convention has been directed, it is satisfactorily established as a general axiom
that free labour is more profitable to the employer, and consequently cheaper,
than slave labour.'

They go on to say,—

' That of all kinds of slave labour, that of imported slaves has been demonstrated to be the most costly and the least productive.'

And they wind up thus :—

' That the advantages of free-labour cultivation cannot be fairly attested or
fully realized under a system of husbandry and general management which
has grown up under the existence of slavery, and which is attested by a waste
of human labour, that, but for monopoly prices, must have absorbed all the
profit of cultivation. That the unrestricted competition of free labour in the
cultivation of sugar would necessarily introduce a new system, by which the
cost of production would be further diminished, and the fall of prices that must
ensue would leave no profit upon slave-grown sugar.'

I will only quote one other passage of three lines from this
report. There was a long debate upon the subject ; many
intelligent witnesses from all parts of the world bore testimony
to that principle, and the committee passed those resolutions
unanimously. I will only read from the report of the discussions a few words of the speech of Mr. Scoble, who was speaking of the difference in the price of sugars which were then in
the market. In alluding to the fact that the price of slave-
sugar was 23s. per cwt., while that of free-grown sugar was
47s., he says :—

' Now, what is it that makes the difference in price between these two
classes of colonial produce but what is usually termed the West Indian monopoly ? Let the monopoly be got rid of, and I will venture to say that free-
labour will compete with slave-labour sugar of any kind.'

That is the testimony of Mr. Scoble, who, I believe, is the
accredited agent of the present London anti-slavery body.

Now, I ask these gentlemen to do that which we Free-
traders do—to have faith in their own principles ; to trust a

great truth, convinced that it will carry them safely, whatever
there may be of apparent difficulty in their way. We, as
Free-traders, do not ask for the free admission of slave-grown
sugar because we wish to consume the produce of slaves
rather than of freemen, but because we object to the infliction
of a monopoly upon the people of England under the pretence
of putting an end to slavery. We deny that that is an effectual
or a just mode of extinguishing slavery. On the contrary, it
is subjecting the British public to a species of oppression and
spoliation second in injustice only to slavery itself. We maintain, with Mr. Scoble and the Anti-Slavery Convention, that
free labour, if placed in competition with slave labour, will be
found cheaper and more productive, and that it will, in the
end, put down slavery and the slave trade, by rendering it
unprofitable to hold our fellow-creatures in bondage. Why,
would it not be a monstrous thing if we found that in the
moral government of this world it was so contrived that a
man should have a premium offered him for doing injustice to
his fellow-man? Plenty and cheapness have been the reward
promised from the beginning of time to those who do well;
but if the greater cheapness and plenty should be the reward
of him who seizes on his fellow-man and compels him to work
with the whip, rather than for the man who offers a fair re-
compense for the willing labourer, I say, if that were found to
be true, it would be at war with all we hold most just, and
which we believe to be true of the moral government of the
universe. If, then, free competition be wanted to overturn
slavery, I ask this anti-slavery body how they can consistently
present petitions to the House of Commons praying that this
free competition shall not be allowed, and therefore that the
very means they recommend for abolishing slavery shall not
be carried into effect in this country? I am willing to believe
many of these individuals to be honest; they have proved
themselves to be disinterested by the labours they have gone
through; but I warn them against being made the uncon-

scious instruments of subtle, designing, and thoroughly selfish men, who have an interest in upholding this monopoly of sugar, which is slavery in another form, for the consumers of sugar here; and who, to carry their base object, will tamper with the feelings of the people of this country, and make use of the old British anti-slavery feeling, in order to carry out their selfish and iniquitous objects.

Now, ladies and gentlemen, before I sit down, I wish to say a word to you on a truly practical part of the question. Some allusion was made by my friend, Mr. Ricardo, to the probability of an election, and the necessity of being prepared for it. I am desirous, particularly in this place, where what we say goes out to the whole world—our own organ, the *League*, conveys every syllable of our speeches to 20,000 persons in all the parishes in the kingdom—I say, I want to dwell especially here upon what I conceive it is necessary that the people of this country should do to carry out the principles of Free Trade. They must simply adopt the plan which Sir Robert Peel recommended to his party—' Register, register, register!' Without a single public meeting or demonstration of any kind at all comparable with this, that party went to work, and in the course of four or five years placed their chief, who had given that good advice, in a majority in the House of Commons. Now, we have infinitely more scope for work than ever he or his supporters had. Are you aware of the number of people who are voluntarily disfranchised in this country at this moment? You will be astonished when I tell you that in the metropolitan boroughs alone there are from 40,000 to 50,000 people who might register and vote for Members of Parliament, if they chose, but who neglect to do so. In every one of the large boroughs, such as Birmingham, Manchester, and Leeds, there are thousands of people entitled to vote for Members of Parliament, but who yet do not make the necessary claim for that purpose. Why, within the walls of the city of London, I will venture to say that there is not one

house which is paying a lower rent than 10*l.* Every man
with a roof over his head there, can, and ought to, be a voter.
How will you carry your Free-trade ticket at the next city of
London election, unless you all register yourselves, for we do
not then intend to go for one, but for all the four Members
together?

I will in a few words state to you, and all our friends in
the country, exactly how we stand at this particular moment.
In about ten weeks the time will have elapsed which will give
the people an opportunity of claiming to vote for the next
year. Then, observe, that in order to have a vote you must
have occupied a 10*l.* house for twelve months previous to the
31st of July, and have paid all rates and taxes due up to the
6th of April, upon or before the 20th of July. Having done
this, you will be entitled to register your names as voters,
and be in a position to exercise the elective franchise the next
year, should there be a dissolution of Parliament, and a contest
for Free Trade. Mark me! By a late decision in the Court
of Common Pleas, every man who rents a room in a house, if
the apartment be a separate tenement—that is, if the lodger
has the key of it, and has ingress and egress at the outer
door when he likes—if that room be rented at 10*l.* a year or
upwards, he will be entitled to a vote; and, if his landlord
pays the rates, it is a sufficient rating, provided his own name
be put down along with his landlord's on the books of the
overseers. Now, that decision alone has given the franchise to
perhaps 1500 or 2000 people in the city of London, and an immense number throughout the whole metropolitan boroughs.
But lodgers who are boarded and lodged in a house, and who
have not a separate room, as is the ordinary way with young
persons, are not entitled to a vote. I wish they were, for I
have no doubt we should get most of them. How is it that
there are 40,000 or 50,000 people in the metropolis, and many
thousands in all large towns, that are not on the electoral
lists? I will tell you why. In the first place, I am sorry to

say that a vast number of people in this country, who would
be shocked and offended if we called them ' slaves,' or did not
compliment them under the title of ' free-born Englishmen,'
will not take the trouble to walk across the street in order to
obtain for themselves votes, even where there is no expense
attending it. In very many cases the difficulty is this, that
in a great number of the smaller class of houses the landlords
owning them compound for the rates, and pay them in a
lump, whether the houses be empty or not, and by so doing
pay a somewhat less amount than they would do if they paid
for each house individually. If a tenant under such circumstances tells the overseers he wishes to be put down in the
rate-book to get a vote, the overseers are required by law to
put their names upon the rate-books with that of their landlords'. That is the condition in which thousands, nay, tens
of thousands, of people in this country are situated who might
have votes for Members of Parliament, if they adopted the
proper means. I do hope that all who hear me, and those
who will read what I am saying, will feel that now the time is   .
come when each individual in his locality will be called on to
make an effort to enrol his own and his neighbours' names on
the register, against a future electoral combat.

Come when it may, our victory will depend on the force we
can bring on paper before we come into the field. It is of no
use going to a contest if we have not previously been to the
registration court. I would counsel our friends, the non-electors
in any borough, and point out to them how much they can do
by looking after their neighbours ; and, when they see a man
just balancing and doubting whether he will or will not claim
to vote, to urge upon him the duty which he owes to the cause
we advocate of having his name placed on the register. If
they do not do so, the time will come when they will bitterly
regret it. It was only the other day that our friend, General
Briggs, at Exeter, where he nobly did the work for us, found
that he could not walk the streets of that city without being

followed by crowds of non-electors, saying, ' I will show you, sir, where there is a man who will give you a vote.' Another would say, ' I have been looking after three votes for you.' A third would exclaim, ' I wish I had a hundred votes, you should have them all.' One honest man who kept a turnpike-gate—and we are often told that turnpike-keepers are misanthropes—positively would not receive toll from the General, stating that as he had not a vote to register for him, he would give him what he could. Persons of this description, if they will take my advice, instead of reserving all their enthusiasm until the time of contest, will during the next ten weeks do their utmost to influence every one of their neighbours whom they can to be enrolled. It is by these means, and not by talking, that the victory will be won. I have over and over again told you that I have no faith in talking; it is not by words, but by deeds, by pursuing a course such as I have been describing, that when the day of battle comes we shall be prepared with a majority on the electoral lists to meet our opponents in that constitutional fight in which the question must be decided ; and if we are true to our principles, and show but ordinary zeal in their behalf, we shall not have another general election without finding a triumphant majority in favour of Free-trade principles.

—◦-◦❖❋❖◦-◦—

FREE TRADE

XI.

LONDON, JULY 3, 1844.

AFTER the narrative which our friend Mr.Villiers has given of the past proceedings of himself and others in the House of Commons, in connection with that great question, the Repeal of the Corn-laws, I am sure it will be as acceptable to you as it will be pleasant to my own feelings to express my gratitude, as I am sure you will allow me to do yours, towards that gentleman especially, who, fortunately for us and the country, took possession six years ago of this question in the Legislature, and who has so nobly and manfully supported it in spite of all sinister influences, in defiance of all those associations which he himself, as a member of the aristocracy, must have had brought to bear upon him. I thank him in your name and in behalf of the country for the consistent course he has followed in advocating this question. He has told us that the progress which he has marked in the House of Commons has been measured by the progress of our agitation out of doors.

Really, when I look back and remember what the Anti-Corn-law League was six years ago, and when I consider the progress which the movement has made since that time, I

cannot help thinking it affords a still greater hope and far
more encouragement to us to proceed than even those more
obvious gains which the figures he has given you respecting
the divisions in the House of Commons are able to demonstrate. I remember quite well, that six years ago we could have
mustered all the members of the Anti-Corn-law League in
one of those stage boxes, and even then I am afraid that at
most of our meetings we should have had a great deal of vacant
space. Our funds were small, collections of 5*., and even at
that low sum there were not very numerous contributors.
Year after year I have seen the progress of this movement,
not merely in Manchester, but in every provincial town, until
I find we are at length landed here in the midst of this
mighty metropolis, and have been during the last six months
holding weekly assemblies in this vast theatre, filled on every
occasion, and to-night as crowded as on any previous meeting.
If this unabated interest of London and the Londoners, in the
midst of so many distracting engagements, such numerous
and inviting temptations—if this attention to our cause is not
proof of the hold which Free-trade principles have on the
public mind, I know not where to go to find evidence which
can possibly prove the fact. Our friend has told you some of
the arguments that are used in the Houses of Parliament, in
opposition to our cause. Now, I am not so jealous of any of
their assertions or arguments as I am of one which I see was
used in the House of Lords last night by his Grace of Richmond. I find he is now continually stating in that august
assembly, that the tenantry of this country arose as one man
to oppose the League. I have myself heard the same assertions from the squirearchy in the House of Commons, and I
have heard it asserted so often, that I confess the repetition
itself, if I had known nothing else upon the subject, would
have made me rather suspect its authenticity; for it very
much reminds me of the schoolboy, whistling his way through
the churchyard to keep his courage up. Why the necessity

for these assertions? Wherefore do the landlords and the dukes now state so continually that the farmers are with them? This must, I suspect, have arisen from some doubts which pervade their minds as to whether the farmers really are to be beguiled and hoodwinked by their professions of protection. But when they tell us that the tenant-farmers rose spontaneously and formed the Anti-League Association, I tell them here, in the most public place in the world, that what they say is not true.

I do not wish to be offensive, and therefore I will use the words 'it is not true' in a logical sense. I say it is untrue, and I will prove my assertion by facts. I will take, for example, the meeting which his Grace of Richmond attended at Steyning, in Sussex, and I will mention facts which cannot be controverted. I know that that meeting was got up by the aristocracy and squirearchy of Sussex, and that if they themselves did not personally go round, and canvass and entreat the farmers to attend, that their land-agents, and land-stewards, and law-stewards did so; that the tenant-farmers were canvassed and pressed to come up to that meeting with just the same earnestness with which they are canvassed for a general election. Nay, more; the carriages and horses,—the vehicles of the landlords, down even to the deer-cart,—were put at the disposal of the farmers, to carry them up to the Steyning meeting. What I say of the Sussex meeting, of my own knowledge, is, I am well assured, a fact as regards almost every assemblage which has been held, purporting to be a spontaneous meeting of the farmers to oppose the League. In some instances dinners were provided for the tenantry at the expense of the landlord. The tenant-farmers were moved by the landlords; they were canvassed by the law-agents and land-agents in every part of the kingdom, often not knowing the business they were going upon, and in much more frequent cases not caring for the object for which they were summoned together. And what I am

telling you now is patent to the whole community; there is
not an individual here from any county in England where
those meetings have been got up, who will not immediately
respond to the truth of what I have stated. [A voice: 'I can
bear you out.'] The land-agent—mark the tribe—is the finger
of the landlord. He has but to point, and the farmer acts
according to his direction, knowing that it is the bidding of
his landlord at secondhand. And who are the men who have
attacked the League at these meetings? Can you show me
one specimen of a *bonâ fide* intelligent, substantial farmer,
like my friend Mr. Lattimore, whom I see sitting behind me;
or like Mr. Josiah Hunt, who addressed us here a short time
back; or those two worthy men who came from Somersetshire
for the same purpose? Can you show me in all the instances
of their meeting, *bonâ fide* respectable, intelligent men, known
to be good farmers in their own locality, men of capital in
the world, who have taken a lead in the movement? You
cannot show me a man of that stamp who has attended a
meeting, and taken the leading part in their proceedings.
But if you ask who the men are that have been placed in the
chair, or put forward to speak upon such occasions, you will
find that a hundred to one they are either agents, auctioneers,
or land-stewards. Who is Mr. Baker, of Writtle, in Essex?
He is the man who has been put forward as the great leader
of the protectionists in that county; it was he who originated
the first meeting, who has written pamphlets and made
speeches upon the subject of protection; and yet, who is this
Mr. Baker, of Writtle? I will undertake to say that he
makes more money by agency and auctioneering than by
farming. You may have seen his name advertised in newspapers, in one column as the author of a pamphlet or the
writer of a letter for the protection societies in favour of the
Corn-law, and in another column advertised as the auctioneer
who is going to sell up some unfortunate farmer who has
been ruined by the Corn-law.

Does his Grace of Richmond or the squirearchy in the House of Commons, after the enlightenment and education which our great peripatetic political university—the League —has diffused through the country, think for a moment that the public will be so gulled by these unfounded assertions in either House of Legislature, as to really believe that the tenant-farmers spontaneously and voluntarily rose up to form anti-league associations, when the facts which I have mentioned are generally known in every county in the kingdom? Why, how can they get up and talk so foolishly! It appears to me that they must be about as cunning as the ostrich, which hides its head in the sand, and thinks that no one can see its unfortunate body because it cannot see it itself. I am jealous of this practice of taking the tenant-farmers' name in vain. They tell us that we have been abusing the farmers, and therefore they have turned against us; but, if there has been one individual in the country who has more constantly stood up for farmers' interests and rights than another, I am the man. I have a right to do so. All my early associations —which we do not easily get rid of—lead me irresistibly to sympathise with the farmers. I was bred in a farm-house myself, and up to the time of my going to school I lived amongst farmers and farm-labourers, and witnessed none other than farming pursuits. I should be utterly unworthy of the class from which I have sprung if I voluntarily entered upon a crusade against one of the most industrious, painstaking, and worst-used classes in the community. I have said scores of times, in all parts of the country, that I believe the tenant-farmers have been more deeply injured by the Corn-laws than any other class of the community. The history of the tenant-farmers—oh, that we could have the history of that class in this country for the last thirty years! Would we could procure a report to be presented to the House of Commons of the number of tenants in this country who have been sold up and ruined during the last thirty years

under the blessed protection of the Corn-laws! It would
form a dark calendar of suffering, not to be equalled by the
history of any other class of men in any other pursuit in this
world. An enemy to farmers! If I am an enemy to the
farmers, at all events I have not feared to trust myself
amongst them. The monopolists did not come to meet me
when I went into the farming districts, and they will not
come to meet me if I go there again: that is the reason why
I have not been lately; and I have often put this question to
the protectionists in the lobby of the House of Commons:
'Will you meet me in your own locality? Will you let your
high-sheriff call a county meeting in any part of the country;
I care not where it is; you shall choose your own county?
Will you meet me in a public meeting in any county in the
kingdom, and there take a vote for or against the Corn-laws?'
No; they will not meet me, because they know they would
be out-voted if they did. The Corn-laws protect farmers!
Why, the farmers pay their rent according to the price of the
produce of their land; and after that well-known fact, you
need not say another word upon the subject. If Corn-laws
keep up the price of food, they maintain the amount of rents
also. The Corn-law is a rent law, and it is nothing else.
But I am jealous of these noble dukes and squires attempting
to make it appear that we are enemies to the farmer. In fact,
I feel it is paying no great compliment to our own knowledge
and intelligence if they suppose that we should have gone on
lumping the landlords along with farmers altogether in the
way in which they lump them. No, no; I began my career
in the House of Commons by a definition of this kind:—You
landlords have called yourselves 'agriculturists;' mind, I do
not denominate you such: you are no more 'agriculturists'
because you own land than a shipowner is a sailor because he
owns ships. When the noble Duke of Richmond gets up in
the House of Peers and says, 'Oh, the Anti-Corn-law League
by their abuse of the agriculturists have set the farmers

against them,' he does not know the language of his own country, and requires to study an English grammar, if he is not aware that an agriculturist means a cultivator of the land. That term may be applied to the tenant-farmer and the farm-labourer; but his Grace of Richmond must change his pursuits, and become a more useful member of society before he will be entitled to be called an agriculturist.

Now, it is not only in the way you have heard pointed out that the Corn-law injures the farmer—it is not merely that the Corn-law has tempted him to make bad bargains by expecting high Act-of-Parliament prices, and then deceived and disappointed him in those prices—that is not the only way in which the Corn-law has worked mischief to the farmer. It has injured him by distracting his attention from other grievances which lie nearer home—which are really of importance—keeping his attention constantly engaged with an *ignis fatuus*, which perpetually escapes his grasp, and which would not benefit him even if he could clutch it. What are the grievances which the farmer feels? He requires a fair adjustment of his rent; he wants a safe tenure for his land; he requires a lease; he must get rid of the game which are nourished in those wide hedge-rows which rob him of the surface of the land, whilst the game devours the produce of his industry and his capital. The farmer wants improvement in his homestead; he requires draining, and a variety of concessions from his landlord: and how is he met when he endeavours to obtain them? He cannot approach the landlord, agent, and steward, and ask for a settlement of any of those grievances; those parties are all in a plot together, and they forthwith tell him, 'This is not the matter you should trouble yourself with: go and oppose the Anti-Corn-law League, or else they will ruin you.' Is there any other class of men who are dealt with in a manner like this? They cannot come to a *bonâ fide* settlement upon any existing grievance, because there is an Act of Parliament pointed to which they are told they must maintain, or else they will all be ruined.

I have often illustrated the folly of this practice to farmers; I do not know whether I have ever done so to you; but if you will allow me, at all events, I will hazard the chance of its being a repetition; for I have found the illustration come home forcibly to the apprehensions of the farmers in the country. I have pointed out the folly of this system in the following manner:—You, as a farmer, deal with your landlord in a manner different from the way in which I transact business with my customers, and they with me. I am a manufacturer, having extensive transactions with linen-drapers throughout the country. I dispose of a bale of goods to a tradesman; I invoice it to him, stating it to be of a certain quality and price, and representing it as an article which he may fairly expect to sell for a certain sum. At the end of half-a-year, my traveller—who is my 'agent,' similar to that of the landlord—goes round to the draper and says, 'I have called for this account;' presenting the invoice. The linen-draper replies, 'Mr. Cobden sold me these goods, promising they were all sound, and they have turned out to be all tender: he stated they were fast colours, and they have every one proved to be fugitive. From what Mr. Cobden stated, I expected to get such-and-such a price, and I have only obtained so-and-so; and, consequently, have incurred a great loss by the sale of the article.' Suppose my traveller—who, as I said before, is my 'agent'—replied to the linendraper, 'Yes, all which you have said is perfectly true; it has been a very bad bargain, and you have lost a great deal of money; but Mr. Cobden is a real linendraper's friend, and he will get a Committee of the House of Commons to inquire into the matter.' Then, still following up the simile of the land-agent, if the commercial-traveller were to present his account, and say, 'In the meantime, pay Mr. Cobden every farthing of that account, for if not, he has got another Act of Parliament,

called the law of distress, by which he is enabled to come
upon your stock, and clear off every farthing in payment of
himself, although no other of your creditors should get a
farthing; but, notwithstanding, Mr. Cobden is a real linen-
draper's friend, and he will get a Committee of the House to
inquire into the subject.' That is precisely the mode in which
farmers deal with their landlords. Do you think that linen-
drapers would ever prosper if they dealt with manufacturers
in that way? They would very soon find themselves where
the farmers are, in fact, too often found—in the hands of an
auctioneer, agent, or valuer. Linendrapers are too sagacious
to manage their business in such a manner as that. I never
will despair that the farmers — the real *bona fide* tenant-
farmers—of this country will not find out—I say they shall find
it out, for we will repeat the fact so often that they shall know
it—how they have been bamboozled and kept from the real
grievances, the real bargains, and actual transactions by which
they should govern their intercourse with landlords by this
hocus-pocus of an Act of Parliament which professes to
benefit them.

What is it that these political landlords tell the farmers at
the present time to do? Is it to petition Parliament to give
them anything different from what they now possess? They are
in distress. Their labourers, numbers of them in every parish,
are standing idle in the market-place, wanting work and getting none. They find themselves threatened with being devoured with poor-rates, and they cannot meet their half-year's
rent. What is it which the political landlords tell the farmers
to do in order to remedy all these grievances? Present petitions to Parliament, praying them to keep things exactly as
they are! That is really what the speeches at the protection
meetings amount to. This attempt at deluding the farmers
is a masterpiece of audacity compared with any previous pretext of the landlords; for in former times, when farmers were
recommended to go to Parliament with a petition for a

Committee to inquire into their condition, it was invariably
with a view of discovering a remedy for their evils; but now all
which these political impostors profess to do, is to persuade the
farmers to keep themselves in the same downward course and
hopeless state in which they at present find themselves. No,
no; I do not despair that the farmers will yet find out this
miserable delusion which has been practised upon them. The
landlords tell me that at the meetings I have held in the
counties I have not had the voice of the farmers with me.
I am perfectly well aware that, in holding a meeting in a
county town, even in the most purely rural district—such as
Wiltshire and Dorsetshire—you cannot prevent the towns-
people from assembling along with the farmers. I am quite
ready to admit that many farmers may have attended those
meetings without holding up their hands one way or the
other. They came, however, and heard our statements, and
that was all I wanted. But mark the inconsistency of these
landlords: one day they come and tell me that the whole
population of the agricultural districts, — the shopkeepers,
mechanics, artisans,—that every man in a county town like
Salisbury, for instance, depends upon the Corn-laws, and
benefits by this protection; and then when, I say, I go down
to such a place and take the voice of the community, including the tradesmen of the town as well as farmers and
farm-labourers, they immediately separate that class of the
community which consists of shopkeepers and residents in
towns, and state, 'We will not take their voices and votes
as decisive in this matter,' though they live in their own
county; but they say, 'It is the farmers and farm-labourers
who alone must be judges between us.'

There is one other argument which has also been employed,
and which I did not expect to hear, even from a duke. I see that
a noble duke tells the House of Lords that the Anti-Corn-law
League wish to repeal the Corn-laws in order that they may
reduce the wages of their workmen. He asserts that the

price of corn governs the rate of wages in this country; that
when bread is high wages are raised, and when it is low
wages are depressed. I say, I did not expect ever to have
heard this allegation made again, even in the House of Lords.
Such, however, was the statement made in that assembly last
night, but which was promptly met by our noble and patriotic
friend Lord Radnor, who is always at his post. It requires a
great amount of moral courage, in an atmosphere like that in
which he was then sitting, in an assembly possessing very
little sympathy for men holding patriotic views and taking
an independent course, to take such a course as he has always
taken; and yet that nobleman is always to be found in the
right place; his courage never fails him; and I must say that
he meets the noble dukes with their fallacies in a most clear
and concise way, and puts his extinguisher upon them in a
most admirable manner. Lord Radnor gave the noble duke
an axiom which should always be borne in mind by you,—
that if the labourer is already sunk so low in wages that he
cannot subsist upon a less sum, that then the price of labour
must rise and fall with the value of corn, because otherwise
your labourers would starve and die off; that, in fact, where
labour has reached its minimum, the labourer is treated upon
precisely the same principle as a horse or beast of burden:
the same quantity of bread is given to him in dear years as
in cheap seasons; just in like manner as you would give as
much oats to a horse when they were dear as you would when
they were cheap, because it is necessary to do so in order to
keep him in working condition, otherwise you would not
obtain his labour. Now, what does this fact prove, except
that the man is reduced to the condition of a slave, where
the wages are not the result of a free bargain between the
employer and the labourer, but where, like the negro in
Cuba and Brazil, he has his rations served out to him—his
red herring and rice—no more and no less, whatever its price
may be.

But will they venture to tell us that this is the condition of the working classes in the manufacturing districts or in the metropolis? [A person in the pit: 'Yes.'] I ask that man who answered 'Yes,' whether he ever knew an instance in London in which the price of labour followed the price of bread? [The person in the pit: 'Yes, in the manufacturing districts.'] I said 'in London.' I will come to the manufacturing districts presently; but let us begin with the metropolis, for I see there are some persons here who require instruction upon this point. In 1839 and 1840 bread was nearly double in price that it was in 1835 and 1836; did the shoemakers, painters, tailors, masons, joiners, or any other operatives in London get an advance of wages in the dear years? Did the porters of London, even, obtain any increase of remuneration? You have in London 100,000 men employed in the capacity of porters in shops and warehouses, in the streets, or upon the river: did any of these 100,000 men ever hear in their lives, or their fathers before them, of wages rising along with the price of bread? What is the mode of proceeding in your Corporation? They fix the wages of many people, such as ticket-porters and watermen, and the rate of hackney-coach fares is also determined either by their orders or by Act of Parliament. Did you ever know of their being altered because there had been a change in the price of corn? Who ever heard of a man stepping into a boat and requesting to be rowed from Westminster to Blackfriars-bridge, and upon arriving at the latter place asking the waterman what his fare was, and being told in reply, 'Why, Sir, it is a dear year; the quartern loaf is up two-pence, and therefore we charge more than we did when bread was cheaper?'

As regards the manufacturing districts, I will tell you what the rule is there. You know that every word of what I am saying is taken down; and I am not speaking here to you only, but for publication, and, if untrue, refutation, in the north of England. If they can contradict my statement,

there are plenty of good friends who would rejoice to do so;
we have, perhaps, one of them now here—I do not think
there are more—who would be glad, if he could, to pick a
hole in my argument. I repeat here what was recently
stated by Mr. Robert Gardner in Lancashire. That gentleman, be it remembered, is a Conservative; the treasurer of a
fund for building ten churches in Manchester, and himself a
subscriber of 1000*l.* to that object; but who, on the Free-
trade principle, nobly threw aside party, and at the last
county election himself proposed Mr. Brown as a candidate
for South Lancashire. What did Mr. Robert Gardner say?
Bear in mind he is one of our largest and oldest manufacturers in Lancashire. He stated on the hustings there,
in the midst of men of his own order, but of different political
views, and who, therefore, would have denied his statement
if they could have done so,—

'I have been engaged extensively in this district for thirty years past, and
I here state as the result of my experience, that, so far from the wages in this
part of Lancashire rising and falling with the price of bread, that there never
has been an instance during my experience when the bread has become dear
and scarce, that wages and employment have not gone down; but whenever
bread has become plentiful and provisions cheap, wages have as constantly
risen, and employment has become more abundant.'

I quote that upon Mr. Gardner's authority; but I pledge my
reputation as a public man and private citizen of this country
to the truth of what that gentleman has stated.

That these scandalous misstatements should have ever again
been repeated, even in the House of Lords—that any one
should have dared to venture upon such a worn-out, miserable
fallacy—surpasses my comprehension. I say here, deliberately,
that instead of the price of corn governing the rate of wages
in the way our opponents state, so far as the north of
England is concerned, the effect is the very opposite; and,
therefore, to say that the Anti-Corn-law League wants a
reduction in the price of food in order to reduce wages,
and acts upon the supposition that wages can be reduced

when food is cheap in the manufacturing districts, is to
charge it with going contrary to all experience. I do not
content myself with arguing upon possibilities. I am not a
duke, you know, and therefore I cannot content myself, like a
duke, with arguing always in the future tense, and saying
what will happen, and then take it for granted that common
plebeians must take my assertions for prophecy or argument;
but I mention facts and experience, the only ground upon
which fallible men can form a judgment of anything; and
therefore I say, if the members of the Anti-Corn-law League
who are manufacturers—although now a very small minority
of that body are manufacturers, I am happy to say—but if
those who are manufacturers want a repeal of the Corn-laws
with the idea that to cheapen food would enable them to
reduce wages, they are the most blind, and apparently the
most besotted class of men that ever existed; for, if one may
trust all experience, the effect of a free trade in corn must
inevitably be to raise the money rate of wages in the north of
England, at the same time that it will give to the working
class their enjoyments, comforts, and the necessaries of life at
a cheaper rate than they have hitherto had them.

You remember our first appearance in London in 1839 and
1840. You did not take much notice of us then: we were
assembled in Brown's Hotel in Palace Yard, in a comparatively small room. The reception you then gave us was a
very cold one. If you had then known as much about the
Corn-laws as you do now, or rather if you had felt as keenly—
for I believe that at that time you knew quite as much as
your fellow-countrymen—if you had felt as you do now, I
believe that by this time we should have had a repeal of the
Corn-laws. What was the state of the north of England
when we first came up to London? Bread was dear enough
to please even his Grace of Richmond. Good wheat, such
as Christians ought to consume, was selling at about 80s. a
quarter. What was then the condition of our manufacturing

districts? Did we come up to London because we wanted labour cheapened, that we might get men out of the agricultural districts, and pull down their wages? Why, a large portion of our own population were in the workhouse or the streets wanting employment, and offering their labour at any rate. One-half the manufactories in Stockport were shut up; and men who were bred to skilful pursuits, worked upon the road at stonebreaking for 7*s.* or 8*s.* a week. Such was the state of things in the manufacturing districts when we first came to London. What was our object in coming here, and what remedy did we propose for that distress? By a free trade in corn to cheapen its price, to lower it materially from the price at which it then was—20*s.* per quarter higher than it now is. Our object then was by this means to enable us to employ our people at good wages. If we had wanted to lower the price of labour, we should have come up to Parliament and asked your noble dukes and squires to keep on the Corn-law; for that was the most effectual way of doing it. No; in London and the manufacturing districts, in all your cities, large towns, and villages, mechanics and operatives, blacksmiths, carpenters, and every class of people, are above that state at which they have rations served out to them like the negroes in Brazil or Cuba: they are superior to that low condition when wages rise and fall with the price of food. If the Duke of Richmond tells me that agricultural labourers are in that state, then I say that this class has reached the lowest point of degradation which men, nominally free but really enslaved by circumstances, ever reached in any Christian country.

For myself, I repudiate the motives falsely attributed to us, of seeking by the repeal of the Corn-laws to reduce wages. I do not urge motive as argument, or as a ground for your confidence. We know nothing of men's motives: they may often be the very worst when we suppose them to be the very best. I say, from the facts I have told you, that the effect of

the repeal of the Corn-laws, if it cheapen the price of food,
will be to lighten distress, and to give a demand for labour by
extending our foreign trade. If it reduce the price of bread,
looking to all past experience, the effect in Lancashire, Yorkshire, and all the manufacturing districts, must be to raise the
money rate of wages; in London and the large towns of agricultural districts leaving the wages at least where they are
now, seeing that wages do not follow the price of food; and
it will give all the people the necessaries of life as cheap as by
nature they were intended to enjoy them.

There was another duke, his Grace of Cleveland, who
applauded a pamphlet written by Mr. Cayley, in which the
writer has taken great liberties with Adam Smith—as Lord
Kinnaird, I think, recently pointed out to you from this place.
Mr. Cayley and his party have taken Adam Smith and tried
to make him a protectionist, and they have done it in this
manner: they took a passage, and with the scissors snipped
and cut away at it, until by paring off the ends of sentences,
and leaving out all the rest of the passage, they managed to
make Adam Smith appear in some sense as a monopolist.
When we referred to the volume itself, we found out their
tricks, and exposed them. I tell you what their argument
reminds me of. An anecdote is told of an atheist who once
asserted that there was no God, and said he would prove it
from Scripture. He selected that passage from the Psalms
which says, 'The fool hath said in his heart there is no God.'
He then cut out the whole of the passage, except the words
'there is no God,' and brought it forward as proof of his
statement. As the Dukes of Richmond and Cleveland have
found out that there is such a work as that of Adam Smith,
I wish they would just read the eighth chapter of his First
Book, where he speaks of wages of labour. I will read an
extract from it to you:—

'The wages of labour do not, in Great Britain, fluctuate with the price of
provisions. Wages vary everywhere from year to year, frequently from

month to month. But in many places the money price of labour remains uniformly the same, sometimes for half a century together. If in these places, therefore, the labouring poor can maintain their families in dear years, they must be at their ease in times of moderate plenty, and in affluence in those of extraordinary cheapness.'

But I will not confine myself to Adam Smith: I will neither take him nor any other writer, but will be guided by experience and facts within our own knowledge, and then we cannot go wrong. I do not think we need argue this matter here to-night; we have come together upon this occasion almost as for a leave-taking. We have had so many delightful meetings in this place, that I cannot help feeling regret that I should have heard our chairman whisper that our weekly meetings are drawing to a close. Depend upon it, we have given an impetus to this question, not merely in England; for in Europe, in America, and every part of the civilised globe, our meetings have excited the greatest attention.

I should not like that we should separate without a distinct enunciation of what our intention is, and, if opponents wish it, what our motives are. In the first place, we want free trade in corn, because we think it just; we ask for the abolition of all restriction upon that article, exclusively, simply because we believe that, if we obtain that, we shall get rid of all other monopolies without any trouble. We do not seek free trade in corn primarily for the purpose of purchasing it at a cheaper money-rate; we require it at the natural price of the world's market, whether it becomes dearer with a free trade—as wool seems to be getting up now, after the abolition of the 1*d.* a pound—or whether it is cheaper, it matters not to us, provided the people of this country have it at its natural price, and every source of supply is freely opened, as nature and nature's God intended it to be;—then, and then only, shall we be satisfied. If they come to motives, we state that we do not believe that free trade in corn will injure the farmer; we are convinced that it will benefit the tenant-farmer as much as any trader or manufacturer in the community. Neither do we believe it

will injure the farm-labourer; we think it will enlarge the
market for his labour, and give him an opportunity of finding
employment, not only on the soil by the improvements which
agriculturists must adopt, but that there will also be a general
rise in wages from the increased demand for employment in
the neighbouring towns, which will give young peasants an
opportunity of choosing between the labour of the field and that
of the towns.   We do not expect that it will injure the landowner, provided he looks merely to his pecuniary interest in the
matter; we have no doubt it will interfere with his political
despotism — that political union which now exists in the
House of Commons, and to a certain extent also, though
terribly shattered, in the counties of this country.   We believe it might interfere with that; and that with free trade
in corn men must look for political power rather by honest
means—to the intelligence and love of their fellow-countrymen—than by the aid of this monopoly, which binds some
men together by depressing and injuring their fellow-citizens.
We are satisfied that those landowners who choose to adopt
the improvement of their estates, and surrender mere political
power by granting long leases to the farmers—who are content to eschew some of their feudal privileges connected with
vert and venison—I mean the feudal privileges of the chase—
if they will increase the productiveness of their estates—if
they choose to attend to their own business—then, I say, free
trade in corn does not necessarily involve pecuniary injury to
the landlords themselves.

If there be a class in the community who may be said to
have a beneficial interest in the Corn-laws—to whom there
would be no compensation from their repeal, if the price of
corn were a little reduced—that class is the clergy of this
country, and they alone.   The Tithe Commutation Act has
fixed their incomes at a certain number of quarters of corn
per annum.   Suppose a clergyman gets 200 quarters of corn
for his tithe, if that corn fetch in the market 40s. a quarter,

it yields him as his annual stipend 400*l.* as the produce of his
tithe; but if the price of wheat be 50*s.* a quarter, then the
clergyman obtains 500*l.* per annum, instead of 400*l.* as
formerly. I am willing to admit, that if the result of Free
Trade causes a reduction in the price of corn to the amount
of 10*s.* per quarter—though I by no means use it as an argument—that it will be productive to him, upon such a supposition, of an uncompensated diminution of his income as a
tithe-owner. He does not spend so much of his stipend in
bread as to obtain from the decrease of its price compensation
for the diminution of his income arising from the same source.
But, I would ask, is this a right position for the clergy of this
country to be placed in? Is it reasonable that they who pray
for ‘cheapness and plenty’ should have an interest in maintaining scarcity and dearness? I will put it to the clergy
of this country whether, with this one fact apparent to the
world, they can, consistently with the retention of their
character of respectability, be found in future assisting Anti-
League meetings in upholding the Corn-laws? Why, they
would not be fit to sit upon a jury for the trial of the question; you might challenge them as interested parties, and
they would, upon the commonest principles of justice, be
excluded the box upon that ground. I appeal to them, as
they love their own reputation, and for the sake of decency,
at least, to stand neutral upon the question: that is all I
require of them.

We believe that Free Trade will increase the demand for
labour of every kind, not merely of the mechanical classes and
those engaged in laborious bodily occupations, but for clerks,
shopmen and warehousemen, giving employment to all those
youths whom you are so desirous of setting out in the world.
O, how anxiously do fathers and mothers consult together
upon this point! What letters do they write soliciting advice and assistance! I have frequently had such epistles
addressed to me: ‘There is our boy, John, just come from

school; he is now fifteen years of age; we do not know where to put him, every trade is so full, we're quite at a loss what to do with him; we can get nothing from Government, for they give everything they have to bestow to the aristocracy.'

Finally, wo believe that Free Trade will not diminish, but, on the contrary, increase the Queen's revenue.

This, ladies and gentlemen, is our faith; these our objects; and this the ground upon which we stand. We believe that we are right: our opponents have acknowledged that we are so; they have confessed that our principles are true; and we will, therefore, stand by the justice of our system. Do not let us be disheartened by the apparent difficulty of our position: I never felt less discouragement in our cause than I do at this moment. Our labours for the next few months may not be quite so noisy as they have been; probably we have had too much talking; but if they are not so loud, be assured they shall be quite as efficient as any labours in which we have hitherto engaged upon this question. The registration throughout the country shall be well and systematically worked. In every locality where you may happen to mix, press upon your fellow-citizens the importance of watching the registration, that your own and your neighbours' names may be placed upon the register, and that you may strike off those irreclaimable monopolists who are not to be brought to the authority of reason upon this question. Let us attend diligently to this duty, and, if they will give us another registration, or even another after that, I have no doubt we shall give a very different account of matters in the House of Commons.

One word more and I have done. In order to keep our question in its true position, do not let us be used, however we may be abused, by any of the existing political parties. I have no objection at all to an alliance, offensive and defensive, with anybody who adopts our principles; but if some men are engaged in the pursuit of one object, and we of another, do not let us think of shutting our eyes, and entering into an arrangement which promises to be a partnership, in which the very first step we take will find us diverging, the one going one way, and the other another.

Political parties are breaking up in this country: I mean the old factions. There never was a period in the history of England when an attempt was made to carry on an opposition with a more intangible line of demarcation than that which separates Whig and Tory at the present moment. I venture to say, looking back upon the history of this country for two hundred years—to the time of Charles I, when party spirit ran so high that men drew their broadswords to decide political questions,—from that time down to the present there never has been a period when there was such an attempt to keep up an opposition against a party in power, without, apparently, one atom of principle or any one great public question on which to support an opposition. There are many other subjects which the politicians of this country take an interest in besides Free Trade; but for none of those questions has the Opposition, as led on now by one nominal chief, the support of the people out of doors. If we give up the ground we have taken upon the Free-trade principles, or surrender one iota of our principles, I know the temper and character of those who have nursed this agitation from its commencement, and by whom it is at this moment carried on, too well to doubt that, if there be the slightest evidence of anything which amounted to a compromise of our principles with any political party, that moment the right arm of every true friend of the League will be paralysed. I ask you, upon this occasion, whatever may happen in party papers, or be spoken in public against us, as Free Traders—and in no other capacity do I prefer the request—that you who have watched over this organisation, who have helped—as you have so continually done by your numbers—to sustain it with your sympathies,—I ask you, whatever you may are, notwithstanding anything which may be put out by a party press—the pens of whose writers are often guided by the intriguers of political faction—to apply but one test to us, namely, are we true as a League to the principles we advocate? If we are, depend upon it, whatever obstacles there may be, if we cling to that truth, we have only to persevere as men have ever done in all great and good objects, and it will be found, that being true to our principles, we shall go on to an ultimate and not very distant triumph.

———:)⟫≫ ✪ ≪⟪(:———

FREE TRADE

XII.

I was thinking, as I sat here, that probably there never have been so many persons assembled under a roof in England, or in Europe, as we have at this great League meeting. And the occasion and the circumstances under which we meet afford the most encouraging symptoms—encouraging, inasmuch as they prove that it is from no transient motive that you have joined together in this great cause—that it is not from the pressure of distress, temporary distress, that you have banded yourselves together—that the cause of Free Trade is, in your minds, something more than a remedy for present evils—that you look at it, under all circumstances, as a great and absorbing truth—and that your minds crave for it with an intellectual and moral craving, which has made it almost a part of the religion of your souls.

I venture to say that this meeting, held under these circumstances, with no pressure or excitement to call you together, will have more weight, more effect upon public opinion, than a score of those assemblies we used to hold, when we were driven together, as it were, under the pressure of local and temporary distress. And quiet as have been those statistical tables that you have heard from our chairman, I venture to say that they will strike more terror into the ranks of the monopolists than the loudest demonstrations or the most brilliant declamation with which we have ever tried to interest you. Upon the subject of this registration there is one thought that occurred to me as our chairman was giving you an account of the proceedings in the county revision. It is this, that the counties are more vulnerable than the small pocket boroughs, if we can rouse the Free Traders of the country into a systematic effort such as we have exercised in the case of South Lancashire. In many of the small boroughs there is no increase in the numbers; there is no extension of houses; the whole property belongs to a neighbouring noble, and you can no more touch the votes which he holds through the property than you can touch the balance in his banker's hands. But the county constituency may be increased indefinitely. It requires a qualification of forty shillings a-year in a freehold property to give a man a vote for a county. I think our landlords made a great mistake when they retained the forty-shilling freehold qualification; and, mark my words, it is a rod in pickle for them. I should not be surprised if it does for us what it did for Catholic emancipation, and what it did for the Reform Bill—give us the means of carrying Free Trade; and if it should, the landlords will very likely try to serve us as they did the forty-shilling freeholders in Ireland, when we have done the work.

The forty-shilling franchise for the county was established nearly five centuries ago. At that time a man, in the constitutional phraseology of the time, was deemed to be a 'yeoman,' and entitled to political rights, provided he had forty shillings a-year clear to spend. That was at that time a subsistence for a man; probably it was equal to the rental of one hundred acres of land. What is it now? With the vast diffusion of wealth among the middle classes, which then did not exist, and among a large portion, I am happy to say, in this district

of the superior class of operatives too, that forty-shilling
franchise is become merely nominal, and is within the reach
of every man who has the spirit to acquire it.   I say, then,
every county where there is a large town population, as in
Lancashire, the West Riding of Yorkshire, South Staffordshire,
North Cheshire, Middlesex, Surrey, Kent, and many other
counties I could name—in fact, every other county bordering
upon the sea-coast, or having manufactures in it—may be
won, and easily won, if the people can be roused to a systematic effort to qualify themselves for the vote in the way in
which the South Lancashire people have reached to the qualification.   We find that counties can be won by that means,
and no other.   It is the custom with many to put their savings
into the savings' banks.   I believe there are fourteen or fifteen
millions or more so deposited.   I would not say a word to
lessen your confidence in that security, but I say there is no
investment so secure as the freehold of the earth, and besides
it is the only investment that gives a vote along with the
property.   We come, then, to this—it costs a man nothing
to have a vote for the county.   He buys his property; sixty
pounds for a cottage is given—thirty or forty pounds in many
of the neighbouring towns will do it; he has then the interest
of his money, he has the property to sell when he wants it,
and he has his vote in the bargain.   Sometimes a parent,
wishing to teach a son to be economical and saving, gives
him a set of nest-eggs in a savings' bank; I say to such a
parent, 'Make your son, at twenty-one, a freeholder; it is an
act of duty, for you make him thereby an independent freeman, and put it in his power to defend himself and his children from political oppression—and you make that man with
60*l.* an equal in the polling-booth to Mr. Scarisbrick, with his
eleven miles in extent of territory, or to Mr. Egerton.   This
must be done.   In order to be on the next year's register, it
requires only that you should be in possession of a freehold
before the 31st of next January.'

We shall probably be told that 'this is very indiscreet—
what is the use of coming out in public and announcing such
a plan as this, when your enemies can take advantage of it as
well as you?' My first answer to that is, that our opponents,
the monopolists, cannot take advantage of it as well as we.
In the first place, very few men are, from connection or prejudice, monopolists, unless their capacity for inquiry or their
sympathies have been blunted by already possessing an undue
share of wealth. In the next place, if they wish to urge upon
others of a rank below them to qualify for a vote, they cannot
trust them with the use of the vote when they have got it.
But, apart from that, I would answer those people who cavil
at this public appeal, and say, 'You will not put salt upon
your enemy's tail—it is much too wise a bird.' They have
been at this work long ago, and they have the worst of it
now. What has been the conduct of the landlords of the
country? Why, they have been long engaged in multiplying
voters upon their estates, making the farmers take their sons,
brothers, nephews, to the register; making them qualify as
many as the rent of the land will cover: they have been
making their land a kind of political capital ever since the
passing of the Reform Bill. You have, then, a new ground
opened to you which has never yet been entered upon, and
from which I expect —in the course of not more than three
years from this time —that every county (if we persevere
as we have in South Lancashire) possessing a large town
population may carry Free Traders as their representatives
to Parliament.

Now, gentlemen, with just these preliminary remarks, I
was going to notice a common objection made to us during
the last two or three months—that the League has been very
quiet of late—that we have been doing nothing. Many people
have said to me, 'When are you going out into the agricultural districts again? I think they will be quite ripe for you
now, for most of your predictions have fallen true, and the

farmers will come and listen.' My answer has been, ' We are better employed at present at home, and the landlords are doing our work very well for us at their agricultural meetings.' What have been the features of the agricultural meetings we had heard of in the last two months? Here is one very striking circumstance, that, from the Duke of Buckingham downwards, every president of an agricultural association has always begun the proceedings of the day by saying, ' We must not introduce political topics in the discussions of this association.' That means, ' It is not convenient to us, the political landlords, to talk about the Corn-laws just now to the farmers'—and so they talk of everything else but the Corn-laws, and a very pretty business they make of their discussions. We hear, in every case in which I have read their reports, of the deplorable state of the agricultural labourers. Now, I beg to premise, from my own personal observation, and much inquiry, that the agricultural labourers, as a class, are better off now than they were when corn was 70s. the quarter in 1839 and 1840. I watched the Poor-law returns during those years, when we had such deep distress in this district, and I found that able-bodied pauperism was increasing faster in the corn-growing counties of Sussex and Kent than it was in these manufacturing districts.

When we called together the conference of ministers from all parts of the country, the accounts they brought from the rural villages were as heartrending as anything we had ever known in these manufacturing districts. You did not hear the clamours from the agricultural districts then, because they were drowned in the concentrated cry from these populous regions; but they were suffering as much as you were suffering. And now, when in this district employment and comparative prosperity have returned upon us, we hear of the state of the agricultural labourers, which has been always bad, always at the lowest level of wretchedness, only because you have ceased to occupy the public mind with your complaints

and your distresses. But, if what they tell us is true, that the
agricultural labourers are so distressed, what becomes of their
plea in the House of Commons, that the Corn-law was passed
and is kept up for the benefit of the agricultural labourers?
After what I have heard from these gentlemen, the squirearchy
in the House of Commons, I should have expected that they
ought to have been the last, upon the institution of agricultural associations, to complain of distress and of the dangers
impending over them in the future—to have said, ' I have a
nostrum in my pocket that will quite prevent distress among
agricultural labourers: have we not got the Corn-law; did
we not pass it upon the pretence of remedying the distress of
the agricultural labourers? Here it is—we have our sliding-
scale, and depend upon it our agricultural labourers have
nothing to fear.' But, instead of that, in no instance do they
ever allude to the Corn-law as either a cause of employment
or as a means of remedying the evil. They never allude to
any Act of Parliament of the kind at all; and they seek, wide
and far, for some other remedy for these distresses.

What are their remedies ? One of the latest declared is the
allotment of land. To hear the outcry that we hear from the
landlords of the country, who, glorifying themselves for having
the idea of giving a patch of land to the labourer, you would
have thought they had resolved all at once to make a present of
a little slice of their estates to the labourers around them ; but
what does it amount to? It is proposed that each cottage
should have a garden attached to it ! The general advice
is, I see, that it should be not more than half an acre, and
some are recommending but a quarter of an acre in extent !
It amounts to this, that the landlords, benevolent souls, are
going to allow the peasantry that live upon their land to have
a garden to their cottages ! Why, there was a law passed in
the reign of Queen Elizabeth ordering that no cottage should
be built in this country without a garden being attached to it.
I do not believe that that law has ever been repealed to this

day; and the landlords, after violating the law, are now taking credit to themselves, and glorifying each other, that they are going to allow their labourers to have a garden to their cottages!

Now, what is the mode in which these gentlemen go to work to benefit the agricultural labourers? They call them together for a ploughing match, then they bring them into the room and give them a glass of wine, and they give a reward of thirty shillings to one man who has ploughed best! Then they inquire who has served twenty-five years in the same place, and, perhaps, they condescend to give him thirty shillings as a reward for good conduct. Then the farmers—the farmers who sit at the table—have their names read over, and prizes are awarded: to one for successfully cultivating turnips, to another for having produced a good fat ox, and to another for having accumulated the greatest quantity of lard upon a pig. And this is the way in which agriculture is to be improved! What should you think if a similar plan was adopted to assist you in your business? Let us suppose that a number of monopolists came down once a year—once a year, mind you, for the lesson is only given once a year, and then it is only about two hours and a half long—that they held a meeting, in which they would have a spinning match or a weaving match. And after they had been into some prize mill to see this spinning and weaving match, they sat down to dinner; and Job Hargreaves or Frank Smith is brought in, stroking his head down all the while as he comes before the squirearchy, and making his very best bow, to receive from the chairman thirty shillings as a reward for having been the best spinner and the best weaver! And, this being disposed of, imagine such a manufacturer getting a prize of five pounds for the best piece of fustian! And another 'ditto, ditto,' for the best yard-wide calico! Then imagine a shopkeeper rising from his seat to the table while the chairman puts on a grave face, and, addressing him in complimentary terms, presents him with

five pounds for having kept during the past year his shop-
floor and his counters in the cleanest state! Then they call up
a manufacturer, and he has an award of five pounds, because
the inspectors had found his mill to be in the best working
condition. Then the merchant rises up, and gets his reward
of five pounds for having been found by the inspectors to have
kept his books in the best order by double entry.

You laugh at all this, and well you may; you cannot
help it. Where is the difference between the absurdity, the
mockery of bringing up men in round frocks to a dinner-table
and giving them thirty shillings, because they had ploughed
well, or hoed well, or harrowed well—bringing up farmers to
give them prizes for having the cleanest field of Swedish
turnips, or for having managed their farm in the best way?
Where is the difference, I ask, between offering these rewards
and the giving out here of such rewards as I have just now
alluded to? Let us suppose, if you can keep your counte-
nances, that such a state of things existed here. Now what
must be the concomitant order of things? It would argue, in
the first place, that the prizemen who were so treated were an
abject and a servile class. It would argue that the trader
who could condescend to be treated so would himself be little
better than a slave. And if you needed such stimulants as
these to make you carry on your business as you ought to do,
where do you think you would be found in the race of industry
as compared with other classes? Where would you be if you
were so childish as to be fondled and dandled by a body of
Members of Parliament? Why, there would not be a country
on the face of the world that you could compete with—that is
evident. You would, like them, be going to these same
parliamentary men, begging them to be your dry nurses, in
order that they might pass an Act of Parliament to protect
you in your trade.

The landlords do not give themselves prizes, but they hold
up their conduct as something deserving of the reward of

public admiration, because they can come forward and tell
us that they make the most of their land, forsooth ! I was
reading just now in this morning's paper a report of Lord
Stanley's speech at the Agricultural Society's meeting on
Tuesday, which, by the magic power of steam, has been
carried to London and brought back to us here in Manchester in two days; and Lord Stanley tells us what must be
done with land.   He says :—

'And I repeat what I have already said on a former occasion in this room,
that there is no investment in the world in which a landlord can so safely, so
usefully, or so profitably invest his capital as in the improvement of his
own farm, by money sunk in draining on security of the land which belongs
to himself.'

Well, what does this amount to?   That it is the interest of
the landlord to make the most of his land.   And he goes on
to say—and he takes some little credit to himself and to his
father for what had been done with his land here in Lancashire.   He says :—

'In this last year we have laid down in deep draining somewhere about
300 miles of drains, at an expense of between 5000l. and 6000l., and, I think,
employed about a million and a half of draining-tiles.'

I believe my friend Mr. Bright here, who has been building a
mill, has during the same time been laying down about a
million and a half of bricks in erecting it; but you would be
astonished, would you not, and I am sure the squirearchy
would be rather puzzled, if Mr. Bright were to get up here
and talk of that as something for which he might glorify
himself, having first of all asserted it to be the most profitable
investment any man could make.   By the way, I wish my
friend here would calculate how much duty his million and
a half of bricks pay to the Government, from which duty
my Lord Stanley and his fellow-landlords have managed
to exempt draining-tiles.

Now, gentlemen, I do not want to say anything rude or
uncivil, and I will not apply my remarks personally to Lord

Stanley; but I will say this, that the whole course of the
conduct of these gentlemen in their exhibitions—the landlords—when they parade to the world what they condescend to
do with their land, is just a gratuitous piece of impertinence
to the rest of the community. What do we care what they
do with their land? Whether they put down draining-tiles
or not, all we say is this, 'If you do not make the most of
your land, it is no reason why we should be starving that you
may grow rushes.' It is a gross humbug, to use no milder
term, on the part of those who come forward at the agricultural meetings, to glorify themselves about the mode in which
they choose to dispose of their private property. There is an
absurd delusion lurking under it. It is intended to make us
believe that we are indebted to them, and must wait until
they choose to supply us with our food; that it is something
like a condescension, or at least an act of favour, on their part,
that they give us their food in exchange for our manufactures.
Now, what is the reason that the land has not been improved
before? Lord Stanley tells us here when these great improvements began, and mark what he says :—

'Even within the last few years—within a much shorter time than that
which I have named, within the last four or five years—I see strides which,
small as they may be compared with what might be done, are gigantic when
compared with what was done before.'

What was 'done before?' What has there been done 'within
the last four or five years?' Lord Stanley gives the credit
to the agricultural associations. Why, what have they been
doing? Up to within the last year, when did they condescend
to talk about the Corn-law? From one end of the kingdom
to the other they were nothing but political clubs, created
for the purpose of drawing the poor tenant-farmers together,
in order that they might be drilled by the land-agent to be
made subservient at a future voting day; and the whole talk
of these agricultural associations was, not about improving
the land, but maintaining protection to British agriculture.

And now, what can these agricultural associations do for agriculture? They meet once a year; they generally have a man in the chair who begins, as Lord Stanley does, by admitting his practical ignorance of the question upon which he is going to dilate; and the chairman is generally the man who occupies three-fourths of the time of the meeting by his speeches. I have watched the proceedings of these associations, and I have observed they have had all sorts of people except farmers in the chair: upon one occasion, in a part of Middlesex, I observed that the late Attorney-General, the present Chief Baron Pollock, was in the chair as president; and I must do him the justice to say (for he is a most candid and excellent man) that he began his opening address by declaring he did not know anything concerning what they had met about. What have these associations done for agriculture? They assemble men together once a year; they bring prize cattle to be exhibited; they bring agricultural implements to be examined. Are improvements only to be sought for once a year in agriculture? Would that do for manufactures? Only think of a commercial meeting once a year to see what our neighbours are doing, where there was any new machinery invented, or which of the hands had discovered some new process in calico printing! Could not farmers see what superior farming was to be seen by riding out any day in the week to look over their neighbours' hedges? Could they not learn where the best breeds of cattle were to be had from the advertisements of those who had them to sell? and could they not get the best agricultural implements by writing for them any day by the penny post, whether they were to be found in Manchester, London, or Ipswich? The thing is a farce; and when my Lord Stanley takes credit to these agricultural associations for having improved agriculture during the last five years, I say it is not due to those agricultural associations, but to the Anti-Corn-law League. It is owing to that that the agriculturists and the landowners have been roused from their lethargic sleep. They are buckling on their armour to meet the coming competition, which competition will do for them what nothing else will do, and what it has done for manufactures—it will make the agriculturists of this country capable of competing with the farmers of any part of the world. They give up the whole case when they talk in this way.

When they tell us what the land might do—and what it ought to do they admit it has not done—they plead guilty to all we have ever alleged against them and their system of Corn-law. I ask them this: can they bring a Member of Parliament, a theorist, into Manchester, with his books in hand, and can he suggest a single improvement in any of our processes of manufacture, whether they are connected with mechanical or chemical science? No. I went the other day into several establishments with one of the most eminent French chemists—a man renowned in Europe: he had nothing to say in visiting the dye-works or the print-works of this neighbourhood, but to express his unqualified admiration of the perfection to which they had brought these arts among us. Can they come here and say, as they say of themselves, in connection with their industry, ' You ought to produce three times as much as you do produce from your machinery, for it is already done in other places which we can name to you ?' No. But what do they say of their own land? I have heard Mr. Ogilvy, who was engaged by Mr. Brooke, of Mere, and other landlords of this and the neighbouring county as superintendent of their estates, declare—and he is willing to go before a Committee of the House of Commons to prove it—that Cheshire, if properly cultivated, is capable of producing three times as much as it now produces from its surface ; and he is willing the statement should be made public upon his authority—and there is not higher authority in the kingdom.

I say, whatever improvement has been made in this respect

it is to the Anti-Corn-law League we are indebted for it; and
more—the most bigoted of our opponents have made the
admission. Whilst they abhor the League and detest its
principles, they have made the admission—'At all events,'
they say, 'you have done good, and are doing good' to agriculture. I passed last year about this time over to Knutsford, where I held a public meeting close to the gates of
Mr. Egerton, of Tatton. As I went from the railway station
across to Knutsford, I rode, at least for five or six miles,
through the estate of that large proprietor, and I saw the
land was in the same state as I believe it was at the time of
the Conquest, growing just about as plentiful a supply of
rushes as of grass. It so happened that, upon the day I was
addressing the meeting upon the racecourse at Knutsford,
Mr. Egerton, of Tatton, was paying a visit to Manchester, to
preside at the Manchester Agricultural Association, and I took
the opportunity of saying, in the course of my remarks, that
I thought a gentleman who had such an extent of territory as
he had might be better employed in exterminating his rushes,
and setting a better example to his neighbours at home, than
in travelling to Manchester to preach up improvements in
agriculture. The other day I met a gentleman who happened
lately to be at Knutsford, and he told me that while sitting at
the inn there came in a number of the neighbouring farmers,
whose conversation turned upon agriculture. In the course of
their conversation one of them remarked, 'What a deal of
draining has been going on here since Cobden was here
blackguarding him about the rushes!' We have indeed given
them a fillip; we have stirred them up a little; but, gentlemen, if the mere alarm of the approach of Free Trade has
done so much for agriculture, what will free trade in corn
itself do for it? 'Why,' they say, 'we should be an exporting country if we only grew as much as we may grow.'
I have no objection to it; if, beside feeding the whole of the
people as they ought to be fed—no short commons—if, besides

feeding them well, they should send four or five millions of
quarters of corn abroad, and bring us back tea and sugar, and
such like matters in addition, we shall have no reason to complain of the British agriculturist. But we do complain, that
whilst they stop our supplies from other countries, under pretence of benefiting agriculture, they at the same time come
before us at these meetings of their own, and plead guilty to
our charge, that under this system of protection they are not
making the most of their land.

I speak my unfeigned conviction—and we have the very
best agriculturists with us in that conviction; men like Lord
Ducie and others, who are agriculturists by profession—when
I say I believe there is no interest in this country that would
receive so much benefit from the repeal of the Corn-laws as
the farmer-tenant interest in this country. And I believe,
when the future historian comes to write the history of agriculture, he will have to state:—' In such a year there was a
stringent Corn-law passed for the protection of agriculture.
From that time agriculture slumbered in England, and it was
not until by the aid of the Anti-Corn-law League the Corn-
law was utterly abolished, that agriculture sprang up to the
full vigour of existence in England, to become what it now
is, like her manufactures, unrivalled in the world.' It is a
gloomy and most discouraging thought that, whilst this
system of Corn-laws alternately starves the people in the
manufacturing districts and then ruins the farmers, it really
in the end confers no permanent benefit upon any class. I
told you in the beginning I did not believe the agricultural
labourer was now so badly off as he was when corn was 70s.
a quarter; but I will tell you where distress in the agricultural districts is now. It is among the tenant-farmers themselves. They are paying rents with wheat at 45s. a quarter,
which they have bargained for at a calculation of wheat being
56s., and, in many cases, 60s. a quarter. It is owing to this
discrepancy in the prices that the tenant-farmers are now

paying rent out of capital; they are discharging their labourers, unable to employ them—and theirs is the real distress now existing in the agricultural districts.

This state of things will not continue, either here or in the agricultural districts. What is the language that drops from the landlords at some of their meetings? It is, ' We shall not very likely have higher prices for corn this year; we must wait for better times; we will give you back ten per cent. this year.' No permanent reduction; and why? Because they know that, by the certain operation of this system, in less than five years from this time, this wheel of fortune, or rather misfortune, will go round again; you will be at the bottom and the farmers at the top, and you will have wheat again at 70s. or 80s. a quarter, causing thus a pretended prosperity among the farmers. As sure as you have had this revolution before, so sure will you have it again. There is nothing in Sir Robert Peel's Corn-law to prevent the recurrence of similar disasters. The law is as complete a bar to legitimate trade in corn as the old law was. I speak in the presence of merchants shipping to every quarter of the globe — men who bring back the produce of every quarter of the globe — and I put it to them whether, with this sliding-scale, they dare to order from a foreign country a single cargo of wheat in exchange for the manufactures which they sell? This being the case—and it is the whole case—you are not stimulating other countries to provide for your future wants, you are laying up no store here or stores abroad, and there will again be a recurrence of the disasters we have so often passed through before.

FREE TRADE

XIII.

LONDON, DECEMBER 11, 1844.

I could not help thinking, as I sat here surveying this vast assemblage, how I wished that all our friends who are scattered over the length and the breadth of this land could be present to-night, to feel their pulses beat in unison with yours, to look you face to face, and join in that triumphant shout, which augurs prosperity to our good cause. We meet here to-night for business. I am almost sorry for it; for we have to give many statistics, which probably are not the most captivating to five thousand people assembled together on this occasion; and, besides, at this time I happen to know that we have a large number of visitors, whom I am especially anxious to see. I am aware that there are many farmers in this assembly, who have come to see the Smithfield Cattle Show, and have been tempted to smuggle themselves into this assembly. I am sorry I cannot give them a farmer's view of our question to-night; but I ask them to look round on this assembly, and then let them, on the day after to-morrow, Friday—it is an ominous day—wend their way to Bond-street, and attend the meeting of the Duke of Richmond's Protection Society; let them remember the scene here—count the odd duke or so, the brace or two of earls, and the half-dozen Members of Parliament, and the score of land-agents and land-valuers—and then, with a vivid recollection of this scene, let them ask themselves which cause is likely ultimately to triumph? I beg of them to compare these two scenes, and to remember that these meetings of such a different character are but types of the comparative merits of our two causes. Then let the tenant-farmer go home and attend to his own business, and not look to dukes or Acts of Parliament to help him. Let him talk about corn-rents, such as the sagacity of the Scotch farmers has secured for nearly twenty years, so soon as it found out the operation of this sliding-scale of corn duties. Let the English farmer put himself on the secure basis of a rent of that description—I mean rent calculated on a certain fixed quantity of corn per annum, fluctuating in price as the value of corn varies in the averages, and then he may bid defiance to all Acts of Parliament. It makes no difference to him, then, what the price may be. He may talk to his landlord about a few other things, such as game and so on, and he will be better employed than in listening to speakers at protection societies, or going to dukes or Members of Parliament.

I believe we have another visitor here to-night. I have had put into my hands a little tract, published by the enemy, and very carefully circulated. On the title-page of this tract—which is addressed to the working classes—there is a quotation from the republican authority, Henry Clay. I am glad they have put his name on the frontispiece, and quoted his sayings; for let the English operatives remember, as my friend Mr. Villiers has already told you, that, since that tract was published, Mr. Henry Clay has been rejected as an aspirant for the Presidency of America. He stood as candidate for that high honour at the hands of three millions of free citizens, on the ground of his being the author and father of the protective system in America. I have watched the

progress of that contest with the greatest anxiety, and received
their newspapers by every packet. There have I seen accounts
of their speeches and processions. The speeches of Henry Clay
and Daniel Webster might have done credit to the Dukes
of Buckingham and Richmond themselves. All the banners
at their processions were inscribed with such mottoes as,—
' Protection to native industry.'   ' Protection against the
pauper labour of Europe.'   ' Stand by native manufactures.'
' Stand by the American system.'   ' Henry Clay and protection to native industry.'   Yes, all this was said to the
American democracy, just as your protection societies are saying it to you in this pamphlet.   And what said three millions
of the American people voting in the ballot-box? Why, they
rejected Henry Clay, and sent him back to his retirement.
I think this protection society, if they have got a large stock
of this tract on hand, will be offering it cheap; it might do
for lighting cigars, probably.

Well, what have you new in London? You have heard
something of what we have been about down in the north;
what is going on among you? I think I have seen some
signs, not of opposition, but of something very like what
I call a diversion. You have had some great meetings here,
professing vast objects, to benefit large classes of people in
London. Mr. Villiers has slightly alluded to that subject;
but I have a word or two additional to say about it. I call
it a ' diversion,' but it is something more; it is rather an
attack by monopolists upon the victims of their own injustice.
When the people in Turkey are suffering under the tyranny
of a Grand Vizier, and are threatening to rise and revenge
themselves upon him, and take his head, it is an old trick
for that functionary to send emissaries among the populace,
who are to point to the bakers' shops, and say, ' The bakers
are selling too high.' The people are then told to go and nail
the bakers' ears against the door-posts. Now, our monopolists
have taken a leaf out of the Turkish Vizier's book. When

we were in great distress and trouble in Manchester and its neighbourhood, and the people were starving in the streets, then it was stated that the manufacturing capitalists were 'grinding the faces of the poor,' and depriving them of bread. Now, when the distress is in the agricultural districts, the landed squires meet the farmers at their agricultural societies' tables, and tell them to go and employ the labourer by laying out more capital upon their farms. It is said that they must drain their land; they do not say a word about the farmer having had his pockets thoroughly drained.

Again, when some distress has fallen upon a large portion of the most defenceless part of your community, I find that a large, a useful, a respectable class of that community, the shopkeepers and dealers in ready-made linen and articles of clothing, are selected by the monopolists as the objects of attack for 'grinding the faces of the poor needle-women.' Now, I stand here to vindicate the character of those traders, and to turn back the charge upon those who assail them. I stand here to vindicate Moses and Son themselves against these attacks. Yes, I say Moses and Son themselves are Christianlike in their character compared with the men who are now assailing them whilst they support this system of the Corn-laws. For there is this difference between Moses and Son and those who vote for Corn-laws, and then affect to pity the poor needle-women : if the former buy cheap, they also sell cheap, and have not by unfair means obtained an Act of Parliament to give them a monopoly. But what shall we say of your landlords of Dorsetshire, who, whilst they are paying 7s. a-week for their labour, have passed an Act of Parliament, by which they are enabled to sell even the very bread that these poor wretches consume at an artificially enhanced and unnatural price? And yet here is a great scheme of charity, forsooth, to atone for this mischief; and you are to have fifty thousand people kept, I suppose, in employment by a society, not of 'middle-women,' but of middle-men, ay, very middling men indeed !

Now, I venture on a prediction : that bubble will burst before
the meeting of Parliament, and they will try and invent some
other.   They will not fail to charge us—or any portion of the
unprivileged class of the community—with being the authors
of their own misdoings. They have set up themselves as being
more benevolent than the rest of the community. My friend
Mr. Villiers was talking of their being charitable, of their
settling everything by alms. But even if they were charitable,
and more so than other people, I agree with him, objecting to
one large portion of the community being dependent upon alms
at the hands of another portion. But I deny that they are such
philanthropists. I roll back the charge they make against us,
and say that the Free-traders—the much-maligned political
economists — are the most truly benevolent people in the
country. We had a meeting two or three months ago in
Suffolk, had we not? There was a great gathering of landowners, noblemen, squires, and clergymen, met together in
a great county assembly in order to—what? To provide for
the distresses of the peasantry of that county by a philanthropic plan. They proposed to raise a subscription; I believe they entered into something like one on the ground ;
they separated then, and what has been done since? How
much has been effected for charity? I will venture here to
say, that there is one Leaguer in Manchester who has given
more money for the parks and pleasure-grounds connected
with that town than all the landowners and gentry of the
county of Suffolk have subscribed for the benefit of the
peasantry.

You will not misunderstand me : we do not come here
to boast, but merely to hurl back these charges which are
made against the great body of the more intelligent portion
of the middle classes of this country, who happen to take
scientific and enlightened views upon what ought to be the
conduct of the Government of this land. They call us 'political economists' and 'hard-hearted utilitarians:' I say the

political economists are the most charitable people in this country; the Free-traders are the most liberal to the poor of this land. I call upon them, if they will have it that the people are to live on charity, at all events, to give us a guarantee that they shall not starve, by really conferring that charity which they propose to bestow upon them. Ay, it is a very convenient thing for them to try and give a bad name to a sort of police who are looking after their proceedings. We avow ourselves to be political economists; and we are so on this ground, that we will not trust our fellow-creatures to the eleemosynary support of any class of the community, because we believe that if we do, we shall leave them in a very hopeless condition indeed. We say, let the Government of the country be conducted on such a principle, that men shall be enabled, by the labour of their own hands, to find an independent subsistence by their wages.

These gentlemen have had another meeting to-day : they are ready in all directions upon every sort of subject except the right one. A gathering took place this morning at Exeter Hall, at which all sorts of men assembled ;—what think you for? To devise means, and to raise a society, to look after ' the health of towns.' They will give you ventilation—air—water—drainage—open courts and alleys—anything in the world but bread. Now, so far as the Lancashire districts go, nothing is clearer—for we have it upon the authority of the Registrar-General's report of deaths in that district —than this : that the mortality of that locality rises and falls, year by year, with the price of food; that this connection may be as clearly traced, as though you had the evidence taken before a coroner's inquest. Upwards of three thousand people more per annum were swept off during the dear years than have died since corn has come down to a more natural price, even in a very limited district of Lancashire. And yet these identical gentlemen, who meet together and form their benevolent societies, will talk to you of air and water, and every-

thing in the world but bread, which is the staff and support
of life. I have no objection to charity—I advocate it strongly;
but I say with my friend, Mr. Villiers, do justice first, and
then let charity follow in its wake. I have no doubt these
individuals may be actuated by very benevolent motives — I
will not charge them here with hypocrisy; but this I do say,
that we shall expect them to meet this question, and not to
shirk it. I am complaining of one section in particular of the
landed aristocracy, who are setting up claims to a superior
benevolence, who are conscience-stricken, I am sure, from
what I know, on this question of the Corn-law, who yet vote
in its support, and who refuse to discuss it, or record their
opinions on the subject. I allude in particular to one
nobleman who acted in this manner in the last session on
Mr. Villiers's motion, notwithstanding he is one who professes
great sympathy for the poor of this country. He did not
attend on that debate, or take a part in the discussion, but
came in at the last moment, at the time of the division, and
voted against that motion. I will mention his name: I refer
to Lord Ashley. Now, I say, let us, at all events, whilst we
admit their good intentions, stipulate that this question shall
be discussed by them in the same way as those relating to
washing and fresh air. Do not let them blink this matter.
What course do they pursue as regards ventilation? They
call in scientific men to help them; they go straightway to
Dr. Southwood Smith and others, and say, ' What is your
plan for remedying this admitted social evil?' and they take
the opinion of scientific men, who have given great attention
to the subject. We ask them, on this question of supplying
the people with food and employment, to call to their councils
scientific men, who have devoted their lives to the investigation
of this question, and who have left on record their opinions in
a permanent form—opinions which have been recognised as
sound and indisputable philosophy all over the world. We
ask them to take Adam Smith, as they have on other

questions taken Southwood Smith; and either prove that he is wrong in his principle for providing food and employment for the people, or vote in accordance with his opinions. It will not be sufficient to wring their hands or wipe their eyes, and fancy that in this intelligent and intellectual age sentimentality will do in the senate; it may do very well in the boarding-school.

Now, what should we say of these same noblemen and gentlemen, who lament over the distress of the people, if they were to refuse to take science, knowledge, experience to their councils, in remedying another class of evils—if they went into a hospital, and found the patients writhing under their bandages after they had just gone through the ordeal of surgical aid from accidents, and these philanthropists were to drive out the surgeons and apothecaries, denouncing them as 'cold-blooded and scientific utilitarians,' and then, after wringing their hands, and turning up the whites of their eyes, set to work and treat these patients after their own fashion? I like these Covent Garden meetings, and I will tell you why; we have a sort of intellectual police here. Byron said this was a canting age, and there is nothing so difficult to meet and grapple with as cant; but I think, if anything has produced a sound, wholesome, and intellectual tone in this metropolis, it has been our great gatherings and discussions within these walls.

There is another meeting to be held to-night, to present a testimonial to Sir Henry Pottinger; I wish to say one word to you about that. First of all, what has Sir Henry Pottinger been doing for these monopolists — I mean the great monopolist merchants and millionaires, including the house of Baring and Co., who have subscribed 50l. in Liverpool towards the testimonial there, and I suppose have contributed here also? I ask, what has that baronet done to induce this determination on the part of the great merchant-princes in the City? I will tell you: he has been

to China, and extorted from the Government of that country
(for the benefit of the Chinese people, I admit) a tariff. But
of what description is it? It is founded on three principles.
The first is, that there shall be no duties whatever laid upon
corn, or provisions of any kind, imported into the Celestial
Empire; nay, even if a ship comes in loaded with provisions,
not only is there no duty upon the cargo, but the ship itself
is exempted from port charges; and it is the only exemption
of the kind in the world. The second principle is, there shall
be no duties for protection. The third is, there shall be
moderate duties for revenue. Why, that is the very tariff
that we, the Anti-Corn-law League, have been contending for
these five years. The difference between us and Sir Henry
Pottinger is this, that whilst he has succeeded by force of
arms in conferring upon the Chinese people that beneficial
tariff, we have failed hitherto by force of argument to extort
a similar boon for the advantage of the English people from
our aristocracy. A further difference is this: that while these
monopolist merchants are ready to offer a demonstration to
Sir Henry Pottinger for his success in China, they have
heaped obloquy, abuse, and opposition on us, for trying un-
successfully to do the same thing here. And why have we
not succeeded? Because we have been opposed and resisted
by these very inconsistent men, who are now shouting and
toasting Free Trade for China. I would ask one question or
two upon this point. Do these gentlemen believe that this
tariff, which Sir Henry Pottinger has obtained for the Chinese
people, will be beneficial to them or not? Judging by all
they have said to us on former occasions, they cannot really
believe it. They have said that low-priced provisions and
free trade in corn would injure the working classes, and lower
their wages. Do they positively imagine that the tariff will
be beneficial to the Chinese? If they do, where is their consistency in refusing to grant the same advantages to their
own fellow-countrymen? But if not, if they suppose that

tariff to be what they have here asserted a similar tariff would
be for Englishmen, then they are no Christians, because they
do not do to the Chinese as they would be done by. I will
leave them on the horns of that dilemma, and let them take
the choice which they will have. There is some little delusion
and fraud practised in the way in which they talk of this
Chinese tariff as a commercial treaty; it is not a commercial
treaty. Sir Henry Pottinger imposed that tariff on the Chinese Government, not as applicable to us, but to the whole
world. What do those monopolists tell us? 'We have no
objection to Free Trade, if you will give us reciprocity from
other countries.' And here they are, ' Hip, hip, hip, hurrah-
ing!' down at the Merchant Taylors' Hall, at this very moment, shouting and glorifying Sir Henry Pottinger because
he has given to the Chinese a tariff without reciprocity with
any country on the face of the earth.

Will Mr. Thomas Baring stand again for the city of London, think you? He said you were a very low set last year,
after he had lost his election. If he should come again, let
me give you one word of advice: go and ask him if he will
give you as good a tariff as Sir Henry Pottinger gave to the
Chinese. If not, let him tell you why he subscribed to this
piece of plate to Sir Henry Pottinger, if he does not think
such a measure would be a good thing for the English too, as
well as for the Chinese. In Manchester we have a good many
of the same kind of monopolists, who have joined in this testimonial; they always do things on a large scale in that town,
and while you have raised a thousand pounds or so here,
pretty nearly three thousand pounds have been subscribed
there, a large portion of it by our monopolist manufacturers,
who are not the most intelligent, numerous, or wealthy class
among us, although they say sometimes they are. They have
joined in this demonstration to Sir Henry Pottinger. A friend
of mine called to ask me to subscribe towards it. I said, ' I
believe Sir Henry Pottinger to be a most worthy man, a great

deal better in every respect than many of those who are joining here in subscriptions for his testimonial; I have no doubt
that he has done excellent service to the Chinese people; and
if they will send over a Sir Henry Pottinger to England, and
if that Chinese Pottinger can succeed by such force of argument (for we want no recourse to arms here)—by the power
of logic, if there be any such in China—as will prevail to
extract from the stony hearts of our landlord monopolists the
same tariff for England as that which our General has given
to the Chinese, I will join with all my heart in subscribing
for a piece of plate for him.'

By the way, gentlemen, we must come to business, notwithstanding.   Our worthy chairman has told you something
of our late proceedings.   Some of our cavilling friends—and
there are a good many of this class : men who seem to be
a little bilious at times, and are always disposed to criticise;
individuals who do not move on themselves, and, not being
gregarious animals, are incapable of helping other people to
move on, and, therefore, who have nothing to do but to sit by
and quarrel with others—these men say, ' This is a new move
of the League, attacking the landlords in their counties; it is
a change in their tactics.'   But we are altering nothing, and
we have not changed a single thing.   I believe every step we
have taken has been necessary, in order to arrive at the present stage of our movement.   We began by lecturing and
distributing tracts, in order to create an enlightened public
opinion; we did that for two or three years necessarily.   We
then commenced operations in the boroughs; and never at
any time was there so much systematic attention, labour, and
expense devoted to the boroughs of this country in the way
of registration as at the present time.   As regards our lectures, we continue them still; only that instead of having
small rooms up three pair of stairs back, as we used to have,
we have magnificent assemblies, as that now before me.   We
distribute our tracts, but in another form; we have our own

organ, the *League* paper, twenty thousand copies of which have gone out every week for the last twelve months. I have no doubt that that journal penetrates into every parish in the United Kingdom, and goes the round of the district.

Now, in addition to what we proposed before, we think we have had a new light; we rather expect that we can disturb the monopolists in their own counties. The first objection that is made to that plan is, that it is a game which two can play at; that the monopolists can adopt the move as well as we can. I have answered that objection before, by saying that we are in the very fortunate predicament of sitting down to play a game at a table where our opponents have possession of all the stakes, and we have nothing to lose. They have played at it for a long time, and won all the counties; my friend Mr. Villiers had not a single county voter the last time he brought forward his motion. There are 152 English and Welsh county members, and I really think it would baffle the arithmetic of my friend, the member for Wolverhampton, to make out clearly that he could carry a majority of the House without having some of them. We are going to try if we cannot get him a few. We have obtained him one already—the largest county in the kingdom; we have secured South Lancashire, and that is the most populous district in the whole kingdom. Lord Francis Egerton sat for that county; he is very powerful, a man of vast property and possessions, and personally respected by all parties. But people are very unfortunate who attack the League. There seems to me something like a fatality hanging over everybody who makes an onslaught upon it.

I am going to mention an anecdote for the benefit of 'Grandmamma,' of the *Morning Herald;* she is wearing to a rather shadowy and attenuated form, and yet she still cackles in a ghost-like tone at us. About two years ago, in the House of Commons, on Mr. Villiers's motion, Lord Francis Egerton rose and spoke, and after saying some pretty little nothings, such as go down in the House of Commons from a lord, but would not be tolerated from anybody else, he wound up his speech by offering very kindly and gratuitously his advice to the gentlemen of the Anti-Corn-law League; and it was to this effect: that they would be good enough to dissolve; that they could do nothing; and, therefore, had better disband themselves; and concluding by saying, that he offered that advice in all kindness to them. Let an election again come for South Lancashire, and Lord Francis Egerton will see who will dissolve first. Somebody has alluded to the Member for Knaresborough (Mr. Ferrand); he was let loose upon us a long time back. When I first went into the House of Commons, in 1841, it appeared to me that he had been sent there on purpose that he might bait me. What has been the fate of that worthy gentleman? Why, that same House of Commons—a large majority of whom hounded him upon me in 1841—last session voted unanimously that his assertions were 'unfounded and calumnious.' That means, in plain Knaresborough language, that he was a slanderer and a ——; I will not give you the other word. There is one other case, which I mention also as a warning and an example to the *Morning Herald.* At the close of the last session, Sir Robert Peel, in speaking upon Mr. Villiers's motion, felt very anxious indeed to retrieve his lost position with the monopolists behind the Treasury benches; and I think he would have stood upon his head, or performed any other feat, to accomplish it. He thought he would have a fling at the League, and therefore he warned us, in his solemn and pompous tones, that we were retarding the progress of Free Trade, and setting the farmers of the country against us by the way in which we had attacked them. Now, mark what I say: it will not be the League that will fall at the hand of the farmers; but I predict it will be Sir Robert Peel, ' the farmers' friend,' whom they will sacrifice.

I have said that we have one county to present to Mr. Villiers; I should be glad to know if he would like to represent

it himself. I have heard but one opinion in Lancashire,—
that, as it is the first county we have to present him, he ought
to have the refusal of it. The monopolists have long played
this game in the counties, and they have worked it out. They
began immediately the Reform Bill was passed; and they
have lynx-like eyes in finding flaws, or discovering the means
of carrying out their own ends. They saw in this Reform
Act the Chandos clause, and they set to work to qualify their
tenant-farmers for the poll, by making brothers, sons, nephews,
uncles—ay, down to the third generation, if they happened
to live upon the farm—all qualify for the same holding, and
swear, if need be, that they were partners in the farm, though
they were no more partners than you are. This they did, and
successfully, and by that means gained the counties. But
there was another clause in the Reform Act, which we of the
middle classes—the unprivileged, industrious men, who live by
our capital and labour—never found out, namely, the 40s.
freehold clause. I will set that against the Chandos clause,
and we will beat them in the counties with it. You have
heard how disproportionately large the number of votes in the
rural districts is to that in the towns. We will rectify the
balance by bidding our friends qualify themselves for the
counties. They do not know how easy a thing it is to do.
I see numbers of people here who have no borough vote at
all—men in fustian jackets—young men living in lodgings.
I will tell them how they may get a county vote, and far
cheaper than a borough vote. It is not so easy for men in
all positions to take a 10l. house, occupy it, furnish it, and
live up to it, with the taxes and expenses that accrue; but to
qualify for the county you have only to invest 50l. or 60l.
(and I have known it done for 35l.) in a freehold which will
produce you 40s. a year, and you will have a vote for the
county. It costs you nothing to keep, and nothing to buy;
for you get interest for your money, and you may sell your
property whenever you are sick of your vote.

Our opponents have been fond of telling us that this is a middle-class agitation. I do not like classes, and therefore have said that we are the best of all classes; but this I believe, that we have enough of the middle class, and the propertied portion of the middle class, to beat the landlords at their own game in all the populous counties in England. Mr. Wilson told you I had been into Yorkshire. Before the 31st of January there will be 2000 new votes qualified for the West Riding of that county. I have a guarantee which I can rely upon, that this will be done. Now, I want you to win Middlesex in like manner. I will tell you where you may gain as many votes in that county as by qualifying now votes. You have a thousand or two of good Free-trade votes that are not on the register; I will be bound to say you have 2000. Look at the case of South Lancashire; you have heard that we have won that county, but we have obtained it without putting in force that 40s. freehold clause. We actually won on the register by the votes that were already in existence, and that were drawn out by that intense contest in May between Mr. Brown and Mr. Entwisle. The revising barrister came round in October and November, and a majority of 1700 was gained by the men who were already entitled to be on the register, but had neglected to put their names on the list. We are going to work now in Lancashire, to induce our friends to qualify there as 40s. freeholders. Our opponents in that district tell us that, although they admit we have won upon the present register, we shall not do so for the future; now I will bet my cause to theirs—and it is the longest odds I know of—that we will make them a thousand worse in the next revision.

I will tell you how you can qualify a thousand or two voters in Middlesex. You have a most important district— Hammersmith, Kensington, Chelsea, and all the surrounding suburbs, which are not in the parliamentary boroughs; Marylebone and Westminster do not extend beyond Pimlico. In

all that district every house paying 50l. of rent—mind, not
50l. of rate, for a house rated upon an average at 40l. will
pay 50l. rent—every one of the tenants of those houses is
entitled to be put on the county list as a voter; for the 50l.
tenant-at-will clause does not confine itself to farmers, but
extends to every dwelling-house within the county; and I
have no doubt in the world that there are 500 or 600 Free-
trade votes in that district that might be on the register,
and ought, and may be, next year. But, then, people must
qualify who have not already done so. There are young men,
clerks, who complain that they have not got the suffrage, and
lodgers have been agitating for votes; I heard them once talk
of forming a 'Lodgers' League,' in order to obtain the franchise. Here is a more reasonable way of getting the suffrage;
the cheapest both to obtain and keep. There is a large class
of mechanics who save their 40l. or 50l.; they have been
accustomed, perhaps, to put it in the savings' bank. I will
not say a word to undervalue that institution; but cottage
property will pay twice as much interest as the savings' bank.
Then, what a privilege it is for a working man to put his
hands in his pockets and walk up and down opposite his own
freehold, and say—'This is my own; I worked for it, and I
have won it.' There are many fathers who have sons just
ripening into maturity, and I know that parents are very apt
to keep their property and the state of their affairs from their
children. My doctrine is, that you cannot give your son
your confidence, or teach him to be intrusted safely with
property, too early. When you have a son just coming to
twenty-one years of age, the best thing you can do, if you
have it in your power, is to give him a qualification for the
county; it accustoms him to the use of property, and to the
exercise of a vote, whilst you are living, and can have some
little judicious control over it, if necessary.

I know some fathers say, 'I could give my son a qualification, but I do not like the expense of the conveyance.' Well,

go to a Free-trade lawyer; you must employ none but professional men of that description in this business. We have drawn out a good many legal patriots already; they have heard the rustling of parchment, and have been caught with the sound. I say, employ no monopolist lawyers; for if you do, they may leave some flaw, by which you will lose your vote, and make it so that it will not be a real *bonâ fide* qualification. They will secure your title to the estate, but it may not be one which will give you a vote; and they will not tell you, but go and inform the opponent's lawyers in the revision court, who will come and object to you. I tell the fathers of these deserving sons to go to a Free-trade lawyer, and employ him to make the conveyance. Now, I will give a bit of advice to the sons. Do you offer to your father to pay the expense of the conveyance yourself. If you will not, and your father will come to me and make me the offer, I will.

Gentlemen, these are the classes that want the qualification; and, by these means, Middlesex may be made perfectly safe against all comers before the next election. For, recollect, besides qualifying, you must take care that your opponents have no bad votes on the list. I have heard of some very wise men who have said that this is an odious plan, very like the Carlton Club proceedings, to disfranchise the people by striking them off the register. If our opponents will not play the game of leaving bad votes on, and will allow no extension of the suffrage in this way on either side, we have no objection; but if they are to take the law into their hands, and strike off our bad votes, and we are not to do the same by theirs, I wonder when we shall win!

Now, when you go home, and begin talking over this with some of your neighbours, who affect to be wiser than other people, they will tell you, 'Notwithstanding all that Cobden has said, the landlords will beat you at this movement.' They will say, 'See how they can split up their

property, and let people have life-rent charges upon it.' As
Mr. Villiers has stated, the estates are not theirs in a great
many instances; I believe four-fifths of the parchments are
not at home; and if they were, whom would they trust with
a *bonâ fide* life-rent charge? Their tenant-farmers have got
the vote already. Will they give it to the agricultural
labourers, think you? The labourer would like those allot-
ments very much. The only difficulty I can foresee is this.
Judging from the accounts I read of their condition in
Dorsetshire and Wiltshire, I should think it is very likely,
when the revising barristers came round, these voters would
be disfranchised, one half of them being in the union workhouse, and the other half in gaol for poaching. No; the
landowners have done their worst. They want money, men,
and zeal in their cause. I believe we have struck the right
nail on the head. We have never yet proposed anything that
has met with so unanimous a response from all parts of the
kingdom upon this subject. It has taken two hours a day, in
Manchester, to read the letters that have come from all parts
of the country, unanimously applauding this plan. I may
tell you, that we have sent out circulars from Manchester to
everybody who has ever subscribed to the League Fund all
over the kingdom; and I need not tell you how many
thousands they amount to. Everywhere, in all parts of
the country, has this question been taken up with the
same enthusiastic spirit. We have received a letter from
Ipswich; we never thought, never dreamt of touching Suffolk; but we had a letter, saying, that it is perfectly easy
for the towns of Suffolk to carry the two divisions of the
county on this plan. We look to the more populous districts
first; we say it will not be necessary to gain the whole of
them; if we obtain North and South Lancashire, the West
Riding of Yorkshire, and Middlesex, the landed monopolists
will give up corn in order to save a great deal more.

There is one other point. Many people may say, 'This is

something not quite legitimate; you cannot go on manufacturing these votes.' We reply, The law and the constitution prescribe it, and we have no alternative. It may be a very bad system, that men should be required to have 40*l.* or 50*l.* laid out on the surface of the earth, in order that they should be represented; but the law prescribes that plan, and there is no help for it. And we say, do not violate the law; conform to it in spirit and in fact; and do so by thousands and tens of thousands, if you can. There is nothing savouring of trick or finesse of any kind in it; you must have a *bond fide* qualification. It will not do now, as it did under the old system, to create fictitious votes; there is now a register, there was none formerly. That is where we will stop them; we will put them through a fine sieve at the registration. No, no; under the old system, when the Lowthers contested Westmoreland against Brougham — the Henry Brougham that was, you know — the contest lasted for fourteen days, and they went on manufacturing collusive and fictitious votes during the whole period, making them as fast as they could poll. The voters went up with their papers, and the day after the polling put them into the fire, or treated them as waste paper. But things are altered now; you must be twelve months on the register, and your name must be hung up at the church doors for a certain period, before you can vote. Therefore we do not intend to win by tricks, for we are quite sure the enemy can beat us at that.

There is one other objection: they will say, you should not tell this; it is very bad tactics. I say, you have nothing to gain by secrecy. There are tens and hundreds of thousands in this country, whose hearts will beat when they see the report of this meeting, and who will read every word of it. Those are our friends. Our opponents will turn their heads away, and will not read what we say. We speak to the sympathising multitude, whose feelings and hearts are with us; and we make an appeal to them; not only to you in Middlesex, but to those who are unqualified throughout the length and breadth of the land. Scotland expects it of you; they say in that country—'Oh! that we had the 40s. franchise here; we could then clear them out of twelve counties in twelve months.' Ireland looks to you, with her 10l. franchise, the same as Scotland. England, wealthy England, with nothing but her nominal franchise of 40s. a year, with such a weapon as this in her hand, and not to be able to beat down this miserable, unintelligent, incapable oligarchy, that is misgoverning her! No, I will not believe it. We will cry aloud, not here only, but on every pedestal on which we can be placed throughout the country, though there is no pinnacle like this to speak from; we will raise our voice everywhere,—' Qualify, qualify, qualify.' Do it, not only for the sake of the toiling millions, and the good of the industrious middle classes, but for the benefit of the aristocracy themselves. Yes, do it especially for their sake, and for that of their dependent, miserable serfs—the agricultural labourers. Do it, I say, especially for the welfare of the landed interest, who, if left to their own thoughtless and misguided ignorance, will bring this country down to what Spain or Sicily is now; and with it will reduce themselves to the same beggary that the Spanish grandees have been brought to. To avert this calamity from them, the ignorant and besotted few, I say again—' Qualify, qualify, qualify!'

———◆◆◆———

FREE TRADE.

XIV.

LONDON, JANUARY 15, 1845.

REALLY I, who have almost lived in public meetings for the last three years, feel well-nigh daunted at this astonishing spectacle. Is there any friend or acquaintance of the Duke of Richmond here? If there be, I hope he will describe to his Grace this scene in Covent Garden Theatre to-night. I do not know how he may be impressed, but I am quite sure that if the Duke of Richmond could call such a meeting as this— ay, even one—in the metropolis, I should abandon in despair all hope of repealing the Corn-laws. But this is only one of many; and when we look back at the numerous gatherings we have had of a similar kind, and when we remember that not one discordant opinion, violation of order, or even breach of etiquette, has occurred at any of our meetings,—why, there is an amount of moral force about these great assemblages which I think it is impossible for any unjust law long to resist.

I appear before you to-night as a kind of connecting link — and a very short one — between two gentlemen who have not so recently presented themselves here as I have: the one (Mr. Milner Gibson) a most able and efficient fellow-labourer in the House of Commons, whose speech you have just heard; and the other (Mr. W. J. Fox), one of the most distinguished and accomplished orators of the age, who will follow me; and I promise you, that, on this occasion, I shall endeavour, in deference to your feelings and in justice to myself, to be very brief in my remarks. Indeed I scarcely know that I should have had any pretence for appearing before you at all, had it not been that we are now preparing for our Parliamentary campaign, and probably, unless I took this occasion, it would be some time before I should have a similar opportunity. And, as we are preparing for our Parliamentary labours, it may be as well, if we can possibly dive into futurity, to try to speculate, at least, upon what the course of proceeding may be, in connection with our question.

Now, I think I can venture, without any great risk of failure, to tell you what will be the course which the Prime Minister will pursue on this question. He will attempt his old arts of mystification. He has acquired somehow, we are told, a great character as a 'financier.' Well, that is a distinction which, amongst men of business, does not place a person always in the very highest grade of respectability. 'A clever financier!' 'He has put the revenue of the country in a satisfactory state!' Yes, he has done so; and how? Why—I hope, to your satisfaction, through the medium of the income-tax. We, as Free-traders, have nothing to do with fiscal regulations here, nor with systems of taxation for revenue; but as I foresee that it will be the policy of the Government, and the Prime Minister in particular, to raise a dust, shuffle the cards, and mix up revenue, taxation, and Free Trade together, I think we cannot do better than begin this year 1845, even at the risk of repetition, by letting the country know what we, the Anti-Corn-law League, really want, and that we are not to be made parties to this or that system of taxation, inasmuch as we ask for nothing which involves any change of taxation of any kind.

I have said again and again—and I reiterate the statement—

that Free Trade means the removal of all protective duties, which are monopoly taxes, paid to individuals, and not to the Government; and that, in order to carry out our principle of Free Trade, to realise all the League wants, and to dissolve our association to-morrow, it does not require that one shilling of taxation should be removed, which goes solely to the Queen's exchequer; but that it will increase the national revenue in proportion as you take away those taxes which we now pay to classes and to individuals. We are told that there is a surplus of revenue; and there is a great boast made of it. The income-tax has been productive. Those men with sharp noses, and ink-bottles at their buttons,—who have gone prying about your houses and at your back-doors, to learn how many dinner-parties you give in a year, and to examine and cross-examine your cooks and foot-boys as to what your style of living may be,—these men have managed to make a very respectable surplus revenue. Now, there seems to be a great contest among different parties who is to have this surplus revenue; that is, what are the taxes which are to be removed? The parties dealing in cotton goods say, ' We must have the tax taken off cotton-wool; ' another class says, ' We want the tax off malt; ' and a third party steps in and says, ' Let us have half the duty taken off tea.' But, although there may be many parties wanting a reduction of taxes, you do not find any class of the community organising themselves against taking off any one tax. Then, how is it that we, who simply desire to remove the tax on bread, meet with such a mighty opposition in the land ? Why, because, as I have just said, the tax that we pay on bread is a tax that goes to the tithe and the landowner, and not to Queen Victoria. Do you think it will do us any more harm to take off a tax that is paid to the squires, than to take off one which goes to her Majesty's exchequer ? It seems to be a principle universally admitted, that when you come to reduce a tax paid to the Queen, it will be a benefit to the community at large—the only question being

which party shall get the most; but when you propose to
reduce the duty on bread, a thousand imaginary dangers are
immediately raised.

Talk to a gentleman about the bread-tax, and he says,
' That is a very complicated question.' Speak about that
other ingredient of the tea-table—tea—and there is not a
gentleman, or gentlewoman, who will not say immediately,
' I think it would be a very good thing indeed to reduce the
tax on tea.' Propose the removal of the tax on bread, and
visions of innumerable dangers rise up directly. ' Why,' it
is said, ' you want to lower the wages of the working man,
and to make us dependent for food on foreigners.' Take the
case of sugar: we, as Free-traders, do not desire to diminish
the Queen's revenue on that article; we simply want to bring
the tax down to a level with the colonial impost on sugar,
that we may have the same duty paid on all, and that the
whole proceeds shall go to the Queen, and none of it to the
owners of estates in the West Indies. Nobody opposes the
reduction of duty on sugar, so far as the Queen gets it; but
if we propose to take away the tax for the protection of the
colonial interest, as it is called, we have a powerful body
arrayed against us, and all the same dangers apprehended
which we find alleged in the case of bread. Gentlemen, this
may serve to illustrate very clearly, to those who are not in
the habit of reasoning upon these matters very closely, what
our object really is. We propose to reduce the taxes paid to
monopolists; and I put it to any person whether it can be
less injurious to the country to pay taxes to individuals who
make no return in the shape of services to the State—who
neither provide army nor navy, nor support police, church, or
any other establishment—to pay taxes to these irresponsible
individuals, than to the Queen's Government, which makes
some return for them? What I wish to guard ourselves
against is this—that Sir Robert Peel shall not mix up our
question of Free Trade with his dexterity in finance. If he

likes to shift the cards, and make an interchange between
tea, cotton, tobacco, malt, and the income-tax, and ply one
interest against the other, it is all very well; let him do so;
it may suit his purpose as a feat in the jugglery of statesmanship. But let it be understood that we have nothing to do
with all this mystification and shuffling. Ours is a very
simple and plain proposition. We say to the right hon.
Baronet, 'Abolish the monopolies which go to enrich that
majority which placed you in power and keeps you there.'
We know he will not attempt it; but we are quite certain
that he will make great professions of being a Free-trader,
notwithstanding.

Oh ! I am more afraid of our friends being taken in by
plausibilities and mystifications than anything else. I wish
we had the Duke of Richmond or his Grace of Buckingham in power for twelve months, that they might be
compelled to avow what they really want, and let us have
a perfect understanding upon the matter. We should not
then be long before we achieved the object of our organisation. Sir Robert Peel will meet Parliament under circumstances which may perhaps call for congratulation in the
Queen's speech. Manufactures and commerce are thriving,
and the revenue is flourishing. Was that ever known when
corn was at an immoderately high price? The present state
of our finances and manufactures is an illustration of the
truth of the Free-trade doctrines. As the chairman has told
you, I have been, during the last two months, paying a visit
to nearly all the principal towns in Lancashire and Yorkshire,
and have seen much prosperity prevailing in those places,
where, four years ago, the people were plunged in the greatest
distress; and I am glad to tell you that I have everywhere
met larger and more enthusiastic meetings than I did in
the time of the greatest crisis of distress. We have passed
through that trying ordeal which I had always dreaded as the
real and difficult test of this agitation: I mean the period

when the manufactures of this country regained a temporary prosperity. We are proof against that trial; we have had larger, more enthusiastic, and more influential meetings than ever we had before; and I am happy to tell you, that, so far as the north of England goes, the present state of prosperity in business is merely having the effect of recruiting the funds of the Anti-Corn-law League.

There is not a working man in the manufacturing districts who has not his eyes opened to the enormous falsehoods which have been told by the monopolists during the last four or five years. You know that the operatives do not deal learnedly in books: they are not all of them great theorists, or philosophers; but they have, nevertheless, a lively faith in what passes under their own noses. These men have seen the prices of provisions high, and they have then found pauperism and starvation in their streets; they have seen them low, and have found the demand for labour immediately increase, and wages rising in every district of Lancashire and Yorkshire, and a state of things prevailing the very opposite of that which was told them by the monopolists. In fact, in some businesses the men now have their employers so completely at their mercy, that they can dictate their own terms to them. We have heard of one gentleman in the north—not one of the Leaguers, but a large employer of labour—who remarked, ' My hands will only work four days a-week now; if we have free trade in corn, and business is as prosperous as you say it would then be, I should not be able to manage them at all.'

I was at Oldham the other day, and, during our proceedings at a public meeting in the Town-hall, a working man rose in the body of the assembly, and begged to say a few words upon the subject for which we were convened; and his statement put the whole question as to the effect of high and low prices on the wages of the operative into so clear a form, that I begged it might be taken down; and I will now give it you

verbatim as he delivered it. I think it is the whole secret,
given in the compass of a nutshell :—

'Joseph Shaw, a working man, in the body of the meeting, said :—Mr.
Chairman and gentlemen, I rise for the purpose of making a few remarks on
the subject of the Corn-laws. I have but once before spoken before a Member
of Parliament, viz. Mr. Hindley, at a public meeting at Leea. I have spoken
once at Ashton and Saddleworth, but never before in Oldham. I have thought
on the subject of the Corn-laws for the last twenty years and more, and I have
ever seen great reason to condemn them. As there is no probability that I
shall ever see Sir Robert Peel, as he never comes down into this neighbourhood,
and I being not able to bear the expense of going to London, I wish you
(addressing Mr. Cobden) to be so kind as to tell him what you have heard a
working man say on the subject of the Corn-laws in a large and respectable
public meeting in the town of Oldham. I am now and have been long of
opinion that the Corn-laws are very injurious to the working classes, and I
will tell you how I prove it. I have been in the habit of observing that when
the prices of food have been high, wages have been low, which sufficiently
accounts for the dreadful state of Stockport and the other manufacturing
towns and districts two or three years since. At that time, when wheat was
up to about 70s. a quarter, the working man would have 25s. per quarter to
pay for it more than now when it is down to 45s., and consequently would
have 25s. less to lay out for clothing and other necessaries for his comfort
during the time he was consuming a quarter of wheat. I have further to state
that, since the prices of eatables have come down, I have seen a deal more
new fustian jackets in our village of Leea than I have seen for four or five
years during the time of high prices; and I will also tell you how I account
for that. When provisions are high, the people have so much to pay for them
that they have little or nothing left to buy clothes with; and when they have
little to buy clothes with, there are few clothes sold; and when there are few
clothes sold, there are too many to sell; and when there are too many to sell,
they are very cheap; and when they are very cheap, there cannot be much
paid for making them: and that, consequently, the manufacturing working
man's wages are reduced, the mills are shut up, business is ruined, and general
distress is spread through the country. But when, as now, the working man
has the said 25s. left in his pocket, he buys more clothing with it (ay, and
other articles of comfort too), and that increases the demand for them, and the
greater the demand, you know, makes them rise in price, and the rising in
price enables the working man to get higher wages and the masters better
profits. This, therefore, is the way I prove that high provisions make lower
wages, and cheap provisions make higher wages.' (Cheers.)

Now, it is not possible that there can be one intelligent
man like this, rising up in a public meeting, and giving so
clear a view of the workings of this system, without there
being a tolerable share of intelligence among his fellow-work-

men in that neighbourhood. One by one these fallacies of our opponents have been by the course of experience cut from under the feet of the monopolists. Now, I do not see that we can do better, at the beginning of the year, than reiterate the grounds on which we advocate our principles, and state again what our profession of faith is. The gentlemen below me, with their pens in their hands, may drop them for the present, for I have stated them over and over again. We do not want free trade in corn to reduce wages; if we, the manufacturers (I speak now of them as a class, but the observation applies to all), wanted to reduce wages, we should keep up the Corn-law, because the price of labour is the lowest when the corn is highest. We do not want it to enable us to compete with foreigners; we do that already. You do not suppose that the Chinese give the manufacturer or merchant who comes from England a higher price for his goods than they will to any other people. Suppose one of the manufacturers who votes for the Corn-law here, sent out his goods to China, and said—'You will give us a little higher price for our longcloths than you give to these Germans or Americans, for we have a Corn-law in England, and I always vote for that side which keeps up the bread-tax; and I hope, therefore, you will give me a higher price.' What would the man with a pigtail say? He would reply, 'If you are such blockheads as to submit to have your bread taxed in your own land, we are not such fools as to give you a higher price for your longcloths than we can get them at from the Germans and Americans.' You compete with foreigners now; and all we say is, that you will be able to do so better if you have your bread at the same price as your competitors have. Then the object of free trade in corn is simply this—to have more trade; and the Oldham operative has shown you how more trade will raise wages. We want increased trade, and that in the articles which will minister most to the comfort of the working man. Every cargo of corn which comes in from

abroad in exchange for manufactured goods, or anything else
—for you cannot get it unless you pay for it with the produce
of labour—will serve the working man in two ways.   In
the first place, he will eat the corn which is thus imported ;
inasmuch as we of the middle, and those of the upper classes,
already get as much as we require, and the poor must eat it,
or it will not be consumed at all.   But it must be paid for as
well as eaten ; and therefore every cargo of corn that comes
to England will benefit the working men in two ways.   They
and their families must eat it all ; and it can only be paid for
by an increased demand for their labour, and that will raise
their wages, whilst it moderates the price of their provisions.
Doubtless it will also be of advantage to other portions of
the community, but it can only benefit them through the
working class—that is, through those who now do not get
enough to eat.

Then we have the farmer's objection to meet, and he
says : 'If you bring in foreign corn, for every quarter of
corn that you so import, we shall have a market for one
quarter less in England.'   That statement proceeds upon the
old assumption, that the people of this country are now sufficiently fed.   The middle classes, I admit, have enough ; and
a great many of the upper classes get much more than is good
for them ; but the working men of this land,—and in that
term I include the Irish, Welsh, Scotch, and the agricultural
poor of England,—I maintain that all these are not half fed :
I mean to say they are not half as well fed as the class to
which I belong, nor as the working classes are in the United
States of America.   I have seen them on both sides of the
Atlantic, and I will vouch for the fact.   We have all heard
of the anecdote of the Irishman in Kentucky : the poor fellow
had gone out to America ; he did not know how to write, and
he asked his master to write a letter for him.   He began it
thus :— 'Dear Murphy, I am very happy and comfortable,
and I have meat once a-day.'   His master said—'What do

you mean? Why, you can have meat three times a-day, and
more if you like.' 'Ah, sure! your honour, that's true; but
they will not believe it at all, at all.' Now, why should
not the working people of this country be allowed to have as
much meat and bread, if they can get it by the produce of
their industry, as the people of America enjoy? It is a hard
penalty to be obliged to send 3000 miles for food; but it
is an atrocity—ay, a fearful violation of Nature's law—if, in
addition to that natural penalty which the Creator himself
has imposed upon us, of sending across the Atlantic for a
sufficient supply of food, men—the owners of the soil in this
country—step in, place obstacles in the way, and prevent the
poorest people in the land from having that food which their
fellow-creatures 3000 miles off are willing to send them.
Then let the people be sufficiently fed, and the introduction
of more corn, cattle, butter, and cheese, will not hurt the
farmer in this country. We of the middle classes, who now
eat his good provisions, and those who are now sufficiently
fed, will continue to be his customers; and all we say is, let
those who now do not obtain enough, get it from abroad in
exchange for the produce of their own honest labour.

The reduction of duty on wool is an illustration of the
truth of what I am now saying. During the last year there
have been about twenty million pounds weight more of
foreign and colonial wool brought into this country than
there was the year before; the penny duty was abolished
totally and immediately, and here is this vast influx of that
article from abroad: and yet the farmers of this country have
been getting from twenty to thirty per cent. more for their
home-grown wool than they did previously. Now, why is
this? Simply because the extension and prosperity of our
manufactures have gone on even in a greater ratio than this
largely-increased importation of wool. So I maintain that,
if you will give freedom to the commerce of this country, and
let loose the energies of the people, their ability to consume

corn and provisions brought from abroad will increase faster
than the quantity imported, whatever it may be. I really feel
almost ashamed to reiterate these truisms to you; but that
they are necessary, the present position of our question proves.
Gentlemen, my firm conviction is, that this measure cannot
be carried in-doors within the House of Commons; that the
next session of Parliament will see no progress made by that
body. We, Free-traders, there, may expose their utter futility
in argument—make them ridiculous, cover them with dis-
grace, in debate; they may talk such stuff that children
would be ashamed of out of the House of Commons; but they
will, notwithstanding, vote for the Corn-law. Yes, it will be
like drawing the kid out of the maw of the wolf, to extort the
repeal of that law from the landowners of this country.

I remember quite well, five years ago, when we first came
up to Parliament to petition the Legislature, a certain noble
earl, who had distinguished himself previously by advocating
a repeal of the Corn-laws, called upon us at Brown's Hotel.
The committee of the deputation had a private interview with
him, during which he asked us what we came to petition for?
We replied, for the total and immediate repeal of the Corn-
laws. His answer was, ' My belief is, that the present Parliament would not pass even a 12s. fixed duty; I am quite
sure they would not pass a 10s.; but as for the total repeal
of the Corn-law, you may as well try to overturn the
monarchy as to accomplish that object.' I do not think any
one would go so far as to tell us that now; I do not suppose
that, if you were to go to Tattersall's, ' Lord George' would
offer you very long odds that this law will last five years
longer. We have done something to shake the old edifice,
but it will require a great deal of battering yet to bring it
down about the ears of its supporters. It will not be done in
the House; it must be done out of it. Neither will it be
effected with the present constituency; you must enlarge it
first. I have done something towards that end since I last

saw you.   I have assisted in bringing four or five thousand
new ' good men and true ' into the electoral list—four or five
thousand that we know of in Lancashire, Yorkshire, and
Cheshire; and I believe there are five or ten times as many
more throughout the country, who have taken the hint we
gave them of getting possession of the electoral franchise for
the counties.   Some people tell you that it is very dangerous
and unconstitutional to invite people to enfranchise themselves
by buying a freehold qualification.   I say, without being revolutionary or boasting of being more democratic than others,
that the sooner the power in this country is transferred from
the landed oligarchy, which has so misused it, and is placed
absolutely—mind, I say ' absolutely'—in the hands of the
intelligent middle and industrious classes, the better for the
condition and destinies of this country.

I hope that every man who has the ability to possess himself of the franchise for a county, will regard it as his solemn
and sacred duty to do so before the 31st of this month.
Recollect what it is we ask you to do : to take into your own
hands the power of doing justice to twenty-seven millions of
people !   When Watt presented himself before George III,
the old monarch asked him what article he made ; and the
immortal inventor of the steam-engine replied, ' Your Majesty,
I make that which kings are fond of—power.'   Now, we seek
to create a higher power in England, by inducing our fellow-
countrymen to place themselves upon the electoral list in the
counties.   We must have not merely the boroughs belonging
to the people ; but give the counties to the towns, which are
their right ; and not the towns to the counties, as they have
been heretofore.   There is not a father of a family, who has
it at all in his power, but ought to place at the disposal of
his son the franchise for a county ; no, not one.   It should
be the parent's first gift to his son, upon his attaining the
age of twenty.   There are many ladies, I am happy to say,
present ; now, it is a very anomalous and singular fact, that

they cannot vote themselves, and yet that they have a power
of conferring votes upon other people. I wish they had the
franchise, for they would often make a much better use of it
than their husbands. The day before yesterday, when I was
in Manchester (for we are brought up now to interchange
visits with each other by the miracle of steam in eight hours
and a half), a lady presented herself to make inquiries how
she could convey a freehold qualification to her son, previous to the 31st of this month; and she received due instructions for the purpose. Now, ladies who feel strongly
on this question—who have the spirit to resent the injustice
that is practised on their fellow-beings—cannot do better
than make a donation of a county vote to their sons, nephews,
grandsons, brothers, or any one upon whom they can bene-
ficially confer that privilege. The time is short; between
this and the 31st of the month, we must induce as many
people to buy new qualifications as will secure the representation of Lancashire, the West Riding of Yorkshire, and
Middlesex. I will guarantee the West Riding of Yorkshire
and Lancashire; will you do the same by Middlesex?

I am quite sure you will do what you can, each in his
own private circle. This is a work which requires no gift of
oratory, or powerful public appeals; it is a labour in which
men can be useful privately and without ostentation. If
there be any in this land who have seen others enduring
probably more labour than their share, and feel anxious to
contribute what they can to this good cause, let them take
up this movement of qualifying for the counties; and in
their several private walks do their best to aid us in carrying out this object. We have begun a new year, and it will
not finish our work; but whether we win this year, the next,
or the year after, in the meantime we are not without our
consolations. When I think of this most odious, wicked, and
oppressive system, and reflect that this nation—so renowned
for its energy, independence, and spirit—is submitting to

have its bread taxed, its industry crippled, its people—the poorest in the land—deprived of the first necessaries of life, I blush that such a country should submit to so vile a degradation. It is, however, consolation to me, and I hope it will be to all of you, that we do not submit to it without doing our best to put an end to the iniquity.

FREE TRADE.

XV.

AGRICULTURAL DISTRESS.

HOUSE OF COMMONS, MARCH 13, 1845.

[On March 13, 1845, Mr. Cobden moved for a Select Committee to inquire into the causes and extent of the alleged agricultural distress, and into the effects of legislative protection upon the interests of landowners, tenant-farmers, and farm-labourers. This motion was opposed on the part of the Government by Mr. Sidney Herbert, on the ground that several such Committees had sat, and had never led to any useful result. The motion was lost by a majority of 92 (121 to 113).]

I AM relieved on this occasion from any necessity to apologise to the other side of the House for this motion having emanated from myself; for I expressed a hope, when I gave my notice, that the subject would be taken up by some one of the hon. Members opposite. I hope, therefore, that in any reply which may be offered to the observations I am about to submit to the consideration of the House, I shall not hear, as I did in the last year, that this motion comes from a suspicious quarter. I will also add, that I have so arranged its terms as to include in it the objects embraced in both the amendments of which notice has been given (Mr. Woodhouse's and Mr. S.

B 2

O'Brien's), and therefore I conclude that the hon. Members
who have given those notices will not think it necessary to
press them, but rather will concur in this motion. Its object
is the appointment of a Select Committee to inquire into the
condition of the agricultural interests, with a view to ascertain how far the law affecting the importation of agricultural
produce has affected those interests.

Now, that there is distress among the farmers I presume
cannot be established upon higher authority than that of those
who profess to be 'the farmers' friends.' I learn from those
hon. Gentlemen who have been paying their respects to the
Prime Minister, that the agriculturists are in a state of great
embarrassment and distress. I find one gentleman from
Norfolk, Mr. Hudson, stating that the farmers in Norfolk
are paying rents out of capital; while Mr. Turner from
Devonshire assured the right hon. Baronet (Sir R. Peel) that
one half of the smaller farmers in that county are insolvent,
that the other half is rapidly hastening to the same condition,
and that, unless some remedial measures are adopted by the
House, they will be plunged into irretrievable poverty. These
accounts from those counties agree with what I hear from
other sources, and I will put it to hon. Members opposite
whether the condition of the farmers in Suffolk, Wiltshire, and
Hampshire is any better. I will put it to county Members
whether, looking to the whole of the south of England, from
the confines of Nottinghamshire to the Land's End, the
farmers are not in a state of embarrassment—whether, as
a rule, that is not their condition. Then, according to every
precedent in the House, this is a fit and proper time to bring
forward this motion; and I will venture to say, that if the
Duke of Buckingham had a seat in this House, he would do
what he, as Lord Chandos, did—move such a resolution.

The distress of the farmer being admitted, the next question that arises is, What is the cause of this distress? Now,
I feel the greater necessity for a committee of inquiry, because

I find a great discrepancy of opinion as to the cause. One
right hon. Gentleman has said that the distress is local, and
moreover that it does not arise from legislation; while the
hon. Member for Dorsetshire (Mr. Bankes) declared that it is
general, and that it does arise from legislation. I am at a
loss, indeed, to understand what this protection to agriculture
means, because I find such contradictory accounts given in
this House by the promoters of it. For instance, nine months
ago the hon. Member for Wolverhampton (Mr. Villiers)
brought forward his motion for the repeal of the Corn-laws;
and the right hon. Gentleman then at the head of the Board
of Trade (Mr. Gladstone) stated in reply to him, that the last
Corn-law had been most successful in its operation, and he
took great credit to the Government for the steadiness of
price obtained under it. As these things were so often dis-
puted, it is as well to give the quotation. The right hon.
Gentleman said,—

'Was there any man who had supported the law in the year 1841, who
could honestly say that he had been disappointed in its working? Could any
one point out a promise or a prediction hazarded in the course of the pro-
tracted debates upon the measure, which promise or prediction had been
subsequently falsified?'

Now, let the House recollect that the right hon. Gentleman
was speaking when wheat was 56s. 8d.; but wheat is at
present 45s. The right hon. Baronet at the head of the
Government said that his legislation on the subject had
nothing to do with wheat being 45s.; but how is the difficulty to be got over, that the head of the Board of Trade,
nine months ago, claimed merit to the Government for having
kept up wheat to that price? These discrepancies in the
Government itself, and between the Government and its
supporters, render it more necessary that this 'protection'
should be inquired into.

I must ask, What does it mean? We have prices now
at 45s. I have been speaking within the last week to the

highest authority in England—one often quoted in this House—and I learned from him that, with another favourable harvest, it was quite likely that wheat would be at 35s. What does this legislation mean, if we are to have prices fluctuating from 56s. to 35s.? Can this be prevented by legislation? That is the question. There is a rank delusion spread abroad among the farmers; and it is the duty of the House to dispel that delusion, and to institute an inquiry into the matter.

But there is a difference of opinion on my own side of the House, and some Members, representing great and powerful interests, think the farmers are suffering because they have this legislative protection. This difference of opinion makes the subject a fit and proper one for inquiry in a Committee; and I am prepared to bring evidence before it, to show that farmers are labouring under great evils—evils that I can connect with the Corn-laws, though they appear to be altogether differently caused.

The first great evil they labour under is a want of capital. No one can deny it; it is notorious. I do not say it disparagingly of the farmers. The farmers of this country are just of the same race as the rest of Englishmen, and, if placed in the same situation, would be as successful men of business and traders and manufacturers as their countrymen; but it is notorious, as a rule, that they are deficient in capital. Hon. Gentlemen acquainted with farming will probably admit that 10l. an acre, on arable land, is a competent capital for carrying on the business of farming successfully; but I have made many inquiries in all parts of the kingdom, and I give it as my decided conviction, that at the present moment the farmers' capital does not average 5l. an acre, taking the whole of England south of the Trent, and including all Wales. Though, of course, there are exceptions in every county—men of large capital—men farming their own land—I am convinced that this is true, as a rule, and I am prepared to back my opinion by witnesses before a Committee. Here, then, is a tract of country comprehending probably 20,000,000 of cultivable acres, and 100,000,000*l.* more capital is wanted for its cultivation.

What is the meaning of 'farming capital'? It means more manuring, more labour, more cattle, larger crops. But let us fancy a country in which there is a deficiency of all those things which ought to be there, and then guess what must be the condition of the labourers wanting employment and food. It may be said that capital would be there, if it were a profitable investment. I admit it; and thus the question comes to be,—How is it, that in a country overflowing with capital—where there is a plethora in every other business—where every other pursuit is abounding with money—when money is going to France for railroads, and to Pennsylvania for bonds—when it is connecting the Atlantic with the Pacific by canals, and diving to the bottom of Mexican mines for investment—it yet finds no employment in the most attractive of all spots, the soil of this country itself?

Admitting the evil, with all its train of fearful consequences, what is the cause of it? There can be no doubt whatever,—it is admitted by the highest authorities, that the cause is this,—there was not security for capital on the land. Capital shrinks instinctively from insecurity of tenure, and we have not in England that security which will warrant men of capital investing their money in the soil. Is it not a matter worthy of consideration, how far this insecurity of tenure is bound up with the 'protection' system of which hon. Members opposite are so enamoured? Suppose it could be shown that they are in a vicious circle; that they have made politics of Corn-laws; that they wanted voters, to retain Corn-laws; that they think the Corn-laws a great mine of wealth, and therefore will have dependent tenants, that they may have votes at elections, and so retain those laws. If they will have dependent voters, they cannot have men of

spirit and of capital. Then their policy reacts upon them ;
if they have not men of skill and capital, they cannot have
protection and employment for the labourer; and then comes
round the vicious termination—pauperism, poor-rates, county-
rates, and all the evils from which they are asking the Prime
Minister to relieve them.

But here I have to quote authorities, and I shall quote
some of the highest consideration with the opposite side of the
House. I will just state the opinion of the hon. Member for
Berkshire (Mr. Pusey), delivered at the meeting of the Suffolk
Agricultural Society. That hon. Gentleman said :—

'He knew this country well, and he knew there was not a place from
Plymouth to Berwick in which the landlords might not make improvements;
but when the tenant was short of money, the landlord generally would be
short of money too. But he would tell them how to find funds. There were
many districts where there was a great superfluity not only of useless but of
mischievous timber; and if they would cut that down which excluded the sun
and air, and fed on the soil, and sell it, they would benefit the farmer by
cutting it down, and they would benefit the farmer and labourer too by laying
out the proceeds in underdraining the soil. There was another mode in which
they might find money. He knew that on some properties a large sum was
spent in the preservation of game. It was not at all unusual for the game to
cost 500l. or 600l. a year; and if this were given up, the money would
employ a hundred able-bodied labourers in improving the property. This was
another fund for the landlords of England to benefit the labourers, and the
farmers at the same time.'

Again, at the Colchester agricultural meeting—

'Mr. Fisher Hobbes was aware that a spirit of improvement was abroad.
Much was said about the tenant-farmers doing more. He agreed they might
do more : the soil of the country was capable of greater production; if he said
one-fourth more, he should be within compass. But that could not be done
by the tenant-farmer alone ; they must have confidence; it must be done by
leases—by draining—by extending the length of fields—by knocking down
hedge-rows, and clearing away trees which now shielded the corn.'

But there was still higher authority. At the late meeting at
Liverpool, Lord Stanley declared—

'I say, and as one connected with the land I feel myself bound to say it,
that a landlord has no right to expect any great and permanent improvement
of his land by the tenant, unless that tenant be secured the repayment of his

outlay, not by the personal character or honour of his landlord, but by a security which no casualties can interfere with—the security granted him by the terms of a lease for years.'

Not only does the want of security prevent capital from flowing to the soil, but it actually hinders the improvement of the land by those who already occupy it. There are many tenants who could improve their land if they were made secure; they either have capital themselves, or their friends can advance it; but with the want of leases, with the want of security, they are deterred from laying out their money. Everything was kept ' from year to year.' It is impossible to farm properly unless money is invested in land for more than a year. A man ought to begin farming with a prospect of waiting eight years before he can see a return for what he must do in the first year or two. Tenants, therefore, are prevented by their landlords from carrying on cultivation properly. They are made servile and dependent, disinclined to improvement, afraid to let the landlord see that they could improve their farms, lest he should pounce on them for an increase of rent. The hon. Member for Lincolnshire (Mr. Christopher) is offended at these expressions; what said that hon. Member on the motion of the hon. Member for Manchester (Mr. Gibson) last year on agricultural statistics ?—

' It was most desirable for the farmer to know the actual quantity of corn grown in this country, as such knowledge would insure steadiness of prices, which was infinitely more valuable to the agriculturist than fluctuating prices. But to ascertain this there was extreme difficulty. They could not leave it to the farmer to make a return of the quantity which he produced, for it was not for his interest to do so. If in any one or two years he produced four quarters per acre on land which had previously grown but three, he might fear lest his landlord would say, "Your land is more productive than I imagined, and I must therefore raise your rent." The interest of the farmers, therefore, would be to underrate, and to furnish low returns.'

Here is a little evidence of the same kind that is to be gathered from the meeting of the South Devon Agricultural Association, where the Rev. C. Johnson said,—

'He knew it had been thought that landlords were ready to avail themselves of such associations, on account of the opportunity it afforded them of diving into their tenants' affairs and opening their eyes. An instance of this occurred to him at a recent ploughing match, where he met a respectable agriculturist whom he well knew, and asked him if he was going to it. He said, "No." "Why!" Because he did not approve of such things. This "why" produced another "why," and the man gave a reason why: Suppose he sent a plough and man, with two superior horses; the landlord at once would say, "This man is doing too well on my estate," and increase the rent.'

I will ask the landed gentry of England what state of things is this, that the farmer dares not appear to have a good pair of horses, or to derive four quarters where the land had formerly produced only three. Hon. Members cheer, but I ask, is it not so? I must say, that the condition of things indicated by those two quotations brings the farmer very near down in point of servility to the ryot of the East. The one takes the utmost care to conceal the amount of his produce; the other suffers the bastinado, rather than tell how much corn is grown. The tenant, indeed, is not afraid of the bastinado, but he is kept in fear of a distress for rent.

This is the state of tenant-farming without a lease, and in England a lease is the exception and not the rule. But even sometimes, when there is a lease or agreement, the case is still worse, for the clauses and covenants are of such an obsolete and preposterous character, that I will defy any man to carry on the business of farming properly under them. I will just read a passage from a Cheshire lease—an actual lease—to show in what sort of way the tenant-farmer is bound down : —

'To pay the landlord 20l. for every statute acre of ground, and so in proportion for a less quantity, that shall be converted into tillage, or used contrary to the appointment before made; and 5l. for every hundredweight of hay, thrave of straw, load of potatoes, or cartload of manure, that shall be sold or taken from the premises during the term; and 10l. for every tree fallen, cut down, or destroyed, cropped, lopped, or topped, or willingly suffered so to be; and 20l. for every servant or other person so hired or admitted as to gain a settlement in the township; and 10l. per statute acre, and so in proportion for a less quantity of the said land, which the tenant shall lot off or underlet, such sums to be paid on demand after every breach, and in default of payment to be considered as reserved rent, and levied by distress and sale, as rent in

arrear may be levied and raised ; and to do six days' boon team work whenever called upon ; and to keep for the landlord one dog, and one cock or hen ;
and to make no marlpit without the landlord's consent first obtained in writing,
after which the same is to be properly filled in ; nor to allow any inmate to
remain on the premises after six days' notice ; nor to keep nor feed any sheep,
except such as are used for the consumption of the family.'

What is such an instrument as this? I will tell the House
what it is. It is a trap for unwary men — a barrier against
capital and intelligence, and a fetter to any free man. No
one can farm under such a lease. The hon. Member for
Shoreham (Sir C. Burrell) cheered ; but if hon. Members
would look into their own leases, though there may not be
the 'cocks and hens, and dogs,' and probably not the 'team-
work,' they will find almost as great absurdities. These
documents are generally taken from old, dusty, antediluvian
remains, that some lawyer's clerk drew from a pigeon-hole,
and copied out for every in-coming tenant ; something that
had been in existence perhaps for five hundred years. You
give men no credit for being able to discover any improvements ; in fact, you tie them down from improving ; you
go upon the assumption that there will be no improvement,
and do your best to prevent it. I do not know why we should
not have leases of land upon terms similar to those in leases
of manufactories, and places of business ; nor do I think
farming can be carried on as it ought to be until then. A
man may take a manufactory, and pay 1000*l.* a-year for it.
An hon. Member near me pays more than 4000*l.* a-year rent
for his manufactory and machinery. Does he covenant as to
the manner in which that machinery is to be worked, and as
to the revolutions of his spindles? No ; his landlord lets to
him the bricks and mortar and machinery. The machinery
was scheduled to him, and, when his lease is over, he must
leave the machinery in the same state as when he found it,
and be paid for the improvements. The Chancellor of the
Exchequer (Mr. Goulburn) cheers that. I want to ask his
opinion on a similar lease for a farm.

I am rather disposed to think that the Anti-Corn-law League will very likely form a joint-stock association, having none but Free-traders in that body, to purchase a joint-stock estate, and have a model farm, taking care to have it in one of the rural counties where they all think there is the greatest need of improvement—perhaps Buckinghamshire; and there establish a model farm, and a model homestead, and model cottages (and I will tell the noble lord, the Member for Newark [Lord J. Manners] that we shall have model gardens, without any outcry about it); but the great object shall be to have a model lease. We shall have as a farmer a man of intelligence, and a man of capital. I am not so unreasonable as to say that you ought to let your land to a man without capital, and to one who is not intelligent; but select such a man, with intelligence and capital, and you cannot give him too wide a scope. You will find such a man, and let him have a farm, and such a lease as my hon. friend took his factory with. He shall do what he likes with the old pasture; if he can make more of it with ploughing it up, he shall do so. If he can grow white crops every year, he shall do so. I know persons who are doing that in more places than one in this country. If he can make any improvement, he shall make it. We will let him the land with a schedule of the state of tillage on the farm, and will bind him to leave the land as good as he found it. It shall be valued; and if in an inferior state when he leaves it, he shall compensate us for it: if it be in a superior state, he shall be compensated accordingly by the association. You will think this something very difficult, but the association will give him possession of the farm, with everything on the soil, whether wild or tame. We will give him absolute control; there shall be no gamekeeper prowling about, and no sporting over his farm. Where is the difficulty? You may take as stringent means as you please to compel the punctual payment of rent; you may take the right of re-entry if the rent be not paid; but take the payment of rent as the sole test of the well-doing of the tenant, and so long as he pays that uniformly, it is the only test you need have; and if he be an intelligent man and a man of capital, you will have the strongest security that he will not waste your property.

I have sometimes heard hon. Gentlemen opposite say, 'It is all very well to propose such leases, but we know many farmers who will not take them.' An hon. Member cheers that. What does that argue? That by a process which the hon. Member for Lincolnshire (Sir John Trollope) has described—that degrading process which renders these tenants servile, hopeless, and dejected — they are satisfied to remain as they are, and do not want to be independent. Hear what Professor Low says on this subject:—

'The argument has again and again been used against the extension of leases, that the tenants themselves set no value on them; but to how different a conclusion ought the existence of such a feeling amongst the tenantry of a country to conduct us! The fact itself shows that the absence of leases may render a tenantry ignorant of the means of employing their own capital with advantage, indisposed to the exertions which improvements demand, and better contented with an easy rent and dependent condition, than with the prospect of an independence to be earned by increased exertion.'

But whilst you have a tenantry in the state described and pictured by the hon. Member for Lincolnshire, what must be the state of our population? The labourers can never be prosperous where the tenantry is degraded. You may go through the length and breadth of the land, and you will find that, where capital is most abundant, and where there is the most intelligence, there you will find the labouring classes the most happy and comfortable. On the other hand, show me an impoverished tenantry, and there I will show you a peasantry in the most hopeless and degraded condition; as in the north of Devonshire, for instance. I have proved that the want of capital is the greatest want among the farmers, and that the want of leases is the cause of the want of capital. You may say, 'You have not connected this with the Corn-laws and the protective system.' I will read to you the opinion of an hon. Gentleman who sits on that (the Opposition) side of the House; it is in a published letter of Mr. Hayter. He said:—

'The more I see of and practise agriculture, the more firmly am I convinced that the whole unemployed labour of the country could, under a better system of husbandry, be advantageously put into operation; and, moreover, that the Corn-laws have been one of the principal causes of the present system of bad farming and consequent pauperism. Nothing short of their entire removal will ever induce the average farmer to rely upon anything else than the Legislature for the payment of his rent, his belief being that all rent is paid by corn, and nothing else than corn; and that the Legislature can, by enacting Corn-laws, create a price which will make his rent easy. The day of their (the Corn-laws) entire abolition ought to be a day of jubilee and rejoicing to every man interested in land.'

I do not stay to collect the causes affecting this matter, and to inquire whether the Corn-law and our protective system have caused the want of leases, or have caused the want of capital. I do not stop to prove this, for this reason:—we have adopted a system of legislation by which we propose to make farming prosperous. I have shown you, after thirty years' trial, what is the condition of the farmers and labourers, and you will not deny any of my statements. It is, then, enough for me, after thirty years' trial, to ask you to go into Committee, and to inquire if something better cannot be devised. I am going, independently of protection, and independently of the Corn-law, to contend that a free trade in corn will be more advantageous to the farmers, and with the farmers I include the labourers; and I beg the attention of the hon. Member for Gloucestershire (Mr. Charteris) and the landowners. I am going to contend that free trade in corn will be more beneficial to these classes than to any other classes. I should have contended so before the tariff, but now I am prepared to do so with ten times more force.

The right hon. Gentleman opposite (Sir R. Peel) has passed a law to enable fat cattle to be imported, and there have been some foreign fat cattle selling in Smithfield Market at 15*l.* or 16*l.* and 1*l.* duty; but he has not taken off the duty on the raw

material. He did not do so with regard to manufactures.
Mr. Huskisson had not done so; but, on the contrary, he
began by taking off the duty on the raw material, without
taking off the duty on foreign manufactures. You (the
Ministers) have begun, on this question, at the opposite end.
I would admit grain free, which should go to make the fat
cattle.

I contend that by this protective system the farmers throughout the country are more injured than any other class of the
community. I will begin with clover. The hon. Member for
North Northamptonshire (Mr. Stafford O'Brien) put a question to the right hon. Baronet the other night, and looked
so alarmed whilst doing so that I wondered what was the
matter. He asked the right hon. Baronet 'if he was going
to admit clover-seed free?' That is to be excluded; and for
whose benefit? I ask that hon. Member or his constituents,
are they in the majority of cases sellers of clover-seed? I will
undertake to say they are not. How many counties are pro-
tected by the sale of clover-seed being secured to them? I
will take Scotland; that country imports it from England;
it does not grow it. I will undertake to say that not ten
counties in the United Kingdom are interested in exporting
clover-seed out of their own borders. There is none in
Ireland.

Take the article of Egyptian beans. I see the hon. Member
for Essex (Sir J. Tyrell) in his seat: in that county they can
grow beans and wheat and wheat and beans alternately, and
send them to Mark-lane; but how is it with the poor lands
of Surrey, and with the poor lands of Wiltshire? Take the
country through, and how many counties are exporters of
beans to market? You are taxing the whole of the farmers
who cannot export beans for the benefit of those few counties
that can grow them. And mark, where you can grow beans.
It is where the soils are better; it is not in one case in ten
that a farmer can grow more than for his own use, or be able

to send any to market; and when that is the case, the farmer
can have no interest in keeping up the price to prevent
importation.

Take oats. How many farmers have oats on the credit
side of their books, as an item to rely on for paying their
rent? They grow oats for feeding their horses; but it is an
exception where they depend on their crop of oats for the
payment of rent. Ireland has just been mulcted by the tax
on clover-seed. Is it a benefit to the farmers who do not sell
oats to place a tax on their import, they having no interest in
keeping up the money price of oats?

Take the article hops. We have a protective duty on hops
for the protection of particular districts, as Kent, Suffolk, and
Surrey; but they in return have to pay for the protection on
other articles which they do not produce.

Take cheese. There is not a farmer but makes his own
cheese for the consumption of his servants; but how many
send it to market? The counties of Chester, Gloucester,
Wilts, and parts of Derbyshire and Leicester, manufacture
this article for sale. Here are four or five counties having an
interest in protecting cheese. But you must recollect that
those counties are heavily taxed in the articles of oats and
beans and corn; for these are the districts where they most
want artificial food for their cattle.

Take the whole of the hilly districts. I hope the hon.
Member for Nottinghamshire (Mr. Knight) is present. He
lives in Derbyshire, and employs himself in rearing good cattle
on the hills; but he is taxed by protection for his oats, or Indian
corn, or beans. That hon. Member told me the other day that
he would like nothing better than to give up the protection on
cattle, if he could only go into the market and purchase his
thousand quarters of black oats free from protective duty.
Take the hilly districts of Wales, or take the Cheviot hills, or
the Grampian hills; they are not benefited by their protection
on these articles; they want provender for their cattle in the

cheapest way they can get it. The only way in which these parts of the country can improve the breed of their stock, and bring their farms into a decent state of fertility, is to have food cheap.

But I will go further, and say that the farmers on the thin soils—I mean the stock farmers in parts of Hertfordshire—farmers of large capital, arable farmers—are deeply interested in having a free importation of food for their cattle, because they have poor land which does not contain or produce the means for its own fertility; and it is only by bringing in artificial food that they can bring their land into a state to grow good crops. I have been favoured with an estimate made by a very experienced and clever farmer in Wiltshire; it is from Mr. Nathaniel Atherton, of Rington. I will read this to the House; and I think that the statements of such men — men of intelligence and experience — ought to be attended to. Mr. Nathaniel Atherton, Rington, Wilts, estimates,—

'That upon 400 acres of land he could increase his profits to the amount of 180*l.*, paying the same rent as at present, provided there was a free importation of foreign grains of all kinds. He would buy 300 quarters of oats at 13*s.*, or the same amount in beans or peas at 14*s.* or 15*s.* a sack, to be fed on the land or in the yard; by which he would grow additional 160 quarters of wheat and 230 quarters of barley, and gain an increased profit of 300*l.* on his sheep and cattle. His plan embraces the employment of an additional capital of 1000*l.*, and he would pay 150*l.* a year more for labour.'

I had an opportunity, the other day, of speaking to an intelligent farmer in Hertfordshire—Mr. Lattimore, of Wheat-hampstead; he stands as high in the Hertfordshire markets as any farmer, as a man of skill, of abundant capital, and of unquestionable intelligence. He told me that he had paid during the last year 230*l.* in enhanced price on the beans and other provender which he had bought for his cattle, in consequence of the restrictions on food of foreign growth, and that this sum amounted to 14*s.* a quarter on all the wheat which he had sold off his farm. With regard to Mr. Atherton

and Mr. Lattimore, they are as decided advocates of free trade
in grain as I am.

I have before told hon. Gentlemen that I have as wide and
extensive an acquaintance with farmers as any Member in
this House. In almost every county I can give them the
names of first-rate farmers who are as much Free-traders as
I am. I told the Secretary of the much-dreaded Anti-
Corn-law League to make me out a list of the names of
subscribers to the League amongst the farmers. There are
upwards of a hundred in England and Scotland, and they
comprise the most intelligent men that are to be found in
the kingdom. I have been into the Lothians myself—into
Haddingtonshire. I went and spent two or three days
amongst the farmers there, and I never met with a more
intelligent or liberal-minded body of men in the kingdom.
They do not want restrictions on corn; they say, 'Let us
have a free importation of linseed-cake and corn, and we can
bear competition with any corn-growers in the world. But
to exclude provender for cattle, and to admit fat cattle duty
free, was one of the greatest absurdities in legislation that
ever was.' We have heard of absurdities in commerce—of
sending coffee from Cuba to the Cape of Good Hope, to bring
it back to this country under the law; but in ten years' time
people will look back with more amazement at our policy,—
that whilst we are sending ships to Ichaboe for manure, we
are excluding oats, and beans, and Indian corn for fattening
our cattle, which would give us a thousand times more
fertilising manure than this which we now send for.

On the last occasion on which I spoke on this subject in
this House I was answered by the right hon. Gentleman the
President of the Board of Trade (Mr. Gladstone), and that
gentleman talked of the Free-traders throwing poor land out of
cultivation, and throwing other land out of tillage into pasture.
I hope that the Anti-Corn-law League will not be reproached
again with any such designs. My belief is, that the upholders

of protection are pursuing the very course to throw land out
of cultivation and to make poor land unproductive. Do not
let the Free-traders be told again that they desire to draw the
labourers from the land that they may reduce the labourers'
wages in factories. If you had abundance of capital employed on your farms, and cultivated the soil with the same
skill that the manufacturers conduct their business, you
would not have population enough to cultivate the land. I
had yesterday a letter from Lord Ducie, and he has given the
same opinion, that if the land were properly cultivated there
would not be sufficient labourers to till it. And yet, whilst
that is the fact, you are chasing your population from village
to village, and passing a law to compel the support of paupers.
You are smuggling the people away and sending them to the
antipodes, whereas if your lands were properly cultivated you
would be trying to lure them back, as the most valuable part
of your possessions. It is by this means only that you can
avert very serious disasters in the agricultural districts.

On the last occasion of my addressing this House, a great
deal was said about disturbing great interests. It was said
that this inquiry could not be gone into, because it would
disturb a great interest. I have no desire to undervalue the
agricultural interest. I have heard it said that the agricultural classes are the greatest consumers of our goods, and that
we had better look after our home trade. Now what sort
of consumers of manufactures do you think the agricultural
labourers could be with the wages they get? Understand
me, I am arguing for a principle which I solemnly believe
will raise the wages of the people. I believe there would be no
men starving on 7s. a week if there were abundance of capital
and skill employed in cultivating the soil. But, I ask, what
is this home consumption of manufactures? I have taken
some pains to ascertain the amount laid out by agricultural
labourers and their families for clothing. It may probably
startle hon. Members when I tell them that we have exported

more goods to Brazil in one year than has been consumed in
a year by the agricultural peasantry and their families. You
know, by the last census, that there are 960,000 agricultural
labourers in England and Wales, and I can undertake to say,
from inquiries I have made, that each of these men does not
spend 30s. a year in manufactures for his whole family, if the
article of shoes be excepted. I say that, with the exception only of shoes, the agricultural labourers of England and
Wales do not spend 1,500,000l. per annum in the purchase of
manufactured goods, clothing, and bedding. Then, I would
ask, what can they pay, on 8s. a week, to the revenue? I
am satisfied, and hon. Members may satisfy themselves, from
the statistical returns on the table, that agricultural labourers
do not pay per head 15s. a year to the revenue; the whole of
their contributions to the revenue do not amount to 700,000l.
a year; and, I ask, when hon. Members opposite have by
their present system brought agriculture to its present pass,
can they have anything to fear from risking a change, or, at
any rate, from risking an inquiry?

On the last occasion that I addressed the House on this
subject, I laboured to prove that we have no reason to fear
foreign competition if restrictions were removed, and I stated
facts to show that. On the present occasion I shall not dwell
on that topic; but still, as many people are possessed with
the idea, that if the ports were opened corn will be to be
had for nothing—and that is one of the favourite fallacies—
I may be allowed to offer a few remarks upon the subject.
People continue to hold this doctrine, and they argue, ' Now
that prices are low, corn is coming in; but if you had not a
duty of 20s. a quarter, is it possible to say what would be the
quantity that would come in?' This is said; but I hope it is
not dishonestly said; I hope the argument is founded on a
confusion between the nominal and the real price of corn.
The price of wheat at Dantzic is now a nominal price. In
January, 1838, wheat at Dantzic was at a nominal price,

there being no one to purchase from England; but in July
and August of that year, when a failure of the harvest here
was apprehended, the price at Dantzic rose, and by the end
of December in the same year the price at Dantzic was double
what it had been in January, and wheat there averaged 40s.
a quarter for the three years 1839, 1840, 1841.   Now I
mention this for the purpose of asking the attention of hon.
Members opposite to it, and I entreat them, with this fact
before them, not to go down and alarm their tenantry about
the danger of foreign competition.   They ought to take an
opposite course—the course which would enable them to
compete with foreigners.   Their present course is the worst
they could take, if they wish to compete with foreigners.

I was about to allude to a case which referred to the hon.
Baronet the Member for Shoreham (Sir C. Burrell), who has
lately let in a new light upon agricultural gentlemen.   The
country was now told that its salvation is to arise from the
cultivation of flax.   This was stated by the Flax Agricultural Improvement Association, Lord Rendlesham president,
of which I have in my hand a report, wherein, after stating
that Her Majesty's Ministers were holding out no hopes of
legislative assistance to the agricultural body, they then called
upon the nation for support them, on the ground that they were
going to remedy the grievances under which the agricultural
interest laboured.   I observe that Mr. Warner, the great
founder of this association, was visiting Sussex lately, and at
a dinner at which the hon. Baronet (Sir C. Burrell) presided,
after the usual loyal toasts, ' Mr. Warner and the cultivation
of flax ' was proposed.   Now, when the hon. Baronet did this,
probably he was not aware that he was furnishing the most
deadly weapon to the lecturers of the Anti-Corn-law League.
The country is told that unless they have a high protective
duty the farmers cannot get a remunerative price for the
wheat they grow.   They have a protective duty of 20s. a
quarter on wheat, and one quarter of wheat was just worth a

hundredweight of flax; yet, although against Polish wheat
they have a protection of 10s., the protective duty on a
hundredweight of flax is just 1d.   Now, I did not hear a
murmur when the right hon. Baronet proposed to take off
that tax of 1d. But we are told that the English agriculturist cannot compete with the foreigner, on account of the
abundance of labour he has the command of, especially in
the case of the serf labour which is employed somewhere up
the Baltic. Now, flax comes from up the Baltic, and yet
they have no protection upon it. Then it is insisted that we
cannot contend against foreign wheat, because it takes so
much labour to raise wheat in this country; yet it takes as
much labour to raise flax. How, then, are we to contend
against foreign flax? Nevertheless, the hon. Baronet undertook to restore prosperity to the country by means of his flax,
which was in this helpless state for want of protection.

The hon. Baronet will forgive me — I am sure he will,
because he looks as if he will—while I allude again to the
subject of leases. The hon. Baronet, on the occasion I have
alluded to, complained that it was a great pity the farmers
did not grow more flax; but it is curious that I should have
since seen it stated in a Brighton paper—the hon. Baronet's
county paper — I do not know how truly—that the hon.
Baronet's own tenants have leases which forbid them to
grow flax. However, it is quite probable the hon. Baronet
does not know what covenants there are in his leases; but,
be that as it may, at any rate it is very common, I know, to
insert in leases a prohibition to cultivate flax. This just shows
the manner in which the landlords carry on the agriculture of
the country. The original notion of the injury done by flax
to the land was derived, I believe, from Virgil, who stated
something to the effect that flax was very scourging to the
land. I have no doubt it was from this source that some
learned lawyer has derived the usual covenant on this subject
in leases.

I have alluded to the condition of the agricultural labourers at the present time; but I feel bound to say, that whilst the farmers are in a worse position than they have been for the last ten years, I believe the agricultural labourers have passed the winter, though it was a five-months' winter, and severe, with less suffering from distress than the previous winters. I mention this because it is a remarkable proof of the degree in which a low price of food is beneficial to the labouring classes. I can demonstrate that in the manufacturing districts, whenever food is dear, wages are low; and that whenever food is low, wages rise. That the manufacturers can prove. Then I stated it as my own opinion, that the agricultural labourers are in a better state than they were in previous winters. But does not that show that the agricultural labourers having only just so much wages as will find them in subsistence, derive benefit from the plenty of the first necessaries of life? Their wages do not rise in the same proportion as the price of food rises, but then neither do their wages fall in the same proportion as the price of food falls. Therefore in all cases the agricultural labourers are in a better state when food is low than when it is high.

Now, I am bound to state, that whatever is the condition of the agricultural labourer, I believe the farmer is not responsible for that condition while he is placed as at present. I have heard many exhortations to the farmer that he must employ more labour. I believe the farmer is very unjustly required to do this. The farmer stands between the landlord and the suffering peasantry. It is rather hard in the landlord to point the farmer out as the cause of the want of employment for labour—as the man to be marked. Lord Hardwicke has lately made an address to the labourers of Haddenham, in which he said,—

'Conciliate your employers, and, if they do not perform their duty to you and themselves, address yourselves to the landlords; and I assure you that you will find us ready to urge our own tenants to the proper cultivation of their farms, and, consequently, to the just employment of the labourer.'

That is the whole question. I think the duty rests with
the landlords, and that it is the landlords, and not the employers, who are in fault. The landlords have absolute power
in the country. There is no doubt about it—they can legislate
for the benefit of the labourers or of themselves, as they
please. If the results of their legislation have failed to secure
due advantages to the labourer, they have no right to call on
the farmers to do their duty, and furnish the labourers with
the means of support. I lately saw a labourer's certificate at
Stowupland, in Suffolk, placed over the chimneypiece in a
labourer's cottage. It was this :—

'West Suffolk Agricultural Association, established 1833, for the advancement of agriculture, and the encouragement of industry and skill, and good
conduct among labourers and servants in husbandry. President, the Duke
of Grafton, Lord Lieutenant of the county.—This is to certify, that a prize
of 1l. was awarded to William Birch, aged 83, labourer, of the parish of
Stowupland, in West Suffolk, September 15, 1840, for having brought up
nine children without relief, except when flour was very dear, and for having
worked on the same farm twenty-eight years. (Signed) Robert Rushbrooke,
Chairman.'

After a severe winter, with little employment to be had, I
congratulate the country that we have fewer agricultural
labourers in the workhouses, and fewer pining in our streets
from want, than in former years; but a bad case at the best
is the condition of the agricultural labourer, and you will
have to look out, before it is too late, how you are to employ
him. The last census shows that you cannot employ your own
labourers in the agricultural districts. How, then, are you to
employ them?   You say, there are too many of them.   That
is an evil which will press on you more and more every year :
what, then, are you to do?   Are you, gentry of England, to
sit with your arms folded, and propose nothing ?   I am only
here to-night because you have proposed nothing. We all
know that the allotment system has been taken up; it is a
plaything; it is a failure, and it is well for some of you
that you have wiser heads to lead you than your own, or

you would shortly be in precisely the same situation as they
are in Ireland; but with this increase to the difficulty of that
situation, that they do contrive to maintain the rights of property there with the aid of the English Exchequer and 20,000
bayonets; but bring your own country into the same condition, and where will be your rents?

What, then, do you propose to do? Nothing this year to
benefit the great mass of the agricultural population! You
admit the farmer's capital is diminished — that he is in a
worse state than he was. How to increase the confidence of
capitalists in the farmers' power of retrieving themselves?
How this is to be done is the question. I cannot believe you
are going to make this a political game. It was well said that
the last election was an agricultural election; and there are
two hundred members sitting behind the right hon. Baronet;
that is the proof of it. Don't quarrel with me because I have
imperfectly stated my case; I have done my best; I ask what
have you done? I tell you this 'protection,' as it is called, has
been a failure. It failed when wheat was 80s. a-quarter, and
you know what was the condition of the farmer in 1817. It
failed when wheat was 60s., and you know what was the condition of the farmer in 1835. And now it has failed again with
the last amendments you have made in the law, for you have
confessed to what is the condition of the agricultural tenantry.
What, then, is the plan you propose? I hope that this question was not made a pretence—a political game—at the last
election; that you have not all come up as mere politicians.
There are politicians in this House who look with ambition—
and probably in their case it is a justifiable ambition—to the
high offices of the State; there may be men here who by
thirty years' devotion to politics have been pressed into a
groove in which it is difficult for them to avoid going forward,
and are, may be, maintaining the same course against their
convictions. I make allowance for them; but the great body
of you came up not as politicians, but as friends of the agri-

cultural interest; and to you I now say, what are you going
to do? You lately heard the right hon. Baronet at the head
of the Government say, that if he could restore protection,
it would not benefit the agricultural interest. Is that your
belief? or are you acting on your convictions, or performing
your duty in this House, by following the right hon. Baronet
into the lobby when he refuses an inquiry and investigation
into the condition of the very men who send you up here?
With mere politicians, I have no right to hope to succeed;
but give me a committee, and I will explode the delusion of
agricultural protection; I will produce such a mass of evidence, and call authorities so convincing, that when the blue-
book shall be sent out, I am convinced that protection will
not live two years.

Protection is a very convenient vehicle for politicians; the
cry of ' protection' won the last election; and politicians looked
to secure honours, emoluments, places by it; but you, the
gentry of England, are not sent up for such objects. Is, then,
that old, tattered and torn flag to be kept up for the politicians, or will you come forward and declare that you are ready
to inquire into the state of the agricultural interests? I cannot think that the gentlemen of England can be content to be
made mere drum-heads, to be sounded by the Prime Minister
of England—to be made to emit notes, but to have no arti-
culate sounds of their own. You, gentlemen of England, the
high aristocracy of England, your forefathers led my forefathers; you may lead us again if you choose; but though—
longer than any other aristocracy—you have kept your power,
while the battle-field and the hunting-field were the tests of
manly vigour, you have not done as the noblesse of France or
the hidalgos of Madrid have done; you have been Englishmen,
not wanting in courage on any call. But this is a new age;
the age of social advancement, not of feudal sports; you belong
to a mercantile age; you cannot have the advantage of commercial rents and retain your feudal privileges too. If you

identify yourselves with the spirit of the age, you may yet do well; for I tell you that the people of this country look to their aristocracy with a deep-rooted prejudice—an hereditary prejudice, I may call it—in their favour; but your power was never got, and you will not keep it by obstructing the spirit of the age in which you live. If you are found obstructing that progressive spirit which is calculated to knit nations more closely together by commercial intercourse; if you give nothing but opposition to schemes which almost give life and breath to inanimate nature, and which it has been decreed shall go on, then you are no longer a national body.

There is a widely-spread suspicion that you have been tampering with the feelings of your tenantry — you may read it in the organ of your party — this is the time to show the people that such a suspicion is groundless. I ask you to go into this committee — I will give you a majority of county members — you shall have a majority of members of the Central Agricultural Protection Association in the committee; and on these terms I ask you to inquire into the causes of the distress of our agricultural population. I trust that neither of those gentlemen who have given notice of amendments will attempt to interfere with me, for I have embraced the substance of their amendments in my motion. I am ready to give those hon. Gentlemen the widest range they please for their inquiries. I only ask that this subject may be fairly investigated. Whether I establish my principle, or you establish yours, good must result from the inquiry; and I do beg and entreat of the honourable, independent country gentlemen in this House, that they will not refuse, on this occasion, to sanction a fair, full, and impartial inquiry.

FREE TRADE.

XVI.

LONDON, JUNE 18, 1845.

I COULD not help thinking, as my friend the chairman (Mr. G. Wilson) was giving you those interesting and somewhat novel statistics, that I am following him at some disadvantage, inasmuch as I fear there is little chance of my being able to communicate anything so new, or even so agreeable, to you as he has done. He has just returned from the north, where he has been making up his accounts; I have just come from a Railway Committee, where I have been on the tread-wheel for the last three weeks—as much a prisoner as though I were in Newgate, and with the disadvantage of being conscious that I am in a place where there is more time wasted than even in that distinguished gaol. Yet even under the roof of St. Stephen's there has been something of late passing of rather a cheering character, and I think I may say, I do bring good news from the House of Commons. It is not such a bad place, after all, especially for agitation. Last year we made a little mistake at the beginning of the session: we laid our heads together, and came to the conclusion that we could employ ourselves better out of doors in visiting some of the counties and rural districts, and agitating a little in the country; this year we have changed our tactics, and we thought that Parliament, after all, was the best place for agitating. You speak with a loud voice when talking on the floor of that House; you are heard all over the world, and, if you have anything to say that hits hard, it is a very long whip, and reaches all over the kingdom.

We determined to confine ourselves during this session to Parliament, and I think the result has shown that it is the best field for our labours. We brought forward a succession of motions. We began with one, in which we challenged our opponents to meet us in Committee and examine the farmers and landowners, to show what benefit the Corn-laws had done them; they refused our proposal, — and I have no doubt the country put the right interpretation upon their motives. Then my friend Mr. Bright, who is an active-minded man, looked about, and thought that, amongst all these burdens upon land, he did not think there was one greater than the game that was eating up its produce. He felt anxious, if possible, to point out to the landowners where they could find a margin in their account-books to turn a penny, and compensate themselves for repealing the Corn-laws by abolishing the Game-laws. And, therefore, he moved for his Committee, and was more lucky than I have been, for he has got it; and I have no doubt that in due time, when the secrets of that prison-house come out at the end of the session, he will be able to show you, from the mouths of the most intelligent farmers in the country, that there is one burden which they consider heavier than all their local taxes, county-rates, high-way-rates, and even their poor-rates—and that is the burden of these excessive game preserves. Then we had our friend Mr. Ward's motion, by way of sweeping the ground clear for Mr. Villiers to pass over with his great annual motion. Mr. Ward proposed that they should give a Committee to inquire what was the amount of these special burdens of which we had heard so much, in order that we might compensate them,

pay them off, and have done with them. They said they
would not have any inquiry made into it.

Now, you who are Londoners know an old trick, called a
'dodge,' which is sometimes practised on the credulous and
the philanthropic in your streets. A mendicant is sometimes
seen walking about with his arm bandaged up; he has a
special burden; it is a grievance, and he makes money by
it. But sometimes, if one of the Mendicity Society's officers
come and ask him to let him undo the bandage to see what
this special damage is, you find these artful dodgers very both
to comply. Now that is the case with our landlords—I mean
the protectionist landlords — only the protectionists; they
have been going about exciting the benevolent feelings of the
community upon the plea that they are labouring under some
serious disadvantage, or great and heavy burden; and when
Mr. Ward comes forward and offers to undo the burden to let
them go free, and take the bandage away, they are like the
impostors in your streets—they take to their heels and run
away.

Those were our motions in the House of Commons; that
was our place of agitation: but I must admit that we have
not done so much for our cause as has been done by our opponents. I must say that I think their motions, resolutions,
and amendments have been of much more importance to us
than anything we could have done. They had the great and
immortal grease debate; and they brought forward their
motion for the relief of farmers by repealing their local
burdens;—and what do you think one of them was? I heard
it with my own ears, or I would not have believed it—that in
the maritime counties, where shipwrecks and accidents occur,
dead bodies are washed on shore, and they have to hold inquests
on them, and the expense is charged to the county-rate. Well,
that is an argument of the great landed interest. Then came
the annual debate, brought forward by Mr. Villiers with his
accustomed talent and earnestness. Now, we heard a rumour

in the House,—for these things are always known, because
they are concocted at clubs—we always know what the dodge
is in the House,—we heard a rumour, before the debate
began, that they did not intend to have any discussion on the
other side: it was determined they would not talk; and I
believe, if my friend Mr. Villiers had not dexterously alluded
in the course of his speech—pointedly alluded—to three of
their county members in such a way that they were forced to
stand up and speak,—I really believe not one of them would
have opened his mouth. But, however, there were three or
four of them that spoke. The most significant part of what
they said was, as an Irishman would say, what they did not
say. They did not say a word about the farmers upon this
occasion; not a syllable about the farmers being interested in
the Corn-laws. But what a change! Three or four years
ago, to my knowledge, they talked of nothing else but the
farmers; how they would stand by them, and how they came
there to protect the interest of the tenant-farmers. I do not
know whether it was our challenge to discuss that point in
Committee, or whether it was from the fact that we happen
to have some of the best and most extensive farmers with
us,—for I find myself just now seated between Mr. Houghton on one side and Mr. Lattimore on the other,—I do not
know whether we may take credit to ourselves, or whether we
ought to give the honour to our excellent agricultural friends
who have come amongst us; but so it is, that nothing is now
said in the House of Commons about the farmers having
an interest in the Corn-laws; nothing is said about special
burdens, for fear we should ask them to undo the bandage.

But the most significant part of that discussion was in
the declarations of opinion by the leading men on both sides
of the House—by Sir Robert Peel and Sir James Graham on
one side, and Lord John Russell on the other. I was very
curious to know what Sir James Graham would say upon the
occasion. He had spoken a few nights before on Lord John

Russell's motion, and he then brought out in a most gratuitous manner,—I feel deeply indebted to him for it, though I did not see that it was quite relevant to the occasion,—but he then brought out voluntarily, from official sources, some of the most startling proofs that I have ever met with in my experience, showing the extensive evils, physically and morally, that arise from scarcity of food, and the great blessings that overspread the country when food is abundant and cheap. He showed, by the statistics of pauperism, crime, disease, and mortality, that all the best interests of our nature are identified with an abundance of the first necessaries of life. My friend Mr. Villiers followed him, and with that promptitude for which he excels, and in which he has no rival, I would venture to say, in the House, he turned to account every fact that the Home Secretary had dropped, and applied them instantly and with immense force as proof of the truth of the doctrine which he had so long been arguing. And when my friend brought forward his motion a few nights afterwards, he again pinned the Home Secretary to the inference which naturally followed from the speech of the previous evening. I was curious to hear what Sir James Graham would say : I listened with great anxiety to what he would say to the public when he spoke upon the subject. I thought he must draw back a little, to please those who sat with blank faces behind him ; but no : he got up and reiterated all he had said before. He stated that he did not withdraw one word of what he had uttered ; that he did not recant one syllable of what he had said ; that those were his principles, and he would abide by them.

Sir Robert Peel followed ; and though he has been going at rather a quick pace lately—I hear somebody calling out '*Punch ;*' well, he is an admirable authority to quote—an excellent commentator, an admirable critic, is *Punch*—he is never wrong, he is infallibly right: *Punch* represented Sir R. Peel as going fast ahead of Lord John Russell on this occasion;—but I must say that, fast as he had been travelling before, he seemed now to have quickened his pace. What a contrast did the speech of Sir Robert Peel present to that which he delivered last year on the same occasion! Then everything was said for the purpose of conciliating the men behind and below him on the same benches; and everything that could be uttered was said to insult the Free-traders: but he had not then had the grease debate, nor had he found out the quality of the men then. He has had a twelvemonths' experience: they have set up for themselves; they have found out their weakness, and, what is more, they have let Sir Robert Peel find it out also; and now he can afford to treat them as he likes. The right hon. Baronet tells them that be intends to carry out the principles of Free Trade gradually and cautiously; but still that they must be carried out:

We had Lord John Russell, and he voted with us. I wish he had done so without any qualification; but, however, as we have got him amongst us, I hope we shall amend him. Lord John Russell proposes a very little fixed duty; but in the same speech in which he propounds this, he tells us he does not approve of a tax on corn: he thinks it is one of the most objectionable taxes that could be raised. Then why does he propose it? He does not intend to keep it; he merely proposes it just to put those people in the wrong who refuse even to put a little tax on corn. I have no doubt next year he will give up that inconsistency, and will be in favour of total repeal.

Well, we came to our vote; and, though we had the verdict in our favour, as far as words could convey it, the votes were against us. But that cannot last long. In this country you must be governed by one of two methods: you must be ruled either by moral or physical force. Moral force means governing according to right principles, when those principles are acknowledged to be true. They may govern by a species of moral force when they can manage to persuade men that,

while they are governing wrong, they are governing right;
but you never can rule by moral force when you yourselves
avow that you are carrying on principles which you believe to
be unjust and untrue.

I think we ought to feel deeply indebted to such meetings as
this, which have stood by this question; which have cheered
on public men in its advocacy; which have aided in disseminating the knowledge that has gone forth from this vast
building, in which we have brought the public mind on both
sides so far to defer to the expression of public opinion as to
show that they are bound to acknowledge the justice of our
principles.

Now, there is but one universal opinion—that it is a question of time. Three or four years ago everybody used to tell
me that it was a species of insanity to think of carrying this
principle of total repeal. Now everybody says, 'There is no
doubt you will effect the total repeal; the only question is as
to the time.' We have narrowed the controversy; we have
reduced it down to one little word. The whole question
hinges upon one monosyllable—'when?' I think the *Times*
newspaper put out a very fair challenge to the League the day
before yesterday, in a very beautiful article, in which it said
we were called upon to argue this question upon that ground;
to show the justice, expediency, and policy of our doctrine of
'immediate repeal.' I have no objection to answer that
appeal; and in doing so, if I am matter-of-fact and dull, you
must bear with me, and that patiently, because I shall be
followed by those who can treat the subject with greater
interest. Mark me, it is quite right, if I am to lay the basis
of a matter-of-fact argument, that I should come first. I will
be the heavy foundation-stone; and here behind me are the
Corinthian capital and the gorgeous pedestal—the architec-
tural beauties that are to grow upon this foundation. It is
right, too, that we should have this kind of variety; because
one of the boasts of the League is this, that we can find

audiences such as could only be assembled in ancient Rome to
witness the brutal conflicts of men, or that can now be found
in Spain to witness the brutish conflicts of animals;—we can
assemble multitudes as great to listen to the dry disquisitions
of political economy.

That is our boast.   Now to our argument.   As Sir Robert
Peel would say, 'there are three ways of dealing with this
question.'   Firstly, you may acknowledge the justice of the
principles of total repeal, and you may defer it until it suits
your party, or until circumstances compel you to abolish
the Corn-laws totally and immediately.   Secondly, you may
abolish it gradually by a vanishing duty, putting an 8*s.* tax,
and sliding off 1*s.* a year till it comes to nothing; that may
be done by an Act of Parliament, and would involve the
principle of a total repeal.   Or, thirdly, you may adopt our
principle of total and immediate repeal.   Now, firstly of the
first.   The policy of our present Government appears to be
this :—'We will acknowledge the principle ; that will stave
off debate.   We could not meet them in debate if we did not
acknowledge the principle ; if we took the same ground as the
Members for Essex, Somerset, and Sussex, we should be rolled
over and over in the mud in debate by these Leaguers, and
be hooted and hissed at the corners of the streets, when we
walked out of the House.'   Well, they give up the principle
of protection.   But they say, 'We will not apply our principle
of Free Trade ; we will tell them, this is not the time ; and
more, we will not tell them (we will take care of that) what is
the time ; that shall be as it suits our party.'   What would be
found in the innermost hearts of these men ? or, if you could
get to their private conferences when they are behind the
scenes, what are they thinking about as to the repeal of the
Corn-law ?   I know it as well as though I were in their hearts.
It is this: they are all agreed that this Corn-law cannot be
maintained—no, not a rag of it—during a period of scarcity
prices, of a famine season, such as we had in 1839, 1840, and

1841. They know it. They are prepared, when such a time comes, to abolish the Corn-laws, and they have made up their minds to it. There is no doubt in the world of it. Is that statesmanlike, think you?

First, for the farmers. They have told them, with all the high authority that belongs to their life and station, that the Corn-laws will be abolished; they tell their tools, the papers, like Grandmamma, to deal out in their diurnal twaddle, the argument that if the Corn-laws are abolished the farmers would be ruined even if they paid no rent. That is the language of Grandmamma of to-day. That is the sort of slip-slop in answer to the admirable article in yesterday's *Times*. How does this work? In the first place, the farmers are told by Sir James Graham and Sir Robert Peel that the Corn-laws must be abolished and Free Trade be established; but it must be done gradually and cautiously. Now, I appeal to my friends Mr. Lattimore and Mr. Houghton, both experienced and able men, whether they could put the farmers in a more disadvantageous position than that in which they are now, under the pretence of benefiting them? They hang them up on the tenter-hooks of suspense. These party newspapers are alarming them with all sorts of raw-head-and-bloody-bone stories of what Free Trade is going to inflict on them; and the Prime Minister is telling them that, notwithstanding all that, he is prepared to carry out Free Trade. Nothing could be worse for the interest of the agriculturists, whether farmers or labourers—for the welfare of any class of capitalists, especially for one having such a vast amount of capital and so large an interest at stake as the farmers—to place them in the position which these pretended friends of theirs do by their present policy. Now, what is that policy morally? They will not deal with this question now, when they can do it calmly and deliberately: they wait for a period of excitement and clamour. They are calculating on repealing these Corn-laws some day when Palace-yard is crowded with famishing

thousands. What is the effect morally of such a proceeding
as that? It is to induce the belief among the people of this
country, that moral influence has no effect whatever on their
legislation. May they not, after such an example as that,
appeal to their countrymen upon any future occasion, when
a body of men shall be found willing to exert themselves
through a period of years, as the League has done, to effect
a great and benign change in our laws,—may they not appeal
to such an example as that, and say, 'What is the use of
your agitation? or what is the use of your printing, passing resolutions, and sending petitions to Parliament? The
League tried that for years; they persevered for seven, eight,
or nine years; but when 10,000 people met in the street,
called aloud in the voice of menace, and threatened with
danger the persons of their legislators, then they yielded, but
never dreamt of doing so till then.'

Now, the second plan of doing this work is the passing a
fixed duty of 8s., and diminishing it 1s. every year. What
is the effect of such a change as that on the farmers? They
begin with a fixed duty of 8s., or any sum you please. The
farmer is told by the land-agent or by the landlord himself,
'Well, we have passed a duty of 8s., but you know you have
only been getting an average protection of 6s. or 7s. for the
last ten years for corn imported; we must try and see what
the effect of this will be. We need not talk anything about
game-laws, under-draining, sub-soil ploughing, clearing away
these hedge-rows, or adjusting rents: wait and see how this
law operates.' The consequence is, nothing is done, but all
must wait. The farmer goes on; next rent-day comes; the
landlord or his agent says, 'Well, Farmer Hobbins, I don't
think much harm is done by this change in the Corn-laws: it
does not seem to have been of so much good to us, after all.
We will wait a year or two; I don't think there will be much
harm.' And so nothing is done: the farmer goes on, in the
meantime, exerting himself to meet the coming danger which

is apprehended when duty is low. What is going on abroad in the meantime? Why, the foreigner is told, as soon as that 8*s.* duty comes down to 2*s.* to 3*s.*, then there will be a wide door opened for grain in England. The foreigner is induced to increase the production every year more and more, expecting to find a market, and when the low duty does come, he is prepared to pour into this country corn, swamping the farmer at the end of this seven or eight years, just as he is now swamped in the month of May or June by an inundation of corn under this sliding scale.

Then we come to our principle of total and immediate repeal. In answer to the word 'when,' we say 'now.' The landlord says it will create a panic, and, in order that that argument may not wear out, they set their newspaper organs to frighten the farmers and keep the argument alive. Well, but what is there to be feared from this total and immediate repeal? We are told there are vast quantities of corn lying somewhere abroad ready to be poured into this market when we repeal the Corn-laws. I think this argument was dealt with so admirably by the *Times* newspaper, that I will just read an extract from its columns of the day before yesterday :—

'Count up every quarter of corn in every one of earth's richest granaries ; track all her winding shores, penetrate every creek and every stream ; measure every diluvial delta and every sheltered valley, the natural fertility of the plains and the artificial productiveness of the hills ; take the sum of all the warehouses, all the heaps, and all the standing crops ; and we entertain no doubt whatever that reasonable and candid men will be astonished above measure at the "universal nakedness of the land." The Baltic and the Euxine, the Gulf of Genoa, the St. Lawrence, the Mississippi, and even the rivers that flow under our feet, are names of terror to some minds, as if they flowed with corn. But rivers of corn are as pure and impossible a fiction as rivers of gold. Once you begin to investigate, to measure, and to count, you find the most formidable accumulations dwindle into a few months' or a few weeks' sustenance for such living and growing multitudes as London, Manchester, or Glasgow. There is not too much corn on earth, nor will there ever be till the mildest and awfullest words that ever were spoken are finally unsaid, which they never will be in this mortal world.'

Now, there is the profoundest philosophy presented in all the charms of poetic language. But I like to go to experience : I never like to deal in the future, or to argue on what will happen ; but let us take the lights of experience to guide us in our paths for the future. We have had occasions in this country, when we have had as sudden a demand for corn all over the world for this country as though we had a total and immediate repeal of the Corn-laws. In 1839, 1840, and 1841, during all those three years, the average price of corn in this country was 67*s.* We ransacked the world for corn during those three years; our merchants sent everywhere for it; we swept over the face of the earth, bribing every nation to send their corn to this rich market, and gain this high price for their produce. I will give you a list of places from which we received corn in one year during that period : from Russia, Sweden, Norway, Denmark, Prussia, Germany, Holland, Belgium, France, Portugal, Spain, Gibraltar, Italy, Malta, Ionian Islands, Turkey, Egypt, Tripoli, Tunis, Algiers, Morocco, Cape of Good Hope, Mauritius, East India Company's territory, Australia, Canada, United States, Chili, and Peru. Every region on the face of the globe — Europe, Asia, America, Africa, and even Australia — were ransacked for corn. How much do you think we got in the course of that year,—bribing the nations of the earth with the high price of 67*s.* a quarter? In 1839 we received in wheat and flour together equivalent to 2,875,605 quarters, about one-eighth of the annual consumption of the wheat of this country. In 1840, when we had given them a year's stimulus, the imports were 2,432,765 quarters of corn. In 1841, 2,783,602 quarters. During those three years we imported 8,091,972 quarters, being on average each year of 2,700,000 quarters. Now, mark me, that corn was sent out for by our merchants with a knowledge that the price in this country for corn was nearly 70*s.* a quarter, and was brought here with the belief and under the conviction that every quarter of it would be ad-

mitted into this country under a 1s. duty. There was, therefore, during those three years virtually a total and immediate
repeal of the Corn-laws ; and you see the result in the supply
for this market.

Now, we say, pass an Act for the total and immediate repeal
of the Corn-laws, and you do not put us in the same position
that we were in during those years in stimulating other countries to send us corn; for now our corn is 46s. a quarter
instead of 67s., as it was then ; and, therefore, if you were not
inundated with corn in those dear seasons, where is the corn
to come from that is to inundate you now ?   No; there is no
such thing as a store of corn abroad in the world; there is
no provision made by people for a contingency that they do
not expect to arise.   There is no cultivator on the face of the
earth that has ever put a plough into the ground, or a yoke
upon his horse, with the idea of producing one bushel of wheat
in order to meet the demands of this country consequent on
the total and immediate repeal of the Corn-laws.   There is no
stock abroad, therefore no supply, except that which has been
provided for a known and expected market; and if we repealed our Corn-law to-morrow, there is literally not a quarter
of wheat provided in order to meet the demands in consequence
of such an abolition of our Corn-laws.

But it is our opponents who want to introduce an unnatural and artificial inundation of corn in this market : they,
by withholding the time, by promising that it shall come, by
telling foreigners abroad that when it does come they can
compete with our farmers, though they do not pay a shilling
of rent,—or, who say to the foreigners, ' Wait until Sir Robert
Peel is pressed on by the cry of distress to repeal the Corn-
laws, and then you may supply all England with corn, for our
farmers cannot compete with you,'—those are the men who
are inviting this inundation of corn; who, not content with
circulating fallacies at home, are trying to spread delusion
through the Ukraine and in the valley of the Mississippi, over

all the face of the habitable globe, and wherever their false
and delusive fallacies can reach.

I have argued this question as though there were only
farmers concerned in it; I have dealt with it with a view to
the interests of the parties supposed to be likely to be injured
by it: but are there no other parties to this question? Why
do we advocate the removal of this bad law?—because it is
destructive to the interests of the great body of the people.
This movement has not taken place—this agitation has not
had its origin or been sustained by the vast proportion of the
intelligent and humane population of this country, because it
is an error in political economy—it is opposed because the
Corn-law is intended to restrict the supply of the food of this
country and to put the nation on short commons. That is
why we oppose this Corn-law; and we do so in the name,
not merely of farmers and landowners, but of the great body
of the people.

If we can show that the law is unjust as respects the
interests of the great majority of the people, then, though
its total and immediate repeal did involve injury to that class
for whose benefit it has been unjustly maintained, it is not
an argument that would weigh one instant with me in op-
posing its total repeal. Whoever said this law was passed
for the great body of the people of this country? We have
never heard any attempt to show that. We have heard it
urged that it was good for the landlords, to compensate them
for the peculiar burdens that I have described just now; but
you know we have found out that that was an imposture:
we sent the Mendicity Society officer after them. We have
heard it maintained that it was for the benefit of the farmer;
but farmers are only 250,000 people out of the 27,000,000
inhabitants of these islands: that is their proportion in Great
Britain; but whoever heard them argue that it was for the
benefit of the great body of the people? They have given up
that case, when they say the law ought to be abolished at

some time; for I maintain that if this law, which has been in existence for the last thirty years, is not a law for the benefit of the people, they never ought to have passed it; and it is a shame to themselves, and they ought to hide their faces for ever, for having maintained it, if it is not for the benefit of the great body of the people.

I say, if it is not for their benefit—and it never was—why on earth should they come forward and say that it should ever be repealed? And if it is to be repealed at all, I say, let it be repealed immediately, as it is an unjust law. They may set up other interests. I believe Sir R. Peel is frequently talking of a due consideration to the great and important interests that have grown up under this law. I plead for the vastly greater and more important interests that have been crushed to the earth under this law. If they want any proof of this, I bring their own Home Secretary, with his Prison Report and the statistical tables, into the witness-box, to prove what the law has done. Now, then, for the sake of that class—the most numerous of all—for the sake of all the un-privileged classes of this country—I plead for the total and immediate repeal of this Corn-law. I do it upon the ground of expediency, as being better at this moment than any other time in which you could repeal the law. I do it on the ground of justice, because I say, if it is not a good law you have not a right to retain it one instant.

What will be the effect on the great body of the people when the time comes at which we believe Government contemplate the repeal of the Corn-law? They are going to repeal it, as I told you — mark my words — at a season of distress. That distress may come; ay, three weeks of showery weather when the wheat is in bloom or ripening would repeal these Corn-laws. But how? We had a taste of it in 1839, 1840, and 1841. Are the people of this country to be subjected to another ordeal before this Corn-law is repealed? What provision is made against that calamity? For here is prob-

ably the most important consideration for us at the present
moment. Divine Providence has repealed the Corn-laws for
this year by an abundance at home. He has in a great
degree repealed the Corn-laws; but He has not given us the
benefit we should have if we had an unlimited range over all
which He designed for the good of His creatures over this
earth's fair surface; but still we have a mitigation by His
bounty of the rigours of the landowners' Corn-law.

Suppose another such reverse to take place as we have
witnessed in this country within the last six years—such a
revolution as the youngest man amongst us has beheld during
the period of his life—or supposing it to come this year, what
provision is made against such a calamity? I have told you
how much corn could be got here in 1839 after our failing
harvest of 1838; but there is no such supply available now,
as those nations are increasing in numbers along the whole of
the maritime districts of Europe. They are wanting more
and more of the corn of the interior. The Atlantic states of
America are increasing, and consuming more and more of the
corn of their interior; and we offer them no inducement to
spread themselves out from the cities—to abandon their premature manufactures—in order to delve, dig, and plough for
us; and they are more and more in a condition to consume all
that they produce.

I heard in the House of Commons, from Mr. Mitchell, a
gentleman himself practically acquainted with the subject,
who in an admirable speech that riveted the attention—as all
practical speeches in that place do, where men will content
themselves with speaking only upon what they do understand—I say, in an address which riveted the attention of
every one in that House, Mr. Mitchell exposed the bankrupt
condition of this country, so far as its future provision of food
goes, looking to the whole world as our resource. We have
now 300,000 quarters of foreign corn in this country. Where
is the supply to come from? Ought we to be called upon to

answer that question? No! but it ought to be answered
by our Government. That is a question which ought to be
thrust upon them. I do not believe they have nerve enough to
bear the responsibility that will be cast upon their shoulders,
if that argument is pressed upon them.

Then look at the position in which our unprivileged middle
classes and capitalists will be placed, as well as the poor, who
first suffer from famine, for want of bread. They are not
allowed to starve in this country: they have a right to claim
relief, and justly so, from those above them; and, if you have
a scarcity, it is the middle classes who will have to support
the lower and working classes, and at the same time maintain
themselves, with a very inferior business to do it with.
Look at our capitalists spreading out their wings. Go down
to the House of Commons; look into the lobbies; go into
one of those groups where I have the misfortune to be at
present. There they are contemplating railways all over the
length and breadth of the land. What would be the effect
of a bad harvest upon those men who have subscribed their
thousands and tens of thousands to some new railway scheme,
and have signed the parliamentary contract? It is all very
fine and plain sailing now when everything is at a premium,
everything is up; get shares to-day, sell them to-morrow,
pay for them the next day, and get 20 per cent. But these
shares will be held by somebody; and if we have a failing
harvest, whenever it comes, then the day of reckoning for
the holders of these shares and scrips will arrive. I would
advise every speculator in railway shares to keep a sharp eye
on the barometer. He should take in two papers—a railway
paper, and the *Mark-lane Express;* and when he has seen the
price of shares, then let him go and observe the price of
wheat in Mark-lane. But if a bad harvest comes, and a rise
in prices takes place, they are a class that will suffer; and not
merely they and their families, but it will entail misery and
disasters on every section of the community. Now, these are

the points that I want to see urged upon the Government at the present moment. Throw on the Government—as a Government, do not let us be misunderstood—throw on them the whole of the responsibility of this state of things.

That is about the completion of my case at present in favour of the total and immediate repeal of the Corn-laws. As the lawyers say,—'Gentlemen, that is my case.' But I want to know, if there is nothing to be said in answer to this, why we should not carry the repeal of the Corn-laws, and carry it now? It is merely partisanship. These men cannot make up their minds to admit that they may have been wrong at some former time. What I want to do is this,— to open a door as wide as possible for the conversion—the avowed conversion—of our opponents. I wish we could burn *Hansard*, and all the debates that have ever taken place, in order to let these statesmen be at liberty to adopt a new course of policy, dictated by their present convictions. But they are afraid of being taunted with having said something different before from what they are ready to say now. We have all said something different before from what we have said now. Have we not all grown wiser? Have we not all learned something by the discussions for seven years? I want to see these men get up in the House of Commons and avow that they have learned something by our discussions in that assembly. I set myself up to teach people years ago; I have been learning more than anybody else every day since; and why should not they make that frank and free admission? If they would make an admission and make a clean breast, and confess that they did not know so much formerly as they do now, they would never be taunted afterwards.

I have only one word to say, before I sit down, upon another subject. I want to see the people of this country feel alive to the ensuing registration. This next registration will, in all probability, decide the fate of the Corn-laws. Most likely we shall have a dissolution next year. I want every man to make that his business as much as he makes his ledger or his counter his business—every man who is convinced that the Corn-law ought to be abolished to feel it his paramount duty to look after his votes and the votes of his neighbours before the next registration. The work begins on the 20th of this month for the counties. This is the time for men to look after their own votes, and to find everybody else they can that have got votes and will support Free Trade. There is another duty: there are a great number of bad votes on the list for counties. Some say we want to disfranchise the people. I do not want to disfranchise any one; but this I do say, that if we are to fight fairly we must fight on equal terms. If we put on false votes, our opponents strike them off: we cannot fight them with our legal votes against their illegal votes, and, therefore, we must strike them off.

I have no hesitation in telling you that there are counties where there are many bad votes. I will be bound to say that in Buckinghamshire, for instance, you will find at the very least 1000. I have heard competent people give a surmise that there are 2000 spurious votes on the register in that county. There they are; nobody looks after them; nobody ever thinks of going and objecting to them. Everybody is afraid, because they hear there is some man they call the Duke of Buckingham. Why, if they would only consider these things a little more rationally, they would see that the Duke of Buckingham, as I assure you, is not a more formidable man in the registration court than any of you here. You, who are Leaguers, consider yourselves as united with a body that can protect you morally, legally, and pecuniarily, against 150 dozen Dukes of Buckingham.

Now, there is East Surrey: what a scandal it will be if that county should return two monopolists at its next election ! There is not one man in 100 in Southwark and Lambeth that is upon county lists, and yet, if you go down into the agricultural districts, you will find one in 30 or 40. It is

one in 30 in the agricultural parts of East Surrey, but only one
in 100 in the metropolitan districts. I say it is the duty of
every man to get himself on the list, and his neighbours
likewise. There are thousands, I believe, qualified to be there
who have not thought of it: it will be a scandal to the people
on that side of the river if they do not see to this. We will
take care of Middlesex; we have it in hand, and will look
after it. There are a few more counties which we will give
you a good account of in due time. I do not consider any
county hopeless.

I will tell you that we have something else in view besides
registration: we will apply our organisation to contesting
counties as well as registration. Why should not the principle of co-operation that we have exercised so long and so
usefully be carried out in the work of contesting counties
where there is a chance of winning them? Why not have in
each parish in every populous county an earnest man who will
devote himself, as far as he can, to bringing persons to vote, and
appealing to their patriotism and good feeling to vote, without
putting the candidate to one shilling expense? I say we can
contest counties, ay, at one per cent. of the expense of that
which it costs our opponents, if we adopt our organisation.
How can monopolists contest a county without expense?
What motives can they appeal to? Where is their organisation? It is gone. They are all backbiting each other in their
counties. One of their Members is accused of voting with Sir
Robert Peel, and another voting against him. When they
meet in Committee they are all pulling each other to pieces
just like so many village gossips.

Bear in mind that the League has a plan in store, by which
we intend to prepare the counties and to contest them; and I
entreat from this place every man interested in this question,
that he will make it his paramount duty, from this time, for
the next two months, to give his attention to the subject
of registration. If we do this, we shall totally repeal the

Corn-laws yet, before a famine comes. In doing so, you will set a glorious example to all future times of the way in which such questions ought to be carried. I really hardly regret, though it has been attended with very heavy sacrifice, that the agitation has lasted so long. If we had carried the repeal of the Corn-laws by a multitudinous shout in 1839, 1840, and 1841, it would have been something like yielding to brute force and clamour; but now, besides the advantage of repealing the Corn-laws—our agitation will have been attended with many other advantages. We have been teaching the people of this country something more, I hope, than the repeal of the Corn-laws.

We have taught the farmers, I trust, to begin to think for themselves; we have made landlords and farmers think of improving their lands; we have taught the middle classes, I hope, that they have a moral power, if they choose to exercise it, and a power of applying it as great as the monopolists, if they will avail themselves of it; but I hope, in addition, that we shall set an example of truth to the working classes, showing them that these questions can be carried by moral means, and that, if they will accomplish anything for their benefit, then they will adopt precisely the same organisation which we have before done to accomplish our object.

FREE TRADE.

XVII.

MANCHESTER, OCTOBER 28, 1845.

MANY as have been the meetings which I have had the honour of addressing in Manchester, yet I think I can truly say that none will lay claim to surpass the present in numbers and intelligence; and, if I look around me on the platform, I am led to the conclusion that for weight, influence, and moral power, this constitutes altogether about one of the strongest meetings I have ever known held in this country. As I came along the street just now, I saw such a rushing and struggling to gain access to this meeting, that I could not help asking myself what it was that we were called together for. You have nothing particular to learn, we have nothing particular to communicate in reference to this cause, and yet there seems to be something in our question which naturally and instinctively draws us together.

I think there is some danger of a misapprehension on the part of some as to the particular object which again draws us together to-night in this building. Our business here to-night is to state the position in which our cause stands at the present moment, to draw some consolation from the particular posture in which we are now placed, and to make some allusion to the dilemma in which our opponents, as many suppose,

x 2

are now placed. We are not met here to-night to exult in the
fallen and menacing condition of our unhappy sister island,
Ireland, whose inhabitants, in consequence of the failure of
the potato crop, and the deficiency of the wheat harvest, seem
to have starvation staring them in the face, and famine impending over them. But, ladies and gentlemen, let it be perfectly understood that we do not meet here to exult over the
calamity in which a large portion of our countrymen are likely
to be placed, or over the scarcity and famine which impend
over our unhappy sister island. The objects for which we
have laboured for seven years have been abundance and
cheapness. ' Plenty' is our motto — ' Plenty always and
everywhere!' And if there be drought, or scarcity, or famine,
here or elsewhere, we, at all events, of all our fellow-countrymen, may fairly claim to stand guiltless of the cause of that
famine and distress. We are told that in a country where
the great bulk of the population are always upon the verge
of famine, where that gaunt spectre now threatens to stalk
through the land — that misery, starvation, and even death,
may be the portion of millions of our fellow-countrymen in
Ireland.

Now, what is the remedy for this? We do not come to
talk about the principle which is applicable to all times and
seasons; but what, I ask, is the natural and obvious remedy,
under existing circumstances, against the gaunt famine that
threatens a country like Ireland? You would say, ' Open
wide the ports, and admit the bread of the whole world to
feed the people.' That is the obvious and natural remedy—
that is the remedy which an enlightened despot would at once
fly to. Witness Russia, witness Turkey, or witness Germany,
Holland, and Belgium; these Governments have not waited,
but when their people have been threatened with want, they
have at once thrown open their ports, and in some cases
stopped exportation, in order to supply their people with
abundance of the first necessaries of life. Why has not our

Government taken a similar course? Why have they waited to learn Christianity from the Turk, or humanity from the Russian? Is it because our Government is less merciful than that of the Mahometan Sultan? Is it that our boasted constitutional power is less humane than that of the despot of Russia? Or is it that our Prime Minister, who holds the responsible position of Sultan in this country—is it because he is afraid that if he takes the step—the obvious and natural and necessary step—he will not have the support of the country in throwing open the ports of this kingdom to foreign corn? If that be his doubt, we meet here to give him all the support which we can give him. I hesitate not to say, that whatever may be the attempts of the aristocracy to thwart the Minister in taking such a 'course, there is popular power enough in the country to support him in that act of humanity. We support him here in this magnificent meeting! What we say, South Lancashire will say whenever he appeals to it. We speak the voice of the West Riding of Yorkshire whenever he chooses; and Middlesex will endorse what we say in this hall.

You have animated the hearts and hopes of this empire; and a Minister having the support of the vast multitude in this country—having their intelligence at his back, which he may have whenever he chooses to draw upon it—I say he is a criminal and a poltroon if he hesitates a whit. He has the power. There is no man, whether he be the Grand Turk, or whether he be a Russian despot—there is no man in the world that has more power than Sir Robert Peel has in this country. His party cannot do without him. Let anybody sit in the House of Commons as we do, opposite to Sir Robert Peel, and watch the proceedings of his party. He comes down to the House night after night. With the exception of his colleague, Sir James Graham, the whole of the side of the House upon which they sit may be called a dreary waste, as far as statesmanship is concerned. Sir James Graham, although I admit

he has manifested great administrative talents, has not exactly
arrived at that state of personal popularity in this country
that he can take Sir Robert Peel's place. Sir Robert Peel
is therefore absolute with his party; and, with the power
he possesses, he must be content to take the responsibility
which attaches to power. I need not tell you that that word
'responsibility' has an ugly and a sinister sound in the ears
of the Prime Minister; but let us be understood. By responsibility, we mean moral responsibility :—he is responsible
to his country, he will be responsible to history, if he fails,
upon this occasion, in taking that step which he is bound
to take to save a large portion of the people of this country
from famine.

Many people now say, 'Admitting that Sir Robert Peel
opens our ports, and foreign corn comes in, that will not
settle the question;' and this is a point that I wish particularly to draw the attention of this meeting to, for I see a
disposition upon the part of many of my friends to throw up
their caps, and consider this question as settled. I do not
exactly see my way to the settlement of this question yet.
I wish I did. I do not think the opening of the ports will
settle this question. We had the ports opened in 1826; but
they passed the sliding-scale in 1828, with all its horrible
iniquities. It is not because Ireland wants feeding that we
shall necessarily have a repeal of the Corn-laws. Ireland has
been in a state of semi-famine for the last thirty years; and
in 1822 you had subscriptions in England—every church was
thrown open—you had 250,000l. raised in England, and sent
to Ireland, to save the two provinces of Connaught and Mun-
ster from a state of actual famine; but nobody said a word
about repealing the Corn-laws then; not the slightest syllable
was said about relieving the people of Ireland by admitting
foreign corn; and what I wish to impress upon you now is
this, that it is not the opening of the ports alone we want,
but we want to set our backs against them to prevent them

from ever being shut again. Do you not think we may find
some arguments nearer home in favour of this principle?
(Cries of ' Yes.') I believe many of you are brought here because you have an idea that things are not looking quite so
promising as they have been in Lancashire. You are not
arrived exactly at that state they are in in Ireland, where
they have commissioners sent over just now, learned doctors,
to see how much the patient will bear, to see how much it
can endure. They have got it upon the rack, and there are
learned doctors round it feeling the pulse, to see if the patient
will live a little longer, or to see whether it should be taken
off the rack. Then the *Standard* newspaper tells us, that even
if the patient is taken off the rack, it shall be put on again
as soon as it will bear it. Now you are not exactly arrived
at that state yet; but what is the price of oatmeal? I believe
that what used to be a guinea is now 35*s.*; and I believe, too,
that flour has advanced fifty per cent. ; that the dozen pounds
of flour which used to cost 1*s.* 8*d.* are now selling at 2*s.* 6*d.*
Am I right? (Loud cries of ' Yes, yes.') Then you have bread
still dearer, because flour makes more than its own weight in
bread; and every man who is now spending half-a-crown in
bread is just getting one-third less for it than he did this time
twelvemonths. Every man will then have one-third less to
spend upon the other things which he uses. We thus come
to the old story again — if he has so much more to spend
in what he eats, he will have less to spend in what he wears;
and if there is more goes to the baker, and through him to
the miller, there will be less to go to the draper and to the
wholesale dealer. You will then have less work, while you
will have more to pay for your food. Then the masters will
cry out at their short profits; then there will be no more
strikes for higher wages. It is the old thing coming round
again, and I believe many of you here have felt it, and that
you are come here to see whether you are likely to get rid of
the cause. It will not be got rid of, however, by throwing

up your caps, because a lord has written a very ambiguous
sort of a letter, or because certain honourable gentlemen make
speeches, the meaning of which you cannot tell, and indeed
they do not appear to comprehend it very clearly themselves.
You must not throw up your caps, and fancy you are going to
have the Corn-law abolished by any such adventitious aid as
that. It will have to be done by your own right arm, if it
is done at all.

We have a new class in this country that I think are more
deeply interested in this question than they have been yet
considered to be. I wonder if we have any people here that
have got any interest in railways? (Loud laughter and
cheers.) I should think, judging by that response, that almost
every lady and gentleman here has a little sympathy in that
direction. Now the railway people have got—a king! Kings
sometimes make speeches, though we never expect much from
kings' speeches. Cobbett once wrote a grammar for the
purpose of teaching statesmen how to write better kings'
speeches; but I do not think that your railway-king has
studied that grammar. You have a 'king,' and he has lately
been railing at the League at Sunderland. He is given to
railing, and he calls the League a 'selfish' body: he denounces
us. I think railway kings and their subjects are more deeply
interested just now in the success of the League than any
other class of the community. Did you ever take a look at
the trains starting from the Leeds or Sheffield station, or out
by Ashton? You who have got shares in railways, just go
and take stock of your business: see who your customers are:
inquire from the secretary or one of the directors how much
they receive for first-class passengers, how much for second-
class, and how much for third-class, and then you will be able
to understand how much you are indebted to the working
classes for the prosperity of your lines. Learn where the
cheap trains go, how much they carry, and how much they
pay; and then just make a little calculation. Here is John

Tomkins, his wife, and seven children; they earn together a
guinea a-week: his wife comes and says, 'John, I'm paying
3s. 2d. more for flour than I did three months ago.' 'Then,'
says John, 'we must give up the trip to Alderley—we shall
not be able to take that.' Go and tell your 'king' this. They
sometimes call him the railway Bonaparte. Recollect that a
man may be a Napoleon among navigators, and only a navi-
gator among statesmen! I am not happy at nick-names, but
I will give him a title. He shall be one of those pasteboard
potentates that shuffle and cut, and win tricks—call him 'the
King of Spades!'

I do not know how it is, but there is nobody who attacks
the League, but you may be almost certain, whatever fame or
reputation he had before—you may take it for granted, I say,
that that man is at the end of his tether, he is just at the
brink of the precipice, and that all his public fame and character goes overboard. We were attacked by an ex-chancellor
once, and what a figure he has been cutting in *Punch* ever
since! Then we have had Ministers attacking us, Prime
Ministers too, who said we should be mad if we persevered for
Free Trade. What is become of them? And, mark my words,
the railway 'king' will turn out only a 'pretender.' Depend
upon it people will soon avoid running their heads against
that stone wall called the Anti-Corn-law League. I wonder
if there is any man who has laid out his money upon railways
that has not bought a county qualification. I cannot imagine
a man showing less calculation or sound foresight than the
man who lays out his 50l. or 100l. in buying a couple of
shares in a railway, rather than upon a freehold qualification.
It is the 40s. qualification that can make railways profitable,
by giving us Free Trade. I like these railways too, and I
will tell you why. They are carrying common sense, that is,
when the railway-king does not travel upon them, into the
agricultural districts. The great proprietor and squire in the
west and south of England have all been anxious to have rail-

ways. For many years they have wanted railways to their
own houses, and they found out that, if they are to have
them, they must come to Lancashire or Yorkshire, for there
was nobody else that had either the money or the wit to make
them. That makes them sympathise with the prosperity of
Lancashire and Yorkshire; they come into contact with business men, and they understand men of business. They are
beginning to feel that railways are the barometer of the state
of trade, as you all will find it out by-and-bye. I like railways; they are drawing us more together; they are teaching
the landowner to feel for the manufacturer, and placing the
manufacturer upon better terms with the landowner. I wish
them to go on; but they cannot prosper unless you have
something to carry upon them. The more trade you have—
the more Free Trade—the more profits will your railways
bring. Nobody objects to railways now; but how was it
twelve years ago with the landlords in this respect? Twelve
years ago, the Marquis of Chandos then, but Duke of Buckingham now, presided at a public meeting at Salthill, near
Windsor, at which the fellows of Eton College and other
great and distinguished men of the county assembled, to
celebrate the first defeat of the Great Western Railway Bill.
What do those gentlemen say now? Why, even the Pope
himself is now in advance on these subjects, and they are only
some ten years in advance of the Pope. Is it not just as
possible that they may be as much mistaken about their true
interests in the matter of Free Trade as they were in the case
of railroads? This is encouraging. Indeed, we are only now
about three or four years in advance of the monopolists with
our arguments.

About three or four years ago we put out placards, stating
that the population of this country was increasing at the rate
of a thousand a day. I was passing by when I heard a man
with a shovel in his hand reading it upon the wall. 'That's
a lie, anyhow!' he said. But that incredible fact at that time

has been so well established, that now even Lord Stanley and
Sir James Graham admit it is true, and are compelled to
acknowledge that it is necessary to make provision for the
large and increasing population. This also is encouraging;
it shows that the principle we contend for is good, and that
we need only continue the efforts hitherto used to set ourselves
free. It begins to be seen now on all hands, that the present
Corn-law cannot stand; but it seems to be very doubtful, at
present, what we shall get instead of it. Are we to have
another Corn-law? Are we to have a sliding-scale or a fixed
duty ? Only think of the number of Corn-laws we have had
during the last few years ! The present has been in operation
three years, and now we are talking of getting rid of it.
Why is it so? Because just now there is a probability of
scarcity ; we want food, and this law, which Sir John Tyrell
tells us is to give us ' plenty, and security for plenty,' stands
in the way of our obtaining it. It is a law at once unnatural,
impolitic, and inexpedient, and meant only to suit the pockets
of those who believe themselves interested in its continuance.
There will be attempts made to cheat us out of the demand
we make, and there is every probability that those attempts
will succeed, unless we, as Free-traders, stand fast to the
principle we have espoused, by showing to our opponents that
we are neither to be used nor abused by the acceptance of
either a sliding scale or a fixed duty. I think we have made
out a sufficient case, and by that we must stand, without any
attempt at compromise.

We do not ask to be benefited at the expense of any other
portion of the community; I have all along repudiated that
idea; but I think we have fully demonstrated that monopoly
is the bane of agriculture ; and Peel says ditto to it. And we
shall continue to labour and to urge this cause, whether the
ports be immediately opened or not, until not the slightest
ground is left to the monopolists, or until every rag and
vestige of the protective system is done away with. We have

told them in the House of Commons that the farmers are
robbing one another, and that position was not controverted,
but must be acquiesced in, by all who are in any way acquainted with the subject. But since the close of Parliament
I have had an opportunity of consulting with many of this
class of men, and have obtained a variety of statistics and
details on the subject, which go to show that the farmer,
instead of being a gainer, is a most material loser by this
so-called system of protection. It has been proved to me,
that the better off the farmer is, the more he suffers by protection. The large stock farmers, as they are called, are more
seriously injured than any other part of the community. They
are consumers of Indian corn, oats, beans, cheese, butter, beer,
and of all other taxed articles, and they are made to pay artificial prices for all these articles for protection. We have
now had thirty years of protection, and during the whole of
this time the farmer has been the dupe of every blockhead
who gave the cry of ' protection !' But it is not enough that
we demonstrate the iniquity and impolicy of these laws, and
the injury they inflict upon all classes of the community. We
may make this clear and unanswerable by the most direct and
logical of processes. There shall not be found a man in the
House of Commons, with any pretension to intellect, who
shall dare to controvert it.

Yet you cannot carry the abolition of this system unless you
are active and energetic in putting yourselves in a position to
have the power of carrying out your principles. Talking will
not do it. I admit we can show our enemies are wrong; but
still you cannot make men do right unless you have the power
to compel men to it. I believe that power is in your hands.
We have done something already by resorting to the constitutional weapons of war which have been already referred to,
the 40s. freeholders. We called upon the West Riding Free-
traders this time twelve months, and we asked them to
qualify 2000 voters, to rescue that county from the grasp

of monopoly; they have nobly responded to that call. They
have put 2300 upon the register. They have converted the
majority that formerly existed in favour of monopoly of 1100,
into a majority of 1600 for Free Trade. Now I ask them not
to rest satisfied there. I ask them to go on again, and by the
same process qualify 2000 more by the 31st of next January;
for if they do that, they will save themselves much trouble
and expense at the next election. An election must come in
twelve months, or a little more. A contest for the West
Riding of Yorkshire will cost each party 10,000l., and by the
expenditure of 1000l. between now and the 31st of January,
our friends may induce as many more to buy freeholds as will
render a contest hopeless, and thus save themselves the expense. I ask them to put themselves in the same position as
South Lancashire. We have a majority of 3000 in South
Lancashire. Mark the extraordinary change that we have
witnessed. In 1841, at the dissolution of the Liberal Government, the Whig committee of that time took the registration
books in hand, and looked at them with the view of contesting the county. They found, if they had contested it, they
would have been in a minority of 2000. Four years have
elapsed; the League took the registrations in hand. South
Lancashire was wholly abandoned by the so-called Whig party.
The League took the registration in hand, and in four years
the minority of 2000 has been converted into a majority of
3000. You will have no contest in South Lancashire. Nobody
will be such a fool upon the side of the monopolists as to
incur the expense of a contest in South Lancashire. We have
a majority in the Manchester polling district alone large
enough to cover the monopolist majority in all the districts
where they have one. We made an appeal to North Cheshire.
We asked them to qualify, to put themselves into a majority;
and they have done so. You will hear the particulars when
the time comes. But I ask them now not to rest satisfied
where they are. I am jealous of North Cheshire. I want to

see the county (for a borough in which I have the honour to
sit), so safe in three months' time, that Mr. Egerton will not
think of coming to contest it. This is easily done. North
Lancashire—ay, we shall make an example of the monopolists
in North Lancashire. There is some pluck in North Cheshire;
but they are a poor, beaten, coward, craven set in North Lancashire. They have no heads. Make light work of them in
North Lancashire. Why, they have turned Lord Stanley and
family to the right-about, and set up their own little champion;
but I think they will have to go and seek the Derby family
to come and help them out of the scrape, for they seem sadly
in want of a leader. Middlesex we have won; South Lancashire, the West Riding of Yorkshire, North Cheshire, South
Staffordshire, North Lancashire. This is nothing but a basis.
This is only the basis of our operations to begin with. Having done what we can down here, we must now appeal to the
country at large to follow our example.

Wherever there is a man above the rank of an unskilled
labourer, whether a shopkeeper, a man of the middle class, or
of the skilled working class, that has not got a county vote,
or is not striving to accumulate enough to get one, let us
point the finger of scorn at him; he is not fit to be a freeman.
It is an avenue by which we may reach the recesses of power,
and possess ourselves of any constitutional rights which we
are entitled to possess. They cry shame upon us for inviting
the people to qualify. Why, the revising barristers everywhere
have not only passed the qualifications that have been made,
and have not only admitted them to be strictly legal and right,
but they have gone out of their way, and said that they considered it honourable for men to purchase property with the
view of acquiring the franchise. For myself and friends, I
may say that we consider it our duty to enlist as many of the
counties as possible in the cause of Free Trade; we have a list
of twenty, and we intend to visit every one of them. We will
have them organised on the plan that has been so successful

in South Lancashire, under the superintendence of our excellent chairman. I mention this to account to our friends for the neglect of many visits we may have been expected to pay in various quarters. They must allow us to proceed with this registration business; for assuredly it is of the utmost importance. There is nothing that will so much alarm the monopolists as to be told that the League has got hold of the counties. What are their pocket boroughs in comparison with South Lancashire, Middlesex, and the West Riding of Yorkshire? With these constituencies to back them, the principles of Free Trade would be found more powerful than all the boroughmongers.

Don't let any friend of the cause, however, entertain the vain hope that a letter from any noble lord will secure the full triumph of the Free Trade cause. This principle for which we have been so long contending will prove successful when the Free-traders are prepared to work out their own redemption, and not before. We have everything to encourage us, however; and I for one believe that the day of our redemption draweth nigh. But we must not relax in our labours; on the contrary, we must be more zealous, more energetic, more laborious than we have ever yet been. When the enemy is wavering, then is the time to press upon him. I call, then, upon all who have any sympathy in our cause, who have any promptings of humanity, or who feel any interest in the well-being of their fellow-men, all who have apprehensions of scarcity or starvation, to come forward with their efforts to avert this horrible destiny, this dreadful and impending visitation.

———⟫⟫⟫ ✿ ⟪⟪⟪———

FREE TRADE.

XVIII.

BIRMINGHAM, NOVEMBER 13, 1845.

[The first indications of the potato disease of 1845, were noticed in the month of August. On Oct. 13, Sir Robert Peel, in a letter to Sir James Graham, said that there was no effectual remedy to impending scarcity, except the removal of 'impediments to import.' On the 31st, a meeting in Dublin, presided over by the Duke of Leinster, memorialised the Lord Lieutenant, to the effect that the Government should, without hesitation or delay, take the most prompt measures for the relief of the Irish people. On Nov. 1, Sir Robert Peel declared that it was impossible 'to maintain the existing restrictions on the free importation of grain.' The majority of the Cabinet were opposed to this step. In consequence, Sir Robert Peel resigned office on Dec. 5, and Lord John Russell was instructed to form a Government. On Dec. 10, Lord John Russell announced that he was unable to form a Government, and Sir Robert Peel resumed office. Lord Stanley (the late Lord Derby) declined to take part in this new Government, the basis of which, though not yet declared, was the gradual abolition of the Corn-laws, Parliament opened on Jan. 22, and on Jan. 27, Sir Robert Peel proposed his plan of a total repeal at the end of three years.]

I FEEL deeply indebted to you for the kind manner in which you have received the announcement of my name, and I may add that I am truly encouraged and gratified by the aspect of the meeting, and the numbers which have assembled here this evening. The greatest gratification next to that which I received from the manner in which the electors of Wolverhampton returned my friend, Mr. Villiers, to Parliament, is that such a tribute has been paid to him by the men

of Birmingham on this occasion, because it will put into his
hands additional weapons in the House of Commons, which I
am sure he will use right manfully for the common benefit of
us all. I did not come here for the purpose of making an
argumentative speech on the subject of commercial freedom,
for all now are made aware, from experience of the results,
how injuriously the restriction of commercial freedom acts,
and the poorest and least informed can see that those consequences which were predicted from the existing system are
approaching. We are now near a state of famine, and this,
as my friend, Mr. Villiers, has already stated, is one of the
results which were frequently predicted as to be expected from
the law which prevented the importation of corn. It was a
prediction which had been made by every enlightened speaker
and writer on the subject, from the time of Lord Grenville's
protest in the House of Lords, in 1815, down to the last pamphlet which had been written in relation to the question. We
have to expect, from time to time, amidst occasional gleams
of happiness and prosperity, such seasons of gloom as that
which we now witness in consequence of the operations of the
Corn-law, for that is its necessary result. A consequence,
which has been well described by my friend, Col. Thompson,
that veteran champion of Free Trade, in one of those graphic
comparisons for which he is so remarkable, when he said
the country, under the influence of the law, was like a bird
fastened with a spiral spring—it might wing its way aloft
for a short time, but only to be again inevitably drawn back
to where it ascended from.

What, then, is to be done? It seems that we have been
deluding ourselves, when we thought that the Government
was going to do something. We, it seems, have not a
Government such as several continental nations enjoy. Are
you not exceedingly gratified that you are not deemed worthy
of as good treatment at the hands of your Government as the
Russians, Turks, and Dutch receive from theirs? When these

Governments find that there is likely to be a scarcity, they do
that which common sense would dictate to any one; which
any community out of Bedlam would do at once, if left to
their own unbiassed judgment. Seeing that there was a prospect of an insufficient supply of food at home, they opened
wide their ports to admit the needed supply from any part
of the world from which it might come. This was precisely
what we expected from our rational Government. What
have thirteen noblemen and gentlemen been lately meeting in
Cabinet Council to discuss? I wish I had the names of the
thirteen notables, for they would be historic curiosities to
be handed down to posterity. What have they been deliberating upon? Was it whether they, from their own rents
and revenues, should make a large purchase of grain or potatoes abroad, in order to supply the wants of the people at
home? Was it whether they should vote a subsidy out of the
public taxes, with which to buy food for a starving people? It
was none of these. The difficulty upon which they solemnly
deliberated was this—whether they should allow the people
of this country to feed themselves?—and it seems they have
decided that they shall not. Rumours reach you—we cannot
tell you how well founded—that there is in the Cabinet a
division on this matter. You are told that Sir Robert Peel
and Sir James Graham have ranged themselves on the one
side, and the Duke of Wellington and Lord Stanley on the
other—that they are thus at variance with one another on this
question, and that the Duke and his party have decided that
you, the people of England, shall not be allowed to feed yourselves. Now this is the question on which we are at issue with
these mighty personages. If I mistake not, you have tried
the metal of the noble warrior before in Birmingham. He is a
man whom we all like to honour, as possessing those qualities
which entitle men to our esteem wherever possessed — high
courage, firmness of resolve, and indomitable perseverance.
But let me remind the noble Duke, that, notwithstanding his

victories on the field, he never yet entered into a contest with Englishmen in which he was not beaten. I say we *shall* feed ourselves. And, now that this battle must and shall be fought, I hope the veteran Duke will live long enough to test the quality of his countrymen again.

But, after all, it is not the Duke who is the Government—it is Sir Robert Peel. We hear in the House of Commons, in the palmy days of prosperity, when Peel brings forward his measures, and dictates to his servile colleagues what his policy shall be, the little word ' I,' repeated over and over again, reminding us that ' I, as Premier, act upon my own responsibility'—that ' I ' do this, and ' I ' do that. If he is the Prime Minister, we hold him responsible for his acts. Now, I see many attempts made to shirk that responsibility, and sometimes in a very shabby manner, by trying to make it appear that we who cry out against this responsibility mean to do him some personal violence. Was ever such a schoolboy trick as that resorted to by a man in his situation? He is fairly ashamed of it now, as are all who sit behind him, and who faithfully supported him in it. But we find the newspapers still dealing with this hypocritical and absurd argument. Why, for my own part, I would not touch a hair of his head, were he ever so much in my power. But what is the meaning of this responsibility on the part of a Minister? The Queen, with us, is not responsible. If we were governed by a Czar, or by a Grand Turk, we would then hold the sovereign responsible. In a system of constitutional government like ours, however, it is the Minister alone who is responsible. None but the Queen can issue an Order in Council for the opening of the ports, and the Queen would have done this long ago, but that she has to wait until Sir Robert Peel chooses to inform her that the Cabinet have consented to her doing so. We, then, as loyal subjects, are only pursuing a constitutional course when we bring him to the bar of public opinion, and declare him responsible for the acts of the Government.

We are told, to be sure, by those who still put forth their
daily nonsense in defence of monopoly, that to admit foreign
corn is not to hit the right way, by which the present difficulties can be surmounted. Instead of enlarging the supply
of food, we are told that certain great public works are to be
undertaken. Railroads are to be constructed, and lands to be
drained in Ireland, and the fisheries are to be promoted, and
all these devices are to be carried through by the instru-
mentality of the public purse. Anything will be done but
the right thing. That reminds me of the old story of the man
who had a horse, which was in the last stage of decline, for
want of sufficient nourishment, and who told his friend that
the horse would not thrive, although he had given him old
shoes, chips, and even oyster-shells. His friend replied to
him, 'Suppose you try corn.' Now we say to those gentlemen
who want to feed the people with pickaxes, shovels, fishing-
nets, and draining-tiles, 'Suppose you try a little corn.' You,
who do not sit in the House of Commons, would be astonished
how reluctantly we bring our opponents' noses to the corn-
crib. Now, mark me. Be prepared in the present emergency,
and constantly on your guard. There will be an effort made to
extract some enormous jobbery out of the anticipated famine.
The landlords in Ireland have not cultivated their lands, their
bogs, and wastes, as they should have done; and now they
will get the Government to do it for them out of the public
taxes, of all which, of course, they will reap the benefit. Now,
be on your guard. I have no objection, after everything else
which should first be resorted to has been done— after the
ports have been thrown open, without let or hindrance—if
charity is to be administered to the Irish people, that it
should rather be bestowed in the shape of payment of wages
than as eleemosynary grants.

I read in the papers of to-day the speech of the King of
Belgium to the Chambers in that country, in which he con-
gratulated them that they have opened the ports for the

admission of foreign corn, and that being done, they are enabled, by a vote of public money, to execute certain public works, to make up for the deficiency in employment, and thereby supply the people with food. In Belgium, you see, they do not expect to feed their people with mere pickaxes and shovels. They first let in the needed supply of foreign corn, and then, by supplying funds for the execution of public works, provide the people with the means of feeding themselves without resorting to charity. Was ever a people so insulted as are the English people by the arguments of the monopolists? What is our present dilemma? It is neither more nor less than the want of food. Now what do people work for? Not for work itself, certainly, but for the food which they are enabled to procure by it. The monopolist writers think, or so pretend, that it is work that is wanted at present. Now work is never wanted but as a means of getting something out of it. We have the highest authority—that of sacred writ itself—for considering work a curse, but a curse which is mercifully sweetened by the rewards of labour. But where are the rewards to come from if there is an insufficient supply of food to meet the wants of the people? The Irish are about to suffer from a famine. It will not confine its effects to those who can work upon railroads, but will also, in all probability, affect every man, woman, and child scattered over the face of that country, and, with the exception of the wealthy portion of the population, the mass of the inhabitants of towns. Those able to work, and those not able, will equally suffer. Are these the people into whose hands, with your supply of food manifestly deficient, you can put pickaxes and shovels, and expect them to work, without holding out to them the prospect of receiving the ample and legitimate reward of labour?

What happened in the spring of 1822, I am afraid, is very likely to happen again. Mark my words, and I speak them in sorrow, that next spring will develope the calamitous result of our present suicidal policy. It was only in the spring after the harvest of 1821 that the evil to which I have just alluded was felt. In the spring of 1822, when the country people had eaten up the potatoes which were left them, they flocked in crowds to the towns for subsistence; for it is in towns that you find ample supplies of food generally accumulated, and in the towns the starving masses had to be fed from the charity of their fellow-countrymen. Depend upon it you will have to feed large masses of the people of Ireland in a like manner out of a public fund before midsummer. But where is the subsistence to come from which you are to administer to them? It is not in this country, and must be procured elsewhere. But does it not behove the Minister of the Crown to see, in the present emergency, that not a moment is lost in accumulating in this country such a stock of food as may not be procurable next spring, when famine presses heavily upon us, for less than double the price which some time ago we would have been called upon to pay for it? Mark how our present rulers are tampering with the existing alarming condition of the country. You behold the organs of the Government giving vent to statements, the object of which is to induce us to believe that the evil does not exist to the extent which has been assigned to it. Is there, then, a deep-laid conspiracy on the part of any one to lead us falsely into the anticipation of evils which there is no real ground to apprehend? That cannot be. Have we not seen that solemn masses have been offered up in Roman Catholic chapels, beseeching the Disposer of all Events that He would graciously avert the impending calamity? Did we not see in yesterday's paper that the primate and bishops of Ireland had ordered prayers to be offered up, to arrest, if possible, the progress of the threatened evil? Have we not had boards of guardians, on more occasions than one, memorialising Government to do what they could to moderate the severity of the apprehended famine? If all this be so, can it, then, be possible that any person or persons have entered into a wide and diabolical conspiracy, for the purpose

of trifling with the most sacred feelings of humanity, or is the
statement of the evil a lamentable and incontrovertible fact?
That statement is unfortunately but too melancholy a truth,
and yet the Government is tampering with this most critical
juncture of our national welfare, and leads us to infer that it is
prepared to do nothing.

Well, then, as Mr. Villiers and Earl Ducie have well advised
you, it is high time for the people to speak out. There have
been scarcely any demonstrations as yet in the country in
favour of the immediate opening of the ports. And why?
Because every one expected that every successive mail from
London would carry to him the welcome decision of the
Cabinet that the ports had been already opened. People did
not choose to waste their strength and their energies in preparing for a demonstration, which was to take place at the end
of a week's time, in favour of an object which they thought
would be accomplished every twenty-four hours. It now
behoves the people of every town to meet, as the people of
Manchester are going to meet, and throw upon the Government the whole responsibility of the present state of things,
and call upon them immediately to open the ports; and, when
once opened, they will never be shut again. That is the true
reason why the ports have not already been opened. If there
had been no Anti-Corn-law League, they would have been
opened a month ago. It is because they know well in the
Cabinet, and because the landlords also well know, that the
question of total and immediate repeal of the Corn-laws is at
stake, that they will risk, like desperate gamblers, all that
may befal us during the next six months, rather than part
with that law.

Well, if they won't open the ports, somebody must make
them. You will be the laughing-stock of all Christendom
if you do not make them: only think of the Dutchman—
think of Mynheer whilst smoking his pipe, and seeing the
ships coming in from America laden with corn for him. How

he will laugh at your stupidity when he sees Englishmen
starving, while Dutchmen are well fed! We are not sunk
quite so low as that yet. But for Sir Robert Peel, what a
critical moment in his fortune has now past! I say past, for
let him do the act at the end of this month, which he ought
to have done ten days ago, still he will not be the same man
that he would have been had he done it then. There is not
even a child in statesmanship that could not have then told
Sir Robert Peel, ' Now is the critical period of your political
fortune—this is the tide of your political life; if you take it
at its flood, you go on to such a fortune as no statesman ever
attained in this country before; but if you miss it—if you
allow the flood to pass by you—you will prove to the world
that you have been all your life a pretender, and a mere hoax
on the credulity of your countrymen.'

We have all been thinking for some time past that Peel
was the man—not the coming man—but the come man.
Everybody began to say, ' Peel is the man for a practical
statesman, to govern a practical people;' and I have no hesitation in saying, that if Sir Robert Peel had taken the course
I have suggested, of boldly bearding the Iron Duke, and at
once dismissing him and his tail from the Cabinet, I have no
hesitation in saying, so far as Lancashire and Yorkshire are
concerned, he would have rallied around him the whole of the
mighty population of those counties as one man in his support. We should have buried Whig or Tory from the moment
we found Sir Robert Peel had abolished the Corn-laws. There
would have been a union of all men and all classes in those
districts in support of the man who had the courage and the
honesty to put an end to this atrocious and long-continued
injustice. But he has not done it, and I venture to prophesy
that he won't do it. Somebody else will have to do it, and
we are not yet so badly off in England but that we may find
somebody willing and able to do the will of the country whenever it is unmistakingly expressed. We are told that it would

be useless to pass a law to admit foreign corn, for there is
none to come in. Then what has the Cabinet been deliberating
about so long? If there was no corn to come in, why did the
Government hold four or five Cabinet Councils to decide whether it should come in or not? Some of the protectionists tell
us, that even if our supply is deficient, the remedy is not to
look to foreign countries, but to our native produce. But that
is not the rule they follow in anything else but corn. I heard
not long ago Mr. Gladstone expound most eloquently the
great importance of permitting the free admission of foreign
lard, flax, hides, and many other things, as being necessary as
the raw materials for our manufactures. Though flax is grown
in England, though we produce hides, and make lard, these
are admitted from abroad; but with regard to corn, the argument is, that we are not to look to foreign countries for an
increased or supplementary supply of that article. And so it
is. It is the corn question upon which the mighty struggle
will be, after all. And I will whisper in your ear the reason
why;—corn is the article upon which rents are fixed, and by
which tithes are regulated. Do not deceive yourselves, and
suppose you will get a free admission of foreign corn—that is,
wheat — except after a considerable struggle. They do not
mind so much about Indian corn. Lord Sandon the other day
wrote from Liverpool, that he has no objection to Indian corn
coming in. And why? It does not regulate tithes, or operate
on fixed rents in this country.

My noble friend, Lord Ducie, was quite right when he said
that the landowner might do as well without Corn-laws as
with them, and the farmer and farm-labourer much better.
But, unfortunately, everybody in the same position is not up
to the light of my noble friend. The squire and landowner
in general think differently from my noble friend, and they
actually hiss him at their agricultural meetings. I tell this as
a specimen of their intelligence. But they only act according
to their own convictions and their own ignorant prejudice.

And here let me remind you, that this country is governed by the ignorance of the country. And I do not say this without proof; for amongst those Members of the majority of the House of Commons who uphold the Corn-law protective principle, there is not a man of anything like average intellect who dares to speak in their favour. You cannot appeal to a single statesman that deserves a moment's regard as such, who has uttered anything like an authoritative dictum in their favour. There is no single writer of eminence who has not repudiated the doctrines of the monopolists. They are condemned alike by all the intelligence of this and of past ages, and yet they rule this country at this time with more tyranny than even the Grand Turk himself governs with. These people, though possessing no intelligence themselves, yet find people to do their work for them. They will find Sir Robert Peel to do it, and that against his own conscientious convictions; for there can be no doubt that Sir R. Peel is at heart as good a Free-trader as I am myself. He has told us so in the House of Commons again and again; nor do I doubt that Sir R. Peel has in his inmost heart the desire to be the man who shall carry out the principles of Free Trade in this country. But he has been tampering with the question in order to adapt his policy to the ignorance of his party, and we see the state into which the country has been brought the while.

We have, however, one consolation—we have run the fox to earth at last, and know he cannot double on us again. The question cannot be dealt with in another session, as it has been when the country has been blessed with her abundant crops, and when trade was good, and the people all employed. If you had seen the jaunty airs Sir Robert Peel gave himself when we talked of Free Trade in past sessions, you would have been amused, if not astonished. But that is all at an end now, and next session we shall have him fairly pinned, and he knows it too. And I can tell you, that if there is one man

who will go up to Parliament next session with a heavier
heart than another, that man is Sir Robert Peel. It is my
belief, that if in the meantime he does not take the step of
throwing open the ports, he will not dare to face us at all next
session. Of this I am quite sure, that if the leading Members
of the Opposition, in another session, take the position they
ought to take—in the van of the people; and, having the
people at their back, stand boldly forth as the advocates of
those sound principles we are met here to support, and will
show themselves ready and determined to apply them as
fairly, as effectually, and as permanently as my honourable
friend, Mr. Villiers, would, and Sir Robert Peel takes his
place in Parliament without first opening the ports, I undertake to say that they will shake him out of office in a week.

But I do not like altogether the idea of giving Peel up.
He is a Lancashire man—and in my part of the country
we are proud of Lancashire men. We used to think that
Sir Robert cast a sheep's eye on the tall chimneys, and that
he had something of a lingering kindness for Lancashire; and
I can tell him it would have been a proud day for the Lancashire men, when they saw a Lancashire man, and the son of a
Lancashire manufacturer, stand forward to rescue the commerce of the country from the shackles of that feudal and
senseless oppression it has so long laboured under. I must
not forget that I am charged with a message from Lancashire
to you. You have already heard what we have done by our
twelve months' labour at the registration. We have secured
that county for the Free-traders; and you have also heard
what we have done in the neighbouring northern counties
with their constituencies of 70,000 or 80,000—constituencies
greater than those of all the counties south of Middlesex put
together. We sent Mr. Hickin to Staffordshire to attend the
last revision—he followed the barrister to every court; and
the result is, we have gained between 1000 and 2000 votes.
The expense of this proceeding has been paid by the League

out of its funds, and when we asked you to contribute your
money to the League, it was with the view of spending it in
the same way for your benefit. I believe South Staffordshire
is safe at the next election for two Free-traders. But we
must not rest there—we must do the same in other counties.
In South Lancashire we have put such a majority of Free-
traders on the registry, that, unless I am much mistaken, our
opponents will not dare to contest another election with us.
I say every man in Birmingham who can afford it must buy a
40*s.* freehold, and so qualify himself to vote for South Staffordshire. In Manchester, we say to every man who has a
good coat on his back, ' You must buy a freehold, and qualify
for the county.' But you have a county nearer here—you are
partly in North Warwickshire as well as Coventry; and if you
qualify, what is to prevent your returning two Free-traders
for that place at the next election ? Shame on you if you
doubt it ! Think of the beauty of the 40*s.* freehold ! Why,
it is the best part of the Reform Bill—it is an inheritance
handed down to us from our ancestors five hundred years ago.
A man for 50*l.* can buy one of these freeholds, and place himself, as regards the county franchise, upon an equality with
the squire who has an estate of 5000*l.* a-year.

The landowners have multiplied their 50*l.* tenants-at-will,
and, do what they will, they cannot stretch out their land like
India-rubber ; but you can make every cobbler's stall, every
butcher's shamble, every stable, the means of conferring the
franchise, and placing its owner on an equality with the man
who holds an estate of 50,000*l.* a-year. I say, too, if you
choose, you can ensure the return of two Free-traders for
Worcestershire. Worcester must also be won. There was a
desultory effort made to gain North Warwickshire the other
day, which ended disgracefully, and which showed the necessity of some local organisation. 'Tis votes, not meetings, that
persuade Sir Robert Peel. In Staffordshire, the revising barrister acknowledged that the League had purged the registry

of an immense number of fictitious votes. The finger of scorn
should be pointed at any of the middle classes in the northern
towns who did not become co-electors. The man is not fit to
be a freeman who, when he could afford it, refuses to pay 50*l.*
for the franchise. Having qualified every man you can, you
must proceed to a systematic purging of the registers. Many
silly persons object to this as disfranchising the people; but
if our opponents strike off our votes, are theirs to remain
untouched? (' No, no.') We should be in such a position as
to be able to tell the Government, ' You must give up the
Corn-laws, or give up a good deal more.'

The aristocracy of this country have the army, the navy,
the colonies, and a large amount of expenditure, at their
disposal. 'Tis a perfect paradise for the aristocracy in this
country, if they knew only how to behave themselves—not as
angels, but as decent, honest, rational men. Whom have they
to govern? Practical, industrious, intelligent men, whose
thoughts centred in their business, and who would gladly
leave to those above them the toil of government, if those
were willing to allow commerce and industry fair play. What
a people for an aristocracy to govern! And yet they risk
all for the sake of a miserable tax on bread, which is of no
earthly benefit even to themselves. Be prepared for a crisis
as to this law, which may come on even before the next dissolution. You will see by the swaying of parties, and the
general agitation of the public mind in the next session, that
some great change is approaching; and when you discover
these symptoms, don't mind who goes out or in, but keep
your eyes steadily fixed on this corn question; and when the
crisis does come, let the multitudinous numbers of Lancashire,
Yorkshire, and Staffordshire be prepared to act with united
strength against the vile fabric of monopoly, over which, when
levelled with the earth, will be driven the ploughshare of peace,
that prosperity may arise out of its ruins.

FREE TRADE.

XIX.

LONDON, DECEMBER 17, 1845.

I THINK some of the protection societies would be glad to have our overflow to-night. If this agitation continues, we shall have to build an edifice as large as St. Paul's to hold the Leaguers. I believe to-day we have had application for 30,000 tickets of admission; we have now many hundreds round this building more than can be accommodated; and we have a great many more inside than can be comfortable. But I feel confidence in the disposition of all good Leaguers to accommodate each other; and I must say that I have seen in front of me every disposition to be quiet; but it is the same to-night as I have observed generally in my great experience at public meetings, that if there is any disturbance it is always amongst the aristocracy upon the platform.

I think this meeting is a sufficient proof of the exciting circumstances under which we meet to-night. I need not say a word. [Mr. Cobden was here interrupted by a slight disturbance arising from the extremely crowded state of the stage.] Some gentlemen at the back of the stage wish to have my assurance that there is no room in front; I can assure them that there is not vacant space for a mouse. I think the aspect of the meeting is a sufficient illustration of the present crisis of our great movement. The manner in which we are gathered together; the excited feeling which animates all present—all indicate that there is something peculiar in the present phase of our movement. I do not know how it is, but if I see other people inclined to throw up their caps and become exceedingly excited, it always makes me feel and look grave; for I always think there is the most danger when people are the least on their guard in this wicked world. Doubtless we have brought our cause to a new position—we have got it into the hands of politicians. The 'ins' and the 'outs' are quarrelling over it. But I am very anxious to impress upon you and our friends throughout the kingdom—for what we say here is read by hundreds and thousands elsewhere—that it is not our business to form Cabinets—to choose individuals who shall carry out our principles; we are not to trust to others to do our work; we are not to feel confident that the work will be done till it is done; and I will tell you when and when only I shall consider it done—when I see the sheet of the Act of Parliament wet from the printer's containing the total abolition of the Corn-laws.

I have always expected in the course of our agitation that we should knock a Government or two on the head before we succeeded. The Government of 1841 can hardly be said to have been killed by the Corn-law; it took the Corn-law as a last desperate dose in order to cure it of a long and lingering disease — but it proved fatal to it. I think we may say, too, that the recent Government has died of the Corn-law; and our business must be, gentlemen, to try and make the fate of the last Government a warning to the next. We do not certainly exactly know yet why Sir Robert Peel ran away from his own law; we have had no explanation. I have been in town for three or four days. I thought when I came from the country I might probably get a little behind the scenes, and learn something about it; but I am as much in the dark now as when I came from Lancashire. I cannot learn why it was that Sir Robert Peel bolted. From what did he run? It was his own law, passed in 1842; it was deliberated upon about six months in 1841. It was not passed at the pressing solicitation of the people for any such law. I know that almost the whole of the people petitioned against it. It was his own handiwork, done in defiance of the people; and now, in 1845, with still the same Parliament, with a majority of 90 to back him, the very men who passed the law being still at his back, he suddenly runs away and leaves his sliding-scale as a legacy to his successors. Gentlemen, if he had carried his own law with him—if he had only carried off his sliding-scale to Tamworth—I do not think we should have made many inquiries about him. But he has left his law, and we do not know how he is going to deal with it in future.

I suppose, when we meet in Parliament, which may be early next month—at all events, the sooner the better—the first thing I shall look to with some degree of interest will be an answer to the question, What is the reason of this sudden dissolution of the Cabinet? I shall await Sir Robert Peel's explanation with very great interest. He will doubtless be able to tell us whether the facts collected by his commissioners in Ireland as well as in England were of such a nature as to impress him with the idea that we are verging on a probable famine in one country, if not in both. If that be the case, I suppose he will also tell us that, so far as he was concerned, he was the advocate in his Cabinet for the suspension of his own handiwork—the sliding-scale. Well, that being the case, I presume, when Parliament meets, he will assist us to do that which he could not accomplish himself with his refractory Cabinet. I expect — I do not know whether I may be rash in expecting it — from Sir Robert Peel straightforward conduct.

There are people who tell us that this Corn-law must not

be suspended suddenly, that it must not be dealt with rashly and precipitately, and that, if we are to have the repeal of the Corn-law, it must be done gradually, step by step. Well, gentlemen, that might have been in the eyes of some a very statesmanlike way of doing it six or seven years ago. Some people would have thought last year, when wheat was at 47s. a quarter, that if a law had been passed then providing for the extinction of the Corn-law in two or three years, that that would have been no very bad measure to have been obtained; but who will propose now to pass a law imposing a fixed duty on corn next spring, to go off 3s. or 4s. the spring after, and 3s. or 4s. the spring after that, till it comes to nothing? That would not suit the exigencies of the present movement. Our wise Legislature, our wise Conservative statesmen, would not deal with this question when they might have dealt with it with some advantage to their own policy. We were pressing on the Government to deal with the Corn-laws last year and the year before, when wheat was at 47s. a quarter, but we were told then we were rash men; that the Corn-law had not had a fair trial; that ours was not the way to deal with it; that we must wait to see how it worked.

Well, now they are seeing how it has worked. But there is no time for temporising now. Nature has stepped in; Providence has interfered, and has inflicted a famine upon the land, and set at nought all the contrivance, delay, and modifications of statesmen. They have but one way of dealing with this question. It is of no use asking us for a feather-bed to drop our aristocracy upon; they might have had a feather-bed, if there had been one to offer them; but there is no feather-bed for them now. They must have the total and immediate repeal of the Corn-laws; not because the League has demanded it; not out of any deference to the Shibboleth of clubs like ours. No, we do not ask them to bow to any such dictation as that: we will not inflict any unnecessary humiliation upon our landowners; but they have put off this good work

so long, until Nature has stepped in, and now they must bow
to the law of nature without any delay.

Gentlemen, we meet Parliament next session—I take it for
granted—with but one proposition before us,—that is, the
immediate and total abolition of the Corn-laws. No Minister
can take office without proposing that measure, whether Sir
Robert Peel or Lord John Russell. I defy them to take office
and come before Parliament without the Queen's Speech proposing that measure. No; we will not exult over them; it
is not our doing, after all; we have prepared the public in
some degree to take advantage of a natural calamity, but
we are not so well prepared as we should have been if they
had given us a year or two more; the potato rot has tripped
up the heels of Sir Robert Peel, but it has also stopped
our registration agents a little. We should like to have
had another year of qualification for counties. If we had had
another year or two, we could have shown the monopolist
landowners that we can transfer power in this country from
the hands of a class totally into the hands of the middle
and industrial classes of this country. We shall go on with
that movement, and I hope it will never stop; but we
shall have to deal with the crisis of the Corn-law question
next session.

The Queen's Speech, within a month of this time, must
recommend the abolition of the Corn-laws. I want to get
into the House of Commons again to have some talk about
that question. Oh ! it is very heavy work, I assure you; it
is heavier work every day to come into these enthusiastic
meetings, and talk of this question, for we meet no opponents.
I do not know how it is, but I have that quality of com-
bativeness, as phrenologists call it, and unless I meet with
some opposition I am as dull as ditch-water. Well, there is
no man to be found at large out of the House of Commons
who can be got in public to say a word in defence of the
Corn-laws; that is, you cannot hear any attempted defence

out of their own protection societies, and you know they are privileged people.

I am anxious to meet them in the House of Commons upon this subject; but it will be an odd scene when we assemble next session, for we shall not know where to sit. There will be such greetings in the lobbies, one asking the other, 'On which side are you going to sit?' And then, the greatest curiosity of all, the greatest subject of interest, will be to see where Sir R. Peel is to sit. I should not wonder if we shall have to find him a chair, and put him in the middle of the floor.

Now, I shall be somewhat interested in witnessing the arguments that will be used by the protectionists in defence of this Corn-law. Recollect, the debate will come on with reference to the exigency of the moment. The Corn-law must be suspended instantly, if Lord John Russell takes office. He will be a bold man if he does. But if he does, I suppose he will either suspend the law the next day by an Order in Council, or he will call us together; and he will throw down his proposition, 'Either you must suspend that Corn-law at once, or I will not hold office a week.' Then the debate will turn as to the necessity of suspending this Corn-law; and we shall have gentlemen getting up from Dorsetshire and Essex, protesting that there is a great abundance of everything in the country, that there is no scarcity at all, no potato rot, and that there is a full average quantity and quality of wheat. [Cheers, and cries of ' Plenty of curry.']

Then I should not wonder, gentlemen, if we were to hear some moral receipts for feeding the people. You know Dr. Buckland has lately been publishing a paper read at Oxford to the Ashmolean Society, I believe, and he has shown that people can live very well on peas, can get on tolerably well upon beans, and, if there is nothing else to be had, they can live pretty well upon mangold-wurzel; and he gives an instance of one good lady who lived, I do not know how many days, by sucking the starch out of her white pocket-handkerchief. Now, mangold-wurzel, starch, and beans, mixed with a little curry-powder, would do very well.

Well, gentlemen, we shall have a division as well as a debate. I should like to see the names of those good men in the House of Commons who will vote against opening the ports—that is, the men who will decree that we shall not be treated as well as the Prussians, the Turks, the Poles, and the Dutchmen; if they outvote us upon that proposition, we shall have a general election. I should like to see some of those curry-powder candidates go down to their constituents. I would advise you to get doses of the curry-powder water ready; a little hot water, and a pinch of curry-powder stirred up, makes a man very comfortable to go to bed with, they say. Try it upon some of the protectionist candidates.

Gentlemen, this is no laughing subject, after all. As my friend, Mr. Villiers, says, it is a question very much between Sir Robert Peel and Lord John Russell now. I have no reason, and I think you will all admit it, to feel any very great respect for Sir Robert Peel; he is the only man in the House of Commons that I can never speak a word to in private without forfeiting my own respect, and the respect of all those men who sit around me. But though I say that, and though I am justified in saying it, yet this I will say, that so deeply have I this question of the Corn-laws at heart, that if Sir Robert Peel will take the same manly, straightforward part that Lord John Russell has taken—if he will avow an intelligible course of action—that is what I want, no mystification—if he will do that, I will as heartily co-operate with him as with any man in the House of Commons.

I should think now the time was come when every statesman, of whatever party, who has a particle of intelligence and conscience, must be anxious to remove this question of supplying the food of the people out of the category of party politics; for see what a fearful state it places the Ministry in. They

maintain a law for the purpose of regulating the supply of
food to the people; if the food falls short, the people assail
the Government as the cause of their scarcity of food: this is
a responsibility that no Government or human power ought to
assume to itself. It is a responsibility that we should never
invest a Government with, if that Government did not assume
to itself the functions of the Deity.

Gentlemen, why should we tax the Government with being
the cause of our suffering when we are visited with a defective
harvest? Why should a Government fly away? Why should
a Prime Minister retire from office because there is a failure
and rot in the potatoes? Suppose we had a devastating flood
that swept away half our houses in a day, we should never
think of charging the Executive Government with being the
cause of our calamities. The Government does not undertake
to build houses, or to keep houses for us. Suppose half of
our mercantile marine was swept away with a hurricane, and
if the whole of it was submerged in the flood, we should never
think of flying at the Government, and making them responsible for such a calamity. On the contrary, if we had
such a dire event by flood or fire happening to the country,
we should instinctively rally round the Government, one helping the other in order to mitigate the horrors of such a
calamity. And why should it be otherwise with supplying
the food of the people? Why, because the Government of
this country,—Ministers and Parliament in this land—have
arrogated to themselves functions which belong not to man,
but to nature—not to laws of Parliament, but to the laws of
Providence—not to regulations of statesmen, but to regulations of the merchants of the world; it is because they have
taken upon themselves superhuman functions that we make
them responsible for divine inflictions.

Then, gentlemen, I hope that every intelligent statesman
in this country will be anxious to get rid of this question of
protection to agriculture. But there is another reason why

our intelligent statesmen ought to wish to bury it so deep
that even its ghost cannot haunt us again—this ragged and
tattered banner of protection—and it is this, that if you
leave a rag of it behind, these protectionist squires will hoist
that ragged standard again.   And my firm conviction is,
that they will find farmers enough to rally round that old
rag—they will have the same organisation, the same union
in the counties between the protectionist squires and their
dupes, the protectionist farmers—that would prove a hindrance to everything like an enlightened and rational government on the part of any Administration.   I say, then,
whether it be Sir Robert Peel, or whether it be Lord John
Russell, put an end to this protective principle; destroy it
altogether; leave no part of it behind.   And the only way
you can do that is by proposing honestly, totally to abolish
the Corn-laws, and the rest of the system will abolish itself
very soon afterwards.

There are terms talked about; they talk of some terms;
they talk of re-adjusting taxation.   I am told Sir Robert Peel
has got a scheme as long as my arm for mixing up a hundred
other things with this Corn-law.   I say we will have no such
mystification of our plain rights.   We have had too much of
his mystification before.   In the north of England, where we
are practical people, we have a prejudice in favour of doing one
thing at a time.   Now, we will abolish the Corn and Provision
Laws if you please; that shall be one thing we will do; and
anything else they propose to do we will take it upon its merits,
as we take the Corn-law upon its demerits.   They propose a
modification of taxation, and I am told that Sir Robert Peel
has some such sop in view to compensate the landowners.   He
has not been a very safe guide hitherto to the landowners of
this country; he has led them into a quagmire with his
leadership.   I predict that if Sir Robert Peel provokes a
discussion upon the subject of taxation in this country, that
he will prove as great an enemy to the landowners as he is

likely to prove, according to their views of the question, in
his advocacy of protection for them.

I warn Ministers, and I warn landowners, and the aristocracy of this country, against forcing upon the attention of
the middle and industrious classes the subject of taxation.
For, great as I consider the grievance of the protective system;
mighty as I consider the fraud and injustice of the Corn-laws,
I verily believe, if you were to bring forward the history of
taxation in this country for the last 150 years, you will find as
black a record against the landowners as even in the Corn-law
itself. I warn them against ripping up the subject of taxation. If they want another League, at the death of this one—if
they want another organisation, and a motive—for you cannot
have these organisations without a motive and principle—
then let them force the middle and industrious classes of
England to understand how they have been cheated, robbed,
and bamboozled upon the subject of taxation; and the end
will be—(now I predict it for the consolation of Sir Robert
Peel and his friends)—if they force a discussion of this
question of taxation; if they make it understood by the
people of this country how the landowners here, 150 years
ago, deprived the sovereign of his feudal rights over them;
how the aristocracy retained their feudal rights over the
minor copyholders; how they made a bargain with the king
to give him 4*s.* in the pound upon their landed rentals, as a
quit charge for having dispensed with these rights of feudal
service from them; if the country understand as well as I
think I understand, how afterwards this landed aristocracy
passed a law to make the valuation of their rental final, the
bargain originally being that they should pay 4*s.* in the pound
of the yearly rateable value of their rental, as it was worth to
let for, and then stopped the progress of the rent by a law,
making the valuation final,—that the land has gone on increasing tenfold in many parts of Scotland, and fivefold in
many parts of England, while the land-tax has remained

the same as it was 150 years ago—if they force us to
understand how they have managed to exempt themselves
from the probate and legacy duty on real property—how they
have managed, sweet innocents that taxed themselves so
heavily, to transmit their estates from sire to son without
taxes or duties, while the tradesman who has accumulated by
thrifty means his small modicum of fortune is subject at his
death to taxes and stamps before his children can inherit his
property; if they force us to understand how they have exempted their tenants' houses from taxes, their tenants' horses
from taxes, their dogs from taxes, their draining-tiles from
taxes—if they force these things to be understood, they will
be making as rueful a bargain as they have already made by
resisting the abolition of the Corn-law.

Do not let them tell me I am talking in a wild, chimerical
strain; they told me so, seven years ago, about this Corn-law.
I remember right well, when we came to London six years
ago, in the spring of 1839, there were three of us in a small
room at Brown's Hotel, in Palace Yard, we were visited by a
nobleman, one who had taken an active part in the advocacy
of a modification of the Corn-laws, but not the total repeal;
he asked us, 'What is it that has brought you to town, and
what do you come to seek?' We said, 'We come to seek the
total and immediate repeal of the Corn-laws.' The nobleman
said, with a most emphatic shake of the head, 'You will overturn the monarchy as soon as you will accomplish that.' Now,
the very same energy, starting from our present vantage-ground,
having our opponents down as we have them now—the same
energy—ay, half the energy, working for seven years—would
enable a sufficient number of the middle and working classes
of this country to qualify for the counties, and might transfer the
power utterly and for ever from the landowners of this country
to the middle and working classes, and they might tax the
land, and tax the large proprietors and rich men of every
kind, as they do in all the countries of Europe but England.

Again and again I warn Sir Robert Peel—I warn the aristocracy of this country—that, on the settlement of this question, they do not force us into a discussion upon the peculiar burthens upon land.

Well, they cannot meet us now with any modification of the law, because—however it might have suited past years to have let them down on a feather-bed, as they call it, to have given a salve to their wounds—the crisis of the potato rot will not wait for it now; they dare not open the question of taxation. What will they attempt to do, then? What can they do? Why, I would advise them as friends, to do justice speedily and promptly; and if we take the repeal of the Corn-laws, and ask no further questions—if we let bygones be bygones—they ought to be abundantly satisfied with the bargain. I am disposed, gentlemen, to ask no questions, to let bygones be bygones. I want no triumph; I want no exaltation. I think no one will accuse us of having crowed over converts, or exulted over repentant sinners. We exist as an association, solely for the object of converting people. It would be a very bad piece of tactics if we ever offered the slightest impediment to an honest conversion to our ranks. We began in a minority of the intelligent people of England. I am willing to admit it, we had to inform the country and to arouse it; we live only to convert; and I am very glad indeed to congratulate you upon having converted some very important allies lately.

I feel very great pleasure in noticing a statement which appears in to-day's paper in the news from Ireland. It is a report of a speech of Mr. O'Connell. We of the Anti-Corn-law League have every reason to feel indebted to Mr. O'Connell for the uniform and consistent course which he has taken in reference to the Corn-laws. From the beginning he has acted and co-operated with us both in our great meetings and in the House of Commons; but I have never considered him as acting here upon English ground. I have always regarded

him as promoting a measure for the benefit of his own countrymen in Ireland, when he has co-operated with us for the
repeal of the Corn-laws; because we have had the best
possible proof, in the continued misery and semi-starvation
of the Irish people, that whatever good the Corn-law may
have done to the landowner in England, it is quite certain
that it has never been of any benefit to the people of
Ireland, a large majority of whom never taste anything
better than lumper potatoes. Then, both upon Irish and
English grounds, I am glad we have an opportunity of
co-operating with Mr. O'Connell. I rejoice that upon this
question, at all events, there cannot be a line of demarcation
drawn between the two countries. Our interests are theirs,
and theirs are ours. They want more bread, God knows, in
Ireland; and if we can help Mr. O'Connell to give it them
they shall have it.

I am not going to talk argumentatively to-night; and I
have but to add, that the times that are coming are just those
that will most require our vigilance and activity. Demonstrations now are comparatively valueless; we shall want you
all next spring. There is a great struggle for that period.
The Duke of Richmond has told us he shall trust to the
hereditary legislators of the country. Well, I might say,—

'Hereditary bondsmen, know ye not!'

I will back the 'hereditary bondsmen' against the hereditary
legislators upon this question. But, no; we have not all the
hereditary legislators opposed to us. I am glad of it; we
have the best of them in our ranks; we always had the best
of them with us. If they have not all joined our club we do
not care about it, so long as they adopt our principles.

I have never been for making this a class question. I have
preached from the first that we would have the co-operation of
the best and most intelligent of all ranks in life—working,
middle, and upper classes. No, no; we will have no war of

classes in this country. It is bad enough that in free and constitutional States you must have your parties; we cannot, in our state of enlightenment, manage our institutions without them; but it shall never be our fault if this question of the Corn-laws becomes a class question, between the middle and working classes on the one side, and the hereditary legislators on the other. No, no; we will save the Duke of Richmond's order from the Duke of Richmond. We have got Lord Morpeth, and we have also Lords Radnor, Ducie, and Kinnaird; and a good many more; and among the rest Earl Grey, our earliest and most tried champion of the aristocracy. This is one proof that ours is not a class question, and that we are not at war with the whole landed aristocracy; but if the Duke of Richmond sets up the Noodles and Doodles of the aristocracy, why, before we have done with them, they shall be as insignificant and more contemptible than the round-frocked peasantry upon his Grace's estate.

This is a question that, during the next three months, will allow of no sleeping: we must be all watching. I have confidence in Lord J. Russell; I think, if you have his word you have his bond. I do not know at this moment whether he will take office or not; but if he does, and has Lord Morpeth and Lord Grey associated with him, you are as safe with them as you are with Lord John Russell himself. I do not know who besides he may have. [A Voice: 'Yourself.'] Yes, I will be the watchman, so long as bad characters are abroad.

But Lord John may have some difficulty, perhaps, in making up a Cabinet as willing to stick to the principles of Free Trade as himself; and he may not find them quite so willing to coerce those refractory legislators as he may wish. We must back him; we must show him the power we can give him to carry this question. They talk of Lord John Russell having made a mistake in putting out that letter to the citizens of London. I have heard some mean and shabby people say, if he had not put out that letter, how much freer

he would have been now. Why, Lord John Russell would
have been nothing now without that letter. The Queen
would not have sent for him without that letter. Lord John
Russell would no more have commanded the people's confidence, or excited their hopes or enthusiasm, without that
letter, any more than Sir Robert Peel himself would have
done. It is a proof not only of the vitality of the principle,
that, without joining the League, he did not join us by the
mere enunciation of a principle which the people quite understand and feel. Lord John Russell, as if by change of a
magic lantern, became from the most obscure the most popular
and prominent man of his day.

Ours is the only party that is now solid, growing, and
consolidated in this country; all that is good of the Whig
party has joined the Free-traders — the Whig party is
nothing without the Free-trade party. The Tory or Conservative party, call them what you will, are broken to atoms
by the disruption in the ranks of their leaders. The League
stands erect and aloft, amidst the ruins of all factions. Let
us hold on to the principle which has made us as strong as we
now find ourselves; let us hold on to it, not turning to the
right or to the left. No man, or body of men, Ministers or
ex-Ministers, have a right to expect it, nor shall they have it;
we will not turn a hair's breadth to keep men in office, or put
them out of office; and if we maintain this ground—ay, for
another six months—then we shall be near that time which
I so long for, when this League shall be dissolved into its
primitive elements by the triumph of its principles.

FREE TRADE

XX.

MANCHESTER, JANUARY 15, 1846.

I SHALL begin the few remarks which I have to offer to this meeting by proposing, contrary to my usual custom, a resolution; and it is, ' That the merchants, manufacturers, and other members of the National Anti-Corn-law League claim no protection whatever for the manufactured products of this country, and desire to see obliterated for ever the few nominally protective duties against foreign manufactures, which still remain upon our statute books.' Gentlemen, if any of you have taken the pains to wade through the reports of the protectionist meetings, as they are called, which have been held lately, you would see that our opponents, at the end of seven years of our agitation, have found out their mistake, and are abandoning the Corn-laws; and now, like unskilful blunderers as they are, they want to take up a new position, just as we are going to achieve the victory. Then they have been telling something very like fibs, when they claimed the Corn-laws as compensation for peculiar burdens. They say now that they want merely protection in common with all other interests, and they now call themselves the advocates of protection to native industry in all its branches; and, by

way of making the appeal to the less-informed portion of the
community, they say that the Anti-Corn-law League are
merely the advocates of free trade in corn, but that we want
to preserve a monopoly in manufactures.

Now, the resolution which I have to submit to you, and
which we will put to this meeting to-night—the largest by
far that I ever saw in this room, and comprising men of every
class and of every calling in this district—let that resolution
decide, once and for ever, whether our opponents can with
truth lay that to our charge henceforth. There is nothing
new in this proposition, for at the very beginning of this
agitation—at the meeting of the Chamber of Commerce—
when that faint voice was raised in that small room in King-
street, in December, 1838, for the total and immediate repeal
of the Corn-laws—when that ball was set in motion which
has been accumulating in strength and velocity ever since,
why, the petition stated fairly that this community wanted
no protection for its own industry. I will read the conclusion
of that admirable petition; it is as follows:—

‘ Holding one of the principles of eternal justice to be the inalienable right
of every man freely to exchange the result of his labour for the productions of
other people, and maintaining the practice of protecting one part of the community at the expense of all other classes to be unsound and unjustifiable,
your petitioners earnestly implore your honourable House to repeal all laws
relating to the importation of foreign corn and other foreign articles of subsistence ; and to carry out to the fullest extent, both as affects agriculture and
manufactures, the true and peaceful principles of Free Trade, by removing all
existing obstacles to the unrestricted employment of industry and capital.’

We have passed similar resolutions at all our great aggregate
meetings of delegates in London ever since that was issued.

I don't put this resolution as an argument or as an appeal
to meet the appeals made in the protection societies' meetings.
I believe that the men who now, in this seventh year of our
discussion, can come forth before their country, and talk as
those men have done—I believe that you might as well preach
to the deaf adder. You cannot convince them. I doubt

whether they have not been living in their shells, like oysters; I doubt whether they know that such a thing is in existence as a railroad, or a penny postage, or even as an heir to the throne. They are in profound ignorance of everything, and incapable of being taught. We don't appeal to them, but to a very large portion of this community, who don't take a very prominent part in this discussion — who may be considered as important lookers-on. Many have been misled by the reiterated assertions of our opponents; and it is at this eleventh hour to convince these men, and to give them an opportunity of joining our ranks, as they will do, that I offer this proof of disinterestedness and the fairness of our proposals. I don't intend to go into an argument to convince any man here that protection to all must be protection to none. If it takes from one man's pocket, and allows him to compensate himself by taking an equivalent from another man's pocket, and if that goes on in a circle through the whole community, it is only a clumsy process of robbing all to enrich none; and simply has this effect, that it ties up the hands of industry in all directions. I need not offer one word to convince you of that. The only motive that I have to say a word is, that what I may here may convince others elsewhere—the men who meet in protection societies. But the arguments I should adduce to an intelligent audience like this, would be spoken in vain to the Members of Parliament who are now the advocates of protection. I shall meet them in less than a week in London, and there I will teach the A B C of this protection. It is of no use trying to teach children words of five syllables, when they have not got out of the alphabet.

Well, what exhibitions these protectionists have been making of themselves! Judging from the length of their speeches, as you see them reported, you might fancy the whole community was in motion. Unfortunately for us, and for the reputation of our countrymen, the men who can utter the drivelling nonsense which we have had exhibited to the

world lately, and the men who can listen to it, are very few in
number. I doubt exceedingly whether all the men who have
attended all the protection meetings, during the last month,
might not very comfortably be put into this hall. But these
protection societies have not only changed their principles,
but it seems they have resolved to change their tactics. They
have now, at the eleventh hour, again resolved that they will
make their body political, and look after the registration.
What simpletons they must have been to have thought that
they could do any good without that! So they have resolved that their societies shall spend their money in precisely
the same way that the League have been expending theirs.
They have hitherto been telling us, in all their meetings and
in all their newspapers, that the League is an unconstitutional body ; that it is an infernal club which aims at corrupt-
ing, at vitiating, and at swamping the registrations; and now,
forsooth, when no good can possibly come of it—when they
most certainly should have wisely abstained from imitating it,
since they cannot do any good, and have kept up the strain
they formerly had, of calling the League an unconstitutional
body, they resolve to rescind their resolution, and to follow
his Grace the Duke of Richmond's advice, and fight us with
our own weapons. Now, I presume, we are a constitutional
body. It is a fortunate thing that we have not got great
Dukes to lead us. But, now, of what force is this resolution ?
Like everything they do, it is farcical—it is unreal. The protection societies, from the beginning, have been nothing but
phantoms. They are not realities; and what is their resolution—
what does it amount to? They resolve that they will look
after the registration. We all know that they have done their
worst in that way already. We all know that these landlords
may really make their acres a kind of electioneering property.
We know right well that their land agents are their electioneering agents. We know that their rent-rolls have been
made their muster-rolls for fighting the battle of protection.

These poor drivelling people say that we buy qualifications,
and present them to our friends; that we bind them down
to vote as we please. We have never bought a vote, and
we never intend to buy a vote or to give one. Should
we not be blockheads to buy votes and give them, when
we have ten thousand persons ready to buy them at our
request?

But I suspect that our protectionist friends have a notion
that there is some plan—some secret, sinister plan—by which
they can put fictitious votes on the register. Now I beg
to tell them that the League is not more powerful to create
votes than it is to detect the flaws in the bad votes of our
opponents; and they may depend on it, if they attempt to
put fictitious voters on the register, that we have our forrets
in every county, and that they will find out the flaws; and
when the registration time comes, we'll have an objection
registered against every one of their fictitious qualifications,
and make them produce their title-deeds, and show that they
have paid for them. Well, we have our protectionist opponents; but how we may congratulate ourselves on the position
which they have given to this question by the discussion that
has been raised everywhere during the last few months! We
cannot enter a steamboat or a railway carriage—nay, we
cannot even go into an omnibus, but the first thing that any
man does, almost before he has deposited his umbrella, is to
ask, 'Well, what is the last news about the Corn-laws?'
Now, we, who remember how difficult it was, at the beginning
of our agitation, to bring men's minds to the discussion of
this question, when we think that every newspaper is now full
of it—the same broad sheet containing, perhaps, a report of
this meeting, and of the miserable drivelling of some hole-
and-corner agricultural gathering—and when we think that
the whole community is engaged in reading the discussion,
and pondering on the several arguments, we can desire no
more. The League might close its doors to-morrow, and its

work might be considered as done, the moment it compels or
induces people to discuss the question.

But the feeling I have alluded to is spreading beyond our
own country. I am glad to hear that in Ireland the question
is attracting attention. You have probably heard that my
friend Mr. Bright and I have received a requisition, signed
by merchants and manufacturers of every grade and party in
Belfast, soliciting us to go there and address them; and I
deeply regret that we cannot put our feet on Irish ground to
advocate this question. To-day I have received a copy of a
requisition to the mayor of Drogheda, calling a meeting for
next Monday, to petition for the total and immediate repeal
of the Corn-laws, and I am glad to notice at the head of that
requisition the name of the Catholic Primate, Dr. Croly, a
man eminent for learning, piety, and moderation; and that
it is also headed by the rest of the Catholic clergy of that
borough. I hope that these examples will not be without
their due effect in another quarter. We have, I believe, the
majority of every religious denomination with us—I mean the
dissenting denominations; we have them almost *en masse*, both
ministers and laymen; and I believe the only body, the only
religious body, which we may not say we have with us as a
body, are the members of the Church of England.

On this point I will just offer this remark: The clergy of
the Church of England have been placed in a most invidious,
and, I think, an unfortunate position, by the mode in which
their tithe commutation charge was fixed some years ago.
My friend Colonel Thompson will recollect it, for he was in
Parliament at the time, and protested against the way in
which the tithe commutation rent-charge was fixed. He said,
with the great foresight he had always shown in the struggle
for the repeal of the Corn-laws, that it would make the clergy
of the Church of England parties to the present Corn-law by
fixing their tithe at a fixed quantity of corn, fluctuating according to the price of the last seven years. Let it be borne

in mind, that every other class of the community may be
directly compensated for the repeal of the Corn-laws—I mean
every class connected with agriculture — except the clergy.
The landlords may be compensated, if prices fall, by an
increased quantity of produce, so also may the farmer and
the labourer; but the clergy of the Church of England receive
a given number of quarters of wheat for their tithe, whatever
the price may be. I think, however, we may draw a favourable conclusion, under all the circumstances, from the fact
that I believe there has not been one clergyman of the Church
of England at all eminent for rank, piety, or learning, who
has come out, notwithstanding the strong temptation of personal interest, to advocate the existing Corn-law. I think
that we may take this as a proof of the very strong appeal
to justice which this question makes, and perhaps augur also
that there is a very strong feeling amongst the great body
of the members of the Church of England in favour of free
trade in corn.

Well, there is one other quarter in which we have seen the
progress of sound principles—I allude to America. We have
received the American President's Message ; we have had also
the report of the Secretary of the Treasury, and both President
Polk and Mr. Secretary Walker have been taking my friend
Colonel Thompson's task out of his hands, and lecturing the
people of America on the subject of Free Trade. I have never
read a better digest of the arguments in favour of Free Trade
than that put forth by Mr. Secretary Walker, and addressed
to the Congress of that country. I augur from all these
things that our question is making rapid progress throughout
the world, and that we are coming to the consummation of
our labours. We are verging now towards the session of
Parliament, and I predict that the question will either receive
its quietus, or that it will lead to the dissolution of this
Parliament ; and then the next will certainly relieve us from
our burden.

Now, many people are found who speculate on what Sir
Robert Peel may do in the approaching session of Parliament.
It is a very hazardous thing, considering that in one week
only you will be as wise as I shall, to venture to make a prediction on this subject. [A cry of ' We are very anxious.']
You are very anxious, no doubt. Well, let us see if we can
speculate a little on futurity, and relieve our anxiety. There
are three courses open to Sir Robert Peel. He may keep the
law as it is; he may totally repeal it; or he may do something between the two by tinkering his scale again, or giving
us a fixed duty. Now, I predict that Sir R. Peel will either
keep the law as it is, or he will propose totally to abolish it.
And I ground my prediction on this, because these are the
only two things that anybody in the country wants him to do.
There are some who want to keep protection as it is; others
want to get rid of it; but nobody wants anything between the
two. He has his choice to make, and I have this opinion of
his sagacity, that, if he changes at all, he will change for total
repeal. But the question is, ' Will he propose total and immediate repeal?' Now, there, if you please, I will forbear to
offer a prediction. But I will venture to give you a reason or
two why I think he ought to take total and immediate repeal.
I don't think that any class is so much interested in having
the Corn-laws totally and immediately repealed as the farming
class. I believe that it is of more importance to the farmers
to have the repeal instantaneous, instead of gradual, than to
any other class of the community. In fact, I observe, in the
report of a recent Oxfordshire protection meeting, given in
to-day's paper, that when Lord Norreys was alluding to the
probability of Sir Robert Peel abolishing the Corn-laws gradually, a farmer of the name of Gillatt cried out, ' We had
better be drowned outright than ducked to death.' Gentlemen, I used to employ another simile—a very humble one, I
admit. I used to say that an old farmer had told me, that if
he was going to cut off his sheep-dog's tail, it would be far

more humane to cut it off all at once than a piece every day
in the week. But now I think that the farmer's simile in
Oxford is the newest and the best that we can use. Nothing
could be more easy than to demonstrate that it is the true
interest of the farmers, if the Corn-law is to be abolished, to
have it abolished instantly. If the Corn-law were abolished
to-morrow, my firm belief is, that instead of wheat falling, it
would have a tendency to rise. That is my firm belief, because speculation has already anticipated Sir Robert Peel, and
wheat has fallen in consequence of that apprehension. I believe that, owing to the scarcity everywhere—I mean in all
parts of Europe—you could not, if you prayed for it, if you
had your own wishing-cap on, and could make your own time
and circumstances—I believe, I say, that you could never find
such an opportunity for abolishing the Corn-laws totally and
immediately as if it were done next week; for it so happens
that the very countries from which, in ordinary times, we
have been supplied, have been afflicted, like ourselves, with
scarcity—that the countries of Europe are competing with us
for the very small surplus existing in America. They have,
in fact, anticipated us in that market, and they have left the
world's markets so bare of corn, that, whatever your necessities
may be, I defy you to have other than high prices of corn
during the next twelve months, though the Corn-law was
abolished to-morrow.

European countries are suffering as we are from the same
evil. They are suffering from scarcity now, owing to their
absurd legislation respecting the article of corn. Europe
altogether has been corrupted by the vicious example of
England in her commercial legislation. There they are,
throughout the continent of Europe, with a population
increasing at the rate of four or five millions a-year, yet
they make it their business, like ourselves, to put barriers in
the way of a sufficiency of food to meet the demand of an
increasing population.

I believe that if you abolish the Corn-law honestly, and adopt Free Trade in its simplicity, there will not be a tariff in Europe that will not be changed in less than five years to follow your example. Well, gentlemen, suppose the Corn-law be not abolished immediately, but that Sir Robert Peel brings in a measure giving you a duty of 5s., 6s., or 7s., and going down 1s. a-year for four or five years, till the whole duty is abolished, what would be the effect of that on foreign countries? They will then exaggerate the importance of this market when the duty is wholly off. They will go on raising supplies, calculating that, when the duty is wholly off, they will have a market for their produce, and high prices to remunerate them; and if, as is very likely and consistent with our experience, we should have a return to abundant seasons, these vast importations would be poured upon our markets, probably just at the time when our prices are low; and they would come here, because they would have no other market, to swamp our markets, and deprive the farmer of the sale of his produce at a remunerating price. But, on the contrary, let the Corn-law be abolished instantly; let foreigners see what the English market is in its natural state, and then they will be able to judge from year to year and from season to season what will be the future demand from this country for foreign corn. There will be no extravagant estimate of what we want—no contingency of bad harvests to speculate upon. The supply will be regulated by the demand, and will reach that state which will be the best security against both gluts and famine. Therefore, for the farmers' sakes, I plead for the immediate abolition of this law. A farmer never can have a fair and equitable understanding or adjustment with his landlord, whether as respects rent, tenure, or game, until this law is wholly removed out of his way. Let the repeal be gradual, and the landlord will say to the farmer, through the land-agent, 'Oh, the duty will be 7s. next year; you have not had more than twelve months' experience of the working of the system yet;' and the farmer goes away without any settlement having been come to.   Another year passes over, and when the farmer presents himself, he is told, 'Oh, the duty will be 5s. this year; I cannot yet tell what the effect will be; you must stop awhile.'   The next year the same thing is repeated, and the end is, that there is no adjustment of any kind between the landlord and tenant.   But put it at once on a natural footing, abolish all restrictions, and the landlord and tenant will be brought to a prompt settlement; they will be placed precisely on the same footing as you are in your manufactures.

Well, I have now spoken on what may be done.   I have told you, too, what I should advocate; but I must say, that whatever is proposed by Sir Robert Peel, we, as Free-traders, have but one course to pursue.   If he proposes a total and immediate and unconditional repeal, we shall throw up our caps for Sir Robert Peel.   If he proposes anything else, then Mr. Villiers will be ready, as he has been on former occasions —to move his amendment for a total and immediate repeal of the Corn-laws.   We are not responsible for what Ministers may do; we are but responsible for the performance of our duty.   We don't offer to do impossibilities; but we will do our utmost to carry out our principles.   But, gentlemen, I tell you honestly, I think less of what this Parliament may do; I care less for their opinions, less for the intentions of the Prime Minister and the Cabinet, than what may be the opinion of a meeting like this and of the people out of doors.   This question will not be carried by Ministers or by the present Parliament; it will be carried, when it is carried, by the will of the nation. We will do nothing that can remove us a hair's breadth from that rock which we have stood upon with so much safety for the last seven years.   All other parties have been on a quicksand, and floated about by every wave, by every tide, and by every wind—some floating to us, others, like fragments scattered over the ocean, without rudder or compass; whilst we

are upon solid ground, and no temptation, whether of parties
or of Ministers, shall ever make us swerve a hair's breadth.
I am anxious to hear now, at the last meeting before we go to
Parliament—before we enter that arena to which all men's
minds will be turned during the next week—I am anxious,
not merely that we should all of us understand each other on
this question, but that we should be considered as occupying
as independent and isolated a position as we did at the first
moment of the formation of this League. We have nothing
to do with Whigs or Tories; we are stronger than either of
them; and if we stick to our principles, we can, if necessary,
beat both. And I hope we perfectly understand now, that
we have not, in the advocacy of this great question, a single
object in view but that which we have honestly avowed from
the beginning. Our opponents may charge us with designs
to do other things. No, gentlemen, I have never encouraged
that.   Some of my friends have said, 'When this work is
done, you will have some influence in the country; you must
do so and so.' I said then, as I say now, 'Every new political
principle must have its special advocates, just as every new
faith has its martyrs.' It is a mistake to suppose that this
organisation can be turned to other purposes. It is a mistake
to suppose that men, prominent in the advocacy of the principle of Free Trade, can with the same force and effect identify
themselves with any other principle hereafter. It will be
enough if the League accomplishes the triumph of the principle we have before us. I have never taken a limited view
of the object or scope of this great principle. I have never
advocated this question very much as a trader.

But I have been accused of looking too much to material
interests. Nevertheless I can say that I have taken as large
and great a view of the effects of this mighty principle as ever
did any man who dreamt over it in his own study. I believe
that the physical gain will be the smallest gain to humanity
from the success of this principle. I look farther; I see in the

Free-trade principle that which shall act on the moral world as the principle of gravitation in the universe,—drawing men together, thrusting aside the antagonism of race, and creed, and language, and uniting us in the bonds of eternal peace. I have looked even farther. I have speculated, and probably dreamt, in the dim future—ay, a thousand years hence—I have speculated on what the effect of the triumph of this principle may be. I believe that the effect will be to change the face of the world, so as to introduce a system of government entirely distinct from that which now prevails. I believe that the desire and the motive for large and mighty empires; for gigantic armies and great navies—for those materials which are used for the destruction of life and the desolation of the rewards of labour—will die away; I believe that such things will cease to be necessary, or to be used when man becomes one family, and freely exchanges the fruits of his labour with his brother man. I believe that, if we could be allowed to reappear on this sublunary scene, we should see, at a far distant period, the governing system of this world revert to something like the municipal system; and I believe that the speculative philosopher of a thousand years hence will date the greatest revolution that ever happened in the world's history from the triumph of the principle which we have met here to advocate. I believe those things; but, whatever may have been my dreams and speculations, I have never obtruded them upon others; I have never acted upon personal or interested motives in this question; I seek no alliance with parties or favour from parties, and I will take none—but, having the feeling I have of the sacredness of the principle, I say that I can never agree to tamper with it. I, at least, will never be suspected of doing otherwise than pursuing it disinterestedly, honestly, and resolutely.

FREE TRADE

XXI.

CORN-LAWS.

HOUSE OF COMMONS, FEBRUARY 27, 1846.

[On Jan. 27, 1846, Sir Robert Peel announced the policy of the Government on the Corn-laws. In three years they were to be repealed. From the passing of the Act, and until Feb. 1, 1849, the maximum duty was to be 10s., which could be levied when corn was under 48s., but should diminish by a shilling per quarter till the price reached 53s., when it should remain at 4s. The duty on barley and oats were to be proportionate; colonial corn to be free, and maize only at a nominal duty. The debate on this proposal lasted twelve nights, and the resolutions were carried on Feb. 27 by a majority of 97 (337 to 240). On June 13, 1846, the Corn Importation Bill was passed in the House of Lords, without a division; and on the same day, Sir Robert Peel's Ministry was defeated on an Irish Coercion Bill, by a majority of 73 (292 to 219).]

I ASSURE the House that it is impossible for me to trespass long upon their notice, but I am anxious to say a few words before the close of this long debate. I have had the good, or the ill, fortune, to listen to many debates upon this subject in this House; and although it has not been my fortune to listen to this, at all events I have had the pleasure of perusing every word of it.

On former occasions I have had to complain, that although the great object and purpose of the Anti-Corn-law motion was to discuss the principle of the Corn-laws, yet that hon. Gentlemen always evaded the question, and tried to discuss every other rather than the particular question before the House; but however much I may have had to complain of that on former occasions, I think it will be admitted that extraneous matter has been introduced into this debate by hon. Gentlemen opposite to a much greater extent than before. It appears to me that one half of the debate has turned upon the conduct of her Majesty's Ministers, and nearly the whole of the other upon the necessity of a dissolution and an appeal to the country. Now, though there may be ground — I will not say there may be just ground — for hon. Gentlemen below the gangway assailing the Ministers for the course they have pursued, yet the country, I assure them, will not sympathise with them in their quarrel with their leaders, nor will it be without some suspicion that the quarrel has been got up to avoid a discussion of principle; for I wish you to bear in mind that, on former occasions, by similar means, hon. Gentlemen did try to avoid that discussion. In 1841 they denounced the leaders of the Whigs as furiously as they denounce the leaders of their own party now; and when I came into Parliament, in the spring of 1841, I must say that I myself, and the members of the Anti-Corn-law League, were as much the objects of their vituperation as the Ministers are now. The country, therefore, will not sympathise with them; and, on the other hand, it will learn whether or not they have introduced these personal topics because they cannot justify the present law.

Now, if hon. Gentlemen opposite have any fear that their present leaders contemplate, after the repeal of the Corn-laws, doing something else which they may think injurious to their party interests, I beg to assure them that they are taking the most effectual means of arming the present Ministers with the power of accomplishing something else, if they wish it; for the more they attack them—the more obloquy they load them with—the more will the country sympathise with them out of doors. Why, you are making the present Ministry the most popular men in the country. If the right hon. Baronet the First Lord of the Treasury were to go into the manufacturing districts of the north, his journey would be one con-

tinued triumph. The right hon. Home Secretary was not
personally very popular two or three years ago. It is a
difficult thing for a Home Secretary in troublesome times to
become popular; but the magnificent contribution the right
hon. Baronet (Sir J. Graham) has given to our good cause,
by his able speeches and authoritative statements of facts, has
sunk deep into the mind of the country; and, spite of the
martyrdom you are inflicting upon him, he has rendered himself so popular that I do not think we could parade any one
in Manchester or Liverpool who would meet with a more
cordial reception. I do not think you (the protectionists) are
pursuing a good party course. I think you are as badly off,
on the score of good judgment and tactics, as ever you were.

I will now, however, draw your attention to the second
topic to which I have referred, and which is of still more
importance. If I understand your position rightly, it is
this—you say, ' We wish for an appeal to the country; if the
country decides that Free Trade shall be the national policy,
we will bow to that decision.' I believe I am fairly inter-
preting your meaning. I tell you then, in the first place, that
if you are believers in the truth and justice of your principles,
you are unworthy advocates of those principles if you would
think of abandoning them on such grounds. If you believe
in the truth of your principles, you should not bow to the
decision of a temporary majority of this House. When I
came into Parliament, in 1841, I met you with a majority of
91 in your favour. Did I then bow to that majority, and
submit to the Corn-law? No; I said I would never cease
my exertions till you abrogated that law. If you have confidence in the truth and justice of your principles, you should
use the same language. You should say, ' It is not one defeat
that shall make us abandon those great principles, which we
consider essential to the welfare and prosperity of the great
mass of the people. No; if we are thrown to the ground
now, we will spring up with renewed determination and

vigour.' You may ' Yes, yes,' that sentiment, but you have
already told me, by your cheers, that you do not intend to do
anything of the kind; and I am conscientiously of opinion
that you are unbelievers in the doctrines you advocate.

But I will assume that you carry out your principles; that
you can force a dissolution; and to this point I wish particularly to draw your attention, and, what is of still more importance, the attention of persons in another place. We have
had some pretty frank allusions — especially in the peroration
of the speech of the hon. Member for Dorsetshire—to what is
to be done in another place, where there is no representative
of the middle classes — no merchant, no manufacturer, no
spinner, no farmer. In that other place, however, what I
now say on the subject of a dissolution may probably be read.
You want a dissolution in order to ascertain the opinion of
the country. Have you ever thought, or considered, or
defined what ' the opinion of the country' means? Do you
think it means a numerical majority of this House? We
shall have that to-night. You are not satisfied with that.
You are preaching the democratic doctrine, that this question
must be referred to the people. Now I want to have well
defined what you mean by ' public opinion.' You will perhaps
say, ' We will abide by the decision of a numerical majority
in this House,' and you will consider that the decision of the
country.

Well, I totally disagree with all those who consider for a
moment that you would obtain a numerical majority in this
House in the event of a dissolution. I ought to know as
much about the state of the representation of this country,
and of the registration, as any man in the House. Probably
no one has given so much attention to that question as I have
done; and I distinctly deny that you have the slightest probability of gaining a numerical majority in this House, if a
dissolution took place to-morrow. Now, I would not have
said this three months ago; on the contrary, at a public

meeting three months ago I distinctly recognised the great probability of a dissolution, in consequence of your having a numerical majority. But your party is broken up. Though you may still have a firm phalanx in Dorsetshire and Buckinghamshire, what has been the effect of the separation from you of the most authoritative and intelligent of your friends? What has been the effect, also, of the defection in the boroughs, and among the population of the north?

I told you, three years ago, that the Conservatives in the towns in the north of England were not the followers of the Duke of Richmond. They were, almost to a man, the followers of that section of the Government represented by the First Lord of the Treasury and the right hon. Home Secretary. Every one acquainted with the towns in the north of England will bear me out when I say that those Conservatives who follow the right hon. Baronet (Sir R. Peel) comprise at least four-fifths of the party, while the remaining one-fifth look up to the Duke of Richmond as their leader, and sympathise with the section below the gangway That large portion of the Conservative party in the north of England has ever been in favour of Free Trade. The language they have used to Free-traders like myself has been this:— 'Sir Robert Peel will do it at the proper time. We have confidence in him, and, when the proper period arrives, he will give us Free Trade.' Then, I say, that in this state of your party I wholly deny the possibility of your gaining a numerical majority.

But I will assume, for the sake of argument, that, in the event of a dissolution of Parliament, you obtained a numerical majority: let us see of what that majority and the minority opposed to you would consist. There are eighteen Representatives in Parliament for this metropolis, and there are two Members for the metropolitan county. We have the whole twenty. They represent 110,000 electors; they represent a population of 2,000,000 of souls. They are the most

intelligent, the most wealthy, the most orderly, and, notwithstanding my acquaintance with the business habits of those in
the north of England, I must add, with respect to business
and mechanical life, the hardest-working people in England.
Do those people express public opinion think you? Why, this
metropolis assumed to itself, centuries ago, the power and
privilege of closing its gates in the face of its Sovereign—a
power which is still retained, and which is exercised on State
occasions. This metropolis is now twenty times as populous,
twenty times as wealthy, twenty times as important in the
world's eye as it was then; and do you think it will be content that you count it as nothing in your estimate of public
opinion?

But turn elsewhere. What says the metropolis of Scotland,
Edinburgh? Do you reckon on having a Member for that
city to vote in the glorious majority you anticipate? Turn to
Dublin. Will you have a Representative for that city with
you? Go to Glasgow, Manchester, Leeds, Birmingham, and
Liverpool; take every town containing 20,000 inhabitants,
and I defy you to show that you can reckon on a single
Representative for any town in the kingdom which has a
population of 20,000, or, at all events, of 25,000. I tell you
that you have not with you now a town containing 25,000
inhabitants in Great Britain. No, no, no; you have neither
Liverpool nor Bristol. That shows you have not weighed
these matters as you are bound to weigh them. Do not be
led away by the men who cheer and halloo here, like the schoolboy whistling in the churchyard to keep up his courage.
Examine these facts, for your leaders that were have weighed
them already; and there are none among you deserving to be
your leaders, unless they have well considered these important
matters.

I repeat that you cannot reckon upon any town of 25,000
inhabitants sending up a Representative to vote with the
great majority you expect to obtain. True, you will have

your pocket boroughs, and your nomination counties. And
I will say a word or two directly as to the county representation ; but I now place before you broadly the situation in
which you will find yourselves after a dissolution. I will
assume that you have a majority, derived from pocket boroughs
and nomination counties, of twenty or thirty Members. But
on this side you will see the Representatives for London, for
South Lancashire, for West Yorkshire, for North Cheshire,
for North Lancashire, and the Members for all the large towns
of Scotland—nay, not one Member will come from any town
in Scotland to vote with you.

Now, what would then be your situation? Why, you
would shrink aghast from the position in which you would
find yourselves. There would be more defections from your
ranks, pledged as you are—steeped to the chin in pledges.
So much alarmed would you be at your position, that you
would cross the floor to join us in larger numbers than you
have ever yet done. I tell you, there would be no safety for
you without it. I say that the Members who came up under
such circumstances to maintain the Corn-laws, from your
Ripons and Stamfords, Woodstocks and Marlboroughs,
would hold those opinions only until they found out what
has been determined by public opinion. They would not
hold them one week longer; for if the country found that
they would not give way to moral force, they might think it
requisite to place them in another Schedule A. Had there
been such an amount of public opinion, as now exists in favour
of the repeal of the Corn-laws, in support of Charles Stuart in
1745, the dynasty of the Stuarts would now have occupied
the throne of these realms. That amount of public opinion
is sufficient to change the constitution of this country ; to
alter your forms of Government ; to do anything, in short,
that public opinion is determined to effect.

But you may probably tell me, that though we have the
electors of the great constituencies I have mentioned in our

favour, the great mass of the people are not with us. That
is a rather democratic sentiment. You never heard me quote
the superior judgment of the working classes in any delibera-
tions in this assembly. You never heard me cant about the
superior claims of the working classes to arbitrate on this
great question ; but you say the mass of the people are not
with us. What evidence is there that this is the case ? Will
you shut your eyes to proofs ? Will you go blindfold against
a stone wall ? You say the petitions presented to this House
have not been honestly signed. I cannot disprove that assertion : it must go for what it is worth ; but we have ten times
as many signatures to our petitions for Corn-law repeal as you
have to your protection petitions. You may assume that the
signatures to those petitions are fictitious. Do so, if you please.
I will give you another test : I will challenge you to the old
Saxon mode of ascertaining what are the opinions of the country, by calling public meetings. Now, if you really entertain
democratic opinions, this is the way in which to elevate the
working man to an equality with his master—ay, to an
equality with the Peer of the realm. Bringing them out into
public assemblies, where every man has an equal vote—assemblies which make laws for the conduct of their own proceedings, and elect their own chairman. Call your public meetings
to support the Corn-laws. I challenge you to call one anywhere. Why, it is not in the manufacturing districts alone
that meetings have been held since the 1st of November last.
Public meetings convened by the authorities have been held
in every large town,—meetings not confined to a particular
class, or consisting of men pledged to particular opinions, but
convened to determine, ay or no, whether the people should
petition for Free Trade or not. These meetings have not been
confined to the manufacturing districts alone ; they have been
held at Exeter, Brighton, and Oxford, and the opinion of the
people was as unanimous at those places as at Bolton, Stockport, and Manchester. Now, cannot you call a public meeting

and test the opinions of the people? Would not one meeting, at all events, be something like a proof that you are practical men, and not disposed to be misled by the chimeras of those hot-headed, half-witted people, who try to deceive you?

I have seen some of your notices calling protection meetings. One was forwarded to me from Epworth in Lancashire, by a gentleman who complained that the notice was so framed that protectionists only could attend, and that no amendment could be proposed. Why, in the purely agricultural district of Haddingtonshire, in the centre of the Lothians, a protection meeting was called about six weeks ago. All the neighbouring nobility and landed proprietors attended; they talked of the British Lion, and of the nation being with them. Soon after, another meeting was held, to petition for the repeal of the Corn-laws. The protectionists fled from the room, the largest room in the place; but it was quite full without them, and resolutions in favour of repeal were adopted. Was this evidence of public opinion? Was it not? Then what will teach you what public opinion is? Must you be tossed in a blanket? Must you be swept out of this House into the Thames? What must be done to convince you that the feeling of the nation is not with you? You will be abandoned to fatuity and destruction if you are left to persons who have so little mercy upon you as to delude you on this question.

I said that I would refer to the county representation. You are pluming yourselves on the result of the recent county elections, and you are reckoning, no doubt, on the attainment of great strength from your purely agricultural counties in the event of a dissolution; but I beg to remind hon. Gentlemen that the county representation under the 50l. tenant-at-will clause of the Reform Act is not the old county representation. We never heard twenty years ago of requisitions being got up to candidates by tenant-farmers. The requisitions were then got up by freeholders. You introduced into the Reform Act, by a great mistake on the part of those who then had the

power to have prevented it, a clause innovating on the old
constitutional custom, and giving tenants-at-will a vote for
counties. Do you mean to tell me that the votes of these
tenants-at-will are an evidence of public opinion? We heard
a definition of tenant-at-will votes, which, with the permission
of the House, I will read. The hon. Member for Dorsetshire
(and I congratulate the Free Traders on his advent here), told
us with great *naïveté*—

> ' He [Mr. Seymer], with his hon. colleague, came forward at the recent
> election for Dorset, in consequence of a requisition signed by the great body
> of the tenant-farmers. Three or four of the largest properties in the county
> were in the hands of Free-traders, and naturally the tenants on those estates
> held back, and refused to sign the requisition, till they knew what were the
> wishes of their landlords; for it was notorious that English tenants generally
> wished to consult the feelings of their landlords. He did not think tenants to
> blame for that. Knowing that their landlords were Free-traders, the tenants
> in question made inquiry, previous to signing, whether those landlords would
> object to their taking the course their consciences dictated; the landowners,
> very much to their credit, said, that this being a farmer's question, they would
> not interfere; and then, almost without exception, the farmers on those pro-
> perties signed the requisition.'

Yes, yes; it is all very well for those who get the consent of
their landlords to vote, but recollect what the hon. Gentleman
says at the commencement of his remarks. He tells us that
he and his colleague were put in nomination in consequence
of a requisition signed by tenant-farmers,—that is, in consequence of a requisition got up by command of the landlords
and signed by the farmers. Now, I put it to you candidly,—
Is it not an understood etiquette in counties that one proprietor who is a candidate should not canvass the tenants on
the estate of another till he has obtained the sanction of the
owner? Am I to understand that the protectionist gentlemen
in a body below the gangway contradict me when I state that
as a point of etiquette in counties, one proprietor, who is a
candidate, does not think it proper to canvass the tenantry on
the estate of another proprietor without first intimating to the
landowner his intention and desire to do so? Well, there are

only two or three faint noes; I think the ayes have it. But, however, this point, at all events, is admitted, that as a rule the farmers vote with the landlords; that the vote goes with the land; nobody denies that the farmer carries the vote. What right, then, have you to call this the opinion of the farmer? You cannot have it both ways. It cannot be both the opinion of the landlord and the opinion of the tenant. What becomes, then, of all those interesting romances in which the Duke of Richmond has indulged in public about the bold, independent, and gallant yeomanry of the country? Why, these are the men who have not the right of using their suffrages. It is your own statement. This country certainly will not be governed by a combination of landlords and tenants. Probably you are not aware on what a very narrow basis this power of yours rests. But I can give you some information on the subject. There are about 150,000 tenants who form the basis of your political power, and who are distributed throughout the counties of this country. Well, let it come to the worst;—carry on the opposition to this measure for three years more; yet there is a plan in operation much maligned by some hon. Gentlemen opposite, and still more maligned in another place, but which, the more the shoe pinches, and the more you wince at it, the more we like it out of doors. Now, I say, we have confronted this difficulty, and are prepared to meet it. We are calling into exercise the true old English forms of the Constitution, of five centuries' antiquity, and we intend that it should countervail this innovation of yours in the Reform Bill. You think that there is something very revolutionary in this. Why, you are the innovators and the revolutionists who introduced this new franchise into the Reform Bill. But I believe that it is perfectly understood by the longest heads among your party that we have a power out of doors to meet this difficulty. You should bear in mind, that less than one-half of the money invested in the savings'-banks, laid out at better interest in the purchase of freeholds, would give qualifications to more persons than your 150,000 tenant-farmers. But you say that the League is purchasing votes and giving away the franchise. No, no; we are not quite so rich as that; but be assured that if you prolong the contest for three or four years (which you cannot do) — if, however, it comes to the worst, we have the means in our power to meet the difficulty, and are prepared to use them. Money has been subscribed to prepare our organisation in every county, and we are prepared to meet the difficulty, and to overcome it. You may think that there is something repulsive to your notions of supremacy in all this. I see a very great advantage, even if the Corn-laws were repealed to-morrow. I think that you cannot too soon widen the basis of our county representation. I say, with respect to a man, whether he be a small shopkeeper or a mechanic, who by his prudence has saved 50*l.* or 100*l.*, and is willing to lay it out in the purchase of a cottage or land bringing in 40*s.* a-year as a freehold, — I say that it is to that man of all others that I would wish to entrust the franchise.

Let it be understood that all this extraneous matter is not of my introducing, for your debate has turned on the question of dissolution. No one can complain of my having, on this question, been guilty of often introducing irrelevant matter; I generally keep close to the argument; but you have chosen to say now that you will not settle the question by argument, and by an appeal to facts and reason in this House; that you will have nothing to do with this House, but that you will go to the country. Now, I have given you some idea of what is your prospect in the country. I do not ask you to take my opinion for it; but as mischief may be averted more from yourselves — more from another place to which allusion has been made, than from others—I do ask you to take these facts home, to study them for yourselves, to look over the registry, to count the population of the towns, and then to come down and say whether you think the public opinion of the country is with you or against you.

So much of the argument has turned on this extraneous question, and what little argument has been addressed to the merits of the case has been so abundantly answered by other persons, that it would be impertinent in me to trespass at too great length on the time of the House. Well, I will tell you what my thoughts were as I sat at home patiently reading these debates. As I read speech after speech, and saw the fallacies which I had knocked on the head seven years ago re-appearing afresh, my thought was, what fun these debates will afford to the men in fustian jackets! All these fallacies are perfectly transparent to these men, and they would laugh at you for putting them forward. Dependence on foreigners! Who in the world could have supposed that that long-buried ghost would come again to light? Drain of gold! Wages rising and falling with the price of bread! Throwing land out of cultivation, and bringing corn here at 25s. per quarter. You forget that the great mass of the people now take a very different view on these questions from what you do. They formerly, seven years ago, did give in, to a certain extent, to your reiterated assertions that wages rise and fall with the price of bread. You had a very fair clap-trap against us (as we happened to be master manufacturers) in saying that we wanted to reduce wages. But the right hon. Baronet at the head of the Government, and the right hon. Baronet the Home Secretary, are not suspected by the English people of having such motives on these questions. The English people have no disinclination to refer to high authorities on these matters. They assume that men high in office have access to accurate information, and they generally suppose that those men have no sinister motive for deceiving the great body of the people on a question like the present. You see I do not underrate the importance of your leaders having declared in favour of Free Trade. On the contrary, I avow that this has

caused the greatest possible accession to the ranks of the
Free-traders. Well, then, the working classes, not believing
that wages rise and fall with the price of bread, when you tell
them that they are to have corn at 25s. a quarter, instead of
being frightened, are rubbing their hands with satisfaction.
They are not frightened at the visions which you present to
their eyes of a big loaf, seeing that they expect to get more
money and bread at half the price. And then the danger of
having your land thrown out of cultivation! Why, what
would the men in smock-frocks in the south of England say
to that? They would say, ' We shall get our land for potato
ground at ½d. a lug, instead of paying 3d. or 4d. for it.' These
fallacies have all been disposed of; and if you lived more in
the world—more in contact with public opinion, and less with
that charmed circle which you think the world, but which is
really anything but the world—if you gave way less to the
excitement of clubs, less to the buoyancy which arises from
talking to each other as to the effect of some smart speech, in
which a Minister has been assailed, you would see that it was
mere child's-play to attempt to baulk the intelligence of the
country on this great question, and you would not have talked
as you have talked for the last eleven days.

Now, with respect to the farmers, I will not deny that you
have a large portion of the farmers clinging to you landlords
on this question. They have been talked to and frightened
by their landlords, as children by their nurses, and they dread
some hideous prospect, or some old bogie, ready to start up
before their eyes. They do not know what is to happen, but
they have not strict and implicit faith in you. They are
afraid lest anything should happen to render them unable to
make terms with the landlords in the matter of rent; or
otherwise they are perfectly easy, and willing to receive Free
Trade to-morrow. They are afraid of how the adjustment
might be conducted; and the question, therefore, I have no
hesitation in saying, is a landlords' question. On this

subject the farmers have had some hints given them in the following paragraph, which appeared some time ago in the *Standard* newspaper :—

'Under what head, then, is the farmer to look for relief? Under the head "rent." The landlord must reduce rent; but the farmer knows, by rather bitter experience, the process by which this reduction must be effected. He must be first himself rendered unable to pay rent, and then the landlord will give way, and not before.'

This is the character given by the *Standard* newspaper of the landlords, and in this consists the great difficulty with the farmers. I do not think that the farmers generally believe all that you have told them. I believe that farms let as high now as ever they did. There is something remarkable in this. Since the right hon. Baronet has proposed his measure, I have directed my attention to this point, because I conceive that it solves much of our difficulty. I have inquired of land agents, land proprietors, lawyers, &c., as to whether land has suffered any depreciation in value in consequence of the proposition on this subject made by the Government. Now, it is remarkable, that though silks have been rendered almost unsaleable, and though the proposed change has produced almost a paralysis in every trade touched, yet land is letting and selling for higher prices than ever. I will give you an example. I will mention a case, and I am at liberty to mention the name. The hon. Member for Somerset will corroborate what I am going to state. Mr. Gordon, a near neighbour of that hon. Member, has had sixty farms, and he made the tenants an offer that he would take their land off their hands on equitable terms at Lady-day; yesterday was the last day for giving notice of accepting his offer, and not one farmer proposed to do so. I think it is not very complimentary to the hon. Member for Somerset. Mr. Gordon is a near neighbour of his, and his tenants of course have been favoured to hear some of those eloquent addresses which the hon. Member has made in Somerset, wherein he has told them that land

will not be worth cultivation at all, or, at least, that there will
be such an avalanche of corn from the Continent and from
America as will quite supersede the cultivation; and yet
these farmers seem to have so little alarm that they are willing to hold their farms at their present rents. Let me read
you, too, the account that is given me by a gentleman in the
City, an eminent solicitor, whom I have known for some
years, and who is largely interested in landed property :—

'I have for many years been connected with the management of landed
property, and with the purchase and letting of estates in several different
counties, and am at this time negotiating for the renewal of leases and letting
of lands in Bedfordshire, Herts, and Essex. In the latter county, the tenant, who
has occupied a farm of 500 acres for fourteen years, under a lease, and who has
always spoken of his rent as somewhat high, and of his own farming as the best in
his own neighbourhood, has now offered a considerable increase of rent (15 per
cent.) for a new lease of fourteen years, and to covenant to underdrain two-
thirds of the farm, the landlord finding draining-tiles; now acknowledging
that the cultivation may be greatly improved, so as to meet the increase of
rent. The farmer has another occupation, and is not, therefore, under any
fear of being without a farm. He is a protectionist in words, and a supporter
of Sir John Tyrell. Under the rumour that this farm might be given up,
there were eight or ten most respectable applicants for it.

'In Hertfordshire, I am at this moment renewing leases upon two large
farms, both with the offer of increased rents, and with covenants for greatly
improved cultivation, particularly as to underdraining.

'In Bedfordshire, upon two moderate-sized farms, the same has been the
result; and on the application for one of them, which the farmer is quitting in
consequence of age and infirmity, the following conversation took place, on the
application to me by an intelligent farmer for the farm :—

'"I understand, Sir, that you have the letting of Mr. L.'s farm, as he is
quitting?"

'"I have."

'"I should like to have the offer of it. My name is ——, and I can refer
you to the clergyman of my parish, and to several gentlemen, for my character
and responsibility."

'"You are, I presume, a farmer?"

'"Yes, Sir; I have one farm, and I should like another, to extend my
occupation, as I have sufficient capital."

'"You know the farm, I presume, and the rent which the present tenant
pays?"

'"Yes, Sir, I know the farm and the rent; and as we are no longer to
have any protection, and the Corn-laws must now be repealed, I hope you will
consider that point in the rent."

'"Pray, as you say that the Corn-laws must be repealed, what, in your judgment, will be the effect?"

'"Why, Sir, the first thing will be the waking up of thousands of farmers who have hitherto been asleep; and we must look to increased efforts and increased production."

'"With respect to rent, I must have a small increase, and I must require covenants for better cultivation, more especially as to underdraining, which must be done very extensively."

'"Sir, my intention is, if I have the farm, to underdrain the whole of it, being allowed tiles."

'"Well, as you are a man of observation, and acquainted with different districts in Bedfordshire, Buckinghamshire, and Herts, tell me whether I am right (so far as your observation goes) in saying that, under improved cultivation, one-third more corn can be grown, and the sample much better?"

'"I have no doubt that you are right."

'"Then, if I am right, what have you to fear from the abolition of the Corn-law?"

'"Nothing at all, Sir."

'This person has hired the farm at an increased rent, and undertaken to underdrain the whole, if required by the landlord so to do.'

Now, hon. Gentlemen must, of course, be better able than I can be to judge from their own experience whether this be a fair statement of the case or not; but I would put it to them, Are any of them prepared to sell their own estates for one farthing less now than they were twelve months ago? But if farmers will take the land at the same rent, and if you will not take less than thirty years' purchase now upon the present rental, where are the proofs that you are in earnest in all that you predict as the consequences of the repeal of the Corn-laws?

Nay, this is a proof that there has been a system of mutual self-delusion, or mutual deception, between you and the farmers. You have preached doctrines which the farmers have affected to believe, but which neither of you have believed at heart. Either you have been doing this jointly, doing it that you might practise upon the credulity of your countrymen, or else you are now pursuing a most unworthy and inconsistent course, because, after telling the farmers at your protection meetings that wheat is to be sold at 30s. to 35s. a quarter, and that they cannot carry on their business in

competition with the Russians and the Poles, even if they
had their land rent free, with what face can you now let your
land to farmers at existing rents?

But the truth is, that you all know — that the country
knows—that there never was a more monstrous delusion than
to suppose that that which goes to increase the trade of the
country and to extend its manufactures and commerce,—that
which adds to our numbers, increases our population, enlarges
the number of your customers, and diminishes your burdens
by multiplying the shoulders that are to bear them, and
giving them increased strength to bear them,—can possibly
tend to diminish the value of land. You may affect the value
of silks; you may affect the value of cottons or woollens:
transitory changes of fashion may do that—changes of taste;
but there is a taste for land inherent in human kind, and
especially is it the desire of Englishmen to possess land; and
therefore, whilst you have a monopoly of that article which
our very instincts lead us to desire to possess, if you see any
process going on by which our commerce and our numbers
are increased, it is impossible to suppose that it can have the
effect of diminishing the value of the article that is in your
hands.

What, then, is the good of this 'protection?' What is
this boasted 'protection?' Why, the country have come to
regard it, as they do witchcraft, as a mere sound and a delusion. They no more regard your precautions against Free
Trade than they regard the horse-shoes that are nailed over
the stables to keep the witches away from the horses. They
do not believe in protection; they have no fear of Free Trade;
and they are laughing to scorn all the arguments by which
you are trying to frighten them.

How can protection, think you, add to the wealth of a
country? Can you by legislation add one farthing to the
wealth of the country? You may, by legislation, in one
evening, destroy the fruits and accumulations of a century

of labour; but I defy you to show me how, by the legislation of this House, you can add one farthing to the wealth of the country. That springs from the industry and intelligence of the people of this country. You cannot guide that intelligence; you cannot do better than leave it to its own instincts. If you attempt by legislation to give any direction to trade or industry, it is a thousand to one that you are doing wrong; and if you happen to be right, it is a work of supererogation, for the parties for whom you legislate would go right without you, and better than with you.

Then, if this is true, why should there be any difference of opinion between us? Hon. Gentlemen may think that I have spoken hardly to them on this occasion; but I want to see them come to a better conclusion on this question. I believe, if they will look the thing in the face, and divest themselves of that crust of prejudice that oppresses them, we shall all be better friends about it. There are but two things that can prevent it: one is, their believing that they have a sinister interest in this question, and therefore not looking into it; and the other is, an incapacity for understanding political economy. I know there are many heads who cannot comprehend and master a proposition in political economy; I believe that study is the highest exercise of the human mind, and that the exact sciences require by no means so hard an effort. But, barring these two accidents—want of capacity, and having a sinister interest—I defy any man to look into this question honestly, and come to any other than one conclusion. Then why should we not agree? I want no triumph in this matter for the Anti-Corn-law League; I want you to put an end, from conviction, to an evil system. Come down to us, and let us hold a Free-trade meeting in our hall at Manchester. Come to us now, protectionists, and let us see whether we cannot do something better for our common country than carrying on this strife of parties. Let us, once for all, recognise this principle,

that we must not tax one another for the benefit of one
another.

Now, I am going to read to you an authority that will
astonish you.   I am going to read you an extract from a
speech of the Duke of Wellington in the House of Lords on
the 17th of April, 1832: it is his opinion on taxation:—

> ' He thought taxes were imposed only for the service of the State. If they
> were necessary for the service of the State, in God's name let them be paid;
> but if they were not necessary, they ought not to be paid, and the Legislature
> ought not to impose them.'

Now, there, that noble Duke, without having had time to
study Adam Smith or Ricardo, by that native sagacity which
is characteristic of his mind, came at once to the marrow of
this question. We must not tax one another for the benefit of
one another. Oh, then, divest the future Prime Minister of this
country of that odious task of having to reconcile rival interests; divest the office, if ever you would have a sagacious
man in power as Prime Minister, divest it of the responsibility
of having to find food for the people!   May you never find a
Prime Minister again to undertake that awful responsibility!
That responsibility belongs to the law of nature; as Burke
said, it belongs to God alone to regulate the supply of the
food of nations. When you shall have seen in three years that
the abolition of these laws is inevitable, as inevitable it is,
you will come forward and join with the Free-traders; for if
you do not, you will have the farmers coming forward and
agitating in conjunction with the League. You are in a position to gain honour in future; you are in a position, especially
the young members among you, who have the capacity to
learn the truth of this question, they are in a position to gain
honour in this struggle; but as you are going on at present
your position is a false one; you are in the wrong groove, and
are every day more and more diverging from the right point.
It may be material for you to get right notions of political
economy; questions of that kind will form a great part of the
world's legislation for a long time to come.

We are on the eve of great changes. Put yourselves in a position to be able to help in the work, and so gather honour and fame where they are to be gained. You belong to the aristocracy of the human kind—not the privileged aristocracy, —I don't mean that, but the aristocracy of improvement and civilisation. We have set an example to the world in all ages; we have given them the representative system. The very rules and regulations of this House have been taken as the model for every representative assembly throughout the whole civilised world; and having besides given them the example of a free press and civil and religious freedom, and every institution that belongs to freedom and civilisation, we are now about giving a still greater example; we are going to set the example of making industry free—to set the example of giving the whole world every advantage of clime, and latitude, and situation, relying ourselves on the freedom of our industry. Yes, we are going to teach the world that other lesson. Don't think there is anything selfish in this, or anything at all discordant with Christian principles. I can prove that we advocate nothing but what is agreeable to the highest behests of Christianity. To buy in the cheapest market, and sell in the dearest. What is the meaning of the maxim? It means that you take the article which you have in the greatest abundance, and with it obtain from others that of which they have the most to spare; so giving to mankind the means of enjoying the fullest abundance of earth's goods, and in doing so, carrying out to the fullest extent the Christian doctrine of ' Doing to all men as ye would they should do unto you.'

FREE TRADE.

XXII.

MANCHESTER, JULY 4, 1846.

[After the repeal of the Corn-laws, the Council of the Anti-Corn-law League resolved on suspending the action of the organisation which they had set in motion, as long as no attempt was made to revive protection.]

Ir this were a meeting for any other purpose than that of business, in the strictest sense of the word, I am quite sure that I should feel more embarrassed at meeting you on this occasion than I have done at any previous time; for I feel myself almost oppressed with the consciousness of the importance of the events we have been passing through lately, and of the great interest which is involved in the present meeting; and I am sure I could not do justice to the feelings which are now affecting me.

We are met here on the present occasion as a meeting of the Council of the League. We have, in the working of this body, as you are aware, an executive committee of gentlemen living in Manchester, and also the Council of the League, consisting of the subscribers of 50l. and upwards. The Executive Council of the League have called you, the Council, together, for the purpose of taking your opinion as to the course we shall now pursue; and I think the importance of that question is such, that I shall confine myself as strictly as possible to business details in what I have to say, because I do not wish to prevent the many gentlemen who have come from

c c 2

distant parts the opportunity of giving their advice and
assistance on this occasion. The Executive Council of the
League in Manchester have talked over the matter repeatedly,
and are now prepared to submit their views; and, as I may as
well put you in possession of what the general purport of all
the resolutions is, I will just explain the substance of the
whole.

We propose to recommend, not that the League shall be
absolutely dissolved in the strict sense of the word, and yet
we propose to take such steps as amount to a virtual dissolution of the League, unless the protectionist party compel us
again to revive our agitation. We propose to ask from you
the authority and instruction to wind up and suspend the
affairs of the League. We recommend that you should pass a
resolution, absolving all those gentlemen who have put their
names down to the large guarantee fund, and paid their first
instalment, from any further liability. We propose that you
shall pass a resolution, authorising the gentlemen in Manchester, who have acted on the Council of the League, in case
they should see any serious efforts made by the monopolists
to revive the system of protection, or to induce Parliament to
retrace its steps, then to request these gentlemen again to call
the League into active existence. Gentlemen, we have thought
that the course by which we shall fulfil our duty to the general
body of subscribers, and likewise our pledges to the public.
We have pledged ourselves not to retire from this agitation,
or disband the League, until the Corn-laws were totally and
immediately abolished. We are, therefore, not competent to
dissolve this League. At the same time I ought to say, that
with reference to our practical operations, it would be exceedingly difficult to draw a line between a total suspension of the
League and a partial suspension. If we continue active operations at all, it must be on a large scale, and at an enormous
expense. I do not think you can draw a distinction between
500l. a week and nothing. We have been spending the last

three years at least 1000*l.* a week. Under these circumstances,
I think it is a fair practical question to consider, what can be
the object gained if we continue the active agitation of the
League.   In two years and a half the Corn-laws will be
abolished by an Act now upon the statute-book; and let us
entertain the supposition that our efforts in agitation out of
doors should be ever so successful, it is hardly possible that in
less than two years and a half we should succeed in altering
the law which now exists; therefore I do not see that any
practical good can result from continuing the agitation in any
form whatever.

Now many people may say, ' Are you safe in disbanding
this great organisation?   Are you safe in taking off your
uniform (if I may use the expression), of casting aside your
weapons of moral warfare?   Will not the protectionists gain
strength and confidence if they see you abandon the field?' I
am of opinion that there is no danger of anything of the kind.
I look upon it that the mere boasting and vapouring of a few
of the less wise part of the protectionist party may be very
well excused by us.   It is quite natural that men who felt
worsted in an argument, and in all the tactics of political
action during the last seven years, should console themselves
with the promise of what they will do the next seven years.
But I hold that you may as soon abolish Magna Charta, or
do away with Trial by Jury, or repeal the Test and Corporation Act, or the Catholic Emancipation Act, as ever re-enact
protection as a principle again in this country.

Some people say we go back in this country.   I maintain
that we never go back after a question has been discussed and
sifted as ours has.   You have never gone back in any of the
great questions; if settled once, they have been settled altogether.   People do say that we went back after the Reform
Act was passed.   I will tell you what we did.   We got hold
of a machine which we did not know how to use, and the
proper use of which we are now learning, but we never went

back. Nobody ever proposed the repeal of one enactment of
the Reform Act. Therefore I hope our friends everywhere will
bear this in mind; and if they should hear a noble lord, or
even a noble duke, talking of what they will do, not let their
nervous system be excited or alarmed. They must raise a
fresh crop of statesmen to carry out their principles, for we
have all the statesmen now on our side of the question. Such
being our position, we have very good grounds for gratulation
on the present occasion. I confess I hardly know whom to
thank, or how to account, for our present position; there
has been such a combination of fortunate accidents, that
I must confess that I am disposed to thank that Providence
which has overruled so many apparently conflicting incidents
for this great and mighty good. I believe we, at all events,
may say, that, humanly speaking, we owe a debt of gratitude
to our gracious Sovereign the Queen. I believe it is not in
strict etiquette to allude to our Queen's personal views and
feelings in any matter, but it is well known that her Majesty's
predilections are strongly in favour of the cause we have been
agitating. Then, there is her late First Minister; along with
our success, we have seen the downfall of that Minister. Some
people say he has lost office by giving us Free Trade. Well,
if he has lost office, he has gained a country. For my part, I
would rather descend into private life with that last measure
of his, which led to his discomfiture, in my hand, than mount
to the highest pinnacle of human power. Among the statesmen, we owe a debt of gratitude to Lord John Russell. Individually, I believe, we owe to him and his firmness, to his
letter, and to his firmness during the intrigues of the last six
months in London—I believe we owe it to his individual firmness that we had the support of the Whig aristocracy at all in
this measure. I am anxious as an individual on this occasion,
that I should lose sight of nobody to whom the country is
indebted for the passing of these measures, because I do feel
there has been a disposition to make one of us a great deal

more a monopolist in this matter than he deserves. ['No, no.']
I speak of myself, and I say, that when I entered upon this
career we found the road very much prepared; the mighty
impediments had been removed by the labours of others; we
had had men preceding us who had been toiling to beat down
great prejudices, and destroy fallacies, and prepare a path for
us which we had simply to macadamise to win our way to
victory. There are many of these men here around me. I
would not forget men who, like the late Mr. Deacon Hume,
Mr. Macgregor, and Mr. Porter, in the privacy of their
closets, furnished the world with statistics, arguments, and
facts, which, after all, have swayed mankind more than any
declamation or appeals to the passions can possibly do. There
is one man especially whom I wish not to forget: it is
Colonel Thompson. Colonel Thompson has made more large
pecuniary sacrifices than any man living for Free Trade, and
we all know his contributions in an intellectual point of view,
which have been invaluable to us — we will not forget the
worthy Colonel amidst our congratulations amongst each
other.

I said I should not detain you with a long speech, and in
fact I cannot do it, for I do feel oppressed with the feelings
which now pervade my mind. I believe we are at an era
which in importance, socially, has not its equal for the last
1800 years. I believe there is no event that has ever happened in the world's history, that in a moral and social point
of view—there is no human event that has happened in the
world more calculated to promote the enduring interests of humanity than the establishment of the principle of Free Trade,
—I don't mean in a pecuniary point of view, or as a principle
applied to England, but we have a principle established now
which is eternal in its truth and universal in its application,
and must be applied in all nations and throughout all times,
and applied not simply to commerce, but to every item of the
tariffs of the world; and if we are not mistaken in thinking

that our principles are true, be assured that those results will
follow, and at no very distant period. Why, it is a world's
revolution, and nothing else; and every meeting we have held
of this League, and this its last meeting probably, may be
looked back upon as the germ of a movement which will
ultimately comprehend the whole world in its embrace. I see
and feel, and have always felt, the great social and moral
importance of this great question. I believe many who have
taken an active part in this question have been influenced
solely by its moral and social consequences.

We have amongst us on this occasion a gentleman who has
come from a neighbouring country, France, an eloquent advocate of Free Trade there, Mons. Duffour Dubergier, the Mayor
of Bordeaux. It is gratifying that we should attract by a
kindred sympathy the visit to our meeting of so distinguished
a man; and I know he will go back, not with fresh emotions
of sympathy towards our cause, for those he has entertained
already, but I have no doubt he will go back inspirited by
what he sees here, and that he will be anxious that France
should not stand long apart from England in this glorious
career, but that we join hand to hand in setting nations the
example of the mutual advantages of peace and prosperity.

Well, this League must dissolve—it must suspend. Our
elements must be scattered. I cannot help saying personally
for myself, that the greatest pleasure I have found in the
course of those proceedings has been in the acquaintances I
have formed with, and the kindness I have received from, the
men connected with this association. If I could ever have
despaired of this country, after the acquaintances which I
have made with the men in connection with this question—
men who will be found the salt of this land in whatever good
is to be accomplished—having known what I do of my fellow-
countrymen in this agitation, I shall never despair of this
moral power to conduct this good ship through whatever
storm may arise, which will save us from anarchy at one

end, or tyranny at the other end of society. I am going to
be egotistical; but I will say that, so far as I myself am concerned—so far as my tastes go—a release from an active life
of agitation will not be unacceptable to me. I ought, in order
to enjoy the full pleasure of an agitator, to be differently constituted; and I don't think nature ever intended me for that
line. I say it most unaffectedly, that I entered upon the
career of agitation without the slightest idea that it would
ever have conducted me to the point to which I have arrived.
I had not the most distant idea of it. I don't think circumstances would have warranted myself in taking the step eight
years ago, if I could have seen what it would lead to. We
got into the groove, and were pushed along, and we found
ourselves carrying a train of good hardy spirits who would not
leave us; and having given us their support, we were impelled
forward in the groove at an accelerated speed, and with a
constantly increased sympathy.

Well, for myself, you will hardly credit it, when I say that
with regard to myself, I have precisely the same feeling now
with respect to the ordeal of public meetings that I had when
I began this agitation. It is a matter of great reluctance and
difficulty for me to appear before an audience at all. Many
people would think that we had our reward in the applause
and *éclat* of public meetings; but I declare upon my honour
that it is not so with me, for the inherent reluctance I have
to address public meetings is so great, that I don't even get
up to present a petition in the House of Commons without
reluctance. I therefore hope I may be believed when I say
that if this agitation terminates now, it will be very acceptable to my feelings; but if there should be the same necessity,
the same feeling which has impelled me to take the part I
have will impel me to a new agitation,—ay, and with tenfold
more vigour, after having had a little time to recruit my
strength.

We are going to dissolve; those good spirits must disband,

and I am not quite sure that it is not wise and proper that it should be so. We have been kept together for seven years without one single dispute, without anything to cause the slightest alienation. We have had the bond of freemasonry and brotherhood so closely knit about us, that I don't think there has been a keen word in the happy family of the Anti-Corn-law League. That is the spirit in which we should break off. Were we to continue our agitation, when the object for which we associated is gone, I am afraid that the demon of discord would be getting in among us. It is in nature so. It is in our moral nature necessary that when an organised body has performed its functions, it must pass into a new state of existence, and become differently organised. We are dispersing our elements to be ready for any other good work, and it is nothing but good works that will be attempted by good Leaguers. Our body will, so to say, perish; but our spirit is abroad, and will pervade all the nations of the earth. It will pervade all the nations of the earth because it is the spirit of truth and justice, and because it is the spirit of peace and good-will amongst men.

FREE TRADE

XXIII.

HOUSE OF COMMONS, MARCH 8, 1849.

[On March 8th, 1849, in the House of Commons, Mr. Disraeli moved for a Committee of the whole House, to take into consideration such measures as might remove the grievances of the owners and occupiers of real property. On this motion, Mr. Hume moved an amendment; and the debate was adjourned to the 15th March, when Mr. Cobden delivered the following speech, in opposition to Mr. Disraeli's motion, which was rejected by a majority of 91 (280 to 189).]

I HAVE been alluded to so frequently in the course of this debate, that I am not willing to allow it to cease without saying a few words. I shall not weary the House by a reference to the speech of the honourable mover of the original motion; I consider that to do so, after the able speech of the right honourable the Chancellor of the Exchequer (Sir Charles Wood), would be to slay the slain. I will not stop to say a word on the jocular misrepresentations which have been made of the speech of the honourable Member for Montrose (Mr. Hume); but I may say that to-morrow I shall probably refer to those misrepresentations, as to the amount of expenditure on our naval and military establishments, which I think are very much calculated to mislead the country.

The plan of the honourable Gentleman opposite has at length been resolved into this—that it is a proposal to lay on between 400,000*l.* and 500,000*l.* of additional taxation on the farmers, on the plea of benefiting them. And this is the proposal which is made in the interest of the tenant-farmers. That is, upon the assumption that it is demonstrated beyond

all possible cavil or contradiction that the local burdens laid
upon property are borne by the owners of property, and not
by the floating capital of the country. If you deny that, of
course you can go to the country with your proposition for
favouring the farmer by reducing the burdens on real property; but is there a human being whose opinion is deserving
a moment's consideration who will deny this proposition, that
if you relieve the burdens upon real property, the relief will
go into the pockets of the owners of that property? Take
this case: Two farms are to let of exactly equal intrinsic
value, as to quality, soil, and situation. One shall be rated at
2s. in the pound to the poor-rate; the other at 8s. Would
you let the two farms for the same rent? I ask even a nod
of assent from the honourable Gentleman opposite. There is
not a farmer or land-agent who would say that the two farms
would let for the same money. Deducting in each case the
amount of the rate, the remainder is the amount of rent in
each. Is not this coming before us under false pretences? It
is altogether very much like a hoax. First of all, the tenant-
farmers are paraded before us. You come in hot haste from
Willis's Rooms with the case of the tenant-farmers. Not a
man is allowed to speak there but a tenant-farmer: by the
way, they are for the most part land-agents. I know the most
of them, because I have met them in the country. But you
come here professing to serve the tenant-farmers, and you try to
raise a quarrel between them and the manufacturers. What was
the peroration of the speech of the hon. Member for Buckinghamshire (Mr. Disraeli)? Was it not an attempt to array the
tenant-farmers against the manufacturers, by the classing the
former under the insidious title of the landed interest. But there
is no difference between the manufacturers and the farmers in
relation to the question before the House. The farmer is a
manufacturer; he hires the land for manufacturing purposes.
But, as farmers and landlords, your interests are antagonistic,
in spite of anything that may be said to the contrary.

I do not wish to set farmers against landlords by saying
that. ['Oh, oh.'] You may cry 'Oh!' but I will be understood
by the farmers as well as by the landlords in this House. As
members of one community I do not say that landlords and
farmers have not common interests in good and equal laws;
but if you come before this House, and ask for a measure to
benefit landlord and tenant exclusively, then I tell you, that
as landlords and tenants your interests are antagonistic—for
the interest of the one is to rent the land as cheap as he can,
and the interest of the other to let it as dear as he can. I say,
then, that it is impossible to combine both in one measure,
so as to give an equal amount of benefit to both interests.
You might as well expect to combine the cotton brokers of
Liverpool, and the cotton spinners of Manchester in one measure, which would be equally advantageous to both. The two
cases are precisely the same. And I do hope the time is not
far distant when these discussions will put the tenant-farmers
in their real position in this country.

I have been accused by honourable Gentlemen with having
said that I considered the farmers had been injured—nay, the
honourable Member for Buckinghamshire went so far as to
say that I was a party to injuring them. I wish honourable
Gentlemen would have the fairness to give the entire context
of what I did say, and not pick out detached words. If they
did so, it would save time and my explanations. What I said
at Manchester was this, that as we carried the principle of
Free Trade with respect to corn, we owed it to the farmer to
carry out the same principles, by removing as far as possible
every impediment to the free employment of capital and labour
upon the soil. The farmer complains of the interference of the
malt-tax with his business, and it is not inconsistent with my
principles to remove that impediment out of his way. I do
this without pretending to any particular affection for the
farmer above other classes. If I did so, I would follow your
error, by attempting to legislate for a particular class. I said

on a former occasion, that I would not enter again into the subject of Free Trade, unless a motion was laid on the table of the House for the purpose of restoring protection to corn. But this motion has been made a protection debate, and we have been challenged by honourable Gentlemen opposite to make good our case; and it has been asserted that we are the authors of all kinds of disasters, not only to the farmers everywhere, but to the labourers, and even to the manufacturers.

I deny the charge, and I bring you to the facts. You complain of the condition of the agricultural labourer—you complain that he is suffering from the low price of provisions. The noble lord the Member for West Sussex (the Earl of March) spoke of the halcyon days of high-priced corn, and how well off the agricultural labourers were then. I have taken pains to inquire into that matter, and I deny that they were better off. Take one of those darling years of which you are so fond—take the year 1847, and compare it with the present time. An agricultural labourer's family, consisting of five persons, if they consumed as much bread as is allowed per head by the Poor-law Unions to out-of-door paupers, should consume ten 4lb. loaves in the week. Then ten loaves in 1847 cost 9d. a loaf, or 7s. 6d. for the whole; they cost now 6d. a loaf, or 5s. for the whole; so that he pays 2s. 6d. less for his bread now than he did in 1847. The reduction of wages generally is about 1s. a week, so that he is a gainer by 1s. 6d. But I will take the extreme case put by the honourable Gentleman opposite, and assume that wages have fallen 2s. a week, and even then it leaves a balance of 6d. a week in his favour, independently of the measures passed in consequence of Free Trade for the reduction of sugar, which conferred a further benefit on the labourer. But take the ordinary case of the labourers and mechanics in towns — take the case of the manufacturing labourers in the north of England and in London — and I maintain that, at the present time, as compared with those high-priced years gone

by for ever, those years for which the noble lord sighs in
vain—the mechanical operatives and labouring population in
our great manufacturing seats save at least from 2*s*. to 3*s*.
a week in their weekly wages, which is tantamount to fifteen
per cent. on their income.

The honourable Member for the North Riding of Yorkshire
(Mr. Cayley) said that we failed in all our predictions, and he
made us appear as if we expected a great many things which
I never expected. He said that we caused a great reduction
of wages. Well, if you say you have reduced wages in the
agricultural districts, I hold that you are good authority for
that statement: but I deny that wages have been reduced in
the manufacturing districts; nay, more, I deny that they
have been reduced in the neighbourhood of those districts.
On the contrary, there has been a tendency to a rise in wages
during the six weeks that the Corn-law has been abolished.
I will state a case which the noble Lord the Member for
Stamford (the Marquis of Granby) will comprehend. Within
a few weeks a body of men for whom he and his brothers
professed great sympathy—the stockingers and glove-makers
of the midland counties—struck for an increase of wages. I
find it stated in the Nottingham newspapers, that they have
had four successive strikes for wages, and that the men gained
the advantage on every occasion — a thing which was not
known for seventy years before — during the whole of which
period there had been a gradual diminution of wages. Take
again the district with which I am connected—take Lancashire. What is the state of things there at the present time
as compared with the days to which the noble lord is so
anxious to go back, and to which you are all anxious to
return? Why, it is in a state of comparative prosperity now.
Look to Bradford, and compare its condition now to the state
it was in twelve months ago, when I accompanied a deputation to the right honourable the Chancellor of the Exchequer,
asking for relief in its behalf.

But I need not confine myself to the manufacturing districts.
I will take the condition of the farmers themselves. I call on
the honourable Member for East Somersetshire (Mr. Miles) to
go over some figures together with me. I admit the farmers
are suffering in certain districts. But I am not going to let
honourable Gentlemen off as to the cause of that distress. Do
honourable Gentlemen forget that the farmers suffered sometimes before? Do they read *Hansard?* Do they recollect the
years 1819, 1820, and 1822, when petitions were presented
every night, and debates and speeches upon them — when
county meetings were held day after day to protest against
the distress and oppression which the agriculturists were
labouring under, and when they showed themselves more
sensible than they did now, for then they always accompanied
their petitions for redress, with a demand for a reduction of
expenditure and taxation? They did not then suffer themselves
to be bamboozled as they do now, when not a word is uttered
by them about a reduction of public expenditure. What do
you think of the year 1821, when Sir E. Knatchbull declared
that all the farmers were nearly ruined in 1820 — that they
were quite ruined in 1821? In 1822 a Committee of Inquiry
was granted to inquire into agricultural distress. Now, bear
in mind, that you had all this time a law which gave you a
monopoly of the wheat market up to the price of 80s. What
said the report of that Committee? Why, it said, ' it must
be admitted that protection could not be carried further than
monopoly, and that the agricultural interest enjoyed a complete monopoly since 1819.' No wheat had been imported
from 1819 to 1822, and yet the agricultural interest was in a
state of universal distress, and even in a state of bankruptcy.
Well, in 1835, you were in the same condition precisely, and
you had a committee which made no report, because no case
could be made out during the time of the sliding-scale. In
1836, again, the Marquis of Chandos made a motion for the
repeal of the malt-tax, and he said that the landlords were

abandoning their mansions to go and live abroad, the farmers
were going to the workhouse, and the labourers, instead of
drinking beer, drank water from the pump. Do you recollect that Mr. Dennett, the Member for Wiltshire, when slily
threatened with the income-tax, said that this was no threat
to the landed interest, for the land was no longer theirs—it
belonged to mortgagees and money-lenders? Well, all this
was during the height of protection—and with this before
you, how can you come and say that, with Free Trade only
in existence for six weeks, we are the cause of the distress
of the farmers?

I believe that this distress has partly arisen in consequence
of our principle of an immediate repeal not being carried out.
I stated my opinion emphatically in 1846, that the farmers
were making a mistake in not having the Corn-law immediately repealed, because I knew that during the three years
that it was to continue a stimulus would be given to the production of wheat all over the world, for the purpose of pouring
it into the market here, when the duty was entirely taken
away. The duty, which was run up to ten shillings, came
down suddenly, and this was partly the cause of the distress.
I believe that the parties who imported this wheat are selling
it now at a loss. But if we are not the cause of the farmer's
distress, who is the cause of it? Let us go back to a time
when farmers were generally doing well. Between the years
1785 and 1790 the farmers had a quiet, steady trade : there
were no complaints then. Why were there now? Why did
not the farmers get the profit now which they got in the
period between the American war and the French revolution?
In 1790 the price of iron and implements of husbandry was
double what it is now ; clothing of every kind was nearly
double ; cotton articles were four or five times their present
price ; salt was double the price at which it is now selling.
Tea, sugar, coffee, soap, fuel, were dearer then than now.
Spices, preserved fruits, and all the moderate luxuries of life

were then dearer than at present. But, on the other hand,
butcher's-meat, bacon, butter, cheese, poultry, and eggs bring
higher prices now than then, so that all the articles in which
the farmer dealt sold as cheap or cheaper then than at present;
while, with the single exception of beer, which we, the Free-
traders, are anxious to put on the same footing, there is no
article of domestic use or implement employed in his business
which the farmer cannot buy cheaper now than in 1790. The
price of labour in the purely agricultural districts has not
changed more than one or two shillings a week, and taking
its productiveness into account, it is far cheaper now than in
1790. Why, then, does the farmer complain now? There is
one little item which you all forget, but which I do not forget,
and that is simply the rent of land, which in any case is
double, and in some places treble, what it was in 1790. I say,
without hesitation or fear of contradiction, that the rent of
agricultural land in England is now double what it was in
1790, and in many cases treble ; while in Scotland it is
generally more than treble.

I am not going to speak to you, now that the Corn-laws
are repealed, in language different from that which I used
when agitating for the repeal of those Corn-laws. I have
never, in the presence of farmers, in any county in England—
and I have met them in open assembly in almost every county
— much as I am charged with telling one story in one place
and another story in another place — I have never dwelt on a
probable reduction of rents as a reason for repealing the Corn-
laws. I have, however, always said that with free trade in
corn, and with moderate prices, if the present rents were to
be maintained, it must be by means of a different system of
managing property from that which you now pursue. You
must have men of capital on your land ; you must let your
land on mercantile principles—you must not be afraid of an
independent and energetic man who will vote as he pleases at
the hustings — you must abandon that modern innovation of

battue shooting, which was not known to your ancestors in
1790. Well, now, you laugh at that. I said before that I
know I was speaking in the presence of landowners and landlords, and I now ask you to deal fairly with me when I tell
you a home truth ; it is, that when you laugh at this battue
shooting, you are doing precisely the contrary of what the
farmers would do if I were speaking about it to them. I
know that farmers regard this system of game preserving
as a very great nuisance,—as a very great hindrance to the
employment of capital. I know an instance of one of the
greatest agitators for Corn-laws, a large landed proprietor, who
has driven some of the best tenants that could be found in
this kingdom—men of capital—from his estates, because he
perseveres in keeping up an inordinate amount of game. I
am not going to be fanatical with you, even on the subject of
game. I never yet met a farmer—I now speak in particular
of the Lothians—who wished to extirpate game. You may
have all the game necessary for exercise ; but if you will keep
up such an amount of game as is necessary for the shooting
of five hundred head in one day—and I have heard of that
being done by a noble lord and some of his friends—let me
tell you that you cannot get men who will pay you in rent,
pay you in game, and pay you also in votes. You must be
content with a money rent. Give up your game, and give up
the votes of your tenants, or you will not be able to retain
your money rent. There is nothing unreasonable, though
there may be something very inconvenient, at this late hour,
in my talking to you in this way. If you come to this House
and parade the distress of the farmer—if, besides, you utter
something like a threat of robbing the Exchequer, and deal
out alarming predictions of what is going to happen if the
farmers are not made to prosper in their business, it becomes
us, who take a different view, to tell you what are the reasons
why the farmers are not more prosperous.

Now, Sir, something has been said about the very painful

ordeal of sending away small farmers who have an insignificant amount of capital. Well, in the first place, it is not very
complimentary to a system of Corn-laws and protection, that
the farmer's trade is the only one in this kingdom in which
capital is deficient. It is overflowing in every other trade. I
defy you to show me any other trade in the kingdom, wholesale or retail, which is not glutting the market. And farming
being the most inviting business of all, is one to which capital
will gladly flow, if you will accept energetic men and men of
capital as tenants. Give such men fair leases, and let them
do what is best for their own prosperity, and capital will
always come to the land in abundance. But what I wish particularly to show you is this—that it is a mistaken humanity
to keep on your estates farmers who are deficient in capital,
and, I should add, intelligence also, if what the honourable
Member for Dorsetshire stated be strictly correct—namely,
that if you went to the farmers of that county and explained
to them what the honourable Member for Buckinghamshire
meant to do for their benefit, they would all, without being
coerced by their landlords, at once say, ' We shall be very
glad if you will take off these local rates, for we feel quite
sure that the landlords will not put the amount into their
pockets, but will take it off our rent.' If such be the real
character of the farmers, I must say that they want intelligence as well as capital.

   What I say on that subject is this, that while you are
looking at the interests of men who are without intelligence
and without capital, you are losing sight of the interests of
the agricultural labourers, who are much more numerous, and
therefore more deserving of consideration, than even these
small farmers. If you have not men of capital on your land,
the labourers cannot be employed. Go to any district—for
example, North Devon or Dorsetshire—where the farmers are
most deficient in capital, and there you will find the poor-
rates highest, and the labourers most depressed. Well, then,

I say, whatever may be the inconvenience of doing so, you must take steps to draw capital to your land. You must invite it—you must tempt it—and if you do so, you will be able to employ your labourers. It is perfectly true, as was stated by the noble lord the Member for West Sussex, that in seasons of depression a number of labourers are thrown out of employment in the agricultural districts; and that while the depression lasts, it tends to raise the amount of the poor-rates, so that it is made to appear that the poor-rate has not a tendency to fall in cheap years, as we maintain it ought to do. But what is the cause of agricultural labourers having been thus thrown out of employment when a depression suddenly arises? It is because the tenantry have made false calculations as to the mode in which they are to carry on a profitable cultivation of the land. Farmers have depended on high prices being maintained by Act of Parliament; and, when those prices fail them, as they always have done from time to time, once in seven or ten years, these men, who have insufficient capital to rest upon, and who have depended upon nothing but artificial prices, break down, and come petitioning Parliament for relief.

Well, then, you must put an end to this state of things. I exhort you to tell the farmers honestly that it is 'a delusion, a mockery, and a snare,' to teach them that you can restore one shilling of protection in this House. I admit that you may tamper with the Navigation Laws. That matter rests with the noble lord and his Government; and, if I were in his place, I would stand or fall by the Navigation Bill without altering a clause. But I tell him in the most amicable spirit, that there will be no agitation for the repeal of the Navigation Laws. The public mind considers the Free-trade question as settled; but the public also expect that the Government will show some vigour in completing the measures of Free Trade, by equalising the duties in the tariff, the duties on coffee, and other articles of general consumption, and by getting rid of the Navigation Laws. They expect the Executive Government to show the same vigour, with a majority of fifty or sixty in this House, as the right honourable Gentleman (Sir Robert Peel) showed in laying the foundation of Free Trade by the repeal of the Corn-laws. The effect of this measure being rejected would not be to create an agitation, but to strike the country with despair of any strong and vigorous administration in the hands of the noble lord.

I say, then, that whatever may be the fate of the Navigation Laws, the Corn question is a different thing. I was always an advocate for confining the public mind to that one question ; I call it the keystone of the arch ; the rest will fall of itself. But if the Government were to propose a 1s. duty on corn —it was a fearful scene in 1815, when the people surrounded this House whilst you were passing the Corn-law; but, depend upon it, you will be surrounded by a totally different class, if you attempt to pass another Corn-law. Now, if you value your own interest, if you value the interest of the farmer,—above all, if you value the interest of your labouring population, dissipate this delusion, which some of you are attempting to propagate ; proclaim, once for all, that any renewal of protection on corn is as impossible as it would be to revoke Magna Charta. Tell them to rely upon their own energies, and that you will co-operate with them. Go to them, and talk to them, and do not come here, talking to the Government or the Prime Minister about reviving protection. Take your proper place, and do your duty alongside of your tenants. Join together in adopting such measures as are suitable to your altered circumstances—and to that which is irrevocable. Don't dream of high prices again. High prices are incompatible with the well-being of this country, and with the interest of the manufacturing population of the large towns. Do you want to follow out the policy of the noble lord the Member for West Sussex, the Earl of March, and to bring us back to the state in which we were in 1839, 1840,

1841, and 1842, the years included in his list of high prices,
and when he says everybody was prosperous? Have you forgotten the state of Stockport, almost a desolation? Have you
forgotten Sheffield, with its 20,000 people existing on the
poor-rates; or Leeds, with its 30,000, in the same condition?
Have you forgotten a state of things in which political excitement almost bordered on insurrection? and would you dare
to bring back such a state of things, and, above all, call
it prosperity? No, you have a fair career before you with
moderate prices, provided you will alter the system on which
you conduct your affairs.

Thirty years ago the manufacturers and merchants of this
country had to go through precisely the same ordeal as you
have now to pass through. Many of you remember what a
revulsion there was within three years after the war in every
article of manufactures. Why, a great number of people were
then ruined by the losses which they sustained through the
stocks which they had on hand. But what occurred gave rise
to a totally different description of trade—a trade aiming at a
large production and small profits; and let me tell you for
your encouragement, that, from 1817 up to the present time,
the fortunes made in manufactures and commerce have not
been realised by selling at high prices, but almost every
successive fortune has been made by selling at lower prices,
though in larger quantities. Now there is abundance of scope
for you to carry out the same thing. I believe we have no
adequate conception of what the amount of production might
be from a limited surface of land, provided only the amount
of capital were sufficient. There is no reason whatever why
I should not live to see the day when a man who lays out
1000l. on fifty acres of land, will be a more independent,
more prosperous, and more useful man, than many farmers
who now occupy five or six hundred acres, with not one
quarter or one-tenth of the capital necessary to carry on the
cultivation.

I sincerely thank the House for having listened to me with
so much attention at this hour of the morning. I should be
sorry if the motion of my honourable friend the Member for
Montrose were ignored in the great discussion which we have
had about local taxes. My honourable friend seems to me to
have very properly met the case as it at present stands. It is
quite clear that the honourable Member for Buckinghamshire
has been put out of court. That is quite certain. When the
farmer reads the Chancellor of the Exchequer's speech—and I
would certainly recommend every farmer in the country to do
so—when he reads that speech, aided by the analysis which I
find in *Punch* to-day—when he sees that the sum total of advantage to the farmer, shown by the speech and the analysis,
is an increase of taxation to the amount of 400,000*l.*, I don't
think he will consider that any boon has been offered to him.
The Chancellor of the Exchequer himself does not, indeed,
promise anything much better. He declares that he cannot
give us any remission of taxation. Well, then, my honourable
friend the Member for Montrose steps in in the most timely
way; and, though now probably, as he has always been, a
little before his time, still he is right. Now, I am quite sure
that you cannot benefit the farmer except by a general reduction of the national expenditure. Let us further tell the landowners that that is the only means of staving off that tendency
to a reduction of rent, which must arise in a transition state,
though I maintain that the value of land will ultimately be
higher under a system of Free Trade than it ever could have
been under protection.

My honourable friend proposes to repeal the malt-tax.
Now, though I am a very great advocate for the repeal of
that tax, yet, being a sober man myself, I do not take such
an interest in the question as some honourable Members do.
But I shall vote for the repeal, chiefly because I wish to
diminish the waste of our national expenditure, and thus, to
find means of reducing taxation. Let there be sufficient

pressure, and the Government will find a way of reducing our costly establishments. I will add, that my own course with regard to the reduction of taxation is supported by that of the noble lord (Lord John Russell), who in 1816, after the war, contended for a reduction of the army below the Government estimate of 99,000 men. The men were voted, but there was an immense excitement against the property-tax, and when it came to be voted, it was rejected by a large majority; hereupon the Secretary at War asked to withdraw his estimates, with a view to their revision, and they were revised and reduced most materially. So, if the Government now was made to take the malt-tax and other taxes in hand, with a view to their reduction, they will soon find it necessary to reduce their estimates; and, therefore, as one very sound reason, do I hope that the House will support the proposition of my honourable friend for a reduction of expenditure.

FREE TRADE

XXIV.

LEEDS, DECEMBER 18, 1849.

[In 1847, Mr. Cobden was returned unopposed for the West Riding of Yorkshire, and sat for that constituency for nearly ten years. For some time after the repeal of the Corn-laws he was absent from England, but on his return he made several speeches on topics of public interest during the year 1849.]

THERE is a peculiar advantage in Members of the House of Commons coming, from time to time, in contact with the people, and especially with their own constituencies. It enables us to take their judgment upon the course which we, their Representatives, have followed in times past; and, what is equally important, it enables us to confer with them as to the line of conduct which we should pursue in future. I was, therefore, anxious to-night to have had the opportunity of listening, at greater length, to the speeches of the inhabitants of Leeds ; and I sincerely regret that my friend, Mr. Baines, and other gentlemen who have spoken, should have curtailed their remarks out of consideration for me, or a desire that I should be heard addressing you instead of them. I think more good would have arisen if they had favoured us, at greater length, with their views and opinions upon the important questions now before us. Amongst the questions which have been launched this evening by our worthy chairman, is one which I fondly hoped I should never again have had the necessity of speaking upon,—I mean the old, worn-out, the disgusting question of protection. Why, I thought

it was dead and buried years ago. It is now eleven years this
very month, and I believe this very week, since the first great
meeting was held in Manchester, from which originated the
Anti-Corn-law League. On that occasion, in December, 1838,
two hundred persons from all parts of the kingdom, assembled,
and many gentlemen here present were at the meeting. For
seven years afterwards there was a continual agitation of the
Free-trade question throughout the country, and I believe
nearly 1000 public meetings were held upon it in every part
of the kingdom. Hundreds of tons' weight of tracts were
printed and distributed upon the subject; debate after debate
took place upon it in Parliament—sometimes scarcely anything else was debated there for months—and now, at the end
of eleven years, we are told that we are to have this question
up again for discussion. And why, and on what ground?
Amongst other pleas why we should have this question again
re-agitated is, that the agriculturists were betrayed, and protection was suddenly abandoned, after seven years of discussion
only! Now, gentlemen, so far as I am concerned, I have
allowed certain people to go about talking in the country, and
talking in the House of Commons, without ever having con-
descended to answer them. Nay, I candidly confess that I felt
the most supreme contempt for all they said. I viewed it as
nothing but the contortions of a body that had lost its head;
just as we read of unfortunate criminals whose limbs writhe and
move by a sort of spasmodic action after they had been de-
capitated. I thought their party, having lost its brains, had
still some muscular action left in it, but I never believed it
was to be treated again as a sentient intelligent body, worthy
the holding a discussion with in this country.

But, gentlemen, I have been told, by those in whose judgment I have confidence, that we have allowed our opponents to
go unanswered too long, and that there is, amongst a very large
portion of the farming class in this country, a belief that, from
our silence, protection is gaining ground again in this country.

Why, let them understand that our silence has been the
result of supreme contempt. In those meetings, which we
read of in the agricultural districts, we hear the reiterated
assertion that the whole country is preparing to go back again
to protection, and I concur with the view taken by our
respected chairman, that we ought, if possible, to prevent the
delusion which is being practised upon the farmers, which
prevents the farmers having an adjustment and arrangement
with their landlords—that we ought, if possible, to put an
end to that delusion here, in order that agriculture may
resume its old course, and the landlord and farmer may come
to some agreement as to terms between each other. Where is
the proof of reaction? I admit that, in some of our rural
villages, where men,—or rather, we ought to call them, old
women—still put horse-shoes over their stable-doors to
keep the witches from their horses—there may, in some of
those parishes, be found men who will gape and cheer when
told that we are going back to protection. But I think there
is somebody else to be consulted before they put on another
bread-tax; and amongst other parties to be consulted, I
calculate the West Riding will have a voice in it. Now,
where is the proof of reaction in the West Riding? We
have in this Riding—the population of which I have the
honour to represent—about 1,400,000 souls, which is about
one-twelfth part of the whole population of England, and a far
larger proportion of its wealth, intelligence, and productive
industry. Well, I presume this community is to have a voice
in this question of the bread-tax. In answer to these village
heroes, these men, who, when they have put their parish in a
turmoil, that vastly resembles a storm in a tea pot, fancy the
whole of England gathered together, when it is nothing but
an agitation of the squire, his agent, and probably a parson
and a doctor. In answer to these protectionist noodles, and
their organs of the press, who are continually telling the
farmers, what they have been telling them now for eleven

years, that they are going to have protection and keep it, I
tell them they never shall have one farthing's worth of protection. These are only a couple of predictions. Some time
or other, I presume, the farmers will wish to have friends who
tell them the truth. Whenever the time comes when the
farmers understand who it is who has been telling them the
truth,—those who say they are going to have protection, or
those who say from this platform they never shall have one
farthing more of Corn-law,—when that time comes, then I
think the age of delusion will be over in the agricultural
districts. I want to know how long they will require before
they make up their minds whether I am right, or those
squires are right. The time will come. I give them seven
years, if they like; only let it be understood, that they remember the promise made on the one side by their own
leaders, and here by the men of the West Riding; and then I
calculate the farmers will throw off their foolish blind guides,
and co-operate with those who have proved themselves to
have some sense and foresight in the matter. What is it
these landlords want to do with you? There is no disguise
about the matter now. When we were agitating the Corn-
law question before, they said their object was plenty, the
same as ours; but what is their cry now? Why, they complain that you get the quartern loaf too cheap, and they want
to raise the price of it to you; and that is the only business
they have in hand. You get a couple of stones of decent flour
now for 3s.; two or three years ago you paid 4s. for a single
stone. Well, those landlords were satisfied when you were
paying 4s. a stone for flour, and now they are dissatisfied
when you get two stones for 3s., and they want to go back
again to the 4s. for the one stone. Will you let them? [Cries
of 'No, no.'] No; you are not Yorkshiremen if you will.
We are told that all parts of the country are in distress and
dissatisfaction. That is the old story again. Because the
landlords feel a little uneasy—they who have been so long

accustomed to consider themselves the whole community—
(I believe many of them think so)—they get up and say the
whole community is suffering from extreme distress.

Now, I say, the West Riding of Yorkshire has been growing more prosperous, and suffering less and less distress, in
proportion as the price of corn, of which those landlords complain, has become more moderate—and, if they can ever return—if they can ever succeed in returning again to the
price I have mentioned, 4s. for the stone of flour, you will
have your town swarming with paupers, your mills stopping
work, and every class in this community suffering distress, as
they were in 1842. And that is what they want to bring
you back to; for, having looked into the matter with attention for ten years past, I declare that I find no period since
the war when the manufacturing interest has been, for two
years together, in a state of moderate prosperity, but the
landlord class in this country have been up in arms, and
declaring they were ruined, and calling out for those measures
which, if successful, must again throw the manufacturing
community into that state of distress from which they had
emerged; and, if we look back to the debates in Parliament,
we find the landlords always assuming, that, because they
were in distress, all the community were in distress likewise.
I remember, in 1822, reading in the debates in the House of
Commons, that Lord Castlereagh himself was obliged to remind the landlords of that day, that, though they were
suffering some inconveniences from the price of corn, the
manufacturing interest was eminently prosperous. Do we
hear complaints now from Manchester, Lancashire, or Yorkshire, Lanark, Nottingham, Staffordshire, Leicester, or Derbyshire? No, they have not been for many years past, both
capitalists and labourers, in a more healthy state than they
are at this moment. Is the revenue falling off? No, the
revenue is flourishing, too. Where, then, are the signs and
symptoms of national distress? It is the danger of rents and

tithes. Well, now, we are told by these protectionist scribes
that there is a reaction, because there have been two or three
elections for places which have returned protectionists, and for
which formerly, they say, Free-traders sat. They talk of
Kidderminster and Reading. That opens up another question. I tell them that the decision of such places as Reading
and Kidderminster will not have a feather's weight in the
scale, in deciding this question of the bread-tax. Let them
see a Member returned for any one of the metropolitan
districts, Edinburgh, Birmingham, Manchester, Liverpool,
Leicester, Derby, Nottingham, Leeds, West Riding, Halifax,
Bradford, Huddersfield. Let any one of these large com-
munities, where the constituencies are free and beyond
corruption and coercion — let them but return one man
pledged to restore one shilling of the Corn-laws from any
one of those great constituencies, then I will admit that there
is reaction. Why, I feel so anxious that the farming class
of this country should be emancipated from this delusion,
and placed in a position to cultivate their land, and to
come to a proper adjustment with their landlords, and that
they shall not be carried away after this *ignis fatuus* any
longer, that, I declare, if they will allow me to offer a test—
which may be called a national test—and if they will promise
to abide by it, I will promise to accept the Chiltern Hundreds
at the opening of Parliament, and come down for re-election;
and, if they can return a Member for the West Riding of
Yorkshire pledged to restore one shilling of Corn-law, in any
shape whatever, then I will give up the whole question. But
do not let them talk to us about these petty boroughs, and,
still less, do not let them talk to us about Ireland. I see
these men's reliance; I have long seen symptoms of this
unholy alliance between the protectionist part of the House
of Commons and the landlordism of Ireland, the very name
of which stinks in the nostrils, not only of the people of
England, but of the whole civilised world. Yes, I see that

the landlords of Ireland are putting forth their strength, and mustering their factions, to restore protection; and, I am told, upon very good authority, that, let a dissolution take place the next year, and ninety at least out of the one hundred and five Irish Members would come up pledged to restore the Corn-law. Well, I say, if the whole of them came up to restore the Corn-law, they could not do it.

That, again, opens up another question—the question of the representation of the people. The representation of Ireland is a mockery and a fraud—rotten, rotten, to the very core. Why, I do not believe, after giving some attention to the matter, that there are more *bonâ fide* voters on the register of Ireland at this moment, entitled to vote, than the 37,000 electors that are upon the register of the West Riding of Yorkshire. It is acknowledged by all parties; nobody will deny it: but I tell the men nominated by landlords, and sent up under pretence of representing the 8,000,000 of the people of Ireland, they shall not decide the question of your bread, and the bread of the people of England. No; they very much mistake the temper of this people if they think that we will submit to a famine law at the hands of the landlord class of Ireland, who have not only brought their own people to beggary, and ruin, and starvation, but they have beggared and ruined themselves at the same time. What were we doing last session? One half of our time was spent either in caring for the paupers of Ireland, or in passing laws to enable the landlords of that country to be extricated, by extra-judicial means, from ruin and bankruptcy, brought on by their own improvidence. And now, what is this class—this bankrupt landlord class—aiming at? Is it to pass a law to prevent corn being brought to Ireland? No, that is not their immediate object; because, in ordinary times, you cannot have Ireland importing food from abroad, for they have nothing with which to pay for it. But if England subscribes its 8,000,000*l.* to fill up the void of starvation in that country, then, indeed, you may buy the Indian corn from America to feed the people. But, in ordinary times, Ireland must be an exporter of corn; and the object of the landlords of Ireland is to prevent you, the people of England, from getting corn from America and Russia, in order that you may be forced to go for corn from Ireland, and thus enable them to extort increased rents from their beggared tenantry. Do they think that Englishmen and Yorkshiremen are going to submit to a transaction like this? No; let the English landlords—that portion of them who are entering upon this new crusade against your bread-basket—let the English landlords enter this unholy alliance with the bankrupt and pauperised landlords of Ireland, and become themselves equally degraded in the eyes of the world—and I much mistake the temper of Englishmen, especially of Yorkshiremen, if you do not make such an example of the conspirators as will make them regret the day that they ever attempted it. Now, we have given them fair notice that we know what they are about, and what their objects are, and that we are perfectly wide awake in Yorkshire. We do not intend that they shall have one shilling more of protection. And something else we do not intend they shall have. There is another thing they are going to do—if we will let them—and which I always suspected they would do. They will try to extort it from us in some other shape; and so the new dodge is, that they shall put their taxes off their shoulders on to yours. There is a society formed in Buckinghamshire, I believe, for the relief of burdens upon real property.

Well, I belong to another association; and it is to relieve the burdens of those who have no property. Their plan is this — that the burdens hitherto put upon the land shall henceforth be paid out of the taxes wrung from the agricultural labourer upon his ounce of tea, and the half-starved needle-woman in London upon her half-pound of sugar. That is the thing, undisguised, and stripped of the transparent veil of mystification that is thrown over it by those new champions of the agricultural interest, who talk to us in strange parables anything but English—I hardly know whether it is Hebrew, or what it is. Yes, all their mystification amounts to this, that the 12,000,000*l.* of local taxes for poor-rates, highway-rates, church-rates, and the rest, shall be, half of them, if they cannot get the whole—they had rather put the whole upon your shoulders—shall be taken off the land, and put upon the Consolidated Fund; that is, taken out of the taxes raised upon the necessaries and comforts of the masses of the people. Well, I tell them I have had my eye upon them from the first, and always expected it; and, mind you, I am afraid we shall have some people joining in this from whom I expected better things. Allusion has been made to-night to my friend Mr. Gisborne, and no one has a higher opinion of his sterling character and racy talent than I have; but, I think, he has got a twist upon this subject of the burdens of real property. He asked, in the speech to which my friend has referred, ' By what right or justice should the whole of these local taxes be laid upon the real property of the country?' My first answer to him is this: Because those burdens have been borne by the real property of the country from two to three centuries at the least. Poor-rates have been nearly three centuries borne by the real property of the country, and the others are nearly as old as our Saxon institutions. Well, these taxes having been borne by the real property of the country for three centuries, this property has changed hands, either by transfer, succession, or in trust, at least a dozen times; the charges have been endorsed upon the title-deeds, and the property has been bought or inherited at so much less in consequence of those charges, and, therefore, the present owner of real property has no right to exemption from those burdens, having bought the property knowing it to be subject to those burdens, and having paid less in consequence. That is my first answer, and I think it is sufficient. But I have another. The poor have the first right to a subsistence from the land, and there is no other security so good as the land itself. Other kinds of property may take wings and fly away. Moveable property has very often been known to 'flit' the day before quarter-day; capital employed in trade may be lost in an unsuccessful venture in China; wages sometimes disappear altogether: and, therefore, the real and true security to which the people of this country should look, is in the soil itself.

But I have another reason why this property should bear these local burdens, and it is this—it is the only property which not only does not diminish in value, but, in a country growing in population and advancing in prosperity, it always increases in value, and without any help from the owners. These gentlemen complain that those rates have increased in amount during a recent period. I will admit, if they like, that those local rates have increased. During the last one hundred years they have increased, I will say, seven millions of money. That is taking an outside view. Well, but the real property upon which those rates are levied—the lands and houses of this country—has increased in value four times as much; and, therefore, they stand in an infinitely better situation now, paying twelve millions of local rates, than ever they did at any former period in the history of this country. I think I have given my friend Mr. Gisborne some fresh points for consideration, showing why the landlords should pay those taxes.

Now, I warn the landlords against the attempt to enter the lists in this country with the whole mass of the population—I warn them, in these days, and in the temper and spirit of the time, from entering upon a new conflict with this population, to try and put on the shoulders of this already overburdened people, those taxes which of right belong to them as a class. Let them bear in mind what Sir Charles Wood, the Chancellor of the Exchequer, told us in the last session of Parliament—that, even including these local rates, and including what

they pay of the general taxation of the country, the landed
proprietors pay a less amount of taxation, in proportion to the
whole amount raised in this country, than any other people of
Europe.   [A voice: 'They ought to pay it all.']   Well, I tell
them that if they renew the struggle with the whole population of this country, whether for the resumption of the bread-
tax, or to transfer the burdens which in justice belong to
them, to the shoulders of the rest of the community, they will
have the question re-agitated in a very different spirit from
what it was before.   Let them take my word for it, they
will never have another agitation carried on with that sub-
serviency to politico-economical argument which was observed
by the Anti-Corn-law League.   It cost me some argument,
as my friends know, to prevent the League from going into
other topics; but, let another agitation arise, a serious one,
such as these individuals would try to persuade their followers
to enter upon—let it be seen that they bring the Parliament
into such a state of confusion that Government is compelled
to dissolve—let it be seen that a protectionist statesman, like
Lord Stanley, is prepared to get into the saddle, and to spur
over the country with his haughty paces—and they will hear
this question argued in a very different manner from what it
was before.   They will have the whole aristocratic system,
under which the country has been governed for the last 150
years, torn to pieces; they will have the law of primogeniture,
and the whole feudal system which exists in this country, and
exists on sufferance only after it has been abolished everywhere
else—they will have these questions brought up in a way
which they, weak and foolish men, little expect,—and let them
once enter the list again, either for another Corn-law, or for
the transference of this taxation upon your shoulders, and I
give them my word of promise that they will come out of the
conflict right happy to abandon not only the Corn-law and
any taxation which they are going to try to avoid, but they
will be glad to escape by a composition of much heavier terms

than that. Bear in mind, when I speak of this question, I
speak of the landlords, and not of the farmers. I treated, on
a former occasion, most tenderly the landlord class. I will
tell you why I did so. I always had more faith in the proprietors than the farmers for repealing the Corn-laws; and,
therefore, I never trod heavily on the toes of the landlords ;
but if this question is to be revived again by the landlord
class, I promise them that I will probe the whole question to
the bottom, and there shall not be a farmer, however dull he
may be, but shall understand right well that they are hum-
bugs who tell them, that, in questions of rent and the revision
of taxation, landowners and farmers, forsooth, row in the same
boat—and I will undertake to satisfy you that when they talk
of the difficulty of cultivating the land under this system of
Free Trade, there is no difficulty whatever, provided the landlords and tenants come to an adjustment according to the
present and future price of corn.

I speak from experience. I stand before you—you may
perhaps be surprised to hear it—but I stand before you as one
of the humblest members of the much-talked-of landlord
interest. I happen to be possessed of a very small estate in
Western Sussex, very near to the Duke of Richmond, and I
am next door neighbour to Lord Egmont, who is the most
notorious personage I know for making foolish speeches at
agricultural meetings, and for overrunning his neighbours'
land as well as his own with game. I wish, instead of
roaming about the country, calling me a republican, at protection meetings, that Lord Egmont would go down to West
Sussex, and cause some of those rabbits and hares to be
destroyed which give some humble people, on land of mine,
the trouble of killing for him. Being myself a landlord, and
possessing land-right in the midst of the greatest landed proprietors, and the most ferocious protectionists, I have had an
opportunity of testing how far it is practicable by reasonable
arrangements with tenants—I have two of them, they are

very small, but they are sufficient to test the principle—I
have had the opportunity of seeing how far it is practicable,
with tenants upon land, not of first-rate quality, to secure
them, in future, as good prospects as in times past, and under
Free Trade, as well as protection. I am not going to tell you
how I did it; but I will promise, before the meeting of
Parliament, I will go into Buckinghamshire—I will have a
public meeting at Buckingham or at Aylesbury, and will
explain the whole case, and give every particular—how the
landlord, instead of bawling for protection, can, by the commonest exercise of judgment, justice, and policy, enable the
whole of his land to be cultivated, just as it was before, and
every farmer and labourer to be in better spirits in future
than in time past.

Now, I am going into Buckinghamshire to tell the farmers
the whole case; and I will tell the whole case, and a little
more; but I am not going to trouble you with it now.
I will turn to the question of the general taxation of the
country. I quite agree with gentlemen who preceded me,
that you will not have the agricultural counties, or their
Members, with you, for the reduction of the general expenditure of the country, until you can make them fully convinced
that you will not let them indemnify themselves from high
taxation by raising the price of your loaf. As soon as they
are satisfied that they must pay their taxes out of the
moderate prices which prevail, they will join with you in
compelling Government to reduce its expenditure. For myself, I can conscientiously declare that, from the moment I
returned from the Continent, two years since, I have always
had the present position of the country in view. I have
always contemplated a transition state, when there would be
pinching and suffering in the agricultural class, in passing
from a vicious system to a sound one; for you cannot be
restored from bad health to good, without going through a
process of languor and suffering; and my great aim has been,

from the moment I returned from the Continent, to try to
ease that transition by reducing the expenditure of the
country, feeling that, if you could, within a few years, cause
a large reduction in the expenditure of the State, you will
give such an impetus to trade and commerce, and so improve
the condition of the mass of the people, that you would aid
very materially in relieving the farmers and labourers from
the inconvenience of that transition state, from which they
cannot escape. It was with that view that I preferred my
budget, and advocated the reduction of our armaments: it is
with that view, coupled with higher motives, that I have
recommended arbitration treaties, to render unnecessary the
vast amount of armaments which are kept up between civilised countries. It is with that view—the view of largely
reducing the expenditure of the State, and giving relief,
especially to the agricultural classes—that I have made myself
the object of the sarcasms of those very parties, by going to
Paris to attend peace meetings. It is with that view that
I have directed attention to our colonies, showing how you
might be carrying out the principle of Free Trade, give to
the colonies self-government, and charge them, at the same
time, with the expense of their own government. There is
not one of these objects that I have taken in hand, in
which I have not had, for a paramount motive, serving of the
agricultural class, in this transition state from protection to
Free Trade.

How, hitherto, have I been requited by them? Have I
had a single aid from any of them? No. At the close of
last Parliament I was taunted by their leader on account of
my want of success. Have you heard them say one word
about the reduction of the expenditure of the country?
Has their leader—if I may call him so—for they have a
plurality—has he ever said one word to indicate the slightest
wish that they desired to reduce the expenditure? No. I
am convinced that it would be distasteful to the landlord

party to have a general reduction of the expenditure, particularly in that great preserve of the landlord class for their younger sons, the army and navy. I believe they are averse to retrenchment — at least, they have done nothing to aid those who wished to accomplish it; and now, I tell them again, as I told them before from this great metropolis of industry, that to a farthing of protection to agriculture they shall not go. And if they will make us pay high taxes to keep up useless establishments, and unnecessary sinecures, and wasteful expenditure, in every department of the State, why, they shall pay their share of that taxation, with wheat at 40s. per quarter.

Gentlemen, allusion has been made to our expenditure for the army, navy, and ordnance. Mr. Marshall has referred to the case of our colonies. He was unfortunate in speaking when the crowd was at the door; but I hope that his facts and his arguments will fully appear reported in the papers, because they went to the very bottom of this question. You cannot materially reduce your expenditure, unless you relieve yourselves from the unnecessary waste of expenditure in the colonies. Sir Robert Peel has, again and again, in his budget speeches, pointed out clearly the vast expenditure in our colonies. He has, again and again, said that two-thirds of our army are either necessary for garrisons in our colonies, or else to supply depots at home to furnish relief for those retiring; or else that thousands of men may be always on the wide ocean, visiting one place or another. He has pointed that out time after time; and he has repeated these things so often, that I have long been of opinion that Sir Robert Peel is anxious to diminish public taxation, by preventing this waste of national resources. He saw the mischief; he would like public opinion to be directed to it; and, if public opinion enabled him to effect a change, I am sure that Sir Robert Peel is the man who would like to accomplish it.

You send drilled Englishmen to serve as policemen to Englishmen in Australia, New Zealand, and the Cape of Good Hope. Do not you think that Englishmen there are quite capable of taking care of themselves, without putting you to the expense of doing it? What have they been doing lately? You have spent two millions of money, in the last four years, to defend the settlers of the Cape of Good Hope against the inroads of the barbarous tribes of Caffres. What is taking place at this very moment? Why, these very men, whom you have treated as children, incapable of defending themselves against a few untaught savages—they have proclaimed your own governor in a state of siege—invested your own troops—refused to allow them even provisions—and sent away a ship under the colours of the Queen; and, in their speeches and letters, the leaders of the anti-convict movement do not hesitate to declare that they are ready to defend their country, if necessary, against the whole force of the English empire. Do not you think there is sufficient pluck about them to defend themselves against a few untutored savages? The same thing is going on in Australia. They quote the example of America; and some of these people are holding their great meetings on the 4th of July, the anniversary of American independence. I do not respect them the less—I respect them the more. I think they would be unworthy of the name of Englishmen, if they did not stand up against their country being made the cesspool for our convict population. But what I want to show is this: that there is not the shadow of pretence for requiring our armies to defend them.

But, besides the colonies, we keep up an enormous amount of force against foreign countries, which, I think, may be diminished; and, I believe, all other countries would be willing to diminish their armed forces, provided a fair and reasonable proposition had been made by our Government to the French Government, to reduce our armaments, if they will reduce in the same proportion. No; they do not do so; but we ferret about, and find some new man-of-war in the French dockyard about to be built, or some new 32-pounder gun going to be made, instead of an old 24-pounder, and we set to work, and make that a reason for increasing our armaments. But, do you think your honourable Member here would conduct his business in such a way as that? Do you not think, if he saw another person in the same branch of business, conducting it with a large amount of waste, which threatened both with destruction; and, if he knew that the work was profitless to the individual who began the system, do you not think that, if he found a rival in his business entering upon such a career as that, he would go and say to him, 'You are entering upon a system which compels me to do the same, and it will lead us both into the *Gazette*, if we don't stop it? Do you not think that we had better abandon it?' Now, this very day, I believe, there has been some sort of consultation, some feeling of pulses, between the directors of two rival railroads, to prevent that waste and competition to which they had been subjected by acting upon the principle which we have adopted in regard to foreign armaments. It is not for protecting ourselves against pirates, or barbarous powers, that you keep those powerful armaments. It is that you may keep upon a level with another nation, whom you are taught to imagine is ready to pounce upon you, like a red Indian, the moment he finds you without your armour on or your sword by your side. I think it is a great mistake to suppose that, in order that you may display a great deal of power to the world, all the power should be put into the shape of cannons, muskets, and ships of war. Do not you think that, in these times of industry, when wealth and commerce are the real tests of a nation's power, coupled with worth and intelligence—do you not see that, if you beat your iron into ploughshares and pruning-hooks, instead of putting it into swords and spears, it will be equally productive of power, and of far more force, if brought into collision with another country, than if you put all your iron

into spears and swords? It is not always necessary to hold up
a scarecrow to frighten your neighbours. I believe a civilised
nation will estimate the power of a country, not by the amount
laid out in armaments, which may perhaps be the means of
weakening that power, but it will measure your strength
by your latent resources—what margin of taxation you have
that you can impose in case of necessity, greater than another
country, to which you are about to be opposed—what is the
spirit of the people, as having confidence in the institutions or
government under which they live — what is the general intelligence of the people—what is, in every respect, their situation and capacity to make an effort, in case an effort were
required? These will be the tests which intelligent people
will apply to countries; not what amount of horse, foot, and
artillery, or how many ships you have afloat.

Look to America. The United States has only one line-of-
battle ship afloat at this moment; and very often she has not
one. She keeps a number of small vessels, and always in
activity—never allowing three or four to stay in harbour, as
ours are, but always running about to see if her merchant
ships require assistance. With only 8,500 soldiers—for that
is all her force—and with but one line-of-battle ship afloat—
is not America at any time prepared to take her stand in the
face of France with 500,000 troops, the finest in the world,
and with a navy three times as large as the American navy?
Is not the United States always able to take the position of
equality? and has she not been even taking very high ground?
And, we see that this nation, with 500,000 soldiers, have
brought their finances into an almost hopeless state, and they
dare not come into collision with a country so lightly taxed,
and with so much elasticity, as the United States; and if all
the Governments of Europe continue this policy, and if the
United States pursues hers, I only hope their Government
may not assume that arrogant tone which it may assume
towards every Government in Europe, which is broken

down by the load of debt and taxes, which are the result of the hideous system to which I have referred.

These are the reasons, I have said, and I say again, that you may return with safety to the expenditure of 1835. Nay, more, you will not stop when you get there. But mark me, with all their sarcasms, they are on the high-road to it, and we will compel them to do it. They will be obliged to return to the expenditure of 1835, and to the budget which I brought forward last year, and in a short time. But how? Why, by such a movement out of doors as I have mentioned, and I wish to see it avoided.

And, last, I come to the point of the greatest importance. I am anxious to see our representative system altered. I am anxious to see it, because it will put an end to this double trial of all public questions—trying it in the House of the Commons, in the face of what are called Representatives of the people, and then coming to the people, and asking them to compel their so-called Representatives to carry out the policy which they wish them to carry out. I say it is a clumsy machine; for, when you are wishful to have it self-acting, you find that the engine will not perform its work. When you have set up your forty-horse steam-engine, you have to call forty horses to do its work. You must not only have an extension of the suffrage, but a re-distribution of the franchise. You must have no such absurdity as the constituency of the West Riding of Yorkshire, with its 36,000 electors, outvoted by a constituency of 150 or 200 electors. I wonder how anybody can believe that such things exist, except those who live in the country, and suffer from the inconveniences of it.

But it is not merely a re-distribution of the franchise, but you must shorten the reckonings of Members of Parliament with those constituencies. Now, do you suppose, if a committee were to sit down to make a constitution, without having the precedent of the present constitution to guide you, anybody would make such an absurd proposition as that a Parliament should sit for seven years without giving an account to their constituents? Nobody would dream of it. Ask your railroad companies, your bank proprietors—any body in the world that has to delegate power to another body—is there on the face of the world an example (except in our Septennial Act) of people giving up their power for seven years' duration? It is no answer to me to say that Parliaments do not last, on an average, more than three years. If we knew that Parliaments only lasted three years, that would be an answer to the question; but men go there expecting that it will last five, six, or seven years, and they act accordingly; and when they come near the end, they begin to go through a process something like a death-bed repentance, and to put their house in order. Yet they do not do it at the end of three years, because when Parliament is dissolved at the end of three years it is only by accident — the decease of the sovereign, or the necessity of testing the opinion of the people; and, therefore, you have no benefit from it.

But, gentlemen, whether you want these or other reforms in Parliament, I reiterate here, what I have said elsewhere— I do not think you will get it by petitioning the House of Commons, or by any other demonstration calling upon the House to reform itself. I tell you why. We have all agreed that we should pursue our agitation by moral means. Well, moral means threaten no noble lords in St. James's Square with brickbats or anything else. They see decent respectable men meeting, and they say, ' They will never lend themselves to anything violent.' They look upon it as a moral demonstration, and they are quite content to let these respectable middle-class demonstrations keep the peace for them and confine themselves to moral force. All this is exceedingly proper. Nothing is so absurd as to think of returning to the time of Burdett and Hunt, bawling after noble lords and breaking

open and firing the houses of your opponents, and getting
knocked upon the head or hung for your pains. But then, if
you do pursue moral means, take care you do use all the moral
means in your power. And that brings me to the doctrine I
have been preaching of late. I say, Qualify yourselves. I
could say more upon it, but I shall not say so much here as
I shall say elsewhere, because I do not think it is meet that
I, as the Member for the West Riding of Yorkshire, should
come here and be carrying on a perpetual canvass with you in
order to get you to qualify yourselves to vote for me. Therefore you will be good enough, if I should be speaking at
Ipswich or Aylesbury on this topic, to apply what you like of
those observations to yourselves. I have calculated that there
are only one in eight of adult males who are qualified to vote
for the counties; seven-eighths have no votes for counties.
If you can take one-eighth out of those seven-eighths and put
them upon the county list, you will have more county voters
added than the whole number of county voters now on the
list.

I do not think that is difficult to be done; and we are
going on rapidly, and we are indebted to a working man,
Mr. James Taylor, of Birmingham, for making the greatest
and best system of reform I know. Oh, if in the days of
Burdett and Hunt, they had had some Mr. Taylor to preach
to them, and say, that for every three-pence you drink you
swallow a yard of land, we should have had a million of
voters qualified. The difference between Mr. Taylor's plan
and the old plan was this: formerly the leaders used to say,
'Come to the House of Commons, make a noise, bawl out,
and tell them you want to get in, and ask them to let you in.'
But Mr. Taylor tells you that 'You have got the key in your
own pocket, make use of it—go to the door, unlock it, and
enter, without asking anybody's permission.' I like this
plan, because it teaches men self-reliance. When allusion
has been made to self-reform—I mean the government of your

own appetites—I am glad to see by the response, not only here, but in London and elsewhere where I go, that the English people are determined so to work out their own emancipation.

I am anxious to see this extension of the suffrage accelerated in every possible way: and I think I have always given every possible evidence of my sincerity by direct votes in the House of Commons, and outside the House by urging men to qualify themselves, and use every means to get a vote. I do it, because I believe the extension of the franchise gives us a better guarantee not only for the safety of our institutions, but for the just administration of our public affairs; and I have latterly felt another motive for wishing for an extension of the franchise, in what I have seen going on upon the Continent within the last eighteen months, which has convinced me that the great masses of mankind are disposed for peace between nations. You have the fact brought out in strong relief that the people themselves, however they may be troubled with internal convulsions, have no desire to go abroad and molest their neighbours. You have seen Louis Philippe driven from the throne. We were told that he kept the French nation at peace; but we find the masses of the people of France only anxious to remain at home, and diminish, if possible, the pressure of taxation.

Where do we look for the black gathering cloud of war? Where do we see it rising? Why, from the despotism of the North, where one man wields the destinies of 40,000,000 of serfs. If we want to know where is the second danger of war and disturbance, it is in that province of Russia—that miserable and degraded country, Austria—next in the stage of despotism and barbarism, and there you see again the greatest danger of war; but in proportion as you find the population governing themselves—as in England, in France, or in America—there you will find that war is not the disposition of the people, and that if Government desire it, the people would put a check upon it. Therefore, for the security of liberty, and also, as I believe, that the people of every country, as they acquire political power, will cultivate the arts of peace, and check the desire of their governments to go to war—it is on these grounds that I wish to see a wide extension of the suffrage, and liberty prevail over despotism throughout the world.

FREE TRADE.

XXV.

It gives me particular pleasure to follow a gentleman who has addressed you in the capacity of a tenant-farmer, one, who to my knowledge, in his own business, by the growth of more corn, and raising more cattle, and employing more labour to a given area of soil, excels most of his neighbours—a man so well entitled to speak to you on the subject of the interests of the agriculturists of this country. We are met here under the denomination of a reform meeting—a parliamentary and financial reform meeting; but it will be known to every one present that the general impression, both here and abroad, is, that this is a meeting for the purpose, so far as I am concerned in the matter, of discussing the question of protection or Free Trade, especially with reference to tenant-farmers' interests in this matter. I remember speaking to an audience in this hall six years ago, and on that occasion going through the arguments necessary to show that the Corn-law was founded upon impolicy and injustice; I remember on that occasion maintaining the proposition that the Corn-law had not proved beneficial to any class of the community, and I ventured to say that the country would be more prosperous without the

F f 2

system of agricultural protection than it had been with it. Well, I am here now to maintain that by every test which can proclaim the prosperity or adversity of a nation, we stand better now without the Corn-law than we did when we had it. [Cheers, and some cries of 'No.'] I am rather glad to see that there are some dissentients from that proposition; our opponents will not say that this is a packed meeting. We have got some protectionists here. And now, if you will only just keep that order which is necessary for any rational proceedings, I will endeavour to make you Free-traders before you leave.

I have said that, by every test which can decide the question of national prosperity or national adversity, we stand in a better position than we did when we had the Corn-law. What are the tests of a nation's prosperity? A declining or an improving revenue is one test. Well, our revenue is better than it was under a Corn-law. Our exports and our imports are better than they were under the Corn-law. Take the question of pauperism. I will not shrink even from the test of pauperism in the agricultural districts; I have the statistics of many of your unions in Buckinghamshire and Bedfordshire, and I warn the protectionist orators, who are going about persuading themselves that they have a case in the matter of pauperism, that when Parliament meets, and Mr. Baines is enabled to bring forward the Poor-law statistics up to the last week (not going to the 'blue books,' and bringing forward the accounts of the previous year), I warn the protectionists that, with regard to the test of pauperism, even in the agricultural districts, it will be seen that things are more favourable now, with bread at a moderate price, than they were in 1847, when prices were to their hearts' content, and the loaf was nearly double the price it is now. Take the state of wages; that is a test of the condition of the people. What are the people earning now, compared with 1847, when the protectionists were so well satisfied with their high prices? Why, as a rule, throughout

the country, there is more money earned now than there was
then; and they are getting the comforts and necessaries of life
in many cases at two-thirds, and in some cases at less than
that, of the prices of 1847. [A Voice: 'It is not so with
the agricultural labourers.'] I will come to them by-and-by.
What I want you to agree with in the outset is that your
labourers are not the nation; and if your agriculture be an
exception to the rule, we must find out the reason why it is
so; we will come to that by-and-by.

I remember quite well, when I came here to see you before,
how my ears used to be dinned by the argument, that if we
had free-trade in corn, the gold would all be drained out of
this country, for that you could not bring in 5,000,000 quarters of grain without being drained of your gold; that the
foreigner would not take anything else in exchange. Why, we
have had between 30,000,000 and 40,000,000 quarters within
these last four years, and the Bank of England was never so
encumbered with gold as it is now. I have spoken of wages,
and I say that in every branch of industry the rate of wages
has improved. You may say that agriculture is an exception.
We will come to that, but I do not make an exception in
favour of any trade in your district; I do not make an exception in the case of the employment of women in your district,
for I have made particular inquiry, and I find, even in the
article of straw-plaiting, that families who could not earn 15s.
in 1847, are now earning 25s. ['No,' and some confusion.]
I say families. I know we have some of the most extensive
manufacturers in this hall. Then there is the lace trade, the
pillow-lace trade, employing a great number of women in
Buckinghamshire. [Renewed confusion, owing to a gentleman
pressing his way towards the platform. A Voice: 'He is a
reporter.'] Well, we are delighted to see the gentlemen of the
press; the more of them the better; what we say here will be
read elsewhere, and we speak for that purpose. I was about
saying, that even the wages of the pillow-lace makers have

advanced, and they are getting their bread at two-thirds the former price. Even the poor chair-makers of this and the adjoining county—a trade that has hardly known what it was to have a revival—are getting better. I repeat it, there is not an exception of any trade in which there is not an advantage gained by the moderate price of food that now prevails. ['Not the lace-makers?'] They are getting more employment.

But I want now to come to the question which interests you in this immediate neighbourhood. If every other great interest of the State is thriving—and no one can deny it—how is it that agriculture is depressed? how is it that the interests of agriculture are found in antagonism with the interests of the rest of the community? Why, these people have been proceeding upon a false system; they have been upon an unsound basis; they have been reckoning upon Act of Parliament prices; they have made their calculations upon Act of Parliament prices, and now they find they are obliged, like other individuals, to be content with natural prices. What is the reason that agriculture cannot thrive as well as other trades? We find meetings called, purporting to be meetings of farmers, complaining of distress; and what is their remedy for that distress? Is it to go and talk like men of business to their landlords, and ask them for fresh terms of agreement, fresh arrangements, that they may have the raw material of their trade—the land—at the natural price, and free from those absurd restrictions that prevent their giving the natural value to it? No. Go to a meeting where there is a landlord in the chair, or a land-agent—his better-half,—and you find them talking, but never as landlords and land-agents, but as farmers, and for farmers. And what do they say? Why, they say, 'We must go to Parliament, and get an Act of Parliament to raise the price of corn, that you may be able to pay us your rents.' That is what it amounts to.

Now, what ought to be the plan pursued by the landlord

and tenant on an occasion like this? The landlord, as Mr.
Disraeli very properly observed yesterday at Great Marlow, is
an individual who has land, which is a raw material, and
nothing more, to dispose of; and the farmer is a capitalist, who
offers to take this raw material, in order that he may work it
up and make a profit by it: in fact, the farmer and the landlord
stand in precisely the same position that the cotton-spinner
and the cotton-merchant stand in. The cotton-spinner buys his
cotton wool from the cotton-merchant, in order that he may
spin it up at a profit. If he can get his raw material cheap, he
can make a profit; and if not, he cannot. But we never hear
of the cotton-spinner and the merchant going together to
Parliament for a law to keep up the price of cotton. I declare, when I find landlord and tenant running about raising
a cry for ' protection,' and going to Parliament for a law to
benefit them by raising the price of corn, I cannot help feeling
humiliated at the spectacle, because it is a proof of want of
intelligence on the one side, and, I fear, want of honesty, too,
on the other.

Now, suppose you were to see a crowd of people running
up and down the streets of Aylesbury, shouting out, ' Protection! protection! oh, give us protection! we are all rowing
in the same boat!' and when you inquired who these people
were, you were told they were the grocers of Aylesbury
and their customers, who were crying out for a law which
would raise the price of all the hogsheads of sugar in the grocers' stores,—would you not say that this was a very curious
combination of the grocers and their customers? Would not
you say that the interest of the men who had the hogsheads
of sugar to sell, and who wished therefore to raise the price,
could not be identical with that of the men who had to buy
the sugar? Yet, that is precisely the position in which the
tenant-farmers and the landowners stand. [Cries of ' No, no,'
and ' Yes.'] Well, will any gentleman rise on this platform,
and explain where I am wrong? Now, the plan I would

recommend the tenant-farmers and the landholders to pursue is precisely the plan which has been adopted by my own tenants and myself. I will explain how I acted in this matter. I promised I would explain my conduct, and I will do so; and if those newspapers that write for protectionist farmers report nothing else of what I may say to-night, I beg them to let their farming readers know what I am now going to say. [A Voice : ' How large are your farms?'] I will tell you all about it. I happen to stand here in the quality of a landlord, filling, as I avowed to you at the beginning, a most insignificant situation in that character.

I possess a small estate in West Sussex, of about 140 acres in extent, and a considerable part of it in wood. It is situated in a purely farming district, in the midst of the largest protectionist proprietors in Sussex; the land is inferior; it has no advantages; it is nearly ten miles distant from a railroad; it has no chimneys or growing manufacturing towns to give it value. Now this is precisely the kind of land which we have been told again and again by Lord John Manners, the Marquis of Granby, and other protectionist landlords, cannot be cultivated at all with wheat at 40s., even if it were given to the cultivator rent-free. This property came into my possession in 1847. [A Voice : ' You got it from the League funds.'] Yes; I am indebted for that estate, and I am proud here to acknowledge it, to the bounty of my countrymen. That estate was the scene of my birth and of my infancy; it was the property of my ancestors; it is by the munificence of my countrymen that this small estate, which had been alienated by my father from necessity, has again come into my hands, and that I am enabled to light up again the hearth of my fathers; and I say that there is no warrior duke who owns a vast domain by the vote of the imperial Parliament who holds his property by a more honourable title than that by which I possess mine.

My first visit to this property, after it came into my

possession, was in 1848. At that time, as you are aware,
prices ranged high in this country; but never expecting
those prices would continue, I thought that the proper time
for every man having an interest in the land to prepare for
the coming competition with the foreigner. I gave orders
that every hedge-row tree upon my estate should be cut down
and removed. I authorised the two occupying tenants upon
the property to remove every fence upon the estate, or, if they
liked, to grub up only a portion of them; but I distinctly said
I would rather not see a hedge remaining on the property,
inasmuch as it was surrounded with woods, and I did not
think fences were necessary. That portion of the land which
required draining, I had instantly drained at my own cost.
The estate, as I have said, was situated in the midst of large
protectionist landowners, who, as a matter of course, were
great game preservers; and it had therefore been particularly
infested with hares and rabbits. I authorised the tenants on
my land to kill the rabbits and hares, and to empower any one
else they pleased to kill them.

So troublesome had been the hares and rabbits on that
little property, that they even entered the gardens and allot-
ments of the labourers; and one of those labourers appeared
before the Committee of the House of Commons on the Game-
laws in 1845, and stated that the rabbits had not only devoured
his vegetables, his cabbages, and his peas, but had actually dug
up his potatoes! At that time—in 1845—the property did
not belong to me; but I took care to explain to this worthy
man, in 1848, when I visited the estate, that if the hares or
rabbits ever troubled him, or the other labourers living upon
my property, that under the present law any man may destroy
hares on his own holding without taking out a licence, and I
advised the labourers to set gins and snares upon their allot-
ments and in their gardens, to catch all the hares and rabbits
they could; and when they caught them, to be sure and put
them in their own pots and eat them themselves. That is the

SPEECHES OF RICHARD COBDEN.

JAN. 9,

way in which I dealt with the game on my property. I must confess that I have no taste whatever for the preservation of such vermin, which I believe to be utterly inconsistent with good farming, and the greatest obstacle to the employment of the labourers. For my own part I would rather see a good fat hog in every sty belonging to my labourers, than have the best game preserve in the country.

That, then, was the course which I took in 1848, to prepare for the coming competition with the foreigner. It was a time when prices ranged high; nothing was settled about rents. In the course of the last year, however, I received a letter from one of my tenants, saying, 'When I took this land from your predecessor, it was upon the calculation of wheat being at 56s. a quarter; it is now little more than 40s., and I should like to have a new arrangement made.' I wrote in reply, 'The proposition you make is reasonable. We will have a new bargain. I am willing to enter upon an arrangement, estimating the future price of wheat at 40s.; but whilst I am willing to take all the disadvantages of low prices, I must have the benefit of good cultivation, and therefore we will estimate the produce of the land to be such as could be grown by good farmers upon the same quality of soil.' Now, from the moment that this reasonable proposition was made, there was not the slightest anxiety of mind on the part of my tenants—not the least difficulty in carrying on their business of farming under a system of Free Trade as well as they had done under the system of protection. From that moment the farmers on this small property felt themselves no longer interested in the matter of Free Trade and protection; and the labourers felt that they had as good a prospect of employment as they had before, and they had no interest in the question of protection. We settled our terms. I have bargained for my rent. It is no business of the public what rent I get. That is my business, and the business of the farmers; but if it is any satisfaction to my protectionist friends, I will admit that I am receiving a reduced rent, notwithstanding that I have drained the land, and given them the game, and removed the hedges, and cleared away every hedge-row tree.

What, then, becomes of the argument that it is impossible to carry on agriculture in this country with wheat at 40s. a quarter? I am getting some rent—and not so very large a reduction from the rent I got before; and it is enough for me to say that the land is being cultivated, and that farmers and labourers are employed and contented.

Now, with regard to a lease, I said to both my tenants, 'Either take the land from year to year, with an agreement binding each of us to submit to arbitration the valuation of unexhausted improvements when you leave the land; or, if you like, take a lease, and I will bind you down to no covenants as to the way in which you are to cultivate the land while you possess it.' What possible excuse, then, can the land-owners in any part of the country have for coming forward and telling us that land cannot be cultivated because wheat is 40s. a quarter? The answer I intend to give to those noble dukes and lords who are running about the country, and who are so angry with me, and are scolding me so lustily, is this— 'Let me have the arranging of the affairs between you and your tenants,—the terms, the rent, and condition of the hold-ings,—and I will undertake to ensure that your land shall be cultivated better than it was before, that farming shall be as profitable to the farmer, that the labourer shall have as full employment, and at as good wages, provided you allow me to enter into the same arrangement that I have made with my own tenants.' But that would not suit these parties. It would make a dry, dull, unprofitable matter of business of what is now made a piece of agitation, which ought to be called moonshine.

Now, if I had been a protectionist, I might have made money by this. I will show you how I should have done so.

When my tenants wrote to me to say there ought to be a fresh agreement between us, what would have been my answer had I been a protectionist? I should have said, 'That is true, my good friends; we will have a meeting at Great Marlow or High Wycombe, and we will petition Parliament to pass a law to protect you.' Well, we should have had a meeting, my tenants would have been invited to attend, and would have shouted, 'We are all rowing in the same boat!' and after two or three hours of dull speeches, you would have had a conclusion with 'three groans for Cobden.' After this meeting was over, my tenants might have gone home, and might have been prepared, until the next audit, to pay their full rents as before. And if I were a protectionist landowner, I should have then wanted some fresh excuse against the next audit-day. Consequently, I should probably have told the farmers to come to the next meeting, at 17, Old Bond-street, to memorialise her Majesty,—for they were not to be told to petition the House of Commons, but to lay their complaints at the foot of the throne. After my poor tenants had done all this, and had gone home, and prepared their rents for the next audit-day, then some fresh excuse must be found, and we might have told the farmers, that instead of memorialising the Queen, they should agitate for a dissolution of Parliament. In this case, we should have been safe in respect to our rents for the next three years, because that is an agitation which would last such a period.

In the meantime what would be the consequence to my tenants with heart-sickening delay, and with the hopelessness inspired into their souls by these dreary, dull, protectionist speeches, telling them that they could not cultivate their land even if no rent were paid; and with the constant drain on their resources to pay their old rents, without amelioration in their holdings, one-half the tenants might be ruined, and I am not sure that a large proportion will not be ruined by the tactics of the protectionists at the present moment. But was

it necessary for any farmer to be ruined if the landlords pursued the same system as myself? This is simply and purely
a rent question. And if the farmers cannot carry on their
business, it is because they pay too high a rent in proportion
to the amount of their produce. I do not say that in many
cases the rents of the landlords might not be excessive, provided the land were cultivated to its full capacity. But that
cannot be done without sufficient capital, and that sufficient
capital cannot be applied without sufficient security, or without a tenant-right, or a lease amounting to tenant-right. We
want to bring the landowner and the tenant together, to con-
front them in their separate capacity as buyers and sellers; so
that they might deal together as other men of business, and
not allow themselves to play this comedy of farmers and landlords crying about for protection, and saying that they are
rowing in the same boat; when, in fact, they are rowing in
two boats, and in opposite directions.

There is a new red-herring thrown across the scent of the
farmers; they are told that protection cannot be had just now;
but in the meantime they must have half the amount of the
local rates thrown on the Consolidated Fund. I am really
astonished that anybody should have the assurance to get up,
and, facing a body of tenant-farmers, make such a proposal
to them for the benefit of the landowners. The local rates at
present are paid on the real property of the country. Such
is the nature of the poor-rates and of the county-rates, &c.
They are not assessed on the tenant's capital. [Hear, and
a cry, ' Mr. Lattimore said they are.'] He said no such
thing. [Some expressions of dissent.] He did not say
that the assessment was on the ploughs and oxen of the
tenantry. It is on the rent of land, and not on the floating
capital; for it is known to everybody that the assessment is
on the rent, and, if the rate is assessed on the rent, why the
tenant charges it to the landlord when he takes his farm. He
calculates what the rates and taxes are, and, if the farm is

highly rated, he pays less rent. Did you ever know a landlord
let his land tithe-free on the same terms as land which had
the tithe on it? At present the rates were laid on the rent
of land, and were ultimately paid by the landlord. I admit
that at first the tenant pays it out of his pocket, but he gets
it again when he pays his rent. But only think of this wise
proposal of the farmers' friend, who says, 'in order to relieve
you tenant-farmers, I will take one half of those 12,000,000l.
of local taxes off, and put it on the Consolidated Fund—that
is to say, on tea, sugar, coffee, tobacco, and other articles
which you tenant-farmers and labourers consume.' There is
a pretty project for benefiting the tenant-farmers!

But there is another scheme; there are two ways of doing
this. The other way is by assessing the rates on the floating
capital of the country. The argument is—why should not the
shopkeepers, the bankers, and the fundholders, be assessed?
But if you allow the bringing in of stock-in-trade to be
assessed, you must bring in the farmers' stock-in-trade to be
assessed. I now ask the farmers in Aylesbury and its neighbourhood, what they would gain if the value of all stock
held upon land within the neighbourhood of Aylesbury were
assessed? Has not Mr. Lattimore told you that the estimated
value of the farming stock of this kingdom is 250,000,000l.,
then I can only say it is five times as much as the capital
invested in the cotton trade, and more than that employed in
the great staple manufactures together; and under such circumstances, how can those landlords tell the farmers that they
would put rates on the floating stock? And is it not, then, a
wise proposal to make to the farmers, to take off half of the
rates, and to put the assessment on the floating capital, of
which the farmer possesses the greater proportion? I am
humiliated when I read of these meetings, in which the
farmers listen and gape at such speeches; and I feel a relief
that it is not my duty to attend at such meetings, and that I
have no landlord to oblige by being present at these meetings.

What is the course, then, which ought to be pursued by the
farmers at the present time? If they had such leaders like
Mr. Lattimore, and the courage to follow him, they would
meet together simply as farmers—as tenant-farmers only. If
it had been a question affecting one of our mechanical trades
in Lancashire and Yorkshire, the persons connected with that
trade would have met together, and would have discussed
among themselves exclusively what should be the course to
be pursued under the circumstances. But the farmers are led
out to parade by land-agents, and land-valuers, and landlords,
who talk in their name, delude them in the face of the country,
and make a lamentable exhibition of them to the rest of the
country. The tenant-farmers should do on the subject of corn
as the manufacturers did in reference to their interests—
they should meet together in one community.

But let me not be misunderstood. I do not say that on
other questions the small squire and tenant-farmer should be
separated. I do not say that the landlords and the farmers
should not go to the same church together, and meet in the
same market. But when the tenant-farmers meet to talk on
the subject of Free Trade, they should meet together alone,
and should exclude every landlord from their council. This I
say in reference to any occasion when the tenant-farmers meet
together to talk about the subject of protection, in which they
have an interest totally distinct from the landlord who lets
them their land; and they should not only exclude the great
landed proprietor, but also the man whose predominant interest is that of the landowner, though he may be at the same
time a tenant-farmer to a subordinate extent. The occupying
tenants are men who employ their capital on the raw material,
as Mr. Disraeli called it, and it was a good term. The tenant-
farmers in this matter of protection have a totally distinct
interest from the landowners, or small squires, or land-agents;
and until they meet in their several localities, totally distinct
from all other classes, they never will have a chance of

arriving at a just appreciation of their own position, or their own difficulties. They never will be able to combine together to get such terms and conditions as are necessary to enable them to carry on their business under the system of Free Trade.

Let me not be misunderstood. I do not say that under a natural state of things all classes have not a common interest in the general prosperity of the country. Let them only act towards each other with fairness, justice, and with honesty, and they would be promoting in the end not only their own, but the general interests of the community. We have come here, I believe, to talk about financial and parliamentary reform, as well as other matters, and as I have been suffering from a cold, as you perhaps are aware, I will leave to other speakers to deal with those general topics, having preferred myself to touch more particularly upon the question concerning the tenant-farmers and the landlord.

LETTER FROM MR. COBDEN

TENANT FARMERS OF ENGLAND.

TO THE FARMING TENANTRY OF THE UNITED KINGDOM.

GENTLEMEN,—The question for you now to determine is, Shall the repeal of the Corn-law be gradual or immediate? Deny it who may, this is the only question that deserves a moment's consideration at your hands. Public opinion has decreed that protection to both agriculture and manufactures shall be abolished; and Ministers and statesmen have at last reluctantly bowed to a power from which there is no appeal. Let no designing or obtuse politicians delude you with the cry that the House of Lords, or a dissolution of Parliament, can prevent the repeal of the Corn-law. All men of average sagacity are now agreed that Free Trade in corn and manufactures is inevitable. How, then, shall we apply this new principle?—timidly and gradually, like children; or boldly and at once, as becomes men and Englishmen? Upon this point, I wish to submit to your consideration a few remarks which I believe to be of the utmost importance to your interests; they are offered in good faith by one who has sprung from your own ranks, and who, although deemed by some to be your enemy, will, I hope, live to be regarded as a promoter of the independence and prosperity of the farming tenantry of the kingdom.

The Government measure proposes to abolish the Corn-law in February, 1849, putting on for the three intervening years a new scale of duties, sliding from 10s. to 4s. The moment this law is passed, the duty will drop from 15s. to 4s. Here will be change the first, fright the first, and with many, I fear, panic the first. But there will be no settlement. You will not be able to foretell whether the duty during the years 1847 and 1848 will be 4s. or 10s. It is quite probable that, in February, 1849, the duty will be 10s.; if so, on the 1st of that month, it will drop again suddenly, from 10s. to 1s. Here will be change the second, fright the second, and, possibly, panic the second. The fall of duty in these two changes would have amounted to, first, from 15s. to 4s.; next, from 10s. to 1s.; making, together, 20s.; but, mark, if the duty were immediately reduced, from 15s. to 1s., the fall would be only 14s. So that, by this clumsy contrivance, you are not only to be kept for three years in a state of suspense and embarrassment, and exposed to double panics, but are liable to a drop of 20s., instead of 14s., duty; you are actually subjected to the shock of the withdrawal of 6s. more of protection!

But this is only a small part of the danger to which you will be exposed by the delay. From the moment that the new Corn-law is passed, foreigners and corn-importers will begin to make preparations for the day of its extinction; they dread a sliding-scale in any shape, owing to former losses, and will keep their eyes steadily fixed upon the 1st of February, 1849.

What a precious policy is this which advertises for three years to all the landowners and speculators of the entire world, offering them a premium to hold back their supplies, and then to pour upon our markets, in one day, a quantity of corn which, but for this contrivance, might have been spread over twelve or eighteen months! And what may your fate be under these probable circumstances? Supposing the crop of 1848 to be abundant in this country, you will be liable, in the spring of 1849, to the sudden and unnatural influx of the corn accumulated by foreigners for this market; thus beating down prices artificially, to the loss of all parties, but more especially of the British farmer.

How different would be the operations of an immediate repeal of the Corn-law! There would then be no stock of foreign corn waiting for the opening of our ports. Nobody expected last year in Poland or America that the English Corn-law would be repealed—nobody prepared for it; not a bushel of grain was raised upon the chance of such an unlooked-for contingency. Is there an intelligent farmer in the kingdom that will not at once exclaim, 'If we are to have a repeal of the Corn-law, give us it this spring, when the foreigner is unprepared for it, and when not a single quarter of corn sown after the news reaches him can be brought to this market in less than eighteen months.'

But the present is, beyond all comparison, the most favourable moment ever known for abolishing the Corn-law. If ever it could be repealed without even temporary inconvenience to the farmer, this is the time. There is a scarcity at present over nearly all the Continent. One-half of Europe is competing for the scanty surplus stock of grain in America. Millions of our countrymen are deprived of their ordinary subsistence by the disease of the potato, and they must be sustained at the public expense upon a superior food. Do what we will, we cannot, during the present year, secure low prices. Abolish the Corn-law to-morrow, and still wheat must rise during the spring and summer. If the farmers had the power of ordering time and circumstances, they could not contrive a juncture more favourable to them than the present for the total and immediate repeal of the Corn-law. Nay, I believe that if the Corn-law could be abolished by a secret edict to-morrow, the farmers would never make the discovery of open ports by any injurious effect produced upon their interests.

I cannot believe that Sir Robert Peel is favourable to the gradual repeal; he supported it by no other argument in his speech than the fear of panic amongst the farmers; but he has told us again and again, in proposing his former alterations in the tariff, that he believes all such changes are less injurious, if suddenly made, than when spread over a period of years. I have the strongest conviction, derived from his own past changes in the tariff, that he is right. Why then should you, in deference to unfounded fears, be deprived of the benefits of experience? If you speak out in favour of an immediate settlement, who will oppose your wishes? Not the Government—they are anxious, so far as public opinion and the exigencies of the moment will allow, to conciliate your favour; not the great landed proprietors, whose interests and yours are in this respect identical, who desire also, on political grounds, to put a period to an agitation, the prolonged duration of which they believe to be injurious, and who would willingly take any step which shall at once consult your interests and dissolve the League.

Let me entreat you to take this subject into your instant and earnest consideration. Do me the justice to believe that I have no other object in view in writing this letter but to serve your interests. If you should be induced to concur in its views, you will avoid the only danger to which, in my opinion, the farmers were ever exposed from the repeal of the Corn-law—that of the transition state. From the first I have always entertained and expressed the conviction that Free Trade, far from permanently injuring the farmers, would ultimately tend to their prosperity and independence. I never disguised from myself, however, the temporary evils to which they might be exposed in the change. But let us unite in seizing the present opportunity, and the triumph of sound principles may be achieved without the bitter ingredient of one particle of injury to any class or individual. From the most exalted personage in the realm down to the humblest peasant, all may witness, with unalloyed pleasure, one of the greatest victories ever achieved over past prejudice and ignorance, whilst each class may derive peculiar gratification at the close of our long domestic struggle. The Sovereign may glory that her reign was reserved for the era of a commercial reformation, more pregnant in beneficial consequences to the destinies of mankind than all the wars of her illustrious ancestors; the landed aristocracy will see in the consummation of our labours an opening for the resumption of their social influence, based upon the only sure foundation—the respect and confidence of the people; whilst to the middle and industrious classes will be presented a constantly widening field for the employment of their peaceful energies, together with greater means and more leisure for that moral amelioration which, I trust, will accompany their improved physical condition.

I have the honour to be,

Gentlemen,

Your obedient Servant,

RICHARD COBDEN.

LONDON,
30th *January,* 1846.

—➤➤➤➤ ◄◆▦◆► ◄◄◄—

FINANCE.

FINANCE.

I.

MANCHESTER, JANUARY 27, 1848.

[On Jan. 4, the *Morning Chronicle* published a letter of the Duke of
Wellington to Sir John Burgoyne, in which the great change which
modern improvement in attack had induced on all systems of national
defence was insisted on. The Duke urged that a large addition must be
made to the military forces of the country, in order to make it secure.
Mr. Cobden, in a meeting at Manchester, where general politics were
discussed, combated this opinion.]

I HAVE, in the first place, to tender you my thanks, and the
thanks of those gentlemen who represent North and South
Lancashire and the West Riding of Yorkshire, for the honour
which you have done us. I believe that a very large proportion of the Members of those divisions of the two counties
are now Free-traders, and, I have no doubt, will be found to
do their duty to the satisfaction of this assembly.

Now, gentlemen, I have been asked a dozen times, I dare
say, what is the object of this meeting. I confess to you that
I do not wish to regard it as a meeting to celebrate past
triumphs, still less to glorify ourselves or one another. I wish
rather that it should be made to show that we are alive to
the future — that, having secured upon the statute-book a

guarantee for free trade in corn, we intend to make that the
prelude to free trade in ships—that we intend to prevent the
West India proprietors from taxing this community for their
advantage—and that, in fact, we intend to carry out in every
article of commerce the principles of Free Trade, which we
have applied to corn.

Now, gentlemen, our esteemed Representative (Mr. Milner
Gibson) has so ably and efficiently anticipated some points
which I intended to refer to in connection with the sugar
question, and other applications of our principles of Free
Trade, that I am relieved from the necessity of repeating
them, and I thank him most heartily for the speech which
he has delivered upon this occasion, which is one of the
ablest that I ever heard in this hall. I believe that the
question of Free Trade, the question of Free Trade in all its
details, is understood by this assembly—that what I have told
you to be the future objects of this meeting has the concur-
rence of every one in this assembly, and I have no doubt
that every Member of Parliament now upon this platform will
aid us in carrying our principles into effect.

But now, gentlemen, I wish to allude to another subject,
and although I deem that subject to have an intimate connection with the question of Free Trade, yet I wish to be
distinctly understood, and I do not for a moment presume
that, in what I am going to say, I shall speak the sentiments
of any Member of Parliament or gentleman beside me. I
speak only for myself, and I wish to be understood as com-
promising no other individual. I allude, as you may probably
anticipate, to the intention which has been announced of
increasing our warlike armaments.

Now, gentlemen, you will bear me out, that throughout the
long agitation for Free Trade, the most earnest men who
co-operated with us were those who constantly advocated
Free Trade, not merely on account of the material advantages
which it would bring to the community, but for the far loftier

motive of securing permanent peace between nations. I believe that it was that consideration which mainly drew to our
ranks that great accession of ministers of religion which gave
so powerful an impetus to our progress at the commencement
of our agitation ; and I, who have known most of the leading
men connected with the struggle, and have had the opportunity of understanding their motives, can say that I believe
that the most earnest, the most persevering, the most devoted
of our coadjutors, have been prompted by those lofty, those
purely moral and religious motives to which I have referred, especially for the object of peace. Well, gentlemen,
I am sure that every one of those men have shared with
me the shock which my feelings sustained, when, within
one short twelvemonths after we had announced our adoption
of Free Trade to the world, we were startled with the
announcement that we were going to increase our warlike
armaments.

I ask, what is the explanation of this ? Probably we may
find it in the Duke of Wellington's letter—in the private
efforts which he announces therein that he has made with the
Government, and to the correspondence which he has had
with Lord John Russell. I may attribute this, then, to the
Duke of Wellington and his letter, and to his persevering
efforts. Well, I do not profess to share the veneration which
some men entertain for successful warriors. But is there
amongst the most ardent admirers of the Duke one man,
possessing the ordinary feelings of humanity, who would not
wish that that letter had never been written or never published ? His Grace has passed the point of the ordinary duration of human existence, and I may say, almost without a
figure of speech, that he is tottering on the verge of the grave.
Is it not a most lamentable spectacle that that hand, which is
no longer capable of wielding a sword, should devote its still
remaining feeble strength to the penning of a letter,—and that
letter may possibly be the last public letter which he may

address to his fellow-countrymen,—which is more calculated
than anything in the present day to create evil passions and
animosities in the breasts of two great and neighbouring
nations? Would it not have been a better employment for
him to have been seen preaching forgiveness and oblivion of
the past, rather than in reviving recollections of Toulon, and
Paris, and Waterloo; and, in fact, doing everything to invite
a brave people to retaliatory measures, to retrieve themselves
from past disasters and injuries? Would it not have been a
more glorious object to contemplate, had he poured the oil
into those wounds which are now almost healed, rather than
have thus applied the cautery—re-opening those wounds, and
leaving to other generations the task of repairing the mischief
which he has perpetrated? I will leave the subject of the
Duke's letter with this remark, which I made when I
read it and came to the conclusion, where he says, 'I am
in my 77th year'—I said, that explains it all, and excuses
it all. We have not to deal with the Duke of Wellington;
we have to deal with those younger men, who want to
make use of his authority to carry out their own special
purposes.

Now, what I wish to impress on you and the people of
England is, that the question before us is not a military, not a
naval question, but a question for civilians to decide. When
we are at war, then the men with red clothes and swords by
their sides may step in to do their work—and, as Sir H. Smith
fitly described it, in a speech which he recently made, a
damnable trade it is. But we are now at peace, and we wish
to reap the fruits of peace, and in order to do so we must
calculate for ourselves the contingency of a possible war.
That is a civilian's question — that is a question for the
decision of the tax-payers who have to pay the cost of a
war. It is a question for the merchant; it is a question for the manufacturer, for the shopkeepers, for the
operatives, for the farmers of this country — ay, and, par-

don me, my Lord Ellesmere, it is a question for the calico-printer.

What is this prospect of a war? Where does it come from? You, I say, are competent to judge on this subject better than military men. You are more impartial; you are disinterested; at all events, your interest does not lie on the side of war. Any man who can read a book giving an account of France—any man who can read a translation from a French newspaper—any man who will take the trouble of studying the statistics of the progress of their commerce and wealth—any man who can study these things, is as competent as a soldier to pronounce an opinion on the probability of a war. I have had better opportunities than any soldier of studying these things, and I say that there never was a time in the history of France and England when there was a greater tendency to a pacific policy in France, and especially towards this kingdom, than there is at the present time. Why, the French people have gone through a process which almost disqualifies them for going to war. They have gone through a social revolution, which has so much equalised property that the tax-payers are equally spread all over the country, and, paying a large portion of the taxes in indirect taxation, they have a direct interest and a most sensitive feeling in the expenditure which would be necessary to go to war. There are in France far more people of property than in England. There are some five or six millions of real proprietors of the soil in France. You have not one-tenth of that number in England. These are all thrifty, painstaking, careful men—all with their little savings, their little hoards of five-franc pieces—all anxious to do something for their children, for there is not a more domestic and affectionate race in the world than the French. I have seen with horror, and shame, and indignation, the way in which some of our newspapers speak of the French people. They have placed us before the community, before the world, in so ignominious, so

degraded a condition—they have marked us as such an ignorant people, to say nothing of our prejudices and want of
Christian charity, that, I say, nothing but an uprising of the
people in multitudinous assemblages like this, and repudiating
the doctrines put forth by those pretending to speak and
write in their behalf, can set us right with the world or with
ourselves.

There is one paper in this city, which I would always wish
to treat with respect, if it will allow me—there is, I say,
one paper here which, I see, last week gravely entered into
this argument, gravely adopted this line of reasoning, that it
is necessary we should have a police in Manchester, and that
we have had a constantly increasing police here to protect
us—against what? thieves, ruffians, pickpockets, and murderers; and, therefore, we must have increasing naval and
military armaments to protect us against the French. Are
the majority of the French people thieves and pickpockets,
ruffians and murderers? If they are, could they exist as an
organised community? And yet they are a community as
orderly as ourselves, for there has been as little tumult in
France during the last five or six years as there has been in
England.

I see that there is another newspaper in London, a weekly
newspaper, which used to write with some degree of credit to
itself, but I presume that it has been panic-stricken,—that it
has lost its wits. That paper tells us that the next war with
France will take place without any declaration of hostilities
on the part of that country, and that, literally, we have to
protect our Queen at Osborne House against these ruffianly
Frenchmen, who may, otherwise, come and carry her off.
What a lesson has our courageous Queen read to these men!
She went over to France, unfriended, unprotected, and threw
herself on shore at the Chateau d'Eu, literally in a bathing-
machine. Now, there is either great courage on one side, or
great cowardice on the other.

But, gentlemen, this is a sort of periodical visitation which we have. I sometimes compare it to the cholera—for I believe that the last infection which we had of this kind came about the time of the cholera. The last time that a cry of this sort was got up, we were threatened with an invasion of the Russians, which my friend (Mr. Milner Gibson) has told you of. Now, I am rather identified with and interested in that invasion of Russia. It was that which made me an author; it was that which made me a public man; and it is quite possible, if it had not been for the insanity of some of the public newspapers—and some of them are just as insane now as they were then—that I should not have come into public life. They then told us that the Russians would be coming over here some foggy day, and that they would land at Yarmouth. If it had not been for that insanity I should never have turned author, never have written pamphlets, but must have been a thrifty, painstaking calico-printer to this day.

Now, again, what I want is, that you should understand a little better about these foreigners. You may remember that about three weeks or a month ago I had occasion to address a few remarks to the electors assembled at Newton, on the occasion of the election of my friend Mr. Henry; and that there I let fall some observations favourable to the reduction of our armaments, and showing how necessary it was that we should reduce our expenditure in that department, in order to enable us to carry out fiscal reform. I little dreamt then, that within a few hours of the time when I was speaking, a large meeting was being held at Rouen, the Manchester of France, at which there were 1800 electors assembled, to promote, at a public dinner, the progress of parliamentary reform, and that a gentleman was there making a speech so similar to my own, that he sent me a newspaper containing a report of it, and expressed his astonishment that two speeches, made without collusion, should have so nearly resembled each other. I will, if you please,

read that gentleman's remarks, and notice the cheers of
the company as I go on. It is Mons. Vicienne who
speaks :—

'How long will it take to turn from theory into practice the very simple
idea that, apart from the precepts of religion, which we do so often quote, but
so seldom practise, and upon the merest calculations of an enlightened self-
interest, nations have a far different mission upon earth than to excite in each
other mutual fear? How long will it be before they discover the selfish objects
of those who have an interest in persuading them that the name of a foreigner
is synonymous with that of enemy? When will they learn that, as children of
the same Father, their real and only enemies, those which they ought to
struggle to destroy, are ignorance, oppression, misery, and superstition?—
[cheers]—that in proclaiming their mutual friendships, they will tend to the
consolidation of peaceful relations with each other? When will they discover
that the maintenance of formidable armaments, in countries whose nationality
is not seriously menaced, inflicts an evil upon all, and confers benefits on none?
[Shouts of "That's true—that's true."] But, better to define my idea, do you
not think that if, confident in the maintenance of an honourable peace, we
were to deduct from the goo millions francs which our army and navy cost us,
so millions to be applied to the education of the people, and a like sum for the
purpose of converting 30,000 soldiers into road-makers; if we gave back to
agriculture and manufactures 50,000 more soldiers, leaving in our pockets the
sum which they cost to pay and support them—think you not that this would
be a good result of the *entente cordiale*, I will not say between the Governments—we know what that is worth—[laughter]—but the nations, which have
no dynastic interests to serve, and do not play at diplomacy. [Cheers.] Do
you not think that this example of common sense and feeling of security given
by us would have its influence upon the other countries of Europe, would lead
to other disarmaments, would facilitate everywhere those fiscal reforms which
are postponed from day to day on the plea of the necessities of the treasury,
and would give to productive industry that capital and labour which are now
diverted into unproductive channels? [Expressions of assent.]'

Now, at the same meeting, another gentleman, an eminent
Member of the Chamber of Deputies, spoke, and said :—

'Heaven grant that the day may come when the world shall be one nation!
God gave us the earth, not to bathe it with blood, but that we might make it
smile with fertility. [Cheers.] Oh! gentlemen, which nation has found the
grandest success in war? What country can exhibit such glorious triumphs as
France, whose soldiers rushed to the field of battle in search of death, or rather
immortality? [Applause.] But after glory comes reverses; we have found
that if war has its immense triumphs, it has also its immense disasters. Besides, what changes are going on around us! If war, during so many ages,
was the rule, and peace the exception, in our day peace ought to be the rule

and war the exception. [Cheers.] See, in fact, what is passing throughout civilised Europe. People are fraternising by their industry, and by those novel means of communication which are almost annihilating distances. In four days you are at the extremity of Germany; in five days you may visit Berlin and Vienna; in seven days you are upon the banks of the Vistula. In a short time we shall be as near to the empire of Russia; already travellers are carrying ideas of liberty into that country, frightening tyranny, which will one day fall from its seat. Enough of conquering! Who would wish again to arm people against each other? Why should they think of the aggrandisement of territory when there are no longer any barriers between nations? [Prolonged cheering.] Let me not be told that this is a dream—a utopia; already we begin to realise it. By their intercourse, nations are beginning to know and understand each other; they are ridding themselves, one and all, of those ancient prejudices and hatreds which have hitherto separated them. Why should they not fraternise together? Why should they be enemies? Are they not the children of one God? Have they not all the same immortal spirit, which is the emanation from heaven? And, upon earth, have they not the same interests to protect and develope? [Prolonged sensation—bravos!] And, I demand of you, if France, warlike and conquering, has seen the nations offering to her the tribute of their acclamations, what a part will she perform in this long peace of the world! [Applause and long interruption.]'

Now, gentlemen, those extracts are very long, but I thought they would interest you—to know what was passing in a popular assembly, representing the active public opinion of the chief manufacturing town of France; and when you see such sentiments as those applauded in the way in which they were in a French assembly, why will you, people of Manchester, believe that the French are that nation of bandits which some of your newspapers would make you believe? I do not mean to say that there may not be prejudices in France to root out; and Heaven knows that we have prejudices enough in England to extirpate; but this I do say, that it is not with a few insignificant brawlers in Paris—men without station, stake, or influence in their country—it is not with those we should attempt to pick a quarrel, but it is rather to such men as those from whose speeches I have quoted that we should hold out the right hand of fellowship.

Now, I will be practical with you on this question of armaments, for I shall not have another opportunity of speaking

to you again before this question comes before the House of
Commons. I have said that it is a question for civilians to
determine—that military and naval men should have no voice
in it—that it is for you only, the tax-payers. Do not let me
be misunderstood. I am not going to enter into the techni-
calities of war. I do not claim for civilians—Heaven forbid I
should—a knowledge of the horrid trade of war. I only contend that, whilst we are in a state of profound peace, it is for
you, the tax-payers, to decide whether you will run the risk of
war, and keep your money in your pockets, or allow an additional number of men in red coats and blue jackets to live in
idleness under the pretence of protecting you. Now, I say
this, that I am for acting justly and fairly, for holding out
the olive-branch to all the world, and I am for taking on
myself, so far as my share goes, all the risk of anything that
may happen to me, without paying for more soldiers and
sailors.

But it is not merely the question, whether you will have
more armaments, that you civilians are competent to decide.
You have already expended this year 17,000,000*l.* sterling in
your armaments, and it is a question on which you are competent to decide, whether the best possible use is made of your
money—whether, for instance, the navy, for which you pay
so largely, is really employed in the way best calculated to
answer the design of those men who profess themselves so
anxious to accomplish it, if you will give them more money—
that is, the protection of your shores. Where do you think all
your great line-of-battle ships go? I have picked up a few
secrets abroad—for you know that I have travelled by water
as well as by land. I venture to say that there is not more
perfect idleness, nor more demoralisation, the consequence of
idleness, going on in the same space on the face of the earth
as in our ships of war, from their want of having something
to do. Where do you find them? Where are those great
line-of-battle ships, of whose payment and equipment you

hear, and which you read of going out of your harbours with
such a display of power? Do they go where we have any
great commerce? Go to Hamburg, and there you will never
see an English man-of-war. Go to the Baltic, where we
carry on so much trade, and you will rarely see one. There
is rough weather, and not many attractions on shore there.
Well, go, then, to America. There is North America, with
which, I suppose, we do one-fifth or one-sixth of the foreign
trade of this country—at least, I hope we shall very shortly
come to that. Do you think any of these great men-of-war
are upon that coast? Why it is the rarest thing indeed for
one to be seen in those waters, and if one does appear there
the fact is recorded in the American newspapers. They do
not go there; for there are no idle people on shore, and the
officers do not like the society they meet with. In fact, the
ships are not wanted there, and they would do more harm
than good if they went there.

Well, then, where do they go? I am trying to get the
information for you. I moved for a return, just before the
close of the last little session of Parliament, which will throw
some light on the subject, and I ask you to keep your eye on
that return. I will tell you what it is. I moved for a return
of the amount of our naval force that has been in the Tagus,
and the waters of Portugal, on the 1st of each month during
the last twelve months — the name of the ships, the comple-
ment of guns, and the number of men. Now, when that
report turns up, I should not be surprised if you see that you
have had a naval force in the Tagus and the Douro, and on
the coast of Portugal, which, in the number of guns, will not
fall much short of the whole American navy. Lisbon is a
pleasant place to be at, as I can vouch, for I have seen it.
The climate is delightful. Geraniums grow in the open
air in the month of January. I do not quarrel with the
taste of the admirals or captains who go and spend twelve
months in the Tagus, if you will let them. But now, I ask,

what are they doing in return for the money which they cost you? Are they promoting, even in the remotest degree, English interests there? Nothing of the kind. Our fleet has been in the Tagus, at the absolute disposal of the Queen of Portugal, positively and literally nothing else. Our papers have avowed that our fleet went there to protect her Majesty of Portugal, and to give her and her Court an asylum, in case the conduct of her people should compel her to seek it.

Now, this is a subject upon which every gentleman, nay, every lady, is competent to judge. I never like to speak disrespectfully of any country, and, therefore, I do not wish to be thought to speak slightingly of Portugal, when I say that it is one of the smallest, poorest, and one of the most decayed and abject of European countries. I am sorry for it, but such is the fact. What in the world has England to gain by going and taking this country under her protection? Is it her commerce that you seek for? Why, you are sure of her commerce, for this simple reason—that you take four-fifths of all her port wine, and if you did not, no one else would drink it. Now, I would not like to be thought capable of using an atrocious sentiment, and what I am about to say I mean only as an illustration of an economical argument; but, positively, if the earthquake which once demolished Lisbon were to come again, and sink the whole of Portugal under the sea, it would be an immense gain to the English people. That, however, is not the fault of Portugal; for our ships go there—to do what? Why, to help the Queen and Government of Portugal to misgovern the people. When they rebel, our forces go on shore and put them down by the strong arm. Why, our statesmen actually undertook to say who should govern Portugal, and to exclude a particular family from all participation in the government. They also stipulated that the Cortes should be elected on constitutional principles. Well, the Cortes was elected, and the people have returned almost every man

favourable to that very statesman whom Lord Palmerston and
Co. said should not have any influence in Portugal.

Now, gentlemen, I ask you just to follow out this question of English interference with Portugal. Understand the
whole subject—the increase of your armaments which is thus
caused; apply your common sense to it. There is a constant
complaint that the English public do not give any attention
to foreign politics. What is the reason of that? It is common sense, and a very sound instinct on the part of the
English people. They turn their heads and eyes from foreign
politics, because they know that they have never done them
any good. But you must do one thing: you must change
from apathy to knowledge; you must superintend your foreign
minister; and when you do that, I undertake to say that you
may save a great deal of money—and that will be one good
result, at all events, in these bad times. What I wish to
bring home to your convictions is this, that if the people in
Brighton—if the old ladies of both sexes there are frightened
lest they should be taken out of their beds some night by the
French—why not bring home the fleet from the Tagus, and
let it cruise in the Channel? I am no sailor, but I feel sure
that no sailor would gainsay this,—that it would be a great
deal better practice, better exercise, better for the crew, for
the condition of the ships, for the quality of the officers and
men, if the fleet were sailing in the Channel, than lying in
demoralising idleness at Lisbon.

Now, gentlemen, if you go into the Mediterranean—if you
follow your ships there — you will find precisely the same
thing going on. Why, the Mediterranean is crowded with
English ships of war—not to look after your commerce: they
can do no good in that way. We have settled that question:
we have repudiated protection. But there you find them,
nevertheless. Leaving Portsmouth, they sail directly for
Malta; and Malta is the great skulking-hole for your navy.
I was at Malta at the commencement of winter, in the month

of November. Whilst I was at Malta, a ship arrived there
from Portsmouth; it had come direct; it had 1000 hands
on board when it left Portsmouth; it came into Valetta
Harbour, when I was there, with 999 people on board, men
and boys, having lost one hand on the passage. Soon after
the arrival of that vessel I started from Valetta, went to
Naples, and from thence to Egypt and Greece, and when I
returned she had never stirred. Her officers had gone on
shore to live in the club, and the lieutenant and other officers
in command found the utmost difficulty for even a pretence of
work. The crew were ordered to hoist up the sails and to let
them down again; and they scrubbed the decks until they
scrubbed the planks almost through. Well, I was introduced
to the American Consul at Malta, and he spoke to me in a
very friendly manner on the subject of our navy. He said,
'We Americans consider your navy to be very slack.' 'Slack!'
I said; 'what do you mean by slack?' 'Why,' he said, 'they
are too idle; they are not sufficiently worked. You cannot
have a crew in good order if they lie for three or four months
in a harbour like this. We have never more than three or
four vessels in the Mediterranean, and rarely one larger than
a frigate; but the instructions which we have from the
Government at Washington are these, — that the American
ships are never to be kept in port at all; that they are to go
from one port to another, to take care of the traders, and
see if there are any pirates, although there are not often any
of them in the Mediterranean. But the vessels are always in
motion, and the American sailors and American ships are in a
better state of discipline and equipment than the English
ships, on account of their idleness.' Now, again, this is a
question on which every man and woman in the country is
competent to form an opinion; and I say that if any one
talks to me about increasing our armaments, I tell them,
if they are frightened in the Channel, let them bring home
those useless ships which are lying in the Tagus and the

Mediterranean.   If they tell me that the ships of war in
the Tagus are lying there for the protection of the Queen
of Portugal, I tell them that her subjects are her proper
protectors.

Now, one word, rather personal to myself, without the
slightest reference to the opinions of the gentlemen around me;
I had been, somehow or another, rather singled out on this
question of armaments.   I dropped a few remarks at Stockport on the subject, in the most harmless and incidental way.
To confess the honest truth, I did not go there to say anything about armaments or taxation; but, in the course of my
speech, as people here can testify, a man shouted out, ' But
ain't taxation something to do with it?' and then, under the
impulse of the moment, I alluded to the army, navy, and
ordnance, as the only item on which a reduction of taxation
can be effected.   The papers in London—I suppose for their
own convenience' sake—tried to make me ridiculous, if they
could, by making me say that I wanted to save the whole
expenditure on the army, navy, and ordnance.   I have no
hesitation in declaring what my opinions are on this subject.
I stated at Stockport, very candidly, what I shall state here—
what I stated in my pamphlets twelve years ago on this
subject—that you cannot have a material reduction in your
armaments until a great change takes place in public opinion
in this country with regard to our foreign policy.   I have
stated that opinion over and over again in my writings.   I
said at Stockport that you cannot reduce that item until there
is a change in public opinion, and the English people abandon
the notion that they are to regulate the affairs of the world.
Indeed, those were my very words at Stockport, as people
here can testify.   I wished to do no injustice—to offer no
factious opposition to Ministers with respect to the maintenance of our armaments.   All I wanted was to invoke
public opinion, as I do now, and as I always will invoke
public opinion.   When the public opinion, the majority of

the influential opinion of the country, is on my side, I shall
be content to see my views carried out. Until that time, I
am content to be on this question, as I have been on others,
in a minority, and in a minority to remain, until I get a
majority.

But, gentlemen, the real and practical question before the
country is not the question of a reduction of armaments. This,
however, has been very carefully mystified. It is not a question, as this paper in Manchester, in its latest number, says,
whether we shall dismantle fleets and leave our arsenals defenceless. That is not the question, and it is dishonest to put
that as the question. The real question is, will we have an
increase of the army, navy, and ordnance? Now, when I
admit that public opinion does not go with me to the extent
which would enable me to carry a great reduction in our
armaments, I at the same time maintain — speaking for the
West Riding of Yorkshire—speaking for Lancashire—speaking for Middlesex — speaking for London — speaking for
Edinburgh — speaking for Glasgow — I say that, on the
question of the increase of our armaments, public opinion is
with me in those places, and against the Ministers. And
if that public opinion is expressed, and expressed through
public meetings, I, for one, have no hesitation in saying that a
large portion of the press has neglected and forsaken its duty
on this question. I say that if public opinion be expressed
in public meetings throughout the country, before the estimates are brought on in the House of Commons, there will
be no increase of our armaments. But whether that manifestation of public opinion take place or not, I—speaking for
myself, as an individual Member of the House of Commons—
say that not one shilling shall be added to the estimates for
our armaments, without my having forced a division of the
House upon it.

I began by identifying this question of our armaments
with the question of Free Trade, and I tell you, in con-

clusion, that the question of Free Trade is jeopardised all over
Europe by the course which it is intended to take. Why,
I receive the papers from Paris, and what do they tell me?
There is a band of Free-traders there associated together;
they publish their weekly organ, as we published our Anti-
Corn-law paper. It is called the *Libre Echange*, and is
edited by my talented and excellent and able friend, M.
Bastiat. That paper, last week, was mourning in sackcloth
and ashes over the course which they there think England
is going to pursue. And what says the organ of the protectionists, the *Moniteur Industriel?* They are deluging,
not only France, but England, with the last week's number
of that paper, in which they leap with exultation at the
condition of this country. 'We told you,' says that journal,
'that England was not sincere on the Free-trade question.
She has no faith in her principles; she sees that other nations
are not following her example, and she is preparing her armaments to take that by force which she thought to take by
fraud.'

Now, I exhort my countrymen everywhere to resist this
attempt to throw odium on our principles, which, if carried
out, the Free-traders believe would bring peace and harmony
among the nations. The most enthusiastic of us never said,
as some of the papers pretend that we did say, that we expected the millennium soon after we had got Free Trade. We
never expected but that we should have to give time to other
nations for the adoption of our principles, precisely as we
required time to adopt them ourselves. But what we did
hope was this: that the Continent of Europe, with eyes
steadily fixed on this country, in connection with this question, would, at all events, not have seen that we were the
first to have doubt as to the tendency of our own principles,
and to be arming against the world when we pretended to be
seeking only their friendship and kindness. We permitted
too many of the good and peaceful men who joined this

agitation to try to make it the harbinger of peace, which it was intended to be; we planted the olivo-tree, never expecting to gather the fruit in a day; but we expected it to yield fruit in good season, and, with Heaven's help and yours, it shall do so yet.

FINANCE.

II.

I MUST bespeak your kindness for keeping silence and order during the meeting, for I am afraid I am so much out of practice, that I shall not make myself heard over this vast audience. I have to move a resolution, which I will read to you. It is :—

'That this meeting resolves to co-operate with the Liverpool Financial Reform Association, and other bodies, in their efforts to reduce the public expenditure to at least the standard of 1835, and to secure a more equitable and economical system of taxation.'

We have often, gentlemen, met in this hall to advocate a cause which has brought upon us the charge of being the farmers' enemies; and now we come forward in another character — we appear here as the farmers' friends. We have been accused of having subjected the agriculturists of this country to a competition with foreigners. They have complained to us that they are more heavily taxed than the foreign farmers. Now, gentlemen, we come forward to offer them the right hand of fellowship and union, to effect a reduction of ten millions in the cost of our Government. I have moved, and in your name I hope it will go forth to the country, that we co-operate with the financial reformers of

Liverpool in their agitation for financial reform, on the condition that we advocate a return to the expenditure of 1835.
In 1835, the affairs of this Government were carried on for
ten millions less of money than they are this year, and I have
ventured to propose, in a letter which may have probably met
the eyes of some of those present, that we should go back to
that expenditure. I have waited three weeks before I should
have the opportunity of saying a word in public in defence of
my views, to see what would be said against that recommendation. I must confess that my opponents have not given me
much to answer. I have heard it said, and it is probably the
most valid argument that can be urged, that the population
has increased since 1835. True, it has; our numbers are 12½
per cent. more than they were then, and our opponents say that
we must allow a larger sum for the government of a greater
number than a smaller; and I admit the argument so far as
civil government goes, and in my plan I allow forty per cent.
more for the civil government than was expended in 1835.
But I deny that thirteen years of duration of peace is an
additional argument why we should have an increase of our
forces. And here I am very glad to call to my aid the
opinion of a statesman who probably will be allowed by our
opponents to be an authority in this matter. Towards the
close of last session of Parliament, Sir R. Inglis, the Member
for the University of Oxford, uttered this extraordinary doctrine—very extraordinary everywhere but at Oxford—that
the longer you remained at peace, the greater the probability
was that you would go to war. His idea seems to be, that
men in time of peace were only being fattened up for a speedy
slaughter. Now, hear what Lord Palmerston said in reply
to him :—

    ' But I look to the general tendency of men's minds towards peace, and
I differ from the hon. Member for the University of Oxford, who thinks that
the long duration of peace renders war more probable : I think, on the contrary, that the duration of peace renders its continuance more likely, and
will make countries more disposed to settle their differences otherwise than
by war.'

It appears that in 1835 we spent 11,600,000*l.* for our army, navy, and ordnance, and I propose that we now shall not expend more than 10,000,000*l.* What I take from the expenditure for warlike purposes in 1835, I add to the civil expenditure in 1848. We spent for purposes of civil government in 1835, 4,300,000*l.*; I allow 5,900,000*l.* for the civil expenditure of the Government now; and taking into account the saving which I contemplate in the cost of collecting the revenue, and in the management of the Crown lands, which I have seen estimated by a financial reformer at something like half a million—taking these into account, I am allowing more than actually we are now expending for the ordinary expenses of the civil government of this country, and thus we get rid altogether of the objection, that increase of population requires an increase of expenditure to govern the people. Then, there has been another argument used also, and it is this: that, during the last year, and the year before, there was a deficiency of revenue. We have spent more than we have received, and we borrow money; and, therefore, even if my financial plan should be carried out, there still will not be the ten millions to dispose of in the remission of taxes. Well, my answer to that is this—and these cunning financiers who meet me with this argument ought to know it—that if the revenue has fallen off during the last year and the year before, it has been because the balance-sheets of our merchants and manufacturers have been equally adverse. The revenue has been deficient because the profits have been annihilated in the trade of every man in the country; but now that you have food at moderate prices, trade revives, and instantly you see the revenue increasing, and next year, perhaps this year —the next year, certainly—will see you with a surplus revenue as certainly as you had a deficiency last year. But I say, gentlemen—and I want to keep the financial reformers to this point, because we must have one simple article of faith, or we cannot march together—I say, give me the expenditure

hack again of 1835, and I will guarantee you the remission
of ten millions of taxation. If you want — if the country
wants to reduce their duty on tea one-half; if you wish to
abolish altogether, the duty upon timber, upon butter, upon
cheese, upon soap, upon paper, upon malt, upon house-win-
dows; if you wish to put an end to a system that curtails
those necessaries and comforts — then raise your voices
throughout the country, simultaneously, for the expenditure
of 1835.

Now, where is the difficulty? Where is the difficulty of
returning to the expenditure of 1835? Why, the whole
question lies in the amount of your warlike armaments. The
whole question is, Will the Government be content to waste
ten millions of money in unproductive services like your
fighting establishments—I mean your fighting establishments
in a time of peace? Will our Government be content with
ten millions? and if not, why not? I want the arguments
—why not? I was asked the other day by an M.P., ' When
are you going into the details to show how you propose to
carry on the Government upon your plan?' My answer was
this : ' I should be a very bad tactician, and but a poor
logician, if, when I have made a proposal that the Government should support its warlike establishments with ten
millions of money, I did not call upon them to give me an
answer, and to show me why they cannot maintain them with
ten millions.' I put them on the defensive. I ask them
whether they have made the most of the money they receive.
How do you think they dispose of the money? Why, you
maintain one hundred and fifty admirals, besides fifty retired
admirals. Well, but how many do you think you employ?
Why, during the heat of the great French war—the greatest
war on record—when you had nearly one thousand pennants
flying, you never employed more than thirty-six admirals at
one time—and at this time you have but fourteen admirals in
active service. With all their ingenuity of putting admirals

to work when they are not wanted, they can only find employment for fourteen. Well, then, I find in the army you have a colonel for every regiment who does the work; and you have another colonel of every regiment, who is the tailor to the regiment—who never goes near it—who never sees it —whom the men would not know if he did go near it; but he supplies clothes to them, and gets the profits of a tailor. These are illustrations how money is wasted. But I won't confine myself to the abuses and waste that occur. I tell you plainly from the outset, that, in order to effect such a reduction of expenditure for your armaments as you require for a relief to the country, a material relief—that will be felt in the homes and at the firesides of the population of this country— you must reduce the number of men. You must be content with a smaller manifestation of brute force in the eyes of the world. You must trust something to Providence—something to your own just intentions—and your good conduct to other nations; and you must rely less upon that costly, that wasteful expenditure, arising from so enormous a display of brute force.

Now, gentlemen, I will bring this matter home to my opponents with a very few figures. How is it we have had this great increase in the cost of our armaments? Has it been only an increase of waste, an increase in the number of admirals, and an increase in the number of colonels? No; it is because you have augmented the number of your men. I hold in my hand a statement made by Lord John Russell in the House of Commons last session. I will quote his own figures. He gives me the increase of the army, navy, and ordnance, since 1835; and in 1835 the number of men in all these services was 135,743; in last year they were 196,063. The increase in the number of men in the army, navy, and ordnance, since 1835, has been 60,320. Now, what has been the increase of the expenditure? In 1835, the total cost for all these services was 11,600,000l. In the present year it is

upwards of 18,000,000*l.* The increase of the men has been
as nearly as possible fifty per cent., and the increase in the
money has been about fifty per cent. also.   It is perfectly
understood when Parliament votes the men, it must vote corresponding establishments in every direction; and, therefore,
while I admit there are abuses, and great waste and mismanagement, I say, if you want a material reduction in the
cost of your armaments, you must at once boldly proceed on
the plan of reducing the number of armed men.

Why should you not reduce them? Why have they been
increased? There has always been a ready excuse for adding
to the force when an augmentation of the army, navy, or
ordnance has been proposed; but what I complain of is, that
when the alleged occasion of the increase has passed away, we
never have a diminution. In 1835, as I have told you, our
armaments were at the lowest point. In 1836, a cry was got
up that the Russians were coming to invade us. I remember
penning a pamphlet, to expose the absurdity of the cry, that
the Russians were preparing to invade the coast of Norfolk
some foggy morning; but that cry was an excuse for an increase in our navy. Then, again, in 1839, after the unfortunate
scenes at Monmouth, in which Frost, Williams, and Jones
were concerned—I suppose I must call it rebellion—there was
immediately a proposal made by Lord John Russell for an
increase of 5000 men to the army. That increase was made
specifically to meet the case of the Chartist riots; but when
tranquillity returned, we never heard a word about reducing
those 5000 men. If you follow step by step the increase in
our armaments, you will find the same course pursued. At
one time, we must needs go and settle affairs in Syria, and we
sent a large fleet to bombard Acre, and fight Ibrahim Pasha,
or some other Pasha. Then we had a quarrel with the French
at Tahiti. Then, in 1845, there was a dispute about the
Oregon boundary. As President Polk talked a great deal
about fighting, and some men in the House of Representatives

uttered more nonsense than usual, our Government proposed
a large increase in the navy, and we had the 'squadron of
evolution' fitted out,—this squadron of evolution that is still
going on with its evolutions. This was as a demonstration
against America; but the Oregon question was settled—the
Tuhiti question is settled—the Chartists, I hope, are now well
employed and comfortable; where, then, is the pretence for
keeping up all these increased armaments? But I have not
forgotten the last excuse. You remember, this time last year,
standing on this platform, I raised my voice in conjunction
with yours—and we stood almost alone—against that wicked
attempt to impose on us by increasing our national defences
to protect us against an invasion from France. By way of
parenthesis, for your encouragement and the encouragement
of the country, let me just remind you of the progress of
opinion since then. We then had to contend against the
increase of our overgrown establishments—we had an up-hill
battle, but we succeeded. Now, here is a proposal before the
country to reduce the cost of our armaments nearly one-half,
and that proposal is receiving more favour with the public
within twelve months than our resistance to an increase of
the armaments did last year.

And why is it? Because, in spite of all the efforts to
mystify the public mind on the subject, events on the Continent have trumpet-tongued declared, that the attempt to
frighten us with the threat of an unprovoked attack from
France, was a vile slander upon that nation. We were told
this time last year, ' It is true the French are quiet now, because Louis Philippe, the Napoleon of Peace, is on the throne ;
but wait till he dies, and you will see how the French people,
that are now kept in by this wise monarch, will break loose
on their neighbours.' Louis Philippe is politically dead ; the
French people were thrown entirely on their own resources—
the bridle on their necks, the bit in their mouths, the masses
were all-powerful, and the Government, on its knees, was

ready to follow them to the utmost bent of their passions.
Has there been amidst that 35,000,000 of people, your next
neighbours, one whisper that could justify the accusations
made against them last year by those wicked alarmists and
panic-mongers whom I will never forgive, or, if I do, I will
never forget to remind them of their wickedness? Has there
been one act of the French people to warrant the imputation
that they wished to come and attack you? But I won't confine myself to that. There were countries nearer home which
everybody supposed the French more likely to attack than to
attempt to conquer England. Has there been the slightest
wish displayed on the part of the French people to make the
Rhine the boundary of their empire? Have they invaded
Belgium? Have they entered Holland? Have they con-
quered Italy? Have they shown the slightest disposition for
conquest in any way? On the contrary, wherever a public
man has sought to conciliate the French people, has he not
addressed them in terms of peace, and promised them, above
all things, that he will follow a pacific policy? Take their
President—a Napoleon Buonaparte—I say nothing of his
fitness to be President of the Republic, that is the affair of the
French people, not ours; but observe, when such an individual
canvasses the French people for their suffrages, how he accosts
them. Does he promise them a war against England, or at
least an invasion of Belgium? What said Louis Napoleon in
his address to the French people?—

'With war, there can be no mitigation of our sufferings. Peace shall,
therefore, be the most cherished object of my desires. At the time of her
first revolution France was warlike, because others compelled her to be so.
She was attacked, and she rolled back the tide of conquest upon her invaders.
But now, that nobody attacks her, she can devote all her resources to peaceful
amelioration, without abandoning a firm and honourable policy.'

Now, does that look as if you had been wisely spending
your money in fortifying yourselves, and keeping up your
enormous standing armaments, because certain parties, who

are interested in clothing regiments, or being admirals, with
nothing to do, choose to tell you that the French people are
a mighty hobgoblin, ready to come over and devour you some
morning. I have dwelt longer on this subject, because what I
stated with reference to the great mass of the French people
last year was perverted; I said that property in France was
more divided than in any other country in the world. I said
there were 8,000,000 or 10,000,000 of real proprietors in
France. The whole soil of that vast empire—and it is the
richest on the surface of Europe—is cut up in small properties,
held in fee-simple by those who cultivate it. And when those
who write in certain aristocratic journals talk of dangers
arising to a country from the minute subdivision of its property, I, am very much disposed to whisper in their ears
whether the lessons of history have not taught us that the
danger is wholly different. Let them point out the nation
that has been ruined because its property was in too many
hands. Does not ruin rather proceed from property being
accumulated by a small number of persons, and the consequent indulgence of luxury and corruption by the few, and
the degradation and misery of the mass? The argument I
drew last year, and which I repeat here now, confirmed by
experience since, is this, that the people in France, being
nearly all proprietors, and having to pay for any war they
may wish to carry on, they will not vote for a war, as they
would have to vote for more taxation. I believe that Louis
Napoleon, Cavaignac, and Guizot, whose book was published
only yesterday, and every man in France, including M. Thiers,
will agree with me, that if there be one passion more predominant than another among the mass of the French people,
it is the desire for peace. But I do not confine myself to
France. I will take Germany; I will take Italy; and I ask,
where, amidst their convulsions—where monarchs have abdi-
cated, where popes and potentates have run away in the dis-
guises of lacqueys, or gone down on their knees before the

mob in their ascendant—where, in all Europe, has there been
among the mass of the people one sign or symptom of a desire
for aggressive war on their neighbours?

Beware of another mystification. One of the most favourite
of the enemy's devices is this—they raise a confusion in your
minds by pointing to the internal disorders in foreign countries, and persuade you it is a state of war. I told you the
people abroad were for peace, and so they are; but when
the revolutions broke out, these fallacy-mongers exclaimed,
' Here's Cobden, just come back from the Continent, tells us
the people are all for peace—now they are all for war.' They
have been in a state of revolution to obtain precisely the same
ends for which this country went through a revolution two
centuries ago. And though in France the gain, even in the
way of practical liberty, has not been so great as in other
countries—for they had a great amount of practical freedom
before their last revolution—yet, when you compare the state
of Germany and Italy with what it was when I was there not
two years ago, I say that, with their convulsions, slight and
evanescent compared with our war against prerogative under
our first Charles, Germany and Italy have gained an amount
of freedom which required ten years' civil war in England to
achieve. I left them in those countries with every newspaper
and every book under the strict control of the censor. I left
them with closed courts of justice administering law, not by
oral testimony in presence of the accused, but by written
documentary evidence. I left them without a representative
form of government, without trial by jury; and now, though
they may blunder and stumble in the path of freedom, they
are at least in the highway for obtaining the same constitutional privileges—as soon as they can use them they may have
them—as we have ourselves. In spite of all the attempts of
the press and public men to cry out ' Reaction,' and applaud
the despots and their soldiers, who are willing to fight for
tyranny, I, in the presence of this great assembly and in their

name, do express sympathy for the people who are struggling
for their liberties. Do not think I am talking to you of
politics foreign to your interests here. It is by studied misrepresentation of what is going on upon the Continent that
our enormous standing armaments are maintained and defended in this country. I say that the progress of constitutional rights on the Continent must be favourable to the
preservation of peace, because I think I have proved to you
that the mass of the people on the Continent, like the mass
of the people in this country, are favourable to peace, and
averse to war. But you have another safeguard. I defy you
to show me how any Government or people on the Continent
can strengthen themselves, even if they chose to carry on a
war of conquest. Let France invade Germany, it only makes
Germany unite like one man—the whole Teutonic race are
united as one man to repel the French. What is their predominant sentiment? The union of Germany, not for aggressive force, but for defensive succour. What is the cry
in Italy? Italian nationality. What is the contest between
Lombardy and Austria? The house of Austria may call Lombardy part of its territory, but there is another race,—the
Latin race say, 'We will not be governed by a Teutonic race;'
and, though the Austrians may keep down the Italians by
Radetski and his 100,000 troops, Lombardy will be a source
of weakness, not of strength, to them. I defy you to show
me any partition where an accession of territory has not been
rather a source of weakness than of strength. Take the very
worst that can happen :—suppose any power on the Continent
is going to attack its neighbour, is there any reason why we
should be armed to the teeth in order to take part in the
struggle? In ancient times, when the people were counted
as nothing, and when sovereigns told out their subjects as a
shepherd would his flock ; when a royal marriage united the
crowns of two kingdoms, and the people of both became the
willing subjects, or even serfs, of the one sovereign, there

might have been danger in an acquisition of territory. But
now that the people count everywhere for something, and we
see on the Continent of Europe great lines of demarcation of
race—the Italian Peninsula, for instance, one; Spain, another;
Germany, another;—and when you find the great mosaic
mass of Austrian dominion broken up, as it were, into Sclaves
and Magyars, I see new limits assigned to conquest. I repeat,
there is no longer any reason to fear that one empire will take
possession, by force of arms, of its neighbour's territory; but,
if it should, the accession of territory would be a source of
weakness, not of strength. Take it at the worst, then; let
the nations of the Continent attack each other; who is coming
to attack you, if you only let their politics alone?

This brings me to another position which has an important bearing on the reduction of our armaments, and that
is, we must let other people manage their own affairs. The
Spaniards, who have very wise maxims, say, ' A fool knows
more of what is going on in his own house than a wise man
does in that of his neighbour.' Now, if we will apply that
to nations, mind our own business, and give foreigners the
credit of being able to manage their own concerns better than
we can do for them, or they with our interference, it will
save us a great deal of money, and they will have their affairs
settled better and sooner than if we intermeddled with them.
But what are we doing? There cannot be a petty squabble
in any country in Europe or the globe, but we must have a
great fleet of line-of-battle ships sent from England to take
part in it. We have just interfered between Naples and
Sicily—what is the consequence? We are detested by both
parties. In all Italy it is the same. They speak of Englishmen with contempt and execration; not because they undervalue our qualities as men—no, they pay us high a tribute
to the qualities of Englishmen as we could desire—but, as a
nation, as a Government, interfering with their politics, from
one end of the Peninsula to the other, the Italians cordially

hate and detest us. So with regard to Spain—we have spent
hundreds of millions on Spain, and what is the present state
of feeling there? I travelled from one end of Spain to the
other, and I never heard the name of the Duke of Wellington
mentioned, although he fought their battles, as we persuade
ourselves—I never saw his portrait or bust through all my
travels, but I saw Napoleon's and his Marshals' everywhere.
At this very moment, Napoleon and France are more popular
in Spain than England and Englishmen. It is the same in
Greece—the same in Portugal. The English people are hated,
because we interfere with their politics. Is not that a very
undignified attitude for a great nation like this to occupy?
If we kept aloof from their squabbles, and contented ourselves
with setting foreigners a good example—if we put our own
houses in order—if we set our mud cabins in Ireland in order
—we should show a great deal more common sense than in
attempting to manage the affairs of other nations when we
are not responsible for their government. But an argument
has been used why we should interfere; and I like to hear it,
for it shows that our opponents are at their last extremity.
They say, 'If we don't interfere, France will interfere;' and
so it is,—we have sent a fleet to Naples, because the French
had a fleet there. I remember, at the last stage of the Anti-
Corn-law agitation, our opponents were driven to this position
—' Free Trade is a very good thing, but you cannot have it
until other countries adopt it too;' and I used to say, ' If Free
Trade be a good thing for us, we will have it : let others take
it, if it be a good thing for them ; if not, let them do without
it.' So I say now, if our constant interference with the affairs
of the Continent be a costly, useless, pernicious policy for us,
and if France—if Austria, choose to adopt that policy and ruin
themselves by it, let them do so, but don't let us follow their
example. This is common sense, although it does not pervade
high quarters in this country.

We have another argument to meet. We are told we must

keep up enormous armaments, because we have got so many
colonies. People tell me I want to abandon our colonies; but
I say, do you intend to hold your colonies by the sword, by
armies, and ships of war? That is not a permanent hold
upon them. I want to retain them by their affections. If you
tell me that our soldiers are kept for their police, I answer,
the English people cannot afford to pay for their police. The
inhabitants of those colonies are a great deal better off than
the mass of the people of England—they are in the possession
of a vast deal more of the comforts of life than the bulk of
those paying taxes here; they have very few of those taxes
that plague us here so much—excise, stamps, and taxes, those
fiscal impediments which beset you every day in your callings,
are hardly known in our colonies. Our colonies are very
able to protect themselves. Every man among them has his
fowling-piece, and, if any savages come to attack them, they
can defend themselves. They have another guarantee—if
civilised men treat savages like men, there is never any occasion to quarrel with them. With regard to our navy, they
tell us it is necessary because of our trade with the colonies. I
should have thought it was just that trade which wanted no
navy at all. It is a sort of coasting trade; our ships are at
home when they get to our colonies. We don't want any
navy to protect our trade with America, which is a colony
emancipated; and we may thank our stars it has broke loose;
it never would have been such a customer if the aristocracy
of England had held that field of patronage for their younger
sons. You don't want a ship of war to protect your trade
with the United States; and last year you exported to them
10,900,000l. of your produce, more by upwards of a million
than you exported to all your colonies together, India excepted. Sir William Molesworth, in that admirable speech of
his on the colonies, showed that, by a better administration,
not by taking away altogether your force from the colonies,
but by an improved system of government, you might save
2,000,000l. per annum.

You have to make up your mind to one thing,—you cannot
afford all this waste. It is not a matter of choice with you.
I tell you, you are spending too much money as a nation. It
is not merely your general taxation—your local taxation likewise oppresses you. Mark me, the greater the cost of your
armaments falling on general taxation, the more you will
have to spend in poor-rates and other taxes. The more you
waste of the capital of the country, the more people will be
wanting employment; and when they want employment, it is
the law of England that the poorest, who are the first to begin
to suffer under a course of national extravagance or decay,
have the right to come to those above them and demand subsistence, under the name of poor-rate; so that, in proportion
as the extravagance of Government increases, poor-rates and
the expenses of a repressive police increase also. You must,
therefore, lessen the national expenditure, or the catastrophe
cannot long be deferred. I have detained you already too
long, but there is one thing I wish to impress upon you
before I sit down. It is of paramount moment to the English
people that we should not allow ourselves to entertain an
undue or exaggerated notion of our own importance as a
nation, or to take a too unfavourable view of other countries.
It is through your national pride that cunning people manage
to extract taxes from you. They persuade you that nothing
can be done abroad unless you do it; and that you are so
superior to all other countries, that your next neighbour,
France, for instance, is nothing but a band of brigands, and,
unless you are constantly on the watch, they will be ready to
pounce upon you and carry off your property. Until, as a
nation, we give credit to other people for being able to work
out their own liberties—unless we believe there is something
of honour and honesty in other countries to shield us from
unjust aggression on their part, we must always be armed to
secure ourselves from the imaginary attacks of our neighbours.
Other nations are far too intelligent to require that we should

always be armed to the teeth, in order to let them know how
strong we are.   I don't believe that the French will come to
attack the English merely because we happen to have a few
less ships of war or a few less regiments than we now possess.
Their Government will look far beyond your manifestation of
force.   They will inquire what is the wealth, the power, the
public spirit of our people; are we a contented nation, attached
to our institutions, governed well, united as one man against
an enemy; and if they see the indications of this latent national power, depend on it they won't wantonly rush into war
with us, even if we don't always go armed to the teeth, and
show ourselves ready for fighting.

Take the case of the United States.   America has three
times, within the last few years, had a misunderstanding with
two of the greatest Powers of the world—twice with England,
once with France.   We had the Maine boundary and the
Oregon territory to settle with the United States, and America had her quarrel with France, arising out of a claim for
compensation of 1,000,000l., which the French Government
refused to pay.   What was the issue of those controversies?
When the claim was refused by France, General Jackson,
then the head of the American Government, published his
declaration, that if the money was not paid forthwith, he
would seize French ships and pay himself.   At that time—
I have it from Americans themselves—the French had three
times the force of ships-of-war that America had; Admiral
Mackau was in the Gulf of Florida with a fleet large enough
to ravage the whole coast of America and bombard her towns;
but did France rush into war with America?   She paid the
money.   Why?   Because she knew well, if she provoked an
unjust war with the United States, their men-of-war were
nothing compared with the force that would swarm out of
every American port when brought into collision with another country.   France knew that America had the largest
mercantile marine; and, though at first the battle might be

to the stronger in an armed fleet, in the end it would be to that country which had the greatest amount of public spirit, and the greatest number of mercantile ships and sailors. What was the case with England? In 1842 there was a talk of war with America, on account of the Maine boundary question. Bear in mind that America never spent more than 1,200,000l. on her navy, in any year of peace previous to 1842. We are spending this year 7,000,000l. or 8,000,000l.; but will anybody tell me that America fared worse in that dispute because her resources in ships-of-war were far inferior to ours? No; but we increased our navy, and we had a squadron of evolution, as it was called. America never mounted a gun at New York to prevent the bombardment of the city; but did she fare the worse? We sent a peer of the realm (Lord Ashburton) to Washington: it was on American soil that the quarrel was adjusted, and rumour does say that America made a very good bargain. It is the spirit of a people, the prosperity of a people, the growing strength, the union, the determination of a people, that command respect.

Now, what I want you as a nation to do, is to believe that other countries will just take the same measure of us that we took of America. They won't come and attack us merely because we reduce our armaments to 10,000,000l. On the contrary, other countries, I believe, will follow our example. I believe, if we are not very quick, France will set us the example. I see General Cavaignac, and all their best men, advocating a reduction of the army. A formal proposal has been made to reduce their army one-half, as the only means of saving the country from financial confusion. Let us encourage these good men in their good work. And, though our Government do not set the example, let us from this Free-Trade-hall tell General Cavaignac and his followers that we will undertake to reduce the cost of our fighting establishments, man for man, as they do theirs. When they tell us

that we are in danger of a collision at any moment with
foreign powers—when they tell us that a couple of drunken
captains of frigates at the Antipodes may suddenly embroil
this country in war with France, and that this is a reason
why we ought always to be armed and prepared for hostile
conflict—I ask you, as reasonable Christian men, why should
we not adopt the proposal which has been made at so many
public meetings, and which I shall submit to the House next
session—to insert a clause in a treaty with foreign nations,
binding each other that in case of collision between two
drunken captains, or a dispute arising from the conduct of
some indiscreet consul at Tahiti—in case of a misunderstanding on any point whatever, each should be bound to submit
the subject-matter of dispute to arbitration—that, instead of
drawing the sword being the point of honour to which nations
shall resort, it shall be to fulfil honourably the treaty by
which the dispute shall be referred to arbitration, and abide
honourably by the decision when pronounced?

To conclude, I tell you, if anything is to be done in this
matter of financial reform, it must be done by the people out
of doors. There never was a time when independent men in
the House of Commons — I mean the very few independent,
both by circumstances and by feeling—of both the two great
parties who have hitherto divided the sway in this country,
were so weak as they are at this moment. And why? Because the party in power is nominally the same party as
ourselves; because their followers mingle more or less with
ourselves, and we are neutralised at every turn, or, at all
events, we find a wet blanket on our shoulders, whenever we
go into the House of Commons. Now, if you want to carry
financial reform, it must be carried precisely in the same way
that Free Trade was carried. You must speak out of doors in
a voice that will be heard and felt in the House of Commons.
The representative system, as we have got it, is a very clumsy
machine. The House of Commons nominally has to look

after the purse-strings of the people, and see that taxes are lightly and equably laid on ; but you are obliged to leave your business, and form financial associations, to compel the House of Commons to do that which it is designed to do, but does not. There is no help for it. We must do it ourselves. I honour that excellent and tried veteran friend of ours — Mr. Hume. I admire his efforts ; I venerate the constancy, the downright pluck, the granite-like hardihood and consistency of the man, who, through good and bad repute, for thirty-seven years, has advocated the people's interest in the most material and useful form. We will back him. We will strengthen his hands, and enable him to do that in future he has not been able to do in times past.

I hope next session we shall have many of the county members voting for retrenchment. I predict you will see many of the county members compelled by their constituents to vote for a reduction of taxation. I wish here to express my sympathy with the farmers in their efforts to get rid of a tax which they consider the most obnoxious of all,—I mean the malt-tax. I crave pardon of the teetotallers. The objection mainly urged against the malt-tax is, that it interferes so much with the business of the farmers. They tell me that not having malt to give cattle is a very great impediment to their feeding. On Monday last, I saw one of the ablest farmers in the country, who told me he bought great quantities of malt-dust, which he mixes as the best ingredient with the food he gives to his lambs. We sympathise with the farmers. We never will tolerate one single shilling by way of protection to corn ; but we will co-operate with them in getting rid of that obnoxious tax—the malt-duty. We owe this to the farmers, and we will try to repay them in kind. We are financial reformers. We have a habit of doing one thing at a time. Perhaps it is weakness ; but I own to it, I can only accomplish one thing at a time. I promise you, and my friends everywhere, that I will never cease the advocacy

of this question until I see the cost of our armaments reduced
to 10,000,000l.; until I see the expenditure of the country
reduced to what it was in 1835, at least. I don't say I will
stop there. But let us understand each other; the least we
intend to do is the reduction of our establishments to the
standard of 1835. I repeat, I won't stop there. I sincerely
believe that, with your assistance, and with the growing tendency for peace throughout the world, we shall not rest with
the horrid waste of 10,000,000l. for our fighting establishment in time of peace. I believe we shall live to see one-half
sufficient; and, with such meetings as this, it will not be long
before it is so.

FINANCE.

III.

HOUSE OF COMMONS, MARCH 8, 1850.

[On March 8, 1850, Mr. Cobden moved the following resolutions :—'That the net expenditure of the Government for the year 1835 (Parliamentary Paper, No. 360, 1847) amounted to 44,422,000l.; that the net expenditure for the year ended the 5th day of January, 1850 (Parliamentary Paper, No. 3, 1850) amounted to 50,851,000l.; the increase of upwards of 6,000,000l. having been caused principally by successive augmentations of our warlike establishments, and outlays for defensive armaments. That no foreign danger, or necessary cost of the civil government, or indispensable disbursements for the services in our dependencies abroad, warrant the continuance of this increase of expenditure. That the taxes required to meet the present expenditure impede the operations of agriculture and manufactures, and diminish the funds for the employment of labour in all branches of productive industry, thereby tending to produce pauperism and crime, and adding to the local and general burdens of the people. That, to diminish these evils, it is expedient that this House take steps to reduce the annual expenditure with all practicable speed to an amount not exceeding the sum which the last fifteen years has been proved to be sufficient for the maintenance of the security, honour, and dignity of the nation.' The resolution was negatived by 183 (272 to 89).]

THE reason why I propose this motion, on this day and at this precise time is, that I am anxious, before we commence voting away the public money, that we should have an opportunity of taking a view of the whole financial interest of the country in order to a large reduction of the expenditure. I know no other way than this of bringing the general view of our finances before the House, for we have a peculiar way of dealing with the finances and expenditure of this country. The House never has brought before it, as in other countries where constitutional laws and usages are in force, a full statement of the whole income and expenditure, with the view of having the sense of the House taken upon both. We have only statements regarding our finances laid before us in detail. After the Government has decided what any particular estimates shall be, they are brought before the House, and the House has then scarcely any other alternative but that of going through the empty form of sanctioning those estimates.

One of the reasons why we are almost uniformly ready to assent to these estimates is, that a refusal to assent to them would be taken as a vote of want of confidence in Ministers, and therefore tantamount to their dismissal. I think, however, that we ought to have the opportunity of discussing the whole of these questions apart from any such considerations. I do not bring forward this motion in a spirit of hostility to the Government. I have not framed it in the shape of an address to the Crown, praying the Crown to adopt a certain course; but I have put it in the shape of a resolution, to the effect that in the opinion of this House it should take steps to reduce the expenditure of the country to the standard of 1835. Now, I must not be misunderstood, as I was on a former occasion, for there are always attempts made to misrepresent any movement of the kind; I must not be accused of meditating an immediate reduction of expenditure to the standard of 1835. I have framed my motion in precisely the same words as last year. I then moved for a reduction of expenditure to a certain amount with all convenient speed, and I make the same motion now. I do not say that we can return to the expenditure of 1835 in one year or in two, but I assume that in the present state of the country, in the state of our domestic affairs, and of our foreign relations, there is no obstacle to a gradual return to the expenditure of 1835, provided the Executive Government has the sanction of this House for resorting to such a course. If events should happen to change the circumstances of the country, there is no reason why we should not next year reverse the decision we may come to in the present.

I only ask you to consider now, whether, in the existing state of our foreign and domestic relations, we are not entitled to expect from the Government a return to the expenditure of 1835 as speedily as possible? I am anxious to bring forward this motion on another ground. We have heard intimations in this House that there will be motions made for a reduction of taxation. Now, I hold it to be self-evident that we can have no large reduction of taxation unless we have a corresponding reduction of expenditure. I know that there are certain parties who think that we may shift the burden of taxation from one shoulder to another, from one class to another, and thereby give relief to the country. I know there are writers who affect considerable scorn of those who merely take the vulgar view which I do,—that we must reduce expenditure in order to reduce taxation. They call such persons as myself vulgar politicians, and argue that more good is to be done by a shifting and a modification of taxes than by what I propose. Now, I have no faith in any such device for relieving the distress of the country. In fact, there is no means of modifying taxation in this way, by which we can relieve one interest without increasing the burden upon another. I defy you to put your hand on any interest of the country that is willing to receive an addition of taxation; and, therefore, if you propose to modify the pressure, by taking it off one to place it on another, you will find as much resistance from those on whom you are going to lay the tax as of assistance from

those who are to be relieved. If we are anxious to effect
a reduction of any tax that presses on the industry of the
country—I do not confine myself to those that press on
trade and commerce, but such, for example, as the malt-tax
or the hop-duty—it is only possible to accomplish this by
entering on such a path as I now point out to you.

I am anxious that, before we come to a vote on the motion
of the hon. Member for the North Riding of Yorkshire (Mr.
Cayley), or on any similar motion, we should first decide
whether or not we are willing to sanction such a reduction
of expenditure as will warrant a reduction of taxation. I do
not take the expenditure of 1835, to which I wish we should
return, as an arbitrary point. I felt anxious, in common
with other gentlemen, for the reduction of the expenditure,
and I looked about to see what were the causes of the increase
of that expenditure. In the course of these inquiries, I naturally turned to the first point from which the increase began.
I went back to 1835, but I took it only as a guide to enable
me to put my finger on some starting-point—a point to rest
my arguments for a reduction upon. And I am doing nothing
new. That was the course always taken by the Whig party;
for a quarter of a century, they always returned to 1792. The
hon. Member for Montrose (Mr. Hume) will bear me out,
that from the close of the war till the time of the Reform
Bill, constant reference was made to 1792 when speaking of
the expenditure. And not merely the Whigs but the Tories
did so. In 1817, Lord Castlereagh, when moving for the
appointment of a committee on this subject, took 1792 as
the point to which chief reference was made in his motion.

I am, therefore, not taking an undue course in fixing on
1835, and am not entitled to be 'pooh-poohed' by those who
have taken the same course on previous occasions. I do not
ask you to go back to 1835, because a certain expenditure
existed in that year; but it is to enable you to satisfy your
own minds as to whether any necessity exists for the increase

that has since taken place, and to show the grounds on which persons resist a gradual return to the expenditure of 1835. And when I speak of 1835, I am equally prepared to take the average of 1835, 1836, and 1837. I hope, therefore, that gentlemen opposite will bear with me while I read a few figures, and ask them to discard altogether from their minds any feelings or prejudices that may arise from differences of opinion on other questions. I wish you to go into the subject as a matter of business, and with a desire to arrive at a conclusion beneficial to those whom you represent in Parliament, and who feel on this question precisely as my own constituents do. I will read the particulars of the expenditure for the years ending the 5th of January, 1836, and the 5th of January, 1850. In 1836, the interest of the funded and unfunded debt was 28,514,000*l.*; last year it was 28,323,000*l.*, making the interest on the debt nearly 200,000*l.* less now than in 1836. The expenditure for the army in 1836 was 6,406,000*l.*; last year, 6,549,000*l.*; for the navy, in 1836, 4,099,000*l.*; last year, 6,942,000*l.*; for the ordnance, in 1836, 1,151,000*l.*; last year, 2,332,000*l.* The civil expenditure of all kinds, in 1836, was 4,225,000*l.*; last year, 6,702,000*l.*—making the whole expenditure of 1836, 44,395,000*l.*, and the whole expenditure of last year, 50,848,000*l.*

When I brought forward my motion last year, taking the finance accounts of 1848, I stated that the increase of expenditure was nearly 10,000,000*l.* as compared with 1835; but the finance accounts of the last year, as compared with the previous year, show a reduction of 3,344,000*l.* We have, therefore, to deal with an expenditure of 50,838,000*l.* against an expenditure of 44,395,000*l.* in 1836, leaving an excess in 1850 of 6,453,000*l.* This was by the last year's finance accounts; but I believe we may assume that in the forthcoming estimates we shall see another reduction of say 1,000,000*l.*, which will bring the excess at the end of the present year, as compared with 1835, to about 5,500,000*l.*

Now, I ask, is not this very satisfactory, and does it not encourage us to pursue the same course which we had already held in this House, viz. pressing on the Exchequer for further and further reductions; for I will venture to say, that if these efforts had not been made in the House, and if they had not been made by gentlemen resident in Liverpool (I mean the Financial Reform Association), the reduction I have referred to would not have been made? We all know that there is an amount of resistance to curtailments in certain quarters, an amount of pressure such as we have just heard on the subject of the brevets, such an amount of importunity from the different professions, that, unless the Executive is backed by this House and the country, it will be impossible to resist the demands made upon us.

Now, then, seeing that we have an excess of expenditure of 5,500,000*l.*, as compared with 1835, how do I propose to reduce that excess so as to return to the expenditure of 44,399,000*l.* in 1835? I wish it to be understood that I am now dealing with an excess of 6,453,000*l.*, and I propose to take 5,823,000*l.* from the amount expended on the army, navy, and ordnance last year, leaving 10,000,000*l.* for those purposes, and the remaining 630,000*l.* I would take from the civil expenditure, from the cost of collection, and from what may be gained by the better management of the Woods and Forests.

To begin with the civil expenditure. I find that last year it amounted to 6,702,000*l.*, while in 1835 it was 4,225,000*l.* Of the different items which make up this expenditure, I find that last year the civil list was 396,000*l.*, and in 1835, 510,000*l.* With regard to the civil list, as appropriated to the service of Her Majesty, I have not one word to offer. The amount settled on the Queen on her accession to the Crown having been given as an equivalent for hereditary revenues, it is my opinion that the Queen has as good a title to that amount during her lifetime as any of our ancient nobility possess to their estates; therefore I must not be misunderstood on this point, after so plain an avowal of my convictions. Nobody ever heard me propose any different arrangement from this, and I do not do so now. There is an impression throughout the country that the Queen has an exorbitant income, because the sum of 395,000*l.* was put down on her civil list; but the country should know that Her Majesty herself had only 60,000*l.* a year at her disposal, the rest going to the expenditure of different departments of Her Majesty's household, to maintain, as it was called, the pomp and state of the Throne. It is on some of these items of expenditure that I should be disposed to raise a question. There are items that I think might, with great credit to the Crown, he transferred to other purposes. Take the case of the buckhounds—a department which costs 6000*l.* or 7000*l.* a year; is it not an absurdity to suppose that such an establishment can add to the dignity of the Crown? Let that sum be taken to pay one of the Queen's judges, the Chief Justice, for example. It would be much more conducive to the dignity of the Crown to spend the money in that way than in throwing it away upon buckhounds, and I question whether it would not be more satisfactory to Her Majesty. The expenditure of items like these does not contribute in the least to the honour and dignity of the Sovereign. We all know that the Queen lives in the affections of her people; but this affection is not attributable to such idle pageants as these,—it is rather due to those quiet domestic virtues that peep out from the retirement of Osborne than to such displays as are supported by this expenditure of the civil list.

But, to pass on to the next item, which is for annuities and pensions for civil services charged by various Acts of Parliament on the Consolidated Fund. Last year it was 464,000*l.*, and in 1835 it was 524,000*l.* These I do not propose to touch, as they are granted under Acts of Parliament, and

those holding them have no doubt made their arrangements
on the faith that they would be theirs for life. But I hope
the House will agree with me that we ought to prevent the
repetition of such things in future. There are a great number
of items under this head that I am tolerably certain never
will be repeated; but it will require vigilant guardianship,
on the part of this House and the country, if they expected
to profit by the demise of these annuities and pensions. It
will be seen from the age of the parties who are recipients
of these pensions, that in all probability there will be a very
considerable and probably rapid diminution of the payments
under this head, and we are all aware that the largest annuity
has lapsed within the last six months. We may, therefore,
expect that something handsome will shortly be got towards
my reductions from the payments that would fall in under
this head.

The next item is for salaries and allowances, which come
under a different category altogether. One thing must have
struck those who look over the accounts under this head,
and that is the great number of commissionerships. I should
very much prefer to a commission, one well-paid responsible
functionary. I cannot understand why, when we give to the
home or foreign ministers such power as we do, we cannot
give to one individual, of good character and talents, the
duties of the most responsible commissionership. The public
business would be better done by one man than by a dozen;
and not only better, but cheaper. Therefore I do hope that
in future we shall have boards transformed into individuals.

The next item is for diplomatic salaries and pensions, being
last year 160,000*l.* and in 1835, 176,000*l.* Here there is
a rich harvest to reap. Our ambassador in France has
10,000*l.* a year, that in Austria 9900*l.* Now, what did the
United States pay for the same services? The hon. Member
for Kent smiles, and I know what is passing in his mind.
He thinks that I am going to be exceedingly democratic in

what I am about to say. Certainly, if I were going to
compare the expenses of the monarchical chief and the elective
chief of a republic, I should be dealing unfairly with my
case; but when we come to speak of the representatives of
two countries living at Paris, one from England and the
other from America, and both exposed to the same necessary
expenses—for of unnecessary expenses I do not speak—then
a comparison may fairly be drawn. Now, our ambassador
at Paris has 10,000*l.* a year; the American ambassador has
2000*l.* Our Austrian ambassador has 9900*l.*; the American
ambassador, 1000*l.* Our Turkish ambassador has 6500*l.*; the
American, 1300*l.* Our Russian ambassador has 6600*l.*; and
the American, 2000*l.* Many of our embassies might be
suppressed altogether, such as those at Hanover and Bavaria.
Gentlemen opposite see all these things as well as I do, and
laugh at them in private, whatever they may say in public.
They never denounce such extravagance in public, unless,
indeed, they sometimes do so for mischief. I believe that
the expenses under the diplomatic head might be reduced at
least one-half.

I next come to the courts of justice, the payments for
which last year amounted to 1,105,000*l.*, and in 1835 to
430,000*l.*, showing an increase of nearly 700,000*l.* The constabulary force in Ireland, amounting to 550,000*l.*, no doubt
adds to the amount under this head, but still there is much
useless expense. I am anxious to see the judges well provided for; but really such salaries as 7000*l.* and 8000*l.*,
especially in Ireland, are out of the question. I find a judge
in Ireland receiving 8000*l.* a year, while the highest judicial
functionary in the world, sitting at Washington, charged
with the settlement of all the international disputes between
the States of the Union, and with the interpretation of the
Constitution itself, had only 1200*l.* a year. Such anomalies
as these should not be allowed to exist. The miscellaneous
charges I find to be 398,000*l.*, and in 1835, 274,000*l.*, these

charges being fixed on the Consolidated Fund. There is
60,000*l.* for commissions in Ireland; but surely these commissions are not to last for ever. Then there are miscellaneous charges on the annual grants of Parliament, these
being last year 3,911,000*l.*, against 2,144,000*l.* in 1835.

I now come to the payment for public works and salaries
of public departments, together with all our colonial and
consular establishments. Under this head there has been
the most extraordinary profligacy of expenditure. The expense of the House we are in, or which we ought to get
into, is a scandal to us. It seems to me, that from the beginning to the end this has been the most melancholy and
disgraceful proceeding the country has ever heard of. We
have adopted for our style the most costly that can be thought
of; and it appears as if we had studied how we could lay
on the greatest expense, in such a way that it could neither
be seen nor appreciated, when we selected the florid Gothic
style for our new Houses. The whole system, the whole
proceedings of the House of Commons in this matter, from
the top pinnacle of the new Houses to the sweeping of the
floors, are characterised by as much disgraceful waste and
extravagance as could be found in any portion of the public
service. In this department of public works, salaries, &c.,
I propose a large saving in the expenditure. I hope that
in this proposal I shall have the co-operation of the hon.
Member for Oxfordshire (Mr. Henley).

Last year I showed the House, that from 1836 to 1848
there had been a continual succession of increases in the expenditure; and that when the special exigencies which caused
the increases had passed away, no return was made to the
old expenditure. I refer to such exigencies as the Oregon
and Maine boundary disputes, Tahiti, Syria, and the like.
We come to the discussion of the subject now with the
advantage of another year's experience. We are another
year further removed from that great crisis of European affairs

which everybody expected was to lead to certain calamitous consequences, in the form of an international war. If there is one consoling remembrance, one drop of sweet in the cup of gall which Europe has drained during the last two or three years, it is this. We have extracted from all that turmoil and convulsion the fact that there is not a disposition, on the part of the bulk of the people of any nation to pass their own frontiers to make war upon any other nation. I speak of the people as distinct from their Governments, because we have always been told that when Louis Philippe should die, the French people are so inclinable to war that they will break the prison bars, and ravage Europe more like wild beasts than human beings. Well, we have now seen that these same people, while having the reins in their own hands, have shown no disposition to carry war into their neighbours' territories. I do not wish the House to assume that the millennium is come, or that there will never be another international war; I do not ask you totally to dismantle your ships, or leave your ports defenceless; but that in which I am anxious you should concur with me is this,— that during the last twelve months events have rather been confirmatory than otherwise of the views I then expressed with reference to the safety of making a gradual reduction of our armaments.

Another point which I considered last year afforded a chance of a great reduction of the army, was the state of our colonial relations. Now since that time a most important event has occurred. The Prime Minister of the Crown has adopted language in reference to the colonies which I have myself often held as to the principle of self-government on the part of those colonies. The noble Lord (Lord John Russell) went the full length of the views which I have ever entertained upon that subject; and has most agreeably surprised me when discussing the constitutions to be established in Australia, and more especially at the Cape of Good Hope.

The noble Lord proposes to give to those colonies the right of framing their own constitution, of levying their own taxes, of determining their own tariff, and of disposing of their own waste lands. The noble Lord has thereby disposed of those vast continents which the English people has held to belong to them, and which they once thought might yield them something to aid and assist them in bearing their burdens and maintaining their position in the country. The noble Lord has given those vast continents to the people who live amidst them. Well, it is perfectly right; but look at the consequences. This House cannot hereafter by legislation give 160 acres of land, which the American Government gives so frequently to those who deserve it, if Parliament even desired to favour the most deserving patriot in Her Majesty's service. I do not complain of that; but what I wish to ask with reference to this question is, did the noble Lord intend to stop there? Is this country to give to the colonies as complete independence as, nay, even greater independence than the separate States of the American Union possess, since they cannot dispose of an acre of waste ground, nor touch their tariff, —are the people of this country, I ask, to be called upon by the same Prime Minister who gives to the colonies the right of governing and taxing themselves to pay and maintain the military police which occupied those colonies? It is utterly impossible, under the altered circumstances arising out of the policy of the Government towards those colonies, that any Minister with a head on his shoulders, after declaring what I have heard declared with reference to Australia, the Cape of Good Hope, New Zealand, and Canada, can permanently impose upon the people of this country the charge of maintaining the military police of those colonies. It is but a military police, and not an army kept up for the defence of the colonies from foreign attack; for this country charges itself with the expense of defending the colonies in the case of war. These military establishments are maintained 10,000 miles away. We send out relief at an enormous expense, and that to maintain a police which the colonists are better able themselves to pay for than are the people of this country.

In assuming that we may make a considerable reduction in the public expenditure by gradually withdrawing our troops from the colonies, let me not be answered by a reference to the case of our arsenals at Gibraltar, Malta, and Ceylon, or in those places where the African race predominated. I confine myself to those colonies where the English race is likely to become indigenous and paramount. What is the object of maintaining these establishments? Is it in order to secure the connection between England and her colonies? Such a ground can hardly be alleged; and yet I know of no other motive, unless it be to preserve the patronage which the system afforded to the Minister. It is for the House to say whether the maintenance of patronage in Downing-street is a sufficient reason for taxing the people of this country. It will be found that, taking into account the force kept in those colonies, the force kept at home for the necessary reliefs, and the number of men always on the ocean on their passage to and fro, there are means of reduction to an amount not much short of 20,000 men.

But since 1835 we are placed in a different position with regard to the army required at home. First, with reference to the means of transport, since the introduction of railways, the same number of troops gives a vast increase of power. We have a piece of very interesting evidence on that subject. General Gordon, Quartermaster-General, stated in his evidence before the Committee on Railways in 1844:—' I should say that this mode of railway conveyance has enabled the army (comparatively to the demand made upon it, a very small one) to do the work of a very large one: you send a battalion of 1000 men from London to Manchester in nine hours; and that same battalion marching would take seventeen days; and they arrive at the end of nine hours just as fresh, or nearly so, as when they started.' What has been the practice of individuals in consequence of the facilities afforded by railways? Men of business keep smaller stocks on hand, because they can be easily supplied from their wholesale dealers. The Committee of last year on the Ordnance Estimates recommended the application of the same principle. There were found to be enormous stores scattered over different parts of the country, and the Committee contended that the Government should avail themselves of the railroads as private individuals do. The Government promised to adopt that regulation; but I want them to understand that they may go a little further, and avail themselves of that mode of communication, and thereby do the same amount of work, in case of need, with a smaller number of troops.

Assuming soldiers to be the proper means of keeping order in this country—though I concur in the opinion which was maintained thirty years ago by the right hon. Gentleman opposite (Sir Robert Peel), that this is a constitutional and civil country, and that the Government ought not to have recourse to military force at all—but assuming that bayonets are necessary to preserve order, one soldier was at this moment, by means of the facilities of railways, more powerful than ten were in 1835. But this is not the only ground why I believe that we possess prospective means of reducing the army. Since 1835, we have very largely increased our armed force in other ways. We have embodied 14,800 pensioners, 9200 dockyard men are enrolled, formed into battalions, and regularly drilled; and there are about 3000 county constabulary. Here is an increase of 26,000 armed men in England, to which I may add an increase of 5000 constabulary in Ireland. All these things form additional ground why I hope to see a gradual reduction of our armed force.

Take the case of Ireland. Ireland has always been the unhappy excuse for keeping up a large army at home. Ireland is now tranquil. Pass your measures for bringing Ireland into closer approximation with this country,—for giving her your own institutions, and a better representative system, —and I believe we shall do more to preserve order there than if we were to send a dozen regiments to that country. Ireland has never been so free from political excitement or disorganisation. That country will soon be brought within a short day's journey of London, and need not be treated in any respect in future but as a province. But there are now in Ireland 25,000 regular troops, to which are to be added the 5000 additional constabulary and upwards of 5000 pensioners, making in all between 35,000 and 36,000 armed men; whereas there were only between 16,000 and 17,000 rank and file in Ireland in 1835. Ireland, then, affords means for a further reduction of the army. But it is not merely by a reduction of the force that I desire to see economy attained.

I cannot speak with practical knowledge of military affairs, but I speak from high military authority when I state that the organisation of the British army is the most extravagant of any army in Europe, and justifies the assertion that it is an army maintained especially for officers. What is the process going on in the army? Last year we withdrew a few thousand drunken men from the service; but the complaint of the country was, that the number of officers ought to have been reduced instead of the number of men. This process is going on again. You have announced it to be your intention to reduce 1800 rank and file, but nothing is said of withdrawing a major, or a second-captain, or a second-lieutenant, from any of the regiments; but all in the higher grades are maintained as before. Great economy might be gained in the army by a different organisation. It does not require one to be a military man to know that.

With regard to the cavalry regiments, more particularly, does the system require change. According to the present mode in which those regiments are organised, they have become the laughing-stock of all the military men in Europe. There is a very distinguished man now in London, a general officer in the service of Austria, and who acquired some celebrity in the war with Hungary. I asked that officer to look over our army list, and just give me some notion how far it corresponded with the system of his own country, which was regarded as a model of organisation, and which does not differ very much from that of Prussia and France. When he saw the number of officers assigned to one of our cavalry regiments he laughed outright. In the light cavalry, in the time of peace, there are eight squadrons of 180 men each, and of about 200 in war. These are commissioned by one colonel, one lieutenant-colonel, two majors, eight captains of the first rank, eight captains of the second rank, sixteen lieutenants of the first rank, and sixteen lieutenants of the second rank, making fifty-two officers in all. This gives one officer to every twenty-eight men. In the English Guards there are thirty-two officers to a regiment of 351, or an officer to every eleven men; in the cavalry and the line there are twenty-seven officers to a regiment of 328 men, or one officer to every twelve men. Put two English regiments into one, and maintain only half the present number of officers, still you would have twenty more English officers than there were in an Austrian regiment. I would recommend the Government to alter this system, if it be only to take away the justification which it affords to the Liverpool and Manchester Reform Association for alleging that the army is kept up for the purpose of serving the aristocracy. Until you remove this fact, no one, either in this country or abroad, will believe that these forces are organised for promoting the interests of the people. If you wished to reduce the army with the greatest economy to the people, and with the least loss of force, you should reduce the number of regiments by amalgamating them, and retain their bayonets at the expense of the officers. While we discharge the men and retain the officers, we shall destroy that which constitutes the strength of the army, and retain that which constitutes all the expense.

With reference to the navy, the expense of that branch of our force has greatly increased since 1835. In 1835, the estimate was 4,494,000*l.* ; and last year the amount was upwards of 6,160,000*l.* I know of nothing to deter us from contemplating a gradual reduction in our marine force. If we compare the British service with that of the United States in maritime matters, we shall find, that whilst the United States have only one line-of-battle ship at sea, wherever their commerce extended, the oceans and seas were visited by a body of small vessels of war, because these were intended to be what a navy should be in time of peace—a police protecting the mercantile marine. But this country keeps up an enormous force of line-of-battle ships which never can be used for the safety of commerce. By using small vessels of war, we might save a deal of expense. But large line-of-battle ships are maintained in order to afford opportunities of preferment to the higher classes.

There are other reasons why the navy might now be reduced which did not exist in 1835. Independently of our regular navy, there is an immense available reserved force in the mercantile steamers of the country, which have been built for maintaining the Post-office communications. Last year a Committee sat to inquire into the practicability of using large merchant steam vessels, in case of necessity, as a means of national defence. The Committee reported that it was practicable to call into use an amount of steam-power, should it be desirable for national defence. The report stated that there were 180 steamers of upwards of 400 tons burden, besides between 700 and 800 smaller vessels, which might all be made available in case of war. Beyond this, there are thirty-five other vessels in the mercantile steam navy, which could all be got ready in the course of a few weeks, if needed.

There were none of these resources in 1835. They have all grown up since.

With respect to the navy in the Mediterranean, I do not see any use in it. The great line-of-battle ships now in the port of Piræus had much better be lying up in ordinary, or on the stocks. I am very much afraid that, as long as we keep up in time of peace that enormous armament, there will always be a disposition, either on the part of the Government, or of the Foreign Minister, or of the Admiral on the station, to bring these ships in some way into action, in order that at the end of the year the estimates might be renewed for the maintenance of that force. We ought to view this question in the way in which the United States has done. The foreign policy of the United States is a lesson to this country. They never arm themselves to the teeth; they never put out their whole strength; they calculate that foreign countries will give them credit for the strength which they have lying latent. The policy of this country is quite the reverse. We seem to think that foreign nations never give us credit for power, unless we display it by having a large number of line-of-battle ships afloat.

Increase the prosperity and happiness of the people by a reduction of taxation, and they will add to their real power quite as much as if they maintain large armies and powerful fleets. Money is the sinews of war; and those nations that are encumbered by an armed force, as is the case at this moment with Austria and France, are in a position to be bullied by a country that has not the tenth part of the force in ships and regiments, but which has an easy exchequer, with a wide margin for expenditure, and which is capable of drawing upon its latent resources. When I say this, I am not for disbanding the army, or dismantling the navy; but I speak in degree, and say that 10,000,000l. of money are enough to be expended upon that army and that navy, upon which 15,000,000l. are now expended.

With respect to the ordnance, it is impossible to deny that
great economy might be gained by better management in
that department. The Committee on the Ordnance Estimates
found it necessary to remonstrate with the Government for
keeping too many stores. By adopting the recommendation
of the Committee, both in the navy and the ordnance, a
saving of fifteen per cent. will be effected, while the stores
will be better manufactured. There will be no further loss on
the sale of stores, which has amounted during the last year to
between fifty and sixty per cent. upon a sum of not less than
500,000*l.* It has been suggested that the sappers, miners,
and engineers, might be usefully employed at the fortresses
abroad—Gibraltar and Malta—instead of the troops of the
line, who might be better employed elsewhere. I believe a
great saving might be effected in the Ordnance department.
Everybody connected with that branch of the service is dissatisfied with it, and requires a reorganization of it. I have
come to the conclusion that in a very few years we may very
largely reduce the military and naval establishments, without
in the slightest degree endangering the peace and security of
the country. What are the 10,000,000*l.* which I propose to
reduce? It is as much as the whole expenditure of the
United States before the Mexican war, and more than the
whole expenditure of Prussia.

'Those who think there is any danger to the defences of the
country in my proposition, I beg to ask whether they do not
see any risk, inconvenience, if not danger, in leaving our
taxation in the state in which it now is? Some one in the
City has written a pamphlet with a view to show that the
country is lightly taxed. It may be perfectly true that there
is more wealth in the country now than during the great
war; but I maintain that wealth does not pay the taxation of
this country. If it did, we should have no rich man in the
City writing a pamphlet to show that taxation is no evil.
Whatever plan you may pursue, you cannot refrain from

altering and abolishing many of those taxes that press upon
the industry of the manufacturing and agricultural interests
of the country.

There is another doctrine recently enunciated—which is,
that the country must not have a remission of taxation, even
if it could be effected by a saving of expenditure, but that
whatever surplus there is must be applied to the reduction of
the National Debt. Whatever may be thought of that doctrine, I am quite content if the country is able to pay the
interest upon the principal of the National Debt. It is a poor
beginning, with a surplus of 2,000,000*l.*, to attempt paying off
a debt of 800,000,000*l.* There should be some grander scheme
than that before talking of paying off a debt of so enormous
an amount. I believe it is proposed to limit the plan to paying off the debt which has been contracted within the last
three or four years. I consider that debt no more pressing in
its nature than any portion of the debt contracted during the
war. It may not be so objectionable, but all the debts were
bad, and happy would it be if we could pay them all. But,
whether the principal were ever paid or not, the country will
never recover the waste which the contracting of those debts
has occasioned.

The right hon. Gentleman the Member for Tamworth (Sir
Robert Peel) in 1842 began a new system—that of reducing
the taxes on industry, and of relieving trade and commerce,
by substituting for duties on the necessaries of life a more
direct system of taxation in the imposition of a tax on income.
It was not enacted in the most desirable shape; but, bad as it
is, I hope we never shall part with it, though I should like to
see some modification of it. Something greater must be done
before we can afford, out of our surplus, to pay any part of
the debt, and at the same time have the means of abolishing
those taxes which more immediately interfere with the
productions of industry.

I humbly submit that both those things must be done; but

Government will be compelled to part with the whole of their surplus of 2,000,000*l.* in relieving those who suffer from indirect taxation, and are clamorous for its remission — not because it takes so much money from their pockets, but because it interferes with the progress of business, whether it be the article of paper or any other that is hampered by the Excise. Whatever Government, therefore, is in power, must contemplate a plan of finance by which it must look to have a much larger surplus than 2,000,000*l.* But how can that be done, if you do not adopt my plan, except it be by some other mode of taxation? I would vote for 10 per cent. direct taxation, if the Government would propose it; but they cannot do that. They can, however, do without it, if they would reduce the expenditure to the standard of 1835. They would then get a present and a growing surplus, and at last a surplus of 10,000,000*l.* from this time. That would be a sum for abolishing something important. If you divide it into two, with half you might convert some part of the debt into terminable annuities, and with the other relieve the industry of the country from the duties on paper, soap, malt, hops, and other articles. Without such a plan, it will be only child's play to look to a surplus.

Is there not less danger, then, in trusting to our good intentions and to Divine Providence, instead of 10,000,000*l.* being expended on our armaments? Is it not better to trust to those elements of security, and have it in our power to relax taxation and give contentment to the people in the way which I have put before the House? It is to enable you to take that course that I ask the House to pass the resolutions I am about to move. It is not a vote of want of confidence—it is, in fact, a vote of confidence; for there is a power that resists improvement in this country. It does not appear in public, but works by covert means, and it requires the counteraction of the House to enable the Government to take any step for the relief of the country. I ask you, then, as I regard the interests of those who sent you here, not to look at this as a party question—not to oppose my motion, because I bring it forward — but to vote upon it *bona fide* and upon its merits, and to go out into the same lobby with me in its favour.

FINANCE.

IV.

INTERNATIONAL REDUCTION OF ARMAMENTS.

HOUSE OF COMMONS, JUNE 17, 1851.

[The discussion to which Mr. Cobden alludes in the commencement of this speech was a motion and division made and taken by Mr. M. T. Bass on the reduction of the Malt-duty by one-half. Mr. Cobden's motion was supported by Mr. Roebuck, Mr. Milner Gibson, and others, and opposed by Mr. Urquhart. It was met by an amicable explanation on Lord Palmerston's part, and was ultimately withdrawn.]

THE resolution which I have now to move is a logical sequence to the discussion in which the House has just been engaged. It has been said, in the course of this discussion, that it is impossible for certain interests to support the present amount of taxation. One of the actuating circumstances that has influenced me in bringing forward this resolution is, that I think it will be so far suited to the present circumstances of the country that it will tend to produce a diminution of burdens and a relief from taxation.

I wish the real scope and purport of my motion to be understood at the outset, so that it may not be misrepresented in the debate. I do not propose, then, to discuss or entertain the amount of the armies maintained upon the Continent.

When I speak of warlike preparations, I allude to naval
preparations and fortifications. Our army is maintained
without reference to the armies of the Continent, and the
armies of the Continent are never framed or maintained with
reference to the army of England. In speaking of armies,
which I regard as the standing curse of the present generation, the matter is usually complicated by questions of a
purely domestic character. I am told that the armies of the
Continent are not kept up by the Governments of those
countries for the sake of meeting foreign enemies, but for
the purpose of repressing their own subjects. · This being the
case, I am asked how I can persuade foreign Governments to
reduce their armies, seeing that they were not kept up from
the apprehension of a foreign foe, but in order to maintain
internal order, as it is called. Now, I believe, if I can succeed in my motion with France, the examples of the two
countries may be at once followed by other countries in the
reduction of their navy, and that, if a reduction in the naval
forces and fortifications of England and France takes place,
other countries may afterwards follow with a reduction in
their armies.

I presume it will be admitted that the maintenance of a
naval force, beyond what is necessary in time of peace for the
protection of commerce, is an evil; but I shall be told it is a
necessary evil. If I ask why, it will be said, ' Because other
countries are armed as well as ourselves.' Well, admitting
that, and assuming that France and England maintain a certain amount of naval force, not for the purpose of protecting
commerce or acting as the police of the seas, but in order to
hold themselves in a menacing attitude towards each other,
that must be an unmitigated evil, and not only a pure waste,
but it would be better and more economical if both voted that
money and threw it into the sea, for both would then save the
labour which was employed upon ships of war, and which
might be more productively occupied. These two countries

will be equally well prepared for warfare with each other if they
reduce their force to one as if they both maintain their force
at twenty, as their relative proportions will remain the same,
and no advantage can be gained, in the event of hostilities, by
keeping up this unnecessary force.

Why do I assume that England arms against France, and
France against England? I am prepared to show that it is
the avowed policy of both countries to arm themselves, so as
to be prepared to meet the armaments provided by the other
country. In the debate in the French Chamber of Deputies
in 1846, when a motion was made for a vote of 100,000,000f.
for a great augmentation of the navy, M. Thiers, who carried
the resolution for this great augmentation, said:—

'There is nothing offensive to England in citing her example, when our navy
is under consideration, any more than there would be in speaking of Prussia,
Austria, or Russia, if we were deliberating upon the strength of our army.
We pay England the compliment of thinking only of her when determining
our naval force; we never heed the ships which sally forth from Trieste or
Venice,—we care only for those that leave Portsmouth or Plymouth.'

I am told that the noble Lord below me was in the Chamber
of Deputies when this speech was made. The noble Viscount
(Palmerston), in the debate on the financial statement in 1848,
said:—

'So far from its affording any cause of offence to France that we should
measure our navy by such a standard, I am sure any one who follows the
debates in the French Chambers, when their naval estimates come under
discussion, must know that they follow the same course,—adopting the natural
and only measure in such cases, namely, the naval force which other nations
may have at the same time.'

In the same debate on the financial statement in 1848, the
noble Lord (John Russell), after showing that the expenditure for the navy in France had increased since 1833 from
2,280,000l. to 3,902,000l., proceeded to observe:—

'I am not alluding at all—it never has been the custom to allude, and I
think we are quite right in that respect—to what may be the military force of

foreign Powers. I do not, therefore, allude at all to the amount of the standing army that is kept up in France, or in Austria, or in Prussia, or in other foreign countries; but so great an increase in naval estimates, I think, does require the attention, and, at all events, should be within the knowledge of the House.'

I have two objections to that policy: first, it is an irritating policy, having a constant tendency to increase the evil, and to which I see no remedy, unless it is in some way met; and secondly, it is a proceeding on exaggerated reports and ideas spread upon the subject of the armaments of the two countries. When these things are exposed, they always bear the trace of great exaggeration. I will mention an instance. Our naval estimates were greatly increased in 1845. The French were alarmed. A Committee of the Chamber of Peers was appointed to inquire into the state of the French navy. They made a report. In that Report they said:—

'We have now to announce the execution of a great scheme which the English Government is pursuing with its usual foresight, and which cannot fail to have a vast influence upon the naval policy of other countries.' (The report then goes on to state that, under the modest pretence of providing steam guard-ships, the British Admiralty is converting eight sailing-vessels into formidable steam batteries, capable of remaining fifteen days at sea; that they will be completed during that year; and that it was expected they would be doubled in the following year.) 'If' (continues the Report) 'we compare the powers of destruction possessed by the broadsides of these floating fortresses with those of the most formidable batteries ever employed by an army upon land for the destruction of fortified places, we shall then know what to think of an armament provided under the modest and defensive guise of steam guard-ships. It is, then, for France an absolute necessity to prepare an armament of a similar character and of equal force, so that we may have nothing to dread in future, in case of a possible misunderstanding with England.'

Now, in that Report it is broadly stated that eight steam guard-ships were being prepared by the British Government against France; and there was some ground for it, inasmuch as eight guard-ships were being altered with screw propellers; but when I sat on the Committee on the Navy in 1848, I found, on examining the authorities of the Admiralty, that

only four of these steam guard-ships were ever completed, and
that, instead of being of the character stated in the Report,
they were only capable of going to sea for four days instead
of fifteen, inasmuch as they were not prepared for carrying
a large supply of coal. I will give another illustration of
how the two countries play at seesaw in this respect. After
the proceedings of England in 1845, and those of France in
1846, Mr. Ward, who was then Secretary of the Admiralty,
came down to the House and proposed again an increase
of our navy, citing the example of France. The proceedings
of France, he said, ought to be a lesson to us, and imposed
a great responsibility upon those who were in power in this
country. But the British Government could not stop there.
They ran the estimate up to 42,000, or, I believe, to 44,000
men. That produced its fruits in France. I hold in my
hand an extract from a Report of the National Assembly
on the Navy in 1849. It says :—

‘ Let us see whether foreign Powers really show us the example of a reduction
of naval armaments. This very spring, England has voted 40,000 men for the
sea service. This vote will amount to 6,000,000l. sterling, without including
the cost of artillery, &c., which is defrayed out of the Ordnance estimates.
We content ourselves with twenty-four vessels of the line afloat, and sixteen in
an advanced state upon the stocks, for our peace establishment ; the English
have seventy afloat, besides those in course of building. With our peace
establishment, such as it was fixed in 1846, we should be one-third inferior in
strength to the English navy.’

But to illustrate this point further I will quote to the House
an extract from a speech of the First Lord of the Admiralty
(Sir Francis Baring). In moving the naval estimates for the
present year, the right hon. Gentleman the First Lord of
the Admiralty said (and it was this remark of the right
hon. Gentleman that has induced me to give notice of this
motion) :—

‘ It was impossible to fix upon what was necessary in their own establishment without looking to the establishments of foreign countries. He might,
however, observe that they had had sufficient proof in the course of the last

year that a gallant, active, and intelligent people, not far from themselves, had not by any means neglected their naval establishments and naval power.'

And the right hon. Gentleman went on to give a description of the naval evolutions at Cherbourg, and that great fortified place was held up to this country, with a formidable account of its preparations. I now hold in my hand a Report of a Commission of the National Assembly for the outlay of 6,800,000*l.* to continue the defensive works at Cherbourg; and it bears date the 11th of April, 1851. It says:—

'If we would be fully alive to the necessity of no longer leaving in a defenceless state the point most important and certainly the most menaced upon the whole coast of the Channel, we have only to listen to the opinion entertained of Cherbourg by the English, and especially by one of their most renowned sailors, Admiral Napier, in his recent letter to the *Times*. We have only, in fact, to cast our eye upon the map, and to observe the vast works which the British Admiralty are now executing at Jersey and Alderney for the purpose of creating a rival establishment to our own. This is the more necessary, inasmuch as the railroads and steam-boats in England are every day increasing, and their powerful means of transportation give to those who possess them the facility of concentrating upon any given point a sudden expedition. We must be on our guard against so powerful an enemy, situate at so short a distance from our shores, and who, by the aid of steam, will be henceforth independent of wind, tides, and currents, which formerly impeded the operations of sailing vessels.'

One of the best things this House has done for a long time was to suspend the other night the works for the fortification of Alderney. These works are a menace and an affront to France, and are meant as a rival to Cherbourg. Now Cherbourg, as every one knows who has sailed along that coast, is a most useful, and valuable, and indispensable port of refuge for merchant ships,—in fact, a breakwater at Cherbourg might have been made by subscription from all the maritime States of Europe, so important is it to all who sail along that coast. But Alderney could mean nothing but a great fortified place, within a few miles of France, intended to menace that country. Now, these fortifications arise out of a panic in England. If any one could get at the profes-

sional springs applied to panic, it would be a most amusing
history. In 1845 the country was led to suppose that we
were to be invaded by some maritime Power. A number
of engineers had a roving commission to go along the coast
and point out places where money could be spent in raising
fortifications, and when they had exhausted the coast of
England they went over to Jersey and Alderney. I have
heard the evidence of some of those gallant gentlemen. One
of them said he went down to Plymouth—he found the people
there expecting their throats would be cut the next day;
and, said he, ' strange as it may appear, I shared their alarm.'
It was understood that this panic had projected our harbours
of refuge, as they were called, upon which it was suggested
that between 4,000,000*l.* and 5,000,000*l.* should be expended.
It was under the same panic that the works at Keyham,
upon which 1,200,000*l.* had been wasted, and the works at
Alderney, which had cost four times as much as the value
of the fee-simple of the whole island, were projected. And
thus it was that France had now an eager rivalry with us.
M. Chevalier, in a pamphlet which he has published on the
subject, endeavouring to stem this torrent of rivalry, said that
while England had projected her fortifications on the coast
of England, France at the same time had projected works
to the extent of between 10,000,000*l.* and 11,000,000*l.* sterling, without including the fortifications of Paris, and he gives
a comparative estimate of the increased expenditure both of
France and England from 1838 to 1847, and shows that
in that period England and France have constantly augmented their naval expenditure to the extent of between
13,000,000*l.* and 14,000,000*l.* sterling, and that both going
on in that neck-and-neck race of rivalry, the two countries
have, in fact, spent nearly the same amount. Now, is there
a remedy for that rivalry? Is it possible to bring human
reason to bear upon that mass of folly? I am sure that
Gentlemen who think it necessary to have a precedent for

what they do, will admit the force of the precedent I am
about to quote. I am not going back to 1787, to the de-
molition of Dunkirk, or to an armed neutrality, or to an
arrangement made for a specific object for any armament,
but there is a case in modern times bearing upon this question.
There was a convention between this country and the United
States to limit the amount of force in the lakes that separate
Canada from America. The convention was this:—

'Arrangements between the United States and Great Britain, between
Richard Rush, Esq., acting as Secretary of the Department of State, and
Charles Bagot, his Britannic Majesty's Envoy Extraordinary, &c., April,
1817.—The naval force to be maintained upon the American lakes by His
Majesty and the Government of the United States shall henceforth be confined to the following vessels on each side, that is:—On Lake Ontario, to one
vessel not exceeding 100 tons burden, and armed with one 18-pound cannon;
on the upper lakes to two vessels, not exceeding like burden each, and armed
with like force; on the waters of Lake Champlain, to one vessel, not exceeding
like burden and armed with like force. All other armed vessels on those lakes
shall be forthwith dismantled, and no other vessels of war shall be built there
or armed. If either party should hereafter be desirous of annulling this stipu-
lation, and should give notice to that effect to the other party, it shall cease
to be binding after the expiration of six months from the date of such notice.
The naval force so to be limited shall be restricted to such services as will
in no respect interfere with the proper duties of the armed vessels of the
other party.'

It was entered into in 1817 at the close of the war with the
United States, in the progress of which, in 1814, the Duke
of Wellington was at Paris, and he then wrote to Sir G.
Murray thus:—

'I have told the Ministers repeatedly that a naval superiority on the lakes
is a *sine quâ non* of success in war on the frontier of Canada, even if our object
should be solely defensive; and I hope that when you are there they will take
care to secure it for you.'

So that, in case of any rupture between England and
America, the occupation of the lakes was considered by that
great authority to be necessary for success in hostilities; and
yet notwithstanding that, immediately after the war, the two
countries had the good sense to limit the amount of force
upon the lakes. And what has been the result of that friendly

convention ? Not only has it had the effect of reducing the
force, but of abolishing it altogether. When I sat on the
Committee I did not find that any vessel was left on the
lakes as an armed force. I would ask, then, whether it is
not possible to devise some plan, if not by actual convention,
as in the case of America, yet by some communication with
a Power like France, and say, ' We are mutually building
so many vessels each in the year; our relative force is as
three to two, and if we increase it tenfold, still the relations
will be the same. Will it not be possible, by a friendly
understanding, to agree that we shall not go on in this
rivalry, but that we shall put a mutual check upon this
mutual injury ?' Lord Auckland stated before the Committee
in 1848 that the amount of force left in the Pacific was
always governed by the force left by other Powers. Now, I
may be told that I am dealing merely with France; but there
are only two countries of any importance as naval Powers,
namely, France and Russia, for America had set an example,
and was out of the question. When California was discovered,
America might have placed two or three line-of-battle ships
off that coast, but she withdrew the only one she had there, and
turned her artisans and shipwrights to construct some of the
most magnificent steam-vessels that were ever seen; and yet
her commerce was extending, as our own is. The hon. Member
for Stafford (Mr. Urquhart) may, perhaps, refer me to Russia;
but I contend that no country that has not a mercantile
marine can be a great naval country. You may build up
a navy as Mehemet Ali has done, and put his fellahs on
board, but if you have not a mercantile marine you never can
become a great naval Power. Russia has, no doubt, a great
number of ships at Cronstadt—I have seen them all—but if
Russia had power she kept it at home; and there may be very
good reasons why she did so, for I have heard remarks from
American skippers lying at Cronstadt to the effect that her
vessels were not much to be admired. She has about 30,000

sailors, but they are men taken from the interior, unac-
customed to sea duty, and are, of course, a complete laughing-
stock to British seamen.   I do not consider that any country
like America or England, carrying on an enormous commerce,
and with 100,000 mercantile sailors, can ever be endangered
by a country having no mercantile marine.   With reference
to our distant stations, at all events America offers no obstacle,
but rather invites us to this course by her example.   France
is the only country that presents herself with any force upon
foreign stations ; and I ask, is it impracticable to carry out
the same rule in regard to France that had been agreed to
with the United States, or are we to go on *ad infinitum*,
wasting our resources, and imposing unnecessary taxes in
order to keep up that waste?   I may be told, probably, that
this is not the proper moment for such a resolution as this.
I think that it is the proper moment.   I believe that nations
are disposed for peace, and I am glad to be able to cite the
opinion of the noble Lord at the head of the Government,
and of the noble Lord the Secretary for Foreign Affairs,
that there is a great disposition on the part of the people
towards maintaining peace.   I hold in my hand also an extract from the most powerful organ of public opinion in
this country—the most powerful vehicle of public opinion in
the world—a paper which certainly everybody would admit
has the best possible opportunity of knowing what the tendency of public opinion is throughout the world—I mean
the *Times* newspaper.   That journal, in a recent leading article,
says :—

    ' Wars of nation against nation are not the evil of the day, but the contests
between classes in the same country.   Europe is already so much governed by
the representatives of tax-payers, that an European war is an affair of im-
probable occurrence.   Even in countries where constitutional government is
not understood, the ruling power would be very slow, for its own sake, to
impose taxes for purposes of war.   England has remained at peace, although
European society has gone through convulsions in the course of the last five
years of which history presents no example since the breaking up of the
Roman empire.'

If there were not a disposition on the part of the people
of the Continent to go to war, where is the use or the necessity of the enormous naval force which France keeps up?
Surely there must be as great a disposition on the part of
that country as of this to reduce the burdens of taxation
by diminishing expenditure. I have conversed with French
statesmen upon this subject, and when I have put it to them,
as I have done to English statesmen, they have admitted that
the plan which I propose would be most desirable for them.
They say that they keep up their navy because England
keeps up hers, but that it would be the greatest possible
relief to them to be able to reduce it. I believe that if our
Government made a friendly proposal to France, it would
be met in an amicable spirit. France does not pretend that
she is as strong as England by sea, and she does not aim
at being thought so, for it is invariably admitted in the
discussions in the French Chamber that she has no pretensions to rival England in the amount of her naval force. I
say, then, that if a friendly proposal of this sort were only
made to France, I fully believe it would be accepted. This
leads me to what I consider the strongest reason why this
system should be abolished, and it is this—that while the
spirit of rivalry is maintained by two countries so equal in
point of resources, taking the army and navy together, it is
impossible that one could ever gain a permanent advantage
over the other. If one were exceedingly weak and the other
strong, and the strong could have some extraordinary motive
to oppress the weaker, I might despair to convince by argument; but the case of England and France is very different.
Whenever England increases her armaments and fortifications France does the same, and *vice versâ*. We are pursuing
a course, therefore, which holds out to neither country a
prospect of any permanent gain. We are not actuated by
motives of ambition or aggression, but are simply acting
for self-defence, and no rational mind in either country

supposes anything else, than that a war between the two
countries must be injurious to both. Every country will
have an interest in putting an end to this mutual rivalry
and hostility by the course which I recommend. I shall be
anxious to hear what the noble Lord says upon this. I do
not ask the noble Lord to do it in any specific form. My
resolution merely says that a communication should be entered
into in a spirit of amity with France. I do not stipulate
for a diplomatic note in this form or that. I shall be perfectly satisfied if I see the attempt made, for the objection
that I have to our system of policy was that there never
had been an attempt made to stay the progress of this
rivalry—there never had been anything done that could by
possibility tend to bring the two countries to an understanding. All I stipulate for is, that diplomacy should put
itself a little more into harmony with the spirit of the times,
and should do that work which the public thought ought
to be the occupation of diplomacy. I shall be told that it
is an affair for public opinion, or for the operation of individual enterprise. Why, public opinion and individual enterprise are doing much to bring England and France together.
Compare the present state of things with that which existed
twenty-five years ago. I remember that at that time there were
but two posts a week between London and Paris, Tuesdays
and Fridays. Down to 1848, thirty-four hours were allowed
for transmitting a post to Paris; we now make the journey in
eleven hours. Where there used to be thousands passing and
repassing, there are now tens of thousands. Formerly, no
man could be heard in our smaller towns and villages speaking
a foreign language, let it be what language it might, but
the rude and vulgar passer-by would call him a Frenchman,
and very likely insult him. We have seen a great change
in all this. In this, the first year of the second half of the
nineteenth century, we have seen a most important change.
We are witnessing now what a few years ago no one could

have predicted as possible. We see men meeting together from all countries of the world, more like the gatherings of nations in former times, when they came up for a great religious festival,—we find men speaking different languages, and bred in different habits, associating in one common temple erected for their reception and gratification. I ask, then, that the Government of the country should put itself in harmony with the spirit of the age, and should endeavour to do something to follow in the wake of what private enterprise and public opinion are achieving. I have the fullest conviction that one step taken in that direction will be attended with important consequences, and will redound to the honour and credit of any Foreign Minister who, casting aside the old and musty maxims of diplomacy, shall step out and take in hand the task which I have humbly submitted to the noble Lord (Palmerston). I beg to move 'An Address to Her Majesty, praying that she will direct the Secretary of State for Foreign Affairs to enter into communication with the Government of France, and endeavour to prevent in future that rivalry of warlike preparations in time of peace which has hitherto been the policy of the two Governments, and to promote, if possible, a mutual reduction of armaments.'

FINANCE.

V.

HOUSE OF COMMONS, DECEMBER 13, 1852.

[On December 3, 1852, Mr. Disraeli made his financial statement. Among other particulars, it proposed to extend the income-tax to Ireland. After a debate extending over five nights, the resolutions of the Chancellor of the Exchequer were rejected by a majority of 19 (305 to 286), and Lord Derby retired from office.]

IF the hon. Gentleman (Mr. Davison) who has just sat down, had offered one word of argument in reply to the speech of the right hon. Gentleman the Member for Halifax (Sir Charles Wood), on Friday evening, I should have felt it my duty to have recurred to the topics he then urged; but as the hon. Gentleman has not ventured to grapple with that speech, the statements contained in it remain unanswered, and that relieves me from the necessity of touching on the principal parts of the Budget of the right hon. Gentleman the Chancellor of the Exchequer (Mr. Disraeli). I wish, however, to refer to one part of the speech of the hon. Gentleman who has just sat down. He represents the city of Belfast; and on a question which touches the taxation of the people of England, I think he would have exercised a sounder discretion if he had remained silent. By the obtrusive activity of the

hon. Gentleman, attention is directed to that on which I
should not have observed if he had been silent — that the
question does not touch his constituents. The hon. Gentleman is an illustration of the evil of what is called an United
Kingdom which is subjected to different modes of taxation in
its different portions. We are now discussing the question of
the house-tax, and the hon. Gentleman cordially concurs in
the proposition which has been made. Now, it is a house-tax
for England and Scotland, and the city of Belfast has no
interest whatever in the matter. We are going to deal with
England—the hon. Gentleman has only himself to thank for
any remarks I may make—and the hon. Gentleman is about
to give his support to an income-tax, which is to be levied
upon the trades and professions in England, and on my constituents in Yorkshire, and upon the manufacturers of linen-
yarn at Leeds and Barnsley. I take this to be an illustration
of the evils and absurdities of the present system. There are
in Belfast, as every one knows, establishments for the manufacture of linen-yarn and linen-cloth, which enter into competition with establishments for a similar manufacture possessed by my constituents in Leeds and in Barnsley. In
Belfast labour is cheaper, the raw material is cheaper, capital
is quite as cheap, and there is little difference in the price of
coal. Now, my constituents pay to the Government 3 per
cent. on the profits of their manufactures, while the constituents of the hon. Gentleman, who are engaged in the same
trade, are exempt from that tax. Is it not evident that my
constituents labour under a great disadvantage in competing
with the constituents of the hon. Gentleman? And since he
has entered into this discussion, I put it to him, whether he
will be ready, by-and-by, to agree to a proposition which is
threatened to be made by my hon. Friend the Member for
Marylebone (Sir B. Hall), to extend the same income-tax to
Ireland as it is to be levied in England? I leave the question
to the consideration of the hon. Gentleman.

With reference to the question which is immediately before the Committee, I will observe, that in some remarks which were made by an hon. Gentleman on Friday night, who spoke before the right hon. Gentleman the Member for Halifax, it was stated that somebody on this side of the House objected to the Budget, because it created an addition to the direct taxation of this country. The hon. Baronet the Member for Hertfordshire (Sir E. Bulwer Lytton), and the hon. Gentleman the Member for Cambridgeshire (Mr. E. Bull), threw out such taunts as these against the Free-traders, and said, ' Now we will put you to the test; carry out your own principles now that we are all Free-traders.' Now, I am prepared to answer the challenge thrown out with regard to the promotion of direct taxation. I say, on the part of the Free-traders, that we do not object to direct taxation, where, in the first place, it is shown to us that it is levied equally on all descriptions of property; and where, in the second place, it is shown that a direct tax is one which will prove beneficial to all the interests of the country. But we do not recognise any right on the part of the representatives of the agricultural districts, or any claim arising out of Free Trade, which entitles them to levy a tax on some particular kind of property in the towns, in order to relieve certain kinds of property in the country from taxation, for that would be a one-sided, partial, and unjust system, and just the kind of system which we have been struggling for the last fourteen years to get rid of by the abolition of the Corn-laws. It would be, in fact, adopting the odious principle of compensation. Our first answer to the taunt from the other side of the House is, that we do not recognise, on the part of Members representing the agricultural districts, any grievances or losses incurred by them which entitle them to ask anybody else to submit to taxes which they do not pay themselves. Hon. Gentlemen opposite seem to doubt this very point themselves. The hon. Baronet the Member for Hertfordshire (Sir Edward Bulwer Lytton) says, that a great deal

depends on the way in which relief is granted. 'Do it graciously,' he said; 'even if you don't grant that the farmers
are distressed, still they think they are, and therefore give
them something, in the way of the abolition of the malt-tax,
which may console them.' This is a very sentimental way
of dealing with a great question, which involves a sum to be
counted by millions, and one which I do not understand. I
deny that there is any distress which entitles them to ask for
compensation. I had a note the other day from one of the
most enterprising and intelligent farmers in the East Lothians,
which I will read to the House, as I believe it will afford not
a bad explanation of the condition of the farming world in
general. He says:—

'The farmers of the Lothians of Scotland, essentially a wheat district, never
were, as a body, in a more flourishing condition; and the demand for land, in
consequence, is beyond parallel for the last thirty years. Every farm that is
to let brings an advanced rent of from 10 to 30 per cent. I have four years
of my lease to run, but have made a new arrangement at an increased rent of
15 per cent. which I begin to pay immediately, and I have always one-fourth
of my land in wheat. Two farms have been let in this parish, within the last
six months, at a similar advance to my own, and an adjoining farm, belonging
to the Marquis of Dalhousie, is at present to let, the factor being in London,
with the offers in his pocket, to show to his Lordship's commissioners; and I
know for a fact that first-rate tenants, men of capital and skill, have offered
30 per cent. increase on the rent which the farm was let nineteen years ago,
when it was advertised for six months, and then let to the highest bidder.
My brother took a farm last week adjoining the one on which he resides
of 225 acres imperial, and for which he pays 20 per cent. increase of rent.
Sheep-farms have brought higher additional rents; but I have said enough
to show you that any talk of agricultural distress is sheer nonsense, and for
myself I have done, and am doing, as well as I could possibly desire. One
of the principal reasons for this is, that where land is properly drained, by a
liberal use of guano and other artificial manures, the crops have been increased
one-half at least, and every acre is made to carry as much corn as can stand.
It costs me as much as 700l. per annum for artificial manures, on a farm of
650 imperial acres. I know several farmers whose outlay in proportion is
greater; but then, in place of four quarters of wheat per acre, we have now
six or seven quarters, and other grains in proportion; while root crops are
also much heavier, and their value per ton is so great or greater than ever—
thanks to the numerous consumers of butchers' meat.'

I mention this in the outset, because I have observed in the

papers this morning a letter written by a Member of the
Cabinet—if he is not a Member of the Cabinet, he is an
exponent of the policy of the Ministry—and he states to his
constituents, that although the Government do not intend to
propose a return to protection, yet that they do intend to
propose compensation, and that the Budget is the first step
towards it, and that the repeal of the malt-tax is peculiarly a
measure of relief to the landed interest.   If such is the case,
I say that we are entering on the old controversy between
town and country, and you compel us to go into this controversy in a spirit that I thought was never to have been
revived.   An hon. Gentleman opposite says, 'Carry out your
principles of direct taxation with regard to the duty on soap
and on paper.'   I say that I am ready to carry out direct
taxation, if you propose a tax which shall be equitable, and
levied on all kinds of property alike; but my objection to the
Budget is, that it does not carry out direct taxation fairly and
equitably.   The proposal now made with regard to the house-
tax is most unjust.   What do you propose?   You have already
imposed a property-tax of 3 per cent. on all land and on all
houses.   You next go to Schedule A, and you lay an additional
house-tax of ninepence in the pound, or 3¾ per cent., making
the tax on houses to be at the rate of 6¾ per cent. as against
3 per cent. on land.   Then you say, 'We want more money
by direct taxation,' and you come with your scheme of compensation, or rather I should call it spoliation; and you go
to Schedule A again, and select houses, and lay on another
ninepence in the pound, or another 3¾ per cent., thus
making the tax 10½ per cent. on houses as against 3 per
cent. on land.

But that is not all; for we all know that in making an
assessment on real property and on houses, you assess houses
at a much fewer number of years' purchase than you do land;
for land is usually assessed at thirty years' purchase, while
houses are only assessed at the utmost at fifteen years'

purchase; and therefore, if you levy the same rate of taxation on both of them, you cause a double pressure of taxation upon houses as compared with land. If you invest 1000*l.* in land, and 1000*l.* in houses, while the one is assessed at thirty years' purchase, and the other at fifteen, if you lay the same tax on both of them, it is, in fact, double on the sum invested in houses, making in the whole 10½ per cent., and that brings the whole amount you levy on houses up to 21 per cent., and that is what you propose to levy on houses as against 3 per cent. on land. That is a great injustice on the part of the Government, and the House will do wrong even to attempt it; for, even if it is carried by a majority, do you think you will ever be able to maintain it? Do you think that the intelligent people of the towns will ever submit to it? Do you think that those centres from which radiate the light and intelligence of the country—— Why, whence do you get your literature and your science? Is it not from the towns? I never heard that we went into country hamlets to seek for such things. I say, if you pass such a law, you cannot expect it will be submitted to; and it would be the worst thing that could happen for you, for you will revive the old controversy between town and country—but not in the old form, when hon. Gentlemen opposite could say it is a contest between cotton-lords and landlords—but they will have every little market-town taking sides against them, for they will all see the injustice that is practised on the owner of house property. Your argument is, that this house-tax would be a tax, not on house property but on rents. I think myself that this, as well as every other tax, would ultimately be felt more or less by everybody. But, at all events, as regards the great proportion of house property, it can be clearly shown that you tax the owners as well as the occupiers, inasmuch as there are a large number of houses in the towns which are owned by those who live in them. Let the House see how the tax will work. You have benefit building societies, whereby frugal

mechanics and humble tradesmen manage, in the shape of
weekly payments, to get together sums of money sufficiently
large to build or purchase houses for themselves, and many of
these houses would be generally 10*l*. houses; and in future
they will be still more numerous than they have been, for I
am glad to say the saving character of this class of society is
increasing, and they are now happily bent on improving their
dwellings. Well, what kind of justice is it to meet these men,
immediately that they have accumulated as much savings as
enables them to become possessors of small houses, with this
inordinate taxation? Your notion of justice is to say that they
shall pay at the rate of 21 per cent. on their investment, in
proportion to the 3 per cent., which is all that is paid by the
owners of the large landed estates. Take another example.
Look at the vast landed property in the metropolis owned by
noblemen, who let it out on building leases. Take Belgrave-
square, for instance. You would find houses built there on
land held on a 99 years' lease, and at a ground-rent of about
50*l*. a year for each house. Well, the person who had put the
bricks and mortar on the ground, or who has bought it, is subjected to this direct taxation, but it does not reach the ground
landlord. He carries off his 20,000*l*. or 30,000*l*. a year, and
is left untouched. Is there any justice in that? Let me
remind you, further, that the householders in towns are subjected to very heavy charges of another kind—to a vast number of local charges, not only for the support of the poor, but
for police-rates, for highway-rates, for lighting, and for every
description of impost; and bear in mind that inequality of
the pressure of the rating, which I alluded to before—that the
smaller number of years' purchase that this house property is
rated at, presses with equal severity on the owners of that
property in assessing it for the local rates, as in the case of
the property and house-tax. Not only, therefore, has this
property higher general taxes to pay, proportionally, but it
has higher taxes to pay for local purposes. You cannot expect

a system of direct taxation, which would work like this, can ever be maintained. And what is this direct tax to be laid on for which we are now discussing—for it is the house-tax which is now before you? It is to be laid on for the purpose of enabling us to remove one-half of the malt-tax. The right hon. Gentleman the Chancellor of the Duchy of Lancaster (Mr. Christopher) has stated, with his usual frankness, what the object of it was. He tells us that the Government are about to take off one-half of the malt-tax for the benefit of the land. The Chancellor of the Exchequer, however, tells us that he makes the proposition in the interest of the consumer.

Well, which are we to believe? I certainly think the Government would do well to come to some understanding with respect to their principles, or, at least, if they cannot agree, that one or the other section of them should engage to be silent. My idea of the malt-tax is precisely that of the Chancellor of the Exchequer—that it is a tax paid by the consumer, but that, undoubtedly, as with all taxes laid on a commodity we produce, the producer is subjected to inconvenience and to loss by it. The illustration which the right hon. Gentleman gave is precisely analogous. The cotton printers protested against the 3½d. per square yard duty on printed cottons, because that duty tended to hamper them in their business, and to diminish the consumption of their goods. I quite agree, therefore, with the right hon. Gentleman, that the consumer will primarily be benefited by the remission of the malt-tax, and also that the producer will be benefited, although to a small extent comparatively. But I have always understood that the great grievance of this tax consists in the Excise regulations which it imposes. This does not affect the farmer, it is true; but in one way it does affect him. An intelligent farmer, with whom I have the honour to be acquainted—one who has been a Free-trader from the time the Anti-Corn-law League began its agitation — I mean Mr. Lattimore of Hertfordshire, who is a model farmer, and admitted to be so by all his neighbours, — Mr. Lattimore was the first who converted me to the importance of repealing the malt-tax, on the ground that it would enable the farmer to feed his cattle with malt. How far this is a valid ground I cannot say; but I have so much faith in Mr. Lattimore's judgment, that I believe it to be a valid ground, and I have always considered the claim of the farmer to the repeal of the tax to be founded upon that fact, if it be a fact. I have, therefore, publicly stated, that if we could by any means produce the necessary revenue without the malt-tax, I would advocate its total remission; but I have at the same time always said this— that I would never be a party to imposing a substitute for the malt-tax. I don't know that you could point out to me any tax, however little objectionable in its form, which I would substitute for the malt-tax, if the amount of revenue it produces is indispensable. And I am not less strongly opposed to removing only one-half of the malt-tax. I voted some two years ago against the proposition of that kind of my hon. friend the Member for Derby (Mr. Bass). My objection to the remission of one-half the malt-tax is on principle. I won't agree to halve an Excise tax, especially the malt-tax. I object, independent of my objection, to the way in which you propose to make up the deficiency. As the right hon. Gentleman (the Chancellor of the Exchequer) has put the case — as the case merely of the consumers — it is open to objections of a serious kind. The right hon. Gentleman says that beer, like bread, is a primary necessary of life; and that idea has been complacently repeated by all the hon. Gentlemen who have spoken on that side since —that it is a necessary of life, indispensable to the health and strength of the labourer. Now, the fact is, that there is a wide difference of opinion on that subject; and I have repeatedly said, both in this House and out of it, that the

great difficulty you have to meet in dealing with the malt-
tax is, that there is a large, a growing, and an influential
body in this country—some of them very fanatical, too—
who hold the opinion, that beer is not only not a necessary
of life, but that it is a very pernicious beverage to the individual, indulgence in which leads to the infliction of serious
evils on the community. You think they are wrong, no doubt;
but you have to deal with that class, which, within my knowledge, is a numerous and a highly influential one among our
constituencies ; and I think that, wrong or right, they are
entitled to be heard in this House. This class is not speaking
wildly, or without considerable authority; and it may not
be amiss if I read to the House what has been said on the
subject by certain persons, begging hon. Gentlemen not to
give way to any lively emotion until they have heard the
names attached to this document.   These persons say :—

'An opinion, handed down from rude and ignorant times, and imbibed by
Englishmen in their youth, has become very general—that the habitual use of
some portion of alcoholic drink, as of wine, beer, or spirits, is beneficial to
health, and even necessary to those subjected to habitual labour.   Anatomy,
physiology, and experience of all ages and countries, when properly examined,
most satisfy every mind, well informed in medical science, that the above
opinion is altogether erroneous.   Man, in ordinary health, like other animals,
requires not any such stimulants, and cannot be benefited by the employment
of any quantity of them, large or small ; nor will their use during his lifetime
increase the aggregate amount of his labour in whatever quantity they are
employed,—they will rather tend to diminish it.'

Now, that is a very strong opinion ; and that ' opinion '
is signed by upwards of seventy of the principal medical
men of the kingdom, amongst whom I find the great names
of Sir Benjamin Brodie, Dr. Chambers, Sir James Clark, Mr.
Barnsby Cooper, Dr. Davies, Mr. Aston Key, Mr. Travers,
and Dr. Ure. I think that, after having got such a declaration as that, I am entitled to say that this question—
whether an increase in the consumption of beer would increase
the health and strength of the people of this country—is,

at least, an open question; and in this direction, therefore,
I claim leave to differ with the Chancellor of the Exchequer
and his friends. And observe that this increased house-tax
would fall on very many thousand professors of 'temperance,'
and that some of you avow your object, in imposing that
tax, is to cheapen the price of beer. The 'teetotallers' among
my constituents would naturally say, 'We don't want to be
relieved from the malt-tax; we have already repealed it, so
far as we are concerned; we are trying, by tracts and lectures,
to induce our fellow-citizens to imitate us; and we think
your Budget unjust, and we won't have it.' And, more than
that, they believe that the consumption of malt is pernicious
to the interests of society, and take pains to persuade their
fellow-subjects that it is so; and yet the Government ask
them to submit to the house-tax, in order that beer may
be cheapened, and that a greater consumption of it may be
occasioned. Had the Chancellor of the Exchequer put his
proposition on any other ground—on the scientific ground,
that the malt-tax was a nuisance to the trader, and that it
prevented the farmer giving desirable food to cattle—all the
principles of political economy would come to his aid, and
we should be compelled to acquiesce in the project. But,
as it is, the obstacles you have to encounter are twofold:
first, that you substitute a partial tax, not levied equally on
property generally; and next, that the malt-tax is to be
reduced to a purpose to which the great bulk of the people
are indifferent, and to which hundreds of thousands—I have
heard them estimated at millions—are wholly opposed, on
strong grounds of moral principle. Such being the case, I
don't think you have the least chance whatever of passing
a house-tax. I don't know what a present majority of the
House may do; but I can tell you, you can't maintain that
tax if you pass it. You have seen lately with the window-
tax, how long-lived is an agitation against an unjust impost;
and, depend upon it, you are embarking in a contest out of

which you will come as disastrously as you have done out
of the battle for Protection—with this difference, that you
will be far more easily beaten. And what is more, you are
going to fight a battle not worth fighting for. I can hardly
bring myself to regard this as an attempt at compensation.
I did not want to allude to the thing; but the statement
of the Chancellor of the Duchy of Lancaster does not leave
me a chance of passing it over, and I have been obliged, in
some respects, to deal with it in that manner. There is
another proposal, in connection with this subject, in regard
to which I think the Chancellor of the Exchequer has really
quite wrecked his character as a financier; and that is the proposal to remit one-half of the hop-duties. I have often had
communications with the growers of hops in Sussex, who have
represented that they wanted the whole duty off, but have
expressed apprehensions, in consequence of the Kent hop-
growers advocating only a removal of half the duty; and I
have comforted them in this way,—'Don't alarm yourself for
a moment; for, after the great doings of Peel, we shall never
have a half-and-half Chancellor of the Exchequer making
two bites at a cherry.' Here is a most exceptional tax—the
only tax you have collected upon the produce in the fields
and gardens of the country—worthy, no doubt, of Persia, or
of Turkey, but too ridiculous for this England of 1852. How
is it collected? Every September the Chancellor of the Exchequer sends a little army of tax-gatherers into half-a-dozen
counties; and every Member of Parliament knows that every
spring he is asked by some unfortunate poor fellow to use
his influence to get for him this temporary employment in
collecting the hop-duty. In September the hops are picked,
carried, and dried, and the Chancellor of the Exchequer
disperses his little army of taxmen over half-a-dozen counties.
They take stock of the hops, and thus an estimate of the
tax is got. It comes sometimes to 200,000*l.* a year, sometimes to 300,000*l.*, sometimes to 400,000*l.* a year; hardly

ever to half a million. Thus it has all the evils that can
attach to any tax: it is cumbrous and costly in its collection;
it is uncertain in amount—no Chancellor of the Exchequer
ever being able to calculate to any positive amount on it;
and it bears with most unequal pressure on different parts of
the country. In some districts, the hops are hardly worth
half the price of hops grown in other districts; and as this
is a tax on the quantity and not on the value, of course it
falls with the severest pressure on the poorest soils and the
poorest quality of hops. Well, is it conceivable that the right
hon. Gentleman, after the experience we have had of the great
works that some of his predecessors have done—after the
Corn-laws had been abolished, and the vast system of Navi-
gation-laws had been done away with—could come down to
the House of Commons, and as a great scheme of finance,
propose such a mockery, the remission of one-half the hop-
duties? I hope the House will never consent to such a
paltry and trifling policy as this. If no one else will make
the motion, I will myself undertake to propose the total
repeal of the hop-duties, and even should that not be carried,
I will still vote against the repeal of only one-half the tax;
for it is far better to keep it as it is, if we cannot get it done
away with altogether.

With regard to the proposed modification of the income-tax,
I feel bound to give the Government every credit for the way
in which they have dealt with that question. I do say it is
most remarkable that a Government supported almost exclusively by county Members—representing territorial interests only—should be the first Government to deal—at all
events, in principle, if not going to the full extent—fairly
with the income-tax, as it relates to trades and professions.
Most assuredly that proposal should have come from a
Government representing this side of the House. My own
opinion is, in spite of all that mathematicians and philosophers may say, that when you are going to levy a tax upon

income and property, you must adopt one of two courses—
either vary the tax upon incomes, making it lighter than the
tax upon property, or take the plan which has been adopted
in the United States, and capitalise the whole property of
the country, whether it is in land, or in capital or stock
engaged in trade—capitalise it all, and levy the same rate on
all. Either you must capitalise all in this way equally, or
you must make a distinction between permanent property and
incomes derived from precarious sources — the practice of
professions—the midnight working of the physician, and the
daily toil of the lawyer—from trades such as that of a farmer,
whose profits depend upon the changing manner in which his
capital fructifies on the soil, and the income of a man who
sleeps while his property fructifies. I repeat that I must
give the Government credit for their intentions to make this
distinction; and I am persuaded that if it is not done by
them, it must very speedily be done by some one else.

But in dealing with this question the old curse of the
party has settled on the right honourable Gentleman, and he
could not deal fairly with it; he was obliged to make a
miserable, paltry attempt to get a special benefit for the
tenant-farmer. Instead of charging the farmer the tax on
one-half of his rent, he proposes to reduce it to one-third.
In the time of Pitt, the farmer paid on three-fourths; Sir R.
Peel reduced the three-fourths to an estimate on one-half of
the rent; and now it is asked to go down to one-third.
Well now, really, I will ask hon. Gentlemen—say, the hon.
Member for Somersetshire (Mr. Miles)—whether they think
farming would be worth following as a trade, if the tenant-
farmer could only get a profit equal to one-third of his
rent? — that the income derived from profit and interest on
his capital — from profit arising out of his own skill and
industry—would altogether only amount to one-third of his
rent? Would it not be better for you to say at once, if that
is so, he ought not to be taxed on his income at all? But

would it not be much nearer the mark to say that it ought to
be equal to the whole rent?

You are proposing to extend the area of the income-tax, so
as to embrace incomes of 50*l.* a year from real property, and
of 100*l.* a year from trades and professions; and, as a principle, I am bound to say that I do not object to an extension
of the area of direct taxation. But I say, too, include all
alike within the area—tax every description of income and
property. Certainly, you are embarrassed in applying the
principle; for you have such an amount of indirect taxation,
comprising seven-eighths of your whole revenue, and which,
no doubt, presses with the greatest severity on smaller incomes, and especially on the labouring classes, that there are
large sections of the community who have a claim to exemption from direct taxation. There is, in fact, no other
ground on which you can resist the application of the principle, that your direct taxation should be universal.

The proposal of the Government is to extend the area of the
tax to incomes of 50*l.* on property, and 100*l.* from trades and
professions. Let us see how this extension to incomes of 50*l.*
and 100*l.* affects the justice of the case, as compared with
what you are going to do towards the farmers. I will put a
case of a farmer with a farm of 250 acres of moderate land,
and paying a rent of 280*l.* a year. By your proposals,
farmers paying rents under 300*l.* a year are exempt from
this tax altogether, because it is proposed that the tax shall
not apply to farmers whose rents are under 300*l.* a year.
If the farmer I speak of farms as he should do in Free-trade
times, he has 2000*l.* or 3000*l.* capital. In fact, 10*l.* an acre
is not so much as he should have; he would be better with
15*l.*; but, at any rate, he should have not less than 10*l.* an
acre. Here, then, would be a man with a capital employed of
2500*l.* paying no income-tax whatever, the Government
assuming that he does not make 100*l.* a year. Let that be
assumed. This farmer goes into the market town, riding his

nag, and looking in fine health and great spirits; and he passes by a lawyer's clerk, who gets 100*l.* a year, and who is subjected to an income-tax of 5½*d.* in the pound. The farmer has 250 acres of land, many labourers employed, stables full of horses, sheds full of cows, pens full of sheep, yards full of stacks; and yet the lawyer's clerk pays, and this farmer does not pay, income-tax.

Now, do not deceive yourselves; do not suppose for a moment that this could last. Is there any judgment or common sense in making such a proposal? Is it not provoking a quarrel with us on the most miserable grounds? You say you want in this way to benefit the farmer; but I do believe, on my honour, unless the farmers are very unlike the rest of their countrymen, that they will not thank you for putting them in this invidious position. They do not want these special exemptions; they want to be regarded as contributors to the revenue on the same footing as the rest of their countrymen.

By your proposal you are widening the operation of the income-tax, so as to embrace a greater number of people who were not included in its range before; you do that on 'principle.' But you have especially framed your measure so as to prevent any new class of farmers from being brought under the range of the tax. Is it worthy of the territorial party? What do you mean by it? Are you always to keep the farmers on your hands as a separate and distinct class? I put it to the farmers—have they not had enough of it themselves? Have they felt it to be their interest to be kept apart as a separate class, to be made political capital of? I thought the example which had been shown in the last few years, in the case of the farmers, of the way in which they have been most ridiculously bamboozled, would have been enough for them; I really thought it would have had the effect of preventing them, or any other class, from being made a separate class for political objects. I never thought we should have had a body of men setting up as friends of the tailors, or friends of the grocers, or friends of the shoemakers. I thought that trade would have been kept out of the arena of politics for ever, after the ridiculous way in which the farmers have been bamboozled; and I sincerely hope that this Budget will be modified and withdrawn, and that farmers will be placed on an equality with other classes, and will be made to pay on their profits just the same as other people. I know the objection that is made to that. You say farmers do not keep books, and that, therefore, they cannot give an account of their profits. Well, here is a good opportunity for making them keep books. You cannot do the farmers a greater service than by inducing them to keep books, and to know exactly what they realise in a year.

No, Sir, I did not expect that on this occasion we should have had these old grievances revived. The Chancellor of the Exchequer has thrown over local burdens, and we were to hear no more about exclusive taxation of that kind; I thought that we were about to get rid of this farming interest altogether; but it seems to me that hon. Gentlemen have not entirely comprehended their position, and do not yet understand what Free Trade is. It seems to me they have confounded two subjects which are not the same— the question of protective duties and the question of direct taxation.

Now they will perhaps excuse me if I give them a little A B C on this matter. I see the hon. Member for Cambridge-shire (Mr. Ball) here. He has not been much accustomed to hear Free-trade speeches. I want to show him and other hon. Gentlemen what it is we have been doing. I beg to inform that hon. Member and other hon. Gentlemen on the same side, that the advocates of Free Trade have not been necessarily the advocates of direct taxation. Direct taxation is indeed a distinct question from that in which we have embarked. We have been opposed to protective duties, and we

have said, 'Give us freedom of exchange with other countries;
do away with the restrictions on our commerce, and we do
not enquire what the effect of that freedom will be on price;
all that we want is to have free access to as great a quantity
of these good things as can be got.' What is running in
the minds of the hon. Member for Cambridgeshire and of
other hon. Gentlemen opposite—I believe the hon. Member
for Cambridgeshire has shed tears on the subject—is sheer
prejudice on this question—that as Free-traders we mean
low prices for everything. Now, what we want is abundance.
We do not say that Free Trade necessarily brings low prices.
It is possible with increased quantities still to advance prices;
for it is possible that the country may be so prosperous under
Free Trade, that whilst you have a greater quantity of anything than you had before, increased demand, in consequence
of the increased prosperity, may arise, so that the demand will
be more than the supply, and you may raise the prices on
some articles. In some articles it has been the case; it has
been so in wool and on meat, and we may not know yet what
effect it may have on wheat itself. But hon. Gentlemen
opposite seem always to proceed on the assumption that the
Free-traders want to reduce prices, and that, therefore, they
ought to have some compensation for those reduced prices.
And then they talk of competition with foreigners; and the
Chancellor of the Exchequer told us that he was going to
prepare a Budget which would enable the industrious classes
of this country to sustain themselves under the pressure of
this unrestricted competition.

Now I thought it had been universally admitted that the
industrious classes were in a much better position under the
competition than they were before under the old system of
restriction. I and my friends do not want commiseration for
the working-classes for the evils which they have suffered in
the progress of Free Trade, for the working-classes themselves
declare that they have derived great advantages from Free-

trade measures. Free Trade has, indeed, conferred great
benefits upon the community at large, and it is intended that
it shall confer upon them still greater advantages. I do not
acknowledge, however, that it is necessary to propose any
remedial measures to benefit anybody against the evils which
are alleged to be caused by Free Trade. The Chancellor of
the Exchequer—who, I think, is not yet very enthusiastic in
the cause of Free-trade principles—has told them that he had
framed a great measure to enable the country to adopt and
conform itself to this new system of commerce. Nobody, that
I am aware of, has asked the Chancellor of the Exchequer for
any such measure. The right hon. Gentleman said that his
proposition would cheapen the necessaries of life ; and, in the
opinion of the Chancellor of the Exchequer, beer seems to
be one of the chief necessaries. Well, how does the right
hon. Gentleman intend to cheapen beer? By raising the
price of lodgings. But are not lodgings as necessary to the
people of this country as beer? If we are competing with
foreigners, which would lower the prices of commodities, I
say that to reduce the price of beer, to raise the price of
lodgings by putting a tax on houses, is not, after all, a
benefit to the people of this country. I do not admit that
the people of this country will come *in formâ pauperis* to this
House for anything of the kind. The truth is, you have
got into a false position by making promises you ought never
to have made. You have tried to appear consistent when
consistency was impossible. But what I am anxious to do
is to see that you do not mix up Free Trade with any
question of compensation. I say the effect of Free Trade
hitherto has been to change a failing revenue into an overflowing exchequer. Free Trade has made the people more
prosperous, has diminished pauperism and crime, and in every
possible way has promoted the prosperity of this country.
Do not come to the House and say we must do something to enable the people to bear up under the load of this

competition. And then hon. Gentlemen opposite ask us to
give a new name to the principle, and to call it 'unrestricted
competition.' I think it is Lord Byron who says a party
has a right to fix the pronunciation of his own name; and
I think Free-traders have a right to put their own name
on their own principles. I never insulted you by calling
you 'Monopolists' when you choose to call yourselves 'Protectionists,' and do not you go out of the good old Saxon
'Free Trade,' and give us this new name—do not call us—
I really cannot pronounce it. How can we call ourselves an
'Unrestricted Competition Party?' You must adopt our
principles, name and all.

Now, one word with regard to the alteration of the tea-
duties. I think that is a question which the late Chancellor
of the Exchequer ought to have dealt with; and I am sure,
that if I had been Chancellor of the Exchequer I should have
done what the present Chancellor of the Exchequer now proposes, four or five years ago. I do not think the right hon.
Gentleman is far wrong in that proposal; but, on the whole,
I doubt whether the Budget is the Budget of the Chancellor
of the Exchequer at all. I do not believe, either, that the
passage in the Speech from the Throne alluding to this
matter, was drawn up by the right hon. Gentleman. I think
the Budget has been cut and snipped away, patched, dovetailed, and swopped away, until at last—as in the Queen's
Speech, when somebody suggested that an 'if' should be put
in, that all parties might be accommodated—so in this case
some one suggested one thing and some another—until at
last, all the bold things that were intended were abandoned,
and what was left was the proposal which has been submitted
to the House. The fact is, that the Budget does not at all
correspond to the magniloquent phrases in which it was introduced by the Chancellor of the Exchequer. It was not at
all worthy of a five hours' speech. Indeed, I humbly conceive
that I could have discharged the duty in about an hour and

twenty-five minutes. But the right hon. Gentleman, I suppose, has done his best.

And now with regard to this controversy as to the direct
taxes. I have long foreseen that this would be discussed. The
hon. Member for West Surrey (Mr. Drummond) stated the other
night that I was consistent in advocating direct taxation, because I have said that such taxation would not be paid, and
that then the public establishments could not be maintained.
I have never said the taxes would not be paid. I have always
had the opinion of the people of England, that they would
pay their just debts under any circumstances; but I have
always said this—if you come to get more of the taxes from
the people in the way of direct taxes, they will come to
scrutinise the expenditure more closely—and I think so still.
The House may depend upon it that we are now entering
upon a controversy as to how the Imperial taxation is to be
raised. When we come to have what the Chancellor of the
Exchequer has promised us, the whole of our accounts of the
taxation brought into a balance-sheet—even the cost of collection—we shall find that our expenditure is approaching to
60,000,000*l.*; that is, about as much as the annual income
from real property in England, and pretty nearly as much
as the trades and professions are assessed to the income-tax.
You will find that the great body of the people will be galled
with the yoke, and that there will be pressure against some
particular tax. Take, as an instance, the paper-duties. Since
I have been in this House, a gentleman has shown me an
American newspaper, printed on paper made out of straw,
at an exceedingly low price. Now, the raw material of that
paper is worth two guineas; but the tax in this country
would be fourteen guineas; and therefore, before a paper-
maker in England can manufacture such paper, he must pay
upon two guineas' worth of raw material fourteen guineas
of taxation. I have also received a letter from Bristol, enclosing specimens of the same paper, and stating that, if it

were not for the Excise regulations, the paper could be manufactured in England quite as well as it is in America. Then,
besides paper, there is the tax on soap. What an abominable
tax is that! Only conceive of an agitation against the Excise
duty on soap. Why, the supporters of the tax would have
it said of them, that they were the advocates of dirt. Then
take the insurance duties. For an insurance from fire to the
amount of 100*l*. you pay 1*s*. 6*d*. for the risk, and Government
makes you pay 3*s*. for the duty. I will not go over the rest,
but their name is legion. But, as they are discussed, you
will feel more and more the necessity of resorting to some
other mode of taxation. It is not merely that you are competing, but the change in the habits of business renders these
obstructions impossible. The greater velocity of business will
render them impossible.

Look at your Customs regulations; there has been an
agitation about them, and you cannot see the end of the
difficulty, except by abolishing custom-houses altogether.
The late Sir Robert Peel effected a reduction of duties upon
a great many articles; and many of us thought that the
reduction of Customs duties would cause a great reduction in
your Custom-house establishments. But no; you cannot
allow articles to pass without examination; if you did, goods
that do pay duty would come in in the guise of those that do
not. For instance, if you allow cotton bales from America
to come in without examination, how soon would these cotton
bales be metamorphosed into tobacco bales? Look at the
magnitude of your transactions. You are receiving from
25,000 to 30,000 bales of cotton a week, and how difficult it
is to examine all of them. How different it was thirty years
ago, when you had not as many hundreds!

Then, suppose any other country, such as America, should
adopt the system of getting rid of these Custom-house regulations, you must adopt their system. You may make up
your minds that, having got rid of protection, with the large

mass of taxation hanging over this country, you are entering
upon a long controversy on the subject of taxation, in the
course of which you will have to deal with many of the duties
to which I have referred; and if the growing surplus of the
revenue does not enable you to abolish these duties, you will
find it necessary, especially in the case of the Excise duties, to
increase the amount of direct taxation. When you do that,
you must make up your minds to come to a fair and honest
system of direct taxation; for there is too much intelligence
and discussion in these days for any party to escape his fair
share of taxation.

This country is adopting the system of Free Trade, and yet
it is extending its colonial empire, and spreading its establishments all over the world; and all the expenses are paid from
the taxation of this little speck of an island. That might
have been very well a hundred years ago, when Adam Smith
had not laid down the law of political economy; but Adam
Smith said, seventy years since, that he did not suppose the
time would ever arrive when protective duties would be
altogether abolished. We have arrived at those days; but they
have entirely changed the aspects of your policy with regard to
your colonial empire, and you ought to make up your minds
to that change. Our colonies must maintain their own
establishments. We cannot keep armies in Canada and elsewhere—we cannot afford it. The taxation of this country,
which impoverished the people, will drive them to those
colonial settlements, where so many inducements to emigration exist.

Twenty-five years hence there will be removed not only
many of the physical but other obstacles in the way of emigration. Emigrants can now perform their voyages in one-
half the time, and at one-half the expense, they could do five
years ago, and they now feel that they are not going into
exile, for many of them have friends or families in our own
colonies or in America, and they go there as on a visit;

but can you suppose, if you allow mismanagement to go on here, that the people will not be eager to go there, to escape the effects of your taxation? That has been the effect of enormous taxation everywhere.

The Chancellor of the Exchequer said the other day that this emigration did not tend to impair the consumptive ability of the country. It may be that the emigration of some 200,000 or 300,000 people may not have impaired the national resources; but what will be the effect if one-half of the population of the country quitted its shores? There is every reason why we should look this question in the face, as the beginning of a movement which will widen in its extent and scope.

I wish the House to consider, when the people of this country have so many burdens of taxation to bear, whether you ought to increase the taxation, as has been done already. We have wasted a great deal of money, and our expenditure is much too large; but it is of no use my saying so, because you call me a Quaker if I do. You have added 1,200,000l. to your expenditure lately; and while we have this large amount of expenditure, let no man in this country expect to escape from taxation. I will not undertake to exempt the 10l. householders from taxation to meet the expenses of our establishments, if they send up to this House Members to vote an increase of those establishments. Already we are spending 16,000,000l. in the expenses of our establishments. Then let the middle class make up their minds that they must pay for this.

We are now, however, dealing particularly with the house-tax, which the Government propose to levy to meet the deficiency arising from the reduction of the malt-tax. If they can show me that there is a deficiency arising from an excess of expenditure, and that expenditure is supported by public opinion out of doors, I will lay that tax upon the shoulders of those who have sent Members to this House. But it is an entirely different thing when the Government propose to create a deficit by reducing the tax upon malt. I say there is no tax I will vote for—I know of no tax I would vote for—in substitution of the malt-tax. It is only in the case of a sufficient surplus that I would vote for the reduction or the abolition of the malt-tax; and that not being the case, I cannot vote for the reduction now proposed.

FINANCE.

VI.

HOUSE OF COMMONS, APRIL 28, 1853.

[In December, 1852, Mr. Disraeli brought forward a Budget, the leading feature of which was a relaxation of the malt-duty, and the substitution of an equivalent to it, in a tax on inhabited houses. The Budget was received unfavourably, the Ministry collapsed, and with it the last attempt to maintain agricultural protection. On April 18, 1853, Mr. Gladstone, Chancellor of the Exchequer in Lord Aberdeen's Administration, proposed his scheme, which contained an extension of the legacy-duty, in a very modified form, to real estate, and the abolition of all duties on 123 articles. It proposed also a gradual abolition of the income-tax. Unfortunately, the aims which Mr. Gladstone had before him were not carried out, for, three days after the Budget resolutions were carried, Prince Menschikoff presented his ultimatum, and those diplomatic negotiations were commenced which ended in the Russian War.]

THE Chancellor of the Exchequer, in his remarkable, nay, his marvellous speech, has dwelt with some emphasis—indeed, with a sort of pathos—on the extent to which the House, by its expenditure, has anticipated the surplus revenue, and the remarks on this subject, I think, have come from the right hon. Gentleman in a tone which seems to invite the special attention of the House to that particular part of his financial statement. I, for my part, rise thus early in the debate with the hope that I may induce the Committee, in taking a review of their public assets and liabilities, in their character of trustees of the people, anxious to do their best for the

interests of those who have intrusted them with the management of their affairs, to pay some attention to the mode in
which that surplus has been appropriated. I am not going to
make a peace oration, nor am I going to blame this Government or the late Government for anything which either has
done in the way of expenditure; those I blame in the matter
are the parties out of doors, who, by their proceedings, have
rendered it almost inevitable that the expenditure I so regret
should be incurred. Nay, I will go even further, and thank
the noble Lord (Aberdeen) at the head of the Government that
he has not taken advantage of the opportunity which many
silly and many, I fear, not over-honest people have given him
to increase the expenditure still more largely. Had the noble
Lord been so disposed, he might, in January last, have proposed an increase to the army of 20,000 men and to the navy
of 10,000 men, and his proposal would have been received
with acclamations—the unhappy Peace party escaping with,
at the very least, a sound drenching under the pump, had
they ventured to raise a murmur of objection. None the less
is it a matter of deep regret that so large and permanent
an increase to our establishments has been forced upon the
Government. For how, let me ask, does the matter stand ?
Since 1851 — I do not go back to 1835 — since 1851, in two
years, we have added to our expenditure for army, navy, and
ordnance, including the militia, the commissariat, and other
outgoings of the same kind, no less a sum than 1,870,000*l.*

What I wish to call the attention of the House to, and particularly that of the hon. Member for North Warwickshire (Mr.
Newdegate), who said that the Manchester school were going to
ruin the aristocracy—what I wish to call their attention to is,
that if they had not since 1851, in those two years, made this
addition to the expenditure, there would be at this moment in
the hands of the Chancellor of the Exchequer a surplus large
enough to enable him to make all the remissions and modifications he proposed to make, without any increase of taxation

whatever. Do not let the hon. Member for North Warwickshire blame the Manchester school for the increased taxation
that he said was going to ruin the aristocracy. I do not for
a moment suggest that nothing should be spent on our armaments; I have been content that 10,000,000*l.* should be
appropriated to that purpose; but the point to which I immediately invite attention is that, under the circumstances to
which I have adverted, not merely has a sum of 15,555,000*l.*
been expended in 1851 on our armaments, but since 1851 a
further sum of 1,870,000*l.* has been appropriated to the same
purpose. No wonder that, under such circumstances, the
Chancellor of the Exchequer should touch in tones of pathos
on the state of the surplus.

The cause of all this expenditure has been the panic which
the public has taken into its head to conceive of a French
invasion. Where is the panic now? So utterly dispersed
that I can find no one who will even admit that he has ever
entertained such a notion, much less that he feels it now.
But, meanwhile, the mischief has been done; the additions to
our expenditure have been made, and the public, who is the
party to blame in the matter, will find that the additional
expenditure it has occasioned will be for years and years to
come an extra burden upon it. These additions to our
establishments, once made, are not to be got rid of in a day;
I will venture to say that the present generation of taxpayers
will not altogether get rid of the additions to the taxation
that they have been instrumental in creating in the course of
the last two years.

Now, what are the items of the Budgets since 1851 for
civil purposes, including the debt, and everything else except
military and naval expenditure? Let the Committee mark
how slightly the amount has varied. In 1851, the expenditure, other than naval and military, was 34,692,000*l.*;
in 1852, 34,731,000*l.*; in 1853, 34,783,000*l.*; so that the
whole increase on the civil expenditure, including the debt,

for all purposes other than naval and military, is only 81,000*l.*
on an amount of 34,000,000*l.*; whereas the increase on the
naval and military expenditure has been 1,870,000*l.* on an
expenditure of 15,000,000*l.*

It must be obvious to every one who wishes to see the
policy carried out which the interests of the country demanded, that, for this purpose, he must grapple with the
naval and military expenditure. What I wish the Committee
to take, along with me, from the outset, is the principle that
the remission of indirect taxation is inevitable. You may
arrive at this result by savings, the growth of a surplus
revenue, of retrenchment, of increased revenue, the product of
the increased prosperity of the country; but, assuredly, if you
eat up such surplus by additions to the naval and military
expenditure, you must, perforce, make up the difference by
increased direct burdens upon property and income. Whoever
holds the reins of power—whoever the Chancellor of the Exchequer may be—whether the right hon. Gentleman below
me, or the right hon. Gentleman opposite, or any one else—
the inevitable rule must be to aim at the reduction of the
Customs and Excise duties, even at the expense of property
and income. The right hon. Gentleman opposite, for example, proposes to take off the malt-tax, an indirect impost,
and to meet the loss, so far as he can, by an additional tax on
houses, which may fairly be considered a direct impost, and
the right hon. Gentleman fell solely in that attempt to find
a substitute for the malt-tax. If the present Government,
powerful as it is, hardly sees its way to a majority large
enough to carry its Budget, its difficulty is the finding
of a direct tax sufficient to enable it to reduce indirect
taxation.

I wish Gentlemen on both sides of the House to consider
that we have come to a time when, if they will be extravagant,
they must be extravagant at the expense of property, and not
at the expense of consumption. In these days, when every

man has, at least on his lips, the profession of deep consideration for the poorer classes, it will never do to leave the main
burden of taxation on consumption. More and more emphatically is it found that the prosperity of the country depends on
the increase of consumption, this means increasing the employment of the masses, and this employment can alone be
fostered by the removal of all impediments in the path of
industry. These impediments, it must be borne in mind,
tended to accumulate with the growth of the population, and
therefore it becomes daily more necessary to provide for their
removal.

The Committee is well aware of the great and just cry of
alarm that has proceeded from our merchants, in consequence
of the obstacles placed in the way of commerce by our Custom-
house regulations. Those regulations were bad enough when
we had to deal with only 30,000,000*l.* or 40,000,000*l.* of exports and imports; they are grievous, utterly insupportable,
now that, instead of from 30,000,000*l.* to 40,000,000*l.*, we
have to deal with from 70,000,000*l.* to 80,000,000*l.* of exports and imports. Further, it is to be considered how enor-
mously the velocity of communication has increased, so that,
by the aid of steam, the traffic which once occupied forty days
on its way to America, now effects its transit in twelve. This
alone is a circumstance imperatively demanding that measures
should be taken, by a reform of the Customs' regulations, to
expedite, and most materially to expedite, the entry and exit
of goods.

As our fiscal regulations now stand, the free bale of cotton
is delayed in its admission, that it may be overhauled so as to
be shown to be not a bale of tobacco, which has 3*s.* per pound
of duty to pay before it passes. But to effect that change
with reference to tobacco, the duty must be reduced to 3*d.* or
6*d.* in the pound, otherwise the object would fail altogether.
I hope there will not be such an increase of smoking in this
country as to enable the revenue from a 3*d.* or 6*d.* duty to be

as much as from a 3s. or 4s. duty ; and the fact is, that there
will be a loss of some millions annually. How are you to
deal with that, except by increasing direct taxation? But
this is not the case with tobacco only, but with other matters.
You must make up your minds to a constant remission of
these taxes. As was stated last year by the right hon. Member for Buckinghamshire (Mr. Disraeli), every year since 1842
has witnessed the constant remission of these indirect taxes.
The right hon. Gentleman has not, indeed, proposed anything
of that sort himself; but there is a self-acting process in the
sugar-duties which was effecting that change even last year.
This will and must go on.

I come now to the practical question before us. There is at
present virtually a deficiency ; because I look upon the remission of indirect taxes as so inevitable, that, though the right
hon. Gentleman has a surplus of 300,000l. or 400,000l., yet he
is obliged to create fresh taxes in order to meet the imperative
demand for the repeal of indirect taxation. The right hon.
Gentleman proposes, then, the continuance of the property
and income tax ; and he has done so with some arguments
very elaborate, very able, and, I may say, very subtle. I
must observe, that the part of the right hon. Gentleman's
speech in which he dealt with the income-tax is, to my mind,
the least satisfactory of all. It was the most declamatory,
and appeared, as all such appeals did, to be the least con-
clusive. The right hon. Gentleman began by an allusion to
Mr. Pitt, and said, that that tax having served its purpose
during the war, it ought therefore not to be used in time of
peace. But, surely, it is time that we had done with that
argument, because there is always this answer to it—that
other taxes did their work also during the war. The Customs
and the Excise were during the war, and, if that were any
reason, they ought to put by that grant of the Custom-house,
as they proposed to do the grant of the income-tax, and let us
remain in repose until we had another war. But no one

proposed that. Why not? Is there anything intrinsically worse in the income-tax than in the tax upon tea and wine? In what way is it worse? Does it give rise to greater oppression in its incidence? Why, how large a proportion of the income of a poor man's family is spent on the ounce or half-ounce of tea which he buys every two or three days! There is the same duty upon his tea, which might be purchased in the bonded warehouse at 10½d. per pound, that there is upon the finest-flavoured pekoe or gunpowder-hyson, that might cost 5s. or 6s. per pound. Is there anything in the income-tax more unequal in its pressure than that? Take, again, the wine duty. The gentleman's bottle of Lafitte, which might cost him 5s. in the cellar of the grower, pays precisely the same duty as the bottle of vin ordinaire, which may be bought in the south of France for 2d. Is there anything in the income-tax more unequal or more unjust than that?

In this way I might go through the whole list of exciseable articles, and I should find that in the most necessary articles of consumption the poor family approached more nearly to the rich family than in any other thing. When we lay a tax upon commodities which enter into the daily consumption of the poor, we may be sure that the mass of the people pay a far larger sum in proportion to their incomes than the rich.

Well, then, why are we to make an exception with respect to the income-tax as compared with the other great taxes which served Mr. Pitt in the time of war? Is it because it offends the law of political economy—because it takes more from the pockets of the people than arrives at the Exchequer? No. I question whether we might not collect direct taxes cheaper than any indirect taxes. Is it because it impedes industry more than indirect taxation? On the contrary, however oppressive it might be felt to be upon other grounds, I have never heard that it interfered with the progress of industry, or impeded commerce in any way whatever. Is it the

demoralisation that flows from it? Does it produce greater
evils than other taxes by demoralising the trader? Does not
the levying of the Excise duty produce more demoralisation
than any direct tax could possibly do? Let us take, for
instance, the case of the tobacco and snuff trade. I remember
being present in the Chamber of Commerce in Manchester
when a deputation, consisting of a great number of tobacco-
manufacturers in Manchester and the neighbourhood, waited
upon them to expose the adulterations which were carried on
in the trade, and to endeavour to induce the Chamber to
interfere to effect some alteration in the duties. Those gentlemen, who were the largest dealers and manufacturers in the
neighbourhood, stated frankly—after exposing all the different
articles with which tobacco was coloured and adulterated, such
as the beard from malt, peat-moss, and things of that kind—
that there was not a man in that neighbourhood who carried
on the tobacco and snuff trade without illegal adulterations,
except Mr. Reed, a gentleman who was present; and Mr.
Reed left the trade, and, though he was nearly forty years of
age, went to Cambridge, and was now in holy orders. Can
you find anything worse than that in the income-tax?

With regard to the criminality arising out of these taxes,
let any one go to one of the maritime counties—inquire of the
chairman of quarter sessions—go to the gaol at Winchester,
or anywhere upon the south coast—and ask what is the number of commitments for smuggling. Let him inquire of the
overseers how many children are left destitute and chargeable
to the parish, because their parents had fled the country for
smuggling. I ask, is there any demoralisation in the income-
tax that can be compared with that? The right hon. Gentleman has alluded to the mode of self-assessment as offering
temptations to fraud, which are in many cases irresistible.
I will suggest whether that might be remedied. I do not
see why any one should be called upon to assess himself at all.
In America, where direct taxation is levied for all the purposes

of the separate States, the taxpayers elect an assessor—an experienced, discreet, sober man of the town or neighbourhood,—and he assesses the value of his neighbour's property. Why should not that system be adopted in England? Then, the assessors having made their assessment, if the party chooses to make oath that he is surcharged, or to produce his books, he would have the same means of redress as in America. The advantage is, that there will be no temptations held out to men to state their property at less than it is.

But there is another thing. It has been found in America that a man has less aversion to an exposure of the amount of his property, when it was known to be only the assessment of others, than he has to expose his own assessment of his property. The consequence is, that you would see, as I have seen in Boston,—I have had the book in my own hands,—a printed list of everybody's assessment in Boston. There is Mr. Abbott Lawrence, for example, figuring away with some 700,000 or 800,000 dollars of personal, and a certain amount of real property. I do not find that there was any grievance complained of there; and, after two or three years of assessment, you arrive at a much better notion of a man's income than when you take his own return, because the people who are appointed assessors are from time to time the changes that are going on in the establishments, the evidences of prosperity, or the reverse. As a rule, we estimate at its true value what the amount of our neighbour's property is. I think that this deserves the attention of the Chancellor of the Exchequer, and I hope that it will be taken into consideration by the public at large.

The right hon. Gentleman has stated that he cannot agree to any modification of the income-tax. Now, I believe that there is one fallacy which runs through the right hon. Gentleman's argument upon that subject, which I should have thought could have scarcely escaped so acute a logician. It all amounts to this,—' Don't show me that you can at all diminish the evil; I'll show you that the evil still remains behind, and therefore I will not allow you to touch it.' Admitting the grievance, as I understand the right hon. Gentleman does, can anybody doubt, if you put trades and professions at 5d., and real property at 7d., that there will not be to some extent a diminution of the injustice? It is true you have terminable annuities besides. It is true that when you come to deal with them and with life-interests, the actuaries may bring you an arithmetical puzzle, which will never work in practice, however well it may look on paper. But the right hon. Gentleman has not told them that they will not be doing some good by mitigating at least the evil which he has admitted. I have no hesitation in confessing, as the result of my experience in the Committee, that there are greater difficulties in the question than I had expected. I have no hesitation in saying so. I went into this question seven or eight years ago, with great confidence as to the practicability of effecting all that was required, but I have found that I was wrong; and my hon. friend, also, the Member for Stoke-upon-Trent, who is a great deal deeper in these mysteries than I am, admitted the same thing. But I cannot say that the right hon. Gentleman has shown good grounds for doing nothing; for, if we were to determine upon doing nothing until we arrived at perfection, why then I am afraid that we must put an end to all sublunary things.

Now, there is one matter with respect to my votes on the income-tax which I think requires a little explanation. In 1842, I resisted Sir R. Peel's attempt to impose the income-tax, and for this avowed reason,—that you were retaining the monopoly on corn, that you were refusing to deal with the sugar-duties, that you were therefore destroying the revenue, and that at the same time you wished him to join in imposing a tax in order to repair the mischief which you were committing. I would act in the same way to-morrow if I were in the same circumstances. In 1848, I voted for Mr. Horsman's

motion for a modification; but I voted against my hon. friend's
the Member for Montrose's motion, to levy the income-tax
only for a year, in order that he might have a committee.
That I did upon the avowed ground that my hon. friend
wanted to unite himself with gentlemen on the other side
of the question, and that he did not want to modify, but to
abolish the tax, while he (Mr. Cobden) wished to preserve the
tax. My hon. friend, however, ultimately obtained his committee, and I cannot say that harm has resulted from it.
Having taken that course in times past, I have the income-
tax now presented to me again without modification by a
Government which I believe will stand or fall by the declaration that they will not agree to any modification. I have at
the same time presented to me another portion of the Budget,
which I believe goes far to redress the inequality which existed in the old income-tax, and which is a bold and honest
proposal. Whatever might be the fate of the Budget, the
right hon. Gentleman and his colleagues, at all events, have
earned for themselves the merit of straightforward and honest
conduct, by dealing with that which defeated Mr. Pitt in the
plenitude of his power, and which no one had attempted to
deal with since—I mean the legacy-duty. I believe that the
right hon. Gentleman the late Chancellor of the Exchequer
was disposed to have recommended that this question should
be dealt with. I am quite sure that it would have been dealt
with by somebody—that public opinion would have done it;
and I must say, looking at the income-tax, coupled with the
legacy-duty, and viewing them as the key-stone of the arch of
this Budget, I shall take them both, and shall take them with
both hands. Though I myself have spoken as strongly as
anybody can speak in this House in favour of the professional
man, as well as in the interest of the mercantile and manufacturing community, I am bound to say that I have not found
in the north of England any very active opposition to the
equal rate of duty laid upon all classes. I believe there is

more feeling of resistance and of suffering under the inquisitorial character of the tax among mercantile men and trading capitalists than there is upon the score of the unjust assessment of the tax. I beg that I may not be misunderstood upon this point. I am only speaking for Lancashire and Yorkshire, and I do not wish it to be thought, from what I say, that there is not among traders and professional men elsewhere a strong feeling against this tax. To be very frank upon this subject, I believe that in Lancashire and Yorkshire there is a feeling among the population that a compensation is afforded by the mode in which the surplus gained from the income-tax is disposed of; I mean by the extension of commerce and the freeing of industry from the fetters that bound it. They submit to the income-tax, therefore, without murmuring, partly from the feeling that it is inevitable, and partly from the belief that they receive some compensation in their trades. That will not operate with professional men, or with small traders in rural districts; but I think that the legacy-duty laid upon real property—although I should wish to view that question *per se*, and not as a compensation, though we are made up of checks and compensations in this country—is, if not an equivalent, at least some compensation, to those very classes, the professional and trading people, and ought to tend to reconcile them to the tax in its present form. I think that the Chancellor of the Exchequer has acted wisely in extending the tax to incomes of 100*l*. As an advocate for direct taxation, I would, as an abstract principle, levy it upon everybody, where the tax could be collected with a profit. When I say 'as an abstract principle,' I am assuming that no other tax existed; but in this country, where so much is already laid upon the mass of the people by indirect taxes, where they paid far more in proportion to their means than the upper classes, it became necessary to compensate them by levying upon the property of those who were richer a direct tax. I do not say that, in the present circumstances of this

country, I would propose to levy the income-tax upon all
wages ; but I think the Chancellor of the Exchequer has
acted very wisely in drawing his line at 100*l.* As I have
before said, the working people of this country pay a very
large amount in indirect taxation. They are sometimes told
of the large amount of Customs and Excise which have been
remitted ; but a great fallacy lurked under that. In point of
fact, we had not by that means diminished the taxes upon the
working people, but we had been very cleverly and industri-
ously shifting the burden ever since the days of Mr. Huskisson
and Mr. Grant. We have taken the load off the head, and put
it on the shoulders ; or we have been strapping it up under
the arms in all kinds of ways, so as to gall less ; but the
burden was borne just as before. Let me give an illustration
of this. The amount of Customs and Excise duties paid in
this country in 1831, which was before the Reform Bill, was
35,680,000*l.* The estimates of Customs and Excise for the
coming year is 35,320,000*l.*, so that there is only 360,000*l.*
less paid now for indirect taxes than in 1831, although during
the interval Customs and Excise duties have been repealed to
the extent of from 12,000,000*l.* to 15,000,000*l.* per annum.
There has been an increase in the population, of course ; but
that does not affect the question to an extent some people
may suppose.

I come now to deal with the question of applying the
income-tax to Ireland, which seems to be the great difficulty
with the Government upon the present occasion. I hope hon.
Gentlemen from Ireland will not suppose that I am anxious
to impose any unjust burdens upon them. I am an advocate
of religious and fiscal equality to the most perfect point. I
have given a proof that, as regards religious equality, whatever might be the odium or passing obloquy which I may
suffer from a partial outbreak of bigotry in this country,
nothing shall induce me to put a fetter upon the consciences
of Roman Catholics. If I could make them so, they should

be as free to exercise the practices and observances of their faith in England as if they were to cross the Atlantic and go to the United States.   I want the same thing in commercial and fiscal questions; but there must be a perfect equality between the two.   I mean that the taxes which are paid in this country must be paid in the other.   I do not want to levy heavy burdens upon either England or Ireland.   If I had my will, they should both pay less than they did now.   But what I say is, that there is no safety for the proper working of the Legislature so long as there are Members sitting in it from parts of the kingdom where the people paid less taxes than in other parts of the kingdom.   I have seen the working of this system for some time, and I will tell the hon. Gentlemen from Ireland what were the symptoms I have observed in consequence of the discrepancy in the amount of taxation.   I have observed that the Irish Members take little interest in Imperial expenditure, unless upon some questions where there is a transfer of taxes from the general Exchequer to some locality in Ireland.   Hence their fights about that bauble, the Lord-Lieutenancy; hence their fights about Kilmainham Hospital, although it is a mere nest of jobbing.   Hon. Gentlemen will allow me to say, that I have had an opportunity of hearing something of Kilmainham, having sat upon a Committee where that matter was brought before us.   And, therefore, I speak with some knowledge of the circumstances of the case.   What is the reason that no statesman has ever dreamt of proposing that the colonies should sit with the mother country in a common Legislature?   It was not because of the space between them, for, now-a-days, travelling was almost as quick as thought; but because the colonies, not paying Imperial taxation, and not being liable for our debt, could not be allowed with safety to us, or with propriety to themselves, to legislate on matters of taxation in which they were not themselves concerned.   What happened on the very last occasion on which I addressed myself to the question

of the Budget? I followed the hon. Member for Belfast
(Mr. Davison), who rose to support a proposition for doubling
the house-tax, and laying on an income-tax upon my constituents at Barnsley and Leeds. Those constituents were
largely engaged in the linen-trade; the hon. Gentleman's
constituents at Belfast were also engaged in the same kind
of trade; and the hon. Gentleman got up and declared his
intention to vote, that taxes from which his own constituents
were free should be laid upon my constituents at Barnsley
and Leeds. But I want to know how that hon. Member is
going to vote now? If he were now to vote against putting
on a similar tax on his profits at Belfast, I want no better
proof that they ought never to allow Members to sit in the
same House representing different interests, where they could
help a Minister to impose taxes on their neighbours on condition that they were not imposed on themselves. How would
the case be if they allowed representatives from the colonies to
sit in this House? An ambitious and unscrupulous Minister
would be sure to make use of them, if they were not possessed
of that virtue which ordinary men have not, for the purpose
of oppressing the English people. The Minister would say,
'Help me in such a case, and I'll help you to prevent England
from putting some tax on Canada.' The consequence might
be, that we should have an irresponsible Government—that
we should have constant *coups-d'état*, until the people rose
and declared for a separation. On the present occasion, the
Government, true to the invariable system of compromise,
has proposed to grant the Members for Ireland a very large
boon indeed, if they will only accept their quota of the income-tax. Now, knowing what I do of the temper of the
people out of doors, I will whisper to the hon. Members,—
'Close with the bargain, and give the Government your vote.'
And why do I say so? Because, if I understand the matter
aright, it is proposed to give the Irish almost as much as they
asked them to pay. I believe that it is almost an equivalent.

But I beg hon. Members for Ireland to look at the exchange, and see how it puts them out of court as the advocates of the poor in Ireland ; because, as I understand the matter, the consolidated annuity-tax is levied upon the poor farmers of Ireland. Of course it is levied one-half upon the landlord and one-half upon the tenant, down to those under 5l. rent. Now, the class of poor tenants above 5l. is to be relieved, according to the proposal of the Government, and an income-tax imposed instead upon all persons having incomes of 100l. a year and upwards. Now, I beg hon. Members to remember, that it is only farmers paying 200l. a year and upwards of rent who would be liable to pay income-tax ; and I will ask them to consider how few farmers there were in Ireland who have rents to that amount. I believe that 100l. a year is considered a very genteel income in Ireland. People there live much cheaper than here ; there are no assessed taxes, and provisions are cheaper. Persons with 100l. a year in Ireland, then, are quite as well, if not better, able to pay income-tax than people of the same class in England. I have heard a great deal said about the amount of English indebtedness to Ireland, and of Irish indebtedness in Ireland. The hon. Member for South Lancashire (Mr. Brown), himself an Irishman, has estimated that Ireland was in England's debt 300,000,000l. The hon. Member for Glasgow (Mr. M'Gregor), who, judging from his name, had some Celtic blood in his veins, has put down the debt at 160,000,000l. ; while the late Mr. O'Connell has put down the amount the other way, and declared that England is indebted to Ireland 60,000,000l. I would say, ' Let the Statute of Limitations apply to both sides. Let Irish Members make up their minds to pay the same taxes as the people of England, and unite with us in advocating retrenchment and economy.' I assure those Members that the thing is inevitable, and that if a dissolution were to take place on the question of the equalisation of taxes — although, no doubt, Ireland would be disposed to avoid taxation, if possible — the thing would be settled without them.

There is another point I wish to refer to, and that is the question respecting licences, which the right hon. Gentleman, I believe, has said is still under consideration. On that question I think the right hon. Gentleman has erred on a matter of principle. I cannot understand on what principle the right hon. Gentleman is going to lay a tax on all traders who deal in tea or tobacco. I can understand why the Excise should require a dealer who sold tea, tobacco, or other articles where surveillance was thought to be necessary, to register themselves, and perhaps pay a nominal fee; but I confess I cannot understand why traders who already pay large taxes should be asked to pay, in addition, an *ad valorem* duty on their rent for licences to carry on their business, and I hope the right hon. Gentleman will alter that part of his plan.

Then, with regard to the advertisement duty, I hope the right hon. Gentleman will not 'make two bites at a cherry' in that matter. I want to see the connection between the press and the Government altogether dissolved. [Laughter.] I know what that laugh refers to. It is an illustration of what I mean to argue. It has been stated that the right hon. Gentleman, in proposing to remit the stamp upon supplements containing only advertisements, would be giving a boon to only one paper; and very free remarks have been passed as to what were his motives in giving that boon to a particular paper. Now, I do not believe the right hon. Gentleman is capable of doing that. I believe that the right hon. Gentleman has with all parties in this House too much credit for sincerity and truthfulness to be supposed capable of being a party to a transaction of this kind; but suspicions are entertained on the subject out of doors,—and how have they arisen? They have arisen because Government were enabled to deal with the tax in a manner which favoured one

particular newspaper. And so with the advertisement duty.
That also keeps up a connection between the Government and
the newspaper press. Certain newspapers want that duty off,
and others want it kept on, and Government are tempted to
watch and weigh the rival influences, and shape their public
course accordingly. I repeat that, in my opinion, the Government should have no connection with the press whatever. I
hope, therefore, that if they adhere to their resolution, and
deal with the advertisement duty at all, they will abolish it
altogether.

And if he deals with the stamp-duty, the right hon.
Gentleman must not — as I believe he is now fully aware—
deal with it in a manner which would merely favour one
newspaper at present, and not more than three or four prospectively. If the right hon. Gentleman should be persuaded
by the proprietors of some large provincial newspapers to
alter his plans, so as to continue the penny stamp on newspapers—allowing supplements to go free, whether they contain news or advertisements, or both together—he would be
falling into an error similar in character, though not so great
in degree, to that into which he fell when he proposed to remit
the stamp on supplements which contained advertisements
only; because, if he did, there would, at the outside, be only
some half-score of newspapers, which were at present in the
habit of publishing supplements, which would at all be benefited by it. And how would it act prospectively? It would
act in the opposite way to that which the right hon. Gentleman has laid down with regard to licences, for in that case he
proposed to levy the tax in proportion to the business which
the parties carried on.

But what will be the effect of the plan to which I have just
referred with regard to newspapers? It will allow a newspaper twice the size of the *Times* to be published with a penny
stamp, while it will impose the same sum of a penny upon the
small struggling paper not half the size of one sheet of the

Times. And I beg hon. Members to mark the effect. The small sheet, having to pay the same tax as the large sheet, will be placed under an immense disadvantage. I have seen in Lancashire, whenever a newspaper publishes a supplement, and gives it to its readers, such is the desire of readers to have a great mass of matter, that all the other papers in the district were obliged also to publish a supplement, or be trampled under foot. If, then, the right hon. Gentleman levies the same stamp upon two sheets as he levies upon one, allowing both news and advertisements to appear in the supplemental sheet, you may depend upon it that the effect will be to destroy all the second and third-rate newspapers. I beg hon. Members opposite to bear this in mind, for I believe that some of the newspapers in their interest are not in the most thriving condition.

I will put this case of the stamp-duty to the test of the Chancellor of the Exchequer's own principles. The right hon. Gentleman said, that if a man kept a gig with two wheels he should pay 15s., but that if he kept a carriage with four wheels he should pay double. But in the case of newspapers he reverses the rule, for he makes the four-in-hand pay only the same tax as a gig. Then, again, with regard to the licensing duty, he proposes an *ad valorem* tax on the rent of a man's shop. If a man happens to have such a prosperous trade that his shop is overflowing with customers, and he is not able to carry on his business on his old premises, does the right hon. Gentleman propose to allow him to open a supplemental shop, and pay only one tax? The question, it will thus be seen, would not bear the test of the right hon. Gentleman's own principles. The right hon. Gentleman must either not touch the stamp-duty at all, or he must be prepared to allow newspapers to be taxed according to weight or size when sent by post, and allow them to be sold on the spot where they are published without a stamp.

With respect to the rest of the Budget, I am glad to find

that the soap-duty is to be abolished. That tax has long
been a standing reproach on this country. It has marked the
hypocrisy of all the pretences to cleanliness, and often, when I
have heard of meetings on sanitary reform, I have thought of
the soap-tax, and felt ashamed of my country. And so with
regard to the paper-duty. You talk of promoting education,
and yet here is a tax on the material by which knowledge is
conveyed. This, also, will stamp us with hypocrisy on that
subject so long as it remains.

I will only add, that I hope this Budget, in its main provisions, will pass this House. I believe, so far as I have had
an opportunity of judging, that it is generally acceptable to
the country. The imposition of the legacy-tax will remove a
sore which has been festering in the minds of the people of
this country for a long time. In the interest of the parties
concerned, I would say, the sooner that tax was put on the
better. I would say, both to the landed gentlemen and the
Irish Members, ' Take on your burdens, and it will be the
better for you in the end.' I am told that the Members of
the other House are looking on with great solemnity. There,
they are in possession; but in the House of Commons many
hon. Members were only expectants. I was breakfasting with
a gentleman of the diplomatic corps the other morning; the
conversation was in French, and my host said it was very easy
to explain why the Chamber of Peers would be favourable to
the tax, and the Commons not: because the one is a *Chambre
des Pairs (Pères)*, and the other is a *Chambre des Fils*.

There is another point which I wish to allude to before I
sit down. I want to be very honest with the House about
the income-tax. They are told that that tax was to continue
till 1860 only. Now, I am sorry that I cannot give my
sanction to that idea. My belief is that we must go on
remitting indirect taxes; and I should not be honest if I said
that I saw any prospect of our being able to do away with the
income-tax in 1860. There are certainly but two ways in

which it could be done. It could only be done either by
substituting some other tax in its place, or by a very large
retrenchment in the amount of our expenditure. Some means
or other must be found available for the Chancellor of the
Exchequer for his meeting the constant demands upon him
for the remission of indirect taxes; and I do not see, therefore,
how we can afford to part with the income-tax. I do not,
however, for a moment doubt the sincerity of the Chancellor
of the Exchequer in the matter. I am quite sure, that if the
right hon. Gentleman is in Parliament in 1860, and holds
a responsible position, he will rather give up his office than
be a party to anything like a breach of faith. But it is
melancholy to think how few of us may be in Parliament in
1860. I hope the right hon. Gentleman and all of us may be
alive then; but, even if they are, who can bind the Parliament that will assemble in 1860? I beg, therefore, to be
understood as not pledging myself in favour of the abrogation
of the income-tax in 1860.

FINANCE.

VII.

HOUSE OF COMMONS, JULY 22, 1864.

[The following speech, recommending the reduction or abandonment of Government manufacturing establishments, as impolitic and wasteful, was the last which Mr. Cobden delivered in Parliament.]

I REGRET that, owing to the necessity which lay on many of us to postpone the notices of Motions which we had on the paper a fortnight ago, I was not able to bring this subject earlier under the notice of the House. The question is important, not only in a financial sense, but in its bearings on the defence and security of the nation. In advocating the view that the Government of the country should not undertake to manufacture for itself that which can be purchased from private producers, I am advancing no new doctrine in this House. On the contrary, this has always been the policy of the House, and the opposite system pursued during the last few years has been in defiance of the reiterated expressions of the opinion of Parliament. I might go back to the celebrated speech of Edmund Burke on economical reform, who so long ago as 1780 laid down, in language which it is impossible to surpass, the reasons why the Government should not resort to the manufacture of its own supplies, but should depend on the competition of individual manufacturers. In 1828, before the Reform era, a Committee of the House of Commons put forth a Report, in which there is a paragraph to this effect :—

'The Committee are not disposed to place implicit reliance on the arguments which have been urged by some public departments against contracts by competition, and in favour of work by themselves. The latter plan occasions the employment of a great many officers, clerks, artificers, and workmen, and not only adds to the patronage, but to the appearance of the importance of a department. Nor can the Committee suffer themselves to feel any prejudice against the contract system, by references to some instances of failure. They believe that most cases of failure may be attributed to negligence or ignorance in the management of contracts, rather than to the system itself.'

Now here is the gist of all I have to say. I shall only amplify this passage, and in doing so, I hope I shall not be accused of more illiberality towards the officials than was exhibited by the Committee of 1818. On various occasions this question has been partially raised in reference to particular articles, and an exceptional ground has always been alleged why we should give, for some special branch of production, a preference to the Government manufactories. The consequence has been, that step by step the departments have taken upon themselves an immense increase of manufacture. I have asked myself how is it, that while we have for twenty years, in our commercial policy, been acting on the principle of unrestricted competition, believing that that is the only way to secure excellence and stability of production, and when the private industry of the country is more equal than ever it was to the demands of the Government, how is it that the departments have been allowed to raise up these gigantic Government monopolies? I believe it is in consequence of the weakness of the Executive Government. For many years past there has, I fear, been very little control exercised by the Treasury over the various departments of the Government; and the rein being loosened, the heads of departments have taken the power into their own hands, and embarked in vast manufacturing undertakings, contrary, as I cannot but believe, to the intention of this House and the country. The result of

my experience is, that there is little use in the House undertaking by Committees to correct the failures of the Executive
Government. By interfering in the management of the details
of the Government, you infallibly do more harm than good.
You lower the Executive in the estimation of the permanent
officials, and you attempt what is impossible, for the departments laugh at the idea of Parliament superintending the
details of the administration. Moreover, the Government,
by allowing Parliament to attempt to control these details,
virtually abandons its own duties and responsibilities. During
the last few years we have had Committees of this House on
ordnance, on plating ships, and on various other branches
of Executive administration connected with the safety and
defence of the country. In early years of my experience in
Parliament, when Sir Robert Peel was Prime Minister, he
would have resisted the appointment of such Committees as
tantamount to a vote of want of confidence. He would have
said, ' If you think the administration is not satisfactorily
conducted by me, then you must find somebody else to undertake it.' My view is, that the House can interfere with great
advantage in prescribing the principles on which the Executive
Government shall be carried on; but beyond that, it is impossible for the Legislature to interfere with advantage in the
details of the administration of the country. The principle
I advocate is, that the Government should not be allowed to
manufacture for itself any article which can be obtained from
private producers in a competitive market; and that, if we
have entered on a false system in this respect, we ought, as
far as possible, to retrace our steps.

To give the House an idea of the extent to which the
system of which I complain has grown, I will quote a few
figures. In 1849-50, I sat upon a Committee to inquire into
the Ordnance, and we found that the whole amount of wages
then paid to artificers and labourers in the United Kingdom
and the Colonies on the Ordnance Votes was 141,330*l*. This

year I find that we have voted in corresponding votes for the
wages of our manufacturing establishments, including the
clothing factories, a sum of 584,000*l.*, being more than four
times the amount of the sum voted in 1849–50. The wages
voted for the gun factory at Woolwich this year were 144,000*l.*,
which exceeded the wages for all the departments in 1849–50.
Down to and including the Crimean war, the British Government never cast an iron cannon, or made shot or shell. Our
ordnance was purchased from the Carron Works in Scotland,
from the Low Moor Company, or from the Gospel Oak Works
of Messrs. Walker. At the outbreak of the Crimean war, my
right hon. friend the Member for Limerick (Mr. Monsell) was
Secretary to the Ordnance, and I am afraid that I must charge
him with having deposited the nest-egg which has produced
the pernicious brood of which I am complaining. From the
evidence given by the right hon. Gentleman himself, in 1854,
I find that he and Captain Boxer, of the Laboratory Department at Woolwich, laid their heads together, and said, ' If we
spend 7000*l.* in putting up machinery, we can make our own
fusees, and bouche our own shells.' That was the beginning
of those acres of costly machinery which may now be seen at
Woolwich. No very long time elapsed before Captain Boxer
said, ' We are now prepared for making fusees, and bouching
faster than we can get shells; therefore, let us make shells;'
and accordingly they laid out 10,000*l.* in the erection of
machinery for casting shells and shot. There is a very interesting narrative in the evidence before the Sebastopol Committee, and I find that the right hon. Gentleman was arraigned
before that Committee for acting without the consent of his
colleagues. I do not blame him for that. We were at war,
and he and Captain Boxer displayed a commendable energy;
but I mention these facts to show you how establishments of
this kind grow. The next step, after setting up machinery
for casting shot and shell, was to erect turning and boring
machinery for making the guns. It was resolved, that instead

of obtaining cast-iron cannon from the Low Moor Company,
they should purchase from that concern solid blocks of iron,
and bore and turn them at Woolwich. Another suggestion
immediately followed:—'We had better cast our own guns
rather than buy these blocks from Low Moor;' and so the
machinery was set up for that. Now came a difficulty. There
are, as I have said, but two or three concerns in England from
which it is safe to buy ordnance, of which the Low Moor
Works are one, and the Gospel Oak Works of Messrs. Walker
another. When casting a 68-pounder at Low Moor, they
not only take selected qualities of their own iron, good as
it is, but they use coal of a particular kind, fresh from the
earth, to smelt it. That firm would not sell pig-iron to the
Woolwich establishment, and the result was, that, having got
the machinery for casting the guns, there was no iron fit to
cast. They went into the market, and purchased the ordinary
kind of pig-iron, and they made about 100 guns; but it is
believed that not one of the 100 ever went into the service.
They were pronounced rotten, and were never used. After
200,000*l*. had been spent in this way, the establishment at
Woolwich for casting guns was abandoned.

Then came the second part of the performance. It had
become necessary that the Government should obtain a supply
of rifled cannon. No sooner did this necessity arise, than
there were men of genius, such as Mr. Whitworth, Sir William
Armstrong, Captain Blakeley, Mr. Lancaster, and Mr. Lynall
Thomas, preparing to supply the want. The reasonable course
would have been to have said to these inventors, 'Go on, and
improve your system. Manufacture some guns, and, to which-
ever is most successful, we will be your customer.' But the
establishment at Woolwich wished to secure the manufacture
of rifled ordnance, and those in authority—some of them in
very high authority—seem to have lost their heads altogether,
and to have gone almost crazy over Sir William Armstrong's
gun. An illustrious Duke is reported to have said, that Sir

William Armstrong's gun could all but speak; and another
eminent officer declared it was equal to anything in the tales
of the *Arabian Nights.* I will venture to offer a suggestion.
When we have in future to make a choice of ordnance, our
high officials in the army should pursue the same course they
do when they hold a court-martial—let the younger officers
speak first—because, when the Commander-in-Chief utters
such an emphatic approbation, it is hardly likely that junior
officers will be found to dissent. I would further suggest,
that the authorities should in these matters follow the commercial system, and not begin to praise and puff an article
before they buy it. The result in this instance was, that Sir
William Armstrong—then Mr. Armstrong—resolved to make
a present of his patent to the War Office. And a very costly
present it was. It was assigned over to the Secretary for War,
and an arrangement was entered into, which to this day I can
hardly understand. It seems that Sir William Armstrong was
to receive, for ten years, a sum of 2000*l.* a year for superintending the working of the patent. That arrangement was
antedated three years, and 6000*l.* was paid down, upon which
he became superintendent of the Royal gun factory, and chief
engineer of the rifled ordnance department. A business was
set up at Elswick, in Northumberland, by the War Office—
an establishment which previously belonged to Sir William
Armstrong—and we made advances in a mysterious manner
to the extent of 85,000*l.* Immediately afterwards our officials
at Woolwich set up a manufactory of the same kind, and
they set it up apparently with a view of controlling the price
at Elswick. It is most amusing to see the *naïveté* with which
the leading men at Woolwich came before the Committee
appointed by this House, and tried to show that they were
producing the gun cheaper at Woolwich than at Elswick,
forgetting that the two were one and the same concern; that
they were both started by the Government with the nation's
capital. The Committee were evidently unable to understand

the accounts of the Woolwich factory, and in their report they
passed a resolution begging them to amend them. I believe
that the right hon. Member for Limerick will admit that this
is a fair statement of the origin and progress of the rifled
Armstrong gun. It was to be made of wrought-iron, was to
be breech-loading, and built up on the coil principle with bars
of forged iron. It is no disparagement to Sir W. Armstrong,
who is a man of great mechanical genius, to say that the
general impression of scientific men has been unfavourable to
his invention; unfavourable to the breech-loading principle,
and unfavourable to the material of which he proposed to construct his gun. But the point to which I desire to call the
especial attention of the House is this, that the Government
set up a manufacture, and installed as its head the author and
patentee of a particular gun. The consequence was, that
Mr. Whitworth, who was then in the field, found that he had
virtually to submit his gun to the inspection and approval of
his great rival. There were other men as well who were candidates, but I mention Mr. Whitworth especially, because
every one who knows him will allow that he is one of the
very foremost practical mechanicians of the age, and everybody will admit, that any system which excluded that gentleman from competition, in a matter to which he had devoted
his attention, must be a wrong system. It was not merely
the mechanicians who were thus excluded. The general impression was, and is, that the great problem to solve is not so
much a pattern of rifling, or a form of gun, as the material
from which a gun is to be made; and we have for the last ten
years been travelling in a direction which will no doubt ultimately land us in this position, that we shall have it in our
power, whenever we find it advantageous, to apply steel to
every purpose for which we now use iron. Mr. Bessemer was
in the field with his invention for cheapening steel. We have
it in evidence before the Committee on Ordnance, from Capt.
Scott, that Mr. Bessemer told him he should have liked the

Government to try his principle of homogeneous metal, which
he and many others believe will be found better than wrought
iron, but that when he found Sir William Armstrong in possession, he gave up the idea.   There is also evidence that the
Messrs. Walker, of Gospel Oak Works, who produced some of
the best cast-iron guns, made the same remark, that, finding
Sir William Armstrong in possession, they should abandon
the manufacture of guns.   Well, a Committee of this House
upon Ordnance was appointed, and sat in 1862-3; and I
must say, that on reading the details of the evidence taken
before it, I was astonished at the levity with which that evidence was allowed to pass into oblivion without having been
brought under the notice of the House.   I call my right hon.
friend the Member for Limerick, who was Chairman of the
Committee, to account for the omission; and the other Members of the Committee are not altogether without blame.   The
evidence adduced before that Committee was of the most
important, and even the most portentous character; for it
transpired that we had between 2500 and 3000 guns upon the
principle of Sir William Armstrong; that there is a confessed
expenditure of 2½ millions on these guns; but I believe it was
very much more; and it was admitted that 100 of these guns,
of the largest size, were made before a trial or experiment was
entered into.   That there may be no cavilling about what the
result of that Committee was, I will read a few words.   The
Duke of Somerset, the head of the Admiralty, in his evidence,
said last year:—

'The whole science of gunnery is in a transition state, and when I was
this year asked what gun I approved for the navy, I was obliged to say that I
really did not know.'

Recollect, this was after nearly 3000 guns had been made on
the Armstrong principle.   His Grace also declared that we
had nothing better now for close quarters than the old
68-pounder made at the Low Moor Works.   And the Com-

mittee report — unanimously, I suppose — that the old 68-pounder is, therefore, the most effective gun in the service against iron plates. The Committee finally say :—

' "The Armstrong 12-pounders, although stated by some of the witnesses to be too complicated a weapon for service, are generally approved ;" but that "the preponderance of opinion seems to be against any breech-loading system for larger guns." '

They recommend that the different systems should be experimented upon. And they also recommend that the accounts of the Woolwich Gun Factory should be kept in a more intelligible manner. [' No.'] These are not their words, but that is their sense. They say they cannot understand the accounts. I would just add a few words from a naval officer who has given considerable attention to this matter. Writing on the 30th of June last, Admiral Halstead thus summed up :—

' The result is, that the largest and most costly fleet of the world, intrusted with the security of the largest maritime empire, has long been presented to all but England's eyes without a gun fit for the special warfare of the day, and with special guns fit for no warfare whatever.'

I ask, is that a satisfactory state of things in which to find ourselves after spending, perhaps, three millions of money, and making nearly 3000 of these guns? Admiral Halstead, in another letter, calls this ' the great blind jump of 1859.' What has been the result of the Committee? The consequence is, that you have had set up at Shoeburyness a stunning competitive contest between Sir William Armstrong and Mr. Whitworth; and thus, after this vast outlay of public money upon the invention of one of the competitors, you are trying which of the two has got the best gun. There might, however, be some consolation in this, if the Armstrong guns were now really being tried against Mr. Whitworth's; but what is the fact? If I am rightly informed, the original gun which we took up and have got in stock — that is, the service gun—is not the gun which Sir William Armstrong is trying.

I am told that the original breech-loader, of which we have
nearly 3000 on hand, has been abandoned in this competition,
and that there is another gun, of an improved construction,
substituted. I saw it stated in a report of the trial in the
Times the other day, that the original breech-loader is withdrawn from the competition. That is not a very consolatory
circumstance in the condition in which we find ourselves.

I beg the House to consider what is meant when we are
told that we have no naval gun. We have 12-pounders for
the field, if we chose to go to war in New Zealand or China;
but you are not to reckon on the contingency of an enemy
landing here to fight you. When I speak of your having no
naval guns, I mean guns to fight with. I observe that
Captain Cowper Coles talks of the Armstrong 110-pounder
as something to do for a chase—or, in nautical phrase, 'to
tickle up a runaway.' Now, let us realise the full force of the
admission, that we have no gun adapted for modern naval
warfare. The hon. Member for Stirling (Mr. Caird) stated
the other day—and we could have no higher authority—that
half the people of this country during the last three years have
been fed with grain and food brought from abroad. We are
in the position of a garrison depending for subsistence upon
our communications being kept open. If, after all your expenditure, you have no guns for your ships to contend with
against an enemy, do you suppose that your foe would be so
foolish as to attempt an invasion with a view of fighting
you on land? No; if they had the command of the sea
they would blockade us, and starve us into submission. Our
life as a nation depends on our having the mastery of
our communications by sea. And yet this is the way in
which those who govern us take care to keep open our
communications.

Well, the whole secret of the failure is this :—The Government do not understand the functions of a buyer; the whole
difficulty of their position arises from their not being able to

fulfil the duty of a purchaser, in a common-sense and judicious manner. The true course to have pursued with all these scientific men, when they came with their improvements in artillery, was to have encouraged them to go on, and to have promised their custom to the most successful, or, perhaps, a very small amount of help at starting. I believe that Sir W. Armstrong only asked for 12,000*l.* to begin with, and that Mr. Bessemer would have commenced making his steel guns with 10,000*l.*; and I have no doubt that for less than 100,000*l.* the Government might have set half-a-dozen establishments to work, competing for the prize of supplying them with guns. That is a matter which the Government will never comprehend till this House insists that they shall buy their commodities, instead of making them. If they are not capable of buying their commodities in the market, do you suppose they are competent to fulfil the far more difficult task of manufacturing them?

I wish to show you the position in which we, as a nation, are placed by these proceedings. We are in danger of seeing foreigners supplied with better armaments than ourselves from our own private workshops. The very individuals whom the Government have rejected and would not have dealings with, have set up manufactories of ordnance for themselves. Mr. Whitworth has founded an ordnance company for the manufacture of guns. I am told that Sir William Armstrong, having closed his connection with the Government at Elswick, and received 65,000*l.* as compensation, has set up a manufactory of guns at Elswick; and, being no longer connected with the Government, I am told that he is actually manufacturing his 600-pounders for foreign countries. Within a quarter of an hour's drive from this spot I saw, a few days ago, an establishment where steel guns — 600-pounders — are being bored; and this firm, which was rejected by the Government, is, I am told, receiving orders for these monster guns by the dozen, while you are in this experimental mood down at Shooburyuess over the 70-pounder and the 110-pounder. I have now said all that I intend to say respecting this gigantic ordnance failure.

Then, as a still further proof of the necessity for the Government to know how to exercise the functions of a buyer, let me refer to small arms as an illustration. Down to about ten years ago, we bought all our muskets from contractors. The Government did not make a rifle even during the Crimean war. I may here remark, that the ordnance supplied during the Crimean war was of a very satisfactory character. The ordnance and small arms were supplied by private contractors to the army and navy, and they were spoken of in the highest terms in the report of the Sebastopol Committee of 1855, which, at the same time, contained condemnations of the commissariat, of the medical, and other departments. As I have said, previous to 1855 we bought our small arms from private contractors. How does the House think the Government managed their purchases? I mention this as an illustration of their incompetency as a buyer. If hon. Members refer to the evidence given before the Small Arms Committee of 1854, they will find that the Government were in the habit of buying their muskets in component parts. They contracted, at Birmingham and Wednesbury and other places, for the stock with one maker, for the barrel with another, for the lock with a third, and so on, until they had about a dozen separate contracts for the component parts of a musket. All those various parts were sent to the Ordnance Depôt, and from that depôt they were given out to a distinct body of contractors, named 'setters-up,' who fitted them together, and made up the musket. Thus they who completed the musket never came into contact with the contractors for the component parts — a system most ingeniously contrived to prevent all improvement. Mr. Whitworth and Mr. Nasmyth, both eminent men, who were examined before the Committee, spoke of the absurdity of this

practice, when large capitalists were ready to undertake to
supply the completed article. The Government complained
that they could not get muskets fast enough, because there
were sometimes strikes among the workmen. They were
asked, in return, 'Why do you not give orders to capitalists,
who will set up machinery for making the entire musket?'
and it was shown that the system of contracting for the
separate parts multiplied the risk of delays from strikes,
because if, for instance, the men struck who made the locks,
they put a stop to the supply of the complete musket. The
Government, however, could not be made to comprehend this ;
and what was the remedy they proposed for the grievance of
which they complained? Instead of improving their mode
of purchasing, they thought it would be easier for them to
manufacture muskets, and therefore the Ordnance Department came before the Committee of 1854 with a plan for
erecting an enormous Government manufactory of rifled small
arms at Enfield. The Committee were decidedly against that
project, and I am glad to see present the hon. Member for
North Warwickshire, who was a member of that Committee.
They said, 'If you wish to see better machinery introduced
for the manufacture of small arms, that is one question ; but
it is quite distinct from the question whether you are to have
a Government factory ;' and, in their report, they speak
decidedly against the Government setting up this enormous
establishment, because, they say, you will thereby extinguish
private trade, which it would be well to preserve for your
future necessities. The result was, that the Government
sent to America to procure machinery. Colonel Colt, the
American, had been in this country for twelve months at that
time, and he had set up his machinery ; but the Government,
rather than encourage a Birmingham or a London house to
enter into the trade to supply them, rushed into what has become the Enfield Rifle Manufactory. That establishment, which
then contained sixty or seventy workpeople, has since grown

into the employment of from 1200 to 1500. I am not about
to contend that the rifle factory at Enfield has, up to the
present time, done its work badly, or that it has not been
profitable. If you set up machinery which is almost self-
acting, and if you give it constant employment, it is not easy
to make a concern otherwise than profitable; but while doing
this, you have been driving out of the trade all those who
would have set up the manufacture upon an independent and
more durable basis. But the future of this establishment
cannot be estimated from the past, for what is now becoming
the fate of the Enfield factory?   You have no longer full
work for it, for you cannot continue to make the one pattern
which you have been continuously at work upon—the pattern
of 1853. A Committee has decided that Mr. Lancaster's rifle
is a better weapon; public competition showed that Mr. Whitworth's was superior; and the consequence has been that the
noble Lord the Member for Haddingtonshire (Lord Elcho)
has moved, in the present session, the rejection of the estimate
for making Enfield rifles, because they were of an inferior
kind, and therefore the manufacture ought to be suspended.
If, then, these rifles are to be discontinued, and others are to
be made, you will be confronted with the difficulties which
await you in every Government manufactory where you are
your own and your only customer. During this transition
period, as your production falls off, the cost of each article
increases, owing to the larger proportion of the permanent
fixed charges which it has to bear. To evade this, and also
in order to find employment for your workpeople, you will
always be liable to the temptation of going on making things
which you do not want, in order to employ the people about
you, and the result will be that you will be overstocked with
articles which your better judgment would induce you not to
buy, if you had to purchase them in the market from private
producers.

    I have said I do not mean to argue that making one article,

and having constant employment, this Enfield establishment
has not paid itself. But here are the balance-sheets relating
to the rifle factory and the gunpowder manufactory adjoining,
which have been laid upon the table, and upon which I wish
to make one or two observations. I see they are signed
'Hartington,' as Under-Secretary for War; but I would
advise the noble Lord not to put his name to any more of
these balance-sheets, as I can assure him they would not pass
the Bankruptcy Court. They are not creditable to him, and
they are still more discreditable to a commercial nation like
this, of which he is a representative. I wish to call attention to some facts connected with these balance-sheets. In
that which is dated the 31st of March, 1863, it is stated that
the articles produced in the year cost at Enfield 199,177*l.*,
while if they had been purchased from the trade the cost
would have been 356,378*l.*, showing a saving of 157,201*l.*
Among the items are 71,590 rifles, for which it was stated
the private trade would charge 63*s.* 1*d.* each. Now, a gentleman who is at the head of the trade in Birmingham informs
me that a tender was actually made this year to the Government to supply rifles at 50*s.* each, or 13*s.* 1*d.* less than it is
said the private trader would charge. Then, again, it is
stated that 13,780 short rifles made at Enfield would have
cost 94*s.* 7*d.* if bought of the private trade. The same gentleman informs me that a contract was made last January for
the Turkish Government, through our War Office, to supply
the same weapons at 65*s.* 9*d.*, or 28*s.* 10*d.* less than is said
here to be the trade cost. Then there are 13,000 carbines
put down as costing 63*s.* 7*d.* in the private trade, but which
this gentleman tells me could have been had for 50*s.* The
amount of these overcharges upon these three items alone is
75,000*l.* It may be objected that the balance-sheet is for
1862-3, while the prices of the private trade which I have
quoted are for this year. I put that point to the gentleman
on whose authority I have spoken, and he said the articles

might have been bad at about the same price last year, if anybody had applied for them.

I find that you can never make the conductors of these Government establishments understand that the capital they have to deal with is really money. How should it be real money to them? It costs them nothing, and, whether they make a profit or a loss, they never find their way into the *Gazette*. Therefore to them it is a myth — it is a reality only to the taxpayers. Throughout the inquiries before Parliamentary Committees upon our Government manufactories, you find yourselves in a difficulty directly you try to make the gentlemen at the head of these establishments understand that they must pay interest for capital, rent for land, as well as allow for depreciation of machinery and plant. There is an immense capital employed in the Enfield Rifle Manufactory. The fixed and floating capital invested in materials, buildings, machinery, and land, appears from the balance-sheet to amount to 350,000*l.* The private manufacturer, of course, in the shape of either rent or interest, would charge himself on the whole of the amount, or if he did not he would soon find himself in the *Gazette*.

There is more than want of self-respect in the departments which publish such accounts. It is an insult and an outrage to private trade to pretend to show by such fallacious balance-sheets how much the articles cost, and how much they would have cost if they had been bought of private traders, and to make it appear that we have had all these rifles for 199,177*l.*, while if we had bought them of private traders we should have had to pay 356,378*l.*, or 157,201*l.* more. The whole amount of wages paid during the year was 135,700*l.*, and we are asked to believe that there has been a saving of 157,201*l.*, as compared with what would have been paid to private manufacturers. Now, we all know that for everything but labour the Government go to the same source of supply as private manufacturers do. They have not as yet established coal or iron mines of their own, and for all raw materials they have to go into the market and buy on the same terms as private establishments buy. Yet the Enfield Rifle Factory professes to have saved more than the whole amount spent in wages during the year! We all remember the story of the two gipsies who sold brooms. Says one of them to the other, 'I can't conceive how you afford to sell your brooms cheaper than I do, for I steal all my materials.' 'Ah!' says the other, 'but I steal the brooms ready-made.' Now I should like to know from the noble Marquis (the Marquis of Hartington), whom I shall persist in holding responsible for these accounts, to which he has appended his name, how he manages this great feat of commercial legerdemain.

Turning over two pages in this Report on the Government Factories, I come to the Waltham Abbey Powder Manufactory. That is an establishment with 160 acres of land, upon which they profess to grow wood for their charcoal, with water-power of immense extent, with large buildings for business and for dwellings, and, of course, with a great amount of machinery. Their business is not a large one. They return themselves as having produced in the year 14,526 barrels of powder, which they value at 34,747*l.* Then, after the usual memorandum, that this is exclusive of interest of capital, depreciation of plant, &c., they show that these 14,526 barrels of gunpowder, if supplied by private makers, would have cost 79,933*l.*, so that they have effected for the Government a saving of 45,185*l.*

Now, I say that, for a country calling itself a commercial nation, to have such accounts published and signed 'Harting-ton,' is monstrous; and it only shows the utter valuelessness of anything that the noble Marquis may say at that table on this subject. The noble Marquis has shown that he possesses too much ability to make these statements on his own authority; but it is clear that he recites anything that is put into his hands, and therefore what he may say at the table is not worth the slightest attention.

Now, let us see how all this is managed. The capital
represented by buildings, water-power, machinery, and rolling
stock is 300,000*l.*, and no interest is charged on that. The
land is worth 20,000*l.*, but there is no item for rent.
Nothing is allowed for rates and taxes, and nothing for
insurance. Now, I asked a very well-informed gentleman
what the custom was in the private trade with regard to the
charge for insurance on a gunpowder manufactory. Of course,
the Royal Exchange or the Phœnix Company would not like
such risks. So I find that private traders are in the habit of
allowing about 25 per cent. for insurance. Nothing of the
sort is allowed for here. Enough has probably been said to show
that the system on which these Government manufactories
are conducted is wholly unsound; that there is an utter
absence of responsibility; that there are none of those motives
for saving money or avoiding losses which private individuals
have; and that, wanting the motives which are necessary for
human action, it is impossible that these establishments can
be carried on properly.

Let me just touch for a minute upon another matter—the
great clothing establishments. Earl De Grey and Ripon, as
the head of the War Department, is not only the largest
manufacturer of ordnance and of small arms, but he is the
most extensive tailor in the world. [Laughter.] You laugh;
but all these tailoring transactions are carried on in his
name, and he is responsible for everything. [Laughter.]
You laugh at the idea that Lord De Grey should overlook all
these details; but is it not a serious thing for the country to
have an immense business of this kind carried on virtually
without control? About ten years ago, the system of clothing
the army was changed, and, instead of clothing-colonels, we
had clothing by contract. For a few years that system continued, and the right hon. Gentleman (General Peel) introduced an improvement in the purchasing department. Down
to this time the custom was to contract for the clothing

by piecemeal, getting the buttons, braiding, and clothing separately; but the gallant officer had contracts made for the whole garment. We were told in evidence before the Army Organisation Committee by the gallant officer, by the Commander-in-Chief, and by another witness, that the system worked very well. But there was a plot all this while to divert the manufacture of army clothing from private makers into the hands of Government officials. The plot was stealthily carried out. A small establishment was first set up at Woolwich for making clothes for the Artillery and Engineers. That establishment was to go no further. Then a small manufactory was started at Vauxhall for making clothing for the Guards.

As one more illustration of the fallacious grounds on which these Government manufactories are established, I will give a brief extract from the evidence given before the Committee on Contracts, which sat in 1858, by Sir Benjamin Hawes, then permanent Under Secretary at the War Office—and we all know that a permanent official often knows more than his chief. He handed in what he was told to give as the cost price of a soldier's garment. There happened to be a man of business on the Committee—my hon. friend the Member for Newcastle-under-Lyne (Mr. Jackson) — and he, mistrusting the calculation, took the subject in hand, and cross-questioned the witness :—

' You have given the Committee the actual cost to the Government of the clothing and the making of the clothing for one man?—Yes. Independent of all departmental charges, and so forth?—Yes. These charges would be plus salaries?—Yes. Plus interest of capital?—Certainly. Plus rent?—Certainly. Plus damage, and every other contingency?—Yes. And carriage, and ink, and pens and paper, and all necessaries for conducting the business?—Yes. Therefore that is not a fair return of what it costs the nation, because, if you have to pay those charges in addition, these prices are not the actual cost to the country?—They are not. So that the return is a fallacious one?—It is not a complete one.'

I will read another extract from the evidence of the same witness. In justice to my late friend, Sir Benjamin Hawes,

I must add that he never contemplated the creation of a
Government clothing establishment on its present gigantic
scale. Alluding to the manufactory of clothing for the
Guards, which had been established the previous year at
Vauxhall, he recommended only a slight extension of the
factory, so as to supply a regiment or two of the Line. He
is asked—

'As I understand you, it is not proposed that that establishment should be
extended so far as to make all the clothing for the army, but only a portion of
the clothing of certain regiments, in order to give you a test as to the price?—
Certainly; I hope never to see a great Government establishment for clothing
the army. The more such establishments are used for the purpose of obtaining
information and obtaining models the better; but I look with some apprehension upon all great Government establishments. . . . It is very desirable that a
Government establishment should produce the minimum, and the private trade
of the country should produce the rest.'

At the very time this evidence was being given, when the
House would have refused to sanction a large extension of the
clothing establishment, the plot was all laid for getting into the
hands of the War Department the manufactory of the clothing
of the whole army, with a slight exception. An enormous
building has been erected at Pimlico—put up, I believe, upon
most costly ground, the item of ground-rent being between
2000*l.* and 3000*l.* a year—and they now make there the
clothing of every regiment, and manufacture everything, with
the exception of the tunics, for about fifty battalions, which
comprise, perhaps, one-tenth of the whole supply of clothing
for the army: I suppose this exception is maintained in order
to enable the noble Marquis to tell this House that the department has not a monopoly. The accounts rendered of this
Clothing Department are most fallacious. I find that about
15,000*l.* a year for fixed charges and interest of money have
never been brought into the account at all, and that there is
no allowance for rates and taxes. Taking into consideration
the waste and fraud to which an establishment for a trade like
that is so peculiarly susceptible, when the materials used are
cut up into pieces, I must say that it is one of the most

unwise and injudicious undertakings that could have been entered into.

I have already said, you never find with respect to those establishments that anything is put down for rates, taxes, lighting, or charges of that kind. There is a fallacy in this. If the tailoring business is carried on by the Government, somebody else is deprived of it, who would have paid rates and taxes, including the income-tax. Let us suppose the extreme case, that all the manufactures of the country were carried on by the Government, and that they were all exempt from taxation, how would the Chancellor of the Exchequer get his revenue?

I now come to the management of the Royal Dockyards, to which the remarks I have made apply with greater force than to any other department. We have had repeated debates on that subject, and Committees and Commissions have reported on it without end. The tendency of our debates during the last few years has been to prevent, if possible, the Admiralty from continuing to make things which we knew were of no use—to prevent them from building wooden ships, when everybody knew that iron ships would be wanted—and great three-deckers, when all scientific men were aware that they would be mere slaughter-houses, if opposed to modern combustible missiles. What, in the meantime, has been the tendency of the Admiralty? The heads of the dockyards have been endeavouring to counteract Parliament by securing votes for timber in every possible way, and even by buying timber with money voted for iron ships, in order that, having the timber on hand, there may be an excuse for using it for the purpose of building obsolete vessels of war.

I have spoken plainly with respect to the right hon. Member for Droitwich (Sir John Pakington) and the noble Lord the Secretary of the Admiralty, and I hardly know which to blame the most for bringing in Estimates which they must have known entailed an improper waste of money.

If I blame the noble Lord most, it is because I know that he knew better. But, after all, there is probably something to be said on the other side. If you will have these enormous establishments employed for one customer only, you are always in danger, in seasons of transition, of having a great number of workpeople thrown out of employment. This operates on the feelings of humane men, who are responsible for their subsistence, and induces them, under the guidance of their feelings, and against their better judgment, to manufacture articles which ought not to be made at all. There is no doubt that we have been spending millions of money on the construction of valueless vessels, and that you have from fifty to a hundred great wooden ships which ought never to have been in existence, and will never be of any use, but which were in great part built because you have a system which compels you to find employment for your men. If, instead of being builders, you had been buyers of ships, does any one suppose that you would have purchased one of those useless and obsolete wooden vessels? I speak to hon. Gentlemen on the other side of the House in the confidence that they will co-operate with me on this occasion. They are said to favour large votes for the military and naval services. But no party in the House is interested in the waste of public money on these establishments. They find me but little disposed to vote money for the army and navy; but I am always for paying the men well, and I would give them more money than they get now, though I should certainly be satisfied with fewer of them; but you cannot indulge in more liberality towards the men while you tolerate the waste and extravagance of keeping up these large manufacturing establishments; for all these charges come under the head of Army and Navy, and swell up, in the eyes of the country, the amount expended on the services.

I wish to ask why we should not take advantage of the present time, when passing from wooden ships to iron ships, and do with

the hulls of vessels what you do with your marine steam-engines
—buy them, keeping up the Government dockyards only, as
far as might be wanted, for repairs.   Where would be the risk
or inconvenience from such a change?   Do you think that the
shipbuilders in private yards could not perform the work as
satisfactorily as the Admiralty?   There are, I believe, at this
moment upwards of 500,000 tons of shipping building in
private yards; and during the last year there have been
building in this country fifteen ships of war, of an aggregate
of nearly 40,000 tons, for the Governments of the following
countries:—Denmark, Italy, Spain, Russia, Turkey, China,
Prussia, Peru, Portugal, and two rams supposed for the Con-
federate States.   With the exception of a small vessel of 500
tons, which is of wood, all these ships, I am told, are being
built of iron.   Do you suppose that the private builders, who
are constructing ships to this enormous extent, cannot build
the hulls of your vessels of war?   Why, you already procure
from private manufacturers the most important part of your
steamers, that which requires the greatest skill and the most
reliable probity in its production.   You get your steam-
engines wholly from private establishments.   I remember
sitting on a Committee upon the Navy in 1848, when we
were just in time to prevent the Government Dockyards from
commencing the construction of steam-engines.   The rule laid
down, and ever since acted upon, was, that the Admiralty
should repair their engines, but not make them.   This has
been found to succeed most admirably; it is the only branch
of your naval construction about which you never hear any
complaint.   No Committees of this House have been called
for, no blue-books have been required, for improving the construction of marine steam-engines.   The difficulties in the
dockyards have been in connection with the building of the
hulls of ships.   Why should not the plan which has worked
so well with the engines be equally applicable to ships?   This
is a most opportune time for making the change, just when

the armour-clad vessels are coming into use. At the present moment you have no means of making iron-plates for the armour-ships, but I have no doubt that, if the House permitted, the authorities of the dockyards would get up plans for having iron rolled in those establishments.

There is an old plea for maintaining these Government establishments on a small scale, upon the ground that you may be able to manufacture a little, so as to serve as a test and a check upon contractors. Such a course might have been to some extent unobjectionable formerly, when there were few competitors; but we live now in a time when such a check is unnecessary; for are not great shipbuilders, great gunmakers, and large tailoring establishments, better checks upon each other, through the force of competition, than you can possibly be upon them? If the accounts in the Government establishments are honestly made out, then you will find that the Government, carrying on a small business without the usual motives for economy, produces things at a very dear rate, and the contractors will expect to be paid at this price, which you say should be the model one. If, on the other hand, the accounts are made out like those to which I have referred, and private producers are expected to compete on such terms, then every respectable manufacturer will throw aside the invitations for contracts with disgust and scorn, and refuse to have anything to do with such departments. But is not the fact of the perfect success of your marine engines, without any such check as is proposed, a sufficient answer to this plea? Surely, the great waste which we know to have been so long taking place is a sufficient motive for a change. I was talking the other day to an eminent practical shipbuilder on this subject, and this is the substance of what he told me :—

'There has been expended in wages to artificers, naval stores, for the building, repairing, and outfitting of the fleet, steam machinery, and ships built by contract, new works, improvements, and repairs in the yards, from 1859 to 1863 inclusive (five years), 24,350,000l. Taking into account the values of all the iron-clads built and building, and giving a large sum for useless constructions of wooden ships, and making a liberal allowance for equipment and repairs, still there will be left more than ten millions out of the above sum, for the expenditure of which a private shipbuilder could assign no rational purpose.'

I remember the noble Lord the Secretary to the Admiralty saying, some time back, that he could not trace several millions of the Estimates in any results to be discovered in the dockyards, and I suppose my friend the shipbuilder has been engaged in a similar search.

It has been said, that if we retain the powers of production in our Government establishments, and a war breaks out, we shall have the means of bringing all these powers to bear on the preparation of our armaments. There is, I think, a great deal more to be said on that score, in favour of my plan of giving the work to private establishments. If our private shipbuilders were employed by our own as well as by foreign Governments, then we should have a dozen or a score of large firms engaged in constructing ships of war, not only for ourselves, but for half the world. In the same way, if the Government merely kept the factory at Woolwich for repairs, or let it, and gave orders to private houses for the supply of their artillery and ammunition, you would have half-a-dozen or half-a-score, as the case might be, of great establishments producing these articles for our own and foreign Governments. In the present very low state of civilisation, in which no country feels itself safe, particularly if a weak Power, but when, fortunately for humanity, there is a principle developing itself in mechanical science, which gives a great advantage to those who act on the defensive, especially against an aggressor from a distance, I am inclined to think there would be constantly a very great demand for munitions of war by foreign countries—South America, for instance; Japan, and others, who would arm themselves, in order to be safe against attack. And I am not prepared to say they would not do well in thus arming themselves, because the stronger a Power is, the less

temptation does it offer to outrage. What, then, if you pursued the course I recommend, would be your position? In
case of a war breaking out, you could prohibit the exportation
of ships of war and munitions of war, and you would be instantly put in exclusive possession of the whole of the resources of all the private establishments which were previously
working, not for you alone, but for foreign Powers as well;
while, on the other hand, the foreign Governments would find
themselves cut off from the supplies on which they had been
relying. I can imagine no contrivance by which you could
place yourself in so advantageous and economical a state of
preparation for war as this.

There is, however, another reason why the two systems of
partially manufacturing for yourself as a Government, and
partly purchasing from private traders, will not harmonise.
The heads of your manufacturing departments must virtually
be the buyers of such commodities as their departments want.
Colonel Dickson, the head of your rifle manufactory at Enfield,
or somebody under him, practically makes all the purchases
of small arms; and there have been repeated complaints from
Birmingham of the unfairness of a rival manufacturer being
constituted the 'viewer' of the rifles supplied by private contract. At Woolwich, there was an extraordinary example of
this state of things, when Sir William Armstrong had to
judge the quality of the productions of his competitors. The
head of a manufacturing department has always an interest in
giving a preference to his own productions or inventions, and
disparaging those of outside rivals. There was the case, for
instance, of Captain Cowper Coles's turret ship. That was
the invention of an outside man; and there is no doubt there
has been an unseen, but a felt reluctance on the part of the
dockyard people, to carry it out speedily. I live near Portsmouth, and have myself observed what has been going on.
It is nearly four years since Captain Coles proposed his plan
to the Government. It is more than two years since they

began to cut down and plate the *Royal Sovereign*, in order to convert it into a turret ship. In the meantime, Mr. Reed comes into power. I will not say a word in disparagement of that gentleman. I have no doubt he is a man of talent. We, who sometimes complain of routine, have no right to object to an outside man stepping into a high place in the service on account of his assumed abilities. Mr. Reed, however, must be more than a man; he must be an angel, if he did not feel that his importance and value at the head of the construction department of the Navy would be enhanced by his producing something which should be better than Captain Cowper Coles's invention, and should be completed earlier. So he sets to work on the *Research*. I am no authority on these matters; but I hear an universal opinion that Mr. Reed's immovable square battery is anything but an improvement on Captain Cowper Coles's revolving turret. The world have decided that question, as is shown by the course taken in America, and by the orders received here from foreign countries. But what are the facts? Mr. Reed's vessel, the *Research*, though designed later than that of Captain Cowper Coles, was launched and at sea considerably in advance of the *Royal Sovereign*. Now, I am not making any attack on individuals; I am only illustrating the working of a system. If, instead of a construction department in your dockyards, you had a buying department, then Mr. Reed, or Admiral Robinson, or whoever were the heads of it, would seek out such men as Captain Cowper Coles, or the hon. Member for Birkenhead (Mr. Laird), and confer with them, would look abroad and avail themselves of inventions and improvements as they arose, without any feelings of rivalry arising from their own personal interest as inventors.

Before I conclude, I must impress on the House the absolute necessity there is for a thorough reform of the buying department of the Government. Do not call it a contract department. That is the old name which was used as an

excuse for ignorance and incompetency, when officials gave
out contracts according to a red-tape rule, taken, perhaps,
from a pigeon-hole, where it had lain for fifty years, and
scarcely to be understood by the modern manufacturer. If a
firm was doing a prosperous business with private customers,
it would have nothing to say to such a contract, and it went
to some one who had nothing better to do, and who hoped he
might possibly make something of it. A person sent me
from Manchester a copy of the specification for a tender for
tarpauling, in which the most minute particulars were set
forth in a tone of dictation, that, if it were not ludicrous from
its ignorance, would be really insulting to any respectable
manufacturer. It was just such a circular as a man of large
business would throw into his waste-paper basket; and it
contained a requirement that the canvas should be sent for
inspection before being tarred. So that, as my correspondent
said, he was expected to send all the canvas from Lancashire
to London, and then to convey it back again; when, if it had
been required that a strip should have been left untarred, it
would have answered the purpose. Why should they not have
devised a means for clearing off part of the tar themselves?
This is a specimen of the way in which the Government contracts are entered into. I would have all that altered. But
my plan involves no disparagement of the services of those
able men now in your employ; you will want all the brains
you have in your constructing department for your buying
department. I have no doubt that Colonel Boxer, Mr. Reed,
and the other heads of the different manufacturing departments, would make most excellent buyers. If they are not
competent for that, I would employ men who are, and I would
pay them on a far higher scale than you pay the heads of your
departments, for you cannot have men fit to be trusted to go
into the market and buy things in the way in which they
ought to be bought, unless they are placed in a position to be
above all temptation. Therefore, I would have men of the

utmost capacity; but I should lay down this condition, and
insist upon it—that if you cannot in England buy what you
want, it is you yourselves who are to blame, and not the
producers of the country. England is now sending abroad
150,000,000*l.* sterling worth of productions every year. There
is not a shilling's worth of that produce that would be bought
here if it could be obtained better and cheaper elsewhere, and
yet it continues to be bought in larger quantities every year.
If you hear anything disparaging to our modern mode of conducting business, that such and such articles are not made so
strong and durable as they were at former times, laugh at all
such shallow criticisms. The manufacturers here produce for
others just what they wish to buy, although, in consequence
of the more rapid changes of fashion, it is certainly not the
habit of our daughters to wear silk dresses of the strength
which were worn by their grandmothers. Then I say, that
if in a country which produces every year 150,000,000*l.*
sterling of manufactured articles for exportation, the Government fail to obtain the 10,000,000*l.* or 15,000,000*l.* sterling
worth of goods which they want, be assured that it arises
entirely from their incapacity to buy them. You must have
men selected for their ability to buy the commodities you
want. If you consult such great wholesale houses as Leaf's
and Morrison's in the City, whose buyers purchase millions'
worth of articles in the course of the year, they will tell
you at once, ' We can do with comparatively inferior men
to sell our goods, but we get the best men we can to buy
them.'

I will conclude with a remark in reference to the present
state of our armaments. When I consider what has been done
in the Armstrong guns, and our armaments generally, I regard it as a deep discredit to the Government of the country,
and of itself it ought to compel a change in the system. You
have invited this disgraceful state of things by undertaking to
do that which you ought never to have attempted. We are

governed in this country—I do not use the word invidiously
—by a class, and it is a very narrow class indeed, which forms
the *personnel* of our Administrations. I do not complain of
that, inasmuch as our manufacturing and trading community
do not seem disposed to educate their sons to compete for the
prizes of official life; but I wish you to bear in mind, that by
such a neglect and mismanagement as you have fallen into in
regard to your artillery and ships, you may produce the most
serious consequences. I know of nothing so calculated some
day to produce a democratic revolution, as for the proud and
combative people of this country to find themselves, in this
vital matter of their defence, sacrificed through the mismanagement and neglect of the class to whom, with so much
liberality, they have confided the care and future destinies
of the country. You have brought this upon yourselves by
undertaking to be producers and manufacturers. I advise you
in future to place yourselves entirely in dependence upon the
private manufacturing resources of the country. If you want
gunpowder, artillery, small arms, or the hulls of ships of war,
let it be known that you depend upon the private enterprise
of the country, and you will get them. At all events, you will
absolve yourselves from the responsibility of undertaking to
do things which you are not competent to do, and you will
be entitled to say to the British people, Our fortunes as a
Government and nation are indissolubly united, and we will
rise or fall, flourish or fade together, according to the energy,
enterprise, and ability of the great body of the manufacturing
and industrious community.

 END OF VOL.

16, BEDFORD STREET, COVENT GARDEN, LONDON.

January, 1870.

MACMILLAN & CO.'S GENERAL CATALOGUE of Works in the Departments of History, Biography, Travels, Poetry, and Belles Lettres. With some short Account or Critical Notice concerning each Book.

SECTION I.

HISTORY, BIOGRAPHY, and TRAVELS.

Baker (Sir Samuel W.).—THE NILE TRIBUTARIES OF ABYSSINIA, and the Sword Hunters of the Hamran Arabs. By SIR SAMUEL W. BAKER, M.A., F.R.G.S. With Portraits, Maps, and Illustrations. Third Edition, 8vo. 21*s*.

Sir Samuel Baker here describes twelve months' exploration, during which he examined the rivers that are tributary to the Nile from Abyssinia, including the Athara, Settite, Royan, Salaam, Angrab, Rahad, Dinder, and the Blue Nile. The interest attached to these portions of Africa differs entirely from that of the White Nile regions, as the whole of Upper Egypt and Abyssinia is capable of development, and is inhabited by races having some degree of civilisation; while Central Africa is peopled by a race of savages, whose future is more problematical.

THE ALBERT N'YANZA Great Basin of the Nile, and Exploration of the Nile Sources. New and cheaper Edition, with Portraits, Maps, and Illustrations. Two vols. crown 8vo. 16*s*.

"Bruce won the source of the Blue Nile; Speke and Grant won the Victoria source of the great White Nile; and I have been permitted to succeed in completing the Nile Sources by the discovery of the great reservoir of the equatorial waters, the Albert N'yanza, from which the river issues as the entire White Nile."—PREFACE.

NEW AND CHEAP EDITION OF THE ALBERT N'YANZA. 1 vol. crown 8vo. With Maps and Illustrations. 7*s*. 6*d*.

A

Baker (Sir Samuel W.) *(continued)*—

CAST UP BY THE SEA; or, The Adventures of NED GREY.
By SIR SAMUEL W. BAKER, M.A., F.R.G.S. Second Edition.
Crown 8vo. cloth gilt, 7s. 6d.

"*A story of adventure by sea and land in the good old style. It appears
to us to be the best book of the kind since 'Masterman Ready,' and it runs
that established favourite very close.*"—PALL MALL GAZETTE.

"*No book written for boys has for a long time created so much interest,
or been so successful. Every parent ought to provide his boy with a copy.*"
DAILY TELEGRAPH.

Barker (Lady).—STATION LIFE IN NEW ZEALAND.
By LADY BARKER. Crown 8vo. 7s. 6d.

"*These letters are the exact account of a lady's experience of the brighter
and less practical side of colonisation. They record the expeditions, adventures, and emergencies diversifying the daily life of the wife of a New
Zealand sheep-farmer; and, as each was written while the novelty and
excitement of the scenes it describes were fresh upon her, they may succeed
in giving here in England an adequate impression of the delight and freedom of an existence so far removed from our own highly-wrought civilisation.*"—PREFACE.

Baxter (R. Dudley, M.A.).—THE TAXATION OF THE
UNITED KINGDOM. By R. DUDLEY BAXTER, M.A. 8vo.
cloth, 4s. 6d.

*The First Part of this work, originally read before the Statistical
Society of London, deals with the Amount of Taxation; the Second Part,
which now constitutes the main portion of the work, is almost entirely new,
and embraces the important questions of Rating, of the relative Taxation
of Land, Personalty, and Industry, and of the direct effect of Taxes upon
Prices. The author trusts that the body of facts here collected may be of
permanent value as a record of the past progress and present condition of
the population of the United Kingdom, independently of the transitory
circumstances of its present Taxation.*

Baxter (R. Dudley, M.A.) *(continued)*—
NATIONAL INCOME. With Coloured Diagrams. 8vo. 3s. 6d.

PART I.—*Classification of the Population, Upper, Middle, and Labour Classes.* II.—*Income of the United Kingdom.*

" *A painstaking and certainly most interesting inquiry.*"—PALL MALL GAZETTE.

Bernard.—FOUR LECTURES ON SUBJECTS CONNECTED WITH DIPLOMACY. By MOUNTAGUE BERNARD, M.A., Chichele Professor of International Law and Diplomacy, Oxford. 8vo. 9s.

Four Lectures, dealing with (1) *The Congress of Westphalia;* (2) *Systems of Policy;* (3) *Diplomacy, Past and Present;* (4) *The Obligations of Treaties.*

Blake.—THE LIFE OF WILLIAM BLAKE, THE ARTIST. By ALEXANDER GILCHRIST. With numerous Illustrations from Blake's designs, and Fac-similes of his studies of the " Book of Job." Two vols. medium 8vo. 32s.

These volumes contain a Life of Blake; Selections from his Writings, including Poems; Letters; Annotated Catalogue of Pictures and Drawings; List, with occasional notes, of Blake's Engravings and Writings. There are appended Engraved Designs by Blake: (1) *The Book of Job, twenty-one photo-lithographs from the originals;* (2) *Songs of Innocence and Experience, sixteen of the original Plates.*

Bright (John, M.P.).—SPEECHES ON QUESTIONS OF PUBLIC POLICY. By JOHN BRIGHT, M.P. Edited by Professor THOROLD ROGERS. Two Vols. 8vo. 25s. Second Edition, with Portrait.

" *I have divided the Speeches contained in these volumes into groups. The materials for selection are so abundant, that I have been constrained to omit many a speech which is worthy of careful perusal. I have*

A 2

naturally given prominence to those subjects with which Mr. Bright has been especially identified, as, for example, India, America, Ireland, and Parliamentary Reform. But nearly every topic of great public interest on which Mr. Bright has spoken is represented in these volumes."

EDITOR'S PREFACE.

AUTHOR'S POPULAR EDITION. Extra fcap. 8vo. cloth. Second Edition. 3*s*. 6*d*.

Bryce.—THE HOLY ROMAN EMPIRE. By JAMES BRYCE, B.C.L., Fellow of Oriel College, Oxford.   [*Reprinting.*

CAMBRIDGE CHARACTERISTICS. *See* MULLINGER.

CHATTERTON : A Biographical Study. BY DANIEL WILSON, LL.D., Professor of History and English in University College, Toronto. Crown 8vo. 6*s*. 6*d*.

The Author here regards Chatterton as a Poet, and as a mere "reader and defacer of stolen literary treasures." Reviewed in this light, he has found much in the old materials capable of being turned to new account; and to these materials research in various directions has enabled him to make some additions.

Clay.—THE PRISON CHAPLAIN. A Memoir of the Rev. JOHN CLAY, B.D., late Chaplain of the Preston Gaol. With Selections from his Reports and Correspondence, and a Sketch of Prison Discipline in England. By his Son, the Rev. W. L. CLAY, M.A. 8vo. 15*s*.

"Few books have appeared of late years better entitled to an attentive perusal. . . . It presents a complete narrative of all that has been done and attempted by various philanthropists for the amelioration of the condition and the improvement of the morals of the criminal classes in the British dominions."—LONDON REVIEW.

Cooper.—ATHEN.E CANTABRIGIENSES. By Charles Henry Cooper, F.S.A., and Thomson Cooper, F.S.A. Vol. I. 8vo., 1500—85, 18s. Vol. II., 1586—1609, 18s.

This elaborate work, which is dedicated by permission to Lord Macaulay, contains lives of the eminent men sent forth by Cambridge, after the fashion of Anthony à Wood, in his famous "Athenæ Oxonienses."

Dilke.—GREATER BRITAIN. A Record of Travel in English-speaking Countries during 1866-7. (America, Australia, India.) By Sir Charles Wentworth Dilke, M.P. Fourth and Cheap Edition. Crown 8vo. 6s.

" Mr. Dilke has written a book which is probably as well worth reading as any book of the same aims and character that ever was written. Its merits are that it is written in a lively and agreeable style, that it implies a great deal of physical pluck, that no page of it fails to show an acute and highly intelligent observer, that it stimulates the imagination as well as the judgment of the reader, and that it is on perhaps the most interesting subject that can attract an Englishman who cares about his country."
SATURDAY REVIEW.

Dürer (Albrecht).—HISTORY OF THE LIFE OF ALBRECHT DÜRER, of Nürnberg. With a Translation of his Letters and Journal, and some account of his works. By Mrs. Charles Heaton. Royal 8vo. bevelled boards, extra gilt. 31s. 6d.

This work contains about Thirty Illustrations, ten of which are productions by the Autotype (carbon) process, and are printed in permanent tints by Messrs. Cundall and Fleming, under license from the Autotype Company, Limited; the rest are Photographs and Woodcuts.

EARLY EGYPTIAN HISTORY FOR THE YOUNG. See "JUVENILE SECTION."

Elliott.—LIFE OF HENRY VENN ELLIOTT, of Brighton. By JOSIAH BATEMAN, M.A., Author of "Life of Daniel Wilson, Bishop of Calcutta," &c. With Portrait, engraved by JEENS. Crown 8vo. 8*s*. 6*d*. Second Edition, with Appendix.

"*A very charming piece of religious biography; no one can read it without both pleasure and profit.*"—BRITISH QUARTERLY REVIEW.

Forbes.—LIFE OF PROFESSOR EDWARD FORBES, F.R.S. By GEORGE WILSON, M.D., F.R.S.E., and ARCHIBALD GEIKIE, F.R.S. 8vo. with Portrait, 14*s*.

"*From the first page to the last the book claims careful reading, as being a full but not overcrowded rehearsal of a most instructive life, and the true picture of a mind that was rare in strength and beauty.*"—EXAMINER.

Freeman.—HISTORY OF FEDERAL GOVERNMENT, from the Foundation of the Achaian League to the Disruption of the United States. By EDWARD A. FREEMAN, M.A. Vol. I. General Introduction. History of the Greek Federations. 8vo. 21*s*.

"*The task Mr. Freeman has undertaken is one of great magnitude and importance. It is also a task of an almost entirely novel character. No other work professing to give the history of a political principle occurs to us, except the slight contributions to the history of representative government that is contained in a course of M. Guizot's lectures . . . . The history of the development of a principle is at least as important as the history of a dynasty, or of a race.*'—SATURDAY REVIEW.

OLD ENGLISH HISTORY FOR CHILDREN. By EDWARD A. FREEMAN, M.A., late Fellow of Trinity College, Oxford. With Five Coloured Maps. Extra fcap. 8vo., half-bound. 6*s*.

"*Its object is to show that clear, accurate, and scientific views of history, or indeed of any subject, may be easily given to children from the very first. . . I have, I hope, shown that it is perfectly easy to teach children from the very first, to distinguish true history alike from legend and from wilful invention, and also to understand the nature of historical authorities, and to weigh one statement against another. . . . . I have throughout striven to connect the history of England with the general history of civilised Europe, and I have especially tried to make the book serve as an incentive to a more accurate study of historical geography."*—PREFACE.

French (George Russell).—SHAKSPEAREANA GENEALOGICA. 8vo. cloth extra, 15s. Uniform with the "Cambridge Shakespeare."

Part I.—Identification of the dramatis personæ in the historical plays, from King John to King Henry VIII.; Notes on Characters in Macbeth and Hamlet; Persons and Places belonging to Warwickshire alluded to. Part II.—The Shakspeare and Arden families and their connexions, with Tables of descent. The present is the first attempt to give a detailed description, in consecutive order, of each of the dramatis personæ in Shakspeare's immortal chronicle-histories, and some of the characters have been, it is believed, herein identified for the first time. A clue is furnished which, followed up with ordinary diligence, may enable any one, with a taste for the pursuit, to trace a distinguished Shakspearean worthy to his lineal representative in the present day.

Galileo.—THE PRIVATE LIFE OF GALILEO. Compiled principally from his Correspondence and that of his eldest daughter, Sister Maria Celeste, Nun in the Franciscan Convent of S. Matthew, in Arcetri. With Portrait. Crown 8vo. 7s. 6d.

It has been the endeavour of the compiler to place before the reader a plain, ungarbled statement of facts; and as a means to this end, to allow Galileo, his friends, and his judges to speak for themselves as far as possible.

Gladstone (Right. Hon. W. E., M.P.).—JUVENTUS MUNDI. The Gods and Men of the Heroic Age. Crown 8vo. cloth extra. With Map. 10s. 6d. Second Edition.

This new work of Mr. Gladstone deals especially with the historic element in Homer, expounding that element, and furnishing by its aid a full account of the Homeric men and the Homeric religion. It starts, after the introductory chapter, with a discussion of the several races then existing in Hellas, including the influence of the Phœnicians and Egyptians. It contains chapters on the Olympian system, with its several deities; on the Ethics and the Polity of the Heroic age; on the geography of Homer; on the characters of the Poems; presenting, in fine, a view of primitive life and primitive society as found in the poems of Homer.

"GLOBE" ATLAS OF EUROPE. Uniform in size with Macmillan's Globe Series, containing 45 Coloured Maps, on a uniform scale and projection; with Plans of London and Paris, and a copious Index. Strongly bound in half-morocco, with flexible back, 9s.

This Atlas includes all the countries of Europe in a series of 48 Maps, drawn on the same scale, with an Alphabetical Index to the situation of more than ten thousand places, and the relation of the various maps and countries to each other is defined in a general Key-map. All the maps being on a uniform scale facilitates the comparison of extent and distance, and conveys a just impression of the relative magnitude of different countries. The size suffices to show the provincial divisions, the railways and main roads, the principal rivers and mountain ranges. "This atlas," writes the British Quarterly, "will be an invaluable boon for the school, the desk, or the traveller's portmanteau."

Guizot.—(Author of "JOHN HALIFAX, GENTLEMAN.")—M. DE BARANTE, A Memoir, Biographical and Autobiographical. By M. GUIZOT. Translated by the Author of "JOHN HALIFAX, GENTLEMAN." Crown 8vo. 6s. 6d.

"*The highest purposes of both history and biography are answered by a memoir so lifelike, so faithful, and so philosophical.*"
                              BRITISH QUARTERLY REVIEW.

HISTORICAL SELECTIONS. Readings from the best Authorities on English and European History. Selected and arranged by E. M. SEWELL and C. M. YONGE. Crown 8vo. 6s.

When young children have acquired the outlines of history from abridgements and catechisms, and it becomes desirable to give a more enlarged view of the subject, in order to render it really useful and interesting, a difficulty often arises as to the choice of books. Two courses are open, either to take a general and consequently dry history of facts, such as Russell's Modern Europe, or to choose some work treating of a particular period or subject, such as the works of Macaulay and Froude. The former course usually renders history uninteresting; the latter is unsatisfactory, because it is not sufficiently comprehensive. To remedy this difficulty, selections, continuous and chronological, have in the present volume been taken from the larger works of Freeman, Milman, Palgrave, and others, which may serve as distinct landmarks of historical reading. "We know of scarcely anything," says the Guardian, *of this volume, "which is so likely to raise to a higher level the average standard of English education."*

Hole.—A GENEALOGICAL STEMMA OF THE KINGS OF ENGLAND AND FRANCE. By the Rev. C. HOLE, M.A., Trinity College, Cambridge. On Sheet, 1s.

The different families are printed in distinguishing colours, thus facilitating reference.

A BRIEF BIOGRAPHICAL DICTIONARY. Compiled and Arranged by the Rev. CHARLES HOLE, M.A. Second Edition. 18mo. neatly and strongly bound in cloth, 4s. 6d.

One of the most comprehensive and accurate Biographical Dictionaries in the world, containing more than 18,000 *persons of all countries, with dates of birth and death, and what they were distinguished for. Extreme care has been bestowed on the verification of the dates ; and thus numerous errors, current in previous works, have been corrected. Its size adapts it for the desk, portmanteau, or pocket.*

"An invaluable addition to our manuals of reference, and, from its moderate price, cannot fail to become as popular as it is useful."—TIMES.

Hozier.—THE SEVEN WEEKS' WAR; Its Antecedents and its Incidents. By H. M. Hozier. With Maps and Plans. Two vols. 8vo. 28s.

This work is based upon letters reprinted by permission from "The Times." For the most part it is a product of a personal eye-witness of some of the most interesting incidents of a war which, for rapidity and decisive results, may claim an almost unrivalled position in history.

THE BRITISH EXPEDITION TO ABYSSINIA. Compiled from Authentic Documents. By Captain Henry M. Hozier, late Assistant Military Secretary to Lord Napier of Magdala. 8vo. 9s.

"Several accounts of the British Expedition have been published. . . . They have, however, been written by those who have not had access to those authentic documents, which cannot be collected directly after the termination of a campaign. . . . . The endeavour of the author of this sketch has been to present to readers a succinct and impartial account of an enterprise which has rarely been equalled in the annals of war."—Preface.

Irving.—THE ANNALS OF OUR TIME. A Diurnal of Events, Social and Political, which have happened in or had relation to the Kingdom of Great Britain, from the Accession of Queen Victoria to the Opening of the present Parliament. By Joseph Irving. 8vo. half-bound. 18s.

"We have before us a trusty and ready guide to the events of the past thirty years, available equally for the statesman, the politician, the public writer, and the general reader. If Mr. Irving's object has been to bring before the reader all the most noteworthy occurrences which have happened since the beginning of Her Majesty's reign, he may justly claim the credit of having done so most briefly, succinctly, and simply, and in such a manner, too, as to furnish him with the details necessary in each case to comprehend the event of which he is in search in an intelligent manner. Reflection will serve to show the great value of such a work as this to the journalist and statesman, and indeed to every one who feels an interest in the progress of the age; and we may add that its value is considerably increased by the addition of that most important of all appendices, an accurate and instructive index."—Times.

Kingsley (Canon).—ON THE ANCIEN REGIME as it Exhibited on the Continent before the FRENCH REVOLUTION. Three Lectures delivered at the Royal Institution. By the Rev. C. KINGSLEY, M.A., formerly Professor of Modern History in the University of Cambridge. Crown 8vo. 6s.

These three lectures discuss severally (1) Caste, (2) Centralisation, (3) The Explosive Forces by which the Revolution was superinduced. The Preface deals at some length with certain political questions of the present day.

THE ROMAN AND THE TEUTON. A Series of Lectures delivered before the University of Cambridge. By Rev. C KINGSLEY, M.A. 8vo. 12s.

CONTENTS :—*Inaugural Lecture ; The Forest Children ; The Dying Empire ; The Human Deluge ; The Gothic Civiliser; Dietrich's End; The Nemesis of the Goths ; Paulus Diaconus ; The Clergy and the Heathen : The Monk a Civiliser ; The Lombard Laws ; The Popes and the Lombards ; The Strategy of Providence.*

Kingsley (Henry, F.R.G.S.).—TALES OF OLD TRAVEL. Re-narrated by HENRY KINGSLEY, F.R.G.S. With Eight Illustrations by HUARD. Crown 8vo. 6s.

CONTENTS :—*Marco Polo ; The Shipwreck of Pelsart ; The Wonderful Adventures of Andrew Battel ; The Wanderings of a Capuchin ; Peter Carder ; The Preservation of the "Terra Nova;" Spitzbergen ; D'Erme- nonville's Acclimatisation Adventure; The Old Slave Trade; Miles Philips ; The Sufferings of Robert Everard ; John Fox ; Alvaro Nunez ; The Foun- dation of an Empire.*

Latham.—BLACK AND WHITE: A Journal of a Three Months' Tour in the United States. By HENRY LATHAM, M.A., Barrister- at-Law. 8vo. 10s. 6d.

" The spirit in which Mr. Latham has written about our brethren in America is commendable in high degree."—ATHENÆUM.

Law.—THE ALPS OF HANNIBAL. By WILLIAM JOHN LAW, M.A., formerly Student of Christ Church, Oxford. Two vols. 8vo. 21*s.*

"*No one can read the work and not acquire a conviction that, in addition to a thorough grasp of a particular topic, its writer has at command a large store of reading and thought upon many cognate points of ancient history and geography.*"—QUARTERLY REVIEW.

Liverpool.—THE LIFE AND ADMINISTRATION OF ROBERT BANKS, SECOND EARL OF LIVERPOOL, K.G. Compiled from Original Family Documents by CHARLES DUKE YONGE, Regius Professor of History and English Literature in Queen's College, Belfast; and Author of "The History of the British Navy," "The History of France under the Bourbons," etc. Three vols. 8vo. 42*s.*

Since the time of Lord Burleigh no one, except the second Pitt, ever enjoyed so long a tenure of power; with the same exception, no one ever held office at so critical a time. . . . Lord Liverpool is the very last minister who has been able fully to carry out his own political views; who has been so strong that in matters of general policy the Opposition could extort no concessions from him which were not sanctioned by his own deliberate judgment. The present work is founded almost entirely on the correspondence left behind him by Lord Liverpool, and now in the possession of Colonel and Lady Catherine Harcourt.

"*Full of information and instruction.*"—FORTNIGHTLY REVIEW.

Maclear.—*See Section,* "ECCLESIASTICAL HISTORY."

Macmillan (Rev. Hugh).—HOLIDAYS ON HIGH LANDS; or, Rambles and Incidents in search of Alpine Plants. By the Rev. HUGH MACMILLAN, Author of "Bible Teachings in Nature," etc. Crown 8vo. cloth. 6*s.*

"*Botanical knowledge is blended with a love of nature, a pious enthusiasm, and a rich felicity of diction not to be met with in any works of kindred character, if we except those of Hugh Miller.*"—DAILY TELEGRAPH.

Macmillan (Rev. Hugh), (*continued*)—

FOOT-NOTES FROM THE PAGE OF NATURE. With numerous Illustrations. Fcap. 8vo. 5s.

"*Those who have derived pleasure and profit from the study of flowers and ferns—subjects, it is pleasing to find, now everywhere popular—by descending lower into the arcana of the vegetable kingdom, will find a still more interesting and delightful field of research in the objects brought under review in the following pages.*"—PREFACE.

BIBLE TEACHINGS IN NATURE. Fourth Edition. Fcap 8vo. 6s.—*See also* "SCIENTIFIC SECTION."

Martin (Frederick).—THE STATESMAN'S YEAR-BOOK :

A Statistical and Historical Account of the States of the Civilised World. Manual for Politician and Merchants for the year 1870. BY FREDERICK MARTIN. *Seventh Annual Publication.* Crown 8vo. 10s. 6d.

The new issue has been entirely re-written, revised, and corrected, on the basis of official reports received direct from the heads of the leading Governments of the World, in reply to letters sent to them by the Editor.

"*Everybody who knows this work is aware that it is a book that is indispensable to writers, financiers, politicians, statesmen, and all who are directly or indirectly interested in the political, social, industrial, commercial, and financial condition of their fellow-creatures at home and abroad. Mr. Martin deserves warm commendation for the care he takes in making 'The Statesman's Year Book' complete and correct.*"
STANDARD.

Martineau.—BIOGRAPHICAL SKETCHES, 1852—1868.

By HARRIET MARTINEAU. Third Edition, with New Preface. Crown 8vo. 8s. 6d.

A Collection of Memoirs under these several sections :—(1) Royal, (2) Politicians, (3) Professional, (4) Scientific, (5) Social, (6) Literary. These Memoirs appeared originally in the columns of the "Daily News."

Masson (Professor).—ESSAYS, BIOGRAPHICAL AND CRITICAL. *See Section headed* "POETRY AND BELLES LETTERS."

LIFE OF JOHN MILTON. Narrated in connexion with the Political, Ecclesiastical, and Literary History of his Time. By DAVID MASSON, M.A., LL.D., Professor of Rhetoric at Edinburgh. Vol. I. with Portraits. 8vo. 18s. Vol. II. In the Press.

It is intended to exhibit Milton's life in its connexions with all the more notable phenomena of the period of British history in which it was cast—its state politics, its ecclesiastical variations, its literature and speculative thought. Commencing in 1608, the Life of Milton proceeds through the last sixteen years of the reign of James I., includes the whole of the reign of Charles I. and the subsequent years of the Commonwealth and the Protectorate, and then, passing the Restoration, extends itself to 1674, or through fourteen years of the new state of things under Charles II. The first volume deals with the life of Milton as extending from 1608 to 1640, which was the period of his education and of his minor poems.

Morison.—THE LIFE AND TIMES OF SAINT BERNARD, Abbot of Clairvaux. By JAMES COTTER MORISON, M.A. New Edition, revised. Crown 8vo. 7s. 6d.

"One of the best contributions in our literature towards a vivid, intelligent, and worthy knowledge of European interests and thoughts and feelings during the twelfth century. A delightful and instructive volume, and one of the best products of the modern historic spirit."
PALL MALL GAZETTE.

Morley (John).—EDMUND BURKE, a Historical Study. By JOHN MORLEY, B.A. Oxon. Crown 8vo. 7s. 6d.

"The style is terse and incisive, and brilliant with epigram and point. It contains pithy aphoristic sentences which Burke himself would not have disowned. But these are not its best features: its sustained power of reasoning, its wide sweep of observation and reflection, its devoted ethical and social tone, stamp it as a work of high excellence, and as such we cordially recommend it to our readers."—SATURDAY REVIEW.

Mullinger.—CAMBRIDGE CHARACTERISTICS IN THE SEVENTEENTH CENTURY. By J. B. MULLINGER, B.A. Crown 8vo. 4*s.* 6*d.*

"*It is a very entertaining and readable book.*"—SATURDAY REVIEW.

"*The chapters on the Cartesian Philosophy and the Cambridge Platonists are admirable.*"—ATHENÆUM.

Palgrave.—HISTORY OF NORMANDY AND OF ENGLAND. By Sir FRANCIS PALGRAVE, Deputy Keeper of Her Majesty's Public Records. Completing the History to the Death of William Rufus. Four vols. 8vo. £4 4*s.*

Volume I. General Relations of Mediæval Europe—The Carlovingian Empire—The Danish Expeditions in the Gauls—And the Establishment of Rollo. Volume II. The Three First Dukes of Normandy; Rollo, Guillaume Longue-Épée, and Richard Sans-Peur—The Carlovingian line supplanted by the Capets. Volume III. Richard Sans-Peur—Richard Le-Bon—Richard III.—Robert Le Diable—William the Conqueror. Volume IV. William Rufus—Accession of Henry Beauclerc.

Palgrave (W. G.).—A NARRATIVE OF A YEAR'S JOURNEY THROUGH CENTRAL AND EASTERN ARABIA, 1862-3. By WILLIAM GIFFORD PALGRAVE, late of the Eighth Regiment Bombay N. I. Fifth and cheaper Edition. With Maps, Plans, and Portrait of Author, engraved on steel by Jeens. Crown 8vo. 6*s.*

"*Considering the extent of our previous ignorance, the amount of his achievements, and the importance of his contributions to our knowledge, we cannot say less of him than was once said of a far greater discoverer. Mr. Palgrave has indeed given a new world to Europe.*"—PALL MALL GAZETTE.

Parkes (Henry).—AUSTRALIAN VIEWS OF ENGLAND. By HENRY PARKES. Crown 8vo. cloth. 3s. 6d.

"*The following letters were written during a residence in England, in the years 1861 and 1862, and were published in the Sydney Morning Herald on the arrival of the monthly mails . . . . On re-perusal, these letters appear to contain views of English life and impressions of English notabilities which, as the views and impressions of an Englishman on his return to his native country after an absence of twenty years, may not be without interest to the English reader. The writer had opportunities of mixing with different classes of the British people, and of hearing opinions on passing events from opposite standpoints of observation.*"—AUTHOR'S PREFACE.

Prichard.—THE ADMINISTRATION OF INDIA. From 1859 to 1868. The First Ten Years of Administration under the Crown. By ILTUDUS THOMAS PRICHARD, Barrister-at-Law. Two vols. Demy 8vo. With Map. 21s.

In these volumes the author has aimed to supply a full, impartial, and independent account of British India between 1859 and 1868—which is in many respects the most important epoch in the history of that country which the present century has seen.

Ralegh.—THE LIFE OF SIR WALTER RALEGH, based upon Contemporary Documents. By EDWARD EDWARDS. Together with Ralegh's Letters, now first collected. With Portrait. Two vols. 8vo. 32s.

"*Mr. Edwards has certainly written the Life of Ralegh from fuller information than any previous biographer. He is intelligent, industrious, sympathetic: and the world has in his two volumes larger means afforded it of knowing Ralegh than it ever possessed before. The new letters and the newly-edited old letters are in themselves a book.*"—PALL MALL GAZETTE.

Robinson (Crabb).—DIARY, REMINISCENCES, AND CORRESPONDENCE OF CRABB ROBINSON. Selected and Edited by Dr. SADLER. With Portrait. Second Edition. Three vols. 8vo. cloth. 36s.

Mr. Crabb Robinson's Diary extends over the greater part of three-quarters of a century. It contains personal reminiscences of some of the most distinguished characters of that period, including Goethe, Wieland, De Quincey, Wordsworth (with whom Mr. Crabb Robinson was on terms of great intimacy), Madame de Staël, Lafayette, Coleridge, Lamb, Milman, &c. &c.: and includes a vast variety of subjects, political, literary, ecclesiastical, and miscellaneous.

Rogers (James E. Thorold).—HISTORICAL GLEANINGS: A Series of Sketches. Montague, Walpole, Adam Smith, Cobbett. By Rev. J. E. T. ROGERS. Crown 8vo. 4s. 6d.

Professor Rogers's object in the following sketches is to present a set of historical facts, grouped round a principal figure. The essays are in the form of lectures.

Smith (Professor Goldwin).— THREE ENGLISH STATESMEN: PYM, CROMWELL, PITT. A Course of Lectures on the Political History of England. By GOLDWIN SMITH, M.A. Extra fcap. 8vo. New and Cheaper Edition. 5s.

"A work which neither historian nor politician can safely afford to neglect."—SATURDAY REVIEW.

Tacitus.—THE HISTORY OF TACITUS, translated into English. By A. J. CHURCH, M.A. and W. J. BRODRIBB, M.A. With a Map and Notes. 8vo. 10s. 6d.

The translators have endeavoured to adhere as closely to the original as was thought consistent with a proper observance of English idiom. At the same time it has been their aim to reproduce the precise expressions of the author. This work is characterised by the Spectator as "a scholarly and faithful translation."

B

THE AGRICOLA AND GERMANIA. Translated into English by
A. J. CHURCH, M.A. and W. J. BRODRIBB, M.A. With Maps
and Notes. Extra fcap. 8vo. 2s. 6d.

*The translators have sought to produce such a version as may satisfy
scholars who demand a faithful rendering of the original, and English
readers who are offended by the baldness and frigidity which commonly
disfigure translations. The treatises are accompanied by introductions,
notes, maps, and a chronological summary. The Athenæum says of
this work that it is "a version at once readable and exact, which may be
perused with pleasure by all, and consulted with advantage by the classical
student."*

Taylor (Rev. Isaac).—WORDS AND PLACES; or
Etymological Illustrations of History, Etymology, and Geography.
By the Rev. ISAAC TAYLOR. Second Edition. Crown 8vo.
12s. 6d.

"*Mr. Taylor has produced a really useful book, and one which stands
alone in our language.*"—SATURDAY REVIEW.

Trench (Archbishop).—GUSTAVUS ADOLPHUS: Social
Aspects of the Thirty Years' War. By R. CHENEVIX TRENCH,
D.D., Archbishop of Dublin. Fcap. 8vo. 2s. 6d.

"*Clear and lucid in style, these lectures will be a treasure to many to
whom the subject is unfamiliar.*"—DUBLIN EVENING MAIL.

Trench (Mrs. R.).—Edited by ARCHBISHOP TRENCH. Remains
of the late Mrs. RICHARD TRENCH. Being Selections from
her Journals, Letters, and other Papers. New and Cheaper Issue,
with Portrait, 8vo. 6s.

*Contains notices and anecdotes illustrating the social life of the period
—extending over a quarter of a century (1799—1827). It includes also
poems and other miscellaneous pieces by Mrs. Trench.*

Trench (Capt. F., F.R.G.S.).—THE RUSSO-INDIAN QUESTION, Historically, Strategically, and Politically considered. By Capt. TRENCH, F.R.G.S. With a Sketch of Central Asiatic Politics and Map of Central Asia. Crown 8vo. 7s. 6d.

"*The Russo-Indian, or Central Asian question has for several obvious reasons been attracting much public attention in England, in Russia, and also on the Continent, within the last year or two. . . . I have thought that the present volume, giving a short sketch of the history of this question from its earliest origin, and condensing much of the most recent and interesting information on the subject, and on its collateral phases, might perhaps be acceptable to those who take an interest in it.*"—AUTHOR's PREFACE.

Trevelyan (G.O., M.P.).—CAWNPORE. Illustrated with Plan. By G. O. TREVELYAN, M.P., Author of "The Competition Wallah." Second Edition. Crown 8vo. 6s.

"*In this book we are not spared one fact of the sad story; but our feelings are not harrowed by the recital of imaginary outrages. It is good for us at home that we have one who tells his tale so well as does Mr. Trevelyan.*"—PALL MALL GAZETTE.

THE COMPETITION WALLAH. New Edition. Crown 8vo. 6s.

"*The earlier letters are especially interesting for their racy descriptions of European life in India. . . . . These that follow are of more serious import, seeking to tell the truth about the Hindoo character and English influences, good and bad, upon it, as well as to suggest some better course of treatment than that hitherto adopted.*"—EXAMINER.

Vaughan (late Rev. Dr. Robert, of the British Quarterly).—MEMOIR OF ROBERT A. VAUGHAN. Author of "Hours with the Mystics." By ROBERT VAUGHAN, D.D. Second Edition, revised and enlarged. Extra fcap. 8vo. 5s.

"*It deserves a place on the same shelf with Stanley's 'Life of Arnold,' and Carlyle's 'Stirling.' Dr. Vaughan has performed his painful but not all unpleasing task with exquisite good taste and feeling.*"—NONCONFORMIST.

B 2

Wagner.—MEMOIR OF THE REV. GEORGE WAGNER, M.A., late Incumbent of St. Stephen's Church, Brighton. By the Rev. J. N. SIMPKINSON, M.A. Third and cheaper Edition, corrected and abridged. 3*s*.

"*A more edifying biography we have rarely met with.*"
LITERARY CHURCHMAN.

Wallace.—THE MALAY ARCHIPELAGO: the Land of the Orang Utan and the Bird of Paradise. A Narrative of Travels with Studies of Man and Nature. By ALFRED RUSSEL WALLACE. With Maps and Illustrations. Second Edition. Two vols. crown 8vo. 24*s*.

"*A carefully and deliberately composed narrative. . . . We advise our readers to do as we have done, read his book through.*"—TIMES.

Ward (Professor).—THE HOUSE OF AUSTRIA IN THE THIRTY YEARS' WAR. Two Lectures, with Notes and Illustrations. By ADOLPHUS W. WARD, M.A., Professor of History in Owens College, Manchester. Extra fcap. 8vo. 2*s*. 6*d*.

"*Very compact and instructive.*"—FORTNIGHTLY REVIEW.

Warren.—AN ESSAY ON GREEK FEDERAL COINAGE. By the Hon. J. LEICESTER WARREN, M.A. 8vo. 2*s*. 6*d*.

"*The present essay is an attempt to illustrate Mr. Freeman's Federal Government by evidence deduced from the coinage of the times and countries therein treated of.*"—PREFACE.

Wilson.—A MEMOIR OF GEORGE WILSON, M.D., F.R.S.E., Regius Professor of Technology in the University of Edinburgh. By his SISTER. New Edition. Crown 8vo. 6*s*.

"*An exquisite and touching portrait of a rare and beautiful spirit.*"
GUARDIAN.

Wilson (Daniel, LL.D.).—PREHISTORIC ANNALS OF SCOTLAND. By DANIEL WILSON, LL.D., Professor of History and English Literature in University College, Toronto. New Edition, with numerous Illustrations. Two vols. demy 8vo. 36s.

This elaborate and learned work is divided into four Parts. Part I. deals with The Primeval or Stone Period: Aboriginal Traces, Sepulchral Memorials, Dwellings, and Catacombs, Temples, Weapons, &c. &c.; Part II., The Bronze Period: The Metallurgic Transition, Primitive Bronze, Personal Ornaments, Religion, Arts, and Domestic Habits, with other topics; Part III., The Iron Period: The Introduction of Iron, The Roman Invasion, Strongholds, &c. &c.; Part IV., The Christian Period: Historical Data, the Norrie's Law Relics, Primitive and Medieval Ecclesiology, Ecclesiastical and Miscellaneous Antiquities. The work is furnished with an elaborate Index.

PREHISTORIC MAN. New Edition, revised and partly re-written, with numerous Illustrations. One vol. 8vo. 21s.

This work, which carries out the principle of the preceding one, but with a wider scope, aims to "view Man, as far as possible, unaffected by those modifying influences which accompany the development of nations and the maturity of a true historic period, in order thereby to ascertain the source from whence such development and maturity proceed." It contains, for example, chapters on the Primeval Transition; Speech; Metals; the Mound-Builders; Primitive Architecture; the American Type; the Red Blood of the West, &c. &c.

SECTION II.

POETRY AND BELLES LETTRES.

Allingham.—LAURENCE BLOOMFIELD IN IRELAND; or, the New Landlord. By WILLIAM ALLINGHAM. New and cheaper issue, with a Preface. Fcap. 8vo. cloth, 4s. 6d.

In the new Preface, the state of Ireland, with special reference to the Church measure, is discussed.

"*It is vital with the national character. . . . It has something of Pope's point and Goldsmith's simplicity, touched to a more modern issue.*"—ATHENÆUM.

Arnold (Matthew).—POEMS. By MATTHEW ARNOLD. Two vols. Extra fcap. 8vo. cloth. 12s. Also sold separately at 6s. each.

Volume I. contains Narrative and Elegiac Poems; Volume II. Dramatic and Lyric Poems. The two volumes comprehend the First and Second Series of the Poems, and the New Poems.

NEW POEMS. Extra fcap. 8vo. 6s. 6s.

In this volume will be found "Empedocles on Etna:" "Thyrsis" (written in commemoration of the late Professor Clough); "Epilogue to Lessing's Laocoön;" "Heine's Grave;" "Obermann once more." All these poems are also included in the Edition (two vols.) above-mentioned.

Arnold (Matthew), (continued)—

ESSAYS IN CRITICISM. New Edition, with Additions. Extra fcap. 8vo. 6s.

CONTENTS :—Preface; The Function of Criticism at the present time; The Literary Influence of Academies; Maurice de Guerin; Eugenie de Guerin; Heinrich Heine; Pagan and Mediæval Religious Sentiment; Joubert; Spinoza and the Bible; Marcus Aurelius.

ASPROMONTE, AND OTHER POEMS. Fcap. 8vo. cloth extra. 4s. 6d.

CONTENTS :—Poems for Italy; Dramatic Lyrics; Miscellaneous.

Barnes (Rev. W.).—POEMS OF RURAL LIFE IN COMMON ENGLISH. By the REV. W. BARNES, Author of "Poems of Rural Life in the Dorset Dialect." Fcap. 8vo. 6s.

"In a high degree pleasant and novel. The book is by no means one which the lovers of descriptive poetry can afford to lose."—ATHENÆUM.

Bell.—ROMANCES AND MINOR POEMS. By HENRY GLASSFORD BELL. Fcap. 8vo. 6s.

"Full of life and genius."—COURT CIRCULAR.

Besant.—STUDIES IN EARLY FRENCH POETRY. By WALTER BESANT, M.A. Crown. 8vo. 8s. 6d.

A sort of impression rests on most minds that French literature begins with the "siècle de Louis Quatorze;" any previous literature being for the most part unknown or ignored. Few know anything of the enormous literary activity that began in the thirteenth century, was carried on by Rutebeuf, Marie de France, Gaston de Foix, Thibault de Champagne, and Lorris; was fostered by Charles of Orleans, by Margaret of Valois, by Francis the First; that gave a crowd of versifiers to France, enriched, strengthened, developed, and fixed the French language, and prepared the way for Corneille and for Racine. The present work aims to afford *information and direction touching the early efforts of France in poetical literature.*

"*In one moderately sized volume he has contrived to introduce us to the very best, if not to all of the early French poets.*"—ATHENÆUM.

Bradshaw.—AN ATTEMPT TO ASCERTAIN THE STATE OF CHAUCER'S WORKS, AS THEY WERE LEFT AT HIS DEATH. With some Notes of their Subsequent History. By HENRY BRADSHAW, of King's College, and the University Library, Cambridge.   [*In the Press.*

Brimley.—ESSAYS BY THE LATE GEORGE BRIMLEY, M.A. Edited by the Rev. W. G. CLARK, M.A. With Portrait. Cheaper Edition. Fcap. 8vo. 3s. 6d.

Essays on literary topics, such as Tennyson's "Poems," Carlyle's "Life of Stirling," "Bleak House," &c., reprinted from Fraser, the Spectator, and like periodicals.

Broome.—THE STRANGER OF SERIPHOS. A Dramatic Poem. By FREDERICK NAPIER BROOME. Fcap. 8vo. 5s.

Founded on the Greek legend of Danae and Perseus.

Clough (Arthur Hugh).—THE POEMS AND PROSE REMAINS OF ARTHUR HUGH CLOUGH. With a Selection from his Letters and a Memoir. Edited by his Wife. With Portrait. Two vols. crown 8vo. 21s. Or Poems separately, as below.

The late Professor Clough is well known as a graceful, tender poet, and as the scholarly translator of Plutarch. The letters possess high interest, not biographical only, but literary—discussing, as they do, the most important questions of the time, always in a genial spirit. The "Remains" include papers on "Retrenchment at Oxford;" on Professor F. W. Newman's book "The Soul;" on Wordsworth; on the Formation of Classical English; on some Modern Poems (Matthew Arnold and the late Alexander Smith), &c. &c.

Clough (Arthur Hugh), (*continued*)—

THE POEMS OF ARTHUR HUGH CLOUGH, sometime Fellow
of Oriel College, Oxford. With a Memoir by F. T. PALGRAVE.
Second Edition. Fcap. 8vo. 6s.

"*From the higher mind of cultivated, all-questioning, but still conservative England, in this our puzzled generation, we do not know of any utterance in literature so characteristic as the poems of Arthur Hugh Clough.*"—FRASER'S MAGAZINE.

Dante.—DANTE'S COMEDY, THE HELL. Translated by
W. M. ROSSETTI. Fcap. 8vo. cloth. 5s.

"*The aim of this translation of Dante may be summed up in one word
—Literality. . . . To follow Dante sentence for sentence, line for line,
word for word—neither more nor less—has been my strenuous endeavour.*"
—AUTHOR'S PREFACE.

De Vere.—THE INFANT BRIDAL, and other Poems. By
AUBREY DE VERE. Fcap. 8vo. 7s. 6d.

"*Mr. De Vere has taken his place among the poets of the day. Pure
and tender feeling, and that polished restraint of style which is called
classical, are the charms of the volume.*"—SPECTATOR.

Doyle (Sir F. H.).—Works by Sir FRANCIS HASTINGS DOYLE,
Professor of Poetry in the University of Oxford :—

THE RETURN OF THE GUARDS, AND OTHER POEMS.
Fcap. 8vo. 7s.

"*Good wine needs no bush, nor good verse a preface; and Sir Francis
Doyle's verse run bright and clear, and smack of a classic vintage. . . .
His chief characteristic, as it is his greatest charm, is the simple manliness
which gives force to all he writes. It is a characteristic in these days rare
enough.*"—EXAMINER.

Doyle (Sir F. H.), (continued)—

LECTURES ON POETRY, delivered before the University of Oxford in 1868. Extra crown 8vo. 3s. 6d.

THREE LECTURES:—(1) *Inaugural*; (2) *Provincial Poetry*; (3) *Dr. Newman's* "*Dream of Gerontius.*"

"*Full of thoughtful discrimination and fine insight: the lecture on 'Provincial Poetry' seems to us singularly true, elegant, and instructive.*"
SPECTATOR.

Evans.—BROTHER FABIAN'S MANUSCRIPT, AND OTHER POEMS. By SEBASTIAN EVANS. Fcap. 8vo. cloth. 6s.

"*In this volume we have full assurance that he has 'the vision and the faculty divine.' . . . Clever and full of kindly humour.*"—GLOBE.

Furnivall.—LE MORTE D'ARTHUR. Edited from the *Harleian* M.S. 2252, in the British Museum. By F. J. FURNIVALL, M.A. With Essay by the late HERBERT COLERIDGE. Fcap. 8vo. 7s. 6d.

Looking to the interest shown by so many thousands in Mr. Tennyson's Arthurian poems, the editor and publishers have thought that the old version would possess considerable interest. It is a reprint of the celebrated Harleian copy; and is accompanied by index and glossary.

Garnett.—IDYLLS AND EPIGRAMS. Chiefly from the Greek Anthology. By RICHARD GARNETT. Fcap. 8vo. 2s. 6d.

"*A charming little book. For English readers, Mr. Garnett's transla-tions will open a new world of thought.*"—WESTMINSTER REVIEW.

GUESSES AT TRUTH. By TWO BROTHERS. With Vignette, Title, and Frontispiece. New Edition, with Memoir. Fcap. 8vo. 6s.

"*The following year was memorable for the commencement of the 'Guesses at Truth.' He and his Oxford brother, living as they did in constant and free interchange of thought on questions of philosophy and literature and art; delighting, each of them, in the epigrammatic terseness which is the charm of the ' Pensées' of Pascal, and the ' Caractères' of La Bruyère—agreed to utter themselves in this form, and the book appeared, anonymously, in two volumes, in 1827."*—MEMOIR.

Hamerton.—A PAINTER'S CAMP. By PHILIP GILBERT HAMERTON. Second Edition, revised. Extra fcap. 8vo. 6s.

BOOK I. *In England;* BOOK II. *In Scotland;* BOOK III. *In France. This is the story of an Artist's encampments and adventures. The headings of a few chapters may serve to convey a notion of the character of the book: A Walk on the Lancashire Moors; the Author his own Housekeeper and Cook; Tents and Boats for the Highlands; The Author encamps on an uninhabited Island; A Lake Voyage; A Gipsy Journey to Glen Coe; Concerning Moonlight and Old Castles; A little French City; A Farm in the Autumois, &c. &c.*

"*His pages sparkle with happy turns of expression, not a few well-told anecdotes, and many observations which are the fruit of attentive study and wise reflection on the complicated phenomena of human life, as well as of unconscious nature.*"—WESTMINSTER REVIEW.

ETCHING AND ETCHERS. A Treatise Critical and Practical. By P. G. HAMERTON. With Original Plates by REMBRANDT, CALLOT, DUJARDIN, PAUL POTTER, &c. Royal 8vo. Half morocco. 31s. 6d.

"*It is a work of which author, printer, and publisher may alike feel proud. It is a work, too, of which none but a genuine artist could by possibility have been the author.*"—SATURDAY REVIEW.

Helps.—REALMAH. By ARTHUR HELPS. Cheap Edition. Crown 8vo. 6s.

Of this work, by the Author of " Friends in Council," the Saturday Review says: " Underneath the form (that of dialogue) is so much shrewdness, fancy, and above all, so much wise kindliness, that we should think all the better of a man or woman who likes the book."

Herschel.—THE ILIAD OF HOMER. Translated into English Hexameters. By Sir JOHN HERSCHEL, Bart. 8vo. 18s.

A version of the Iliad in English Hexameters. The question of Homeric translation is fully discussed in the Preface.

" *It is admirable, not only for many intrinsic merits, but as a great man's tribute to Genius.*"—ILLUSTRATED LONDON NEWS.

HIATUS : the Void in Modern Education. Its Cause and Antidote. By OUTIS. 8vo. 8s. 6d.

The main object of this Essay is to point out how the emotional element which underlies the Fine Arts is disregarded and undeveloped at this time so far as (despite a pretence at filling it up) to constitute an Educational Hiatus.

HYMNI ECCLESI.E. See "THEOLOGICAL SECTION."

Kennedy.—LEGENDARY FICTIONS OF THE IRISH CELTS. Collected and Narrated by PATRICK KENNEDY. Crown 8vo. 7s. 6d.

" *A very admirable popular selection of the Irish fairy stories and legends, in which those who are familiar with Mr. Croker's, and other selections of the same kind, will find much that is fresh, and full of the peculiar vivacity and humour, and sometimes even of the ideal beauty, of the true Celtic Legend.*"—SPECTATOR.

Kingsley (Canon).—*See also* "HISTORIC SECTION," "WORKS OF FICTION," *and* "PHILOSOPHY;" *also* "JUVENILE BOOKS," *and* "THEOLOGY."

THE SAINTS' TRAGEDY : or, The True Story of Elizabeth of Hungary. By the Rev. CHARLES KINGSLEY. With a Preface by the Rev. F. D. MAURICE. Third Edition. Fcap. 8vo. 5s.

ANDROMEDA, AND OTHER POEMS. Third Edition. Fcap. 8vo. 5s.

Kingsley (Canon), *(continued)*—

PHAETHON; or, Loose Thoughts for Loose Thinkers. Third Edition. Crown 8vo. 2*s.*

Kingsley (Henry).—*See* "WORKS OF FICTION."

Lowell.—UNDER THE WILLOWS, AND OTHER POEMS By JAMES RUSSELL LOWELL. Fcap. 8vo. 6*s.*

"*Under the Willows is one of the most admirable bits of idyllic work, short as it is, or perhaps because it is short, that have been done in our generation.*"—SATURDAY REVIEW.

Masson (Professor).—ESSAYS, BIOGRAPHICAL AND CRITICAL. Chiefly on the British Poets. By DAVID MASSON, LL.D., Professor of Rhetoric in the University of Edinburgh. 8vo. 12*s.* 6*d.*

"*Distinguished by a remarkable power of analysis, a clear statement of the actual facts on which speculation is based, and an appropriate beauty of Language. These essays should be popular with serious men.*" ATHENÆUM.

BRITISH NOVELISTS AND THEIR STYLES. Being a Critical Sketch of the History of British Prose Fiction. Crown 8vo. 7*s.* 6*d.*

"*Valuable for its lucid analysis of fundamental principles, its breadth of view, and sustained animation of style.*"—SPECTATOR.

MRS. JERNINGHAM'S JOURNAL. Extra fcap. 8vo. 3*s.* 6*d.* A Poem of the boudoir or domestic class, purporting to be the journal of a newly-married lady.

"*One quality in the piece, sufficient of itself to claim a moment's attention, is that it is unique—original, indeed, is not too strong a word—in the manner of its conception and execution.*"—PALL MALL GAZETTE.

Mistral (F.).—MIRELLE: a Pastoral Epic of Provence. Translated by H. CRICHTON. Extra fcap. 8vo. 6s.

"This is a capital translation of the elegant and richly-coloured pastoral epic poem of M. Mistral which, in 1859, he dedicated in enthusiastic terms to Lamartine. . . . . . It would be hard to overpraise the sweetness and pleasing freshness of this charming epic."—ATHENÆUM.

Myers (Ernest).—THE PURITANS. By ERNEST MYERS. Extra fcap. 8vo. cloth. 2s. 6d.

"It is not too much to call it a really grand poem, stately and dignified, and showing not only a high poetic mind, but also great power over poetic expression."—LITERARY CHURCHMAN.

Myers (F. W. H.)—ST. PAUL. A Poem. By F. W. H. MYERS. Second Edition. Extra fcap. 8vo. 2s. 6d.

"It breathes throughout the spirit of St. Paul, and with a singular stately melody of verse."—FORTNIGHTLY REVIEW.

Nettleship. — ESSAYS ON ROBERT BROWNING'S POETRY. By JOHN T. NETTLESHIP. Extra fcap. 8vo. 6s. 6d.

Noel.—BEATRICE, AND OTHER POEMS. By the Hon. RODEN NOEL. Fcap. 8vo. 6s.

"Beatrice is in many respects a noble poem; it displays a splendour of landscape painting, a strong definite precision of highly-coloured description, which has not often been surpassed."—PALL MALL GAZETTE.

Norton.—THE LADY OF LA GARAYE. By the Hon. Mrs. NORTON. With Vignette and Frontispiece. Sixth Edition Fcap. 8vo. 4s. 6d.

"There is no lack of vigour, no faltering of power, plenty of passion, much bright description, much musical verse. . . . Full of thoughts well-expressed, and may be classed among her best works."—TIMES.

Orwell.—THE BISHOP'S WALK AND THE BISHOP'S TIMES. Poems on the days of Archbishop Leighton and the Scottish Covenant. By ORWELL. Fcap. 8vo. 5s.

"*Pure taste and faultless precision of language, the fruits of deep thought, insight into human nature, and lively sympathy.*"—NONCONFORMIST.

Palgrave (Francis T.).—ESSAYS ON ART. By FRANCIS TURNER PALGRAVE, M.A., late Fellow of Exeter College, Oxford. Extra fcap. 8vo. 6s.

Mulready—Dyce—Holman Hunt—Herbert—Poetry, Prose, ana Sensationalism in Art—Sculpture in England—The Albert Cross, &c.

SHAKESPEARE'S SONNETS AND SONGS. Edited by F. T. PALGRAVE. Gem Edition. With Vignette Title by JEENS. 3s. 6d.

"*For minute elegance no volume could possibly excel the 'Gem Edition.'*"—SCOTSMAN.

Patmore.—Works by COVENTRY PATMORE :—

THE ANGEL IN THE HOUSE.

BOOK I. *The Betrothal*; BOOK II. *The Espousals*; BOOK III. *Faithful for Ever.* With *Tamerton Church Tower.* Two vols. fcap. 8vo. 12s.

** A New and Cheap Edition in one vol. 18mo., *beautifully printed on toned paper, price 2s. 6d.*

THE VICTORIES OF LOVE. Fcap. 8vo. 4s. 6d.

The intrinsic merit of his poem will secure it a permanent place in literature. . . . Mr. Patmore has fully earned a place in the catalogue of poets by the finished idealisation of domestic life."—SATURDAY REVIEW.

Rossetti.—Works by CHRISTINA ROSSETTI :—

GOBLIN MARKET, AND OTHER POEMS. With two Designs by D. G. ROSSETTI. Second Edition. Fcap. 8vo. 5*s*.

"*She handles her little marvel with that rare poetic discrimination which neither exhausts it of its simple wonders by pushing symbolism too far, nor keeps those wonders in the merely fabulous and capricious stage. In fact she has produced a true children's poem, which is far more delightful to the mature than to children, though it would be delightful to all.*"— SPECTATOR.

THE PRINCE'S PROGRESS, AND OTHER POEMS. With two Designs by D. G. ROSSETTI. Fcap. 8vo. 6*s*.

"*Miss Rossetti's poems are of the kind which recalls Shelley's definition of Poetry as the record of the best and happiest moments of the best and happiest minds. . . . They are like the piping of a bird on the spray in the sunshine, or the quaint singing with which a child amuses itself when it forgets that anybody is listening.*"—SATURDAY REVIEW.

Rossetti (W. M.).—DANTE'S HELL. *See* "DANTE."

FINE ART, chiefly Contemporary. By WILLIAM M. ROSSETTI. Crown 8vo. 10*s*. 6*d*.

This volume consists of Criticism on Contemporary Art, reprinted from Fraser, The Saturday Review, The Pall Mall Gazette, and other publications.

Roby.—STORY OF A HOUSEHOLD, AND OTHER POEMS. By MARY K. ROBY. Fcap. 8vo. 5*s*.

Shairp (Principal).—KILMAHOE, a Highland Pastoral, with other Poems. By JOHN CAMPBELL SHAIRP. Fcap. 8vo. 5*s*.

"*Kilmahoe is a Highland Pastoral, redolent of the warm soft air of the Western Lochs and Moors, sketched out with remarkable grace and picturesqueness.*"—SATURDAY REVIEW.

Smith.—Works by ALEXANDER SMITH :—

A LIFE DRAMA, AND OTHER POEMS. Fcap. 8vo. 2s. 6d.

CITY POEMS. Fcap. 8vo. 5s.

EDWIN OF DEIRA. Second Edition. Fcap. 8vo. 5s.

"*A poem which is marked by the strength, sustained sweetness, and compact texture of real life.*"—NORTH BRITISH REVIEW.

Smith.—POEMS. By CATHERINE BARNARD SMITH. Fcap. 8vo. 5s.

"*Wealthy in feeling, meaning, finish, and grace; not without passion, which is suppressed, but the keener for that.*"—ATHENÆUM.

Smith (Rev. Walter).—HYMNS OF CHRIST AND THE CHRISTIAN LIFE. By the Rev. WALTER C. SMITH, M.A. Fcap. 8vo. 6s.

"*These are among the sweetest sacred poems we have read for a long time. With no profuse imagery, expressing a range of feeling and expression by no means uncommon, they are true and devoted, and their pathos is profound and simple.*"—NONCONFORMIST.

Stratford de Redcliffe (Viscount).—SHADOWS OF THE PAST, in Verse. By VISCOUNT STRATFORD DE REDCLIFFE. Crown 8vo. 10s. 6d.

"*The vigorous words of one who has acted vigorously. They combine the fervour of politician and poet.*"—GUARDIAN.

Trench.—Works by R. CHENEVIX TRENCH, D.D., Archbishop of Dublin. See also Sections "PHILOSOPHY," "THEOLOGY," &c.

POEMS. Collected and arranged anew. Fcap. 8vo. 7s. 6d.

ELEGIAC POEMS. Third Edition. Fcap. 8vo. 2s. 6d.

Trench (Archbishop), (continued)—

CALDERON'S LIFE'S A DREAM : The Great Theatre of the
World. With an Essay on his Life and Genius. Fcap. 8vo.
4s. 6d.

HOUSEHOLD BOOK OF ENGLISH POETRY. Selected and
arranged, with Notes, by R. C. TRENCH, D.D., Archbishop of
Dublin. Extra fcap. 8vo. 5s. 6d.

*This volume is called a " Household Book," by this name implying that
it is a book for all—that there is nothing in it to prevent it from being
confidently placed in the hands of every member of the household. Specimens of all classes of poetry are given, including selections from living
authors. The Editor has aimed to produce a book " which the emigrant,
finding room for little not absolutely necessary, might yet find room for
in his trunk, and the traveller in his knapsack, and that on some narrow
shelves where there are few books this might be one."*

" The Archbishop has conferred in this delightful volume an important
gift on the whole English-speaking population of the world."—PALL
MALL GAZETTE.

SACRED LATIN POETRY, Chiefly Lyrical. Selected and arranged
for Use. Second Edition, Corrected and Improved. Fcap. 8vo.
7s.

" The aim of the present volume is to offer to members of our English
Church a collection of the best sacred Latin poetry, such as they shall be
able entirely and heartily to accept and approve—a collection, that is, in which
they shall not be evermore liable to be offended, and to have the current of
their sympathies checked, by coming upon that which, however beautiful as
poetry, out of higher respects they must reject and condemn—in which, too,
they shall not fear that snares are being laid for them, to entangle them
unawares in admiration for ought which is inconsistent with their faith
and fealty to their own spiritual mother."—PREFACE.

Turner.—SONNETS. By the Rev. CHARLES TENNYSON
TURNER. Dedicated to his brother, the Poet Laureate. Fcap.
8vo. 4s. 6d.

"*The Sonnets are dedicated to Mr. Tennyson by his brother, and have,
independently of their merits, an interest of association. They both love to
write in simple expressive Saxon; both love to touch their imagery in
epithets rather than in formal similes; both have a delicate perception
of rythmical movement, and thus Mr. Turner has occasional lines which,
for phrase and music, might be ascribed to his brother. . . He knows the
haunts of the wild rose, the shady nooks where light quivers through the
leaves, the ruralities, in short, of the land of imagination.*"—ATHENÆUM.

SMALL TABLEAUX. Fcap. 8vo. 4s. 6d.

"*These brief poems have not only a peculiar kind of interest for the
student of English poetry, but are intrinsically delightful, and will reward
a careful and frequent perusal. Full of naiveté, piety, love, and knowledge
of natural objects, and each expressing a single and generally a simple
subject by means of minute and original pictorial touches, these sonnets
have a place of their own.*"—PALL MALL GAZETTE.

Vittoria Colonna.—LIFE AND POEMS. By Mrs. HENRY
ROSCOE. Crown 8vo. 9s.

*The life of Vittoria Colonna, the celebrated Marchesa di Pescara, has
received but cursory notice from any English writer, though in every
history of Italy her name is mentioned with great honour among the poets
of the sixteenth century. "In three hundred and fifty years," says her
biographer Visconti, "there has been no other Italian lady who can be
compared to her."*

"*It is written with good taste, with quick and intelligent sympathy,
occasionally with a real freshness and charm of style.*"—PALL MALL
GAZETTE.

Webster.—Works by AUGUSTA WEBSTER :—

DRAMATIC STUDIES. Extra fcap. 8vo. 5s.

" *A volume as strongly marked by perfect taste as by poetic power.*"
NONCONFORMIST.

PROMETHEUS BOUND OF ÆSCHYLUS. Literally translated into English Verse. Extra fcap. 8vo. 3s. 6d.

" *Closeness and simplicity combined with literary skill.*"—ATHENÆUM.

MEDEA OF EURIPIDES. Literally translated into English Verse. Extra fcap. 8vo. 3s. 6d.

" *Mrs. Webster's translation surpasses our utmost expectations. It is a photograph of the original without any of that harshness which so often accompanies a photograph.*"—WESTMINSTER REVIEW.

A WOMAN SOLD, AND OTHER POEMS. Crown 8vo. 7s. 6d.

" *Mrs. Webster has shown us that she is able to draw admirably from the life; that she can observe with subtlety, and render her observations with delicacy; that she can impersonate complex conceptions, and venture into which few living writers can follow her.*"—GUARDIAN.

Woolner.—MY BEAUTIFUL LADY. By THOMAS WOOLNER. With a Vignette by ARTHUR HUGHES. *Third Edition.* Fcap. 8vo. 5s.

" *It is clearly the product of no idle hour, but a highly-conceived and faithfully-executed task, self-imposed, and prompted by that inward yearning to utter great thoughts, and a wealth of passionate feeling which is poetic genius. No man can read this poem without being struck by the power and finish of the workmanship, so to speak, as well as by the chastened and unpretending loftiness of thought which pervades the whole.*"
GLOBE.

WORDS FROM THE POETS. Selected by the Editor of " Rays of Sunlight." With a Vignette and Frontispiece. 18mo. Extra cloth gilt. 2s. 6d. *Cheaper Edition,* 18mo. limp, 1s.

GLOBE EDITIONS.

Under the title GLOBE EDITIONS, the Publishers are
issuing a uniform Series of Standard English Authors,
carefully edited, clearly and elegantly printed on toned
paper, strongly bound, and at a small cost. The names of
the Editors whom they have been fortunate enough to
secure constitute an indisputable guarantee as to the
character of the Series. The greatest care has been taken
to ensure accuracy of text; adequate notes, elucidating
historical, literary, and philological points, have been supplied; and, to the older Authors, glossaries are appended.
The series is especially adapted to Students of our national
Literature; while the small price places good editions of
certain books, hitherto popularly inaccessible, within the
reach of all.

Shakespeare.—THE COMPLETE WORKS OF WILLIAM
   SHAKESPEARE. Edited by W. G. CLARK and W. ALDIS
   WRIGHT. Ninety-first Thousand. Globe 8vo. 3s. 6d.

   "*A marvel of beauty, cheapness, and compactness. The whole works—
   plays, poems, and sonnets—are contained in one small volume: yet the
   page is perfectly clear and readable. . . . For the busy man, above all
   for the working Student, the Globe Edition is the best of all existing
   Shakespeare books.*"—ATHENÆUM.

Morte D'Arthur.—SIR THOMAS MALORY'S BOOK OF KING ARTHUR AND OF HIS NOBLE KNIGHTS OF THE ROUND TABLE. The Edition of CAXTON, revised for Modern Use. With an Introduction by SIR EDWARD STRACHEY, Bart. Globe 8vo. 3s. 6d. Third Edition.

"*It is with the most perfect confidence that we recommend this edition of the old romance to every class of readers.*"—PALL MALL GAZETTE.

Scott.—THE POETICAL WORKS OF SIR WALTER SCOTT. With Biographical Essay, by F. T. PALGRAVE. Globe 8vo. 3s. 6d. New Edition.

"*As a popular edition it leaves nothing to be desired. The want of such an one has long been felt, combining real excellence with cheapness.*" SPECTATOR.

Burns.—THE POETICAL WORKS AND LETTERS OF ROBERT BURNS. Edited, with Life, by ALEXANDER SMITH. Globe 8vo. 3s. 6d. Second Edition.

"*The works of the bard have never been offered in such a complete form in a single volume.*"—GLASGOW DAILY HERALD.
"*Admirable in all respects.*"—SPECTATOR.

Robinson Crusoe.—THE ADVENTURES OF ROBINSON CRUSOE. By DEFOE. Edited, from the Original Edition, by J. W. CLARK, M.A., Fellow of Trinity College, Cambridge. With Introduction by HENRY KINGSLEY. Globe 8vo. 3s. 6d.

"*The Globe Edition of Robinson Crusoe is a book to have and to keep. It is printed after the original editions, with the quaint old spelling, and is published in admirable style as regards type, paper, and binding. A well-written and genial biographical introduction, by Mr. Henry Kingsley, is likewise an attractive feature of this edition.*"—MORNING STAR.

Goldsmith.—GOLDSMITH'S MISCELLANEOUS WORKS. With Biographical Essay by Professor MASSON. Globe 8vo. 3*s.* 6*d.*

This edition includes the whole of Goldsmith's Miscellaneous Works—the Vicar of Wakefield, Plays, Poems, &c. Of the memoir the SCOTSMAN *newspaper writes: " Such an admirable compendium of the facts of Goldsmith's life, and so careful and minute a delineation of the mixed traits of his peculiar character, as to be a very model of a literary biography."*

Pope.—THE POETICAL WORKS OF ALEXANDER POPE. Edited, with Memoir and Notes, by Professor WARD. Globe 8vo. 3*s.* 6*d.*

" The book is handsome and handy. . . . The notes are many, and the matter of them is rich in interest."—ATHENÆUM.

Spenser. — THE COMPLETE WORKS OF EDMUND SPENSER. Edited from the Original Editions and Manuscripts, by R. MORRIS, Member of the Council of the Philological Society. With a Memoir by J. W. HALES, M.A., late Fellow of Christ's College, Cambridge, Member of the Council of the Philological Society. Globe 8vo. 3*s.* 6*d.*

" A complete and clearly printed edition of the whole works of Spenser, carefully collated with the originals, with copious glossary, worthy—and higher praise it needs not—of the beautiful Globe Series. The work is edited with all the care to noble a poet deserves."—DAILY NEWS.

. Other Standard Works are in the Press.

. The Volumes of this Series may also be had in a variety of morocco and calf bindings at very moderate Prices.

GOLDEN TREASURY SERIES.

Uniformly printed in 18mo., with Vignette Titles by Sir Noel Paton, T. Woolner, W. Holman Hunt, J. E. Millais, Arthur Hughes, &c. Engraved on Steel by Jeens. Bound in extra cloth, 4s. 6d. each volume. Also kept in morocco.

" Messrs. Macmillan have, in their Golden Treasury Series especially, provided editions of standard works, volumes of selected poetry, and original compositions, which entitle this series to be called classical. Nothing can be better than the literary execution, nothing more elegant than the material workmanship."—British Quarterly Review.

THE GOLDEN TREASURY OF THE BEST SONGS AND LYRICAL POEMS IN THE ENGLISH LANGUAGE.
Selected and arranged, with Notes, by Francis Turner Palgrave.

" This delightful little volume, the Golden Treasury, which contains many of the best original lyrical pieces and songs in our language, grouped with care and skill, so as to illustrate each other like the pictures in a well-arranged gallery."—Quarterly Review.

THE CHILDREN'S GARLAND FROM THE BEST POETS.
Selected and arranged by Coventry Patmore.

" It includes specimens of all the great masters in the art of poetry, selected with the matured judgment of a man concentrated on obtaining insight into the feelings and tastes of childhood, and desirous to awaken its finest impulses, to cultivate its keenest sensibilities."—Morning Post.

THE BOOK OF PRAISE. From the Best English Hymn Writers. Selected and arranged by Sir ROUNDELL PALMER. *A New and Enlarged Edition.*

"*All previous compilations of this kind must undeniably for the present give place to the Book of Praise. . . . The selection has been made throughout with sound judgment and critical taste. The pains involved in this compilation must have been immense, embracing, as it does, every writer of note in this special province of English literature, and ranging over the most widely divergent tracts of religious thought.*"—SATURDAY REVIEW.

THE FAIRY BOOK; the Best Popular Fairy Stories. Selected and rendered anew by the Author of "JOHN HALIFAX, GENTLEMAN."

"*A delightful selection, in a delightful external form; full of the physical splendour and vast opulence of proper fairy tales.*"—SPECTATOR.

THE BALLAD BOOK. A Selection of the Choicest British Ballads. Edited by WILLIAM ALLINGHAM.

"*His taste as a judge of old poetry will be found, by all acquainted with the various readings of old English ballads, true enough to justify his undertaking so critical a task.*"—SATURDAY REVIEW.

THE JEST BOOK. The Choicest Anecdotes and Sayings. Selected and arranged by MARK LEMON.

"*The fullest and best jest book that has yet appeared.*"—SATURDAY REVIEW.

BACON'S ESSAYS AND COLOURS OF GOOD AND EVIL. With Notes and Glossarial Index. By W. ALDIS WRIGHT, M.A.

"*The beautiful little edition of Bacon's Essays, now before us, does credit to the taste and scholarship of Mr. Aldis Wright. . . . It puts the reader in possession of all the essential literary facts and chronology necessary for reading the Essays in connexion with Bacon's life and times.*"—SPECTATOR.

"*By far the most complete as well as the most elegant edition we possess.*"—WESTMINSTER REVIEW.

D

THE PILGRIM'S PROGRESS from this World to that which is to come. By JOHN BUNYAN.

"*A beautiful and scholarly reprint.*"—SPECTATOR.

THE SUNDAY BOOK OF POETRY FOR THE YOUNG. Selected and arranged by C. F. ALEXANDER.

"*A well-selected volume of sacred poetry.*"—SPECTATOR.

A BOOK OF GOLDEN DEEDS of all Times and all Countries. Gathered and narrated anew. By the Author of "THE HEIR OF REDCLYFFE."

"*. . . To the young, for whom it is especially intended, as a most interesting collection of thrilling tales well told; and to their elders, as a useful hand-book of reference, and a pleasant one to take up when their wish is to while away a weary half-hour. We have seen no prettier gift-book for a long time.*"—ATHENÆUM.

THE POETICAL WORKS OF ROBERT BURNS. Edited, with Biographical Memoir, Notes, and Glossary, by ALEXANDER SMITH. Two Vols.

"*Beyond all question this is the most beautiful edition of Burns yet out.*"—EDINBURGH DAILY REVIEW.

THE ADVENTURES OF ROBINSON CRUSOE. Edited from the Original Edition by J. W. CLARK, M.A., Fellow of Trinity College, Cambridge.

"*Mutilated and modified editions of this English classic are so much the rule, that a cheap and pretty copy of it, rigidly exact to the original, will be a prize to many book-buyers.*"—EXAMINER.

THE REPUBLIC OF PLATO. Translated into ENGLISH, with Notes, by J. Ll. DAVIES, M.A. and D. J. VAUGHAN, M.A.

"*A dainty and cheap little edition.*"—EXAMINER.

THE SONG BOOK. Words and Tunes from the best Poets and Musicians. Selected and arranged by JOHN HULLAH, Professor of Vocal Music in King's College, London.

"*A choice collection of the sterling songs of England, Scotland, and Ireland, with the music of each prefixed to the words. How much true wholesome pleasure such a book can diffuse, and will diffuse, we trust, through many thousand families.*"—EXAMINER.

LA LYRE FRANCAISE. Selected and arranged, with Notes, by GUSTAVE MASSON, French Master in Harrow School.

A selection of the best French songs and lyrical pieces.

TOM BROWN'S SCHOOL DAYS. By an OLD BOY.

"*A perfect gem of a book. The best and most healthy book about boys for boys that ever was written.*"—ILLUSTRATED TIMES.

A BOOK OF WORTHIES. Gathered from the Old Histories and written anew by the Author of "THE HEIR OF REDCLYFFE." With Vignette.

"*An admirable edition to an admirable series.*"

WESTMINSTER REVIEW.